HUMAN LEARNING

Second Edition

Thomas H. Leahey

Virginia Commonwealth University

Richard J. Harris

Kansas State University

PRENTICE HALL, Englewood Cliffs, New Jersey 07632

Library of Congress Cataloging-in-Publication Data

Leahey, Thomas Hardy.
    Human learning / Thomas H. Leahey, Richard J. Harris. -- 2nd ed.
        p.   cm.
    Includes bibliographies and index.
    ISBN 0-13-445214-3
    1. Learning, Psychology of.   2. Learning--Physiological aspects.
I. Harris, Richard Jackson.   II. Title.
    [DNLM: 1. Behavior.   2. Cognition.   3. Learning--physiology.
4. Memory.   BF 318 L434h]
BF318.L37 1989
153.1--dc19
DNLM/DLC
for Library of Congress   88-26568
                                                               CIP

To William F. Brewer
mentor, friend, and teacher,
and a truly scholarly cognitive psychologist

He modeled for us
not only a scholar's quest for knowledge through research,
but also a scholar's commitment and excitement
in communicating this knowledge in the classroom.

Editorial/production supervision and interior design: Kathleen Schiaparelli
Cover design: Diane Saxe
Manufacturing buyer: Ray Keating

 © 1989, 1985 by Prentice-Hall, Inc.
A Division of Simon & Schuster
Englewood Cliffs, New Jersey 07632

Printed in the United States of America

10 9 8 7 6 5 4 3 2 1

ISBN 0-13-445214-3

Prentice-Hall International (UK) Limited, *London*
Prentice-Hall of Australia Pty. Limited, *Sydney*
Prentice-Hall Canada Inc., *Toronto*
Prentice-Hall Hispanoamericana, S.A., *Mexico*
Prentice-Hall of India Private Limited, *New Delhi*
Prentice-Hall of Japan, Inc., *Tokyo*
Simon & Schuster Asia Pte. Ltd., *Singapore*
Editora Prentice-Hall do Brasil, Ltda., *Rio de Janeiro*

CONTENTS

PREFACE

In the second edition of *Human Learning* we have tried to preserve what we believe to be the virtues of the first edition—focus on human beings, comprehensiveness, relevance, and inclusion of biology—while making organizational and substantive changes that we hope have improved our text.

First of all, we have updated our chapters to include current research across the whole field of human—and, where important, animal—learning. We have also remedied omissions in the first edition that were brought to our attention by reviewers; for example, our neglect of research in verbal learning, now included in chapter 3.

Second, we have included some substantial new material. Chapter 1 has been completely rewritten to be less historical and provide a better introduction to the deeper issues underlying theorizing about human learning. Material has been added on the new connectionist/parallel-distributed-processing approach to cognition that has seized the attention of, and stirred excitement among, psychologists, computer scientists, philosophers, and biologists. Most importantly, we have included a whole new section on the neurophysiological bases of learning, one of the hottest and rapidly advancing areas in all of learning psychology. While it seems likely that some of the theories about the physiology of learning presented here will be out of date by the time our book is in print—things are changing so fast—we thought it important that students know something about this important area.

Finally, we have reorganized the last third of the text. In particular, our old chapter 10, on the biology of learning, has been divided into two chapters. Chapter 10 now covers general issues in the biology of learning, the neurophysiology of learning, and human evolution, with a focus on the evolution of human intelligence. Chapter 11 focuses exclusively on sociobiology, both human and animal. Some teachers and students found the old biology chapter to be too long, and some of the material peripheral to their conception of what should be in a human learning text. We have thus placed the most traditional learning material in chapter 10, making it easier for such teachers to skip the social material in chapter 11.

We both found useful the thoughtful reviews of prepublication reviewers:

Peter Derks, College of William and Mary
William C. Gordon, University of New Mexico
Glenn E. Meyer, Lewis and Clark College

It is our earnest hope that teachers, students, and readers will find our new edition to be an improvement on the old, and will find it useful, instructive, and readable. We hope, too, that you will become as intrigued and excited by the study of human learning as we are.

Thomas H. Leahey
Richard J. Harris

PROCESSIONAL: INTRODUCTION

LEARNING IN HISTORY

How people learn is a question much older than organized psychology. Philosophers and biologists have wondered and investigated how people perceive, know, and learn ever since the time of the ancient Greeks. Their ideas shaped and continue to shape how psychologists study learning and the theories they have constructed to explain learning. Therefore, it is important to trace and understand how learning was thought about before there was psychology.

Learning and Philosophy

Like all sciences, psychology was originally part of philosophy and inherited many of its problems and proposed solutions from the parent discipline. With regard to learning, two philosophical problems are most important—the problem of how we know, and the problem of other minds.

One subdiscipline of philosophy is **epistemology,** concerned with the nature of human knowledge. The epistemologist wants to know what knowledge is, how to distinguish knowledge from opinion and falsehood, how people acquire knowledge, and how they use it. Obviously, learning is part of epistemology, and the psychology of learning has inherited from epistemology a set of orientations to knowledge and its acquisition, that is, learning.

Perhaps the oldest theory of knowledge is the **copy theory** of cognition originally proposed by the Greek philosophers Alcmaeon, Empedocles, and Democritus in the fourth and fifth centuries B.C. According to copy theory we perceive an object, and the act of perception creates a mental copy of the object in our minds. We know only the copy, because it exists in our minds and we are directly acquainted with it; we know about the object only indirectly, via the copy. The psychological plausibility of the copy theory derives first from the fact that we have mental images of objects, that is, internal copies, and we can clearly use them to think. For example, if I ask you what you ate for breakfast this morning, you would probably answer the question by summoning up an image of the breakfast table and seeing all you ate laid out before your mind's eye. In addition, we distinguish between our sensations and objects, generally feeling quite certain about our sensations, but willing to doubt if the sensations exactly correspond to an exterior object. For example, you might "see" a ladybug on a tree, although closer inspection might reveal it to be a spot of red paint. In this case, you would admit you had been wrong about the ladybug, but you would insist that you had seen a red spot, even though it wasn't an insect. In other words, we are quite sure about our sensations—that is, the images in our minds—even though we are prepared to admit that these sensations may not correspond to how things really are. Because epistemology is about knowledge, it might seem, then, that knowledge—what we are certain of—concerns the copies of objects in our heads, not objects themselves.

Unfortunately, this leaves us in a disquieting situation, one that made many philosophers search for a better epistemology. The problem created by the copy theory is the problem of **skepticism:** Is it possible to know the world at all? If we can be mistaken about something as simple as the ladybug, might we not be mistaken about *everything*? Our mental copies might never correspond to reality, so that we could not know reality. If so, knowledge would not be worth much, being only about sensations in our heads, and never about anything outside us. The copy theory, therefore, is flawed, and a better epistemology is desirable.

From the standpoint of the psychology of learning, three answers to the skeptical problem are important: realism, idealism, and pragmatism.

The skeptical problem lies in questioning the resemblance of the mental copy of the real object. The skeptic points out that the representation may not resemble the object, and that since we only know the copy, there is no way to verify if the copy is accurate. One answer to the skeptic is to reject the copy theory and propose **realism.** Realism restores knowledge of the real world by eliminating the copy. According to the realist we know objects directly, without the intervention of any mental representation. It was first proposed by the eighteenth-century Scottish philosopher Thomas Reid. Since according to Reid the realist view is the one ordinary people believe without philosophical tutoring, his school of philosophy is called the Scottish common sense school. The philosophical problem with realism has always been the problem of error. If, as the realist says, we know the world directly, how is it that we make mistakes, thinking that what we see is a ladybug when it is really a spot of paint?

Returning to the skeptical challenge, we can see another, perhaps more drastic, way of answering the skeptic, first suggested by the Greek philosopher Plato, and then developed by a number of philosophers in the eighteenth and nineteenth centuries. The skeptical problem is the possible lack of correspondence between object and representation; the realist solved the problem by eliminating the representation: The *idealist* solves the problem by eliminating the object! If ideas—representations—are all that exist, then there is no skeptical problem, because our knowledge is of ideas, not things. The audacious proposal of the idealist can be supported by serious arguments, but doing so would take us far afield into abstruse realms of philosophy.

The realist and the idealist accept the skeptical challenge and abandon the copy theory for theories of cognition that do not rely on copies. The **pragmatist** sticks with the copy theory and attacks the skeptic. The force of the skeptic's argument depends on an absolute conception of knowledge. If we assume that knowledge must be perfectly and absolutely true now and forever, the skeptic's point is disquieting: If we can be wrong about one thing—the ladybug and the spot of paint—then we can be wrong about everything. The pragmatist simply replies that being wrong about one thing does not mean that one is wrong about everything; most of the time our beliefs work out.

Hidden in this attractively simple response, however, is a drastic revision in our conception of knowledge. Because we can be wrong, the pragmatist says, we must hold all beliefs as provisional: as not absolutely *true*. What we call knowledge is just the set of beliefs we find most useful in living our lives, and this set of beliefs is open to change. Today's truths will turn out to be tomorrow's falsehoods if they no longer help us adequately lead our lives. Truth, says the pragmatist, is always relative and never absolute. In short, the pragmatist concedes that the skeptic is correct: What we think we know might turn out to be false. But the pragmatist refuses to draw the conclusion that knowledge is impossible, for pragmatists believe that knowledge is what works, and that to ask more of knowledge is foolish.

Each of these views will find a place among the learning theorists discussed in this book. The copy theory will be found in the later theory of E.C. Tolman, one of the two greatest learning theorists of the behaviorist era. It is also found in the representational theory of knowledge of contemporary cognitive psychology. Cognitive science draws a strong parallel between the workings of a computer and the workings of the human mind. Computers represent the world internally and perform computations on the representations. Thus, holds the cognitive scientist, people form representations of the world and think with them.

Realism will be found in the radical behaviorism of B. F. Skinner. Skinner denounces the copy theory of knowledge as part of his general denunciation of mentalistic theorizing in psychology. Instead, Skinner believes that the environment controls us directly, without any intervention of mental processes. If there are no representations, then there are no mental processes to operate on them, and we may safely delete reference to them from scientific psychology.

There are no outright idealists in psychology today, but idealism's influence is real nevertheless. The great contribution of idealism to epistemology was pointing out that the environment does not simply impose itself on us. The tendency of both copy theorists and realists is to think that objects make impressions on the mind the way a signet ring leaves an impression in soft wax. The idealist, however, rejects this passive view of human perception, holding that every perception is an act of interpretation. A simple example is the Necker cube.

We cannot see the Necker cube for what it is, namely a flat arrangement of lines on paper. We see it as a cube, having three dimensions. Furthermore, we can see it in two ways, because there are two equally plausible interpretations of the lines. The idealist is right in insisting that the world as we experience it depends on how our minds interpret sensory input; however, we need not follow the idealist to the extreme of denying the existence of the world altogether. A view accepting the constructive nature of perception—the idealist lesson—is incorporated in the constructivist view of perception and memory in cognitive psychology, and in Jean Piaget's genetic epistemology.

Finally, pragmatism is the working philosophy of most psychologists. The philosophy of pragmatism was propounded and developed by three of the founders of American psychology, Charles S. Peirce, William James, and John Dewey. The working psychologist may ignore the ultimate philosophical import of his theories. If the copy theory is a correct account of human cognition, then that is what the psychologist must be concerned with, no matter the consequences for absolute truth. The psychologist is, then, a natural pragmatist, concerned with how people in fact learn. At the same time, a philosopher might decide that epistemology must rest on the best psychological account of real human thinking. In modern cognitive science, the pragmatist-psychologist and some philosophers have come together to pursue *naturalized epistemology*, an account of knowledge resting upon psychological research instead of on philosophical speculation.

The problem of other minds was first raised by the philosopher Rene Descartes in the seventeenth century. Each of us is directly aware of our own consciousness, that is, one's mind. We do not have direct access to anyone else's mind. Therefore, the question arises: How do I know anyone other than myself has a mind? Obviously, we do attribute mentality to other people, but on what basis do we do so?

Descartes argued that the behavioral sign from which we may infer the existence of mind in another creature is *language*. Descartes believed that the one distinct function of the mind is thinking. Thinking produces thoughts. Language expresses thoughts. Therefore, language use implies thinking, which in turn implies a mind that thinks. It is important to separate two aspects of Descartes' argument. First, he asserts that postulation of mind in another is an inference from behavior; then he proposes a particular—and very strict—behavioral criterion for the attribution of mind, use of language.

At first glance, Descartes' worry seems like a pointless philosopher's puzzle, but in fact it bears on profoundly important issues with deep moral ramifications. Consider, for example, the question of whether or not to discontinue life support for a comatose patient. Our concern is to avoid destroying a human mind, and we look for signs that a mind is present in the patient's body. Similar considerations may arise in controversies over abortion: At what point in fetal development is a mind present that it is impermissible to destroy? (Note, by the way, that Descartes' criterion could condone even infanticide; Descartes himself believed animals feel no pain.) In cases of insanity we similarly look for signs of mind in deciding how to treat, or perhaps forcibly institutionalize, someone who may be "mindless."

The problem of other minds has thrice proved important to the psychology of learning. Descartes' criterion clearly denies that animals have minds, for they do not possess language. In the nineteenth century, acceptance of evolution undermined Descartes' radical separation of human and animal. Because humans evolved gradually from the lower animals, it began to seem implausible that animals have no minds at all, and psychologists began to work on the problem of how to attribute mind to animals. This problem directly led to the importance of learning to scientific psychology, and we will discuss it in more detail later. Animals are also involved in the second way the problem of other minds has affected psychology of learning. In 1748 another French philosopher, Julien Offroy de La Mettrie, challenged Descartes' denial that animals have minds by proposing teaching apes the language of the deaf; if they could acquire language, La Mettrie said, they would become "perfect little gentlemen," the equal of humans. La Mettrie never undertook his project, but in the 1960s, prompted by a revival of Cartesian thinking, psychologists did, and their findings have proved most controversial, as we shall see in Chapter 12. Finally, today's hi-tech computer raises the problem of other minds in yet another way. We call computers "electronic brains": Do they, *can* they, have minds? Contemporary cognitive science is built on the premise of a close similarity between human and computer intelligence, and this belief rests on the assumption that computers have minds, rightly defined.

Learning and Biology

As we shall see in more detail in Chapter 10, biology is important to the psychology of learning in two quite different ways. To begin with, learning must involve some change to the nervous system of the organism. As far back as the Middle Ages, philosopher-physicians tried to use physiological theories to bolster their epistemologies; for example, by positing "animal spirits" in the nervous system and brain that embody the internal copies of a perceived object. Thinking and memory then could be described as the movement of the spirit-copies around various specialized organs of the brain. Such theories were speculative, but not much more so than the twentieth-century search for the "engram," the neural trace of each memory. To some extent, it is only since publication of the first edition of this book that serious progress on the neuropsychology of learning has been made, and we include it here for the first time.

Another old philosophical problem introduces the second way biology is relevant to the psychology of learning. The ancient inventors of the copy theory were **empiricists,** who believed that knowledge is rooted solely in experience. Our minds receive "impressions" of objects, almost as if they are clay tablets to be written on by experience. Idealists resisted this notion by insisting on the activity of mind and by conceiving perceptions as constructions by the mind. Another response to empiricism often, but not necessarily, linked to idealism is **nativism.** The nativist, beginning with Plato, believes that at least some knowledge (Plato believed *all*) is innate; that is, present in some form at birth. Nativists do not believe babies possess knowledge in the full sense, only that some ideas are present in an undeveloped form and emerge from native endowment as human development unfolds.

For a long time this nature/nurture problem was only marginally scientific. Knowledge of human genetics was nonexistent, and humans were seen as distinct from the rest of the animal world. However, in the nineteenth century, Gregor Mendel invented modern genetics, and Charles Darwin showed that human beings had evolved from simpler animals. Modern biology thus revived the nature/nurture question by implying that perhaps human beings have a particular innate nature shaped by natural selection and inherited through our genes. Psychology of learning is deeply touched by the new nature/nurture debate. For—it seems—what is innate cannot be learned, and what is learned cannot be innate. Thus, to the extent that there is a human nature, learning is limited in scope and influence, while to the extent that there is no human nature, people can be shaped by the environment into anything the environment wishes. Not surprisingly, most psychologists of learning tend to be empiricists, elevating learning into the supreme creator of human behavior. However, in the last decade or so new nativists have come along, insisting that because human beings have evolved, their behavior is created by genes and environment acting together.

Learning and Early Psychology

The European founders of psychology, such as Wilhelm Wundt, who established the first recognized laboratory of psychology anywhere, conceived of psychology as the science concerned with conscious experience. Not surprisingly, then, early psychology focused on the areas of sensation, attention, and perception. Although learning and memory were not ignored, they were not psychology's central concern. One exception to this was the research on human memory of Hermann Ebbinghaus, who founded one important means of studying human learning, *verbal learning.*

In 1879 Ebbinghaus began to use himself as the only subject in the first experimental investigations of learning and memory. Although he does not say so explicitly, it is clear that Ebbinghaus' research program was built on **associationism.** By the nineteenth century, most philosophical psychologists thought of the mind as a sort of tinkertoy arrangement. Your mind is full of ideas: "Horse," "boy," "telephone," "Ebbinghaus," and so on. Associationists believe that these ideas are connected to one another by a kind of mental thread—Ebbinghaus' term—that is, an *association.*

You may have heard of *free-association tests*: "Say the first word that comes to your mind when I say _____." Likely free associates would be boy–girl, horse–rider, telephone–call, Ebbinghaus–memory. According to the associationists, when you learn something you learn an idea (for example, the idea of "associationism") and tie it, or associate it, to other ideas you already have. Thus, you learn to associate, for a multiple-choice test perhaps, "associationism" with "Ebbinghaus" and "mental thread." Pushing this theory as far as it can go, associationists argue that mind and behavior are just collections of ideas or responses linked by association, and that the basic problem of the psychology of learning is finding out how people learn to associate ideas.

Ebbinghaus was the first person to use experiments to find out how ideas and associations are learned. His most important achievement was thinking of an experimental procedure to substitute for philosophical speculation. Ebbinghaus saw that in starting out in a new field, as memory then was, he would have to simplify the problem to be solved. Most of our learning is both complex and haphazard. You sit down in your chemistry class and listen to the lecture. The material you must learn is complicated; you do not have time to ask yourself, "How am I learning this?" So a simple, controllable bit of learning is needed for scientific study.

How and what you learn will also be affected by irrelevant influences such as time of day, interest in chemistry, and the attractive student in the next row. To avoid such complications, Ebbinghaus simplifed the material to be learned and introduced experimental control.

To simplify the material, Ebbinghaus invented the **nonsense syllable,** constructed by placing a vowel between two consonants: TOB, SAB, GEN, and so on. They were easy to make up and produced a large amount of learnable material. Being meaningless, they simplifed the process of learning to sheer memorization, ruling out such factors as motivation, interest, and relevance to what has already been learned. Ebbinghaus believed they would reveal the processes of learning, retention, and forgetting, unclouded by any other mental processes. They also resemble the associationists' **simple ideas,** the basic copies in the mind.

To impose experimental control, Ebbinghaus would compose lists of syllables to be presented to himself at a constant rate of speed, and at consistent times of the day. The whole procedure was easily quantifiable: Ebbinghaus could measure how long it took him to learn or relearn lists of syllables as he changed independent variables. He hoped to discover scientific laws that govern the process of learning and, thus, to transform at least part of psychology from a branch of philosophy into a branch of experimental science.

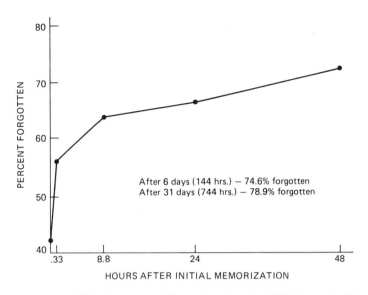

After 6 days (144 hrs.) — 74.6% forgotten
After 31 days (744 hrs.) — 78.9% forgotten

HOURS AFTER INITIAL MEMORIZATION

FIGURE 1-1   Ebbinghaus curve of forgetting. (Based on Ebbinghaus, *On Memory*, 1885)

One of the most obvious facts about memory is that the longer ago we learned something, the harder it is to remember. On the basis of personal experience we can say no more than that—hardly a scientific statement. But Ebbinghaus' experimental approach made it possible to frame the question more precisely and receive a quantitative answer. In a series of experiments, Ebbinghaus learned by heart eight lists of 13 nonsense syllables each; later, after differing amounts of time (20 minutes, 1 hour, 8.8 hours, 1 day, 2 days, 6 days, or 31 days), he learned them by heart again. Consequently, Ebbinghaus could ask precisely, in terms of difficulty of relearning: How much of a list of nonsense syllables is forgotten at a given time?

Figure 1–1 illustrates the results of Ebbinghaus' experiments; it shows the percent of material forgotten as a function of hours after initial learning. Most forgetting takes place quickly. Only an hour after learning, more than 55 percent of the nonsense syllables have been forgotten, while the additional loss past 8.8 hours is only 14 percent after 31 days. Common sense told us only that we forget over time. Ebbinghaus showed exactly how forgetting takes place, rapidly at first and then more slowly; moreover, he managed to quantify the rate of forgetting.

Ebbinghaus' invention of the nonsense syllable learning experiment also enabled him to investigate precisely other common sense hypotheses. He asked, What is the effect of amount of material on learning? He quanitified amount as nonsense syllable list-length, and obtained quantitative results showing (not surprisingly) that the longer the list the longer it takes to learn. He compared learning a list of nonsense syllables to learning a stanza of poetry from Byron's *Don Juan*, and found that learning the poem was easier, notwithstanding the fact that the poem contained many more syllables than the lists. This demonstrates that the more organized material is, the easier it is to learn. Nonsense syllables are meaningless and the list has no structure; poetry is made of meaningful words put together with controlled structure of grammar, meter, and rhyme. This discovery of Ebbinghaus', and his finding that the number of syllables he could hold in his mind at one time was seven, are important to memory researchers today. Ebbinghaus also showed that the more a list is repeated, the better it is remembered after one day.

Ebbinghaus could also use his experimental method to scientifically answer questions raised by philosophical associationists. So, for example, philosophers had argued over whether, if three ideas a, b, and c are presented in a series one at a time, will a and c be associated, or if only a and b and b and c will be associated. Ebbinghaus experimented on this heretofore speculative question. He learned lists, scrambled them in various ways, and then relearned them. He found relearning was always easier despite the scrambling. He concluded from this that syllables do get associated not only with their immediate successors but also with their remoter fellow list members, although the farther apart two syllables are, the weaker the association is. His conclusion follows, because if only adjacent pais were associated, then learning a, b, c, d, e, and f will not make it easier a day later to learn a, c, e, d, b, f, since none of the new pairs is the same.

Despite Ebbinghaus' study of memory, learning did not become a central problem for psychology until evolution began to be integrated into psychology in Great Britain and the United States. Evolution revived the problem of other minds and made it central to psychology. Descartes, by making language the mark of mind, had drawn a sharp line between humans and animals; Descartes' line coincided neatly with the old religious-creationist view that men and women have souls but animals do not. Evolution, however, erased Descartes' line, and it made drawing a new line between mind and mechanism more difficult than ever before.

Descartes had said that animals were mere machines, physiological devices without thought or feeling. Humans were machines inhabited by conscious souls, revealing thought through language. But evolution taught that humans were evolved from simpler animals, implying either that people were machines or that animals possessed minds. In the nineteenth century, and for several decades of the twentieth, it seemed easier to claim that animals had minds. For people of the nineteenth century, the prototypical machines were the watch and the steam engine. What is characteristic about the behavior of such machines is their blindness to the environment. A watch just runs on until it runs down, relentlessly and unchangingly telling the time, keeping the seconds, minutes, and hours. Left unattended by an engineer, a steam engine could overheat and blow up. It is apt to call a watch or a steam engine a "mindless machine." People, by contrast, adjusted their behavior to the environment, responding to changes in circumstances with changes in behavior. Moreover, inspection of the animal world suggested that many animals adjusted their behavior to the environment, although perhaps not as well as humans.

Thus, the early comparative psychologists of the nineteenth century set out in search of an animal mind, confidence that animals were not mere machines. Generally, they agreed that the mark of the mind was not language, as Descartes had maintained, but *learning*, the ability of creatures to change their behavior to adapt to the environment. Having erased Descartes' old line between mind and machine, evolution suggested the new one of learning. Just as species adapt physically to the environment by evolving over generations, so organisms adapt psychologically to the environment by learning over time. Learning became the central problem of psychology: Learning was the outward sign of mind—and psychology is the study of the mind—and learning was an important biological process, being no less than the means by which individuals (the subjects of psychological research) adapted to their environments.

However, the continuity of humans and animal proved to be a two-edged sword. The early comparative psychologists happily inferred mind from behavior, but they did not actually *see* mind. As their researches progressed, moreover, they found signs of adaptive behavior in some very simple organisms. Cockroaches, after all, can locate food and then return to it night after night. Now while a watch can't match this simple feat, we might be hard-pressed to justify attributing mentality to a cockroach, and if we refuse to attribute mentality to the cockroach who is capable of learning, what becomes of learning as the mark of mind? The early comparative psychologists thus wrestled with the problem of other minds, caught— to change metaphor—on the slippery slope of phylogenetic continuity. Continuity could be used to argue that both humans and animals have minds, with the animal mind a simpler version of the human. On the other hand, continuity might be used to argue that humans and animals are both machines, with the human machine a more complex version of the animal. In the end, as we shall see later in the text, the latter view won out, as psychologists became convinced that machines could learn.

One might have expected that just as evolution revivified and reshaped the problem of other minds, it would have revived and reshaped the nature/nurture question. However, it did not, because of the overriding influence of associationism.

The man who first applied evolution to psychology was Herbert Spencer in his book *Principles of Psychology*, written five years *before* Darwin published his *Origin of Species* in 1859. Spencer was a follower of the French evolutionary theorist J.B. Lamarck, who, among other things, believed that physical characteristics acquired by parents during their own lifetime could be passed on to their offspring. To Lamarck, Spencer added associationism. Like other associationists, Spencer believed that the mind registered sensations and that learning consisted in building up associations between them. Associationism implied an extremely strong form of phylogenetic continuity: Human minds were not merely continuous with animal minds; they were virtually identical to animal minds. According to associationism, the sole difference between human and animal minds lay in the number of associations they can make; otherwise they are the same. Associationism greatly simplified the nature/nurture issue. The only possible thing that might be innate were certain associations, or reflexes, possessed at birth and perhaps differing between species. Spencer, following Lamarck, believed that some associations highly learned in one generation might become heritable in subsequent generations.

Spencer's views were important to the first generations of psychologists of learning, the *behaviorists*. Spencer's paradigm makes learning the master process in all psychology. Everything that a person becomes is created by associative learning, either in one's own lifetime of learning or in one's ancestors' lifetimes of learning. Species differences are trivial and may be ignored, because learning is the same in all species—association-formation— and what innate properties any species possesses can be no more than a few prelearned associations. Finally, these conclusions suggest an attractive research strategy. Because learning is the same in all species, including human beings, and differences between species are unimportant, then we can discover the principles of learning by studying one convenient animal— the rat, as things turned out—knowing that the principles would be the same throughout the animal kingdom. The difficulties of experimentally studying learning in humans could be bypassed. Thus Spencer at once laid the foundation for behaviorism and buried the nature/nurture problem.

BASIC ISSUES

Because learning is such a large and complex field, with many subfields and sub-subfields, we have chosen to organize our text around four basic issues in the psychology of learning. Each part of this text is devoted to one issue and the research and theory flowing from its consideration. Now, we will very briefly present each issue, the first three of which arise naturally from the history of learning just presented.

Learning and Behavior

As comparative psychologists wrestled with the problem of animal mind in the late nineteenth and early twentieth century, some of them concluded that the question was a waste of time. Why, they began to say, argue about something no one can see? We can see behavior, and we can see the environment, and we can see that behavior adjusts itself to the environment. The study of learning might then be the study of *how* behavior adjusts itself to the environment, without dragging in attributions of mind to animals. More radically, one might apply the same strategy to human learning, too, linking behavior to environment without mediation by mind. The view that psychology can be done entirely in terms of environment and behavior—of stimulus and response—is **behaviorism.** Although it is an historical oversimplification, for our purposes there are three sorts of behaviorists—methodological behaviorists, radical behaviorists, and mediational behaviorists.

Methodological behaviorists acknowledge that consciousness exists but believe that because it is private—locked up in each person's head—it cannot be studied by science, and must be left to poets and philosophers. Their answer to the problem of other minds is to place it outside science and treat animals and people on an equal footing, as objects to be studied from outside. The term *methodological behaviorism* describes their viewpoint, because they say that the scientific *method* demands that we study only *behavior*. While they exclude reference to consciousness from psychological science, methodological behaviorists permit reference to unseen theoretical entities, provided they are defined in terms of behavior. The formal behaviorists of Chapter 3 are within this tradition, and we will see that, although they refused to talk about consciousness, they constructed elaborate theories of learning that referred to hidden mechanism behind behavior change.

A diametrically opposite school of behaviorism is *radical* behaviorism. Radical behaviorists recognize that private conscious events may cause behavior: When you have a headache (private conscious experience), you take a pain reliever (behavior). The problem of other minds cannot be dodged by science, according to radical behaviorists, and consciousness must be made part of the psychology of learning. On the other hand, radical behaviorists reject reference to unseen machinery used to explain learning. If the machinery cannot, in principle, be seen by anyone, then it does not exist and is mythical; science does not deal in myths, and so should not deal with unseen processes lying behind behavior. Note that private experiences are observed, albeit by a tiny audience of one. The radical behaviorist wants to keep myth out of science, not consciousness. Conversely, if theoretical terms referring to hidden machinery are defined solely in terms of behavior, then we don't need them because we can just talk about the behaviors, not their made-up labels. In any event, the radical behaviorist says that we should not go beyond what we can observe—including private consciousness—in our science of learning.

Mediational behaviorism developed out of methodological behaviorism's attempts to study human learning. As we will see, studies of human learning showed that in some respects humans learned rather differently from animals, and mediational behaviorists tried to capture the difference with the concept of *mediation*. Animals learned, they held, in a very simple way, associating responses (R) directly to stimuli (S), that is S → R. People, however, learned by responding covertly to the environment, and controlling their overt responses with symbolic stimuli: S → (r→s) → R. The little r→ s connection is called a *mediator* because it occurs covertly between and links an environmental stimulus with an overt motor response. This move allowed behaviorists to keep their familiar S→R formula from animal learning yet talk about human cognitive processes such as memory and thinking. It remained a species of methodological behaviorism, however, because the mediational links were generally not conscious, but were theoretical entities read into the organism by theoreticians. Mediational behaviorism formed an historical bridge to cognitive science, which brings us to our second issue.

Learning and Cognition

A watch is a mindless machine. But is a computer a mindless machine? Based on the Spencerian paradigm of evolution and phylogenetic continuity, the behaviorists made animals—usually rats—their model for human behavior. Contemporary cognitive science rests on a different model not available to the older behaviorists, namely the computer. Clearly, computers do adjust themselves to their environment. The daughter of one of the authors of this text has a toy called a Petster, a mechanical cat with a microchip for a brain, and unlike a watch it responds differentially to a series of clapped command stimuli. Computers possess well-specified internal processes by which they take in, store, and work on information, and by which they make decisions. The cognitive scientist believes that the human mind is rather like a computer, accepting input through perception, storing it in memory, processing it in thought, and acting on it in making decisions. They believe that computers do possess—or at least, can possess—minds like ours.

Cognitive scientists are a new class of methodological mediational behaviorsts. Like the methodological behaviorist they neglect consciousness and propose unconscious machinery behind thought and behavior. Like the mediational behaviorist, they believe that symbolic processes mediate between stimulus and response, although their formula is not S→ (r→s) → R but Input→ (information processing)→ R. The mediational behaviorist believed that internal processes were miniature S-R connections because S-R language was the only scientifically rigorous language available in psychology. The cognitive scientist, on the other hand, has available the rigorous processing language of the computer, and is therefore not constrained by the S-R paradigm. On the analogy of human and computer, cognitive science has built a large and flourishing enterprise, the dominant form of learning theory today.

Cognitive scientists are like behaviorists in another respect: They neglect biology.

Learning and Biology

Behaviorists neglected both of the ways biology relates to learning. They believed that the laws of learning are derived from the facts of behavior, so that the internal story of what physiology underlay learning was unimportant. They knew, of course, that there is such a story, but regarded behavior study and the discovery of behavior principles as worthy autonomous ends in themselves. Having inherited Spencer's associative evolutionism, they believed that the nature/nurture debate had been decisively resolved in favor of nurture. Cognitive scientists share the same biases. Because the computations of thought may be carried out by different computers with different electronic architecture, they believe that likewise the computations of thought may be carried out by brain "wetware" as well as computer hardware. The essence of thought for cognitive science lies in the computations themselves, not the device that carries them out. Again, they realize there is a neurophysiological story behind every thought, but they regard it as psychologically unimportant. With regard to the nature/nurture question, the important fact is that computers don't evolve: They are created. Hence, cognitive scientists, caught up in the excitement of breaking the human computer code, have simply ignored evolution and its possible relevance to learning.

However, in recent years the concerns of biology have made themselves felt again. Brain science is perhaps the most important science of its time, the way physics was in the 1930s and 1940s. Enormous strides have been made in recent years in understanding how the brain works, and scientists studying the brain—working as it were up from brain to behavior—have begun to propose their own ideas about how learning and memory operate. Some neuroscientists now believe that the brain does not compute the way a computer does, suggesting that perhaps the parallel between brain and computer, and between computer mind and human mind, has been overdrawn.

More urgent and visible have been the claims of evolutionary biologists. They believe that the psychology of each species is importantly unique, implying that the search for general principles of learning and cognition may be misguided. They have proposed exciting and controversial theories of behavior, especially social behavior, that challenge the long dominance of psychology by the nurturist Spencerian paradigm. The new evolutionary biologists of behavior see behavior from the standpoint of Darwinian evolutionary theory, and they try to show how the dispositions and patterns of learning of evolved species have been shaped by evolutionary history and the competition to reproduce. Long dormant, the nature/nurture debate has heated up again.

Learning and Development

It seems only a short way from not having learned a list of nonsense syllables to having learned them. It seems a long way from being two years old to being 20 years old. In the latter case, part of the difference is physical maturation: The 20-year-old is physically very different from the two-year-old. But what about the psychological distance? Some psychologists, including behaviorists and cognitive scientists, believe that the enormous psychological difference between child and adult is solely the result of learning. The adult knows much more than the child, has learned much more. In this view, the child is like a lump of clay slowly shaped by the environment into adult form. Or, to use the cognitive metaphor, the baby is a factory-fresh computer to be slowly programmed by its parents and teachers. Rejecting this view, a smaller number of psychologists believe that in addition to learning and maturation, children possess an inner drive to develop into the adult. For these psychologists, the child is not a lump of clay or a computer passively waiting to be shaped and programmed, but is an active learner, spontaneously moving forward from simple forms of childish learning and cognition to the sophisticated modes of the adult.

This second camp of psychologists are *developmentalists*, and include such well-known theorists as Sigmund Freud, Erik Erikson, Jean Piaget, and Lawrence Kohlberg. Although they differ on the details of development, each of them asserts that long-term human change cannot be explained by maturation and learning alone. Each of them postulates at least one autonomous, inner-directed, developmental process that guides learning at each stage of development.

These are the issues around which we have organized the book. In chapters 2–4 we will study the older tradition in learning, the animal-based models of the behaviorists. In chapters 5–9 we will examine the more recent computer-inspired models of cognitive science. In chapters 10 and 11 we will see what contribution biologists have to make to the study of learning. And in chapters 12 and 13 we will inquire into whether or not development is separate from learning. Throughout, we will keep our focus on human learning and the human condition.

SUGGESTED READING

For more information on the place of learning in the history of psychology, see Thomas H. Leahey, *A history of psychology: Main currents in psychological thought*, 2nd ed. (Englewood Cliffs, N.J.: Prentice-Hall, 1987).

2

FUNDAMENTALS
OF CONDITIONING

INTRODUCTION

Learning and Conditioning: Behavioral Psychology

Regardless of their differences, behaviorists built their theories of learning primarily on studies of animal behavior, and then moved on to study or theorize about human conditioning. Believing that there are few important differences in how different species learn, behaviorists have done with animals what cannot be ethically done with humans—studied them under totally controlled conditions. From their animal work they have extrapolated to the human case, sometimes doing actual conditioning studies with human subjects, sometimes just speculating about human behavior.

Kinds of Conditioning

We intuitively distinguish involuntary reflexes and voluntary acts. A reflex is an immediate response to some stimulus over which we have little if any control. We possess many reflexes, many of which we never even think about: Our pupils enlarge in the dark, get smaller in sunlight; if someone brushes a finger against our bare feet, our toes contract (in babies they spread out); if wind suddenly blows in our face, we blink. Emotional responses often are reflexive: In grade school, when the local bully hit us we felt afraid; going to the dentist makes us feel queasy; erotic stimuli arouse us. While we may stand up to the bully, see the dentist, and not attend pornographic films, our basic emotional reactions usually remain, showing them to be deeply rooted reflexes.

Over against reflexes we set voluntary behavior: We choose to fight (or run away from) the bully; we choose to see (or avoid seeing) the dentist; we choose to attend (or not attend) pornographic films. To common sense, these two kinds of behavior are quite different. Reflexes have to do with extremely simple muscle-responses and gut feelings, while voluntary behavior concerns how we choose to live our lives. We make different kinds of moral and legal judgments about reflexes and voluntary acts. We do not blame soldiers for being afraid of battle, but we punish them severely for running away. We may exonerate the criminal whom we judge insane—He "had to do it." He "couldn't help himself!"

From the beginning, the psychology of learning has usually maintained the same distinction, speaking of two types of conditioning. Historically, the two forms of learning were brought into the laboratory at the close of the nineteenth century by two widely separated scientists. But the basic strategy behind each research program was the same: Isolate a simple form of learning that is subject to experimental control and map out its parameters and limits in animal subjects.

In each case the hope was that by breaking down complex learned behaviors into simpler parts—something more easily achieved with animals than with humans—the elementary processes of learning would be revealed. After the parts were understood, psychologists could put the pieces back together, so to speak, and explain complex, perhaps uniquely, human behavior as an assemblage of simpler parts with animal foundations.

PAVLOVIAN CONDITIONING

Pavlov's Research Program

The scientific study of reflexes began in Russia with a serendipitous discovery by Ivan Petrovich Pavlov (1849–1936). Pavlov was a brilliant physiologist, whose study of the digestive system won him a Nobel Prize in 1904. In the course of that work, part of which involved surgically bringing the opening of the salivary gland to the outside of a dog's skin and watching the secretion of saliva when food was presented, Pavlov noticed a curious thing. After being used as a subject for some time, a dog would not only salivate when food was presented, but would also salivate to previously neutral stimuli—the sight of the experimenter who fed it, for example. Pavlov saw that not only are there innate reflexes (put food in a dog's mouth and it salivates) but there are also learned reflexes (the dog salivates at the sight of food or at the sight of the experimenter). The learned reflexes Pavlov originally called **psychical** (as opposed to biological) reflexes, and he soon came to focus his research on them, abandoning the term "psychical" and bringing both unlearned and learned reflexes into the province of physiology.

Pavlov's basic conceptions came from the founder of Russian physiology. I.M. Sechenov (1829–1905), mixed with associationism. Sechenov (1863) espoused an extreme form of the sensory-motor conception of the nervous system, believing that all behavior is reflex behavior caused by some external stimulus. The sensory-motor view of the brain meshes conveniently with associationism, because learning can be thought of as acquiring new reflexes by association of stimulus and response.

Pavlov's achievement was harnessing associationism and the reflex theory to a particular experimental setting, as Ebbinghaus also did. Pavlov saw that his "psychical secretions" were the outcome of associative learning; the food, which already elicited salivation became associated with the experimenter, who then elicited salivation. As an experimental physiologist, Pavlov knew how to put careful controls on his happenstance discovery, creating a rigorous experimental paradigm. Pavlov went to great lengths to control the experimental conditions, building a special laboratory which, to ensure exclusion of uncontrolled stimuli, had thick glass windows, specially separated rooms, a foundation embedded in sand, and a straw-filled moat! The dogs were kept in a harness (see Fig. 2–1), and from another room the experimenter could control stimulus presentations and count the drops of saliva produced in the dog's mouth. When Pavlov's experimental setup allowed complete control of the animal's environment and produced an objective quantitative measure of learning, his brilliant research program could begin.

Before considering these experiments, however, we must develop some Pavlovian terminology. A stimulus that biologically elicits a reflex (food placed in the mouth, a puff of air at the eye) does so reliably and unconditionally, and so is called an **unconditional stimulus,** abbreviated

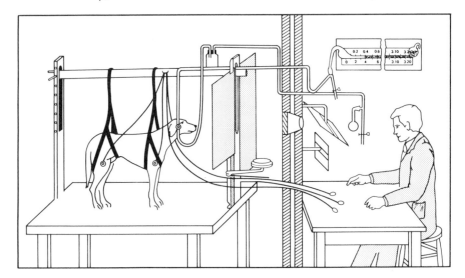

FIGURE 2-1   Diagram illustrating experimentation on the dog. (From Pavlov, 1928, p. 271)

US. The biologically elicited reflex is, therefore, an **unconditional response,** or UR. A stimulus that through pairing with a US comes to elicit a response usually almost identical with the UR is called a **conditional*** **stimulus,** for its ability to elicit the UR is *conditional* on pairing with the US and other conditions elucidated by Pavlov; it is abbreviated CS. The reflex elicited by a CS is a **conditional response,** or CR. Finally, the US is often called a **reinforcer,** since its pairing with the CS strengthens (reinforces) the power of the CS to elicit the CR.

Basic Phenomena of Pavlovian Conditioning

Relations between CS and US.   One of the primary laws of association is **contiguity,** which says that two ideas will get associated if they occur in the mind at the same time. Translated into Pavlov's hypothetical brain-theory, it says that stimuli set up centers of activity in the cerebrum, and that centers regularly activated together will become linked, so that when one center is activated, the other will be, too. Given Pavlov's experimental paradigm, the law of contiguity may be readily investigated by controlling when we present CS and US in relation to each other. Pavlov employed two US's—food, which elicited salivation as part of digestion, and mild acid, which elicited salivation as a defensive reflex. He used many CS's—the clicking of a metronome, musical tones, odors, the sound of bubbling water, though he did not use the famous bell. We will here assume the US is food (appetitive conditioning) and the CS is a musical note, or tone.

From the law of contiguity we might expect exact *simultaneous* presentation of US and CS to be most effective. Oddly, such pairings produced no conditioning, as also happens when the US is presented, however briefly, before the CS begins (*backward conditioning*). Instead, the CS must begin slightly *before* the US and overlap with it. If the CS begins and ends before the US, it is called *trace conditioning*, which is extremely difficult to establish. The fact that CS and US must overlap to create a CR supports the law of contiguity, but the finding that the onset of the CS must precede the US suggests that CS's become effective only if they act as signals to the organism (Pavlov, 1927).

One other kind of CS-US arrangement was investigated by Pavlov. Suppose the CS starts well before the US is presented, perhaps 30 seconds before, and overlaps US onset. This is called *delay conditioning*; it is like the standard procedure except that the CS begins far before the US. In this case a CR gets established, but it changes as CS-US pairings proceed. At first, the dog begins to salivate as soon as the CS begins, but as trials continue, the salivation does not begin until a little before the US is scheduled to arrive. This finding suggested to Pavlov (1927) that time itself

---

*Although time has sanctioned the mistranslation of the Russian word *ooslovny* as condition*ed*, the proper translation should always have been condition*al*, which expresses Pavlov's idea much more clearly. In any case, US and CS have become the regular tokens for unconditioned and conditioned stimuli.

could act as a CS. The tone alone no longer was the CS eliciting the salivation CR, but it was the *compound stimulus* of tone *plus* a certain passage of time.

Other compound stimuli were investigated by Pavlov. He found one could condition two or more CS's at the same time, for example, pairing a light and a tone with food. An old law of association was *vividness*: A given idea will get mostly associated with concurrent vivid ideas, rather than with weak ones. Pavlov's work bore this out. If the two CS's were about equal in intensity, and if they were presented alone, after conditioning, each would elicit the CR. But if one were stronger than the other, a bright light and a dim tone, for instance, only the more vivid stimulus became a CS. This phenomenon, when one CS of a compound is much more powerful than the others, is called *overshadowing*.

Excitation and inhibition. The conditioning of a distinct positive response, such as salivation, Pavlov (1927) called conditioning of **excitation.** The US naturally excites the brain center controlling the UR, and, after several pairings, so does the CS. Pavlov also believed that the action of CR's could be **inhibited** as well as excited.

If we return to delay conditioning we see inhibition in action. After many CS-US pairings, the CR occurred only near the end of the CS interval, near the anticipated time of the US. Why then did the earlier CR's to the start of the CS disappear? Was the first part of the tone simply disconnected, disassociated from the CR? Pavlov thought not. He believed that the early part of the tone actively *inhibited* the CR from taking place. As evidence, Pavlov pointed to *disinhibition*: If, during the early stages of the CS, before any CR would occur, a wholly new stimulus is introduced, such as a light flash, the CR would occur. Now if the CR had simply been disconnected from the early CS, the light would not cause salivation, any more than it would outside the laboratory. But the unexpected appearance of salivation when the light flashed during the CS indicated to Pavlov that the light interfered with the cortical process, specifically, inhibition, thus releasing the suppressed CR to the tone.

Pavlov (1927) distinguished several kinds of inhibition, the most important of which is *extinction*. What happens if we present an established CS alone, without further reinforcement? The CR occurs for a while, slowly weakens, and finally falls to zero: No saliva appears when the tone is sounded. It seems plausible to say here that the CS has been disassociated from the CR, even that the CS is no longer a CS but a neutral stimulus, and there is no CR—the reflex has literally extinguished.

But further investigation reveals that the CS-CR association is still present, only inhibited by the extinction procedure. In the first place, if we simply put the animal aside for some time, even as little as 20 minutes, and present the CS again, salivation appears. The conditional reflex has spontaneously recovered. This indicates that the reflex was not unlearned by extinction, but was actively inhibited; it also indicates that inhibition is a temporary state, abating with time. Another kind of evidence also supports Pavlov's argument. Suppose we continue extinction well beyond the point at which zero salivation occurs, presenting the CS over and over. If extinction were simply unlearning the conditional reflex, additional unreinforced pairings would have no effect: Once a CS has become a neutral stimulus, it makes no sense to say it has become "more neutral" still. Instead, Pavlov found that the longer extinction continued past zero, the longer it took for the CR to spontaneously recover, indicating that additional reinforced pairings deepened and so prolonged the inhibition of the CR.

Higher order conditioning.   What happens when we take an established CS (CS_1) and pair it with a new, neutral stimulus? Will the new stimulus become a CS eliciting a CR of salivation? Pavlov found that in the right conditions it could, and called it *secondary conditional reflex*; the building of a new CS on old CS's is called **higher order conditioning.** If CS_2 is presented before, and not overlapping with CS_1, then CS_2 will come to elicit a CR. On the other hand, if CS_1 and CS_2 overlap, *conditional inhibition* occurs. The dog will salivate to CS_1 alone, but will not salivate to CS_1 and CS_2. CS_1 has been reinforced, and so a CR remains until extinction occurs, but the compound stimulus $CS_1 + CS_2$ has never been reinforced, and so the CS_1-CR reflex is inhibited by the presence of CS_2.

How far can higher order conditioning be pushed? Can we build CS_3 on CS_2 and CS_4 on CS_3? Pavlov found that in alimentary conditioning he could go no further than secondary conditioning, and with defensive conditioning he could go no further than third-order conditioning. Pavlov's finding has not been overturned.

Generalization and discrimination.   Another law of association is *similarity*: Similar ideas are easily associated. Pavlov found that CR's occur not just to the trained CS, but to similar stimuli, too. Suppose we have trained a dog to salivate to a tone of 1000 cycles per second, and then present tones near or far from 1000 cycles, either above or below. We find that the CR occurs to the related tones, and that the closer the new tone is to the original CS, the greater the CR; the farther away, the less the CR. The extension of a CR to stimuli similar to the CS is called **generalization,** and the gradual weakening of the CR as the test stimuli increasingly differ from the CS is called the *generalization gradient.* Pavlov experimented with many different kinds of CS's and replicated the same finding over many stimulus dimensions.

On the other hand, we can set excitation and inhibition against one another to produce **stimulus discrimination.** Suppose we condition salivation to a CS (CS +) of a luminous circle presented on a screen before the dog's eyes (Pavlov, 1927). If we then present ellipses varying from near-circular to extremely elliptical, we find a generalization gradient. However, right after presenting the CS, we repeatedly present an extreme ellipse alone and never reinforce it. Inhibition will build up to the ellipse (CS−). We have created stimulus discrimination. The animal responds to CS+, and does not respond to CS−.

Knowing about generalization, we can now ask the following question.

Suppose we continue the discrimination procedure while making successive CS−'s more and more circular? The generalization gradients of excitation and inhibition will begin to clash: CS−, being like a circle, will to some degree elicit salivation, while as an ellipse it will elicit inhibition; CS+, being similar to an ellipse, will to some degree elicit inhibition, while as a circle it will elicit salivation. As CS− increasingly resembles CS+, the antagonistic tendencies will agonizingly clash. Pushed far enough, Pavlov's dog "presented all the symptoms of acute neurosis." It squealed, it wiggled, it tore at the apparatus and barked violently. All conditioning vanished and had to be started over (Pavlov, 1927, p. 291). These results indicated to Pavlov that psychopathology is learned by conditioning and should be "undoable" by new conditioning.

While our brief survey has not exhausted all of Pavlov's research, it has presented the fundamental procedures, findings, and terminology of Pavlovian conditioning, many of which also apply to instrumental conditioning. We have also seen how a firm conception of the theoretical problems in an area, given to Pavlov by associationism and the reflex conception of the brain, plus a well-defined and controllable exemplar of research, discovered in Pavlov's "psychical reflexes," led to the beautiful development of a research program.

Pavlovian Conditioning of Humans

Behaviorists eagerly adopted Pavlov's objective method—here was sound experimental procedure yielding quantitative results with no nonsense about consciousness and introspection. But the behaviorists' interests were altogether different from Pavlov's. They were interested in finding regularity in behavior, and Pavlov's method let them do that. But they did not care at all about supposed brain-functions. They were *behavior-theorists*, not physiologists, questing after knowledge of adaptive behavior, not after the inferred secrets of brain function. They therefore took Pavlovian conditioning as a fact, and Pavlov's technique as a proven method, and went on from there, for which Pavlov himself (Pavlov, 1941) reproved them.

The behaviorists, even when they experimented on animals, really aimed at explaining human behavior. It is no surprise, therefore, that it was American psychologists, not Pavlov, who applied his method to human beings. The most famous application of Pavlov's method to a human being was carried out by the founder of behaviorism himself, John B. Watson (1878–1958), with Rosalie Rayner, his lover who was soon to be his second wife (Watson & Rayner, 1920). Watson wanted to unravel human emotional life, and used classical conditioning to do so.

Watson (1930) believed that all human behavior was reflexive, and his studies with Rayner were designed to support his thesis. Watson and Rayner stated that in newborns there are a few emotional UR's (fear, rage, and love) elicited by a few US's (noise, frustration, patting, and rocking). The complex emotional patterns of the adult or older child, such as fearing the I.R.S., raging at the Ayatollah, loving one's spouse, had to be learned, specifically through Pavlovian conditioning—they were CR's and CS's. Emotional CR's Watson and Rayner called *CER*'s, **conditioned emotional reactions.**

To demonstrate this, Watson and Rayner secured a nine-month-old baby, "Albert B.," as a subject, and investigated the CER of fear. First, they determined for a wide range of stimuli that Albert was not afraid of them, that is, that they elicited no fear UR or CER. Then they found a reliable elicitor (US) of fear, striking a hammer on a steel bar. Albert would check his breathing, start, and finally cry.

At 11 months, Albert was presented with a tame white rat he was known to approach. This time, when he touched the rat, the US was applied—the bar was struck. After a total of seven pairings (spaced over a week), the rat was presented alone and proved to be a CS: "The instant the rat was shown the baby began to cry. Almost instantly he turned sharply to the left, fell over on the left side, raised himself on all fours and began to crawl away . . . rapidly . . ." (Watson & Rayner, 1920, p. 5, italics deleted). A CER had been established.

Five days later, Albert's CER was tested for generalization. Albert still showed fear to the rat, considerable fear to a rabbit and a fur coat, less to a dog, Watson's hair, a Santa Claus mask, and cotton balls, and none at all to his blocks. So generalization of the CER was shown. Watson did, however, have to keep "freshening up" the CR with new reinforcement. Even without freshening, the CER lasted at least a month, when Albert was removed from the hospital where his mother worked, and the tests ended.

Contrary to popular belief (B. Harris, 1979), Watson and Rayner never undid their conditioning. It is to be hoped that the CER weakened completely. Watson and Rayner had intended to "cure" Albert, however, and they list three of the later important techniques of behavior modification they would have used: implosion (extinction), counter-conditioning (pair the CS with a pleasant US), and modeling.

Watson and Rayner demonstrated Pavlovian conditioning in a young human being—although doubts about the validity of their results have recently been expressed (Samelson, 1980). Many other studies on children and adults also were carried out, but the Watson—Rayner study exemplifies the others, and is one of the most widely cited works in all of psychology.

Early Theory of Pavlovian Conditioning

Pavlov explained conditioning in terms of his speculative theory of brain function, in which CS's and US's set up centers of activity in the brain that became linked in either an excitatory or inhibitory way. More psychologically, his regarding of the CS as a signal suggests that CS's tell the organism that a US is about to occur, triggering behavior adapted to that US anticipating current theories of Pavlovian conditioning as an adaptive process based on information processing of US and CS.

However, within the behaviorist tradition the accepted theory of Pavlovian conditioning was the *stimulus substitution* or *reflex transfer* account (Holland, 1984). According to this theory, control of the unconditioned reflex got transferred to the CS as it was paired with the US, so that in the future the CS could be substituted for the US, as it had the same effect of the animal. The reflex transfer theory may be diagrammed thus

$$\text{Before Conditioning:} \quad \text{US} \longrightarrow \text{elicits} \longrightarrow \text{UR}$$
$$\text{After Conditioning:} \quad \text{CS} \longrightarrow \text{elicits} \longrightarrow \text{CR}$$

with the assumption that the UR and the CR are identical or nearly identical responses, as in salivary conditioning. In terms of associationism, the stimulus substitution view holds that, although US and CS are paired, an association is formed not between them, but between the CS and the UR, with the UR renamed "CR." Or, in terms of S-R learning theory, Pavlovian conditioning involves S-R learning between CS and CR, not S-S learning between CS and US.

INSTRUMENTAL CONDITIONING

Thorndike's Research Program

Just a few years before Pavlov discovered his "psychical reflexes," an American psychologist named Edward Lee Thorndike (1874–1949) began his own experimental researches into what he called **trial-and-error learning.** Today, this other kind of learning is usually called *instrumental* or *operant learning*, because instead of being completely passive, like Pavlov's harnessed dogs, organisms in this kind of experiment must *operate* on the environment in some way to get rewarded.

While Thorndike also was influenced by associationism, his research program was quite different from Pavlov's. To begin with, Thorndike was a psychologist, not a physiologist, and was consequently interested in behavior change itself instead of in the light thrown by learning on cerebral functioning. Moreover, the intellectual tradition out of which Thorndike came was American functionalism, not physiological reflexology. The functionalists were interested in the individual Darwinian question: How does the organism's mind adapt it to the demands of its environment? Finally, the specific context in which Thorndike worked was Anglo-American comparative or, as it was called then, animal psychology.

Animal psychologists wanted to be able to establish the relative mental abilities of different animal species. The work began with Darwin's friend George Romanes (1848–1894) and his 1882 book *Animal Intelligence.* Romanes employed what has come to be called the *anecdotal method.* He collected stories (anecdotes) about the behavior of animals, often pets, in different situations. He then sifted through the stories and attempted to reconstruct the mental processes of the animals involved, aiming at a relative assessment of the intelligence of each species.

But Thorndike (1911) was highly critical of the anecdotal method. It tended, he believed, to overestimate the abilities of animals. One tends to notice only when animals are being clever, not when they are being ordinary or even stupid; in the case of pets, the tendency to see only the best will be especially marked. Worse, the anecdotal method, with its attendant reconstruction of the animal's thought processes, was easily given to anthropomorphism. If we watch an animal solving a problem, we tend to put ourselves in its place and project onto the animal the thoughts we would have while doing the same thing. Thorndike observed, as had Pavlov, that experimentation was needed to gather conservative, objective scientific data about this area of psychology.

But Pavlov was a physiologist studying their reflexes of the brain, and Thorndike was a functionalist psychologist studying the adaptation of individual organisms to their environment. Thus, their methodologies diverged sharply. Pavlov's research exemplar was admirably suited to studying nervous reflexes: Start with a US that already elicits a reflex and pair it with a CS to create a new, learned reflex. What Thorndike needed was an environment, more controlled than a pet-owner's back yard, that could present a set problem to an animal. In short, he needed to invent a controlled but challenging environment to which a subject would have to adapt. He hit on a solution with his famous *puzzle-boxes*.

Basic Phenomena of Trial-and-Error Conditioning

Less well established than the famous Pavlov, Thorndike, a graduate student at Harvard, set up his laboratory in William James' basement. However, he did most of his work at Columbia University, where he gained a job even before graduating. Thorndike constructed a number of puzzle-boxes (see Fig. 2–2) in which he placed one of his subjects, a kitten or a

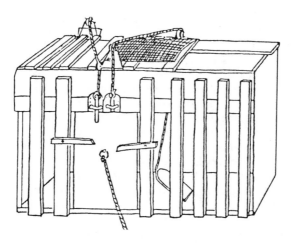

FIGURE 2-2   One of Thorndike's puzzle-boxes. (From Thorndike, 1911, p. 30)

dog (he also experimented with chicks placed in a maze). As you can see, the puzzle-box is a sort of cage so constructed that the door can be opened by the animal from the inside, providing it learns to make a correct response. Thorndike designed many variations of his boxes, but most required the animal to operate a string dangling in the box, which in turn ran over a pulley and opened the door, releasing the animal, who was then fed before being placed back in the box. Thorndike wanted to know exactly how the subject learns the correct response. He described what happens in a box in which the cat must pull a loop or button on the end of the string.

> The cat that is clawing all over the box in her impulsive struggle will probably claw the string or loop or button so as to open the door. And gradually all the other nonsuccessful impulses will be stamped out and the particular impulse leading to the successful act will be stamped in by the resulting pleasure, until, after many trials, the cat will, when put in the box, immediately claw the button or loop in a definite way. (Thorndike, 1911, p. 36)

Thorndike conceived his study as one of association-formation, and interpreted his animals' behaviors in terms of associationism:

> Starting, then, with its store of instinctive impulses, the cat hits upon the successful movement, and gradually associates it with the sense-impression of the interior of the box until the connection is perfect, so that it performs the act as soon as confronted with the sense-impression. (Thorndike, 1911, p. 38)

The phrase *trial-and-error*, or perhaps more exactly *trial-and-success*, learning aptly describes what these animals did in the puzzle-boxes. Placed inside, they try out (or, as Skinner called it later, *emit*) a variety of familiar behaviors. In cats, it was likely to try squeezing through the bars, clawing at the cage, sticking its paws between the bars. Eventually, the cat is likely to scratch at the loop of string and so pull on it, finding its efforts rewarded: The door opens and it escapes, only to be caught by Thorndike and placed back in the box. As these events are repeated, the useless behaviors die away, or extinguish, and the correct behavior is done soon after entering the cage; the cat has learned the correct response needed to escape.

Thorndike's description of his cats' struggles meshes with our own intuitions of how we learn our own nonreflexive, voluntary behaviors. Confronted by a new situation, we try out a number of reactions. Eventually, we hit on a behavior that works (unless we give up). Later, when we meet the situation again, or one like it, we know what to do. In short, both Thorndike's cats and people slowly *adapt* to the environment. This kind of learning is not reflexive. Pavlov could initially *make* his dogs salivate by presenting the US, but there is no stimulus that Thorndike could have presented that would have forced the cats, zombie-like, to walk over to and pull the dangling cord leading to escape. In a sense, a US forces a subject to make the correct, reinforced response; the dog salivates and is fed. In trial-and-error learning, however, we must await for the correct response to occur, and then pounce on it with reinforcement.

Theory of Trial-and-Error Conditioning

Thorndike began his research program seeking to understand how the mind adapts an organism to its environment. He ended up, however, seeing learning as a far simpler affair, probably not involving mind at all. He showed that animals, or at least cats, dogs, and chicks, do not learn by imitation, nor do they reason and have memory. Instead, he found himself driven to the conclusion that although association is real enough, what is associated is not ideas at all, but simply situations (S) and responses (R). Learning, Thorndike concluded, consisted only in changing the degree of control a certain stimulus exerts over a given response, by either rewarding or punishing the connection. Thorndike states this in his famous **law of effect,** the basic law of instrumental learning:

> The Law of Effect is that: Of several responses made to the same situation, those which are accompanied or closely followed by satisfaction to the animal will, other things being equal, be more firmly connected with the situation, so that, when it recurs, they will be more likely to recur; those which are accompanied or closely followed by discomfort to the animal will, other things being equal, have their connections with that situation weakened, so that, when it recurs, they will be less likely to occur. The greater the satisfaction or discomfort, the greater the strengthening or weakening of the bond. (Thorndike, 1911, p. 244)

As Thorndike moved into his first love, education, he extended his S-R psychology to human beings (Thorndike, 1928), but it was never as influential as Clark Hull's S-R psychology (see Chapter 3).

The specifics of Thorndike's shared exemplar, the puzzle-box, also had a limited influence. Although the puzzle-box exerted more experimental control than the natural environment of the anecdotalists, it really did not give the experimenter much to manipulate besides the intricacy of the release mechanism. Therefore, later behaviorists used other specific experimental arrangements, first the maze and then, the triumphant exemplar of operant learning, the Skinner box. Despite their differences, the spirit of each device remains Thorndikian—provide a controlled environment in which an animal is rewarded for the specific response you want the animal to learn.

Pavlov and Thorndike, between them, laid the experimental foundations of behavioral psychology. Each provided a first experimental technique for investigating the laws of association in animals, reasoning that in this way the laws could be clearly worked out for later application to complex human behavior. Each elucidated important fundamental laws and phenomena of learning; Thorndike the law of effect, and Pavlov the phenomena of extinction, spontaneous recovery, generalization, discrimination, and inhibition, that by and large apply to operant conditioning as well as classical conditioning (Hearst, 1975).

FUNDAMENTAL CONTROVERSIES

Two Kinds of Learning or One?

Although we have found the distinction between Pavlovian and instrumental conditioning to be intuitive and comfortable, current research has shown that the two kinds of conditioning are more similar than we thought. We can most easily approach the problem through a simple thought experiment. Suppose I subject you to a typical classical conditioning procedure involving the eyeblink reflex. Holding your head fixed in a stand, I sound a tone and mechanically puff air into your face. If I do this a few times, I find that when I sound the tone you blink your eye. We can analyze this as an experiment in classical conditioning. We start with an unconditional reflex between a US (puff of air) and a UR (eyeblink), and pair the US with a neutral CS (the tone), finding that you acquire a CR (eyeblink). This appears a straightforward example of Pavlovian conditioning.

But is it? Suppose instead of the above procedure I had told you, "When the tone sounds, you'll shortly find your eye puffed at with air." In all likelihood, to avoid the unpleasant air in your eye, you would blink voluntarily when you heard the tone. The following US would not elicit the reflex, the eye already being closed. So there need be no US-CS pairing at all for "conditioning" to occur, since eyeblinks are voluntary as well as reflexive behaviors.

If we return to the original experiment, then, we find it can be analyzed as instrumental conditioning. You find the air puff aversive and close your eye for the "reward" of ending your pain. The law of effect seems to operate—you learn to blink your eye for the "satisfaction" of ending the uncomfortable blast of air. Such ambiguity between what is Pavlovian and what is instrumental learning has grown since the 1970s.

While a number of criteria have been advanced to separate Pavlovian and instrumental learning (see Hearst, 1975, for a review), two of these, one substantive and one procedural, have been most frequently defended. Substantively, it has been proposed that different *kinds of responses*, mediated by different nervous systems, are conditionable only by one kind of procedure or the other. Thus, Pavlovian conditioning applies only to the glandular and smooth muscle responses of the autonomic nervous system, instrumental conditioning applies only to the striated muscle, and "skeletal" responses of the somatic nervous system.

But eyelid movement is a "skeletal" response, and it is best conditioned by Pavlovian procedures. On the other hand, instrumental control of autonomic processes has proved possible, and indeed has become famous as "biofeedback." People have learned to modulate their heart rate, blood pressure, and brain alpha waves simply by being hooked up to devices that tell them if their heart rate is high or low, blood pressure high or low, or alpha wave production high or low. People do not necessarily learn direct control over these "involuntary" responses, however, using instead little tricks that lead to the rewarded bodily change. Hence, one might alter one's heart rate by indulging in sexual fantasies, or salivate by thinking of food. In these cases, an instrumental behavior has been learned that happens to lead to a change in a Pavlovian response. Consequently, animals have been given curare, which suppresses all skeletal activity, and then have been rewarded for changes in smooth-muscle activity.

Thus, it seems we cannot distinguish instrumental and Pavlovian learning on the basis of the responses each produces. This leaves us with the procedural distinction. In Pavlovian conditioning the experimenter presents US and CS together, quite independent of, and indeed before, any response occurs. In instrumental conditioning, on the other hand, the reward follows and, more importantly, is *contingent on* some response—the reward is given only when the desired response occurs (the cat must pull the string to escape).

But as Hearst (1975) points out, even this simple procedural distinction is often blurred in practice. Skinner has studied what he calls "superstitious behavior." Food is delivered at regular intervals to a pigeon walking around in a chamber. What happens is that each reward strengthens the behavior occurring when it's delivered, and after a few rewards, the pigeon is behaving very oddly indeed, trying to do all the behaviors it has been "rewarded" for. However, the food delivery did not actually depend on what the pigeon did, any more than food delivery depended on what Pavlov's dog did. Nevertheless, Skinner regards superstitious behavior as an example of operant, not Pavlovian conditioning. Is he right?

How muddy the waters have become is shown by considering that instrumental and Pavlovian conditioning always go on at the same time. After pressing a bar to get food in a Skinner box, the animal eats food (US) in the box (CS) and so we should not be surprised to find that the animal begins to salivate when we put the creature in the box for a new day of training. Similarly, a dog, Pavlovianly conditioned to salivate to the sound of a metronome, would, if simply released in the room, run to the machine, jump up to it, and wag its tail—all operant behaviors (Hearst, 1975).

The interaction of Pavlovian and instrumental conditioning is powerfully demonstrated by auto-shaping (Brown & Jenkins, 1968), which we will look at again in Chapter 10. Here, a pigeon is put in a Skinner box with a key that can be lighted up. Then we simply put food in the cup and light the key at the same time. We find that after some pairings of US (food) and CS (light), the pigeon will peck the key when it's lighted even though it does not have to in order to get fed. The behavior of pigeons during auto-shaping is just like that of pigeons being taught to peck a key in order to be rewarded with food. So, we find operant behavior controlled by simple, "classical" US-CS pairings. Auto-shaped key-pecks even violate the law of effect, as a variation on this experiment shows. If the pigeon's pecking at the key is made to block delivery of food, while not pecking would produce food, the pigeon pecks the key anyway! This is called *auto-maintenance*. Auto-shaping is now regarded as a form of Pavlovian conditioning. Food is a US that elicits a UR of pecking. The lighting of the response key is a CS that is paired with the US, and eventually elicits pecking—now a CR—by itself.

Of course, as the psychophysicist S.S. Stevens has remarked, just because the exact borderline between night and day may be hard to pinpoint does not mean we should not distinguish them, and similarly the distinction between Pavlovian and instrumental conditioning may be defended as useful if a little fuzzy.

Do Humans Condition?

Asking whether humans condition may be surprising, since we have already discussed some studies of human conditioning, but William Brewer (1974) has suggested that the picture is not so simple. Obviously, if we reward people for some activity, or pair US's and CS's, their behavior will change. But as scientists, we want to know *why* behavior changes, not just record that it does.

From the time of Thorndike, most behaviorists have believed in the *automatic action of reinforcers*. As Thorndike put it, reward and punishment simply stamp in or stamp out the responses they follow. A subject does not have to be aware of the connection between one's behavior and its consequences, or of the regular pairing of US and CS, for conditioning to occur. The action of reinforcers was held to be direct and automatic, unmediated by consciousness or thought (Postman & Sassenrath, 1961), which behaviorists were trying to throw out of psychology anyway. In the behaviorist view, then, the mental state of a person is simply irrelevant to behavior, which is instead the outcome of stimuli and reinforcers in one's environment.

On the other hand, cognitive psychologists like Brewer contend that when a subject learns something, or "conditions," what really happens is that the subject figures out what's going on in the experiment and then acts appropriately. In the cognitive view, then, what changes during a person's "conditioning" is his or her conscious mental state, with behavior changing because the subject has "solved" the experiment. Therefore, it should be possible to create and extinguish CR's and instrumental responses by directly manipulating subjects' mental states, without actually doing any conditioning. Or it should be possible to fool people about what's really going on in an experiment so that they do not condition despite manipulation of stimuli or reinforcers, or learn associations other than those of CS and US, or response and reward. In general, the cognitive hypothesis maintains that beliefs about the environment are more important in regulating behavior than the actual environment.

Brewer (1974) reviewed over 200 studies done by others that tested the automatic action of the reinforcers view against the cognitive view. To illustrate the findings on this dispute we will just look at the results from two traditional areas of learning, one Pavlovian, and the other instrumental.

Autonomic conditioning. As an example of Pavlovian conditioning of an autonomic response, we will consider conditioning the galvanic skin response (GSR). When you are frightened or aroused, you sweat, changing the ability of your skin to conduct electricity; lie detectors use this fact to detect the bodily arousal that should accompany the stress of lying. Electric shock produces the GSR response, and we can pair a tone (CS) with the shock (US) to condition a conditional GSR. Many such studies have been carried out.

What if we simply tell subjects that when they hear the tone they will be shocked, without ever doing it? The result is that subjects acquire a conditional GSR. On the other hand, already conditioned subjects who are told the shocks will no longer follow the CS show immediate extinction, at least in those subjects who believe us; however, many don't. Studies that follow the usual conditioning procedures and then ask the subjects if they figured out the CS-US connection found that only those who had figured out the connection displayed any conditioning.

More sophisticated experiments fool the subject about what is going on. For example, in one experiment subjects heard a repeated series of five tones, the last of which was either high or low. The high tone was accompanied by shock; the low tone was not. From Pavlov's work, we would expect this to condition a GSR to the high tone, but not to the low tone. After they heard each series of tones, the subjects had to say which of the last four tones was most like the first. Finally, half the subjects were told they were just in a sensory discrimination experiment, and were not told about the shock–last-tone relation. Although *all* subjects in fact received US-CS pairings, *only* those who had been told about the last-tone–shock connection acquired a conditional GSR.

Motor conditioning.   As an example of motor response learning, we will select finger-withdrawal conditioning. In this kind of experiment, subjects rest their fingers, palm down, on an electrode. A tone is sounded and the subject is shocked. Subjects soon learn to avoid the shock.

Behaviorists take nothing for granted, and one investigator showed that people will lift their finger when instructed to do so to avoid shock, even if they never get shocked. Similar experiments were done with eyeblink conditioning, except that *five* studies had to be done to convince behaviorists that subjects can blink when told to! Like the GSR studies, telling the subjects the shocks will stop produces immediate extinction, and only subjects who are aware of the shock-tone relation do condition.

Subjects in finger-withdrawal conditioning have also been fooled by instructions. After we condition subjects by ordinary means, suppose we turn their hand over and present the tone? Will they withdraw their finger, making the opposite motor response from what they had learned, or will they move their finger in the same way as before, pressing their finger into the electrode? By and large, about 75 percent of subjects make the new flexion response that gets their finger off the electrode, 5 percent press their fingers into the electrode, and 20 percent make no response.

With this established finding in mind, let us consider an experiment in which subjects' beliefs are manipulated. One group is put through the above procedure. Another group receives the same conditioning, but is told that what they are expected to learn is a particular muscle movement—

withdrawing the finger up, with palm down. Finally, the last group is conditioned, but in the second half of the experiment they are lied to about the location of the electrode, so that in trying to avoid the shock they will actually be pressing their finger into the electrode. The first, or standard, group produced the usual results just described. In the group told they were learning a simple muscle reflex, only about one-third gave responses away from the electrode in the second part of the experiment when they turned their hands over. The third group gave *all* their responses into the electrode. We see here that what subjects think the experimenter wants them to do is generally more powerful than actually getting shocked.

Conclusion.   These are only a few of the studies Brewer (1974) reviewed to challenge the view that human beings condition automatically without the intervention of mental processes. Exactly if and when people condition without awareness is an open issue. Some experiments have been done to support Brewer's position (Solanto & Katkin, 1979). Others support the finding that only aware subjects learn, but interpret this as an outcome, not a cause of physiological learning (Maltzman, 1977, 1979; Pendery &

BOX 2–1   Pavlov on Madison Avenue[*]

Joel S. Dubow, communication's research manager at the Coca-Cola Company says "We nominate Pavlov as the father of modern advertising. Pavlov took a neutral object and, by associating it with a meaningful object, made it a symbol of something else; he imbued it with imagery, he gave it added value. That is what we try to do in modern advertising."

Whether Coke's "Pavlovian" advertising techniques work or not, they cannot work the way Mr. Dubow thinks. In the first place, as we've just learned, it is unlikely that humans classically condition at all; Brewer's (1974) view is now the consensus (Fox, 1983). Even Mr. Dubow's own description of conditioning is cognitive and unbehavioristic; he is not really describing conditioning at all, even if the thinks he is.

Moreover, Mr. Dubow is still clinging to the outmoded stimulus-substitution theory of classical conditioning, which explained conditioning as a process in which the CS comes to be a substitute for the US. But as we will see in Chapter 4, the stimulus-substitution theory has been replaced by a cognitive theory of the CS coming to be a signal preparing the learner to adapt to the coming US. So a "neutral object" in an advertisement will not become a "symbol" of a "meaningful object" through classical conditioning.

As we will see in several later chapters, advertisers often use psychological methods and themes in producing an ad campaign. In the present case, the method is not properly understood and the theory is out of date. Again, we do not mean Coke's ads are ineffective, only that like so many psychological phenomena, they don't work the way we used to think.

[*] See John Koten, "Marketing: Coca-Cola Turns to Pavlov." *Wall Street Journal*, Thursday, January 19, 1984, p. 33.

Maltzman, 1977; Maltzman, Raskin, & Wolff, 1979); still others have attempted to assimilate Brewer's challenging findings into standard behavior theories (Galizio, 1979). Despite Brewer's review, advertisers believe people condition—and even believe in the old stimulus—substitution theory of conditioning; see Box 2–1.

In conclusion, it is interesting to observe that the studies Brewer reviews, almost all of which support the cognitive position, go back as early as 1919 and were produced in all the following decades up into the 1970s, right through the dominance of behavioral theories in the field of learning. This shows the power of tradition. If research programs are going well, then occasional challenging results are either quietly ignored, called interesting phenomena to be shelved for later study, or explained away. Only when an alternative view emerges, as cognitive theory emerged in the 1960s to rival behavior theory, do old problems appear significant. Not until the 1970s did anyone assemble the separate pieces into a picture disquieting to behaviorists.

SUGGESTED READINGS

Biographies of the major figures in this chapter are available. *Pavlov*: B.P. Babkin, *Pavlov* (Chicago: University of Chicago Press, 1949); *Watson*: David Cohen, *J.B. Watson* (London: Routledge & Kegan Paul, 1979); *Thorndike*: G. Joncich, *The Same Positivist* (Middletown, Conn.: Wesleyan University Press, 1968). Broader treatments of all three figures as well as early behaviorism can be found in T.H. Leahey, *A History of Psychology*, 2nd ed. (Englewood Cliffs, N.J.: Prentice-Hall, 1987).

3

TRADITIONAL
THEORIES
OF CONDITIONING

INTRODUCTION

Having reviewed the fundamental research that began the behavioral psychology of learning, we will now turn to the theoreticians who built their ideas on Pavlov's and Thorndike's work. The 1930s and 1940s were known as "The Golden Age of Theory" in American psychology. During that time, behaviorism was the dominant school of psychology, and learning was the core of psychology. The field of learning was contested by the three theoreticians that are the subject of this chapter: Edwin R. Guthrie (1886–1959), Clark L. Hull (1884–1952), and Edward Chace Tolman (1886–1959). Their critic and most influential successor, B. F. Skinner, will be treated in the following chapter.

None of the three theories discussed in this chapter has survived in anything like its original form, but retain influence through their author's students and by having made certain topics in the psychology of learning centrally important. We will therefore focus only on the general orientation of each theory, citing references for the student who wishes more detail.

KEEPING ISSUES ALIVE: GUTHRIE'S STRICT ASSOCIATIONISM

Guthrie did relatively little research, producing a primarily theoretical program, which was the least influential of the big-three theories of the Golden Age. Guthrie was not nearly as systematic as Hull, or even Tolman. But his theory did raise several important issues. Certain theoretical and empirical problems are endemic to the psychology of learning, and Guthrie forcefully drew attention to three that are still extant today.

Two Kinds of Learning or One?

We have already examined some recent evidence casting doubt on the instrumental conditioning Pavlovian conditioning dichotomy. Already in the 1930s Guthrie's theory was based on the premise that there is only one kind of learning (Guthrie, 1940). The single learning process Guthrie recognized was the forming of simple associations between stimuli and movements. These associations are not to be identified with either Pavlovian or instrumental conditioning, but were held by Guthrie to underlie both.

Guthrie believed in strict association by immediate simultaneous contiguity. That is, in a learning situation you learn a connection between whatever stimuli are present at a given moment and the behaviors that are occurring at the same time. As Guthrie put it, "Stimuli which are acting at the time of a response tend on their recurrence to evoke that response" (Guthrie, 1933, p. 365). This is his one fundamental law of learning, superseding Pavlov's cortical account of Pavlovian conditioning and Thorndike's law of effect in instrumental learning. Guthrie always sought the simplest theory possible, and he believed that bare association by contiguity could account for all learning.

Applying this idea to Pavlovian conditioning, Guthrie had to face Pavlov's showing that simultaneous presentation of US and CS resulted in little or no conditioning. The best arrangement Pavlov found was for the CS to precede and overlap the US. This appears inconsistent with Guthrie's insistence on simultaneous association.

But Guthrie had an ingenious explanation, subsequently invoked by other psychologists who in other situations needed to fill gaps between S's and R's. As Guthrie (1930, 1952) saw it, every stimulus, even an apparently neutral CS, provokes some response or series of responses. Sound a tone and a dog may flex an ear to listen, shift his posture, or turn his head. All these responses in turn produce stimuli, which themselves produce responses, which produce stimuli, etc. . . . So any stimulus, even a CS, initiates a chain of R—S—R—S . . . connections. Thus, when Pavlov sounded a tone, the CS created in the dog certain movements, which in turn produced stimuli present when the US subsequently occurred, and it is these *movement-produced stimuli* that get conditioned to the CR. So the real CS in Pavlov's experiment is not the CS he administered, but the stimuli it evoked, and simultaneously present when salivation occurs.

Guthrie's reasoning also gave a clever account of generalization. Generalization appears to be inconsistent with Guthrie's associationism: If a dog has learned to salivate to a 1000-cycle-per-second tone, why does it also salivate to a 900-cycle-per-second tone? The 900-Hz (Hertz, or cycle) tone was never coupled with salivating, and so under Guthrie's theory ought not be associated with salivating. But Guthrie argued that listening to a 900-Hz tone was quite like listening to a 1000-Hz tone, and therefore elicited many of the same movement-produced stimuli; it is these identical movement-produced stimuli that elicit the "generalized CR" (Guthrie, 1952).

Having briefly reviewed Guthrie's analysis of Pavlovian conditioning, we will turn to Thorndike's puzzle-boxes, with which Guthrie was quite familiar. They had been the object of his one extensive piece of research (Guthrie & Horton, 1946; also fully reported in Guthrie, 1952). Guthrie was very tough on the law of effect and the terms *reward* and *punishment* (Guthrie, 1934). The law of effect seemed to him to be unscientific, for it let one thing (the reward or punishment) affect another thing that had already occurred. This appears to be backward causation, because we say the reward strengthens a *past event*, the response. Guthrie thought causes had to precede effects. Reward and punishment were, Guthrie believed, unscientific "moral" terms used by people in power to describe the effects they wish to have on another's behavior.

Now, remember a cat struggling to escape from a puzzle-box. At some point the cat bumps into or claws at a vertical lever (in Guthrie's boxes) that opens the door and allows the cat to escape. Thorndike saw here the effect of reward (escape) on behavior (the cat learns to work the lever to get out). Guthrie's view was quite different. The box is a distinct stimulus-situation in which responses are occurring, and by Guthrie's law of learning each time a response occurs it gets conditioned to the box-stimuli. Moreover, as each response occurs it *replaces* the S-R bond between the previous response and the box-stimuli. At some point the cat makes a response that operates the lever; say it rubs against the lever with its left shoulder. The door flies open, and the cat flies out.

Thus, the *last response* to occur in the presence of and, therefore, be conditioned to, the box stimuli was rubbing the lever with the left shoulder; after that the cat left the box, so no *new* responses could occur that would get conditioned to the box stimuli, and so replace the lever-rubbing response. When the cat is placed back in the box, the stimuli conditioned to the rub-lever-with-shoulder response elicits that response and the cat escapes once more. In Guthrie's (1934, 1939) account, the lever-rub is not stamped in by reward at all. Escape simply ensures that no new responses will occur in the box that would get conditioned to the box-stimuli, breaking the bond with lever-rubbing.

We find, then, that Guthrie was able to interpret plausibly both Pavlovian and instrumental conditioning as the outcome of a single process of constantly associating current responses with current stimuli. His single-process theory failed to carry the day, however, succumbing to the traditional distinction of "reflexive" and "voluntary" learning. But we have seen how that distinction is itself in danger of dissolving and being replaced by a new one-process view in which the organism learns relations between environmental stimuli (for example, Rescorla, 1975). Modern one-process theorists have not adopted Guthrie's theory, but they owe him something for having kept the issue alive for many years.

Gradual, or One-Trial Learning?

Careful study of Guthrie's description of puzzle-box learning reveals another startling feature of his theory, namely that learning takes place all at once, on one trial (Guthrie, 1939). The cat rubs the lever, bonding together S and R, and escapes—the S-R bond is complete; all that subsequent escapes do is to continue to ensure that no new *R* gets conditioned to the box stimuli.

Guthrie's position seems outrageously absurd. Anyone who has learned to hit a golf ball, pitch a baseball, drive a car, or type knows that it took a long time—often unbearably long—to master. It appears ridiculous to say we learned these things all at once.

But Guthrie would reply that these are complex activities. In the jargon of his era, Guthrie was a militantly *molecular* theorist, claiming that a psychologist should not study whole acts. A psychologist who studies swinging a golf club was called *molar*. Instead, a molecular psychologist studied specific muscle movements such as all the muscle activity taking place when swinging a golf club. In Guthrie's theory, then, it is not an act that gets conditioned to stimuli but whatever movements are happening in their presence. To state what the cat learned in Guthrie's puzzle-box was not to push the lever, or even to rub the lever with the left shoulder, but it learned those *exact* muscle movements that were going on when the door opened, and that associative conditioning took place on one trial.

Objecting that it takes a long time to learn to drive a golf ball is not a tenable objection, for golfing is a complex series of muscle movements, not just one response, and each movement must be learned and linked properly into the chain of movements we call "driving a golf ball." Moreover, our movements keep conditioning to new stimuli, since the second tee isn't exactly like the first. (Maybe this is why golfers hit better at a driving range than on the course, since the stimulus situation is always the same at the range, and why we are told to keep our eye on the ball, since at least the ball looks much the same from "trial-to-trial"—and golfers certainly find it a trial!) In Guthrie's scheme of things, essentially, we learn particular muscle responses on one trial, but it may take many trials to learn and coordinate all the muscle responses that assemble together into a complex act.

To give any empirical support to Guthrie's theory, it is obvious the researcher cannot study a complex act. Guthrie himself tried to do so in his puzzle-box studies (Guthrie, 1952). He and his colleagues photographed cats at the moment they activated the lever and escaped. They found that a cat's subsequent responses varied only a little from trial to trial, indicating that it had learned, and retained, the first trial's movements.

But an even more precise study was carried out by Virginia Voeks (1954) on a simple human reflexive movement, the eyeblink. Specifically, Voeks compared Guthrie's theory to that of Hull, who held the common sense view (mathematically expressed) that learning a habit, however simple, is a gradual affair, each reinforcement adding a little bit to the strength of the habit. Previous studies had supported Hull. If 20 subjects are put through a conditioned eyeblink experiment and we plot trial-by-trial the total number of eyeblinks given to the CS on each trial, we find that total rises slowly and finally levels off.

Adopting Guthrie's molecular strategy, however, Voeks argued that group data are misleading. Suppose one-trial learning does occur. Then, on each trial a given subject either learns or does not learn. One subject may learn on the first trial, another on the third; three may learn on the fourth trial and so on. Adding their responses together we would see "evidence" of gradual learning: trial 1, 1 blink; trial, 2, 1 blink; trial 3, 2 blinks; trial 4, 5 blinks, and so on. Each subject would learn to blink on a given trial, and blink on every subsequent trial (all or none learning). However, since as we go from trial to trial *more* subjects condition (and blink ever after), the total number of blinks rises slowly and gradually, seeming to show gradual learning. Voeks looked at the behavior of each subject in her study and found that for most of them, once the blink CR occurred it occurred on every trial thereafter, just as Guthrie's theory predicted. But when she pooled the data, "gradual learning" appeared, an illusion created by adding up everyone's responses.

Despite her acute reasoning and novel treatment of learning data, Voeks' experiment did not convince psychologists of the correctness of Guthrie's theory. But it did at least teach them the perils of mistaking group results for individual learning processes. Since psychologists want to understand individual learning, Voek's study stands as a permanent reminder to pay attention to what individual people do.

Forgetting: Decay or Interference?

Psychologists of learning and memory must study not only how responses are learned and material acquired, but also how responses are lost and previously remembered material forgotten. We have already seen Pavlov addressing the problem of unlearning or forgetting in his studies of extinction. He suggested that CR's that no longer occur are still present, only inhibited, to reoccur when the inhibition lifts. Pavlov's theory of inhibition somewhat resembles Freud's theory of repression, which claims that when we "forget" something we have really only forced it into the unconscious so that we do not have to think about it, as when a boy represses his Oedipal wish to kill his father. In both inhibition and repression, things are not forgotten; they are suppressed. Thorndike, on the other hand, originally maintained in his law of effect that punishment weakens S-R connections, eventually stamping them out. In Thorndike's view things can be unlearned or forgotten, not just repressed. The effect of punishment is still controversial, and we will come to it again in the next chapter.

Guthrie's (1930) view was different from any of these. In the puzzle-box, for instance, Guthrie claimed that reward, that is, escape, works because it prevents new responses from occurring to the stimuli present when the crucial response was made and conditioned. Guthrie argued from his stand-point of strict associationism that old responses, or S-R connections, get lost not because of inhibition or punishment, but by being *replaced* by new responses to the same situation, creating new S-R connections. So if we don't let the puzzle-box door open when the cat presses the lever as it has learned to, new responses will occur in the presence of the puzzle-box stimuli, replacing the old learned S-R connection. If we let the cat escape after making some new responses, say, rearing on its hind legs, that response will be associated with the puzzle-box stimuli and will recur on the next trial.

Guthrie's argument anticipates a modern issue in the cognitive theory of memory: Do we forget things simply because memories weaken over time (decay theory) or because new learning overlays old learning, making it harder to recall the old material (interference theory)? Guthrie's theory is an interference theory because he did not think S-R bonds, once acquired, naturally weaken with age, but are instead broken by new learning. We will return to this issue in its cognitive form in Chapters 5–6.

Guthrie's Legacy

Of the three major theories of the Golden Age, Guthrie's theory was the least elaborated and the least influential. The amount of research done to support it was small compared to Hull's or Tolman's theories, and it was criticized for its looseness, informality, and lack of systemic rigor (Mueller & Schoenfeld, 1954).

Two other illustrative difficulties deserve mention. First, Guthrie's account of reinforcement as something that protects the most recent response from being unlearned is implausible. It seems to work for the puzzle-box, where escape indeed releases the animal. But so would a trap door opening under the cat when it pushed the lever; but surely, when placed back in the box, pushing the lever is the last thing the cat would do (Hilgard & Bower, 1975). The second problem concerns Guthrie's molecularism. Consider the experiments on finger withdrawal conditioning (Chapter 2). Subjects first learned to lift their finger to avoid shock. When they turned their hands over they did not repeat the same muscle movement, as Guthrie would have expected, but instead made the opposite movement, curling their finger toward the palm (Wickens, 1938). This shows that people learn such acts as "get finger away from shock," not simple muscle movements such as "flex finger extensor muscle."

Despite these problems, and the recently discovered fact that he tripped over the cat (Box 3–1), we have seen several areas in which Guthrie's

---

BOX 3–1   How Guthrie Tripped Over the Cat[*]

As mentioned in the text, Guthrie's major experiment was a modification of Thorndike's work with puzzle-boxes. Cats were placed in a box that had a tall, thin rod projecting from the floor, and if the cat rubbed against the rod the door of the box opened allowing the animal to escape. The results of the experiment were offered as support for Guthrie's views. The rubbing behavior was stereotyped, occurring in the same form on trial after trial, indicating first-trial learning (since no subsequent modification of behavior occurred), and indicating learning without reward.

However, like all behaviorists, Guthrie ignored the species-specific behavior of his subject. Cats—great, small, and domestic—share a common form of greeting behavior. The tail is raised, the back is arched, and the animal rubs against the greeted cat as it walks by. Should the target animal be far away, the greeter displaces the greeting on to some convenient object such as a tree. Domestic cats typically regard people as conspecifics (that is, fellow cats) and, as any cat owner knows, perform the greeting on human legs, or on door posts or furniture.

In his research on cats, Guthrie, along with as many as eight other people, observed the cat's behavior in full view of the cat. Recently, Bruce Moore and Susan Stuttard have shown that Guthrie tripped over this part of feline nature. Guthrie's results were an artifact of the situation and the cat's innate greeting response. Moore and Stuttard reproduced Guthrie's experiment except that bar-rubbing opened no doors and whether a person was present or not was varied. They found that when a person was present, the bar was rubbed; when absent, the bar was not rubbed. And the rubbing was quite stereotyped, as we would expect of a genetically programmed behavior.

It was typical of behaviorists to ignore animal nature and to believe that any behavior an animal manifested, aside from a few reflexes, must have been learned. They disagreed about how learning worked, but not its power and ubiquity. We will see later in this text that not only did Guthrie trip over the cat, but that Hull, Tolman, and Skinner tripped over their rats and pigeons.

[*] Read Bruce Moore and Susan Studdard, "Professor Guthrie and *Felis domesticus*, or: Tripping Over the Cat." *Science*, 1979, *205*, 1031–1033.

---

theory offered novel analyses of problems in learning, and raised issues that might otherwise have been ignored. His theory also gave rise to a sophisticated and highly technical theory of learning called *stimulus sampling theory* (beginning with Estes, 1950). Stimulus sampling theory attempts to quantify the way in which stimulus elements in a situation get conditioned to responses when accompanied by reinforcement. Guthrie's beliefs in association by contiguity, in all-or-none one-trial learning, and in forgetting as interference, are given elegant formulation in Estes' work (see Robbins, 1980, for a review). Even if it did not really develop a research program, Guthrie's theory was provocative and different.

PROMOTING MATHEMATICS AND MECHANISM: HULL'S LOGICAL BEHAVIORISM

The Research Program of Clark L. Hull

Guthrie's theory was simple and he never worked it out in systematic detail; Hull's theory was fearsomely complex and systematically stated as a network of axioms, corollaries, and theorems expressed in mathematical and logical form. Where Guthrie seemed content with qualitative interpretations of learning, Hull aimed at exact quantification carried out to many decimal places. The student who opens Hull's *A Behavior System* (1952) finds this as early as page 6:

$$D = D' \times \eta$$

where

$$D' = 37.824 \times 10 - 27.496 \, lh + 4.001$$

and

$$\eta = 1 - 0.00001045h^{2.4826}$$

The student is likely to give up all hope of learning about learning. But all Hull states here is that one's motivational state, or drive D, is a component of three factors: D', which increases the longer you go without food; h, which is hours of food deprivation; and η (the Greek letter *eta*), representing the slow weakening effect of starvation. Hull has just dressed up the commonplace notion—that motivation increases until you get too weak to move—with logico-mathematical clothes.

Don E. Dulany (see Leahey, 1980a) has called Hull's school **logical behaviorism.** While all the behaviorists of the Golden Age aspired to systematic formal theory, only Hull achieved it, and he set the standard for others to emulate. More particularly, Hull believed that a good scientific theory should be stated as a set of logically expressed axioms from which observable consequences, that it, predictions, could be deduced. In his view, the scientist then constructed an experiment to test the predictions, and should they fail, the theory would have to be changed.

For example, one of the fundamental postulates of Hull's system as set forth in 1943 was

$$_sE_R = {_sH_R} \times D$$

What this says is that the tendency to make a given response, *reaction potential* or $_sE_R$, is a function of motivation, *drive* or D, multiplied by how well the response has been learned, *habit strength* or $_sH_R$. Hull's proposed axiom is based on common sense, for it says you will only give a response if you have learned it as a habit ($_sH_R$ is positive) and are motivated to give the response (D is positive). Should you either not know what to do ($_sH_R$ is 0) or not be motivated (D is 0), you will not respond ($_sE_R$ is 0).

Testing the axiom is relatively straightforward, at least if we do not try to put exact numbers on the theoretical terms. As our response we might choose pressing a bar in a Skinner box to get food, and as our measure of the strength of the response ($_sE_R$) we can use how quickly the bar is pressed after our subject, a rat, is released into the box, assuming quite reasonably that the more quickly the bar is pressed the stronger is the response tendency; $_sE_R$ is our dependent variable, and we can manipulate our independent variables $_sH_R$ and D to see if they affect $_sE_R$ in the right way.

To manipulate D we simply compare well-fed animals (D is zero) to animals of moderate drive strength (for example, 12 hours without food) and animals of high drive strength (24 hours without food). We cross the drive factor with $_sH_R$. Contrary to Guthrie, Hull believed that learning, the acquisition of habits, is a gradual affair, and he expressed this by saying that habit strength grows slowly to a limit as an organism's responses are reinforced. More precisely, $_sH_R$ is a positive function of the number of reinforced responses. So we manipulate $_sH_R$ by having some rats never learn the bar-press response ($_sH_R$ is zero), some learn it moderately well (50 reinforced presses) and some very well (100 reinforced presses).

We can infer from the equation that those animals who have no motivation (D is zero) will not respond no matter how well they have learned the bar press; neither will animals respond who have not learned the response ($_sH_R$ is zero) regardless of their drive state. Other groups will respond to the bar with varying degrees of swiftness, with the fastest responding (highest $_sE_R$) coming from the group that combines the longest food deprivation with the best-learned habit. Experiments along these general lines were carried out (Hull, Felsinger, Gladstone, & Yamaguchi, 1947), although they were aimed at actually quantifying Hull's theoretical terms.

Hull's system was open to change. For example, it doesn't take research—though research was done—to see that other important factors should determine reaction strength besides drive and habit strength. Surely you, or any organism, will work harder for a large reward than for a small one, and will react more strongly to powerful than to weak stimuli. These considerations were duly incorporated into Hull's revised system (Hull, 1952) as *incentive motivation* (K) and *stimulus-intensity dynamism* (V), respectively. The revised equation constituting reaction potential became

$$_sE_R = D \times V \times K \times {_sH_R}$$

Logical behaviorism evolved as a research program through the 1930s and 1940s as Hull modified his theory in the light of new data and theoretical reflection. Nevertheless certain ideas were central to Hull's program. To begin with, Hull's theory was an S-R theory. He believed there was only one kind of learning (Hull, 1937), in which responses are attached to controlling stimuli. For Hull, every response had its eliciting stimulus, however hard to find. When it was impossible to find an external stimulus for some response, Hull (1930b, 1931) argued there had to be internal, covert stimuli controlling it. Hull's search for nonobservable stimuli to control otherwise inexplicable responses shows that the basic S-R formula was an idea not to be abandoned.

Not only did every response have to have a stimulus, but Hull also believed only stimuli could control behavior. Motivation presents a problem here: How can food deprivation, in which nothing actually happens to an organism, act as a stimulus? Hull (1930b, 1931) supposed that food deprivation, or any other motivation-producing circumstance, created internal stimuli, such as hunger pangs, that could be associated with responses leading to reduction of the drive. In fact, Hull believed that all learning depended on drive reduction—that is, he accepted the law of effect. This belief led to controversies with Tolman's informational psychology (see below), and apparent refutation when electrical stimulation of the brain was discovered (Box 3–2).

You may have wondered why some of Hull's theoretical terms are bracketed by S and R ($_sH_R$, and $_sE_R$) and others are not (D, V, K). Hull used in his thinking about learning something called *intervening variables*, a characteristic of formal as opposed to radical behaviorism. An actual observed response is a *dependent variable*, because we assume that its occurrence depends on environmental conditions. The conditions that affect behavior are called *independent variables*, because we can manipulate them independently of the organism. Hull believed that when learning takes place something inside the organism changes, linking up stimulus and response. These changes are *intervening variables*, because they intervene between the independent and dependent variables, that is, between stimulus and response, and so we have $_sE_R$ and $_sH_R$. D, V, and K are not intervening variables; they refer directly to something outside the organism—how many hours we have not fed it, how strong a CS or US is, how large a reward is. Use of intervening variables sets Hull and Tolman off quite sharply from B. F. Skinner. Hull and Tolman, whatever their other differences, tried to infer what happens inside an organism when it learns; Skinner sees in this an invitation to myth-making.

Hull's deepest commitment as a scientist was somewhat obscured by his axiomatic theory and its widespread influence. Hull believed that living organisms—including human beings—were nothing but complicated machines, whose behavior patterns could be described with mathematical precision, hence his faith in quantified, axiomatic theory. Believing that organisms are machines also implied that it should be possible to build machines capable of behaving like animals and, ultimately, like human beings. Fascinated with machinery all his life—he originally wanted to be an engineer—Hull tried to build simple machines capable of replicating the basic phenomena of S-R learning. He occasionally published accounts of his machines (see Hull & Baernstein, 1929), and demonstrated one during his presidential address to the American Psychological Association (Hull, 1937). However, for personal reasons that remain obscure and because his axiom theory was so widely hailed as psychology's salvation (L. J. Smith, 1986), he did not pursue the construction of learning machines after 1936. Nevertheless,

---

BOX 3–2   Reinforcement Without Reward?

In Hull's theory of learning, acquisition of a habit depended on reduction of a motivational drive, a position Tolman effectively attacked in his latent learning experiments. In 1954 a new kind of reinforcer was discovered that could powerfully change behavior without reward or long-term benefit to the learner—electrical stimulation of the brain (Olds & Milner, 1954; Olds, 1960). Electrodes could be planted in certain areas of the brain, and rats would work hard for stimulation of their brains; they would drive themselves to exhaustion, ignoring hunger and thirst, just to get a jolt from the electrode; stimulation to certain other areas is aversive.

More limited studies have been done with human patients undergoing brain surgery (Delgado, 1976). These patients report feelings of intense pleasure, sometimes sexual, when the "pleasure centers" of the brain are stimulated. Cases of chronic pain and some forms of epilepsy have been treated by long-term implantation of electrodes (Delgado, 1976; Sem-Jacobsen, 1976). If rat behavior and human self-report may be integrated, we find that sheer pleasure—completely divorced from any biological imperative—is quite reinforcing on its own.

Besides its theoretical interest, electrical stimulation of the brain raises serious ethical issues because it holds out the threat, or promise, of physical *control* of the mind (Delgado, 1969). While its advocates, such as Delgado, see in physical mind-control the promise of a "psychocivilized society," most people fear it as a threat. Long-term electrode implanting was nightmarishly portrayed in Michael Crichton's novel *The Terminal Man*, later made into a popular movie.

In our increasingly technological age, when computers have become pocket-size, citizens must weigh the good and evil of electrical stimulation of the brain. It may cure epilepsy and relieve chronic pain, but could it lead to routine implants, first in criminals, who might be aversively shocked for criminal acts or even thoughts, then in the retarded, to promote learning efficiency, and perhaps finally in anyone who rubs the authorities the wrong way?

---

his belief that organisms are machines was basic to his construction of mathematical learning theories and continued to shape his theorizing for the rest of his life (L. J. Smith, 1986).

The final central feature of Hull's program is his commitment to *continuity theory* in learning. Guthrie argued that learning always occurs all at once, on one trial. Opposed to Guthrie's all-or-none view was Hull's belief that habit strength grows a little bit at a time, continuously as rewards are given, until learning is complete. Hullians regarded results like Guthrie's and Horton's, and Voeks' as unrepresentative of learning in general.

These, along with a commitment to logical theory, are the central ideas of Hull's research program. Surrounding them were the explicit postulates and defined theoretical terms that were always open to change. New terms such as V and K could be added, old ones could be redefined, and postulates could be revised, as when Hull's student Spence altered $_sE_R = D \times V \times K \times _sH_R$ to $_sE_R = (D + K) \times V \times _sH_R$. But undisturbed by all these changes were logical behaviorism's commitment to S-R theory, continuity, intervening variables, and the drive-reduction theory of learning.

The Legacy of Logical Behaviorism

Not long after Hull's death in 1952, his theory was subjected to some severe criticism. It was argued that Hull's predictions could not really be logically derived from his theory (Cotton, 1955), that it could not account for certain maze-learning experiments with rats that suggested they could reason (Deutsch, 1956), and that Hull's theory was just too simple to explain human behavior (Ginsberg, 1954). The most scathing and influential critique was that of Koch (1954), who showed that Hull's formal system was a logical mess; that he did not practice what he preached, for example, ignoring contrary data available while writing his postulates; and that his quantificational program was ill-conceived and doomed from the start. For Koch, Hull's usefulness lay in his failure, demonstrating the impossibility of Hull's heroic, or foolhardy, system-building.

In any case, the stream of influence from Hull's theory divided after World War II. Those of his students, colleagues, and admirers who wanted to study human learning largely abandoned the formal and quantificational aspects of logical behaviorism, while retaining a commitment to Hull's S-R theory. Their hypotheses were stated rather informally, and in this respect they merged into a mass of eclectic behaviorists dominating American psychology in the 1950s. They also augmented the S-R formula by elaborating the idea of central, covert mediating responses, S-r-s-R, to handle certain special problems of human learning. Both trends will be discussed later in this chapter.

Hull's major student, Kenneth Spence, continued to study animal learning, and his influence has been long lasting. While moving away from Hull's excessive quantification, Spence remained a powerful spokesperson for formal theories (see Spence, 1944, 1956). Because our topic is human learning, we will pass over the important contributions of Spence and his students to animal learning. The interested student can get a good discussion of their work in Hilgard and Bower (1975). We will move on to Hull's formidable rival, a devilishly clever experimenter and charming writer named E. C. Tolman.

DEFENDING INTENTION AND COGNITION: TOLMAN'S PURPOSIVE BEHAVIORISM

The Research Program of E. C. Tolman

Tolman (1959) himself tells us that both his system and his research were based on hunch and common sense. His research program was not guided by formal deductions from postulates like Hull's, or by a single law of learning, like Guthrie's. Rather, it appears that in designing an experiment Tolman asked himself what *he* would do in the rat's position as opposed to what a Hullian or Guthriean rat would do. Tolman was gratified to learn that rats were generally as common-sensical as he was. Especially in reading his occasional attempts to formalize his theory (see Tolman, 1932, 1938, 1959), one senses that technical formulae and a playful, occasionally bizarre vocabulary ("means-ends-readiness," "sign-gestalt-expectation") are being used to express straightforward common sense.

In Tolman's case, therefore, formal statements of his theory are even less important than in Hull's case. Central to Tolman's theory are two ideas that, more than anyone else, he kept alive during the behaviorist era: **purpose** and **cognition.**

Tolman always maintained that behavior and learning are a "getting toward" or a "getting away." That is, behavior is purposive; it is oriented toward a goal, be it securing something good or avoiding something bad. In Tolman's view no psychology could dispense with reference to purposes, and in common sense we tend to agree with him.

But purposes were viewed askance by other important behaviorists, who thought "purpose" to be too vague and mentalistic for scientific psychology. Instead, Guthrie, Watson, and even Hull sought a more mechanistic account of behavior. Guthrie wanted to understand learning as the acquisition of *muscle-movements*, such as twitching a finger, not as the learning of purposeful acts, such as removing a finger from the source of an electrical shock. In the old-fashioned jargon, Guthrie was a molecular theorist, believing that scientific psychology studied movements, not acts.

Tolman was the supreme molar theorist because of his commitment to purpose. Because behavior for Tolman was guided by goals, the proper level of analysis is of the acts that lead to the goal, not of the muscle twitches that happen to be involved at the moment. So, for example, a rat that has learned to walk through a maze could also swim through it when it was filled with water, even though the muscle responses were different in each case (MacFarlane, 1930). Moreover, simply pulling a rat through a maze in a basket can result in learning, even though no R's have occurred to be reinforced and learned (McNamara, Long, & Wike, 1956). These results support Tolman's contention that the proper study of psychologists is an organism's goals and the acts it can mobilize to reach them.

The molecular-mechanistic versus molar-purposive issue is profound and important, involving much more than interpreting rat maze-learning behavior. Consider a game of tennis. In a molecular-mechanistic account all that happens is a series of physical events: A ball is propelled through different trajectories because of the muscle movements two organisms use to strike the ball. The psychologist could only talk about the fluctuating strengths of $_sE_R$'s under changing stimulus conditions. The psychologist could *not* talk about strategies for winning, and could not even account for the end of the match except to say that when the ball fell on the outside of a certain line the behavior exchange ended. But of course we, and Tolman, reject such a view. Tolman would talk about a player's purpose—winning—and we could discuss a player's game as a set of meaningful acts aimed at the goal of winning. A purposive, molar account respects the human world of meaning and purpose; a molecular-mechanistic account reduces them to muscular twitches and glandular secretions. Nor is this issue dead with Guthrie, Tolman, and Hull. It is very much alive in debates over Skinner's theory, cognitive science, and sociobiology.

The other notion central to Tolman's program was *cognition*. Tolman believed that an organism learns *about* its environment; it doesn't just learn to react to it. In the last chapter we questioned if human beings really condition, or if their behavior is determined by thinking. Tolman (1932, p. 330) wrote in a similar vein that a conditioned response will occur only if an organism "believes" that the old response-reinforcement contingencies hold. Subsequently, Seward and Levy (1949) demonstrated in animals the kind of "instant extinction" Tolman's theory predicts, which we also found in Brewer's review of human research.

Seward and Levy trained rats to run from a start box down an alleyway to a goal box containing food. Then they simply placed the rat in the goal box several times without feeding it. The rats, "knowing" that food was no longer in the goal box, now generally did not run down the alley when placed in the start box. As others had shown with humans, Seward and Levy showed that extinction in animals can occur even without the occurrence of nonreinforced R's. This is contrary to Hull's theory, in which $_sH_R$ must be lowered by nonreinforcement of a response, but is expected by Tolman's cognitive theory.

Nor were beliefs the only cognitive processes Tolman attributed to rats. His associate I. Krechevsky (later David Krech) showed that rats seemed to act on hypotheses. Krechevsky (1932) found that in certain kinds of mazes rats would systematically try different modes of behavior. Thus, a rat might try all right turns, then all left turns, then alternating left and right, as if it were formulating hypotheses and then trying them out, rather than engaging in a random trial-and-error process (see also Tolman, 1948).

Tolman's cognitive emphasis led him to reject the law of effect. S-R reinforcement theories like Thorndike's and Hull's say that what causes learning to occur, or be "stamped in," is pleasure or pain-avoidance. Rather, Tolman stressed the cognitive role of reinforcement as a signal to the organism.

Tolman, Hall, and Bretnall (1932) offered a disproof of the law of effect, in which introductory psychology students learned a punchboard maze. In front of them was placed a board with many sets of pairs of holes. The subjects inserted a metal stylus into one of each pair of holes, one of which was "correct," the other "incorrect," and they had to pass through the maze by repeatedly inserting the stylus in sequential pairs of holes until they did it once without choosing a "wrong" hole.

For our purposes, the important groups are as follows:

Bell-right—when the subject inserted the stylus into the *correct* hole of each pair, an electrical circuit closed and rang a bell.

Bell-wrong—when the subject inserted the stylus into the *incorrect* hole of each pair the bell rang.

Bell-right-shock—when the subject chose the *correct* hole, not only did the bell ring, but the subject also received a painful electric shock through the stylus.

Bell-wrong-shock—when the subject chose the *incorrect* hole, not only did the bell ring, but the subject was shocked.

The results were that the *bell-right* group made the fewest errors followed very closely by the *bell-right-shock* group. Many more errors were made by the *bell-wrong* group, and many more still by the *bell-wrong-shock* group.

Let us first discuss the effects of the bell. The bell is a supposedly neutral stimulus of no reinforcing value, yet it acted to "emphasize," in Tolman's words, whatever response it followed. So, regardless of shock, both *bell-wrong* groups learned more slowly than the *bell-right* groups. As Tolman put it, the bell exerted a "baleful fascination" on his subjects, who had some trouble learning to choose the hole that did *not* ring the bell.

Turning to the shock, we find that it acted contrary to the law of effect. Subjects in the *bell-right-shock* group were learning to *receive* shocks, not avoid them, as suggested by the law of effect. Indeed, their rate of learning was not significantly different from the *bell-right* group. On the other hand, the *bell-wrong-shock* group was learning to avoid shocks, since for them every error resulted in a shock. But the shock did not make them learn faster; in fact, they were the slowest of all the groups. The shock seemed to act as an emphasizer that impeded learning rather than helped it. Tolman's result was not a fluke, because more recent research, has shown consistently that the information value of reinforcers is more important than their supposed reward or punishment value (see Estes, 1972).

Although Tolman championed the scientific respectability of purpose and cognition throughout his career, his treatment of them changed. In his earliest writings, Tolman took a realistic approach to purpose and cognition, claiming that they were directly observable aspects of behavior. He contrasted his view with the traditional Cartesian belief that when one sees an animal striving for a goal one could infer an inner purpose behind the striving, and maintained instead that the striving simply *was* purpose, openly visible and not inferred. In the mid-1930s Tolman seemed briefly to abandon the reality of purposes and cognitions, and flirted with physiological reductionism. Finally, however, Tolman developed the representational view for which he was best known. He abandoned realism and accepted the copy theory, arguing that learning consists of building representations of the environment—cognitive maps—that are consulted by an organism when it behaves.

Tolman's Cognitive Maps vs. Hull's Habit Family Hierarchy

Although Tolman was an unsystematic theorist, he was a wonderfully clever experimenter, and he loved to devise experiments to show that Hull's S-R theory of learning was simplistic, and that animals really did possess intentions and thoughts. Some of the most famous of these experiments concerned maze-learning. Hull said that when an animal learned a maze it learned a chain of S-R connections, learning which way to turn at each choice point. Tolman, in contrast, held that animals learn maps that they use to plan their route through the maze.

Hull's habit family hierarchy. Perhaps because it appeared in Hull's writing very early (Hull, 1930a) and so was not inextricable from the later axiomatic theory, his **habit-family hierarchy** proved to be a flexible and durable concept of widespread application. While the formal system generated much animal research, the habit-family hierarchy has been a useful tool to behaviorists concerned with human learning.

The idea is really quite simple, and is inherent in any S-R psychology. Recall what a cat does when placed in a puzzle-box by Thorndike. The situation calls forth many responses: The cat reaches through the slats, claws at the walls, pushes its head against the door, and eventually pulls the string and escapes. In trial-and-error learning a single stimulus situation calls forth a series of responses, one at a time, until the correct one is executed and reinforced. Adopting S-R terminology, we can say that the situation elicits several responses, but each S-R connection is of a different strength. We may note this

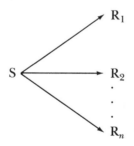

and call it a *divergent habit-family hierarchy*. There is a family of habits diverging from a single stimulus arranged in a hierarchy of strengths.

What happens in trial-and-error learning is this (Hull, 1930a, 1934). A situation calls forth a hierarchy of responses, and the one with the strongest $_SH_R$ occurs first. If the response is not reinforced, the S-R bond, that is, the habit strength, weakens. When it weakens enough, it becomes weaker than the next habit in the hierarchy, which now is tried out. If it fails, too, it will weaken until the third response takes over. The trial-and-error process continues until the incorrect responses are extinguished and the correct response occurs and is reinforced. Subsequent reinforcements strengthen the response until it is the strongest response in a remade habit-family hierarchy.

Just as one stimulus may elicit many responses, so many stimuli may tend to elicit the same response in a *convergent* hierarchy:

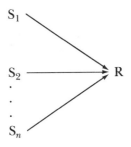

The phenomenon of stimulus generalization can be thought of as a convergent hierarchy: Many related stimuli evoke a CR with differing strengths. Learning involves changes in the S-R connection strengths of convergent and divergent hierarchies.

Tolman's cognitive maps. Tolman's theory was well summed up in his paper "Cognitive Maps in Rats and Men" (1948). In it, Tolman contrasted the S-R view, in which learning consists in establishing S-R connections by reward and breaking them by punishment, with his own view in which organisms selectively take in information from the environment and work it over into a map of their world. It is this cognitive map that controls behavior for Tolman, not blind reactions to external and internal stimuli.

The most famous kind of research that addresses this question, as well as the role of reinforcement in learning, is research on **latent learning** (see reviews by Thistlethwaite, 1951; MacCorquodale & Meehl, 1954). The classic experiments were Blodgett's (1929) and Tolman's and Honzik's (1930). In these experiments some rats learned to negotiate a maze for food reward in the goal box, while others simply wandered around the maze for several trials before food was introduced in the goal box. According to reinforcement theory, learning will not take place without reward—the first group of rats should learn because they are rewarded for learning, and the second group should not begin to learn until reinforcement begins. According to Tolman, even the rats just wandering the maze are learning about their environment—building up a *cognitive map*—even though that learning may not be apparent. Since the food box is not yet a goal, the wandering rats will not head right to it like the rewarded rats.

An S-R reinforcement theory predicts for this experiment that the always rewarded group will learn the maze in some number of trials, for example 12; the wandering group will only *begin* to learn when food is introduced, for example, on the eleventh try, and should take 12 trials beyond that to master the maze. Tolman's theory maintains that after ten trips through the maze even the nonrewarded rats will have learned

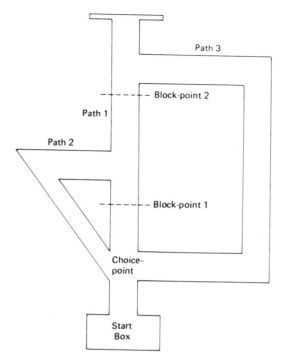

FIGURE 3-1 Tolman-Honzik maze.

its layout, and when food is introduced on trial 11 they will do just as well as the rewarded group, their "latent learning" being immediately transformed by purpose into goal-directed performance. Most of the many experiments designed to test latent learning supported Tolman's prediction.

After enough tinkering, Hull's theory was adjusted to "predict" latent learning, but such tinkering has the appearance of defensive rationalization. Tolman's theory is the simpler and more appealing, and he had other research designed to challenge the fundamental S-R idea of the habit-family hierarchy.

We have seen how Hull's habit-family hierarchy is able to give a plausible account of trial-and-error learning. Tolman, however, was able to design experiments in which the hierarchy leads to predictions contrary to intelligent common sense, and thus to Tolman's cognitive-map theory. One of the simpler experiments is shown in Figure 3–1, where a maze used by Tolman and Honzik (Tolman, 1933) is schematically shown.

By suitable placing of blockades, we can force rats to run from start through the different paths to the goal, where they are fed. The crucial choice-point is just down the path from the start box, where the rat must choose path 1, path 2, or path 3. According to Hull, after learning, the stimuli at the choice-point evoke a divergent hierarchy (shown below) such that path 1 is preferred to path 2, which is preferred to path 3.

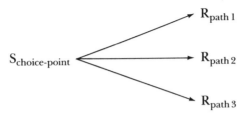

This is quite reasonable, since rats, like people, won't work any harder than they have to for a given reward. We can also justify it on more technical Hullian grounds because Hull's is an S-R chaining theory. Running down a maze path is, in Hull's theory, a chain of responses ultimately rewarded by the terminal reinforced response. The longer the behavior chain, the weaker is its first link. Therefore, since the chain of response links is longest along path 3, the initial turn-right response will be weaker than the turn-left or straight-ahead response. Similarly, the turn-left response will be weaker than the straight-ahead response.

After the rats have learned the three paths, we introduce a barrier at block-point 1. What will a Hullian rat do after bumping its nose on the barrier? It will retreat to the choice-point and execute the next habit in its hierarchy, running, successfully as it turns out, down path 2. Now suppose, instead of blocking at point 1, we block at point 2. The Hullian rat will retreat to the choice-point and again execute its second strongest habit, running down path 2, only to be thwarted again. S-R path 2 now being eliminated, it will return to the choice-point and finally and successfully run down path 3.

But a Tolman rat would behave differently. What it learned to begin with was a map of the environment, rather like Figure 3–1 itself. Now you, and the rat, can see on the diagram that if there is a barrier at choice-point 2, then there is no point in taking path 2, since only path 3 will get you to the goal box. Therefore, the Tolman rat will return to the choice-point and immediately choose path 3. Of course when the block is at point 1, the Tolman rat will choose the shorter path 2, being just as common-sensically lazy as the rest of us.

Unsurprisingly, Tolman's research found most rats to be Tolman rats, and so did most outside research. This kind of finding is powerful evidence that the S-R connection formula and its associated habit-family are hard put to account for all learning by animals or humans.

The Legacy of Purposive Behaviorism

Tolman was a resourceful and clever experimenter, able to challenge effectively S-R psychologies with uncomfortable data. But his own theory was never set out in a systematic enough way for others to use it as well as he did. As he conceded in 1959, his research program was really guided by his own common sense and his own hunches, and these do not travel well to even the closest associates. He seems to have had more fun than most psychologists of learning (Tolman, 1959), but his influence is hard to trace. When a psychologist, all too rarely, follows common sense, is he or she doing it on one's own or following Tolman? Tolman did not have the kind of neo-Tolmanians who followed him the way neo-Hullians followed Hull.

Nevertheless, Tolman did keep open a line of theorizing that without him would perhaps have vanished. He upheld a cognitive account of learning while most psychologists were S-R connectionists. So even though his direct influence on them has not been great, cognitively oriented psychologists such as today's human-information-processing psychologists pay homage to Tolman as their precursor.

THE LEGACY OF FORMAL BEHAVIORISM

Guthrie, Hull, and Tolman, each in his own way, influenced the psychology of learning. But the overall impact of the Golden Age of Theory is harder to make out. For our purposes two influences are paramount.

First, the grand battle of the theorists convinced one psychologist that theories were useless at best, positive burdens at worst. B. F. Skinner (1950) argued that psychology did not really need theories at all, and he proposed his atheoretical approach instead. His radical behaviorism has been so successful that today radical behaviorism is the only behaviorism.

On the other hand, many psychologists considered the grand theories to be dinosaurs, impressive but unwieldy, which should be replaced by newer ways of theorizing. Two new theories did evolve to replace the formal dinosaurs. Many psychologists simply reduced the scope of their theorizing, occupying themselves with relatively specific kinds of animal and human behavior. These mini-theorists, often called *modelers*, proposed small theories in their particular problem areas and refused to think about the laws of all mammalian behavior. This method of constructing theoretical models of specific behaviors has been characteristic both of much of learning theory in the 1950s and the information-processing psychology of the 1960s and 1970s.

Other psychologists were reluctant to abandon the broad claims of the big learning theories, especially those psychologists concerned with social learning and clinical intervention. They wanted some scientific base for thinking about aggression, moral learning, and psychotherapy, but saw that the fine details of the grand theories, especially Hull's, were simply unworkable. So they "liberalized" the theory, which meant including new concepts to help deal with human learning, and giving up mathematical precision for informal theorizing about significant problems.

HUMAN LEARNING

Throughout the 1930s, 1940s, and 1950s, psychologists influenced by the major theorists—especially Hull—continued to experiment on human learning. Their approach was generally S-R in nature but unconstrained by Hull's mania for quantification and his system of axioms. We will look at three areas of human learning in this tradition: problem solving, mediation theory, and verbal learning.

Problem Solving

Habit-family hierarchies are flexible, and Hull used them to give speculative S-R accounts of mentalistic ideas such as knowledge, purpose, and direction of behavior (Hull, 1930b, 1931). However, it was left to followers such as Irving Maltzman (1955) to extend Hull's account to human thinking, and to carry out supporting research, for example, Maltzman & Morrisett (1952, 1953a, 1953b) on the topic of anagram solution set learning.

Almost everyone has played with anagrams at one time or another: You are given the letters of a scrambled word and try to rearrange the letters to recover the original word. Anagrams provide cheap and simple problems that psychologists can pose to research subjects, studying mental *set*; it is one of the oldest ideas in experimental psychology, dating back to the turn of the century. Problem-solving behavior is not random, but has a definite direction. In the case of anagrams you can see a set at work when a subject solves a series of anagrams all scrambled in the same order. After doing a few, the subject no longer tries different letter combinations, but immediately applies the correct unscrambling order. The subject has acquired a disposition, or set, to solve the problem in a given way. Sets can be useful or they can be detrimental as when they make us persistently apply old solutions to new and different problems. This danger can be seen, for example, in generals who are "still fighting the last war," sending cavalry up against tanks, as the leaders of the valiant Poles did in World War II. A mental set can be a deadly problem.

Mental sets appear to challenge behaviorism because they show that problem solving need not involve random trial and error, but may have a definite direction. Maltzman, however, argued that sets are just mental habits. We may analyze the solution of one anagram as a trial-and-error process analogous to figuring out a puzzle-box. We are given the letters N-O-P-D-S and we try out different letter-orders until we get PONDS, the successful R finally rising to the top of our habit-family hierarchy to the stimulus N-O-P-D-S.

Maltzman accounted for "mental" set in the Hullian framework by treating anagrams having the same soltuion as a class of stimuli that can be conditioned to a class of responses. In the above anagram, N-O-P-D-S, the letters of the target word PONDS were placed in the order 32145. After doing several 32145 anagrams, you could do the next one right away—you would have acquired the response-set for unscrambling 32145 anagrams. In S-R notation we might write the set as a habit:

$$S \xrightarrow{\quad 32145 \quad} R_{(321)45}$$

where S_{32145} represents the class of 32145 anagrams and $R_{(321)45}$ represents the response of unscrambling them into the right order by reversing the first three letters.

Of course, other sets could be learned. Suppose all the target words were closely related in meaning, for example, RIVER, BROOK, CREEK, FOGGY—all (wet) nature words. Even if the scrambling order were different for each anagram, knowing it was a nature word would facilitate solving it, that is, it would be a set:

$$S_{nature} \longrightarrow R_{nature}$$

Suppose that in a series of anagrams both sets were present: PONDS is a nature target word and its anagram N-O-P-D-S is in 32145 order. In this case, according to Hullian theory, *both* sets, as habits, should be acquired, setting up a convergent habit-family hierarchy:

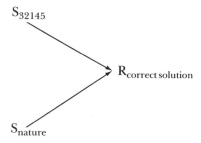

$$S_{32145}$$
$$R_{correct\,solution}$$
$$S_{nature}$$

In Hullian theory, two $_sH_R$'s converging on the same terminal R will *summate*, so that the strength of the compound R will be greater than either S-R habit alone. In terms of anagram solving, the letters N-O-P-D-S will be more readily solves if it has been preceded by a series of anagrams containing both nature and 32145 (order) sets than by either of these sets alone.

Hullian habits can also interact subtractively. If you learn a set of anagrams havings two sets converging on one solution, you acquire the summation of two $_sH_R$'s. If, however, you move on to anagrams having only one of the sets, the number of solutions should decrease, as one habit is no longer operable.

Maltzman and Morrisett (1953a) tested these predictions as well as some others we will pass over. In the *learning* phase of the experiment, ten subjects ($N = 70$) in seven different groups learned 20 five-letter anagrams that embodied the *nature set* (N), the order set 32145 (*O*), or both (*ON*). Then in the test phase subjects solved 15 anagrams that had two solutions each, one adhering to the learned set, the other not. For example, L-D-I-E-F can be unscrambled as FIELD, a nature word, or FILED, not a nature word. K-A-B-E-R can be unscrambled BAKER, if you follow the 32145 order, or BREAK or BRAKE, if you use another order. Finally, E-I-F-L-D, is a compound set anagram, since the 32145 order unscrambled yields FIELD, while the other solution is FILED.

To illustrate the principles discussed here, the important groups are *O-O* and *N-N*, the control groups involving only one set in both learning and test phases; *ON-ON*, the group that learns and is tested on the compound

TABLE 3–1   Mean Set Solutions in the Test
Phase in the Anagram Problem-
Solving Experiment of Maltzman
and Morrisett (1953a)

O-O	N-N	ON-ON	ON-O	ON-N
73.3	55.3	87.3	61.3	63.3

sets; and *ON-N* and *ON-O*, groups in which the compound habit is learned, and then one habit becomes inapplicable in the test phase. The mean percent of set solutions in the test phase for each group is shown in Table 3–1.

We see that in a general way the Hullian predictions have been borne out. The compound habit group shows more set solutions than any other group, as we expected from the convergent hierarchy set up during training. And in those groups where a habit learned during training can be applied in the test phase, there is a drop in number of set solutions, to be expected from the removal of one of the converging habit acquired during the learning phase.

On the other hand, there are some inconsistent results. Removal of one $_sH_R$ from a converging hierarchy leaves a single habit, either $S_N{\rightarrow}R_N$ or $S_O{\rightarrow}R_O$, but the *ON-N* group has more set solutions than the *N-N* group, and the *ON-O* group has fewer set solutions than *O-O* group. This is surprising since in both cases the remaining habit in training is identical to the one habit acquired by the control groups, leading us to expect that both control and experimental groups should give the same number of set solutions on the test phase.

However, these difficulties are quantitative only, the general predictions having been confirmed. Results like this were typical of later logical behaviorist research, especially in human learning. The theory could explain broad aspects of learning but failed in the quantitative predictions so important to Hull. Consequently, neo-Hullians gradually abandoned Hull's obsession with mathematical precision and they used Hull's theory more informally, as Maltzman did. This retreat from quantification was especially great in those psychologists of learning, Maltzman among them, who applied Hull's approach to human problems.

Thinking as Mediation

S-R psychologists concerned with human behavior found that they had trouble accounting for human thought within Hull's system. People can symbolize their environment, and act on the symbols—think—before behaving. Although Hull did not exploit the idea, he suggested the concept of mediation that his followers used to explain human thinking. Two notions of Hull's suggested the idea of mediation. First was his concept of the *pure stimulus act*. If you ask a man how he ties his shoes, he will very likely make shoe-tying movements with his hands, and will simultaneously describe his movements. The purpose of the hand movements, Hull believed, was purely to provide a stimulus to verbal behavior, and so was a pure stimulus act.

A second source of the concept of mediation was Hull's discussion of anticipatory goal-response errors. As a rat approached the goal of a maze, Hull observed that it was increasingly likely to make a mistaken movement identical to the last movement into the goal box. So, for example, if the last movement was a turn to the right, rats were increasingly likely to turn mistakenly to the right the closer they were to the goal; this is an anticipatory goal-response error, for it anticipates the final correct turn. Hull proposed that such errors occur because of unobserved *fractional anticipatory goal responses*. In the goal box, various behaviors, such as salivation, get associated with the goal. As the rat gets closer to the goal on later trials, these covert responses occur and stimulate the terminal response to occur too soon. Using lowercase letters to designate the covert responses we can write this concept in S-R language: S→r→s→R. The choice-point stimuli elicit the covert response (for example, salivation) whose stimulus properties trigger the too-early goal turn.

Hull's presentation of these ideas was completely peripheralistic. That is, they were conceived as actual miniature behaviors which provide stimuli that trigger subsequent responses. However, it is easy to imagine both pure stimulus acts and r-s links as central mental or brain processes. So one might imagine in mental imagery tying one's shoe, and r-s connections might be internal copies of overt S-R links. If so, then the covert behaviors in the brain, the r-s processes, would *mediate* between external stimulus and overt response. Various of Hull's followers interested in human behavior developed exactly this view (Goss, 1961; Kjeldergaard, 1968). Such neo-behaviorists accept Hull's S-R framework, but elaborate on it by considering the existence and influence of covert, mediating s-r processes that take place in the brain and intervene between a received stimulus (S) and an overt response (R). One of the most widely cited studies in experimental child psychology concerns human discrimination learning and how it develops.

Hull's foremost pupil, Kenneth Spence, intensively studied animal discrimination learning, but unlike Hull, he suspected that his theory of animal discrimination learning might not apply to human beings because of our verbal abilities. Some of Spence's students, especially Howard and Tracy Kendler, set out to investigate Spence's hunch.

Consider the discrimination problem pictured in Figure 3–2. We may require an organism to discriminate the stimuli shown under Preshift Training, rewarding responses (say, bar-pressing) only to the stimuli marked "+," and not those marked "−." Soon the organism will only press the bar when (+) stimuli are present and not otherwise. This is so far only simple discrimination learning as described earlier. After this initial learning, we then change the contingencies of reinforcement as shown under Postshift Training in one of two ways, each without informing the organism of the change, but simply requiring a new discrimination to be learned. In either case the reinforced responses are marked (+); the nonreinforced

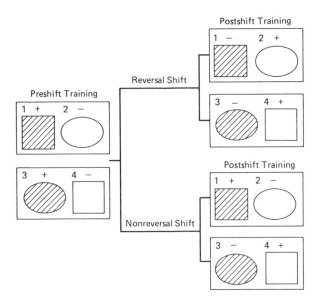

FIGURE 3-2   Discrimination shift learning experiment involving a comparison between a reversal and a nonreversal shift. For each pair of stimuli, plus (+) indicates reinforcement follows a response to that stimulus; minus (−) indicates nonreinforcement.

ones marked (−). The point of the experiment is to find out which kind of shift in contingencies will be more easily learned.

According to Hull's theory, as modified by Spence, what the learner acquires during preshift training is a set of S-R associations. The learner must learn to bar-press (R) to stimuli 1 and 3, but not to bar-press (−R) to stimuli 2 and 4. Four S-R habits are learned: (1) $S_1 \rightarrow R$; (2) $S_2 \rightarrow -R$; (3) $S_2 \rightarrow R$; (4) $S_4 \rightarrow -R$. Given these four habits, a learner should find the extradimensional shift easier. For in an extradimensional shift two habits are still correct, (1) $S_1 \rightarrow R$ and (2) $S_2 \rightarrow -R$, while two habits must be unlearned and replaced: (3) $S_3 \rightarrow R$ is incorrect and must be replaced by $S_3 \rightarrow -R$, and (4) $S \rightarrow -R$ is incorrect and must be replaced by $S_4 \rightarrow R$. In a reversal shift, however, all the earlier habits must be unlearned and replaced with new ones.

Research on this problem revealed an interesting pattern. Animals in a discrimination shift procedure behaved as predicted by the simple S-R model, finding nonreversal shifts easier than reversal shifts. However, college students responded to the shifts the opposite way, preferring reversal to nonreversal shifts. Further, when children were the subjects, it was found that the younger the child the more he or she behaved according to S-R theory, that is, like animals. These findings present an anomaly for Hullian theory. Hull's laws of S-R learning were found not to be the same across different species or even across members of the same species at different ages.

Howard and Tracy Kendler (1962) proposed a mediational analysis of these findings. They suggested that the usual S-R laws, now called *single-stage* S-R laws, applied to animal learning, but that humans possess central and developing cognitive processes—including, most importantly, language—that modify the laws of learning. These central responses *mediate* between environmental stimuli and overt response. According to this model, an environmental stimulus elicits a central, covert symbolic response: $S \rightarrow r$. This central response has covert stimulus properties: $r \rightarrow s$. These stimulus properties then control overt behavior: $s \rightarrow R$. Thus, any cognitively mediated behavior is an associative chain of stimulus-response events some of which are covert: $S \rightarrow r \rightarrow s \rightarrow R$. It is assumed that central responses ($r \rightarrow s$) obey the same behavioral laws as overt responses ($S \rightarrow R$). According to this scheme, the brain functions like the body, only covertly.

The mediational apparatus may be used to explain the apparently anomalous behavior of the college students. The adult subject makes a mediational response (r) to the stimuli to be discriminated. We may regard these responses as implicit labels for the stimuli that categorize them according to the two stimulus dimensions defining the four stimuli. In Figure 3–2, two dimensions, brightness and shape, define the stimuli. The subject learns to make the mediational response "brightness" to the stimuli, because this is the dimension relevant to the preshift training where stippled figures are reinforced and white ones are not. The mediational association $r_{brightness} - s_{brightness}$ controls the terminal overt response: to press the lever when black stimuli are present. We may write what is learned as follows in S-R language.

$$S \rightarrow r \longrightarrow s \longrightarrow R$$
brightness   brightness   black (press lever)

What happens after each possible shift? In the reversal shift, brightness is still the relevant stimulus dimension, so the mediational response is correct, and all the subject must learn is a new terminal response, pressing the lever when the white stimuli are present:

$$S \rightarrow r \longrightarrow s \longrightarrow R$$
brightness   brightness   white (press lever)

However, when the shift is a nonreversal one, the terminal responses are wrong and the mediational response must learn the S-R chain:

$$S \rightarrow r \longrightarrow s \longrightarrow R$$
shape   shape   circle (press lever)

There is more to learn in the nonreversal shift, and so it naturally takes longer.

In general the neo-Hullian regards development as the accumulation of learning. Human cognitive development is different from animal learning because human beings possess symbolic, mediating responses; nevertheless, mediators follow the usual laws of conditioning, and the development of thinking can be explained as the learning of a large number of mediating s-r connections.

Verbal Learning

With his invention of the serial-learning method, Ebbinghaus founded a sturdy line of research into human learning and memory. New methods were added to Ebbinghaus' theory by later researchers. In 1894 Mary Calkins described the method of *paired associate* learning, in which instead of being presented with a serial list of items to be remembered, subjects are presented with pairs of items to be associated, learning to say the response word or nonsense syllable when presented later with the stimulus word or nonsense syllable. (In her pioneering study, Calkins used colors as stimulus items.) Remarkably, in the same year (1894) the third major method in verbal learning, *free recall*, was introduced by E. A. Kirkpatrick. In this technique, subjects are presented with a list of words all at once, and then are asked to recall as many as possible in any order. With some variation, serial learning, paired-associate learning, and free recall were the mainstays of verbal-learning research for 75 years (Kausler, 1974).

Theoretically, the early students of verbal learning continued Ebbinghaus' eclectic associationism, couching their investigations in the classical terms of vividness, recency, and contiguity. However, in the 1930s and 1940s, theories of verbal learning were increasingly dominated by the major behaviorist theories we have reviewed, especially Hull's, so that by the end of World War II the fields of animal and human learning had effectively merged (McGeoch & Irion, 1952; Horton & Turnage, 1976).

Verbal learning was very easy to interpret in S-R terms. Serial learning was treated as the creation of an S-R chain. Each item was both a response and the stimulus for producing the next item: S→R(S)→R(S)→R(S) . . . and so on until the end of the list. Because in serial learning the response and stimulus functions of each word or syllable are mixed up together, S-R theorists preferred the paired-associate paradigm, in which the stimulus and response are clearly separated. Each item in paired-associate learning can be thought of as an S-R pair; for example, in the item VOC-KAS, VOC is the stimulus to which the subject must learn to respond "KAS." Free recall was interpreted as forming responses to the context stimuli in the experimental situation. The idea was that as each word was presented to the subject, he or she would repeat it silently, building up an association between the saying of the word (R) and the experiment room stimuli. The list as a whole would then be learned as a divergent habit family hierarchy in which the central controlling *S* was the experimental context and the R's were the words in the list.

An enormous amount of research on verbal learning was done within the S-R framework from 1930 to 1970. To give some idea of it, we will look at one important phenomenon found in both serial and free-recall paradigms, the *serial position effect*. In serial learning, Ebbinghaus and others found that the middle items of the list took longest to learn compared either to the earlier or later items, with the greatest difficulty being with the items just after the middle one. In free recall, it was found that people were most likely to recall the first items in a list (primacy effect) and the last items in the list (recency effect). These findings received a great deal of interest among investigators of verbal learning, and they also have received explanations in terms of information-processing cognitive psychology, as we shall see later.

Serial learning.   Lepley (1934) and Hull himself (1935) provided the standard S-R analysis of the serial position effect; although it was modified somewhat by Hull's student Hovland (1938a,b) it remained unchallenged until the 1950s. Consider a list consisting of nine items: a-b-c-d-e-f-g-h-i. The excitatory stimulus for the production of response *a* is the experimental situation. The excitatory stimulus for response *b* is the stimulus properties of saying *a*. The excitatory stimulus for *c* is a compound stimulus consisting of the stimulus properties of *b* plus the trace of *a*. The excitatory stimulus for *d* is the convergent compound of traces of *a*, *b*, and saying *c*, and so on until *i*. Observe, however, that traces of earlier responses are linked to several later items, not just the correct one. So, the compound stimulus for *e* is made up of excitatory traces from items *a* through *d*, but these same traces are also linked to response *f* as well. In order to correctly learn the list, one must *inhibit* the incorrect excitatory S-R links. Thus, the S-R link of *a* to *b* is correct, but the link of *a* to *c* is not, and must be inhibited. It now follows that the middle of the list will be hardest to learn. An early item like *b* will have no excitatory incorrect links to it, and increasingly weak stimulus links to *c*, *d*, *e*, *f*, *g*, *h*, and *i* to be inhibited. An end item like *i* will have no inappropriate stimulus links at all, and increasingly inappropriate triggering links from *a*, *b*, *c*, *d*, *e*, *f*, and *h*. A middle item like *d* will have relatively strong links to items on both sides of it to be inhibited, and will therefore be hardest to learn. In sum, the most inhibition will have to be learned at the exact middle of the list, with increasingly less necessary inhibition at either end of the list, and the serial position effect is the result.

Although the Lepley-Hull-Hovland theory provides a general explanation of the serial-position curve, it runs into certain difficulties. For example, it fails to explain why the serial-position effect is asymmetrical, with the hardest to learn item being not the middle one but one shortly after it. As a result, alternative S-R explanations were proposed. To pick just one, Ribback and Underwood (1950) proposed that association formation is anchored at the first item in a list and at the last item, and proceeds as subjects establish associative chains working inward from each anchor. Because backward associations are weaker than forward ones, the chain anchored by the end item builds up more slowly, so that when the chains meet and the list is learned, the meeting point is not the middle item but one shortly after it. By 1970, when information-processing theories of learning supplanted S-R ones, there were several S-R theories of the serial-position effect, none of them entirely satisfactory.

Free recall.   The serial-position effect in free recall was given an S-R explanation by Postman and Keppel (1968). The recency effect was explained by noting that the early items in a list are likely to be rehearsed more than later items. Thus, they are paired more frequently with the experimental context, so that the S-R bonds between them and the contextual *S* will be stronger than for later items. The recency effect was explained in rather Guthrean terms. The items at the end of the list are followed by few (and in the case of the last item, no) later items. Thus, there is little or no new learning to interfere with the S-R connections between the context *S* and the last items. Lack of interference also helps explain the primacy effect, since the early items do not have to compete with already-being-rehearsed items, the way later items do. As we shall see, this Guthrean notion of interference plays an important role in information-processing explanations of the serial-position effect in free recall.

SUGGESTED READINGS

Broad views of the Golden Age of Theory may be had from T. Leahey, *A History of Psychology* 2nd ed. (Englewood Cliffs, N.J.: Prentice-Hall, 1987), and from Sigmund Koch (ed.) *Psychology: A Study of a Science* (New York: McGraw-Hill, 1959). Volume 2 of Koch's work contain the theories presented here, plus others, and are reviewed by the participants themselves.

4

CONTEMPORARY THEORIES OF CONDITIONING

RADICAL BEHAVIORISM: PHILOSOPHY

The thinkers of the Golden Age of theory wore themselves out disputing the field of learning. Then a new voice arose calling for an end to theories. B. F. Skinner (1950) argued that theories, while they might be fun, got in the way of the real job of the psychology of learning—collecting hard facts about behavior change. Skinner would heartily agree with the character in many detective stories who challenges the sleuth by saying, "But this is mere theory. What we need are facts."

Skinner (1974) distinguishes his research program, the experimental analysis of behavior, from the philosophy of mind and science that justify and are justified by his empirical findings. Skinner's philosophy is **radical behaviorism.** Like the behaviorism of Guthrie, Hull, or Tolman, it takes behavior as psychology's subject matter. Radical behaviorism, however, goes much further than formal behaviorism in the implications it draws from this idea. In fact, Skinner's central idea is so simple, yet so challenging to common sense, that it is difficult to grasp.

Every day, each of us tries to explain the behavior of people we know or of public figures. We ask, "Why did Bill break up with Susan?" "Why did that Congressman take a bribe?" We generally try to explain these things by appealing to causes *inside* the person. So we might say that Bill "felt threatened" by Susan's academic excellence; or that the Congressman is "greedy." We do not *see* Bill's insecurity or the Congressman's greed, but we infer it from their behavior and then use it to explain their actions.

In a more sophisticated way, most psychologists, including the formal behaviorists, do the same thing. Tolman did not see little maps in the rats' brains. Rather, he inferred them from their maze-running behavior, and then explained their maze-running as based on having acquired maps. Hull, similarly, did not see little $_sH_R$'s and D's in rats; he inferred them from what he did to the rats—reinforcements for $_sH_R$ and food deprivation for D—and then explained their behavior as an outcome of the joint action of $_sH_R$ and D, namely $_sE_R = {_sH_R} \times D$. Within both common sense and the scientific study of learning, people try to explain behavior in terms of internal causes or purposes.

It is precisely this that Skinner's radical behaviorism repudiates. According to Skinner, "greed," "cognitive map," and "$_sH_R$" are equally unscientific and mythical. We do not *observe* any of these things. Instead, we *infer* them from behavior, thus leaving the realm of facts—behavior—for the realm of fiction—mental or hypothetical concepts.

Skinner insists on sticking to what we can observe, describing behavior precisely and scientifically, and refraining from unnecessary inferences. Why do we say, "Congressman X is greedy?" Because we see him or her take bribes. Skinner says we should forget about "greed"—a mythical mental concept—and just say, "Congressman X tends to take bribes," which precisely describes such behavior and makes no inference past the facts. Similarly, a Hullian would say, "$_sH_r$ is high" because a rat has received 500 reinforcements. Skinner says that inventing $_sH_R$ is needless—just say, "This rat has received 500 reinforcements." A Tolmanian would say, "This rat has a cognitive map," because the rodent chose the smart route in the Tolman-Honzik maze. Skinner says that inventing the cognitive map is needless. Just say, "This rat chose route 3 over route 2 in the Tolman-Honzik maze."

Skinner's philosophy of radical behaviorism is that the causes of behavior and learning lie entirely in the environment rather than in the organism itself. Observable behavior is a lawful function of environmental changes, and the job of the psychologist is to understand that function without inventing mental or other hypothetical entities to intervene between environment and behavior. Skinner hopes to do for psychology what Newton did for physics. Before Newton, many people believed angels pushed the planets around their orbits; Newton's laws of motion showed the angels to be unnecessary and therefore probably mythical. Before Skinner, people believed the mind controls behavior; Skinner hopes to show the mind to be a myth.

Radical behaviorism says that behavior is a lawful function of environmental variables. This belief dictates a research program aimed at discovering such functional relationships or natural laws. That program is the experimental analysis of behavior.

RADICAL BEHAVIORISM: THE EXPERIMENTAL
ANALYSIS OF BEHAVIOR

The Skinner Box

Prior to Skinner's initial work (Skinner, 1938) the most popular experimental setting in learning research was the maze, whether a simple straight alley or a replica of the complex, royal Hampton Court maze in England. Skinner, however, believed that maze learning was not a representative behavior. Most notably, maze learning requires the imposition of separate learning trials: The rat is placed in the start box, navigates the maze, is picked up, and replaced in the start box. But real-life behavior—which is what psychologists of learning ultimately want to understand—is not chopped up into discrete and separate trials. One bit of action leads immediately to another as long as we are awake. So Skinner looked for an experimental arrangement that would keep the virtues of experimenting—control and precise manipulability of the environment—without artificially segmenting the free flow of behavior.

In his desire to achieve the most general account of behavior possible, Skinner made another important decision, namely, to study the acquisition of an *arbitrary* behavior. Skinner feared that many of the responses studied by other psychologists, such as Pavlov's salivation or Watson's conditioned fear, raised the possibility that whatever laws emerged from research on these or similar responses would be valid only for such responses and could not be generalized to other behaviors. Skinner believed that if he studied an arbitrary behavior, one not tied to a specific reinforcer or eliciting circumstance, any discovered regularities in its acquisition would be of general validity.

Putting these requirements together we see that Skinner desired a methodology that would be rigorously experimental, that would produce results of wide generality, without interfering with the natural flow of behavior. What he hit upon has become famous as the "Skinner box," although he prefers to call it "an experimental space," and it quickly eclipsed all competitors as the favored methodology in animal learning research, even among psychologists who are not radical behaviorists.

There are two main kinds of Skinner boxes, one for rats, Skinner's original subjects, and one for pigeons, his favorite subjects in later years. Both boxes are usually made of clear plastic on three walls, some with a shock grid on the floor, and are just large enough to hold the subject comfortably and allow it to move around. The fourth wall contains a magazine that can dispense food or water to a feeding cup, a speaker, a light or lights for discriminative stimuli, and the manipulandum that the subject must operate to get food or water. The manipulandum for the rat is a horizontal lever sticking out of the wall; for pigeons it is a lighted key or keys set into the wall. Operation of the manipulandum activates recording devices and the food or water magazine. Figure 4–1 shows the chamber for a rat (Fig. 4–1a) and for a pigeon (Fig. 4–1b).

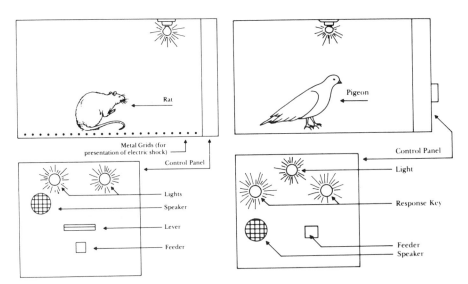

a. The Rat-Conditioning Chamber. *Diagram of a standard conditioning chamber for rats (a) and a rat's-eye view of the control panel housed in the chamber (b).*

b. The Pigeon-Conditioning Chamber. *Diagram of a standard conditioning chamber for pigeons (c), and a bird's-eye view of the control panel housed in the chamber (d).*

FIGURE 4-1   The Skinner box. (Reproduced from *Psychology of Learning and Behavior* by Barry Schwartz, by permission of W. W. Norton & Company, Inc. Copyright © 1984 by W. W. Norton & Company, Inc.)

With one exception, these boxes meet Skinner's requirements. Once placed in the box, animals move about freely and need not be handled until an experiment is over, so that separate trials are not imposed. For the rat, bar-pressing is an arbitrary behavior unlikely to occur in the wild and, therefore, unlikely to be closely tied with a special set of circumstances. In the case of the pigeon, pecking a lighted key appears to be an arbitrary behavior, but it really is not, because pecking is how wild pigeons get their food and drink. Consequently, to get a more arbitrary behavior in a new type of Skinner box, pigeons must work a foot-treadle for reinforcement. But just as Guthrie's difficulties with the cat's greeting response, this short-coming of the key-peck did not become apparent for more than 20 years.

In addition to meeting Skinner's theoretical requirements, Skinner boxes have practical virtues. Bar-presses and key-pecks are easily defined and counted, allowing precise quantification of behavioral laws. A good dependent variable—response rate—is easily calculated and graphed, directly revealing the impact of experimental manipulations. Finally, data collection can be automated, removing much of the drudgery from research. Because there are no experimental trials, the experimenter need not be

BOX 4–1 Biofeedback

Earlier in this text we learned how Neal Miller's demonstration of the operant conditioning of autonomic functions helped undermine the distinction between operant and classical conditioning. Not long after, psychologists applied similar techniques to human beings, and in 1969 coined the term **biofeedback** to name the learned, voluntary control of bodily states. In biofeedback learning, subjects are hooked to a device that signals when a certain bodily process is being altered. By using these signals the subjects learn to produce the change at will.

While "biofeedback" designates the learned control of any ordinarily involuntary physiological state or activity (Blanchard & Epstein, 1978; Yates, 1980), the most famous example is the control of one of the brain's four known brain waves, the *alpha* wave. Because of concurrent popular interest in "altered states of consciousness," and because early reports of subjects in the learned alpha state resembled reports of mystic meditation, alpha-wave feedback became famous. Demonstrations were given on television talk shows, and alpha-wave biofeedback devices were advertised in the back of *Psychology Today*, a popular journal where alpha-wave biofeedback made its first splash in 1968.

Unfortunately for its enthusiasts early claims that subjects in alpha biofeedback experiments were learning to alter, and presumably raise, their consciousness have not panned out. There is good evidence that now subjects learn to produce alpha waves unfocussing their eyes—which hardly seems a likely path to enlightenment.

Nevertheless, biofeedback training has been applied to many clinical problems, from alcoholism to sexual dysfunctions, from dental hygiene to blindness (Yates, 1980), although the effectiveness of such applications has been questioned, and how biofeedback works, if it does, remains mysterious (Yates, 1980). In a debate familiar to students of learning, it is still unclear whether the biofeedback signal that subjects use to monitor the bodily function they are trying to control is an operant reinforcer (Black, Cott, & Pavloski, 1977) or an informational signal (Lazarus, 1977). Until these controversies are resolved, anyone contemplating biofeedback training or investing over a hundred dollars in an alpha-wave signaler should proceed with caution, reading, for example, *A Biofeedback Primer* (Blanchard & Epstein, 1978) which, while positive, is not over-enthusiastic.

present after putting the animal in the box. The control panel can be linked to simple computers that record and plot each response and control discriminative stimuli and reinforcement delivery. Skinner's shared exemplar has also provided the inspiration for various human applications. These range from teaching machines to behavior therapy. One application—biofeedback—for a while seemed to open a technological Western doorway to *satori*. See Box 4–1.

The Contingencies of Reinforcement

Skinner believes that in order to describe scientifically the acquisition, retention, and loss of a piece of behavior one must be able to specify three things: the response itself, the setting in which the response is most likely to occur, and the reinforcer responsible for acquisition and maintenance of the response. These three things Skinner (1969) calls the **contingencies of reinforcement.**

The Response

Two kinds of learning.   Skinner has always been one of the most influential advocates of the view that there are two kinds of learning corresponding to two kinds of responses, *respondents* and *operants*. Respondent behavior was studied by Pavlov. A respondent is a response that is unconditionally *elicited* by some particular stimulus, a US. Operant behavior was studied by Thorndike. An operant is a response that simply occurs for no observable reason; as Skinner explains, an operant is a response that is simply emitted, not reflexively elicited. An operant *operates on* the environment, and the result of the operation—reinforcement, punishment, or nothing—determines whether the response will become more or less likely to occur.

Defining the operant.   Because behavior is observable, it seems at first glance easy to define a particular operant behavior. But this ease is altogether illusory, and Skinner has been careful to avoid the pitfalls into which other behaviorists have stumbled.

The major pitfall of behaviorism has been defining responses as particular movements, as Guthrie and Hull did. It is tempting to define the operant a rat learns in a Skinner box as a paw push of the lever, that is, as a particular movement made by the rat.

But doing this leads to serious difficulties that may be best illustrated with respect to language, an important topic to Skinner. In the first place, the same physical response can have different meanings. For example, the response "Fire!" means very different things when shouted by a patron in a theater and when shouted by the captain of a firing squad. In the second place, several physically different responses may mean the same thing. For example, "George Washington," "The first President of the U.S.," "The father of his country," and "The man on the one-dollar bill" all designate the same person.

Thus, one of the important criticisms of behaviorism has always been that in reducing action to mere physical movement, the meaning and significance of behavior is lost. Tolman tried to get around this difficulty by leaving purpose in animals, ascribing the significance of behavior to the purpose behind it, be that purpose avoiding a finger shock in Wickens' (1938) experiment, or getting fed at the end of a maze.

But Skinner thought purposes too mentalistic because we cannot see them or describe them directly. So in his characteristic way Skinner moved the meaning and significance of behavior out of the organism's invisible mind and into its visible environment. Skinner, therefore, defines an operant in terms of the setting in which it occurs and in terms of the reinforcer that maintains it.

We can illustrate this definition first with the Skinner box and then apply it to human language. We could teach a hungry and thirsty rat to press one bar for water and another for food. While the movements involved in pressing each bar might be identical, Skinner would identify two different operants, each controlled by its consequence, or reinforcer. Here is a laboratory analogue to the case of "Fire!" For the firing squad or the audience the shout creates different reactions and different consequences for the speaker, and so, despite the similarity of the vocal movements and sounds, we may identify two different operants. In our human example, of course, the operants are distinguished by setting as well as by consequences.

On the other hand, in a standard Skinner box the rat could press the lever in many ways—with the right paw, left paw, both paws; with the nose, by biting it and pushing down, etc. But all these movements achieve the same end, namely, depressing the lever and closing an electrical switch that delivers food. Therefore, since the setting and the consequence of all these movements are the same, we identify only *one* operant, lever-pressing, or even switch-closure. As Schwartz (1984) points out, an operant exists only for the experimenter, not for the learner. The learner may do many things, but the Skinnerian counts only one thing—switch-closure. Applying this example to language, Skinner would identify only one operant in the various phrases that designate George Washington. Each phrase is different, but the discriminative stimulus for each is the same.

Skinner, then, defines an operant not as a single behavior, but rather as a *class of behaviors*, all controlled by the same setting and consequences, that is, by the same contingencies of reinforcement.

Shaping.   Precisely because operants are emitted and not elicited, there is no way we can make them occur. If we put a naive rat in a Skinner box we might have to wait days before it pressed the lever and got reinforced. Similarly, if parents waited until their child said, "Mother, I am thirsty and would like some juice," before responding, they would have a long and fuss-filled wait. Both experimenters and parents, therefore, resort to *shaping*, to leading the organism to make the correct response.

The basic idea behind shaping is the law of effect—an animal will be more likely to do that for which it has just been rewarded. We place our naive rat in the Skinner box. It wanders around the cage, and when it goes into the end near the bar we press a button and food is delivered in the tray. As a result, the rat will spend more time near the control panel. Next we require a little more. At some point while hanging around the control panel the rat will align itself facing the bar. We reinforce it. Soon the rat is facing the bar most of the time. So we require a little more, that the rat touch the bar before we reinforce it. Now that we have gotten it to touch the bar, the rat is likely to press it sometime, and the *terminal response* of bar-pressing will have been acquired.

Shaping, therefore, is the gradual molding of diffuse behavior into a well-defined operant. Just as the sculptor shapes clay, so the experimenter shapes the behavior of animals into the form he or she wants it to take. Similarly, parents respond to imperfect "ma-ma's" and badly pronounced "juice's" when their children are two, but successively require better responses as the children get older. Thus, the parent, albeit not always successfully, tries to shape a fussing baby into a civilized adult.

Having discussed operant responses, we will turn now to the environmental factors that control emission of operants, the **setting** and the **reinforcer.**

The Setting

Both common sense and psychologists of learning agree that behavior is controlled by its setting. We act very differently with friends, with parents, with professors or deans, in the gym, in bed, or in the army. Beginning with Pavlov, psychologists have studied the controlling effect of the situation as *the stimulus control of behavior*. We have already studied how Pavlov discovered and elaborated on stimulus generalization—the tendency of a response learned in one setting to occur in similar ones—and stimulus discrimination—the capacity of an organism to respond to one stimulus but not to another.

These processes also apply to operant behaviors. An operant trained to one discriminative stimulus, for example a 1000-Hz tone, will generalize to tones close to 1000 Hz, the rate of response declining as new tones depart from 1000 Hz. We can create a *discriminated operant* by reinforcing a lever-press in the presence of a 1000-Hz tone, but withholding reinforcement to a 2000-Hz tone. Soon the animal will use the lever only when the 1000-Hz tone is sounding.

The fact that generalization and discrimination apply to the wider field of instrumental behavior, as well as to classical responses, gives radical behaviorists the hope that even complex behaviors, not obviously under stimulus control, can be explained if only the search is conducted thoroughly enough. So, for example, much of child development might be explained as the outcome of generalization and discrimination. Children must learn to act appropriately in certain settings (parents are fond of saying things like, "This is the dining room, not a gymnasium!") and this is discrimination learning. At the same time children must apply what they learn in school to new situations—being able to add not just 2 + 2 but also 432 + 182— and this is generalization.

In discussing Pavlov's study of discrimination learning we spoke of discrimination as setting the processes of inhibition and generalization against one another. So a nonreinforced CS becomes an active inhibitor of the response, while the reinforced CS becomes an elicitor. This is also normally the case in operant conditioning. A discriminative stimulus that signals reinforcement (S^+) increases response rate, while a nonreinforced discriminative stimulus (S^-) reduces the rate.

However, it has proved possible in operant conditioning to create discriminations in which the subject almost never responds to S^-, so that it never acquires negative, inhibitory properties, remaining a truly neutral stimulus. This technique is called *fading* (Terrace, 1963a,b).

Terrace first trained pigeons to peck a red key to obtain reinforcement; the red key became a S^+. Then he turned the light on the key off for 1 second. Pigeons generally do not peck dark keys, so they resumed responding when the light came back on. Then Terrace gradually increased the duration of the dark interval to 30 seconds. The change was so gradual that the pigeons rarely pecked the darkened key. Thus, an errorless discrimination was established between the red S^+ and the dark S^-. Then Terrace *faded* in a new S^- by very dimly illuminating the key during its darkened interval with a green light. Because the key was still mostly dark, it remained an S^-, not being pecked. Very gradually Terrace again increased the green illumination until it was just as bright as the red S^+. Nevertheless, the green key became an S^-, and a new discrimination was established between green and red, with few if any errors being made.

In his second experiment, Terrace showed that the fading procedure was much more efficient than the usual method of discrimination learning, which may involve hundreds or even thousands of keypecks to S^- and various emotional reactions of rage and frustration.

However learning takes place, it is through the process of discrimination and generalization, in the radical behaviorists' view, that the setting comes to exert control over behavior. Learning involves not only the acquisition of a new response, but also learning when that response will be reinforced and when it will not be—discrimination—and learning to transfer the new response to similar situations—generalization.

The Reinforcer

Kinds of reinforcement. A **reinforcer** is anything that strengthens the behavior that leads to it. More technically, a reinforcement is any event that increases the probability, that is, raises the response rate, of the operant upon which it is contingent. Between them, the setting and the reinforcer determine what behavior will occur when.

There are two types of reinforcement, **positive reinforcement** and **negative reinforcement.** Positive reinforcement corresponds to what common sense calls *reward*. Positive reinforcement is an event that, when it follows an operant response, increases the likelihood that that response will recur. Obvious examples of positive reinforcers are food, water, sex, and money, although, as we will discover shortly, almost anything an organism does can be a positive reinforcer.

Negative reinforcement is an event whose *termination*, when it occurs following an operant response, increases the likelihood that the response will recur. A negative reinforcer is typically a noxious stimulus that an animal will learn to avoid. So, for example, if a rat is placed in a box divided into two compartments by a low wall and is shocked in one compartment, and jumps the wall into the safe compartment, we can say that the jump was *negatively reinforced* by the termination of shock. Obviously, the rat will quickly learn to jump the barrier whenever placed in the electrified

compartment. An example of everyday negative reinforcement is nagging—
your mother nags at you to clean up your room until you do so, and
then she stops her nagging, hoping you will keep your room clean. Torture
may also be regarded as negative reinforcement—"Tell us what we want
to know and then we will stop!"

One of the two most common confusions in all psychology (the other
being confusing schizophrenia with multiple personality disorder) is to
identify negative reinforcement with punishment. This happens because
"negative reinforcement" sounds like the opposite of "positive reinforcement," as punishment is the opposite of reward, and because the stimuli
used to engender negative reinforcement are frequently the same used
in punishment.

But punishment is not a reinforcer at all, since its aim is the *reduction*
of the frequency of some behavior. Punishment may be defined as an
event, following an operant response, that reduces (or attempts to reduce)
the likelihood of that response being repeated. The difference between
negative reinforcement and punishment may be painfully illustrated by
the Inquisition (Le Roy Ladurie, 1978). If a heretic is put on the rack as
a consequence of being a heretic, this is punishment, for the pain follows
the offensive behavior and aims to reduce it. If, on the other hand, the
heretic is put on the rack to obtain the names of other heretics, this is
negative reinforcement. For the pain will cease when the desired behavior
occurs, and the Inquisitor hopes it will lead to further confessions.

To our list of behavior controllers—positive reinforcement, negative
reinforcement, and punishment—we may add *extinction*. Extinction (already
familiar from Pavlov's research) like punishment aims at the reduction of
some response rate, but it does this by withdrawing previously available
reinforcement.

Which means of controlling behavior works best is controversial, even
among behaviorists. Punishment is the traditional favorite among govern-
ments and parents alike. Typically, the citizen or child is allowed to emit
behaviors except for a few that are punished. Negative reinforcement is
also popular, whether as parental nagging or as government harassment.

Positive reinforcement mostly occurs in praise, raises, and government
contracts, but in a day when most raises depend on union threats and
the cost of living, it is unclear if they are really rewards for any individual's
behavior. Extinction—simply ignoring an unpleasant behavior until it goes
away—is probably the least-used technique.

Skinner himself has been a consistent opponent of punishment as a
behavior controller. In the first place, Skinner maintains that punishment
is generally ineffective. It does not really "unlearn" behavior; it just temporarily suppresses it. The high recidivism rates of American convicts may
support his view. In the second place (and this shortcoming applies to
negative reinforcement as well), aversive stimuli create unfortunate emotional side effects. Punishment or its threat produces anger, hostility, anxiety, and aggression even in animals. Since happiness consists in getting
what you want, Skinner advocates thoroughgoing and careful use of positive
reinforcement by parents and by society. People can be shaped into accept-

able behaviors by proper application of rewards, and, as a direct consequence, they will be made happy by receiving rewards.

However, there have always been those who dispute Skinner's negative evaluation of punishment (for example, Solomon, 1964). They argue that punishment can be effective, but that it is generally badly used. For instance, it is well established that delaying the consequences of an act, whether reward or punishment, attenuates the reinforcing or punishing effects and does little to strengthen or weaken the behavior. But in most human cases punishment is long delayed, as when a mother waits for father to get home to spank his naughty boy. And, of course, criminals do not go to jail until months, even years, after their crimes were committed.

Likewise, to be effective, punishment must be reasonably severe—which rarely happens to children. Finally, punishment is most effective if alternative, rewarded behaviors are available, but all too often neither children nor criminals are taught such alternatives.

Ultimately, the choice of whether or not parents and society should use punishment depends on ethics as much as on science. Can we in good conscience eliminate the legal system that creates the delay between crime and incarceration? If imprisonment is too weak to be an effective punishment do we return to whips, to the severing of noses and ears? Capital "punishment" is, of course, not punishment at all because it does not reduce the strength of the operant that led to the crime, except in the sense that it reduces all operant strengths to zero.

Similarly, we must ask how much pain are we willing to inflict on a child to get it to behave? While Skinner's critics may be technically right about the effectiveness of punishment, Skinner is probably right about punishment as it is actually used and as we may morally use it.

Primary and secondary reinforcement.   In Chapter 2 we discussed higher order classical conditioning, in which an established CS can be paired with a neutral CS until the new CS elicits the same response as the established CS. The same phenomenon occurs in operant conditioning, where it creates a secondary, or conditioned, reinforcer.

A primary reinforcer, like a US, is a reinforcer whose reinforcement value is biologically established. Food is a US in classical conditioning and a primary reinforcer in operant conditioning. We can create new reinforcers by pairing a neutral stimulus with a primary reinforcer, whether as a CS in classical conditioning or as an S^+ in operant conditioning. The new stimulus then acquires reinforcing powers. We can use it to reward and establish some new behavior. Of course, primary reinforcement must sometimes be forthcoming, otherwise the secondary reinforcer would lose its value through extinction.

As it is obvious that most human behavior is neither taught nor maintained by primary reinforcement, the concept of secondary reinforcement is of special importance in accounting for human learning. Parents, teachers, and employers do not run around popping food into the mouths of those who please them, but they do dispense praise, gold stars, and bonuses. Behaviorists treat all these as secondary reinforcers, assuming, even when they cannot prove it, that these acquired their reinforcing properties through higher order conditioning.

Relativity of reinforcement. A student of Skinner's, David Premack (1959, 1962, 1965a), offers an interesting extension of the notion of secondary reinforcement. He proposes what has come to be called the principle of **relativity of reinforcers.**

The basic idea is simple and commonsensical. A person or other animal engages in many activities and does some more frequently than others. So activity *A* is more frequent than activity *B*, which is more frequent than *C*, and so on: $A > B > C > D$. . . . Premack says simply that any activity higher on the scale can be used to reinforce any activity lower on the scale. Eating is more common than lever-pressing in a naive rat, and so we can use the opportunity to eat to reinforce bar-pressing. A child may prefer playing baseball to reading, and so we can use access to baseball as a reinforcer for reading.

Premack's suggestion is useful in two ways. First, it reminds us of individual differences. At least in people, what is reinforcing for one person may not be reinforcing for another. A shy, introverted child may read more than play baseball, and a teacher concerned with the child's loneliness may make access to books contingent on playing with other children.

Second, Premack's principle offers concrete guidance to the behavior modifier. It points out that for any given low-level behavior you wish to strengthen there must be many potential reinforcers, and it tells how to locate and use them.

Theoretically, Premack's idea suggests that the distinction between primary and secondary reinforcement is too simple. Instead of two categories of reinforcers there is a continuum, from the most powerful and general, such as food and water, to the weakest and most idiosyncratic. In any event, the relativity of reinforcers helps extend the behaviorists' analysis of human behavior by showing how reinforcers are everywhere in behavior, not just in objects, and that what is in one context a behavior to be reinforced by a stronger one, may in another context become itself a reinforcer.

Patterns of Reinforcement

The patterns of reinforcement effect. Because he (Skinner, 1959) wanted to economize on the costs of feeding his experimental subjects, Skinner (1938) made an interesting discovery, one that was made independently by Humphreys (1939). Instead of reinforcing every bar-press his subject made, Skinner reinforced only some of the responses. In the developed jargon of learning psychology, Skinner shifted from *continuous reinforcement*, in which every response is reinforced; to *partial reinforcement*, in which only some of the responses are reinforced on one schedule or another.

Skinner found that when an animal was on a partial reinforcement schedule it took longer for a learned bar-press response to extinguish than if it had been on a continuous reinforcement schedule. Particularly in the light of Hullian theory, this finding appeared paradoxical. Suppose we compare two hypothetical rats, both of which have made 500 bar-presses, but one rat has been continuously reinforced while the other has been only partially reinforced, receiving one reinforcement every ten presses. Because habit strength grows with the number of reinforcements, we would expect the continually reinforced rat, who has received 500 reinforcers, to have a stronger, more resistant habit than the partially reinforced rat, who has received only 50 reinforcements. The opposite, however, is the case.

This greater resistance of partially reinforced responses is called the **partial reinforcement effect,** and it is a reliable and robust phenomenon. Practically, it has proved to be of great value to behavior modifiers, because it provides a reliable means of strengthening a behavior and preparing it for the real world, where people get less attention than in an institution, be it a school, a prison, or a mental hospital. The partial reinforcement effect indicates that positive learned behaviors should transfer to the real world if they are at least occasionally reinforced.

Of course, the effect has its drawbacks. If a child learns to whine and fuss to get things from its parents, and the parents decide to ignore the behavior to get it to go away, then they will have to possess great fortitude and resistance to aversive stimuli. For, if they give in occasionally, they put their child on a partial reinforcement schedule and will wind up with more persistent whining than if they simply indulged the child for a while when it was an infant and then stopped cold.

Theoretically, the partial reinforcement effect has proven controversial. Two main theories have been offered to explain it. The first one, the discrimination theory, Capaldi (1966, 1971), says that it is easy for a continuously reinforced animal to tell when extinction begins, because the shift from continuous reinforcement to no reinforcement is abrupt and obvious. But to a partially reinforced animal the onset of extinction is much less obvious, and so, instead of quickly giving up responding, it keeps pressing the bar for no reward.

The second theory, the expectancy theory, (Amsel, 1958, 1962, 1967) says that when an animal expects a reinforcement but it does not occur, this event is frustrating and aversive. In a sense, failure to get an expected reward is punishing. Now the partially reinforced animal has learned to live with this kind of frustration, but the continuously reinforced animal, having never experienced nonreward, has not. Consequently, when extinction begins, the punishing effect of nonreward is much greater for the continuously reinforced animal, and it quickly stops responding, while the partially reinforced animal, feeling less punished, will continue the response longer.

Schedules of Reinforcement

Once the idea of partial reinforcement was in hand, it opened up a new research program. It became possible to manipulate systematically the schedule on which reinforcement was delivered to the learning organism and to observe the effect of each schedule on the response rate. Such a program occasioned Skinner's most massive empirical work (Ferster & Skinner, 1957) and has remained a prime focus of research among radical behaviorists ever since. While the number of schedules investigated by Ferster and Skinner is quite large, and new ones have been invented since, there are four basic schedules of reinforcement—**fixed ratio, variable ratio, fixed interval,** and **variable interval.**

Fixed ratio.   In a ratio schedule, delivery of reinforcement depends on the number of times the learner makes the response. In a fixed ratio (FR) schedule, there is a fixed number of responses that must be made before the reward will be forthcoming. Continuous reinforcement is an FR1 schedule, because there is a fixed ratio of one reinforcer per response. In an FR5 schedule only every fifth response is reinforced, whereas in FR8 every eighth response is reinforced, and so on.

Variable ratio.   In a variable ratio schedule, it is still the number of responses that determines delivery of reinforcement, but in this case the ratio changes from reinforcement to reinforcement. So, for example, reinforcement might be delivered after the fifth response, then the second, then the tenth, twelfth, third, and so on. In some cases the ratios may go through a regular cycle; for example, reinforcing the third response, then the tenth, then the fifth, then the seventh, and then back to the third, the tenth, and so forth.

Fixed interval.   In an interval schedule, delivery of reinforcement depends on the passage of time. After a reinforced response, some interval of time passes during which reinforcement is unavailable; after the interval is over, the next response is reinforced which begins the nonreinforcement interval again. In a fixed interval schedule, the nonreinforcement period is the same every time. For example, a FI30″ schedule would impose a 30-second interval of nonreinforcement, while a FI2′ schedule would impose a two-minute wait, and so on.

Variable interval.   By now you should be able to guess what this is. A variable interval schedule is an interval schedule in which the period of nonreinforcement is different after each reinforced response.
    Ratio schedules typically produce higher rates of responding than interval schedules. Variable schedules produce a steadier rate of response than fixed schedules. This is because fixed schedules produce what is called the *post-reinforcement pause*: After reinforcement the animal does not respond at all for a while, then begins to respond slowly, and finally more quickly. Such acceleration is especially pronounced in FI schedules, when the animal may be responding quite frantically at the time of reinforcement.

Humans and schedules of reinforcement.   When we think of applying schedules of reinforcement to interpreting human behavior there are only two obvious examples. Workers who are paid on a piece-work basis, in which the amount of pay depends on the number of items built, may be on a fixed-ratio schedule—a certain number of pieces yields a fixed return. Slot machines are a more obvious analogue, right down to the response of lever-pressing. These machines pay off at random, on a variable schedule, and produce steady, persistent responding that is highly resistant to extinction.

Other interpretations of natural human schedules are more dubious. Is a person who gets paid every Friday on a fixed-interval schedule, as appears at first glance? Probably not. In the case of animals, the reinforcement, on whatever schedule, reinforces the immediately preceding response. This would make the paycheck reinforce the behavior of going to the payroll office and picking up the check. If people behaved exactly like animals, we would hang around the payroll office all Friday, periodically asking if the check had arrived, and never going to work. In any case, there is growing evidence from the laboratory that people are not very sensitive to actual schedules of reinforcement.

There is a body of data (for example, Baron, Kaufman, & Stauber, 1969) that shows that:

1. Human subjects on a given schedule of reinforcement do not exhibit the characteristic behavior associated with that schedule unless they are instructed as to the schedule in effect.
2. Instructions induce behavior appropriate to the described schedule even when subjects receive no reinforcement.
3. Instructions induce behavior appropriate to the described schedule, even if some *other* schedule is really in effect.

An example shows the difficulty of directly applying operant learning laws to human behavior, even in the laboratory. Weiner (1970) explored the effects of certain kinds of instructions on extinction following partial reinforcement. Subjects sat alone in a room and pressed a key that operated a digital counter on an FR3 schedule: Three presses yielded a one-digit advance on the counter. Subjects were told that at the end of the session they would receive as many pennies as there were digits on the counter. The five subjects in the first of three groups were told that 700 pennies were the most they could earn. The five subjects in the second group were told they could earn 999 pennies. The five subjects in the last group were given no instructions about how much they could earn. In all cases the objective situation was the same—after the counter got to 700, extinction was begun and lasted for two hours.

The results were that the first group extinguished quite quickly, two subjects making no response after 700, and the others very few responses past 700. Subjects in the second group persisted longer, but completely extinguished after a while. Subjects in the third group showed little, if any, slowing of their response rates during extinction. Weiner comes to the stunning (at least for a behaviorist) conclusion that his study (and many others done by radical behaviorists) shows that people can follow instructions!

These studies further support Brewer's (1974) argument that human behavior is determined less by the objective manipulations to which experimenters subject their subjects than by what the subjects believe is happening. This means that objective schedules of reinforcement may not be very useful to our understanding of human learning. In fact, some animal researchers (Jenkins, 1970, for example) have suggested that, because of their inapplicability to the natural environment and the complexity of long-term schedules of reinforcement, exhaustive study of animal learning under various schedules of reinforcement is a waste of time.

Conclusion

For Skinner, analysis of the contingencies of reinforcement completely exhausts what a psychologist may scientifically say about a piece of behavior. Skinner sometimes calls this approach *functional analysis*, because it aims at uncovering lawful functional relationships that hold between behavior and its environmental determinants.

The response itself is the *dependent variable*, usually quantified by measuring the rate of response. The things in the environment the experimenter manipulates—discriminative stimuli; kind, quality, and quantity of reinforcer; schedule of reinforcement; and hours of reinforcer deprivation—are the *independent variables* of which the dependent variable is a function. The research program dictated by Skinner's framework is clear: Exert total control over the learner's environment by controlling all the independent variables, and then systematically manipulate the independent variables, observing the consequent changes in behavior, the dependent variable. Properly done, functional and causal laws linking the dependent variable to its antecedent independent variables will emerge.

In the perspective of radical behaviorism, the organism, animal or human, is reduced to a *locus of variables* (Skinner, 1969). A person is no more than a place where independent variables come together and interact to determine the dependent variable—behavior. In radical behaviorism there is no need to look inside the organism for the causes of behavior; they lie in the environment, in the independent variables. Even physiological explanations of behavior may be ignored, for, however the nervous system works, the facts of behavior remain, and Skinner insists we can hunt for the laws of behavior without worrying about why, physiologically, they are true.

Another important way of looking at radical behaviorism and the experimental analysis of behavior is by comparing them to Darwin's theory of natural selection, as Skinner often does (Skinner, 1969). Darwinian theory states that species' offspring are variants on their parents—new combinations of genes and mutations of genes—each quite different from the other. Out of this variation nature selects some favorable traits and rejects harmful ones; animals with the good traits live while those with the bad traits die. Finally, the successful variants grow up and pass their successful traits on to their offspring. Variation, selection, and retention are the three processes of evolution, and, for Skinner, of learning.

An organism emits many different behaviors (variation). Some of these are reinforced; others are not reinforced or are even punished (selection). Reinforced behaviors are learned (retention). Darwin's theory of natural selection eliminated the need for God or any other supernatural principle to give direction and purpose to evolution, by reducing evolution to blind variation, natural selection, and genetic retention. In the same way, Skinner hopes to eliminate the need for a mind or inner purpose to account for learning, by reducing learning to blind emission of operant behaviors, selection by reinforcement, and retention of learned behaviors.

RADICAL BEHAVIORISM: EXTENSION TO HUMANS

Especially since World War II, Skinner's major preoccupation has been extending the results of his animal research and his philosophy of radical behaviorism to human behavior. Two problems in particular have occupied him: understanding language and scientifically designing cultures.

Verbal Behavior

As a would-be writer (Skinner, 1976), Skinner has a keen interest in language. He worked for years on the problem of language, and his operant analysis was finally published in 1957 as *Verbal Behavior*. He treats language as a complex set of operant responses shaped by a child's parents, teachers, and peers, being brought under the control of stimulus and reinforcement. This is in strong contrast to the traditional, Cartesian account of language as a unique human possession that sets people—who have free souls—apart from merely mechanical animals. Skinner's book is lengthy, complex, and full of novel terminology. To illustrate the approach and show one of its difficulties, we will briefly consider one operant class distinguished by Skinner, the *tact*, which has nothing to do with polite public behavior.

What Skinner calls a tact we might intuitively call a naming response; it deals with the ancient philosophical problem of universal concept terms (see Leahey, 1987). The problem is this: How does a child learn to categorize correctly the objects in its world as cats, dogs, toys, cars, and so forth? As every parent knows, it takes a long time for children to label correctly what they see. One child known to the author had a pet gerbil, and at the age of two the youngster called all furry animals, even big dogs, "Gerbil!"

Skinner views such class names—or universal terms as opposed to the individuals that make up the class—as *discriminated operants*. Applying contingencies analysis, let us select one operant, the class-name, or *tact*, "cat." The discriminative stimulus controlling emission of "cat" is, of course, some cat the child sees. Stimulus generalization comes into play, for since all cats resemble each other, learning to label a few cats "Cat!" will generalize to new cats. The reinforcement control is through praise for correct responses of "cat" to cats, and corrections of incorrect responses of "cat" to other animals. In this way, shaping takes place, and soon the child will say "cat" only to cats.

This is Skinner's whole analysis; being a realist, he does not bring in mental images of cats, or "the idea of the cat," or "the concept of the cat," or any other unobservable mental entity. For Skinner, a class-label, a tact, is no more than a type of verbal operant that refers to its controlling stimulus. It makes con*tact* with the environment, hence its name.

While Skinner's analysis of class names, or tacts, is unusual, it has some plausibility. Its difficulties emerge when we try "tacting" our own behavior. Skinner faces up to the difficulty of accounting for utterences such as, "I am looking for my glasses." This utterence has elements of the tact about it for it names the object of my search. But the object is not present to control my speech, and Skinner cannot allow that I have an image of my glasses to which I am referring. Instead Skinner (1957) maintains that the stimulus control of the verbal operant "I am looking for my glasses" is the observation of my searching behavior. The meaning of the statement does not derive from any idea in my mind, but instead means, "When I have behaved in this way in the past, I have found my glasses and have then stopped behaving this way." Simply put, according to Skinner when you ask me what I am doing, I observe my own behavior, see myself rummaging around in my desk, and am moved to say as a result of my observations, "I am looking for my glasses."

As an otherwise sympathetic observer (Malcolm, 1964) has observed, Skinner's description of such sentences is "weird." If you asked me what I am doing and I uttered the real meaning of "I am looking for my glasses," namely, "Well, since I'm rummaging around in my desk, I must be looking for my glasses," you would think that I was either joking or behaving like a radical behaviorist who takes his theory too seriously—or perhaps an alien who had read only Skinner's works as preparation for visiting Earth.

On the empirical front, difficulties have arisen in showing that speech is under operant control. Beginning in the mid-1950s, various researchers (Greenspoon, 1955; Verplanck, 1955) tried to show that verbal behavior follows the laws of reinforcement and extinction. In Verplanck's study, for example, undergraduate student experimenters modified subjects' opinion-giving statements. The experimenters talked to subjects and were only to agree, disagree, or keep silent when opinions were given, refraining from nodding, smiling, asking questions, and so forth. They talked to their subjects for 30 minutes, which was divided into learning phases, when they agreed with opinions, and extinction phases, when they kept silent (in some groups) or disagreed (in other groups). The results were that the frequency of emission of opinions rose when they were reinforced and fell when they were extinguished.

However, Azrin, Holz, Ulrich, and Goldiamond (1961) showed that Verplanck's data were suspect. In the course of replicating Verplanck's study (as a class exercise), they discovered that many of the experimenters had violated the procedures; for example, by participating in the conversation through nods, smiles, and questions, or had been unable to finish the study because the subjects quit during extinction.

Using undergraduate classes, they replicated Verplanck again, except that one class was told what Verplanck told his student-experimenters—

that agreement increases verbal operant rate and disagreement depresses it—while the other class was told just the *opposite*. Each class reported data confirming what it was told to expect. Covert questioning by a student who the class members did not know was working for Azrin and colleagues showed that most of the students has simply made up their data, while nearly all the rest cheated during the experimental sessions.

Finally, four professional experimenters, well-drilled in animal behavior shaping and scientifically aware of the importance of negative results (one suspects they were Azrin, Holz, Ulrich, and Goldiamond themselves), tried to condition 12 subjects. None could complete an experimental session of 30 minutes because each of the 12 subjects got up and left the room before ten minutes were up. As we discovered before, we again find great difficulties in extending the theories and methods of behaviorism to human beings.

Scientific Design of Cultures

During World War II, Skinner (1960) worked on a bizarre project, building a pigeon-guided missile! He designed a missile that contained pigeons in the warhead; their pecking at an image of their target operated flaps on the missile and guided it home. While the kamikaze pigeons performed well in dry runs, the Navy found the project a bit laughable, and Skinner lost his funding. It is ironic that the same military problem—guiding weapons to their targets—helped produce computers and the information-processing psychology that is radical behaviorism's main rival today. But at the time Skinner was most impressed by the degree of behavioral control he had established over the pigeons. In the aftermath of his project's failure he wrote a novel, *Walden II* (1948b), which reveals his postwar obsession, the idea of constructing a scientifically managed society. *Walden II* describes Skinner's fictional utopia, whereas other works (for example, Skinner, 1972) argue that this utopia can actually be attained through behavioral technology.

Through these works the same ideas run like distinct threads. Skinner maintains that existing societies are badly managed, mainly because we believe in myths such as free will. People are no freer than pigeons, Skinner asserts, and to deny that our behavior is controlled is to deny scientific truth. Instead, Skinner asks us to accept that we are just as mechanical as pigeons and rats, and apply the established laws of learning to ourselves. If we do this, Skinner concludes, society will be much better managed, and everyone will be happy under the control of positive reinforcement.

Walden II and Skinner's vision of a remade Western culture are the fruits of his psychology of learning; he maintains that what we have learned in the laboratory of behavior should be applied to the problems of society in the same way that we apply what we have learned from physics and chemistry. While no one has seriously tried to remake Western society along Skinnerian lines, applying behavior modification to social and individual problems has been tried in many settings.

CRITIQUE OF RADICAL BEHAVIORISM

A thinker as radical and aggressive as B. F. Skinner has naturally been heavily criticized on a number of fronts. His analysis of language has been termed folk psychology masquerading as science (Chomsky, 1959). His attacks on mentalism have been found confusing and overdrawn (Dennett, 1978). His atheoretical approach to science has been reproached as simplistic, narrow, and restrictive (Shimp, 1984). However, in the context of the psychology of learning, perhaps the most interesting critique has been the finding that applying reinforcement theory to human beings may be dangerous. William Brewer, as we saw earlier in this text, raised the question of whether or not humans condition. Barry Schwartz (1982) has experimentally demonstrated that when humans are subjected to reinforcement contingencies their motivation declines, their creativity evaporates, and they fall into rigid, stereotyped patterns of behavior.

What happens if we reinforce people for solving problems? Behavior theory would predict improvement in their success at problem solving. However, there is evidence that reward actually undermines cognitive abilities by diminishing their intrinsic attractiveness; it turns fun into work (Lepper & Greene, 1978). Moreover, an elegant series of experiments by B. Schwartz (1982) demonstrates that reward not only undermines intrinsic motivation, but actually damages thinking, almost turning it off.

Schwartz adapted a pigeon experiment for use with undergraduate students. Subjects sat at a display panel containing a 5-by-5 matrix of electric lamps with the top left light illuminated. There was also a response console with two levers, one for each hand, and a digital counter that showed how many reinforcements—later translated into money—they had received. A certain sequence of lever presses was rewarded. When the left lever was pressed the light went out on the display panel and the one below it was lighted. When the right lever was pressed, the light was extinguished and the one to the right was lighted. The rewarded sequence of lever presses brought the light from the upper left corner to the lower right corner; the subject, however, was told nothing about the display panel.

In the first experiment, the rewarded sequence was any series of presses such that each lever was pressed exactly four times. However, subjects quickly fell into a stereotyped sequence of responses. Moreover, they believed their pattern of responses to be the only correct one. That is, each subject confused a sequence *sufficient* to get a reward—the one he or she had used—with the sequence *necessary* to get the reward, which could be *any* sequence of four presses to each key.

In the critical experiment, naive and experienced subjects were again compared, with four groups defined within naive and experienced subjects: One-fourth were reinforced for correct response sequences as before; one-fourth were reinforced only for figuring out the rule that defined the correct response sequence; one-fourth were reinforced for correct sequences *and* were paid a bonus for finding the rule; and the remaining one-fourth received neither reinforcement nor bonuses. All subjects had to solve four problems of varying difficulty, in the same order.

Naive subjects performed equally well under all reinforcement and bonus conditions. Experienced subjects uniformly performed more poorly than naive subjects, especially when they were receiving reinforcement for correct sequences of key presses. The specific deficit induced by reinforcement is that reinforced experienced subjects tried out many fewer hypotheses per block of 50 trials than other subjects. Schwartz suggests that reinforcement induces a passive approach to problems, that pretraining and reinforcement "switches off their active intelligence" (B. Schwartz, 1982, p. 41). Finally, we should note that reinforcement is both damaging and unnecessary; naive subjects who received no payoffs at all did just as well as subjects receiving both reward and rule-finding bonuses.

Schwartz worries—and we should join him—about the effect of behavior modification programs in schools. These programs typically involve reinforcing particular desirable behaviors, and are in widespread use. But if Schwartz's findings are correct, the reinforcement techniques are unnecessary and dangerous. Reinforcement for particular behaviors seems to undermine intrinsic motivation, to short-circuit human problem-solving skills, and to strengthen the confirmation bias already so entrenched. If we want creative scientists, we had better be careful about using reward systems in school.

Finally, Schwartz's research underlines an important and perennial problem of psychology as a science. Unlike the ideas of physicists, psychologists' ideas can affect their subjects' behavior. Society adopts psychological concepts—"Freudian slip" is a household word, and *behavior modification* is used in prisons, hospitals, schools, and workplaces—and so psychology changes the way people behave. In this way, psychological theories can produce self-fulfilling data by changing human nature. As Schwartz puts it:

> It may be that as more components of the natural environment are subjected to modification by applied reinforcement theory, and more components of human behavior are thus controlled by reinforcement contingencies, a point will be reached at which virtually all human behavior will look like operant behavior. If this point is reached, it will tell us not that reinforcement theory has captured something general and essential about human nature, but that it has produced something general in human nature. (B. Schwartz, 1982, p. 58)

BEYOND RADICAL BEHAVIORISM: RECENT ISSUES AND THEORIES

In the last decade the study of animal learning outside the circle of radical behaviorism has flourished. The field of conditioning is in ferment, with old issues revived, new ones raised, and novel theories proposed. In this section we will look at one old issue revived—What is learned?—at one new one tackled—What is the relation of conditioning to the individual organism's survival?—and at a range of new theories.

What Is Learned?

Learning and Performance

One issue that divided Hull and Tolman was the question of what is learned—Hull's S-R connections or Tolman's cognitive maps? Both Tolman and Hull distinguished between learning—what an animal knows—from performance—what an animal does with its learning, and both took their problem to be explaining learning rather than performance. Although a great deal of research was generated by this controversy, it abated in the 1950s. Howard Kendler (1952) influentially argued that the only differences between Hull and Tolman were ways of talking about behavior, so that there was no substantive issue at stake. Because we cannot see what animals have learned, only what they do, arguing about what animals learn is futile, Kendler argued. The similar influence of Skinner caused the *what is learned* debate to lose its urgency, and the *learning/performance* distinction its importance. However, several phenomena, some only recently discovered, demonstrate that learning is not always straightforwardly translated into performance, so reviving the controversy—now several controversies—over learning and performance.

Three interesting phenomena of Pavlovian conditioning illustrate how learning may not be directly reflected in performance. The first is *latent inhibition*. Suppose an animal is exposed several times to a possible CS, for example a tone, without being paired with a US. If we now put the animal through a standard conditioning experiment, pairing the CS with a US, we find that it is more difficult to get conditioning to the preexposed CS than to a novel stimulus. Calling the phenomenon latent inhibition is misleading, because it suggests that the preexposed CS is hard to associate to the US because it has acquired inhibitory properties. That this is not the case is shown when we try to make the preexposed stimulus an inhibitory CS. If it were already inhibitory, such learning should be quite easy, but in fact it is not; it is just as difficult to make the preexposed CS inhibitory as it is to make it excitatory (Schwartz, 1984). Latent inhibition demonstrates the difference between learning and performance, because after mere exposure to the CS we do not see the animal behave any differently toward it: It looks as if the animal has learned nothing. However, when we later try to condition the CS, we find that simple exposure has indeed changed the organism's response to the CS.

Another Pavlovian phenomenon that shows how learning does not always manifest itself in performance is *sensory preconditioning*. Suppose we simply pair two CS's together without a US. Will the animal associate the two? As with latent inhibition, the animal does not immediately demonstrate any changed response to either stimulus, so we need further investigation to answer the question. In one experiment (Rescorla, 1984) rats initially drank two solutions containing water mixed with two harmless chemicals that could be tasted. Let us call one solution the AB solution and the other the CD solution. Then, half the rats drank a solution made with chemical A and were made sick by injection of a nausea-producing drug;

in this situation, taste *A* is a CS, the nausea is a UR, the chemical-producing nausea is the US, and as a CR the animal will avoid drinking the *A*-flavored water. The other half of the rats had the same experience with taste *C*. What we find is that rats sickened with *A* will now avoid a pure *B* solution, but will drink the *C* or *D* solutions, whereas rats sickened to *C* will avoid *D* but not *A* or *B*. It appears that during the initial exposure to the joint solutions, rats learned to associate the tastes—even though such an association was not manifest in their behavior—so that when one member of the pair became a nausea-evoking CS, so did the other. More generally, sensory preconditioning almost always results when we simply pair two stimuli, and then make one a Pavlovian CS: The other becomes an effective CS, too. The important point here is that the initial association formation is not manifested in behavior right away.

A third phenomenon showing that learning and performance are separable comes in a modification of the auto-shaping paradigm followed by some higher-order conditioning (Rescorla, 1984). Recall that in the standard auto-shaping experiment, food is presented to a pigeon in a Skinner box coincident with lighting the response key. Even though the pigeon does not have to peck the key to get grain, it comes to do so anyway. In a variant on this experiment, a tone was presented when the grain was delivered. Naturally a pigeon cannot peck a tone, and in fact manifests no particular response to the tone as pairings continue. So it appears as if nothing has been learned. However, if we now pair the tone with lighting the key—higher-order conditioning—we find that the pigeon auto-shapes to the key. So, even though it was not apparent at the time, the tone got associated with the grain, becoming a CS for the grain, providing the foundation for higher-order learning.

These three phenomena demonstrate very clearly that learning is not always directly and immediately manifested in performance. Learning takes place within organisms, and performance is in turn based on what is learned, and the learning may not reveal itself in behavior until it is useful to the animal to do so. The large issue of what is learned has been intensively investigated recently, and we will examine three specific questions: Is Pavlovian conditioning S-S or S-R? Do Pavlovian and instrumental learning depend only on contiguity of stimuli and responses, or is something more required? And, finally, is conditioning merely associative, or is perhaps something more cognitive involved?

The Nature of Association

The standard stimulus-substitution account of Pavlovian conditioning assumes that the CS gets associated with the UR and comes to elicit a response just like it, the CR; this is thus an S-R theory of learning, embodied, for example, in Hullian and neo-Hullian theories of learning. However, it is possible that pairing CS and US creates an association between them rather than between CS and UR. After learning, when the CS is presented alone it activates an internal representation of the US, and this internal representation in turn elicits the CR. In this scheme, learning is S-S, because two stimuli, the US and the CS, get associated. We have seen how in sensory preconditioning two neutral stimuli can become associated, demonstrating conclusively that S-S learning does occur. The stimulus substitution theory cannot be entirely correct, although other complex experiments show that S-R conditioning can occur too (B. Schwartz, 1984). Apparently, both S-S and S-R associations can be formed.

Recently, N. J. Mackintosh (1985) has put the S-S vs. S-R controversy in a broader context borrowed from philosophy via human cognitive psychology. Philosophers have long distinguished *knowing how* from *knowing that*. Most of us know how to ride a bicycle, but few of us could explain the physical and physiological principles involved: We *know how* to ride a bike, but we do not *know* the principles *that* we use to do so. On the other hand, a physicist might know very well the physical principles involved in making a 20-foot jump shot in basketball but be unable to make such a shot. Cognitive psychologists refer to "knowing how" as *procedural learning*, and "knowing that" as *declarative learning*. In these terms, Tolman emphasized declarative learning, for he always emphasized that organisms learn about the environment, not just how to respond to it, whereas Guthrie and especially Hull emphasized procedural learning, seeing learning as acquiring responses to environmental stimuli. Thus S-S conditioning is a form of declarative learning, whereas S-R learning is procedural learning. These new terms help us see that arguing about whether learning is S-S *or* S-R is a mistake, for both occur and both are important, so that both deserve study.

Contiguity and Contingency

In the spirit of associationism, most traditional learning theorists assumed that contiguity of stimuli (in S-S theories) or of stimulus and response (in S-R theories) were all that were required for conditioning to take place. Conditioning was seen as a rather mechanical process that occurred automatically when *S* was paired with *S* or *S* with *R*. Theories differed over the role of reinforcement, Guthrie and Tolman believing that associations were formed in the absence of reinforcement, while Hull and Skinner seeing reinforcement as a necessary catalyst that creates the associative bond. However, several findings have questioned the role of sheer contiguity as the sufficient condition for conditioning, showing that what really matters is a *contingency* between CS and US in Pavlovian conditioning, and between response and reinforcement in instrumental learning.

The most dramatic evidence of that contiguity alone is insufficient for association formation is the phenomenon of *blocking* (Kamin, 1968, 1969). In a blocking experiment we first create a Pavlovian response in the usual way, say by pairing a tone (CS) with footshock (US) in rats. The tone itself becomes a fear-producing stimulus, as demonstrated by *conditioned suppression*: The rat is taught to bar-press for food, and after it has learned this response we occasionally present the conditioned tone CS. Because the tone elicits fear from the Pavlovian conditioning, the bar-pressing is briefly suppressed following its presentation. Suppose now we return to Pavlovian conditioning and further pair the tone CS with shock, only now we add another CS presented with the tone, for example, a light flash. Observe that the light flash and the shock are contiguous, just as the tone and the shock always have been. If contiguity theory is correct, presentation of the lightflash with the shock should make the lightflash a fear-producing CS. But it does not: Previous and continued pairing of the first CS *blocks* the formation of any association with the lightflash.

Examination of *unblocking* experiments will help us see what is going on here (B. Schwartz, 1984). An unblocking experiment proceeds just as a blocking experiment until the introduction of the second CS, when the US is changed. To continue our example, after the fear conditioning of the rat to the tone is complete, we begin to pair the tone with a lightflash and with *two shocks at a time*. In this case blocking does not occur, and the lightflash becomes fear producing. In a related experiment, rats were first conditioned with the tone to pairs of shocks, and then when the second CS was introduced, both were paired with just one shock. In this case, too, blocking did not occur.

The current view among animal-learning theorists is that stimuli become CS's only to the extent that they *predict* the US (Rescorla, 1968, 1985; Rescorla & Holland, 1982). In the blocking experiment, the lightflash does not condition and become a CS because despite perfect contiguity between it and the US, it does not help the animal predict the US, because it is perfectly predicted already by the original tone CS. Another way to state this is to say the animal learns to ignore the lightflash because it does nothing to help the animal cope with shock (Mackintosh, 1978; Wagner, 1978). If a stimulus is going to become a CS, there must be a unique predictive *contingency* between it and the US; contiguity alone is insufficient. The importance of contingency is underscored by the unblocking experiments. In them, the second CS does predict something new, a change in the nature of the US. The contingency between the new CS and the change in the US is helpful to the animal in preparing for shock, so the contingency is noted and unblocking occurs. Pavlovian conditioning is not the mechanically automatic process associationism suggests it should be, but it is a more complex process involving the animal computing contingencies between environmental events, and learning to behave accordingly.

Turning to instrumental conditioning, we find that despite his reference to the *contingencies* of reinforcement, Skinner, in fact, attributes the power of the law of effect to simple *contiguity* between a response and the reinforcement, or nonreinforcement, that follows it. That Skinner relies on contiguity can be seen best in his concept of *superstitious behavior* (Skinner, 1948a; Schwartz, 1978). In inducing superstitious behavior the experimenter randomly delivers reinforcement to a subject (Skinner used pigeons), which is not actually dependent on the behavior taking place at the moment of reward. *Whatever* the animal is doing would then be "reinforced" at that moment. What Skinner found was that his pigeons would acquire and persist in giving those behaviors that had been followed by reinforcement. For example, a pigeon might happen to be turning around when food was delivered, and would tend to repeat this response in the future, performing an action, turning around, that has no obvious rational connection to food gathering. This action might look like a superstitious ritual to an observer who did not know about the initial reinforcement the pigeon had received for turning around.

So, simply because of the contiguity between an irrelevant response and reinforcement, the response has been learned and will be repeated. Skinner believes human superstitions are acquired in the same way. A black cat crosses your path and a minute later you trip and fall. It is easy to attribute your pain to "bad luck" and the causally irrelevant black cat. Not only superstitions but also human depression may result from reinforcements that cannot be controlled.

One of the most dramatic findings to emerge from the controversy between the contiguity and contingency accounts of reinforcement is the phenomenon of *learned helplessness* (Seligman, 1975; Maier & Seligman, 1976). Two dogs are placed in harnesses and subjected to identical periodic electrical shocks. One dog can terminate the shock by pressing a lever in front of its nose; the other dog, his yoked companion, has no control over the shock. When the first dog receives a shock, the second one does too. When the first dog stops the shock by pressing the lever, the shock stops for the second dog too. Both dogs receive identical patterns of shock and nonshock. The only difference is that the first dog can control its shocks, and naturally learns to do so, while the second dog is a helpless victim—what does the animal learn?

What the second dog learns is revealed in the second phase of the experiment when each animal must learn to jump a barrier to avoid receiving a shock. The first canine, like any normal dog that had never before been exposed to shock, quickly learns to jump the hurdle and avoids being shocked. The second dog, however, who was helpless during the first phase of the experiment, remains helpless even now when action could relieve its suffering. The creature whines and yelps, but after a while it becomes totally passive, simply accepting the shocks without complaint or any attempt to avoid them. It has *learned* to be *helpless*. A pious observer might even say that the second dog has acquired the resignation to the will of God, or of the gods, that most religions try to teach.

How does this dreary finding reflect on the contiguity-contingency debate? Remember that the two dogs received exactly the *same* pattern of shock and nonshock in phase 1. A contiguity view of learning would say that the first dog learned to press the lever because it was followed by negative reinforcement while the second dog learned "superstitiously" to act passive in the face of shock. A contingency analysis would say that the first dog learned that what it did made a difference—that it could avoid shock through effective action, learning that appropriately transferred to the hurdle-jumping phase of the experiment. But the second dog learned literally to be helpless—that there was no connection between what it did and shock, that there was no point even in wasting its energy whining and yelping—and so remained helpless even in the new situation of phase 2.

To test these hypotheses Maier (1970) repeated the original experiment, except that this time the first dog learned to be master of its fate by standing rigidly still to terminate the shock. The creature's companion remained helpless as in the standard experiment. Now, if the first dog learned simply, "Stand still to avoid shock," we would expect it to stand still in the hurdle-jumping phase of the experiment. But these dogs did not act passively—they learned to jump the hurdle—while the yoked dogs were again rendered helpless. So it appears that reinforcement works because of contingency between action and reward, not just because reward happens to follow a behavior. Organisms can tell when their activities affect their lives and when they do not.

The learned-helplessness phenomenon has had considerable impact on the theory and treatment of human depression. It has been theorized that perhaps human depressives have had experiences similar to the learned-helplessness dogs, and have similarly concluded that nothing they do will be effective in getting what they want, falling into the misery and stupor of depression. Normal people, on the other hand, believe in their mastery of the world, behave effectively, and are reasonably happy. Research has shown that this picture is only partly correct. One experiment (Alloy & Abramson, 1982) exposed subject to sequences of events (sequences of flashing lights) and asked them to predict the next event in the sequence. Some of the sequences were orderly and the next event predictable, some were merely random, so the next event was not predictable. It was expected that depressives would feel always unable to predict the next event, for they always feel out of control. Normals, on the other hand, should be able to tell when the lights were random and prediction was impossible from when prediction was possible, given an orderly set of lights. What happened was that depressives were able to tell random from nonrandom sequences, whereas normals always thought the sequences were predictable. The depressives were in touch with reality, the normals out of touch. It appears that being normally happy depends, as one depressive has said, on being a foolish cockeyed optimist. Depressives know better. They would agree with the cartoon character who told his psychiatrist, "I don't mind being in touch with reality, but I don't want to live there."

In both Pavlovian and instrumental learning, then, learning depends on contingency, not contiguity. Hence, CS's must uniquely predict US's for Pavlovian conditioning to happen, and reinforcement must be truly contingent on behavior for instrumental learning to occur. Contiguity is still important as a variable affecting the strength of conditioning (Rescorla, 1985)—it still helps for CS and US to be near one another—but we now know it is not the major cause of conditioning; contingency is.

Expectancies

So far, even recent accounts of conditioning assume that learning is based on association of stimuli and responses, or of stimuli and other stimuli, even when the traditional assumptions of associationism have been modified. More radically, however, we might ask if principles of association, no matter how modern and sophisticated, can account for all the phenomena of conditioning. Certainly Tolman did not think so, and he introduced nonassociative elements into his theory of conditioning, including purposes, cognitive maps, and expectancies. Recent research suggests that Tolman's insight was correct, that learning involves more than associative conditioning. A good example comes from the study of escape and avoidance learning.

We may begin here by recalling J. B. Watson's demonstration of classically conditioned fear in his unfortunate subject Little Albert. We say that not only did Albert exhibit fear when he saw the rat—the rat CS having acquired the fear-arousing properties of the loud clanging of the bar, the UCS—but he also attempted to get away from the rat. That is, he tried to *escape* from the now fear-producing stimulus. Moreover, he would, of course, try to *avoid* the rat. Doubtless he would not go places where he would be likely to see the rat, and if he caught signs of a rat's presence he would get away.

Now the motor behaviors of escape and avoidance are operant responses, and so we need to ask how they are acquired and how they are reinforced.

The usual laboratory experiment for studying escape and avoidance learning involves a shuttlebox. A shuttlebox is a container separated into two compartments by a divider that the subject, typically a dog, can jump over. One compartment is the "shock" side equipped with an electrified floor; the other compartment is the nonelectrified "safe" side. Escape learning takes place when we place the dog in the electrified side and turn on the shock. The dog will act fearful and distressed, and after a number of such trials will learn to jump the barrier to the safe side. After the response is learned, the length of time between shock onset and the escape response shortens until the jump is made as soon as shock begins. If we provide a discriminative stimulus, or *cue*, that signals that shock is about to begin, the animal will learn to avoid the shock by jumping when the signal occurs. At first the dog simply *escaped* shock; now it has learned to *avoid* it just as Little Albert learned to escape and then avoid the white rat.

The most influential account of escape and avoidance learning was the *two-process theory* advocated by neo-Hullians. This theory holds that first classical and then operant conditioning are involved in escape and avoidance learning. First, a classically conditioned CER of fear is acquired to stimuli predicting onset of shock, specifically the shock signal. As a result, a learned or secondary drive is set up, in which the CS comes to elicit fear just as shock does. Both escape and avoidance are acquired and maintained by negative reinforcement. Jumping the barrier to the safe side terminates shock in the case of escape, or conditioned fear in the case of avoidance.

The two-process theory is a simple and direct application of standard conditioning principles to a new situation. Much of its appeal to applied behavior analysts derives from its easy extension to a class of human neuroses, namely, the phobias. Fear, whether of punishment or loss of love, is a socialization tool employed by most parents, and it seems plausible to root adult phobias in childhood escape and avoidance situations. We may imagine the 40-year-old Little Albert presenting himself for psychotherapy because of his irrational fear of rats and white furry objects. In this way, Freud's insight that adult behavior is determined by childhood experience is retained, while the unconscious is demystified and replaced by simple conditioning.

A more direct therapy than psychoanalysis' "talking cure" is also suggested by the two-process analysis of escape and avoidance learning. What happens when we simply prevent the animal from jumping to the safe side, perhaps by raising the barrier, and present the avoidance signal but not follow it with shock? We observe extinction: The CS occurs but no US follows, and the avoidance response disappears, even when we lower the barrier and the response can be made in later trials.

Such "therapy" is not only effective but also appears to be an extension and confirmation of learning principles, showing how fear is learned and unlearned according to the laws of conditioning. However, things are not so simple. A bit of reflection shows that every avoidance trial is an extinction trial, because if the subject avoids the shock by jumping when the CS is presented, there is a CS not followed by the US, and extinction should occur. But it is almost invariably the case that an avoidance response once learned will occur on every trial for as long as the experimenter has the patience to go on. We know, of course, that phobias once established rarely go away by themselves.

This and some other problems with the two-process theory have led to something we have come to expect by now, the introduction of a cognitive theory of avoidance learning (Seligman & Johnston, 1973). Like the two-process theory, the cognitive theory says that the first step in avoidance learning is classical conditioning. The shock elicits fear and muscle responses that eventually lead to escape. However, once the animal figures out the contingencies operating in the shuttle box, Tolman-like *expectancies* develop. The dog comes to expect that it will be shocked when the signal comes on and, more importantly, it expects that it can avoid shock by jumping the barrier. According to the cognitive theory, an expectancy is confirmed and strengthened whenever it proves true, as it does every time the animal makes a successful avoidance response, for it does indeed not get shocked. Nonshock, which ought to extinguish an operant response, confirms a cognitive expectancy; naturally, extinction of the jumping response, under the control of the expectancy, does not extinguish. Blocking the avoidance response without delivering shock quickly disconforms the expectancy, and so the animal quits jumping. Seligman and Johnston have shown that paying attention to a subject's beliefs provides a more satisfactory account of escape and avoidance learning than does a theory that ignores them.

Learning and Survival

Biologists and psychologists are coming to recognize that learning should be viewed within the context of evolution. In this view, learning is a biological process, and we find that learning is guided by instinct, whereas instinct may be transformed by learning (Gould & Marler, 1987). We will have a great deal more to say about this in Chapters 10 and 11, but in order to conclude our discussion of current issues in conditioning, we will present a few examples of how conditioning is shaped and guided by instinct, and discuss the consequences of viewing learning not as a machine process of plugging together stimulus and response, but as a flexible strategy organisms use to survive.

A sensory preconditioning experiment performed by Holland (1981) illustrates how instinct guides an animal's learning. In the sensory preconditioning phase, Holland exposed rats to pairings of a tone with a flavor in their water. In the conditioning phase, he paired the same tone with chemically induced nausea. In tests, Holland found that the rats showed no aversion to the tone, but considerable aversion to the flavor. Besides supporting an S-S theory of Pavlovian conditioning (Rescorla, 1984), Holland's finding reveals the control of learning by instinct. Rats seem to know innately that an external stimulus like a tone cannot cause an internal effect like nausea, so they do not associate the tone with nausea even though it is directly paired with nausea; the tone does not, and it appears cannot, become a CS in such circumstances. On the other hand, it is likely that something eaten or drunk could cause nausea, so the aversion is directed to the flavor associated with the tone. It becomes the CS even though it has never been directly paired with nausea. Instinct tells the rat what kinds of associations to make, and what kinds not to make.

Instances of Pavlovian conditioning in which the CS determines the nature of the CR (Rescorla, 1975) may also reveal the role of instinct in shaping learned behavior. For example, if we pair a tone or a light with footshock, a rat will in the future freeze or run away from the CS. On the other hand, if we shock the rat with a prod, the rat will bury the prod rather than freeze or run away (Holland, 1984). Different CS's will have different effects even if paired with the same US, depending on the animal's inherited ability to cope with different kinds of stimuli. Sometimes, innate associations may override the usual principles of conditioning. As we have seen, backward conditioning is essentially impossible to bring about. This is natural, for if we regard CS's as signposts telling animals what to expect, then a sign that follows a turn in the road is not very useful (B. Schwartz, 1984). However, if we signal a footshock with a tone, and right after the tone throw a rubber hedgehog in the rat's cage, the rat will later avoid the hedgehog rather than the tone, even with just one such trial (Staddon, 1985). Even though the hedgehog comes after the tone, its lifelike properties make it a far more likely natural CS than a tone, and rats backward-condition to it, ignoring the signaling tone CS.

The most dramatic evidence that conditioning is a biologically adaptive process comes from studies of compensatory CR's in Pavlovian conditioning, in which the CR is not just different from the UR, but is its opposite. One result of shock is heartrate acceleration. If we pair a tone with shock a few times, we find that it too elicits heartrate acceleration, a standard Pavlovian response wherein the CR is like the UR. However, as pairings continue, the CR shifts from being heartrate acceleration to heartrate deceleration (Obrist, Sutterer, & Howard, 1972).

Compensatory responses like these are especially common when the US is a drug; the CR is usually the physiological opposite of the UR brought about by the drug US. These findings have led to an intriguing hypothesis about drug addiction: that it is a primarily *learned* phenomenon. This hypothesis is based on the observation that in conditioning with a drug as the US, the acquired CR is the opposite of the UR. This makes adaptive sense, because the CS acts as a signal warning of imminent drug delivery (the US), and the body prepares itself by altering its physiology (the CR) in directions opposite to the effects of the drug (the UR). As a result, over trials, the actual effect of the drug becomes weaker and weaker.

Now consider a person taking heroin. Initially, the drug creates a pleasurable high. However, certain stimuli regularly precede drug use—most immediately the sight of the hypodermic, but also the user's regular haunts and friends. These stimuli come to act as CS's, signaling drug delivery, and a preparatory CR appears and strengthens over time. So increasing doses are needed to experience any high at all, as the net drug effect diminishes; the addict—for such he or she has become—may overdose in time. Moreover, the CR is the opposite of the UR—the wretched craving of the addict for more heroin, making life miserable without the drug.

If this hypothesis is correct, then certain implications for drug rehabilitation become apparent. For example, in animal studies, drug tolerance has been extinguished by presenting the cues (CS's) that formerly signaled drug delivery, without administering the drug (US). So perhaps the best way to treat drug addicts is in their home community, where familiar places and people may be experienced without heroin. Removing addicts to a remote treatment center may be ineffective, as their eventual return home will return them to CS's that will elicit an unextinguished CR, and a probable return to the heroin habit.

As B. Schwartz (1984) points out, learning, to be advantageous to the organism, must be adaptive. Now, it is not very adaptive to elevate your heart rate just before a stimulus will occur that in turn will elevate it even more. The functional and adaptive thing to do would be to lower heart rate when the CS signal occurs, to minimize the impact of the shock on your system.

Thus, it seems that even in classical conditioning, more than blind, stupid reflexive learning takes place: Organisms learn about the world from their experience, and what they learn provides the basis for adaptive action.

Recent Theories of Conditioning

In the ferment of work on contemporary animal conditioning, several new theories of conditioning have been proposed. Because our interest is primarily in human learning, we will only briefly describe some of the new theories. In any event, we will find that animal-learning theories are coming to resemble current theories in cognitive psychology.

Learning as Inference

J. E. R. Staddon (1984, 1985) regards learning as a joint process of selection and variation. He distinguishes between principles of behavioral variation and principles of behavioral selection (Staddon, 1975; Staddon & Simmelhag, 1971). Skinner focused his theorizing exclusively on the principles of selection, leaving mysterious why certain behaviors are emitted at all. Clearly, behavior is seldom random, even before reinforcement occurs. Any cat owner would have been able to predict the behaviors of a cat in Thorndike's puzzle-boxes. The situation of being in a small box brings out certain feline behaviors, and other situations evoke different behaviors. We need to pay attention to the principles that account for the kinds of behaviors that naturally occur in a given situation, and these Staddon calls the principles of behavioral variation. The principles of selection then choose among the alternatives thrown up by the principles of variation in a process similar to evolution by natural selection.

So far, Staddon's theory is a reasonable extension of Skinner's own selectionism, adding principles of variation to Skinner's principles of selection. However, Staddon's theory incorporates the findings on the importance of contingency in conditioning and on the biological guidedness of learning, so that he regards learning as more cognitive and as more constrained than does Skinner. Staddon (1985) calls animals *inference engines*, "using built-in rules to anticipate, identify, and react appropriately to events of biological importance," p. 288. Staddon identifies two kinds of built-in rules. The first are the classic general rules of association that are valid for all species in all ecological situations. For example, as causes usually precede effects by brief intervals, animals quite rightly usually associate a US with a CS that occurs just before it. The second kind of rules are species and ecology specific, helping a particular kind of animal cope with its particular environment. For example, because a hedgehog is a more likely threat to a rat than a tone is, rats, as we have seen, backward-condition to a plastic hedgehog, ignoring the tone CS that just precedes shock. In this case, a rat-specific rule overwhelms the general rule of half-second contiguity.

Associationism

Many theorists regard learning as a process of building associations between perceived events, and between events and behaviors. Prominent among them is Robert Rescorla (but see also, for example, Pearce & Hall, 1980). In response to the findings of phenomena such as blocking that show that in order for a stimulus to become a CS in Pavlovian conditioning (Rescorla, 1968), Rescorla produced a very influential mathematical theory of Pavlovian conditioning (Rescorla & Wagner, 1972; Rescorla, 1975, 1978, 1985) viewing it as an associative process by which CS's and US's get linked to the degree that the CS predicts the US (see also Granger & Schlimmer, 1986). Rescorla recognizes that S-R procedural associations can be learned (Rescorla, 1985), his theory is primarily an S-S declarative-learning theory, in the broad spirit of Tolman. His theory also has a mildly cognitive flavor, for he talks about CS's and US's being encoded into mental representations, so that when the CS recurs it activates a representation of the US, which in turn triggers the CR.

Rescorla has recently applied his associative conception of Pavlovian conditioning to instrumental conditioning (Rescorla & Holland, 1982; Rescorla, 1985; Colwill & Rescorla, 1986). In the classic S-R conception of instrumental learning, the reinforcer was regarded as a catalyst for the formation of an S-R association. In chemistry, a catalyst is a substance that affects or controls a chemical reaction without itself becoming involved in the final product of the reaction. The law of effect states a similar role for reward in instrumental learning. What is learned in the Thorndike or Hull S-R theory is a linkage between stimulus and response. All reinforcement does is cause R's to get associated to certain S's, but it does not become part of the S-R association. Tolman challenged this theory when he insisted that during instrumental learning animals learn about the world as well as how to respond to the world.

Rescorla has revived Tolman's objection in a different way, by asserting that the key association in instrumental learning is between the response and the reinforcer. Rescorla has demonstrated that response-outcome associations are learned (Colwill & Rescorla, 1986). In one experiment, rats learned to bar-press for food pellets and to pull a chain for sucrose pellets, or the reverse. Then, one of the outcomes became freely available, and was made poisonous, so that the rats learned to avoid it. It was found subsequently that the rats refused to make whichever response had previously been reinforced for the now poisoned outcome. If reinforcement had merely been a catalyst during the original instrumental conditioning, the rats should have made the same responses as before, learning now instrumentally that pulling the chain (or pressing the bar) led to a noxious outcome. Rescorla has experimentally demonstrated the obvious, perhaps: No one would work for a reinforcer lately found to be revolting. But Tolman always asserted the claims of common sense against the excesses of S-R theory. In any event, Tolman's point is made, that animals learn about the world, not just to respond to it, even in instrumental conditioning. Rescorla himself regards instrumental conditioning as a variant on Pavlovian conditioning in which the animal itself generates the CS with its response, and the behavioral CS is then associated with the following reinforcing US.

Attention

Another class of theories (see, for example, Mackintosh, 1978) treats conditioning as a matter of changing how an organism comes to pay attention or ceases to pay attention to different stimuli. For example, Pavlovian conditioning may be regarded as the animal learning to pay attention to a usually unattended CS because that CS is followed by a US, which directs attention to the CS signal. Blocking occurs because, as the already established and attended-to CS effectively signals the US, the new CS is simply ignored. In unblocking, because the US does change, the new CS is attended to.

Latent inhibition occurs because, when a stimulus occurs with no significant following event, the animal learns to ignore it. Other conditioning phenomena can be given similar interpretations (Lubow & Schnur, 1981).

Cognitive Maps

The existence of Tolman-like cognitive maps has been demonstrated in creatures as simple as honeybees (Gould & Marler, 1987). Bees forage for nectar over about a four-square-kilometer range centered on their hive. In an experiment, bees were first trained to go to a feeding site about 150 meters north-northwest of the hive. Then one day the workers were caught as they emerged from the hive to go to the feeding site, and they were transported in the dark to a release site 125 meters northeast of the hive. If the bees simply had learned to get to the feeding site by flying north-northwest, they would then fly off from the new release site at the same compass bearing, missing the feeder completely. If they had learned Hullian rules relating environmental landmarks (stimuli) to flight directions (responses) connecting the hive and the feeder, then like a Hullian rat in the Tolman-Honzik maze, they would have worked their way back from the release site to the hive, and thence to the feeder. Finally, if, like real rats, bees learn cognitive maps, then they should be able to get their bearings at the release site, figure out how to get to the feeder, and fly directly to it. This is in fact what they did.

Information Processing

Finally, theories borrowed from information-processing cognitive psychology have been applied to animals (see Wagner, 1978; Riley, Cook, & Lamb, 1981; Honig & Thompson, 1982; Staddon, 1984; B. Schwartz, 1984; Shimp, 1984). To sample this work, we shall briefly discuss work on short-term memory in pigeons and rats.

The paradigm used to study short-term memory in pigeons is called *delayed matching to sample*, on which several variations are possible; we will discuss just two. Imagine a pigeon Skinner box with a row of four possible keys to peck. In a delayed-matching-to-sample procedure we light one of the keys, say with a green light; this is the *sample*. Then there is a variable *memory interval* when no keys are lighted. When the memory interval is over we present a pair of *test stimuli* by lighting two of the keys, one with the same color as before—green in our example—and one with another color, say red. The animal is reinforced for pecking the same color key as presented in the sample. The position of the correct key in the test phase is chosen at random, so the pigeon cannot simply learn always to press one of the keys on the basis of position.

Pigeons can perform this task, although their ability to do so declines (as does human short-term memory in analogous tasks) as the memory interval increases. It appears that pigeons can remember the sample for a period of time and can base their test response on memory. However, interesting questions now arise. For example, why does the pigeon's performance decline as the memory interval gets longer? Borrowing from theorizing about human memory, two possibilities present themselves: decay and interference. First, the memory of the sample might simply *decay*, so that the longer the memory interval, the weaker the trace and the poorer the performance. On the other hand, new experiences in the box might *interfere* with the stored memory, making it harder to retrieve the memory of the sample. That the latter occurs in pigeons is suggested by the finding that when we turn off the room lights during the memory interval, test performance is intact over very long times (B. Schwartz, 1984).

Another question about pigeon short-term memory is to ask exactly what is stored during the memory interval. One might think it is just a visual image trace of the sample stimulus, so that in the test phase the pigeon simply pecks the same colored light as its image. However, delayed *symbolic* or *conditional* matching undermines this simple hypothesis. In symbolic, or conditional, matching to sample, the test stimuli are different from the sample stimuli. For example, the test pair might be horizontal and vertical lines, with the pigeon reinforced for pecking the vertical lines when the sample was green, horizontal lines when the sample was red. Although a trace might still be involved, clearly there is more involved in delayed symbolic matching to sample than merely matching up a trace with a new stimulus. Some sort of rule must be learned of the sort, "If sample is green, peck the vertical lines."

This conclusion is underscored by a the results of a clever experiment by Stonebreaker (1981, described by Honig & Thompson, 1982). In this experiment, the memory interval was followed by either the standard matching test stimuli or by a conditional test pair. The pigeon was told which to expect by a signal given just after the sample; a circle meant a standard test, and a triangle signaled a conditional test. Occasionally, a *probe test* was given, in which the test was the opposite of the one that had been signaled. Performance was good on trials when the test matched the signal, but was dismal on probe trials. The finding strongly suggests that when the signal was given the animal decided on what the correct response would be at test, and stored this information in memory. Thus, on probe trials the pigeon was not ready with the correct response and performed poorly. If the pigeon simply held a trace of the sample stimulus and used it at the time of the test to choose the correct response, the probe trials should have given it no trouble. Pigeons also seem able to control their short-term stores, as evidence by *directed forgetting* experiments in which a sample is sometimes followed by a signal to forget it. Tests after forgetting signals produce very poor results, suggesting that the animal did dump memory of the sample when signaled.

Short-term memory in rats is studied in the multiarm radial maze. A radial maze consists of a central platform form which radiate numerous arms, each of which is baited with food. The best thing for a rat to do is visit each arm once. It might adopt two memory strategies for accomplishing this task. On the one hand, it might try to remember which arms it had already visited, and not visit those arms. In this case, the list of visited arms held in memory would increase through the experiment, and the number of mistakes would thereby increase. On the other hand, the rat might initially put in memory a list of arms not yet visited, and only visit arms on that list, deleting arms as it visited them. In this case, the list to be remembered would get shorter during the experiment, and mistakes should decrease. As it happens, rats seem to adopt the former strategy (Honig & Thompson, 1982).

SUGGESTED READINGS

An outstanding book on contemporary animal learning research and theory is Barry Schwartz's *Psychology of learning and behavior* (New York: Norton, 1984). It covers both Skinnerian and non-Skinnerian approaches and findings. For discussion of Skinner's theory in historical and philosophical context, see Thomas H. Leahey, *A history of psychology*, 2nd ed. (Englewood Cliffs, N.J.: Prentice-Hall, 1987).

5

MEMORY AND INFORMATION PROCESSING I: PERCEPTUAL AND WORKING MEMORY PROCESSES

INTRODUCTION

During WWII scientists actually built a device that earlier generations had dreamed of: a digital computer. After the war, as the modern computer age began, psychologists found in computers and computer programming a new conceptual basis for psychology. Computers accept information, store and process that information, make decisions, and generate output. In short, computers seemed to think.

It became attractive to view humans and computers alike as information-processing devices studied by psychologists on the one hand and computer scientists on the other. The marriage of cognitive psychologists and computer scientists created a new field called *cognitive science*, the study of computational devices both of silicon and steel and of nerve and tissue (Stillings and others, 1987).

It is very common to distinguish cognitive psychology from behavioral psychology, but we believe things are not so simple. Clearly, cognitive psychology and radical behaviorism are quite different, since Skinner does not tolerate the postulation of any inner psychological entities, whether it be Freud's ego or a cognitive psychologist's long-term memory. However, both Tolman and Hull postulated inferred entities that controlled behavior, cognitive maps, and mediating responses; neo-Hullians have proved eager to embrace cognitive concepts in studying human development (Chapter 13), and we have already found some animal behaviorists talking in cognitive terms.

Cognitive psychology has created an entirely new vocabulary for discussing learning. Stimulus becomes input; behavior, output; response mediators, levels of information processing. This new vocabulary is so different, in fact, that many colleges and universities have separate courses with separate texts in Learning and Cognitive Psychology. However, the basic question of cognitive psychology is the same as human learning, namely, How does the environment modify the behavior of people? While the specific answers cognitive psychologists give are different from behaviorists', their quest is the same.

In this section we will present the cognitive view of learning beginning with the simplest and best understood information processes, then moving to the deeper, harder to study and less well-known ones. Chapter 5 opens the section by discussing the initial stages of information processing—what happens to stimuli (input) as they are registered and prepared for storage. In Chapter 6 the subject is long-term memory, the processes and representations involved in storing, maintaining, and retrieving learned information. Chapter 7 takes up the topic of language, perhaps humans' most important cognitive tool. Chapter 8 examines comprehension, the understanding of complex linguistic information. Finally, Chapter 9 surveys work on thinking, including reasoning, problem solving, and scientific thinking.

Most human experiences, whether studying for a test, sizing up a new acquaintance at a party, or listening to a commercial on television, involve processing information. It is difficult to separate perception, memory, comprehension, language, problem solving, and decision making. Thus, our discussion of each problem will necessarily have frequent allusion to other topics. In all cases, both applications in our daily lives and theoretical conceptual principles will be stressed.

AN OVERVIEW
OF THE INFORMATION-PROCESSING SYSTEM

Before examining the various processes that occur when we take in and interpret information, it is useful to have some general understanding of the information-processing system. Figure 5–1 schematically illustrates a general conceptual view of the most characteristic way that most contemporary cognitive psychologists view the information-processing system. Much of this conceptualization is traceable to the model of Atkinson and Shiffrin (1968), who developed an extensive description of such a model. What is presented below is very much in the tradition of Atkinson and Shiffrin, without necessarily adhering to all the details and assumptions of their theory.

Generally, with some important exceptions to be discussed later, processing proceeds from left to right in Figure 5–1. Environmental input comes into sensory memory, which holds information for a very short time (about 0.5 to 1.0 seconds in the visual system), just long enough for us to select what to attend to for further processing. Our sensory memory contains everything impinging on our senses, including not only voices we hear and colors we see, but also background distractions we "tune out," that is, those we do not send on for further processing.

Attention and pattern recognition occur to help identify and select information for further processing. Though we will discuss these processes in more detail later in the chapter, one important paradox should be introduced here. Although we said earlier that information is generally processed left to right in Figure 5–1, sometimes the processes of attention and pattern recognition must draw on material "farther along" in the information-processing chain, specifically, knowledge from long-term memory. For example, we choose to attend to one conversation rather than another at a party because the material being discussed in one interests us more than that being discussed in the other. To make this decision about attention, we must draw on information already in long-term memory. Such anecdotal examples and experimental evidence pointing in the same direction have been used to argue against Atkinson-Shiffrin-type models, sometimes labeled "multistore" models because of their postulation of three different memory stores (see Figure 5–1). For now, however, we will ignore this anomaly in our left-to-right linear processing of information, but we will return to this important theoretical issue near the end of Chapter 6.

Material in working memory includes everything we are thinking about right now. This material comes from two basic sources: the external environment (new sensory information) and previously learned information retrieved from long-term memory. Both types of information interact in working memory in ways discussed at length later in the book. To give a brief informal example, suppose you are introduced to someone new, Laura, whom you have never seen before. That is new information coming in through your senses through sensory memory to working memory. However, let us suppose, as frequently happens, that Laura reminds you very much of someone else you already know, Jane. Thus, information about Jane is retrieved from long-term memory to mingle in working memory with new information about Laura. Sometimes the information about the two people may become very confused, with some important ramifications we shall explore later.

Material may be retained in working memory only a very short time (some experiments suggest 15 to 30 seconds), unless it continues to be processed in some way. This could occur by repeating (rehearsing) the material over to yourself, as when you look up a phone number and repeat it to yourself while you dial the phone. It could also be retained in working memory indefinitely by continuing to think about it for some reason, for example, when solving a problem. If we make a response (verbal or behavioral), it must be from working memory, not sensory memory, which is too short-lived and unprocessed, and not long-term memory, which is not in immediate consciousness.

If we want to remember something for the future, we generally seek to encode it somehow into long-term memory. If it is thus encoded successfully, we can forget about it for the moment, knowing we can retrieve it later when we need it. If it is not encoded and we do not continue to process it in working memory, it is quickly and permanently forgotten. For example, in the case of the phone number, we rehearse it only long enough to dial the phone. The importance of encoding in memory can hardly be overstated. Most popular books on how to improve one's memory are really about how to encode information more efficiently. If material is encoded well, it can more likely be readily retrieved. On the other hand, if it is not encoded accurately or at all, even the best retrieval strategies are probably doomed to failure. Encoding and its sister set of processes, retrieval, are both places where memory can go wrong.

A consistent and recurring issue in information processing is the juxtaposition of *top-down* (conceptually-driven) and *bottom-up* (data-driven) processes. Bottom-up processes refer to the processing of the actual environmental stimuli with the course and character of that processing determined only by the nature of those stimuli (data) themselves. Although such "pure processing" is perhaps the lay person's view of how we perceive and comprehend information, it almost never occurs in the real world or even in the laboratory. This is so because we typically have top-down (conceptually-driven) processing going on simultaneously. Such processing involves expectations about what the data will hold, based on our past experiences and knowledge in long-term memory. Such expectations inevitably color our interpretation of those data and prevent us from doing purely data-driven processing. We will see examples of simultaneous top-down and bottom-up processes occurring at several different levels of information processing throughout the next few chapters.

An important distinction to make when discussing cognitive processes is differentiating *serial* and *parallel* processes. Processes done serially are performed sequentially, one after the other, while those done in parallel are performed simultaneously, or are at least partially overlapping in time. For example, if you scan a list of words to see if the letter T occurs in any of them and then scan the list again to see if the letter P occurs, you are performing the two scanning processes serially. If you scan the list once, looking for either a T or a P, you may likely be performing the operations in parallel.

While the difference between serial and parallel processing is often neither as easy to identify nor as conceptually distinct as the above example might suggest, it is a useful distinction to make in studying the covert processes of cognition. It is often possible to infer whether processes must have occurred serially or in parallel, especially through the use of reaction-time methodology, which is discussed later.

At this point we will begin examining each of the separate memory stores and sets of processes that occur as we comprehend and remember information. In general, the coverage of topics in the next two chapters will proceed from left to right as in Figure 5–1.

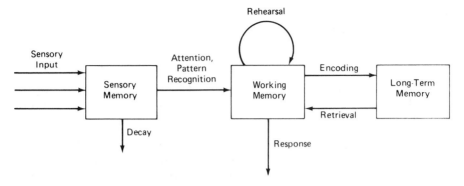

FIGURE 5-1 Overview of information-processing system.

SENSORY MEMORY

The most immediately perceptual store of memory is **sensory memory,** also sometimes called the *sensory registers* or *sensory information store*. Its function is merely to hold information very briefly, just long enough for it to be selectively attended to and identified for further processing in working memory. The material in sensory memory is completely unorganized and is basically a perceptual copy of objects and events in the world. Material decays very rapidly from sensory memory (about 0.5 to 1.0 second for vision and 3.0 to 4.0 seconds for hearing), unless it is selected for further processing. Although we generally are not conscious of information while it is in sensory memory, you can informally demonstrate its existence by quickly waving your arm from side to side in front of your face. You continue to see a very faint copy or shadow of your arm for a fraction of a second after it has sped by. This is the *icon*, or visual sensory memory representation. Another example of the icon is the ribbon of light that you see in a dark room immediately after waving a flashlight.

Although information in sensory memory is not generally open to introspection, its existence was convincingly demonstrated many years ago in a clever experiment by George Sperling (1960). When an array of 12 letters (three rows of four each) was flashed on a screen for 50 milliseconds (one-twentieth of a second), subjects were barely aware of their presence yet could consistently report three to four letters accurately. While this result appeared to reflect the actual processing capacity, Sperling demonstrated that many more letters had in fact entered sensory memory. To do so, Sperling used a high-, middle-, or low-pitched tone to indicate to the subject to report only the top, middle, or bottom line of the array. Using this "partial-report" method, subjects could report about 75 percent of the letters correctly, as opposed to half that many when the whole-report ("repeat all the letters") method was used. This suggests, then, that the limits of sensory memory are temporal, not visual, and that considerable information is there, but decays very rapidly, faster than the time it takes to report it. In the case of the visual system, decay from sensory memory is essentially complete in one second or less.

In another study, Sperling (1960) showed that the accuracy of recall of the letters decreased substantially if the tone signaling which line to recall was delayed even for a fraction of a second. In fact, if it is delayed as much as a second, the number of letters recalled was down to the equivalent of four out of twelve, the number reported under the whole-report procedure.

The faster we can transfer information from sensory to working memory, the more efficiently we can process information. There is some evidence that dyslexics may make this transfer more slowly than normals, with their icons lasting 30 to 50 milliseconds longer than normal (Stanley, 1975). This longer-than-optimal duration could make reading considerably more difficult, because of the potential interference and confusion among icons.

The Sperling effect was replicated in a study using the auditory system, with one important difference (Darwin, Turvey, & Crowder, 1972). The auditory sensory memory, or *echo*, lasts for several seconds, with recall under partial report being superior to that under whole report for up to four seconds. The auditory sensory memory is critical for understanding speech. Sounds early in a word must remain in sensory memory long enough to be mentally combined with the later sounds.

At least in theory, there must be a sensory memory for other senses beside vision and hearing, though these have not really received much examination.

The fact that information decays so rapidly from sensory memory is actually an adaptive feature of our information-processing system, since we might experience double images in the visual system or confusing echoes in the auditory system if everything we had perceived in the last few seconds remained in our sensory memory. There are, in fact, a fortunate (or unfortunate, depending on your point of view) few people who have icons that persist for very long periods of time and can be recalled at will. This is called *eidetic imagery* (or sometimes photographic memory) and is a truly remarkable ability. See Box 5–1 for the story of one person with this ability.

Not everyone accepts that sensory memory necessarily passively copies all incoming stimulus information with no interpretation whatsoever. For example, Merikle (1980) argued that different aspects of stimuli (for example, location, identity) are encoded at different rates and do not require the postulation of a separate sensory memory. He replicated Sperling's study using mixed arrays of numbers and letters. Cuing by category ("recall the numbers") was just as effective as cuing by position ("recall the top line"). If sensory memory is entirely precategorical (that is, information is not yet organized into categories), such categorical cuing would not have been effective. Evidence such as this has begun to question the necessity of postulating a qualitatively separate sensory memory of pure and unanalyzed sensory information.

BOX 5–1   Eidetic Imagery

There are a small number of children, and a much smaller number of adults, who possess an unusual ability to maintain visual images for much longer periods of time than most of us are able to. This is called "eidetic imagery" (or sometimes, less precisely, "photographic memory"). It may be viewed as the ability to retain icons from sensory memory far longer than the usual second or so that they last. One of the most striking "eidetikers" ever studied is "Elizabeth," a very exceptional woman studied by Charles Stromeyer (1970; Stromeyer & Psotka, 1970). Elizabeth was a very intelligent young artist and teacher at Harvard. She could mentally project an exact image of a picture onto the canvas or any other surface she was looking at. She could also retrieve images of pages of textbooks she had read and copy them in writing from memory. In an effort to determine the limits of her eidetic abilities, Stromeyer tested Elizabeth with computer-generated random-dot stereograms. A normal person can look through a stereoscope at a pair of stereograms, a different one with each eye; the machine allows the eyes to fuse the two patterns and thus see some figure emerge from the combination. Elizabeth, however, could do this without the stereoscope! She looked at a 10,000-dot pattern for one minute with one eye. Then she looked at another pattern with the other eye and superimposed the eidetic image retained from the first pattern over the second pattern, thus causing the figure to emerge.

In later studies Elizabeth showed other amazing eidetic feats, including retaining an eidetic image of a million-dot pattern for at least four hours and a kinetic image of ten seconds from a Laurel and Hardy movie one week later. For some reason we do not understand, eidetic imagery is much more common in children than adults (Haber, 1979). Why it disappears with development remains a mystery, though it might be related to the development of cognitive and literate skills, which may supplant functions performed earlier in development by imagery. Although Haber and Stromeyer have taken great pains to demonstrate that eidetic imagery is different from both afterimages and imagery in memory, the extreme rarity of people with Elizabeth's abilities has led others to question the existence of eidetic imagery as a qualitatively separate phenomenon (Holding, 1979; Lieblich, 1979.)

ATTENTION

The purpose of sensory memory is to hold information just long enough for some of it to be selected for further processing in working memory. For this to occur, it must be attended to and we must start to recognize patterns. It is to these processes that we now turn, in examining how material is selected from sensory memory for further processing. Let's begin by examining **attention.**

General Issues

Attention is another one of those many psychological topics that everyone has intuitions about, but no one knows exactly how to define precisely. Although discussed by William James (1890) and even earlier by the German introspectionists, it was long ignored in the behaviorist era as being too mentalistic and unobservable to be worthy of study in scientific psychology. In the 1950s and 1960s, however, there arose a resurgence of interest in studying attention, primarily by several British researchers, notably Donald Broadbent (1958); Anne Treisman (1964); and Colin Cherry (1953). Since then, and especially in the last ten years, the problem has received intense study, though many unanswered questions remain.

One of the most fundamental issues in studying attention involves a basic paradox common in information processing. While attention seems to be an early process in the sequence of processing information (that is, we must attend to something before it can be processed too deeply), the variables affecting how we choose what we attend to sometimes require extensive processing before that "early" decision is made. How to resolve this tension between the top-down and bottom-up processes is both a continuing theme and conflict within this area of cognitive psychology.

To return to our earlier example, suppose that you are at a party and suddenly turn your head to begin attending to a new conversation because you've just heard your name spoken in that conversation. Even though you were not consciously attending to it, you must have been unconsciously processing meaningful elements of that unattended conversation to some degree, in order to be able to recognize your own name. The top-down process of drawing on knowledge from long-term memory, specifically the knowledge of what your name is, has interacted with the bottom-up processes of understanding the words spoken by the other people in the conversation.

Generally, attention has been conceptualized in two ways. First of all, it has often been considered as a state of concentrating on something. In this tradition, William James (1890) called attention the "focalization of consciousness." As a state, it has some similarities to other psychological states such as emotions like anxiety or happiness, which are not directly observable, but rather must be inferred from behavior.

An alternative, though not necessarily totally inconsistent, way to conceptualize attention is as processing capacity, which can be allocated in a variety of ways to different stimuli and activities (see Kahneman, 1973). The concept of time-sharing is useful here. A finite amount of capacity (attention) exists that may be allocated or time-shared among the various stimuli and activities demanding attention. It is as if you had 12 cookies to give to 12 children. They could all be given to one especially hungry child, distributed two each to six children, or one each to all 12 children.

Selectivity in Attention

How we select activities to attend to and how we determine how many stimuli we can process simultaneously depends on a variety of factors.

First of all, the number of sources is important. It is harder to pay attention to five people talking than it is to one. Secondly, the similarity of sources is important. For example, some people find that they can study well with instrumental music in the background, but not with vocal music. The latter, being linguistic, is similar enough to reading to interfere, while purely instrumental music is not. To develop the example a bit further, if you are solving algebra problems rather than reading, you may be able to work them to vocal music, because here there is only one linguistic stimulus. One of the most highly interfering tasks known is the "shadowing" task used in many laboratory experiments studying attention. This requires you to "shadow" or repeat a message as it comes into your ear through earphones. Because the content of the message you shadow and the words you speak are identical, this is very difficult, though practice improves performance considerably. The task can be made even more difficult by giving delayed auditory feedback (DAF), which involves hearing in one ear the recording of what you just spoke a few seconds earlier, all the while repeating the message heard in the other ear. In this case, the DAF message is in your own voice, thus increasing the similarity of sources and making the task more difficult.

The complexity of sources or tasks is another important variable. It is much easier to pay attention to several simple stimuli or simultaneously perform more than one simple task than it is if the stimuli or tasks are complex. For example, you may be able to read *TV Guide*, watch *Dallas*, and talk to your roommate about dinner simultaneously, but watching a complex documentary on television or reading your psychology textbook would each require all your attention for that single activity. Some people, especially children, have trouble selecting a single source to attend to. See Box 5–2 for a discussion of a disorder of selective attention.

BOX 5–2   Attention Deficit Disorder

According to the American Psychiatric Association (1980), about 3 percent of preadolescent children in the United States, 90 percent of them boys, suffer from Attention Deficit Disorder, a condition that makes selective attention very difficult because the child is unable to "turn-off" the irrelevant messages (Koppel, 1979). The condition may or may not occur with associated hyperactivity. Although it is not correlated with intelligence, such children often perform poorly in school, because they are easily distracted and do not listen well, due to their inability to focus their attention on one activity to the exclusion of others. Sometimes children may lose major symptoms of this disorder as they grow older, though they may persist. Drug therapy using Ritalin has been shown to help many children, probably by stimulating part of the brain involved in controlling attention; in addition, behavior modification, sometimes in combination with drug therapy, is sometimes useful (Gittelman-Klein, Klein, Abikoff, Katz, Gloisten, & Kates, 1976).

Automaticity

Unpredictable sources tend to capture our attention, whereas highly predictable ones do not require it. Sometimes very predictable stimuli are not really noticed until they stop; for example, a whirring heater or air-conditioner or a continuing conversation goes unnoticed until it stops, at which time attention immediately is drawn to it. In this case the cessation of the stimulus is the unpredictable and, thus, attention-capturing event. Gradual habituation occurs to continual, highly predictable stimuli; that is, we gradually allocate less and less attention to it until we may not even be consciously aware of its presence.

Perhaps the most important variable in determining the allocation of attention is the degree of **automaticity**. Shiffrin and Schneider (1977) and others have made the distinction between automatic and controlled (or deliberate) processes. *Automatic* processes do not require much allocation of attention and can be executed in parallel with other cognitive processes or activities. For example, we can often drive and carry on a conversation simultaneously because little if any attention must be allocated to the motor activity. If, however, unusually demanding conditions arise while driving, we may have to cease the conversation to devote full attention to the driving activity, which now becomes a *controlled*, no longer automatic, process. Controlled processes must generally be executed serially because they require so much attention, while automatic processes may be executed in parallel.

As a controlled task becomes habitual, it becomes greatly overlearned and eventually may become automatic. Amateur or professional musicians may recall the first thrill of realizing that their hands moved to the right piano keys or guitar frets without conscious attention to the finger movement. Another good illustration of automatic versus deliberate processes comes in the area of sports. A skilled basketball player is not consciously worrying about placement of the feet at most times, whereas a beginner might be very preoccupied with such considerations and not able to devote much attention to larger considerations such as overall game strategy. Much of the process of learning skills like sports or musical performance may be seen as increasing the automaticity of more and more of the specific motor and cognitive skills involved. Box 5–3 further explores the information processing involved in skill learning.

Apparently the limits of what tasks can become automatic are less than we might think. For example, Spelke, Hirst, and Neisser (1976) trained subjects for several weeks in the formidable job of taking dictation and reading an unrelated story aloud simultaneously. While these are both tasks that normally are highly controlled, with several weeks of intensive practice the subjects acquired a high enough degree of automaticity to carry them out simultaneously with little apparent interference. This suggests that attentional limits in the area of automaticity may be due more to limited practice than any inherent cognitive limits on such processing. Our minds may be capable of a lot more than we suspect, given sufficient practice of the right kind.

BOX 5–3   Declarative Versus Procedural Knowledge

A useful distinction was made in Chapter 4 between declarative and procedural knowledge (J. R. Anderson, 1976, 1985). Declarative knowledge ("knowing that") consists of information that typically can be communicated verbally. Most studies of memory and cognition over the years have been studying declarative knowledge. On the other hand, procedural knowledge ("knowing how") is a skill. It is often, though not necessarily, motor in character: typing, riding a bicycle, driving a car, dribbling a basketball, or playing a piano. Procedural knowledge, especially that which is involved in motor skills, is not readily expressible verbally. If you don't find yourself convinced of this, try to write a description of how to ride a bicycle.

Procedural knowledge may also be entirely internal, such as our knowledge of how to apply linguistic rules in speaking or our knowledge of how to use certain strategies in decision making or problem solving. Such knowledge is often applied implicitly without our being able to verbalize the rule we are using. For example, the four-year-old child, if not the adult, may be unaware consciously of the set of linguistic rules that tell whether to add /d/, /t/, or /əd/ sound to form a past tense in English. Try for yourself to verbalize the rule that tells when to add each of the three sounds. Even if you cannot articulate the rule, you can probably apply it correctly; for example, to make past-tense forms of the nonsense verbs *gurge*, *gurch*, and *gurt*.

Anderson (1985) distinguished three stages of skill learning. While these are probably not clearly serial and separable in all cases, the taxonomy is useful in understanding the general process. First is the *cognitive* stage, which involves an internal, probably declarative, representation of what the learner must do. For instance, when you memorize the steps in starting a car, shooting a basketball, or conjugating a verb, you are forming a mental representation of this appropriate procedural knowledge, even though the knowledge at that point may be declarative, in that you are learning specific information.

The second stage is the *associative* stage, where the declarative knowledge is translated into procedural knowledge. Errors made in learning in the cognitive stage are detected and eliminated, and connections among the elements required for successful performance are strengthened.

Finally, the *autonomous* stage occurs, in gradual evolution from the associative stage. Here the procedure becomes faster and more automatic. The less attention that must be allocated to the task, the more automatic it becomes.

Models of Attention

The earliest contemporary psychological model of attention was Broadbent's (1958) filter model. This proposed that there are different information "channels" coming through our senses into our information-processing system. The "filter" selects one of these channels for further processing and tunes the other out. The basis for this selection was thought to be perceptual, often based on gross physical characteristics, such as overall voice quality or loudness. While this model has much intuitive appeal (we speak of "tuning someone out"), there are numerous anecdotal and experimental counter-examples, showing that we do perceive some, though usually very limited, information from the unattended channels. In the example discussed earlier, we "perk up our ears" and start attending to another conversation at a party when we hear our name or some other very salient stimulus spoken. This suggests that we must be monitoring the unattended source at some level rather than totally filtering it out. To account for such cases, Anne Treisman (1964) modified Broadbent's filter model. Instead of a filter, she proposed an attenuator that "turns down" the unattended channels, somewhat as we would turn down a television set to the point that we would perceive something especially interesting but otherwise would not attend to it. This still leaves unexplained what determines when something is important enough to be perceived from an unattended channel.

Beginning with Kahneman (1973), some people began to think of attention in a very different sort of way, as a limited set of processes or resources to be allocated. Shiffrin and Schneider's (1977) distinction of automatic and controlled processes arose from this new way of thinking about attention. These **capacity** models focus on describing the processing differences between these two types of processes.

In a recent review of the current status of the attention-research literature, Johnston and Dark (1986) suggested that contemporary theories of attention fall into two global categories, theories that view attention as a causal mechanism and those that see attentional phenomena as consequences of other processes. Those in the former category generally distinguish between automatic and controlled processes. Schneider and Shiffrin (1977) are clearly in this tradition, but there are many other models as well (Broadbent, 1982; LaBerge, 1975; Marcel, 1983; Posner & Snyder, 1975b; Schneider, Dumais, & Shiffrin, 1984; Treisman & Gelade, 1980). The particular theories of this type differ primarily in terms of how the two types of processing interact.

The second major class of attention theories sees attention as a consequence of priming activities of some other processing. For example, attention is directed one way rather than another by the presence of some stimulus (somebody shouts "fire" in a classroom and our attention is turned from the teacher to the shouter). This view was discussed by William James (1890), and more recently such a view has been proposed by Hochberg (1978) and Neisser (1976). More extensive reviews of theories of attention may be found in Broadbent (1982), Johnston and Dark (1986), and Shiffrin (1985).

PATTERN RECOGNITION

Besides attending to a stimulus, we must start to analyze and identify it in order to begin processing it in working memory. *Pattern recognition* is a basic problem in human information processing. It concerns the question of how we recognize environmental stimuli as exemplars of concepts already in memory. This is part of the more general set of processes of attaching meaning to information that we process.

Pattern recognition is a very general phenomenon, cutting across all sensory modalities, including everything from how we recognize a certain letter we read as a *T* or understand someone's speech as containing the sound /*p*/ to how we recognize Rover as a dog or recognize a certain social interchange as one of that class of events of "getting dumped" in a dating relationship.

There are three general classes of models of pattern recognition: template matching, prototypes, and feature analysis. Which class of models one chooses carries implications both for processes used in pattern recognition and for the form of the representation of information in long-term memory.

Template Matching

In many ways **template-matching** is the most straightforward and intuitively appealing of the three classes of models. This approach says that we store mental copies of environmental stimuli in our memory, and that pattern recognition proceeds by matching up the external stimuli with these stored mental copies called *templates*. This model postulates something like police fingerprint files, where a suspect's fingerprints are checked with a computer file of other prints until a match is recognized or all prints have been checked. Another example of a template-matching system is a bank's method of identifying and matching checks by matching the characters printed in the corner of the check with those stored in its memory. In both cases the stored template is an exact match with the stimulus.

In spite of the practicality of such a system for fingerprints and check processing, template matching fails as a model of human pattern recognition. For one reason, we would have to have an enormously large number of templates to match up with every possible stimulus, including all the possible variations on a basic theme.

Figure 5–2 shows several possible variations of even a trivially simple stimulus like the letter *X*. An *X* that was slightly larger, smaller, tilted, elongated, flattened, or stylized would not match one's stored template of an *X*. Even modifying the theory to include some preprocessing operations to reduce, enlarge, or rotate the retinal image before comparing it to the stored template cannot adequately deal with the variety of stimuli that are still recognized as members of the same class. For example, how do we recognize as members of the class "dog" such breeds as German shepherds, chihuahuas, fox terriers, collies, and any other number of canines, while at the same time recognizing that physically similar wolves, coyotes, and cats belong to other categories?

Frequently it is very small features that distinguish the different categories, while much grosser physical differences occur across members of the same category. For example, only a tiny mark differentiates an *O* from a *Q*, while a cursive *Q* (*Ձ*), though also a *Q*, looks much less like a *Q* than an *O* does.

FIGURE 5-2   Examples of stimuli recognized as "X."

Moreover, sometimes we recognize an instance of a category even when we have never seen that particular stimulus before; for example, a mutt is still recognized as a dog even if we've never seen that particular type of dog before. Clearly, some more abstract type of model than template matching is required to account for pattern recognition.

Prototypes

The **prototype** model of pattern recognition says that what is stored is not an exact copy of each stimulus, but rather an abstracted general instance. This prototype represents no particular object in that class, but contains key features present in all or most instances. The pattern-recognition process recognizes a match if enough of the properties of the stimulus match the properties of the prototype. Memory about particular instances of subclasses may be stored as the prototype plus information about variations and special features; this would be a much more parsimonious and economical system than storing separate templates for each example.

A prototype theory has intuitive appeal and support in that we often seem to have truly general ideas about what a dog, a criminal, or a party is like, without necessarily storing information about any particular instance. Still, defining exactly what is contained and is not contained in the prototype is difficult and far from obvious. Recent work in schema theory (see Chapter 8) is a promising approach to describing prototypes.

Feature Analysis

The third class of theories of pattern recognition is **feature analysis.** With this type of theory, the input is analyzed into specific perceptual attributes called *features.* After such analysis, the resultant list of features is examined for a possible match to the concept identified by that particular list of features.

Such a model has both intuitive and experimental support. Many concepts and classes of stimuli are defined, at least in part, by distinctive features. For example, a break in a certain place in the circle distinguishes a *C* from an *O*, vibration in the throat differentiates an /s/ from a /z/ sound, and such features as warm-bloodedness and the presence of feathers distinguish birds from reptiles. Because features may be combined in so many possible ways, feature-analysis models get around the problem of the template-matching model having to store such a large number of templates. Although feature-analysis models are sometimes criticized for not clearly specifying how all those features are organized and structured, there are obviously many possibilities for combination. Further, features have the advantage of greater specificity than prototypes.

There is also evidence supporting feature analysis from physiological studies, going back to the pioneering studies of Hubel and Wiesel (1962, 1968) of single-cell recording of neurons in the eye and visual cortex of cats and monkeys. There are cells at various places in the visual pathways and in several layers of the visual cortex in the occipital lobe of the brain that fire in response to very specific types of stimuli that are well characterized by features. For example, one cell might fire in response to a vertical line, another only to a moving vertical line, and another to a moving small, dark, round object. It would appear that certain combinations of features are the triggering stimulus for certain neurons to fire. The brain's analysis of the firing patterns of all these neurons then recognizes the object.

Gestalt Principles of Organization

Besides the identification of features and the use of prototypes, there are also a number of more holistic principles that operate in pattern recognition and perception more generally. These are often called **Gestalt principles,** from the German word meaning "configuration" or "whole." These principles include *closure, similarity, proximity, good continuation,* and *common fate,* and they are illustrated in Figure 5–3. Closure involves a mental "filling in the blanks" to complete some sort of unit. Looking at a follow-the-dots picture and seeing the figure illustrates this principle. Our minds tend to impose organization and interpretation on all incoming input; closure is one way of doing so.

The principles of similarity and proximity involve perceiving elements that are similar in character or close together in space or time as belonging to a unit. For example, what do you see between the following parentheses? (XXXOOO) If you said something like "three X's and three O's" you were probably grouping the three similar elements in proximity with one another into a unit.

Good continuation involves the perception of a line or other element as continuing through an intersecting line; see Figure 5–3. The straight line (arrow) is perceived as continuing across the curved lines (heart) rather than as turning the corner and becoming the curved line, though both interpretations are equally consistent with the retinal image.

These principles applied to movement occur in the principle of common fate, where elements that move in similar patterns are perceived as a unit. This is a very important principle in choreography, employed in dance or marching bands. If every other person in a line of marchers or

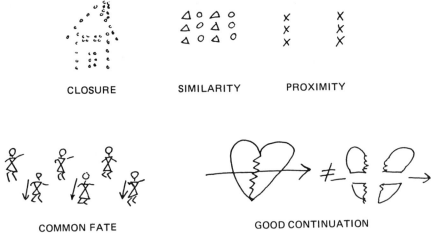

FIGURE 5-3 Gestalt principles of organization.

dancers steps forward at the same time, they are perceived as one group, while those who stay behind are perceived as a separate group.

Whatever emerges as an eventual definitive model of pattern recognition must somehow incorporate such holistic principles, as well as very fine-tuned analytical processes like feature analysis.

Speech Perception

Now that we have examined the basic problem of pattern recognition and looked at the major theoretical explanations, let's examine in detail one of the most important but also most complex problems in pattern recognition—how we understand speech. Before beginning, we must first have a little background knowledge of the nature of speech sounds. Then we will examine how these sounds are perceived. Finally, we will examine the rules specifying how phonemes are to be combined and the role of suprasegmental cues like intonation and stress in the speech-perception process.

On an intuitive level any word or sentence may be analyzed into a chain of discrete sounds called *phonemes*, the smallest acoustic units of language that can make a meaningful psychological difference in that language. For example, the word *bit* is made up of three phonemes. By substituting the first phoneme /p/ for /b/, the meaning of the resulting sequence of three phonemes is changed; *pit* instead of *bit*. (Note: letters between slashes represent the phonemes, not the written letters.) Incidentally, there is not always exactly one phoneme in the pronunciation for each letter in the spelling. For example, *date* only has three phonemes, and the sounds spelled *th* or *sh* in English typically are in fact only one phoneme each. It is the phonemes, not the letters, that we must consider in examining speech perception.

Perception of phonemes. Although with a little practice you may be able to identify the sequence of phonemes in any sample of coherent speech, there is, perhaps surprisingly, no machine that can do this nearly as well as people. This is because the same phoneme is not always perceived for a given sequence of acoustic sounds. For example, the physical sound is not identical every time the phoneme /b/ is understood. If such were the case, it would be a relatively simple matter for the brain to perceive the sound and record the information, which it would then immediately identify as a particular phoneme /b/, perhaps using a template-matching theory discussed earlier. A sequence of sounds like this could thus be identified and eventually be put together into words.

There are several reasons why speech perception cannot possibly occur in this way, however. One reason is that the acoustic speech stimulus changes depending on the pitch, intensity, and voice quality of the speaker. A four-year-old girl, a gruff old man, and an operatic soprano are not emitting the same physical stimulus for the sound that anyone hearing any of them interprets as the phoneme /m/. For that matter, none of the three says the sound exactly the same way every time one of them says it.

Similarly, we can usually understand different dialects of English quite readily even though the actual sequence of phonemes may be quite different. For example, in standard American English the word *water* is pronounced [WAH-der], whereas in standard British English it is more like [WAU-tuh]. Even with three out of the four phonemes different, these sounds are still clearly identifiable by most people on either side of the Atlantic as the word *water*, especially if it occurs in an appropriate meaningful context.

Although computer scientists have so far been unable to program a machine to analyze and interpret reliably a wide range of phonemes from real speech, human listeners can do so quickly and easily. Spoken speech can be followed as fast as 400 words per minute, about 30 phonemes per second. This is quicker than the fastest rate that we can pick out individual sounds in any other sequence of sounds; thirty separate sounds per second of most anything else except natural language is perceived only as "white noise," that is, like static on the radio.

Other evidence also indicates that the sequence of phonemes heard in a word or syllable is not a succession of physically separate sounds. Single phonemes can be spliced from spoken speech by cutting a tape where the boundaries between the phonemes appear to be. Such detached "phonemes" are only identified about 80 percent as accurately as the same phonemes in either normal spoken language or in a group of phonemes that are pronounceable but do not make an identifiable word (*bup*, *jiz*). This suggests that part of how we identify the phoneme /p/ comes not only from the part of sound clearly identified as the phoneme /p/, but also from the surrounding vowels and the transitions between phonemes.

Another series of speech-splicing experiments have produced even more surprising and compelling evidence. Take the syllable /pee/ and splice it to separate the part of the tape containing the /p/ and that containing the /ee/. If the /p/ part of the tape is then spliced to a recording of the vowel /o͞o/, the resulting string is understood as /po͞o/. So far, so good. However, if the same cutting /p/ from /peel/ is spliced to /ah/, the resulting syllable is consistently heard as /kah/ (Schatz, 1954). Even more surprising are results indicating that nothing may be perceived as something! For example, the word *slit* was recorded and then 75 milliseconds of time, less than a tenth of a second, spliced in between the /s/ and the /l/ phoneme. The resulting word perceived was *split*, that is, the pause was heard as /p/ (Liberman, Harris, Eimas, Lisker, & Bastian, 1961)! Similarly, a 75-millisecond pause inserted after the /s/ in *sore* caused the word to be heard as *store* (Bastian, Eimas, & Liberman, 1961). Typically, taking recorded speech and cutting it into pieces and splicing the phonemes back together in a different but meaningful order does not produce intelligible speech, but only gibberish or, at best, misperceived phonemes such as the *split*-for-*slit* example above.

How then do we understand speech at all, given that phonemes are perceived as other phonemes, pauses are perceived as phonemes, and so on? The fact is there is no generally accepted theory of speech perception that produces the "right answer" to this question, and scientists from several disciplines are busily working on this very difficult question. However, we can identify certain kinds of acoustic cues that are definitely involved in understanding language.

One type of acoustic cue is the particular sound that *always* occurs in a sequence of sounds heard as a given phoneme. Although this type of cue is the exception and not the rule, there are nevertheless some such invariant cues, especially in certain consonants called *fricatives* (/s/, /z/, /f/, and /v/). These sounds always have some kind of rush of air out of the mouth, slightly different for each consonant, but always the same for that particular consonant. Unlike consonants like /b/ and /p/, fricatives constrict, but do not completely stop, the flow of air through the mouth.

A more typical but far more complex type of cue occurs in the transition from consonant to vowel, precisely the type of information that is obliterated by cutting a tape of *pah* into /p/ and /a/. On an electronic recording of the frequencies and intensities of your speech (speech spectrogram), it is impossible to identify definitively a point where a consonant ends and the following vowel begins. One critical variable in determining what consonant is heard is called *voice onset time*, the amount of time between the stopping of the flow of air from the lungs in a consonant such as /p/ or /b/ and the resonance of the air in the mouth which is heard as the succeeding vowel. For example, much of the acoustic difference between /b/ and /p/ is that the voice onset time is only 0.001 second following /b/, but is 0.058 second following /p/. This difference in time causes one sequence of sounds to be heard as containing a /b/ and the other a /p/.

In normal speech the difference in voice onset time may be even less, but there we have contextual cues to help identify the words. There is even some evidence that newborns may be able to discriminate between the sounds /b/ and /p/, suggesting that infants can identify the differences in voice onset time (Eimas, Siqueland, Jusczyk, & Vigorito, 1971). The ability to hear such a subtle discrimination may be a part of the innate perceptual system for language processing present in all of us.

One often overlooked way that spoken language is more complex than written language is that there are no consistent physical boundaries among words or phrases comparable to the spaces between words or sentences in writing. Although there are sometimes clear pauses between phonemes, such pauses do not necessarily occur at word boundaries more often than at other places in normal rapid speech. Consider listening to someone speaking a foreign language you do not understand. Can you pick out the word boundaries?

In comprehension, there are segmentation ambiguities that occur precisely because such acoustic cues of spacing are absent; these ambiguities may be bases for humor. Consider the symbol below.

This is a *round tuit*, which you give to someone who always says he or she will do such-and-such "as soon as I get a round tuit!" Similarly, there is the case of the little girl who named her cross-eyed teddy bear "Gladly." When questioned by her parents about this unusual name, she replied that she named it after the animal they sang about in church: "Gladly, the cross-eyed bear."

Every language uses a different subset of all the possible phonemes available. While there is a high degree of overlap, any two languages contain certain sounds that do not occur in the other and thus are especially difficult for speakers of the other language. People have been aware of such differences since ancient times and have even used them to their own advantages. For example, *Judges* 12:5–6 in the Old Testament relates the following story:

> And when any of the fugitives of Ephraim said, "Let me go over,"the men of Gilead said to him, "Are you an Ephraimite?" When he said, "No," they said to him, "Then say *shibboleth*, and he said *sibboleth*, for he could not pronounce it right [because the /sh/ phoneme did not exist in the Ephraimite language]; then they seized him and slew him at the fords of the Jordan.

Sometimes whole sets of sounds may be present in one language but absent in another. For example, French, Polish, and Portuguese have nasal vowels that do not occur in English, German, Spanish, or Italian. German, Dutch, Welsh, Polish, and some Scottish dialects of English have one or more fricative consonants spoken far back in the throat (for example, the last phoneme of *loch* or *Bach*). Some languages, including Arabic, cockney English, and many American Indian languages, contain consonants that involve stopping or constricting the air stream very far back in the throat. American English does in fact contain a related sound, the phoneme spelled by *t* in words like *carton* and *mountain*. This is not a /t/ or /d/ in most American dialects, though in British English it is pronounced /t/.

Phonological rules. Besides the knowledge of phonemes themselves, we also have knowledge of the phonological rules of our language; these are the implicit directions that tell how to combine phonemes into possible words in that language. Sometimes certain phonemes are permitted, but only in certain places and under certain conditions. For example, the final consonant in *sing* (which is not /n/ or /g/ or a combination of them) is very common in English at the end of a syllable, but never occurs at the beginning of one; in fact, it is very difficult for an English-speaker to pronounce in such a position, though some languages allow it; for example, *Nguyen* is a common name in Vietnamese. Similarly, the sound spelled by *s* in *measure* and *ge* in *rouge* cannot begin a word in English, except possibly for loan words from other languages, though it very commonly begins French words. Moreover, English contains a constraint that the *schwa* /ə/ sound, the vowel spelled by *e* in *women*, *ai* in *curtain*, *o* in *lemon*, and so forth, may occur only in unstressed syllables. Some languages—Arabic or French—allow it in stressed syllables, and the resulting sequence, even if it contains only phonemes that occur in English, sounds very unlike English, simply because of the stressed schwa vowel. Still another example involves consonant blends. English allows only certain consonants to follow /s/. Thus /st/, /sk/, and /sp/ are allowed but not /sd/, /sg/ or /sb/, although the latter three are pronounceable and occur frequently at the beginning of Italian words.

Suprasegmentals. Besides phonemes and phonological rules for combining them, there is a whole class of additional and very important sound cues in language, the **suprasegmental** (prosodic) factors such as *stress*, *pitch*, *pause*, and *intonation*. The most important suprasegmental in English is *stress*, which often can make the meaningful difference between two words. For example, IN-sult and PER-mit are nouns, while in-SULT and per-MIT are verbs; the phonemes are the same in both cases, but each member of the pair stresses a different syllable. Differential stress in a sentence can also distinguish an adjective-noun combination and a proper name. Consider the spoken sentence RON LIVED IN THE WHITE HOUSE. If *house* is stressed it may be the place next door, while if *white* is stressed it is most likely 1600 Pennsylvania Avenue, and Ron is President Ronald Reagan.

Compared to many languages, English has a high degree of differential stress. Where these stresses occur is determined by some fairly regular, though highly complex, rules. This is a very difficult aspect of English for speakers of languages such as French or Japanese, where differential stress is much less marked. Similarly, it is a reason that makes song lyrics, which depend heavily on differential stress, difficult to translate from a heavily stressed language to a lightly stressed one, or vice versa. It also is one reason that an otherwise fluent speaker of a second language may appear to have "an accent" if, for example, a Parisian speaks English with the comparatively even stress of French. For a more detailed discussion of different "rhythms"of different languages, see Box 5–4.

Another suprasegmental cue is *pitch*, or *tone*. While in English and

---

BOX 5–4 Stress-Timed Versus Syllable-Timed Languages

You may have noticed that different languages appear to have characteristic overall rhythms. English, for example, is a *stress-timed* language, whereby the time between two heavily stressed syllables is about the same, regardless of how many unstressed syllables intervene. For example, in the sentences below, all would typically be spoken with heavy stress on *John's* and the first syllable of *banker*, with the same amount of time in between in all four cases:

> *John's a banker.*
> *John's not a banker.*
> *John's not a rich banker.*
> *John's not a very rich banker.*

In English, unstressed syllables tend to be reduced to schwa /ə/, but only if they are unstressed. In the sentence *Sue went to the store*, the vowel in the preposition *to* is normally pronounced /ə/, even though we would say the vowel in the word *to* spoken alone as / o͞o/. Speakers of languages that do not use schwa, such as Spanish or Portuguese, often mispronounce English by speaking "too precisely," that is, not reducing the unstressed vowels to schwa. This is one factor that makes them appear to have a "foreign accent."

In contrast to stress-timed languages such as English or Portuguese are the *syllable-timed* languages like Spanish, French, or Turkish. In these there are an approximately constant number of syllables per unit of time, regardless of the stress. Such languages often have relatively less differential stress than do the stress-timed languages—though differential stress does still exist—and more precise pronunciation of every sound. To speakers of languages like English, a syllable-timed language often sounds very regular, staccato, and mechanical. Speaking Spanish with a stress-timed rhythm and reducing lightly stressed vowels to schwa is a giveaway of a North American accent.

---

most other modern European languages it makes no difference within a given syllable what pitch is used, in many so-called tonal languages such as Chinese, Vietnamese, and many American Indian Languages, pitch can distinguish one word from another! For example, in the northern dialect of Vietnamese, there are six distinct tones, that is, six different pitch patterns with which a given syllable may be spoken. For example, the word *ba* may mean "three," "to hug," "grandmother," "bane," "dregs," or "haphazardly," depending on the pitch with which it is spoken. It is small wonder that such languages pose difficulties for the English speaker to learn!

Pitch is important in English, however, insofar as it combines with stress to produce characteristic *intonation* patterns, which are used to indicate the speech act (statement, question, exclamation) of an utterance. For example, statements in English typically have an intonation pattern of the highest pitch toward the end of the sentence, but then falling at the very end. On the other hand, yes-no questions end with a rising intonation, with the highest pitch near the end. Intonation patterns carry such strong information that even a declarative sentence becomes a question if spoken with a rising intonation: *This is a good job?*

In addition, stress is important in that any word receiving particularly heavy stress is interpreted as being emphasized in some way, which can radically alter the meaning of the sentence. Stressing different words implies different sorts of contrasts, as in the following example.

a Drive to the *park* (not downtown).
b *Drive* to the park (don't walk).

Another suprasegmental cue is *pause*. Although we have already discussed the voice onset time difference between phonemes, pause may also be important between syllables. For example, depending on whether the

---

BOX 5–5   Graze Seem Use Sick

"Omen Do Wrench"

Oak if my you womb
Were dew buff hello roman
Do tyranny ankle hope lay,
Wears hell dumb absurd
Add as courage inward
Andrew's geyser knock loud he halt hay.

"Gin Gulp Else"

Gin gulp else, gin gulp else,
Gin gulp wall dew hay,
Owe it phone add hiss tour eye
Done new won oar soap inks lay.

"Hiss Slanders Yule Lamb"

Hiss slanders Yule lamb,
Hiss slanders mile lamb,
Thumb gal leaf horn yeah
Tooth anew yore guile inn.
Farm thumb rid wooed far wrist,
Tooth her gulls dream what terse,
Hiss slanders mate fur ruin mean.

The fact that these chains of unrelated words can sound like meaningful song lyrics, even when the phonemes are not quite "correct," suggests the powerful contribution of suprasegmental cues, specifically intonation, in speech perception.

---

long pause comes before or after the /t/, a particular sequence of phonemes may be heard as *night rate* or *nitrate*.

To fully appreciate the contributions of suprasegmental cues to the understanding of language, consider an example of how an appropriate intonation pattern can suggest meaning even when the phonemes are incorrect. If Box 5–5 is read as what it appears to be, that is, a list of unrelated words, it will make no sense. However, if read, or better, *sung*, with a certain intonation pattern, it is recognized as three familiar songs.

Any adequate theory of comprehension will have to include how we perceive phonemes and suprasegmental cues in speech. The pattern recognition process involves the recognition of sounds, but much more than that. Speech perception remains one of the most complicated puzzles facing psychologists (Pisoni, 1978).

Now that we have completed our look at attention and pattern recognition, those processes that select information in sensory memory for further processing, let's look at working memory, where some further processing occurs.

WORKING MEMORY

After some material has been selected for further processing, it comes to the memory store that is variously called *short-term memory, short-term store, working memory, immediate memory, active memory,* or *primary memory*. Each of these labels highlights a different aspect of this limited-capacity memory store. It contains all the information that we are thinking about and "working on" right now; hence the term *working memory*. In this sense it is our current consciousness, where information is held just enough for a decision to be made about further processing, especially encoding for long-term memory storage. All the information that we are thinking about right now includes both information activated from long-term memory and new stimulus information entering through perceptual senses and sensory memory; hence the term *active memory*.

Material in working memory does not stay in this state of activation very long unless it is continually being used in some way; hence the term *short-term memory* (or *store*), which emphasizes this transient character. Of course, if material is actively attended to, rehearsed, or otherwise thought about, it can remain in working memory indefinitely. For example, if you look up a number in the phone book and hold it in your working memory by repeating it to yourself while you walk across the room to dial the phone, that will hold the numbers there.

Limited Capacity and Rapid Decay

One of the most important aspects of working memory is its **limited capacity.** There is only so much that we can think about at one time. Measuring exactly what this amount is is more difficult than you might expect, however. As we have already seen, there are clearly attentional limits on what we can process. George Miller (1956) showed many years ago that the so-called memory span was about 7 ± 2 numbers in a digit-span task; that is, you hear a list of numbers read and immediately afterward must repeat them. It is no coincidence that local phone numbers are exactly seven digits long; anything more would be much more difficult to remember for a few seconds without encoding into long-term memory.

The metaphor is often used of a series of slots (called the *rehearsal buffer*) in working memory. As new material is processed and/or old material retrieved from long-term memory, these slots are filled one-by-one until there is no remaining space in the rehearsal buffer. Once this happens, in order for new material to be added to working memory, something currently there must be "bumped," either through forgetting or encoding and transfer to long-term memory, out of immediate consciousness. This metaphor reflects the intuitive feeling we often have that our mind is so full that there is no room for even one more piece of information without something already there being pushed out.

If information is not attended to or processed in some way, it decays from working memory in 15 to 30 seconds, a phenomenon first demonstrated by Brown (1958) and Peterson and Peterson (1959), in milestone working memory studies. Subjects were presented with a consonant trigram (for example, NKX), followed by a retention interval of 3 to 18 seconds, after which they were to recall the letters. While this task is trivially easy if one is allowed to rehearse during this interval, the experimenters tried to prevent this from occurring by having the subjects spend the retention interval counting backwards by threes from a given three-digit number. This task was intended to keep them from rehearsing the letters, thus measuring the curve of "pure decay" in working memory. They found that, while recall was about 80 percent correct at a three-second interval, it had dropped to between 10 percent and 15 percent by 18 seconds. They concluded from this that the decay function of material in working memory falls very sharply. Although it might at first sound unfortunate, this rapid-decay property is actually very adaptive; it keeps our mind from becoming cluttered with unnecessary information we have already finished thinking about.

While Miller's so-called magical number of 7 ± 2 "bits" of information has generally been demonstrated as the memory span for a wide variety of materials, there is a tremendous amount of variation of what can be put into each of those seven bits. For example, we can hold seven numbers in our working memory, but also seven words, seven pictures, or sometimes even seven sentences. In fact, the bits may be made considerably larger through the processes of *chunking*, by which we combine pieces of information together to allow them to take up less space in working memory. For example, you might chunk the words *rabbit*, *hat*, and *hamburger* from three bits into one by encoding them as one coherent image of a rabbit wearing a baseball cap and chomping on a Big Mac. Similarly, you might chunk the 16 letters TWAFDRAIDSERASOB into the five units TWA, FDR, AIDS, ERA, and SOB. The issue of chunking is discussed further in the discussion of mnemonics in Chapter 6.

Rehearsal

Another important process that occurs in working memory is **rehearsal,** the temporary activation or recycling of information through memory. Rehearsal may be of two sorts, either *maintenance* or *elaborative* rehearsal. Maintenance rehearsal merely holds information in working memory long enough for it to be acted upon in some way. For instance, when you look up a phone number, it may serve your needs adequately to repeat it over to yourself while you dial the phone; you make no effort to encode it into long-term memory. Often in such cases a brief maintenance in working memory is all that is required.

In fact, it is very difficult to prevent people from rehearsing or to accurately assess rehearsal efforts. The Brown-Peterson task of having people count backward by threes has been frequently used in working memory studies. While this is fairly effective in diverting attention and effort to the counting rather than the rehearsal, there is still some evidence that people often may manage to slip in a few rehearsals during the counting task. Although other tasks have been developed that may be somewhat more effective at preventing rehearsal, for example, the detection of a sound in a sea of noise (Reitman, 1971, 1974; Shiffrin, 1973), it is very difficult, if not impossible, to be absolutely sure that someone is not rehearsing.

Rehearsal has been used to explain the primacy effect of the so-called *serial position curve* (Figure 5–4), that is, relatively good memory for the first few items in a list. Early items in the list have received more rehearsal, both because there has been more time to practice them and because when they were presented there was less information competing for the limited resources available for rehearsal. The recency part of the serial position curve—relatively good memory for the last few items in the list—is explained by the fact that the last items are still in working memory simply because

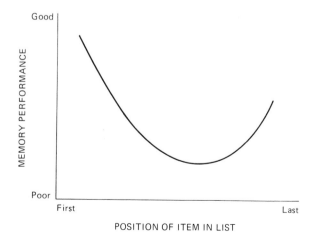

FIGURE 5-4 Serial position curve.

they have not yet had time to decay. Very often studies examining long-term memory will have a brief interfering task immediately after presentation of the to-be-remembered material and before the response task; this exists purely to insure that none of the material will remain in working memory and thus that anything retained must have been encoded into long-term memory and been retrieved from there during recall.

In contrast to maintenance rehearsal, elaborative rehearsal helps transfer information to long-term memory. Rather than merely repeat the to-be-remembered information, elaborative rehearsal relates it to other concepts already in long-term memory and develops new associations among those concepts. An example would be learning the concept of *reinforcement* by relating it to concepts already learned (for example, response, contingency, operant conditioning, punishment, behavior) and by generating examples of its application, such as animal training or child-rearing. Elaborative rehearsal is very helpful in learning class material for exams. It is also helpful for your teachers, as illustrated in Box 5–6, which discusses learning the names of students in a class.

Finally, a lot of rehearsal done all at once (the equivalent of cramming) improves memory for the information studied. However, the rate at which memory for that information deteriorates is the same as for more poorly learned information. The poorly learned material is forgotten sooner (because it starts out as a weaker memory), but the rate of forgetting is the same as for the better-learned material "crammed" in a very short amount of time.

BOX 5–6   Learning Names of Students in a Class

At the beginning of every semester a teacher is faced with the task of learning the names of all the new students. Employing maintenance and elaborative rehearsal and other techniques from memory research, I (RJH) am now able to learn the names of almost all the students in my classes (up to 50 or so per class) during the first three or four class meetings. Below are some "secrets" of the trade.

1. Collect information on each student the first day (address, phone, major, year in school, interests, hometown, career goals).

2. Rehearse names frequently, at least before and after each class, until names are learned. This ensures familiarity with the names and starts associating the names with the other information, which serves to elaborate the memory network around that name.

3. Call the roll the first few classes until names are learned. Go through slowly to concentrate on associating the name and the face.

4. During the first few classes, maintain good eye contact and think about making the faces familiar. Once the faces and the names are both familiar independently, associating the two is much easier.

5. Elaborate the concept of each student by associating the name or face with information collected the first day or actions observed in class.

a. Notice the place where the student generally sits in the room.
b. Notice the general physical appearance, especially very salient physical characteristics or those that strongly remind you of someone else you know.
c. Take note of unusual names or cases where a student uses a middle name or nickname. Such information can serve to distinguish that student from others.
d. Remember comments made in class, especially insofar as they relate to information given on the first day; for example, mentioning a two-year-old child in class discussion and writing "learning how to toilet train a child" as an interest.
e. Remember behavior in class, as it might be reflected in information given. For example, Fred might mention "girls" as an interest and Cheryl might mention "Fred." Two people in the class might not be able to keep their eyes off each other the first day; thus, you have learned who Fred and Cheryl are.
f. Look for similarities of the students to people you know; try to remember possible prior contacts with the student. ("I remember seeing her in the animal lab last semester.")
g. Use mnemonic techniques to associate the face with the name or other information, for example, "Save a seat for Donna Sweet" (because she's always late), "Lefty Hefty" for a left-handed fellow named John Hefty. If you've already associated together all the information about the student, all it takes is linking one piece of that information to the physical appearance.
h. Once the rich network of information about the student is learned, in addition to having observed him or her a couple of class periods, it is fairly easy to make some connection between these visual and informational domains.

6. Use every possible opportunity to connect these two knowledge domains.
a. Call the roll as long as necessary and concentrate on the face while rehearsing the name.
b. Take advantage of individual contacts (students talking to you individually after class) and watch the names as students hand in papers.

By contrast, consider rehearsal of an event in our lives. Whenever we think about something that has happened to us, we are rehearsing that event. If the event was interesting, the rehearsal will be frequent and spread over time. Each time we rehearse the event, we refresh, or reinstate, the memory for that event. Because the rehearsal is spread over time, that rehearsal should slow the rate of forgetting for that event. Such slowing of forgetting through frequent rehearsal has been demonstrated in studies of memory for naturally occurring events (Thompson, 1982).

Encoding

Although material in working memory has not been as extensively processed as has most encoded material in long-term memory, it has been partially analyzed and interpreted with a variety of encoding involved. Acoustic or phonetic encoding is very common in working memory, and for a long time psychologists thought that was the only (or at least the predominant) method of encoding. While we now know this is not completely true, acoustic encoding is still a very important form of memory representation in working memory. Evidence of its importance is documented by studies that show, for example, the letters *C* and *T* are more likely to be confused in working memory than *C* and *O*, even when they are presented visually (Conrad, 1964; Wickelgren, 1965). Such results suggest that subjects are recoding the visual symbols to acoustic representations, thus explaining why the similar-sounding *C* and *T* are more easily confused than the different-sounding (though visually similar) *C* and *O*.

In spite of the great importance of acoustic encoding, there is ample evidence of visual and especially semantic encoding in working memory as well. For example, the Stroop color-word task requires one to name the color ink in which names of colors are written (for instance, the word GREEN written in blue ink). When you try to name the colors, the meanings of the words interfere, because it is hard not to semantically encode information in working memory, even when we consciously try to ignore such information as totally irrelevant to the task at hand. Another example of semantic encoding in working memory is shown in the way we semantically cluster words in a free-recall task; for example, remembering all the animal words together, the clothing words together, and the food words together, when animal, clothing, and food words had been all mixed together in the acquisition list.

Working memory is important in ways far beyond the instances of simple learning and memory we have discussed so far. Box 5–7 presents an extended application of working memory to musical performance.

Forgetting

The explanations offered for forgetting from working memory generally cluster around two general phenomena. On the one hand, forgetting is said to occur due to the decay of the memory over time. This type of explanation uses the notion of the strength of memory. In this view, a strong memory is more likely to be retrieved than a weak memory. Thus, forgetting results from the weakening of a memory over time. This type of explanation would be very appealing if we were to find that the underlying physiological correlate of working memory is some sort of transient change whereby a neuron or set of neurons is temporarily altered in some way and then takes some time to restore to its initial state (see Chapter 10).

The other class of explanations uses the concept of interference. Material is forgotten because other material that is similar is some way interfered by replacing or distorting it. Interference may be *retroactive*, which means it occurs after the original learning. For example, if you are meeting people at a party and first are introduced to Marilyn Smith and soon after Marylou Schmidt, you may call Marilyn "Marylou" because of retroactive interference. If you did the reverse, that is, called Marylou "Marilyn," that would

BOX 5–7 Working Memory and Musical Sight-Reading

An interesting application of information-processing research to musical performance was made by Thomas Wolf (1976), who is both a cognitive psychologist and a professional flutist. He examined the skill of sight-reading, the act of reading music and immediately performing it. Like oral reading, this skill makes heavy use of working memory, since the notes of music must be held in working memory for a few seconds before they are played on the piano (or on the flute, or sung, or whatever). This is a very different use of memory from that of the musician who memorizes the whole piece and performs from rote memory. In his study of professional pianists, Wolf found that most of them were either excellent sight readers or excellent memorizers, but seldom highly skilled at both. Either technique could lead to excellent performance, but for entirely different reasons: Either the working or long-term memory store (but not both) is highly developed.

Wolf identified several factors involved in sight-reading ability. During sight-reading the information on the written music is chunked into units in working memory. The skilled musician can draw on knowledge of music theory as well as one's performance experience to chunk those visual stimuli into larger and more useful units; for example, coding all the notes in both clefs for a whole measure as one chunk, whereas the less accomplished musician might have to code every note, every key signature, and every tempo indicator as a separate chunk.

This offers a scientific argument for the importance of studying music theory, at least for its usefulness in sight-reading. Wolf's subjects reported that there were vast differences in difficulty of sight-reading different types of music, with the most predictable genres of music being the easiest and the least predictable the most difficult. For example, baroque chamber music is quite easy, because there is so much similarity in the different parts of a given piece. The constraints on composition at that time were so great that the predictability is much greater than, say, atonal twentieth-century music, which follows many fewer "rules." Thus, the latter is far more difficult to sight-read because the chunks of information in working memory must be much smaller. There is also a lot less redundancy involved in the modern music.

Wolf illustrates this point with a compelling anecdote about the discovery of a misprinted note in a Brahms capriccio (opus 76, no. 2). One of Wolf's pianist subjects reported that a student of his, upon arriving at a certain C# major chord, played a G instead of the G# that would normally occur in a C# major triad. When her startled teacher stopped her, the student replied that that was what was written on the page, which was true. In later checking other editions of the piece, it was found that they all had the same "misprint," assuming Brahms must have really meant a G# rather than a G in that C# major chord. Apparently few, if indeed anyone, had ever caught his error before, since everyone had apparently been playing the chord with the predictable G# instead of the written G-natural. This suggests that in sight-reading, we don't really read everything, but rather read some of the input and construct the rest drawing on knowledge from long-term memory, perhaps in the forms of schemata (see Chapter 8).

be *proactive* interference, because the interfering material came first and hindered the learning of something else later. There is much experimental evidence that both types of interference occur.

There is probably some truth to both the decay and interference explanations. While interference can be demonstrated fairly easily, it is difficult in principle to design an experiment to once and for all definitively test the two predictions. This is because any test of decay involves allowing time for the decay to occur. However, it is difficult to be sure that no interfering activity is occurring during that time. No matter what you ask the subject to think about, there is no assurance that whatever is going through his or her mind is not in some way interfering with the material to be tested.

Memory Scanning

Many operations may be performed in working memory, including those where we are not consciously aware of all the subprocesses. Such operations were nicely illustrated in an important series of experiments by Saul Sternberg (1966, 1975). Sternberg decided to study working memory by using reaction time instead of the more traditional memory measures. The time measured was then used to infer the nonobservable processes that must have occurred.

The task chosen by Sternberg was a very simple one. Subjects learned some materials arbitrarily included in the set to be learned, for example, the numbers 74926. After this "positive set" had been learned, the subjects were presented with another item and asked to indicate "yes" or "no" to show whether or not the new item was in the positive set. With practice, subjects can generally do many trials of this task quite rapidly with an error rate under 5 percent. Using digits as stimuli, Sternberg varied the size of the positive set and found that the mean RT increased linearly with set size, as if each additional item that must be searched added a constant amount of extra time (38 milliseconds, to be exact) to scan in working memory.

Furthermore, the slope (rate of increase) was the same for positive ("yes") and negative ("no") responses. This is somewhat counterintuitive, as negative responses require searching the entire set, because all members must be checked before being sure there is no match. With the positive responses, however, one ought to be able to stop scanning on the average halfway through the list (position of the test digit was systematically varied across all positions). One does not need to keep searching after a match has been found, yet that appears to be exactly what happens in this task. Based on these data, Sternberg posited a *serial exhaustive search* model, which says that we check each member of the positive set in turn, and check the entire set, *even if we have already found a match*. This speed of search is very rapid, at a rate of 25 to 30 items per second, and is thus not open to introspection.

Sternberg has replicated this basic finding of equal slopes for positive and negative responses with a wide variety of stimuli (letters, words, shapes, colors, numerals), with the slopes varying depending on the complexity of the stimulus. For a discussion of alternative models and interpretations, see Glass (1984).

This line of research is clearly basic research with no apparent and obvious application in the "real world." Yet this work has had many applications probably not initially envisioned by Sternberg. For example, processing deficits in special populations may be more precisely identified. Schizophrenics, alcoholics, and those high on marijuana show higher y-intercepts but the same slopes as normal people. This shows that the memory deficit from the drug or pathology is due to increased encoding or response time but not increased search time. On the other hand, some elderly and brain-damaged retarded show steeper slopes, indicating a longer search time. This ability to identify memory deficits more precisely vastly improves diagnosis of problems. Tasks like Sternberg's are increasingly being tested and incorporated into intelligence testing as well (see E. Hunt, 1983).

CONCLUSION

We have now completed our examination of the perceptual and working memory aspects of information processing. In the next chapter we shall turn to long-term memory, and the encoding and retrieval processes involved with it.

Even though long-term memory is probably the sort of memory that you primarily think of when someone talks about remembering, it is not the only important component of information processing. All of the prior steps we have discussed in this chapter must occur before material is ever encoded in long-term memory, much less retrieved from there. Material must be attended to and patterns recognized and it must be passed onto working memory for initial processing. If it "survives" all these hurdles, it may pass on to more permanent memory.

Conceptualizing working memory and long-term memory as qualitatively separate memory stores, as represented in Figure 5–1 and Atkinson and Shiffrin (1968), is not the only possible framework for conceptualizing memory, however. After we have examined long-term memory in the next chapter, we shall return to the examination of some alternative theoretical frameworks.

SUGGESTED READINGS

The topics in this chapter are covered in more detail in several excellent cognitive psychology texts. Particularly recommended are J. R. Anderson (1985), Best (1986), Bourne, Dominowski, Loftus, and Healy (1986), Glass and Holyoak (1986), Howard (1983), and Matlin (1983). Anderson takes the most computed-oriented approach, while Howard, Best, and Matlin are quite eclectic. Best has an excellent chapter on attention, and Howard has a good one on working memory and the best one on speech perception, an often-neglected topic in texts. Both Anderson and Bourne and colleagues pay particular attention to applications.

6

MEMORY
AND INFORMATION
PROCESSING II:
LONG-TERM MEMORY

In discussing working memory, we have already begun to consider aspects of long-term memory, especially in processes of encoding material for storage in long-term memory. In this chapter we will continue to examine this more permanent store of memory. In doing so, there are many facets to consider: encoding and retrieval processes relating long-term to working memory, the structure of information in long-term memory, and processes for searching through that information structure. Such issues will be examined here. Not only is it difficult to consider long-term memory totally apart from working memory, but it is also difficult to consider it in isolation from other issues and problems in language and cognition. Thus, we will continue to mention attention, pattern recognition, and working memory. Toward the end of the chapter we will look at alternative conceptualizations of the whole memory system and a detailed application of memory principles to the problem of eyewitness identification.

TAXONOMIES OF MEMORY

In considering long-term (permanent) memory, it is helpful to examine some classifications of different types of long-term memory. The best-known distinction is between **episodic** and **semantic** memory. We will begin by looking at this historic dichotomy and then turn to a more complex contemporary alternative.

Endel Tulving (1972) first made the distinction between episodic and semantic memory in long-term storage. While semantic memory is all the general information that we have in our long-term memories, episodic memory is information about particular memories associated with the time and place that we learned that information. For example, remembering that people frequently have eggs for breakfast and that eggs come from chickens is semantic memory. Remembering that you had a fried egg and toast for breakfast this morning while you crammed for your Abnormal Psychology exam is episodic memory. Remembering that Bismarck is the capital of North Dakota is semantic memory; remembering that you first learned this on a cold, snowy December day when your fifth-grade teacher made you stay after school and write "Bismarck is the capital of North Dakota" 50 times is episodic memory.

Episodic and semantic memories may be related. For example, one result of traveling can be to accumulate episodic memories to relate to previously learned semantic memories. For example, before I (RJH) ever visited Brazil, I knew that Rio de Janeiro was a large coastal city in a beautiful setting where rugged mountains meet the Atlantic Ocean and Guanabara Bay. I also knew that popular tourist spots there included Copacabana Beach, the cable car up Mt. Sugarloaf, and the Christ statue on Mt. Corcovado. Now, however, my semantic memory of that information is supplemented by episodic information of the wave that knocked me in the surf at Copacabana, the lunch I had with my friends at the halfway stop on Sugarloaf, and the cold wind blowing at the top of Corcovado as we savored the magnificent view of Rio on that early spring afternoon.

Tulving argued that most memory research up to 1972 tested episodic memory, specific information learned at a particular time, that is, in a memory experiment (such as, "Was this word on the list or wasn't it?"). Also important, Tulving said, was semantic memory, all the knowledge that we have and can retrieve at will, even though we don't remember exactly when and where we learned it. Since then, cognitive psychologists have increasingly turned to studying semantic memory, though episodic memory is still widely researched as well.

Recently, however, others have noted the need to further subdivide memory. For example, the burgeoning research in autobiographical memory (Rubin, 1986) has highlighted the need to separate memories of personal experiences from memories of experimental events like learning a list of words. In Tulving's dichotomy, both of these classes would have to be considered episodic memory, yet they have a very different character.

In response to such concerns, Brewer (1986) presented a considerably more elaborate taxonomy of memory along four dimensions. First are the *types of input*: ego-self (personal and autobiographical memory), visual-spatial (memory for objects and places), visual-temporal (memory for events and actions), and semantic (facts and knowledge). Across these four types of input are crossed the form of representation (imaginal or nonimaginal) and conditions of acquisition (single-instance or repeated). Single instances produce representations of particular events or facts, whereas repeated inputs produce generic representations of classes of situations (for example, what a job interview is like, how baseball is played, or how one makes airline reservations). Such generic representations will be considered further in the discussion of schema theory in Chapter 8.

THE QUESTION OF REPRESENTATION

One of the central issues in the study of permanent memory is that of *representation*; that is, in what form is the information in memory? While this is a very basic question that was long debated by philosophers before the emergence of scientific psychology, it is also a very complex one. In examining the issue here, we will concentrate on looking at some sample forms of representation that have been proposed and studied. We will begin by examining imagery and then looking at some more complex models of how information is represented in memory. While the question of representation involves the development of some highly complex models, the question of the form in which we encode information in memory is also a highly practical issue. See Box 6–1 for one example of its everyday relevance.

Analogue and analytic representations. The form of the information stored in long-term memory may be either **analogue** or **analytic** (abstract) representations. An analogue representation physically resembles what it represents in some important way. Such similarities may be very thorough and detailed or contain only one or two superficial similarities. One clear example of an analogue representation is a map, which physically resembles the territory it represents in the relative locations of places, while remaining very different in other ways, such as size, color, and amount of detail.

Other examples of analogue representations include physical models, graphs, drawings, and thermometers. Such representations may have partially analytic characteristics, as when a map shows rainfall amounts or population densities in terms of different colors to represent different quantities. Assignment of these colors to different rainfall amounts is largely arbitrary and bears little physical resemblance to those amounts of rainfall.

In contrast to analogue representations are *analytic* representations, which are totally abstract and arbitrary, with the representation bearing no physical resemblance to its referent at all. The most complex and pervasive analytic representational system is language, which is entirely analytic, with the exception of onomatopoeic words like "meow" and "ding dong." A dog has no more relation to the word "dog," "chien," "perro," "cachorro," or "Hund" than to "truck" or "idea." Other examples of analytic codes include mathematics, formal logic, musical notation, computer languages, and propositions.

Language will be discussed in more detail in the next chapter and will not be further considered here. Rather, let us now turn to examining one of the most important types of analogue mental representations, namely imagery.

BOX 6–1 Memory Representations of Medication Instructions

The type of cognitive representation that you form in your memory can have important consequences. Ruth Day (1986) studied the effects of the type of representation that people have of bus schedules, recipes, and medication instructions. For example, most medications are given with rather confusing instructions like "4 tablets per day," "Take one three times a day," or "Take one before bedtime." Such instructions are especially confusing to people, including many elderly, who take multiple pills on different schedules daily. Day tested people's comprehension of several different forms of instructions and representations of such information in the context of answering a real-world task such as: "How many of pill X would you have to take along for an overnight trip?" She found that this question was answered much better when the information was represented as a matrix (see Fig. 6–1) than when represented as a list of instructions for each pill. In this case, a poor or confusing representation of information in memory may not only lead to less efficient processing but actually could have life-and-death consequences if medication is forgotten or taken in the wrong dosage.

FIGURE 6-1 Sample daily medication schedule.

MEDICATION	TIME OF DAY			
	BREAKFAST	NOON	DINNER	BEDTIME
A	X	X	X	
B	X			X
C				X
D		X		X
E	X		X	

Imagery

What is imagery? Imagery has been discussed by philosophers for centuries and was a major area of inquiry among the nineteenth-century German introspectionists (see Chapter 1), the earliest experimental psychologists. However, because of its mentalistic character, imagery fell out of favor during the behaviorist era and was only "rediscovered" in the 1960s. It has been a very active area of research ever since. (See Block, 1981; Kieras, 1978; Kosslyn, 1983; Marschark, Richman, Yuille, & Hunt, 1987, for reviews).

Although imagery is most often discussed in terms of *visual* examples, it is not exclusively a visual phenomenon. Imagery, in fact, occurs in all sense modalities. *Auditory* imagery is clearly illustrated by one's mental response to the request "think of the sound a cow makes" or "think of the first few notes of Beethoven's *Fifth Symphony*." *Olfactory* imagery occurs when we image the smell of a turkey cooking in the oven; this may be followed by *taste* imagery imagining how it would subsequently taste. When we imagine how velvet would feel on the skin or imagine the touch of another person in an anticipated sexual encounter, we use *tactile* imagery. *Kinesthetic* imagery is even involved in some forms of relaxation training, where people are taught to put their bodies in a relaxed state and become sensitive to kinesthetic feedback from muscles that may be tense or relaxed (for example, "Imagine how your lungs feel as you breathe all the tension from your stomach to your lungs and then exhale it from your body").

Imagery is often discussed in terms of the metaphor "pictures in the head." Such a metaphor is useful in certain ways but may be misleading in others, even within the visual modality. Imagery, unlike pictures, is very dynamic and constructive with a high degree of plasticity. We can image moving objects, changing events, and things and situations we have never actually seen or experienced. The mental imagery of our minds has a richer store of special effects than directors Steven Spielberg or George Lucas will ever create in their motion pictures.

In a very general sense, imagery is a major reason that we can remember the past and anticipate the future. Some sort of imagery code is almost certainly at the base of the earliest instances of memory in children, such as when an infant moves an arm to indicate "bye-bye" to an adult. Upon doing this act, the child's mind must contain some mental representation of an adult making such a motion to indicate that he or she was leaving.

Indeed, a child's conception of time must rely on imagery in conceptualizing the past and future, as well as imagining hypothetical present events. Perhaps the earliest concrete evidence of this is the demonstration of the attainment of object permanence by a child of ten months. If a child sees a toy covered up with a blanket and immediately removes the blanket to reach the toy, that child must have had some representation, perhaps an image, of that toy in mind after it had been covered. If that had not occurred, the child would have presumably stopped looking for the toy or, indeed, doing any other behavior that reflected a memory of the missing toy. This is, in fact, the way that infants six months or younger behave.

Imagery can be used in problem solving as a means of assessing and testing out possible solutions and restructuring a problem (see Chapter 9). This occurs in ill-defined real-world problems such as trying to figure out how to rearrange the furniture in your living room to increase the available seating to facilitate conversation. It is certainly easier to rearrange the furniture through visual imagery first before doing so in reality. Similarly, it is easier to decide what meal to prepare for a dinner party if you have visually imagined the appearance of the dish, and used the senses of taste and smell to imagine those properties.

Imagery may be useful in problem solving in ways beyond such purposive imagining. Shepard (1978) reports several examples of scientific and literary discoveries made through the use of visual imagery. For example, the German chemist Kekule frequently used the visual imagery of "dancing atoms" linking together to form molecules. In one such reverie the atoms united to form a ring, which Kekule immediately recognized as the long elusive structure of benzene, a discovery that became central to all organic chemistry.

Imagery can be used to perform different types of operations. One of the most studied operations is the mental rotation of figures such as letters and three-dimensional block patterns (Cooper & Shepard, 1973; Shepard & Feng, 1972; Shepard & Metzler, 1971). For example, in one study subjects saw a picture of some sort of three-dimensional block pattern and were asked to judge if one pattern was a rotation of the first pattern or not (Shepard & Metzler, 1971). The time it took to identify a match correctly was a linear function of the number of degrees of rotation separating the two figures. Researchers argued from this result that subjects were mentally rotating the first figure until they produced a match with the second figure.

Imagery is frequently used as a means of encoding information for transfer to long-term memory. Some types of information are more amenable to imagery encoding than others. Allan Paivio (1971, 1975; Begg & Paivio, 1969; Paivio & Begg, 1981) has proposed the *dual-coding* theory to account for why concrete information is typically remembered better than abstract information. For example, in a serial-learning task, subjects remember words like *chicken, piano,* or *truck* better than equally frequent but abstract words like *liberty, idea,* or *happiness.* The same effect has been demonstrated with sentences (Begg & Paivio, 1969). Paivio postulates that concrete words have a readily available imagery code that abstract words lack. Therefore abstract words must be encoded as the words themselves, or perhaps as abstract propositions. Concrete words may be encoded in these ways as well, but they also have an additional memory code available to them, namely, visual imagery. This accounts for their greater memorability. Although abstract words could conceivably be encoded by visual imagery, and no doubt are on occasion, it is a considerably less efficient code than it is for the concrete words.

Imagery is often useful in comprehension of language. One type of language where imagery may be especially important is metaphorical language. If you hear, for example, "The reporters torpedoed difficult questions at the President" or "Bill is an octopus on a date," part of the process of interpreting metaphors might involve the use of imagery in a creative and even surrealistic fusion of two entire domains of knowledge. For example, one might picture, upon hearing "Bill is an octopus on a date," a man with several arms with suckers on them wrapped around a woman. For further discussion of this issue see Harris, Lahey, and Marsalek (1980) and Riechmann and Coste (1980).

Cognitive maps.   One way that we all use imagery is in our use of **cognitive maps** (or mental maps). We have image representations of places that we are familiar with and use these to find our way around or give someone else directions. However, these cognitive maps are not merely internalized aerial photographs of the environment. In an early milestone book on cognitive maps, K. Lynch (1960) identified several elements of mental maps. *Paths* are channels along which people move (streets, walkways, railroads). *Edges* are linear elements other than paths (shores, boundaries of neighborhoods). *Districts* are areas having some common identifiable character (parks, neighborhoods). *Nodes* are important focal areas (junctions, path crossings, or plazas). *Landmarks* are points of reference (towers, signs, or buildings).

The general axes of orientation are important in cognitive maps. While the most common type of axis is a grid system (city blocks, NSEW directions, and so forth), some geographical areas, especially coastal and mountainous regions, use different axes. For example, in areas near large bodies of water, people often figure mental maps in terms of distance away from the shore. This may be especially confusing if that body of water has an unexpected orientation in that area. For instance, the normally north-south Pacific coast runs roughly east-west between Santa Barbara and Los Angeles. In mountainous areas, a perpendicular grid system is useless, because the paths are consistently curving. Someone moving from hilly Boston or Pittsburgh to the flat and perpendicular American Midwest at first has a difficult time thinking and speaking in terms like north, south, east, and west. Similarly, a Midwesterner has difficulty understanding directions like, "Follow the highway for three miles, then bear to the right and follow the road a ways down the hollow, till you get to a little past the red barn, where you veer to the left . . . ."

Another important characteristic of cognitive maps is their mobile quality; they are not purely static images. When Linde and Labov (1975) asked New Yorkers to describe the layout of their apartments, 97 percent of them gave a "tour," including the information in the form of "mobile vectors" such as, "you keep walking straight ahead, turn right at the kitchen," or "go from the bathroom into the bedroom." Very few used a static "aerial view" cognitive map.

Like most memory representations, cognitive maps include *inferred* and *constructed* information as well as information mentally reproduced. We draw on stored knowledge about what typical rooms, cities, or countrysides are like. We assume that the room has four straight walls, a ceiling, and at least one door unless we are told otherwise. This knowledge may occasionally be misleading if the environment in question is an unusual one. For example, most people would answer that Reno, Nevada, is east of Los Angeles, although in fact it is west. However, we draw on our schematic information (see Chapter 8) that Nevada is east of California. Although this is generally true, not everything in Nevada is east of everything in California.

We may acquire our initial cognitive map information from one of two sources: maps or navigation (Thorndyke & Hayes-Roth, 1982). Information acquired from maps is survey knowledge and is very similar to the map itself, including shapes, locations of objects, and easily estimated straight-line distances. In contrast, knowledge acquired from navigation, that is, actual experience traveling through that environment, is more episodic and procedural (see Box 5–3). We remember specific routes with associated landmarks, but the information is organized around the routes we travel. In many ways knowledge from navigation is probably stronger and more useful than knowledge from maps, but it is much harder to acquire.

Although imagery is one major type of representation of information in memory, much of the emphasis in the study of the representation issue in recent years has been on the development of more global structural models that describe how information in memory is coded and organized. Most of these models have focused primarily on semantic memory.

One of the major aims of the research in semantic memory since Tulving's landmark paper has been the attempt to discover the structure of the knowledge in semantic memory. In exactly what form is that information stored? How is it organized? How do we search through it when we try to retrieve information from long-term memory? It probably will not surprise you to learn that a definitive answer to these questions has not emerged, though we have learned quite a bit. It is helpful to look briefly at some types of structures that have been posited for semantic memory and some of their implications.

Network Models of Semantic Memory

One general class of models is the network models (see J. R. Anderson, 1976; Collins & Loftus, 1975; Collins & Quillian, 1969; Anderson & Bower, 1973). These models posit the existence of "nodes" (concepts), which are related to each other in various ways, depending on the particular model. Probably the best-known model is the earliest one (Collins & Quillian, 1969). They posited a branching network of subordinate and superordinate nodes (concepts) hierarchically arranged. Information about the various nodes is stored as attributes at each node. Each attribute applies to that node but also to all those nodes below it in the hierarchy. For example, such information as "has feathers" and "is two-legged" is stored at the node "bird" and thus does not need to be stored at each of the many specific bird nodes subordinate to "bird."

More recent network models have focused on specifying the character of the relationships between the various nodes and have also explored different types of organization other than hierarchical. Most of these recent models take the structure of language (see Chapter 7) more seriously. Thus, we will defer further discussion until later.

One advantage of network models, or indeed of most models of semantic memory, is that they allow for individual differences. Each person's hierarchy of information may be slightly different, or perhaps substantially so. For example, the typical urban American, especially from the East or West Coast, may divide the superordinate class "farm animals" into subordinate classes like horses, cows, pigs, sheep, and chickens, with no further differentiation within each subordinate class.

On the other hand, the farmer or rancher would require further subdivisions; a class "livestock" could be divided into dairy and beef cattle, beef cattle could be divided into Angus, Herefords, Charolais, and Simmentals, subclasses that would have little meaning or use to the New York apartment dweller.

The failure to subcategorize concepts within one's semantic memory can have some important social and political consequences when certain types of semantic memory organizations are characteristic of whole cultures. For example, North Americans' failure to distinguish subordinate classes of Moslems (Sunni and Shi'ite) makes it difficult for them to fully understand the dynamics behind certain Middle Eastern conflicts, such as Lebanon, the Iran-Iraq war of the 1980s, and neighboring countries' diverse reactions to the Iranian Revolution of 1979 and its aftermath.

Latin Americans consistently resent the North American's failure to develop subordinate categories of "Latin America" to recognize the tremendous social, cultural, and political differences that exist there (Brazil is a Portuguese-speaking, industrialized, multiethnic society; Peru and Bolivia are largely Indian and rural; Argentina prides itself on being the most European country in South America). Though both countries are in Central America, Costa Rica is an ethnically white, highly literate, and stable democratic society, while nearby Guatemala is largely Indian, poor, and feudal, having seldom ever known real democracy.

Feature Comparison Model of Semantic Memory

An alternative conception of the structure of semantic memory was proposed by Smith, Shoben, and Rips (1974; see also E. E. Smith, 1978). Instead of claiming that concepts were stored in hierarchies of networks, Smith and others (1974) proposed that each concept contains lists of features, corresponding to its common attributes (for example, a bird has feathers, can fly, has two legs, is warm-blooded). These features are of two types: **defining** and **characteristic.** *Defining* features are those that absolutely must be present for the example to be a member of that concept. For example, a bird *must* have feathers; otherwise it isn't a bird. *Characteristic* features, on the other hand, are attributes that are typically, but not necessarily, present. For instance, birds typically can fly, but there are exceptions (penguins and ostriches). In fact, characteristic features are much more numerous than defining features when considering real-world concepts. (See the discussion of fuzzy sets in Chapter 7.)

Smith and others (1974) proposed different sorts of processes in verifying the truth of a sentence. Specifically, they proposed a two-stage process. Consider the following example:

(1) A canary is a bird.
(2) A chicken is a bird.
(3) A bat is a bird.
(4) A table is a bird.

A subject sees (1), for example, and retrieves the concepts "canary" and "bird" and begins comparing both the defining and characteristic features of each to determine if there is a sufficient match to respond "true." In this case subjects would quickly find such a match and could immediately reply "true." Similarly, for (4), there is such a clear mismatch between "table" and "bird" that the subject can quickly respond "false."

The other two cases are more complex, however. With either (2) or (3) the subject will probably find an intermediate degree of matching on defining and characteristic features. In such cases, that is, when the match is intermediate, a second stage of processing must be initiated, namely, a comparison on the basis of the defining features only. Thus, one would compare only on the attributes that a bird *must have*, not those it usually has but may not. After this second stage of comparison, (2) could be answered "true" and (3) could be answered "false."

Even though "bat" and "bird" share many characteristic features (can fly, are small), when compared on defining features only, the match is poor. The model proposed by Smith and others (1974) nicely explains the so-called "typicality" effect, where it takes longer to verify the truth of category membership of less typical instances ("turkey" as opposed to "robin"). This is a robust and consistent finding that had always posed problems for the simple network model of Collins and Quillian.

Feature-comparison also has its drawbacks, however, most notably the criticism that it does not deal seriously enough with the question of the organization of all the features. Positing collections of features all through semantic memory could be very uneconomical if they are not organized in some way. See E. E. Smith (1978) and Chang (1986) for reviews of semantic memory models.

One important aspect of meaning that has not been considered seriously by any of these models is meaning's flexibility. Though *piano* generally has but one meaning, different aspects of its meaning are more salient in some situations than others. For example, a comment like "Help me move the piano" highlights its "heavy furniture" aspect, whereas "You play the piano beautifully" highlights its "musical" aspect (Barclay, Bransford, Franks, McCarrell, & Nitsch, 1974). While both features are present in both contexts, each is present to a different degree. Schoen (1986, 1988) explored this aspect of semantic flexibility more thoroughly and argued that all models of semantic memory must eventually deal with the phenomenon.

Parallel Distributed Processing (PDP) Models

One of the newest approaches to the study of memory and cognition is the *parallel distributed processing* (PDP), or connectionist, model, developed most extensively by the PDP Research group (see McClelland & Rumelhart, 1986, and Rumelhart & McClelland, 1986, for readings on the topic). The PDP models attempt to address the complexity of cognitive processing with a class of models generalizable across a wide variety of tasks and problems. They recognize that multiple cognitive operations may be done in *parallel* (simultaneously) and are *distributed* across an extensive processing network (McClelland, 1988).

The basic components of PDP models are units and connections between those units, not unlike earlier models like Collins and Quillian (1969) or J. R. Anderson (1976), except that there are no assumptions that the complex networks need be hierarchical in nature. Nor are the units thought to map onto ordinary language concepts, as in the earlier associative models. Instead, PDP models are *subsymbolic* and should not be thought of as processing meaningful information. In PDP models, the form of the representation in memory is not a passive recording or data structure but rather a pattern of activation, either excitatory or inhibitory, and cognitive processing occurs through the propagation of activation patterns. Knowledge is thus not encoded at a particular "place" by some "thing" but rather is encoded in connection strengths, and learning occurs through modification of these connections. This activity is seen as directly modelling the neural interconnections in the brain.

The PDP models describe the robust incremental learning that occurs in a wide variety of situations, such as perception, memory, and motor skills. Their great generality has the advantage of being adaptable to a wide variety of situations, each of which has its own unique constraints for its own domain. The PDP models are not without criticism, however (Massaro, 1988). At least in principle, one of the hopes of connectionist models is to be able to bridge the conceptual gap across cognitive psychology, computer science, and neuroscience. These three domains have for some time all been studying thinking but each largely from its own perspective. The connectionist-network structure is quite consistent with what neuroscience knows about the nervous system and what the computer scientist is able to program an artificial intelligence program to perform.

Now let us turn from examining the representation of information in memory to a focus on the processes involved in using that information. Most memory processes fall into the two major classes of *encoding* and *retrieval*.

ENCODING AND RETRIEVAL PROCESSES

Although we have mentioned encoding quite a bit so far, we have not discussed much how **encoding** and **retrieval** are so intimately related, especially insofar as the way the methods of encoding can affect the ease of retrieval. The next section will examine encoding, specifically focussing on its implications for retrieval.

Before examining different encoding and retrieval processes, let us look first at the different ways that memory has been measured. Next, we will look at the constructive memory strategies known as *mnemonics*. Following that, we will investigate the role that contextual variables play in encoding and retrieval; what your surrounding environment and mental state are when your memory is at work makes a lot of difference. Finally, we will focus a bit on forgetting; that is, the failure of encoding and/or retrieval.

Ways of Measuring Memory

How do we measure memory? What kinds of dependent variables can be used to make inferences about structure and process in long-term memory?

When we test someone's memory, there is a variety of measures that we may use. Many of them fall into two general categories: **recall** and **recognition.** Though both have been developed and widely used in studying episodic memory, they have some applications to semantic memory as well. Both recall and recognition have several variations, but the overall distinction has proven a useful one. The basic difference is that in recall, one must both generate the response *and* recognize that it is correct, while in recognition memory the response is already generated and all we are asked to do is judge whether or not it is the correct response.

Recall.   Recall may either be **free recall** or some form of **cued recall.** In total free recall we are given no cues or hints to help us remember the desired information. An extreme form of this might be a history test question that asks: "Tell all that you know about World War II." Perhaps more realistically, an attorney might ask a witness, "Tell me what you remember about the night of the murder." Because there are no potentially biasing cues present, recalled information is less subject to distortion than more structured memory tasks. Unfortunately, there is a tradeoff, in that there is also less total accurate information remembered. Thus, quality is high but quantity is low (Lipton, 1977).

In contrast, cued recall is generally easier, since there is some sort of cue present to aid retrieval, but the cue may bias the reconstruction of the response. Any kind of memory situation where someone gives us a "hint" is a cued-recall task. Cued recall has been studied extensively in the psychological literature using paired-associate learning tasks and various forms of completion tasks. An actor learning lines for a play is also practicing a cued recall task, where each preceding line acts as the cue for the next line.

Recognition.   In contrast to recall measures, **recognition memory** presents some pregenerated stimulus for the person to judge whether or not it is accurate. Like recall, there are two general kinds of recognition. The first kind, often called *yes-no* or *old-new recognition*, presents some item and asks you to indicate, "Yes, I remember that" or "No, I don't remember it." There are two important factors involved in this type of recognition memory. Most obviously, there is the *strength* parameter, that is, how strong the memory ("trace") of the information is. Generally, a strong memory is going to be recognized more accurately than a weaker memory.

However, strength is not the only relevant dimension. There is also a *criterion*, that is, how sure you have to be in order to say, "Yes, that's it." Upon examining a recognition-memory item and your own memory trace of that information, a decision must be made. If there is a strong and obvious match or mismatch, the decision is easy, but how about the middle ground? For example, if you are looking at a suspect and are asked to indicate whether he was the man who mugged you, how sure do you have to be before you say "yes," given that your fragmentary memories somewhat match the characteristics of the suspect in front of you? If a "yes" decision meant sending a suspect to life in prison, you might set a more stringent criterion than you would in a more trivial situation with a memory of equivalent strength and match to the recognition-memory item.

Besides yes-no recognition, we also have *forced-choice recognition* memory, perhaps best exemplified by the multiple-choice test, where you must choose one answer from among several but where one, and only one, is correct. The difficulty of forced-choice recognition memory may be greatly altered depending on the nature of the distractors, the wrong answers in which the correct item is embedded. Consider the relative difficulty of the two multiple-choice test items below:

(5) The capital of Burkina Faso is
     a. Los Angeles, b. Mexico City, c. Tokyo, d. Ouagadougou
     e. All of the above.
(6) The capital of Mali is
     a. Timbuktu, b. Bamako, c. Niamey, d. Abidjan, e. Conakry.

One could easily answer (5) correctly with no knowledge whatsoever of Burkina Faso, while (6) could be difficult even for someone quite knowledgeable about West Africa. (Incidentally, the answers to (5) and (6) are *d.* and *b.*, respectively.)

Implicit memory.   While the two traditional types of memory measures (recall and recognition) typically require conscious recollection of remembered material, other measures may test memory more indirectly by measuring performance on some task that may implicitly reveal the effects of memory. For example, subjects may be asked to identify the word in the fragment D_L_H_N; performance on this task is greatly affected by some priming task like seeing the word "porpoise" (Graf & Schacter, 1985; Roediger & Blaxton, 1987; Tulving, Schacter, & Stark, 1982; Weldon & Roediger, 1987). Implicit memory tasks may sometimes be sensitive to differences not picked up by recall and recognition tasks.

In an excellent review of historical and current uses of implicit memory measures, Schacter (1987) concluded that implicit memory measures have yielded somewhat different results than those obtained from more traditional measures. Schacter argued that models of memory must take such data into account and examine reasons why implicit memory measures often produce different results than do explicit memory measures.

Reaction time.   A very different type of implicit memory measure is **reaction time** (RT). This measure has the advantage of being a concrete and quantitative measure of very covert and unobservable cognitive *processes* of thought. This is in contrast to recall or recognition, which measures only the remembered *products* of thought processes. The general logic of RT, going back to Donders (1868), is that a longer time reflects either more complex processes or a greater number of processes than a shorter time reflects. To understand further how RT is used, an example will be discussed in detail, with emphasis on the logic behind this measure.

Consider a situation like those discussed previously (questions 1 through 4 on page 138), where the subjects are asked to verify a sentence as being true or false and their time to do so is measured. Usually such sentences are very simple, and the reaction times themselves short, often measured in milliseconds. Suppose we find, for example, that it takes significantly longer to answer true to (2) than to (1), and significantly longer to answer false to (3) than to (4). Researchers studying semantic memory concluded that the relatively longer times to verify (2) and (3) were obtained because those statements were more difficult than (1) and (4), requiring a more extensive search of features stored in semantic memory about the two concepts in each statement. This can be a window to view the otherwise unobservable cognitive processes of searching knowledge structures in memory. It can be used to infer what the structure of memory is like. Such logic was employed extensively in the research used to support and build the network models of semantic memory discussed earlier in the chapter.

Now that we have examined some ways of measuring memory, let us turn to examining encoding and retrieval more directly, beginning with the memory strategies called *mnemonics*.

Mnemonics

Probably the most promising way to work on improving your memory is by improving your encoding strategies. One, though by no means the only, way to do this is to use **mnemonics,** strategies for more efficient encoding. Mnemonics are the products of conscious decisions to organize and chunk information into larger and more meaningful units for the purpose of remembering it better. During the S-R era mnemonics occupied a much maligned position of being considered somewhat devious and underhanded "tricks" for remembering, if one had to stoop to using less-than-pure methods of learning. Happily, mnemonics are now recognized as frequently useful and eminently respectable strategies.

Let us examine some types of mnemonics to better understand what they do and how they work. Sometimes they may add an additional memory code to the original code, allowing two, instead of one, avenues of retrieval. For example, if you make up a little song to help you remember something, this gives you two possible ways to retrieve that information later—either remember the words, or remember the tune and use that to retrieve or reconstruct the words. This is why advertising jingles are so durable in memory.

Mnemonics are perhaps at their most useful when they impose meaning on a rote series of items that otherwise would have little or no meaning. For instance, it may seem arbitrary whether to set the clocks ahead or behind in the spring and fall, but if you remember that maxim "spring ahead and fall behind," the direction seems less capricious because it has been linked meaningfully (through the use of the second meanings of *spring* and *fall*) to the season to which it belongs.

To take another similar example, suppose you want to remember the words spelled with "ei" that are exceptions to the "I before E except after C" rule of English spelling. You could memorize a list of words, or you could make a meaningful sentence out of them, thus chunking them all together in one (more or less) coherent semantic unit (for example, "*Either* the *weird sheik* will *inveigle* his *weighty neighbor* on the *heights* or *neither* of them will *feign seizures* in *their leisure* time"). Mnemonics may also be used to remember spelling of those few troublesome words that continually elude us ("The Double-C Double-M Motel gives good accommodations" to remind us that "accommodation" has two *C*'s, two *M*'s and an *O* after the *M*'s). Try to make the mnemonic as meaningful as possible and as closely related as possible to all aspects of the to-be-remembered information.

Series of numbers may also be learned using mnemonics (remember 539–4079 because the 5 people born in 1939 were 40 years old in 1979. A long sequence of numbers can be memorized by creating a sentence where each successive word has the exact number of letters as the next number in the sequence (for instance, remembering that the value of e, the base of the natural logarithms, equals 2.718281828 with the sentence, "It enables a dumbbell to memorize a quantity of numerals"). To recall the value of e, simply retrieve the sentence and count the number of letters in each successive word. It is, of course, recommended that you construct mnemonic sentences with words that you know how to spell!

There are more elaborate mnemonic systems. The *method of loci* has been around since ancient times, reported in Cicero's *De Oratore* to have been used by the Greek poet Simonides (Yates, 1966). This involves learning a list of items by associating them in sequence with different positions in some very familiar spatial network. For example, you might use visual imagery to remember a shopping list by associating milk with your front door (a milk carton hanging on the doorknob); eggs with the sidewalk (eggs rolling up the walk toward your house); coffee with the street corner (coffee flowing into the sewer at the intersection), and so on. To retrieve the information, simply retrace your familiar route and "pick up" the images left there earlier.

The *pegword system* involves learning a system of associations in advance and then using these to "peg" items to be learned on. One popular system involves the associations 1 = bun, 2 = shoe, 3 = tree, 4 = door, 5 = hive, 6 = sticks, 7 = heaven, 8 = gate, 9 = line, 10 = hen. Notice that these are made easier to learn initially because of the auxiliary code of rhyme. To use the pegword system, associate the first item to be learned with a bun, the second with a shoe, and so on. To retrieve, simply count through the numbers and retrieve the associated images. The same pegword associations, once learned, may be reused any number of times.

A highly developed use of mnemonics can have valuable practical benefits and is not limited to people with exceptional ability. A Boulder, Colorado, waiter and college student, John Conrad, developed his own mnemonic system for remembering customers' dinner orders, associating the entree with the person's face and afterward associating the side dishes and salads they had ordered (Singular, 1982). He perfected this system up to the point where he could take orders from a party of 19 without writing anything down and without making any errors. His extraordinary skill captured the attention of his customers and helped him win lucrative tips. His co-workers were so impressed that they asked him to teach them his system, as did University of Colorado psychologists interested in studying memory. These studies revealed Conrad to be highly organized and systematic; intellectually, he was probably only average. Some even more extraordinary memory feats are discussed in Box 6–2.

BOX 6–2 Amazing Feats of Memory

While most research on memory has been done on "normal" people, usually college students, there are occasional reports of outstanding memory feats by other individuals. Neisser (1982) collected and commented on several of these reports. While it is often difficult to draw general conclusions from such anecdotal evidence, the tantalizing fact remains that these astounding memory feats are possible, at least in some people in some circumstances. At the very least they provide important counter-examples that any theory of memory cannot totally ignore.

While many professional musicians have exceptional memories, astounding even among these was Arturo Toscanini (Marek, 1975). Toscanini apparently had rote-memorized every note of every instrumental part for around 250 symphonic works and about 100 operas. He could apply this knowledge in a most impressive fashion. One anecdote reports a bassoonist discovering just before a performance that the lowest note on his instrument was broken. Upon hearing this, Toscanini thought for a moment and replied that there was no problem, since that note did not occur anywhere in the repertoire of that evening's concert! He could also, at will, sit down and correctly write from memory any instrumental part from a huge collection of works.

One of the most astounding memory feats was Stratton's (1917) reporting of the Jews called "Shass Pollaks," who memorized all the thousands of pages of the Babylonian Talmud. They not only could recite each page from memory but could also tell exactly what word was in any given position on any given page.

Some preliterate societies have oral traditions that often place a high value on an extensive memory for past history of the community or the nation. This can be seen, for example, in the *griots*, the oral historians of the West African forest societies (D'Azevedo, 1962; Haley, 1976). With our easy access to reading and recorded written history, it is hard to imagine the high value placed on such oral memory; thus, the memory feats of these oral historians seem entirely amazing. With the motivation and circumstances of their situation, however, such feats may have been within the reach of many.

Why do mnemonics work?   On the surface, mnemonics might appear to make learning more difficult, since usually some additional information must be learned beyond what one is trying to master (the pegword associations, the sentence chunking the *ei*-words). However, if done well, learning this extra information can actually make learning the target information easier, because it increases the meaningfulness of the information. The more meaning something has, the easier it is to remember.

Mnemonics are not very helpful in learning material that is already meaningful, but they are quite useful in learning arbitrary, verbatim information where elements are not particularly associated with other elements or where a specific and arbitrary order must be learned.

Mnemonics take advantage of our natural information-processing tendency to impose structure and organization on material that we process. It is natural, not exceptional, to try to make meaningful something that does not have much meaning. The more links we can establish between the material we are trying to learn and information already in our long-term memory, the more potential avenues we have to retrieve the information when we need it. This same principle applies to your studies, in that it is easier to learn and remember information if you have made connections of that information with knowledge already in your memory. If you find it difficult to make such connections, it will probably be difficult to remember that information.

Many, though by no means all, mnemonics make use of visual imagery in one way or another. This draws on our naturally large capacity for picture memory. Visual images tend to be among the easiest units of information to remember. They also have the advantage of allowing us to combine elements within an image. For example, the logo for a product to use on basement walls to seal out water once used a seal (animal) splashing in water under the label "water seal." This combines one aspect of the function of the product (water) with its specific function (sealing) plus an additional meaning (the animal seal) of the same sound. Such information-processing principles are known and used by advertisers. See Alesandrini (1983) for a complete discussion of the use of imagery in advertising strategy. Box 6–3 develops an application of imagery mnemonics to second-language vocabulary learning.

Contextual Variables in Encoding and Retrieval

Memory and cognition research has frequently been curiously silent about contextual, especially social-personality, variables. However, this situation is rapidly changing; several recent books and papers have looked at encoding more broadly and even tried to integrate personality and social variables like attitude, empathy, and mood into existing theories of cognition (Bower, 1981; Fiske & Taylor, 1984; Hastie, 1983; Izard, Kagan, & Zajonc, 1984; Nisbett & Ross, 1980; Wyer & Carlston, 1979).

Encoding specificity.   One important basic construct pointed out some years ago by Thomson and Tulving (1970) and Tulving and Thomson

---

BOX 6–3 Application of Mnemonics to Second-language Learning

Atkinson (1975; Atkinson & Raugh, 1975) developed a key-word method for second-language vocabulary learning, frequently a process of tedious rote memory for language students. The idea is to provide a key word relating the pronunciation of a word with its English translation. An image is then constructed using the key word and the English equivalent of the to-be-learned word. For example, to learn the Spanish word "pato" (duck), one might use the key word "pot" and image a duck with a pot on its head. Thus, one could remember "pato" by thinking of a duck, remembering the image, retrieving "pot" from the image, and associating "pot" with "pato." An experimental group using this method was shown to be superior to a control group in a vocabulary test six weeks after learning. In fact, it was so successful that it was implemented in Russian classes at Stanford University. Computers were programmed to present the word, its translation, and the key word. The student then formed his or her own image.

(1973) is **encoding specificity.** This principle says that the probability of recall at test time depends on the similarity of the context of encoding at study to the context of retrieval at test time. To illustrate this, if you hear the list of words "January, March, June, July, September, October, December, Mary, Alice, Joanne, Linda, Cathy, Ann" and are then asked for the seven girls' names, you may find it difficult to find all seven. The word "June" at study appeared in the context of months and was probably encoded as a month, not as a girl's name, the context at retrieval. Similarly, Anderson and Ortony (1975) gave subjects the sentence: "The container held the apples" or "The container held the cola." They found that "basket" was an effective cue for the former but not for the latter, and "bottle" exactly the reverse. Unlike the "June" example, container does not have two separate meanings here, but is vague as to the type of container. Thus, the material held therein serves to encode the information about the container as more like either a basket or a bottle, and it is easier to recall in the same context.

State-dependent learning.   Encoding specificity is related to the concept of *state-dependent learning*, which derives from the literature on the effects of drugs. Information learned in one state of mind (such as while intoxicated) is less accessible for retrieval while one is in other states of mind. Thus, it may be easier to recognize someone when you are drunk if you originally met that person while in a similar state of inebriation, though this does not, of course, mean that memory is enhanced by alcohol. In fact, it is depressed overall; state-dependent learning merely suggests that it may not be as far depressed when intoxicated again as during subsequent sober moments (Goodwin, Powell, Bremer, Hoine, & Stern, 1969).

Perhaps the most dramatic demonstration of state-dependent memory occurred in a study where divers learned a list of words either on land or underwater. Words learned on land were recalled better on land and those learned underwater were recalled better underwater (Godden & Baddeley, 1975).

The same logic is invoked in forensic hypnosis, when witnesses are hypnotized and put into a mental state more similar to that which they were in when they observed the critical crime. The hope is that, in this similar state, they will remember information about the crime that had been previously irretrievable. The fact that memory deteriorates under stress may be due in part to the stress-inducing environment at retrieval being very different from the relaxed conditions at encoding (Jones, 1979).

In an extension of the state-dependent learning research to personality variables, Bower (1981) has demonstrated *mood-dependent learning*. For example, happy subjects remembered words learned in another happy moment better than words learned in a sad moment, while the reverse was true for subjects in a sad mood. When recalling childhood events, people remembered more happy moments when they were in a happy mood and more sad ones when they were in a sad mood. In another study, subjects read a story with a happy and a sad character. They identified more with the character that matched their own mood; the next day, when in a neutral mood, they recalled more information about that character than about the other one.

The similarity of emotional states at learning and recall can facilitate retrieval in normal adults (Bower, Monteiro, & Gilligan, 1978; Mecklenbrauker & Hager, 1984), children (Bartlett, Burleson, & Santrock, 1982; Bartlett & Santrock, 1979), and even manic-depressives (Weingartner, Cohen, Murphy, Martello, & Gerdt, 1981). However, the phenomenon is not universal and tends to occur especially in more difficult tasks where the to-be-remembered material is not readily available (See Isen, 1984, and Gilligan & Bower, 1984 for reviews). When it does occur, the effects are stronger with happy than with sad moods.

Another issue in interpreting this research involves the concern that the induction of moods in laboratory studies typically occurs in ways very different from the onset of feelings in the "real world." Many use Velten's (1968) technique of reading several happy or sad self-statements, though other studies have used hypnosis or manipulating success/failure on a prior task. All of these are somewhat artificial and often highly verbal, quite unlike a situation, where we might, for example, see a movie and be suddenly filled with emotion, remembering similar experiences of our own that had been forgotten for years. Emotion can be a powerful retrieval cue, probably in far more complex and important ways than these studies have yet revealed.

At least one study, however, suggests that this effect in the laboratory does transfer to the real world. Clark and Teasdale (1982) asked clinically depressed patients to recall personal experiences twice in a day, during times of more or less natural depression. Like the laboratory studies, these researchers found that patients recalled more sad experiences when more depressed and, beyond that, rated the same experiences as less happy than in moods of lesser depression. Thus, Clark and Teasdale concluded that mood affected both the selective retrieval of information and the interpretation of the pleasantness of that information after it has entered working memory.

Several studies of memory have used diaries to examine the effect of the pleasantness or unpleasantness of recorded personal events on recall for those events. In those studies, no attempt was made to manipulate the subjects' mood during recall. Under those "neutral" conditions, events with high affect (that is, very pleasant or very unpleasant events) were recalled better than events with neutral affect (Thompson, 1982, 1985b; Thomson, 1930). Interestingly, the effect of the pleasantness of the event is different when subjects attempt to recall the date (rather than the content) of the event. Pleasant events are dated much more accurately than unpleasant events, with neutral events in between (Thompson, 1982). Thompson speculated that we are much more likely to deliberately associate a date with a pleasant event than with an unpleasant one—and he referred to the result as "the red-letter-day effect."

Bower argued that emotions, as well as information, are coded in memory. During retrieval, one's memory network is entered at the point of the event being remembered but also at the point of emotion. Activation (discussed later in the chapter) spreads outward from both points. When the activation spreading from both points meets, it comes together to make a strongly activated memory that is then recalled. The whole area of the role of emotions in memory is just beginning to be studied in cognitive psychology. Later findings could have important ramifications for counseling and clinical psychology, especially for the process of developing tools for helping clients to remember long-forgotten events and their associated affect. The retrieval of such memories could be very instrumental in helping someone work through personal problems. Box 6–4 discusses a case study of one person's memory for some very important conversations.

FORGETTING

Through our examination of encoding and retrieval, we have implicitly considered **forgetting,** since the failure to either encode or to retrieve effectively will naturally lead to forgetting. Now, however, we will focus more specifically on forgetting from long-term memory. There are several possible reasons why we may forget something that we had apparently learned previously.

Failure to Encode

One major reason for forgetting is that the material was never encoded properly to begin with. While we may have used the material in working memory, there was perhaps not enough elaborative rehearsal or active rehearsal strategies to transfer it to long-term memory. This may occur, for example, when you fail to remember information on a test because you never encoded it when studying, that is, never learned it to begin with.

BOX 6–4   John Dean's Watergate Memory

In an interesting and insightful application of memory research, Neisser (1981) studied former Nixon presidential counselor John Dean's memory for Watergate conversations of the early 1970s by comparing his courtroom testimony about these conversations with the actual transcripts of the conversations as covertly taped by President Nixon. This offered an unusual opportunity to test the accuracy of verbatim recall in a natural setting, in that there was a tape recording of the original conversation made without the subject's knowledge. Neisser found that, as laboratory studies have shown, verbatim memory was very poor. However, he also found, unlike laboratory studies, that "gist" memory was not all that good either. Neisser, however, argued that Dean's memory was in fact quite good at a still more abstract level, that he "captures the 'tenor,' though not the gist, of what went on" (Neisser, 1982, p. 150). Distortions tended to be in the direction of details and intrusions from other conversations. They also were somewhat distorted by "ego needs" of Dean himself; memory errors tended to somewhat enhance his own importance in the conversations. Nonetheless, Neisser concludes that overall Dean captured the "theme and spirit" of the Watergate conversations quite well. This abstract level of memory is a topic that has not yet been explored much in research.

Retrieval Failure

Sometimes the forgetting is due not to failure to encode but rather from failure to access the material in long-term memory. A book that is in the library but misplaced on the wrong shelf is nearly impossible to find, unless one stumbles upon it serendipitously. So it is sometimes with "lost" memories.

Issues discussed earlier in regard to encoding specificity are very important here. It is easier to retrieve information if the context at retrieval is similar to that which was present at encoding. Again we see that effective encoding is the best way to ensure effective retrieval.

The selection of an appropriate retrieval cue is critical to the retrieval process. What is an effective retrieval cue for one person might be ineffective to another person trying to retrieve the same information. For example, if you try to remember all the states of the United States and all the provinces of Canada that begin with the letter M, there are many possible retrieval cues you could use. If you have good visual memory and imagery ability, you might imagine a map of North America and start scanning east to west for states and provinces starting with M. Another retrieval cue might be to imagine combinations of letters (MA . . . ME . . . etc.), which may form official abbreviations. Still another approach would be to retrieve a previously learned alphabetical list. Other strategies include retrieving by regions (New England, Rocky Mountains, Prairie provinces). One sports-minded student reported retrieving the names by recalling different collegiate athletic conferences! Whatever strategy one uses, failure to retrieve the eight states and one province starting with *M* would not necessarily mean that those names had not been learned, only that they could not be retrieved.

The Freudian defense mechanism of *repression* would explain retrieval failure by saying that some threatening event was unconsciously expelled from our consciousness because of its anxiety-evoking nature. We cannot access this memory because of the defensive barriers that have been erected to prevent it from becoming conscious. Therapy, especially in the psychoanalytic tradition, tries to break down the barriers to allow retrieval of the repressed memory, in order to start the healing process.

Decay and Interference

The *decay-interference* issue, discussed in the section on working memory in the last chapter, is also relevant to long-term memory. As with working memory, there is ample demonstration of forgetting due to interference (both proactive and retroactive), but it is far more difficult to demonstrate unequivocally the existence of decay. Clearly, we remember less with the passage of more time; whether this is due purely to decay, that is, the passage of time, is much less clear.

Over the last few decades the prevailing view has been that anything we have ever learned is still in our long-term memory somewhere and that forgetting occurs because of retrieval failure: We can't find the information, much like the library book that is in the library but on the wrong shelf and thus is never found.

Much of the evidence for this permanence of memory has come from case studies from the brain stimulation neurosurgery by Wilder Penfield (1969; Penfield & Roberts, 1959). Penfield reported some very dramatic case studies of neurosurgical patients who, when under local anesthesia with their brain electrically stimulated during the course of neurosurgery, reported long-forgotten memories from early childhood. However, in an important paper reexamining Penfield's findings, along with other arguments from hypnosis and psychoanalysis, Loftus and Loftus (1980) concluded that this permanence hypothesis is a severe overinterpretation of some case-study data, which may in fact have been reflecting reconstruction, based on other memories, rather than actual retrieval.

Systematic Partial Forgetting

Sometimes we remember some material but forget where we learned it; for example, we recall that Jane would miss the party Saturday but we can't remember who told us that. This has been labeled "source amnesia" and has sometimes been attributed to the aging process. Craik and McIntyre (1986) reported some studies to investigate this question. Young and old adults were presented with 30 "Canadian trivia questions" either on overhead transparencies or spoken by the experimenter. A week later subjects were tested for this knowledge but also were asked whether the fact was presented visually or auditorily. In terms of the information, recall by young and old adults was about the same (on one measure even better in the older adults). However, in the source recall younger adults did much better than the older ones (89 percent vs. 56 percent). A second study had young and old subjects learn obscure "fictitious facts"; for example, that Jane Fonda's favorite color is blue; subjects were later tested after varying intervals. Again, older subjects showed considerable source amnesia, especially at the longer delays. Craik and McIntyre concluded that source amnesia is not true amnesia but rather is a natural part of the aging process.

Amnesia

Perhaps the most dramatic form of forgetting is **amnesia,** which will be discussed in detail in Chapter 10.

ALTERNATIVE CONCEPTUALIZATIONS OF MEMORY

Now that we have examined the basic phenomena of memory, it is time to step back and take another broad look at memory. Although we have largely been assuming an Atkinson-Shiffrin type of multistore model, as described at the beginning of the last chapter (see Figure 5–1), there is considerable evidence that such a qualitative separation of working and long-term memory may not be warranted. While no other approach has been so completely developed or widely accepted, there are other frameworks for conceptualizing memory, the best-known being the levels-of-processing approach, which we now will examine.

The Levels (Depth) Metaphor

Craik and Lockhart (1972; see also Craik & Tulving, 1975) proposed an alternative metaphor for conceptualizing memory. Instead of discrete memory stores like working and long-term memory, they proposed that memory involves different **levels of processing,** with trace persistence being a function of how deeply the analysis has proceeded. For example, processing speech only to the point of understanding what language the speaker is using or how loud or soft the speech is would be a very shallow level of processing, while understanding the content thoroughly, including all its implications and nuances, would be a very deep level. Memory is thus viewed as the natural residues of both the transient products of sensory analyses and the much more durable traces of semantic (meaningful) processing.

Familiar memory phenomena may be reinterpreted using a levels-of-processing framework. For example, forgetting due to what might otherwise be described as a failure to transfer from working to long-term memory occurs because the analysis during comprehension has not proceeded to a sufficiently deep level. Rehearsal or continued attention to the material is reconceptualized as recirculation of the material, which may occur at any level by continued attention to the analysis at that particular level.

The well-documented superiority of intentional over incidental learning (we remember something better if we try to remember it than if we see it accidently for other reasons) is reinterpreted by saying that in intentional learning we have processed the material to a deeper level and it is this, rather than an intention to remember as such, that accounts for the better performance. If subjects can be induced to process material deeply, even though they are not expecting a memory test, incidental recall is much improved. This finding suggested that depth of processing, not the intention to remember, is the critical factor.

Some of the strongest evidence for a multistore approach to memory has come from the physiological domain. It is often argued that working memory processes are primarily electrical, perhaps in the form of reverberating circuits of neuronal firings, while long-term memory involves structural biochemical changes. For this reason long-term memory is more permanent, while working memory is ephemeral. This, however, is probably an oversimplification (see Lewis, 1979; Loftus & Loftus, 1980).

As insightful as it has been, there are some criticisms of the levels-of-processing approach (Baddeley, 1978), many of them centering around the vagueness of its constructs. See Craik (1979) for a summary of this debate.

One major criticism is that there is no independent measure of depth of processing. In most studies using this framework, two tasks are chosen intuitively as differing in depth of processing. It is also sometimes defined by what is remembered better. Shallow processes are usually done faster than deeper ones, but there may be some exceptions; for example, deciding if the word "rabbit" fits the CVCCVC pattern by most definitions would be shallow processing, since it is totally nonsemantic, but it is not trivially easy. Lockhart and Craik (1978) admit this problem but defend the approach by saying that levels-of-processing was intended to be a framework, not a theory, and that it can still have heuristic (discovery) value even without an independent measure of depth. As a parallel, they argue that the concept of reinforcement has been useful in psychology, even though there is no independent measure of its effectiveness beyond its operational definition of increasing the probability of the response recurrence.

A related concern comes from the fact that, especially within semantic processing, there is no real consensus on what constitutes deep versus shallow processing. For example, people very readily draw inferences from all that they hear or read (see Chapter 8; see also Harris, 1981; Harris & Monaco, 1978; Singer, 1984). In a sense this would seem like a deep level of processing; however, to stop people from drawing such inferences requires considerable effort to invoke a metalinguistic monitor to stop such natural processes from occurring. Is such a monitor relatively deep or shallow processing? The answer is not clear. Perhaps depth of processing is not a linear dimension.

There is also evidence that under some conditions we remember information from so-called shallow processing very well, such as the way people remember certain kinds of thematically irrelevant comments verbatim, such as jokes and offhand comments in a lecture or conversation (see Keenan, MacWhinney, & Mayhew, 1977; Kintsch & Bates, 1977; MacWhinney, Keenan, & Reinke, 1982).

BOX 6–5 Memory Metaphors

The way we talk about something may actually affect the way we conceptualize it. Roediger (1980) offers a fascinating survey of the metaphors used to discuss memory. Like most basically abstract and unobservable concepts, memory is typically described in concrete, though metaphorical, terms. In examining these metaphors, Roediger concludes that the majority of them have been some sort of spatial metaphor, usually combined with some action of searching through this space. While the most popular and prevalent of these spatial search metaphors is probably the computer metaphor, there have been many others as well, including the wax tablet, rooms in a house, switchboard, workbench, acid bath, dictionary, pushdown stack, conveyor belt, subway map, leaky bucket, and even a cow's stomach!

While the spatial-search metaphors predominate, they are not the only metaphors used to discuss memory. For example, all the network models of semantic memory use a more structural metaphor, and there are several more dynamic metaphors, such as construction, levels of processing, and signal detection.

Though metaphors are certainly often insightful, perhaps even essential, to discuss such an abstract concept as memory, it is also good to examine them critically, for they can guide our thinking into excessively rigid modes of conceptualizing. For example, Roediger warns against thinking of memory so much as spatial storage and search that we do not take seriously enough its other characteristics not included in or consistent with this particular metaphor. Craik and Lockhart's levels of processing or Collins and Loftus' spreading activation are two examples of popular alternative metaphors to spatial storage and search conceptualizations. However, each of these (and indeed any metaphor) has its dangers and limits.

In a very different approach to the metaphors of memory, Larsen (1987) argues that the archaeology metaphor was central to Freud and the entire psychoanalytic tradition. Memories are "pieces" of experience and knowledge to be "excavated" out of the dirt of the past. This notion of memory as self-contained "things" to be found in a matrix of irrelevant material is inconsistent with the thrust of most current research and thinking. Memory is inextricably a part of its context, not isolated bits of information as many earlier memory researchers conceptualized it.

Surprisingly enough, Larsen does not recommend a wholesale discarding of the archaeology metaphor of memory. Instead, he argues that recent thinking in archaeology is coming to realize that archaeological relics embedded in the soil are not isolated from the context either, but rather are lodged in a matrix of material holding rich information about the times and circumstances when it was laid down.

In spite of its definitional and precision problems, the metaphor of levels of processing continues to be very influential in offering an alternative way to think about memory from the traditional multistore model.

Spreading Activation

Another useful metaphor for looking at memory is the notion of **spreading activation** (J. R. Anderson, 1984; Collins & Loftus, 1975). Instead of speaking of two separate memory stores, with information retrieved from long-term to working memory, we may say that this information is *activated* or brought into a state of activation. When we enter our memory to search for information, this activation spreads from the node of entry to related concepts stored close by. The more nodes there are in that area, the more diffuse the activation and probably the longer the time required to retrieve the information. Such activation may or may not be a conscious process. In fact, the concept of spreading activation may eventually be useful in describing other areas in psychology. For example, psychoanalysis may be viewed as an attempt to activate previously dormant concepts and relations among those concepts in the patient's mind.

The concept of activation has important implications for structural aspects of memory discussed early in the chapter. How the activation spreads through memory from the entry point will be determined in part by the structure of that particular individual's memory. Instead of positing separate working and long-term memory stores, activation theorists often argue that what we are thinking about at the moment are the highly activated concepts, while nonactivated concepts remain in (long-term) memory until needed and activated.

The use of different models and metaphors to describe memory can each be helpful and lend insight in different ways, even if none of them is totally "correct." Over the years memory has been described using all sorts of metaphors; some others are discussed in Box 6–5.

To complete our discussion of long-term-memory, we turn now to a detailed examination of one practical application of many of the memory principles we have studied in the last two chapters—eyewitness memory.

EYEWITNESS MEMORY

The popular viewpoint seems to be that eyewitness testimony is nearly infallible. To say that there is an eyewitness to a crime is considered practically the equivalent of saying the whole event was recorded on videotape. This section applies some of the principles of memory discussed above to the problem of eyewitness memory. While this problem was considered in psychology as far back as Hugo Münsterberg's (1908) book, *On the Witness Stand*, it has only been rediscovered in the last decade (Clifford & Lloyd-Bostock, 1983; Loftus 1979; Sheehan, 1982; Wells & Loftus, 1984; Yarmey, 1979).

Eyewitness identification may be considered a recognition memory problem with four possible outcomes. Someone could be guilty and be correctly recognized as guilty. Someone could be innocent and be correctly not recognized. As well as these two correct recognitions, there are two types of errors, analogous to the two types of errors in statistical inference, where one falsely rejects a true null hypothesis or fails to reject a false null hypothesis (Type I and Type II). Someone could be guilty but not be recognized; therefore, the guilty party might go free. On the other hand, the person could be innocent but falsely recognized as guilty (false alarm). Part of the philosophy of the legal system of many democratic countries is the desire to minimize the false alarm type of error, assuming that it is better to set an occasional guilty person free than to risk punishing someone who is innocent.

What Is Eyewitness Memory Like?

Many factors can affect eyewitness memory for a criminal act (Buckhout, 1974). One major factor is the delay between the crime and the identification. Frequently, an identification lineup is days, if not weeks or months, after the crime, allowing much opportunity for decay and retroactive interference to occur in memory.

Secondly, many situational factors frequently contribute to the event's not being deeply processed at the time of occurrence. For example, most crimes that are observed happen very quickly and are totally unexpected. There is little time to reorient one's attention; by the time one has done so, the criminal is often gone and the crime is over, as in a car wreck or purse snatching. In one mock assault study (Buckhout, 1974), subjects estimated that the event they had witnessed had taken 2.5 times as long as it in fact had (81 seconds versus 34 seconds). Typically, the observer has no previous knowledge of the criminal and thus can make no quick recognition or relate to other information in long-term memory. Moreover, crimes often occur in settings with poor lighting (at night, in shadows) with a poor angle for viewing the event.

Third, several factors about the observer contribute to less-than-perfect memory for eyewitness events. Often the observer is under extreme stress, especially if one feels in any personal danger, which is often the case when witnessing a crime in progress (Kassin, 1984; Loftus & Messo, 1987). One's own prejudices enter in the way we process information; we are more likely to recognize an assailant as a member of another racial group than our own. Additionally, many otherwise upstanding and conscientious citizens develop some strong motivation to be heroes, to prove themselves right, to ensure that someone is convicted, or to be important. Such motivations can do strange things to one's information processing.

A number of creative and clever studies have demonstrated that eyewitness memory is frequently very poor. For example, Buckhout (1974) and his colleagues had 141 students in a class witness a staged assault on the professor; seven weeks later students looked at a lineup of six photos. Sixty percent (including the professor who was attacked) chose the wrong man! Twenty-five percent chose one innocent bystander, who happened to have the misfortune to be sitting in the front of the class that day. This is not unlike a pretrial questioning situation where a witness may have previously seen a suspect being led in and thus be more likely to recognize the suspect later, without realizing that the previous encounter had occurred a few minutes earlier in the police station rather than last week at the scene of the crime.

People place great faith in eyewitness testimony in spite of its demonstrated fallibility. For example, Elizabeth Loftus (1974) presented the same evidence in a simulated robbery-murder case to three groups of subjects. In two of the groups some of the evidence was presented as having come from an eyewitness, though in one of those two groups additional evidence was presented discrediting the eyewitness by showing his vision was too poor to have possibly recognized anyone at that distance. While in the control (no eyewitness) group, only 18 percent of the subject-jurors voted to convict, 72 percent of the eyewitness group did. Most surprising, however, was the eyewitness-discredited group, where 68 percent voted to convict, suggesting that the mere fact there was an eyewitness carried more weight than expert testimony discrediting it.

Expert testimony of a different nature may, however, be useful. In a later study, Loftus (1980a) did show that expert testimony about the general fallibility of eyewitness testimony led to fewer verdicts of conviction by juror-subjects (see also Hosch, 1980; Hosch, Beck, & McIntyre, 1980; Wells, Lindsay, & Tousignant, 1980). There is considerable debate among psychologists and legal scholars today about the usefulness and advisability of whether psychologists should testify about the fallibility of eyewitness memory. See Loftus (1983) and McCloskey and Egeth (1983) for further discussion of this issue.

In what may prove to be a landmark state court decision, *Kansas* vs. *Warren* (1981, Vol. 230, #52,753) ordered a new trial in a case where the court had not allowed the expert testimony of Elizabeth Loftus warning of the fallibility of eyewitness testimony. While not insisting that the expert be heard, the court ordered a new trial for the defendant because the instructions given the jury did not specifically enough discuss the fallibility of eyewitness testimony.

While eyewitnesses can often be discredited, either through specific cross-examination or through general expert testimony about the fallibility of such testimony, most eyewitnesses to crimes never enter a courtroom and are never cross-examined, because a large majority of criminal cases are settled by plea bargaining. The mere presence of an eyewitness carries a lot of weight in arranging such pleas.

The Question Matters

In a careful study of several important variables in eyewitness memory, Lipton (1977) showed subjects a film of a robbery and shooting in a park and questioned them immediately afterward or one week later. He was interested in the effects of time and type of question on both accuracy and quantity of information. In terms of delay, he found a slight (4.3 percent) decrease in accuracy in the group tested one week later but a much greater decrease (18 percent) in the quantity recalled. It made no difference whether the testimony was in written or oral form.

Lipton used several types of questions, ranging from very open-ended to highly structured (multiple-choice) questions. He also varied the bias of some of the structured questions. Results generally showed that the most open-ended questions elicited the most accurate information, but the smallest quantity of it. On the other hand, multiple-choice questions elicited more information, but it was less accurate. Biased questions elicited more information than neutral questions but that information was highly subject to reconstructive bias. In conclusion, the style of questioning has enormous impact on how much an eyewitness remembers and how accurate those memories are. Such effects are applicable even beyond the problem of eyewitness memory (see Box 6–6).

Over the past decade, Elizabeth Loftus and her associates at the University of Washington have conducted an important research program in eyewitness memory. Her typical method has been to show subjects a film of a crime or auto accident and then question them afterward about their recollection of the incident. She has demonstrated tremendous biasing effects of the wording of the question on eyewitness memory. For example, asking subjects what happened when the car "came to the yield sign" when in fact it was a stop sign increased the number of subjects who later falsely

---

BOX 6–6   Being an Eyewitness to Yourself

The subject of how the form of a question influences memory has ramifications beyond the eyewitness memory problem. The wording that a doctor or counselor would use to question a person about his or her physical or psychological condition could greatly affect their responses and even their selfperception. This may be an even greater problem than with eyewitness testimony, since what is being remembered is often very subjective and ambiguous to begin with, for example, one's feelings or reactions to others. Consider how differently you might answer each question in each pair below:

1.   Do you feel threatened by your boss?
     Don't you feel threatened by your boss?
2.   Do you occasionally have sinus trouble?
     Do you frequently have sinus trouble?
3.   Are you often very anxious when talking in front of a group?
     Are you often unable to cope when talking in front of a group?

In such cases, as with eyewitness memory, the form of the question can structure our response and even alter our comprehension and memory of our own state of mind or body. This application awaits careful laboratory study.

remembered that there had been a yield sign (Loftus, Miller, & Burns, 1978; Schooler, Gerhard, & Loftus, 1986).

Sometimes such an alteration may be even more subtle yet still have strong effects. For example, Loftus and Palmer (1974) asked subjects either

(7) Did you see the broken headlight? or
(8) Did you see a broken headlight?

after they had viewed a film of an auto accident in which there was no broken headlight. Twice as many subjects questioned with (7) responded "yes" as those questioned with (8). While (8) is a neutral question, (7) actually says something like, "There was a broken headlight; did you see it?", and it perhaps carries an implication that one is unobservant if one did not see it.

Such biasing effects of questions can permanently alter the character of eyewitness memory. In the same set of studies, Loftus and Palmer questioned subjects with either

(9) About how fast were the cars going when they smashed into each other?

or the same sentence with "smashed" replaced by "hit." The speed estimates were faster by subjects questioned with "smashed" than those questioned with "hit" (41 mph versus 34 mph), though, interestingly enough, both were significant overestimates.

One week later, subjects were asked if they had seen any broken glass in the film (there was none); more "smashed" subjects falsely reported that they had seen it than did "hit" subjects. Apparently broken glass is very consistent with one's knowledge about what happens when cars smash into each other. The wording of the question thus helps guide reconstruction through the activation and retrieval of relevant knowledge from long-term memory. Slightly different knowledge is activated to remember an accident of "smashing" than one with "hitting."

Loftus has also demonstrated that such reconstructive biases can affect the verdict that jurors arrive at as well as the information they remember. Kasprzyk, Montano, and Loftus (1975) had subjects read excerpts from a trial about an ambiguous waterfront incident. The lawyer's questions were either neutral, (10) or biased, (11). Almost twice as many subjects in the biased group voted to convict (41 percent versus 22 percent).

(10) How much of the incident did you see?
(11) How much of the fight did you see?

There can also be biasing effects from testimony by the witnesses. For example, in simulated-courtroom studies (Harris, 1978; Harris, Teske, & Ginns, 1975) a witness either stated something directly (12) or merely implied it (13). In both cases subjects remembered that the witness had stated the information

(12) I walked away without taking any money.

(13) I was able to walk away without taking any money.

unequivocally. Lawyers and juries should be aware of such information-processing tendencies.

Although Loftus argues that the underlying memory representation has been altered by subsequent misleading information and that warning subjects of this possibility has at best very limited effect (Greene, Flynn, & Loftus, 1982), others suggest that a more accurate representation may still exist. For example, Hammersley and Read (1986) presented evidence to argue that, while a misleading and inaccurate memory representation may exist after the introduction of false information, the original accurate representation may also still be present and retrievable given the right conditions. One week after reading both an original story and an inaccurate summary of it, Hammersley and Read's subjects retained parallel memory representations, one accurate and one misleading. The accuracy of reported memory depended on which of those representations was accessed during retrieval.

A Rebuttal to Loftus

When evaluating the import of Loftus' research, it is important to note that eyewitness memory was generally studied using laboratory simulations. For obvious reasons, it is very difficult to do such a study in the real world, though some such studies have been done (see Brigham, Maas, Snyder, & Spaulding, 1982; Krafka & Penrod, 1985). At least one such study (Yuille & Cutshall, 1986) produced results strikingly different from those of Loftus. Twenty-one people were eyewitnesses to an actual shooting incident on a main street in mid-afternoon in Burnaby, British Columbia. There was one death and one serious injury in the incident. All witnesses were interviewed by the local Royal Canadian Mounted Police, and 13 of them agreed to a research interview four or five months later.

Contrary to Loftus' findings, Yuille and Cutshall's eyewitnesses showed highly accurate memory, which changed little in amount or accuracy of recall over five months. The subjects resisted attempts to mislead them through the wording of the questions (for example, "Did you see the busted headlight?" when there was none), and were clearly not greatly debilitated in remembering due to the high stress level of the actual crime situation. Some errors were made over time, however, especially personal details such as age, height, weight, and color of clothing. Yuille and Cutshall concluded that eyewitness memory, though certainly not perfect, is much better than laboratory simulations by Loftus would suggest. As to reasons for the differences, they suggest that the extremely high level of salience of the event (having life-and-death consequences) is important. Another important factor may be the chance for active involvement of at least some eyewitnesses to a real crime; we tend to remember events better in which we participate, as compared to those we only observe.

Conclusion

What may we conclude from this examination of eyewitness memory? While Yuille and Cutshall have shown that eyewitness memory is not necessarily as subject to distortion in the real world as earlier work had suggested, Loftus' work shows that under the right conditions, it *can* be so distorted. This alone is cause for concern, especially since often eyewitness testimony is about all that a court case is based on. However, all parties involved must bear in mind that eyewitness memory is highly subject to distortion by reconstructive errors, stemming both from a failure to encode the event accurately at the time it occurred or from the distortion introduced in the questioning process by the wording of the questions. Courtroom procedural rules rather tightly prescribe the sort of questions that may or may not be asked of a witness on the stand, and many, though not all, of the blatantly biasing questions would not be allowed. Control of pretrial questioning, however, is much less regulated, and this is as far as most eyewitnesses ever get. Even those who do come to trial have already been through the potentially distorting influence of the pretrial questioning.

Ellison and Buckhout (1981) suggest three ways of reducing the bias of an eyewitness in a police lineup. First, do not assume that confidence in a choice and accuracy are correlated, as evidence suggests they are not (Deffenbacher, 1980). People more sure are not necessarily more likely to be right. Second, making sure the witness understands that the guilty party may not be in the lineup will help ensure that they set a recognition criterion high enough to avoid false recognitions. Third, composing a lineup of plausible distractors ("innocents") will help avoid biases coming into play.

In an article in the *University of Pennsylvania Law Review* Levine and Tapp (1973, p. 1130) very aptly describe our minds as eyewitnesses:

> The mind is not a mirror which reflects the external world, but an organism with its own needs, values, and capacities—its own vision of "reality" through which the outside world is interpreted.

Indeed, this is an excellent statement about information processing and memory in general.

MEMORY AS CONSTRUCTION AND RECONSTRUCTION

Throughout this chapter and the last, we have examined questions in the psychology of information processing. The major byproduct of information processing is memory. Whenever we process any information more than extremely superficially, we are necessarily encoding it, though usually to a less-than-perfect degree. Encoding involves processes of *constructing* a memory representation, that is, we build something in our memory to represent that information we have been thinking about. Such construction may be very conscious and deliberate, as in the use of mnemonics, or it may be completely unconscious and accidental, as in the impression you take away of someone you meet in a social encounter when you are not even aware of forming a judgment. When you have cause to think about that information again, you retrieve the relevant information from long-term memory and set about to *reconstruct* the original input ("Let's see, what were the freedoms guaranteed in the Bill of Rights?" "What does Mary Jones look like and what did she tell me when I saw her last week?"). In this process of reconstruction, we have the remains, perhaps very fragmentary, of our original constructed memory representation, plus all the information that we have added to it through subsequent experiences and during the processes of reconstruction.

This reconstructive character of memory was discussed at length by pioneering British psychologist Sir Frederick Bartlett (1932) in his book *Remembering*, but it was not studied widely in American psychology until the last decade or two. More recently, the emphasis has shifted some to *construction* (see Spiro, 1980) and its implications for memory.

F. Smith (1985) argues that most of cognitive psychology has tended to think of information processing as a "shunting of information" between the real world and the brain. Rather, he suggests that the fundamental and ongoing activity of the brain is the "creation of worlds." Thought involves constructing these worlds, and learning involves elaborating and modifying them. Rather than containing primarily "information," the brain "contains nothing less than a *theory of the world*, . . . an interpreted summary of all past experience" (p. 199). The key is interpretation. The mind is not primarily a repository of information in long-term memory banks but rather is constantly interacting with the world. Learning, then, occurs not so much from the acquisition of new information into the mind but rather from the modification of the internalized theory of the world, which may only very imperfectly correspond with that world itself. Smith argues that the traditional "shunting of information" view of memory is subtly reflected in educational systems that stress the acquisition of information rather than the construction of ideas and arguments.

The ideas of construction and reconstruction in memory have many actual and potential applications, some of which will be discussed later in this book. Look at Box 6–7 for a brief account of the way an actor constructs a memory for a character being portrayed on the stage and then uses this constructed memory to cover a forgotten line during a performance.

Before we can deal further with construction and reconstruction, we need to examine our most abstract and analytic representational system— language—in more detail. Particularly in our society, so much of our information comes to us in the form of language that we must understand something of its structure and character. This will be the focus of the next chapter, after which we will return to the questions of construction and reconstruction, viewed through the eyes of schema theory, a promising contemporary approach to information processing.

BOX 6-7   Information Processing on the Stage

The information-processing system may be useful in understanding the job of an actor in creating a character. Learning the lines and actions for a part is a real-world analogue of the laboratory paired-associate learning task. In fact, many actors learn their lines by taping the other actors' lines and leaving blank spots on the tape for them to say their lines in practice.

More abstract but more significant, however, is the issue of an actor creating a character on stage. Learning the lines of the dialogue, though certainly not trivial, is one of the most superficial parts of an actor's preparation for a role. He or she must also "create the character" and learn to think and react as that character does. What this really involves is a creation of second working and long-term memory stores, this time for the character instead of oneself.

Some directors go so far as to ask their actors to write a biography of their character, building up a long-term memory of events and influences that could have happened prior to the raising of the curtain on Act 1.

By constructing such a mind of the character, not only can the actor come across more convincingly in the role, but unforeseen circumstances can be handled much more adeptly, thus obeying every director's cardinal maxim of "stay in character." For example, if the roof of the theater suddenly starts leaking at center stage one night, an actress could respond from her own working memory by asking, "What's going on here? This isn't supposed to happen!" Or she could respond in the character of the part she is playing by observing, "It looks like the kids let the tub run over again."

Of course this response would only be appropriate in certain contexts; the line above would sound pretty bizarre if the setting of the play were a ranchstyle house or the family contained no children. Such a parallel memory store also allows the actor to cover for missed or bungled lines of oneself or others. As long as the actor responds from the working memory of the character and not that of the actor, the audience will probably never know there was a missed line.

To a lesser extent this principle of creating a character, specifically the working and long-term memory of the character, is useful to a teacher (Harris, 1977b). A teacher can create a character that he or she feels would be the most effective teacher. This character would have a lot of characteristics of the person but probably some that were not characteristic at all. For example, a rather shy teacher might create a teacher character that was somewhat less shy, figuring that a high degree of shyness would diminish one's effectiveness as a teacher. Keeping this "teacher persona" in mind, the teacher could respond from the working memory of this created teacher character when approached by a student.

SUGGESTED READINGS

The topic of memory is covered extensively in all of the cognition texts mentioned at the end of Chapter 5. In addition, there are several good brief texts on memory, including Howe (1983), Zechmeister and Nyberg (1982), Stern (1985), Klatzky (1980), Wingfield and Byrnes (1981), and Seamon (1980). For the most comprehensive cognitive science approach, see Stillings and others (1987).

Neisser's (1982) *Memory Observed* is a fascinating and highly readable anthology of papers about memory in natural settings. For a more rigorous set of research studies and conceptual papers on natural memory, see Rubin (1986). Luria's *The Mind of a Mnemonist* (1968) offers an engrossing case study of one exceptional individual.

For further reading on eyewitness testimony, see Loftus (1979), Yarmey (1979), or Wells and Loftus' (1984) book of readings.

There are also two thorough but highly readable nontextbook introductions to memory: Elizabeth Loftus' (1980b) *Memory* and Alan Baddeley's (1982) *Your Memory: A User's Guide*. Both are based on solid research but present the material in a fascinating manner fully comprehensible to the reasonably intelligent layperson.

7

LANGUAGE

As highly evolved as we humans are compared to other species, we tend to rely heavily on language, our most abstract representational system. This chapter will deal with language, though we shall see in the next chapter that many of the principles of language comprehension also operate in the comprehension of nonlinguistic information. When people say that they "know" a language, what is it that they know? In fact, it is many types of information, including elements such as sounds, letters, words, meanings, sentences, and grammatical constituents and rules for combining these elements. Generally, the information that we possess when we know a language may be grouped into four general categories, or components: the **phonological** (sound) component, the **semantic** (meaning) component, the **syntactic** (structural) component, and the **pragmatic** (contextual) component. Each of these components includes both elements of information and rules about how those elements may and may not be combined and used together. In this chapter we will look at these components and their ramifications for the processing of language. Finally, we shall discuss the psychology of reading and writing.

The **phonological** (sound) component of language includes (1) the perceived speech sounds, phonemes, and the suprasegmental cues in speech and (2) the implicit phonological rules for how these sounds may be combined. This component of language was discussed in Chapter 5, as an example of complex pattern recognition. Thus, we will not discuss it further here, except to note that any adequate theory of comprehension will have to include how we perceive phonemes and suprasegmental cues in speech and how we use phonological rules. However, the phonological component is only one of four components that any such comprehension theory must consider. It is the other three that we will now examine.

SEMANTICS

A second component of language is meaning, or **semantics.** In a sense this facet of language is central, for if there were no meaning to be communicated or understood, there would be little reason for any structure, sounds, or context. Because it is so difficult to isolate and identify, however, meaning is in many ways the most difficult aspect of language to study.

Word Meaning

One major concern in semantics is the meaning of individual words. Every word has come to have a particular meaning. Many, if not most, words may have more than one completely distinct meaning (river *bank* versus money *bank*). In fact, however, ambiguity is more potential than real in the normal usage of language. For example, the context would typically make it perfectly clear which sense of *bank* was intended. Occasionally, of course, genuine confusion does result because of the ambiguity of some word, and such ambiguity can be the source of humor. Often the so-called punch line of a joke is the information that the earlier, and normally most likely, interpretation of some word or words was, in fact, incorrect, as in (1):

(1)   The bells were peeling; in fact, the whole tower needed painting badly.

See Box 7–1 for some entertaining examples of lexical ambiguity in newspaper headlines.

Presupposition.   The semantics of even single words that are not ambiguous can be quite complex. For instance, there are many verbs that carry as part of their meaning a *presupposition* about whether the speaker believes some other piece of information to be true (Kiparsky & Kiparsky,

---

BOX 7–1   Lexical Ambiguity in the Headlines

"Boy gets in line for liver"
"Preacher shocked at Senator's sex position"
"Politician stoned at rally"
"Hookers appeal to Mayor"
"Heavy TV watchers tend to be obese"

1970; Harris, 1974). A presupposition is something that the speaker assumes to be true; it is a necessary precondition to a statement being either true or false. For example,

(2) Janice regretted that Elaine had left.

This presupposes that the speaker of sentence (2) believes the information in the subordinate clause, namely, that Elaine had left, to be true. Indeed, if Elaine has not left, (2) would not be either true or false; it would just be strange. Consider the weirdness of (3) and (4), that follow. While both (3) and (4) suggest that

(3) Eric knew the unicorns were real.
(4) Eric was sure that unicorns were real.

Eric is a little weird for believing that unicorns were real, (3) suggests as well that the speaker is also a little weird and holds the same strange belief. (A possible exception would be if heavy unnatural stress were laid on *knew* to make it sound ironic, but that possibility will be ignored at present.)

Sometimes what a word asserts directly versus what it presupposes can be the basis of the difference of two contrasting words. For example, *accuse* presupposes that the act in question is considered bad by the speaker while it asserts that a particular person was responsible. In contrast, the otherwise similar verb *criticize* presupposes that a particular person is responsible and asserts that the act was bad (Fillmore, 1971). If a presupposition is violated, absurdity (as opposed to falsehood) results.

(5) Bill accused Jim of rescuing the little girl.
(6) Bill criticized Betty Crocker for shooting Abraham Lincoln.

While (5) presupposes that the act is bad, it seems odd that the speaker would think it bad to rescue a little girl; thus, a presupposition of *accuse* appears to be violated. In (6), the presupposition of responsibility appears to be violated, since Betty Crocker did not shoot Abraham Lincoln, and it seems highly unlikely anyone would believe she did.

Fuzzy sets. When examined closely, even what at first appear to be very clearly defined semantic concepts or classes become "fuzzy," or difficult to define precisely. A good example is *furniture*. What constitutes a piece of furniture? Most would agree that objects like beds, couches, chairs, tables, and dressers are furniture, but how about grandfather clocks, end tables, card tables, ping-pong tables, wastebaskets, rugs, footstools, floor lamps, table lamps, vases, pillows, flower pots, plant stands, built-in bookshelves, pianos, cellos, music stands, typewriters, coasters, trunks, and picture frames? Is the class furniture defined by size (for example, a grandfather clock is a piece of furniture, but an alarm clock isn't), by position (all things that sit on the floor are pieces of furniture while those that sit on tables or hang on walls aren't), or by object class (plants and flower pots are not furniture, even if a six-foot plant sits in a two-foot diameter pot on the floor)? Everyone has his or her own conceptions of what is and is not furniture, and each definition may be slightly different from all the others. For this reason we say that furniture is a *fuzzy set*. Fuzzy sets are very common, being the rule rather than the exception.

A similar example involves differentiating between a *glass*, a *cup*, and a *mug*. People typically classify based on physical attributes, such as cups having handles and sitting on saucers (but then what about paper and styrofoam cups—why aren't they glasses?). If mugs also have handles but are thicker and don't take saucers, is there a certain thickness after which a cup becomes a mug? If a glass can be of many shapes (tumblers, wine glasses, shot glasses, juice glasses) but must have no handle and be made of either plastic or glass, then why is an object the same size, shape, and thickness but made of paper called a cup instead of a glass? One final complication: Does what we call a drinking vessel in part depend on what drink is in it? If a paper cup is filled with cola or beer, is it still a cup of cola or a cup of beer, or has it become a glass (or perhaps a glass of cola in a cup!)?

If we have coffee in a large, transparent glass vessel with no handle or saucer, is it still a glass? Clearly glasses, cups, and mugs, like furniture, are all fuzzy sets, but, surprisingly, we are usually able to comprehend and converse about them with little confusion. In fact, we can construct categories whenever we need them; such categories may sometimes contain objectively very disparate members; for example, a class of situations (party, class, club meeting) in which one might make new friends (Barsalou, 1983). There might be very few, if any, concrete attributes common to all instances of some class, but yet we would be able to construct a category and use it; for example, in trying to structure one's life in such a way as to make new friends.

The fuzzy set issue is not a purely academic one, but manifests itself in some serious social problems. For example, physicians and legal scholars are discovering that the concept *death* is a very fuzzy set. Such issues as euthanasia, organ transplants, and reviving someone after a brief heart stoppage underline the importance of defining death more precisely. Similarly, the abortion debate issue can be posed as: When does personhood begin? If a first-trimester fetus is in fact a person, then aborting it is murder; if it is not, then the abortion is merely a surgical procedure. "*Person* is a fuzzy set in that an egg and sperm are not persons, but a baby at birth is; just where in between does the entity enter the class *person*?

Negation.   One semantically interesting type of word is a *negation*. This may be expressed directly by a negative word, like *not, no one, never,* or *none,* by negative prefixes (*un-, dis-, im-, in-*), or even by certain words that have an inherent negation in their meaning (*abolish, subtract, lose, refrain from, forget, fail, prevent*). Most psychological research has found that, other things being equal, a negative statement is typically more difficult to comprehend or remember than a corresponding affirmative one. However, this may depend considerably on the context. Negatives are often used to deny something and tend to be reasonable only if such a denial is plausible (Wason, 1965; Johnson-Laird & Tridgell, 1972). Thus, sentence (7) below seems a reasonable negation because someone could easily assert that a bat was a bird, but (8), though a true statement, is somewhat bizarre in that it is hard to imagine the need to ever assert it; who would ever think a table *was* a bird?

(7) A bat is not a bird.
(8) A table is not a bird.

Sometimes a negation can be ambiguous as to exactly what it is negating, that is, its *scope*. Example (9) below is ambiguous in that Dolly may have done something else to the microphone, Dolly may have turned on something else, or somebody else may have turned on the microphone. Some languages, like German, could more easily clarify just what was being negated by placement of the negative particle *not* (German: *nicht*). In English we usually have to depend on the context to clarify it, although we can more narrowly specify the scope using a more formal style in the following examples.

(9)   Dolly did not turn on the microphone.
(10) It wasn't Dolly who turned on the microphone.
(11) It wasn't the microphone that Dolly turned on.
(12) What Dolly did to the microphone was not to turn it on.

Context. A curious fact about the meaning of certain words is that their meaning is partly determined by surrounding words or even by nonverbal context. One type of word for which this is true are *quantifiers*, words like *many, few,* and *several*. For example, consider (13) and (14).

(13) Many people earned over $10,000 last year.
(14) Many people were killed by tornadoes last year.

How many people would have to have earned over $10,000 to make (13) true, and how many would have to have died in tornadoes to make (14) true? For most people, "many" killed by tornadoes is not nearly as many as "many" earning over $10,000. Thus, *many* has meaning only in relation to what it is modifying and what the person using it expected; it means "many" relative to what might be expected. Hence, something as "purely linguistic" as word meaning can, in fact, be defined in part by psychological factors.

Another type of context-dependent word meaning involves *deictic* words, that is, words that take on their meaning only by relating to a context. For example, demonstrative adjectives such as *this, that, these,* and *those* mean nothing more than *the* unless there is a near or far context to point to in order to discriminate, for example, *these* people from *those* people. Consider the silliness of sitting in an office and saying (15), unless there happen to be pictures of ostriches or real birds within sight.

(15) These ostriches are pretty.

Other examples of deictic words include *here* and *there*, verb tense, time adverbs and verbs like *come* and *go* and *bring* and *take*. For instance, whether one uses *come* or *go* depends on where he or she is in relation to the movement described. If one is in Kansas, one can say (16) but typically not (17), while a speaker in Washington could say (17) but not (16), in describing the same Presidential visit.

(16) The President came to Kansas.
(17) The President went to Kansas.

People remember, or misremember, deictic words as having been spoken from the rememberer's own perspective (Brewer & Harris, 1974).

Sometimes one language will have one word to cover two different ideas, while another language will have two separate words. For example, in American English the word *rent* can refer either to what the landlord or the tenant does in a rental transaction, while in a sales transaction we

---

BOX 7–2   Embarrassments in International Marketing

General Motors did not understand for a while why its popular Chevrolet Nova was not selling in Puerto Rico. When someone finally pointed out that *Nova* in Spanish means "it doesn't go (run)," the name was changed to "Caribe" and sales improved. For similar reasons, AMC's Matador did not do well in Latin America, but then an imported car named "Killer" or "Murderer" probably wouldn't sell too well in the United States!

The company that is now the Exxon Corporation made some preliminary plans several years ago to change the firm name to "Enco," short for "Energy Company." While this sounded very appropriate in English, in Japanese the word "enco" means "flat tire," hardly a good name for a company of service stations. Thus, that name was dropped too.

A certain brand of toothpaste did not sell well in Buenos Aires, quite possibly because "Colgate" in Argentinian Spanish means "go hang yourself!" A type of Brazilian bank account was marketed under its Portuguese acronym PIS, which would not market well to North America, nor would the Japanese Mypee Shampoo or Bluebird Drops candy or the Mexican Bimbo bread. Some products actually marketed in the United States include Calpis (a Japanese soft drink pronounced "cow-piss"), Pfanni (a German dumpling mix), and Superglans (a Dutch carwax) (Aman, 1982). Slogans can also cause problems. The unfortunate translation of "Come alive, you're in the Pepsi generation" in Thai was "Pepsi brings your ancestors back from the dead."

distinguish between *buy* and *sell*. In German, however, there are two corresponding words for the two senses of *rent* (*mieten* and *vermieten*), as exists in British English (*let* and *rent*). English has one word, *know*, which can mean either to know a piece of information or to be acquainted with someone. French, Spanish, Portuguese, and German have two separate verbs for these two senses of *know* (*savoir-connaître*, *saber-conocer*, *saber-conhecer*, and *wissen-kennen*, respectively). On the other hand, Romance languages have one verb (*faire, hacer, fazer*), which means both *make* and *do* in English. Translation across languages, and even across dialects, can be fraught with peril. See Boxes 7–2 and 7–3 for further discussion of this issue.

Lest you think that ambiguous or unclear word meaning is an interesting but not terribly consequential issue, see Box 7–4 for an explanation of one of history's most devastating events as lexical ambiguity.

Metaphor. Another important but often overlooked aspect of meaning is the figurative level, or *metaphor*. Very often language is intended nonliterally and very clearly so. Metaphor is widely used in all types of language and is even a part of the way we think (Lakoff & Johnson, 1980). It is frequently present in sports (18), persuasive rhetoric (19), informal name-calling (20), literature (21), and counseling (22) (see sentences below). Any eventual theory of semantics will have to explain how we comprehend figurative as well as literal meaning.

BOX 7–3 Subtle Translation Differences

Sometimes the same word can mean something slightly, or considerably, different in another dialect or language. Consider, for example, the many differences between British and American English. For example, what Americans call "cookies" and "apartments" the English call "biscuits" and "flats." If you talk about your "pants" in London, you may receive a few titters, since the word refers to underwear in Britain; "trousers" are what you wear over your underwear. "Chips" in Chicago are "crisps" in London, while "chips" in Britain are "french fries" on the other side of the Atlantic. If a woman says "I'm easy," it means "I don't care" in Britain, but something else altogether in America. In the U.K. (but not the U.S.!) "rubbers" means "erasers."

There are differences in connotations as well. For example, the word "toilet" means approximately the same on both sides of the Atlantic, but whereas it is the standard word for public bathrooms in Britain, in America it has slightly crude connotations, and terms like "restroom" or "comfort station" are favored.

The outskirts of large cities in Brazil have facilities called "motels," which look somewhat like American buildings of the same name and where you can rent rooms overnight. However, the resemblance in terms of purpose is superficial. Brazilian motels are explicitly for clandestine sexual encounters between people not married to each other; travelers seeking only overnight lodging stay in similar-looking places called hotels.

BOX 7–4   The Semantics of Hiroshima

Coughlin (1953) speculates that the mistranslation of the Japanese word *mokusatsu* may have been partly responsible for the bombing of Hiroshima.
"The literal translation of *mokusatsu* is 'to kill with silence.' Denotatively, this can mean two things to a Japanese: (1) to ignore or (2) to withhold from comment. When Premier Suzuki confronted the press on July 28, 1945, in response to the Potsdam Declaration of the Allies, which demanded the unconditional surrender of the Japanese armed forces at the end of World War II, he announced that the Japanese cabinet was holding to a policy of *mokusatsu*. Testimony after the war from Japanese cabinet officials indicated that Suzuki's intended meaning was 'to withhold from comment' until the Allies' ultimatum was communicated to the Japanese government through official channels. To do otherwise would have meant acting upon unofficial, perhaps erroneous information that was transmitted over radio. Japanese translators at the Domei News Agency, however, chose the 'ignore' meaning. Thus, the Allies received the message, 'The Japanese government *ignores* the demand to surrender.' Not only was the denotative meaning erroneous, but the connotations associated with being 'ignored' are usually quite negative. The atom bomb was dropped a week later on Hiroshima, killing approximately 70,000 people. Is it not plausible that a single reaction to this mistranslation played a part in the final decision to unleash history's most awesome weapon?" (Rothwell, 1982, p. 27)

---

(18) The Mets creamed the Phillies.
(19) This Administration is bleeding the state dry.
(20) Tim is a real pain in the butt.
(21) ". . . suffer the slings and arrows of outrageous fortune. . . ."
(22) I know I keep my feelings all locked up inside.

So far we have considered the semantic aspect of language only in regard to the meaning of single words. In fact, another important fact of the semantic component of language is the meaning of a sentence or utterance as a whole. This may be referred to as its *propositional meaning*, and it will be considered more carefully after a look at syntax.

SYNTAX

The next aspect of language is **syntax,** or structure. This involves rules for describing how words, or, more precisely, abstract grammatical constituents like subjects, predicates, noun phrases, and other elements may be put together to form an acceptable sentence in a given language.

Syntax, as the linguist and psychologist deal with it, is descriptive; it attempts to identify rules actually used in real language. It is not intended to be normative or prescriptive, that is, what we *should* do. Contrary to what might be your memories of eighth-grade English class, the interest in psychology is not on coercing people to say *isn't* instead of *ain't* or *brought* instead of *brung*. The scientist studying language is interested in how people actually talk, not how someone thinks they *should* talk.

Surface and Deep Structure

Any sentence may be broken down into grammatical constituents, or structural units, such as noun, verb, and modifier. Such an analysis of a sentence is its *surface structure*. For example, the surface structure of (23) below is noun–verb–adjective–infinitive. A very large number of different words could be plugged into each of these "slots," but they would have to conform to the type of word allowed there. For example, the word *the* could not be inserted in the adjective position, nor the word *friendly* in the noun position. The sentence diagramming you learned back in junior high and the grammar drills you labored through studying a foreign language were basically surface structure exercises, training you to identify the surface syntactic constituents. Syntactic knowledge is in some sense implicit in a school child, since he or she would have to possess it to be able to speak intelligibly at all, but this knowledge is certainly not at a conscious level. To come to such a level, it must be carefully, even laboriously, taught.

(23) Henry is easy to please.
(24) Henry is eager to please.

Surface structure is not the only possible level of analysis, however. There is a deeper level, pointed out by the linguist Noam Chomsky (1957, 1965a), called the *deep*, or sometimes the *underlying*, structure. Let's go back to (23) and make a companion to it (24). Both (23) and (24) have the identical surface structure. They do, of course, contain one word different from the other, and that changes the meaning somewhat, but it is structure, not meaning, which is of concern here. Although the two sentences have identical surface structures, there is something very different about them syntactically, specifically the relation of the noun *Henry* to the verb *please*. In (24) *Henry* is the deep-structure subject of *please*, while in (23) *Henry* is the deep-structure object. In one case he is doing the pleasing; in the other he is being pleased. We might say that *Henry* is the agent or actor in (24) and the acted-upon in (23) (cf. Fillmore, 1968). Nowhere in the surface structure of noun–verb–adjective–infinitive is this important distinction captured.

Even though you may have never before thought about differences like the contrast between the syntax of (23) and (24), you must have in some sense "known" that knowledge in order to be able to speak and understand such sentences correctly, that is, to know whether Henry was doing the pleasing or being pleased. This also has ramifications for language acquisition in children. If part of what children must know about a language involves deep-structure relationships, there is no way they could learn that purely by imitating surface structures of parents. Language acquisition will be discussed further in Chapter 12.

The importance of deep-structure relationships can be further illustrated with an additional example (25), which has one surface structure (noun–verb–adjective–infinitive), but two possible deep structures, depending on whether the chicken is the deep-structure subject or object of *eat*.

(25)   The chicken is ready to eat.

On the other hand, there are cases where one deep structure may have different alternative surface structures, such as the active and passive versions of the same idea (26) and (27). Here the same deep structure can be realized into either of two surface structures.

(26)   Robin Hood rescued the princess.
(27)   The princess was rescued by Robin Hood.

See Box 7–5 for some humorous examples of how multiple surface or deep structures can lead to multiple meanings, some quite different from what was intended!

Linguistic studies of syntax, especially those of Noam Chomsky and his followers studying *transformational grammar*, have identified many grammatical rules called *transformations* that move constituents of sentences

---

BOX 7–5   Syntactic Ambiguity

Surface Structure Ambiguity

Headlines: "Police Kill Man with Club"
"Professor Gives Talk on Mars"
"Criticisms about Council Members Growing Ugly"
Sign in gym: "I will be taking people out of lockers who haven't paid their rental fee."
Report in newspaper: "She saw sexual intercourse taking place between two trees in the park."

Deep Structure Ambiguity

Sign at bank: "Drive through window"
Signs: "SLOW MEN WORKING"
"SLOW CHILDREN CROSSING"
"FOR BATHROOM USE STAIRS"
Headlines: "Man Eating Fish Mistakenly Sold as Pet"
"Group Studies Changing Hospital to Jail"
"UFO Talks at University"
"All Ohio Condemned to Face Death"
"Deer Kill 100,000"

around in different orders and add or delete elements. For example, transformations can turn an action sentence to a passive sentence (*Jason bought the car* to *The car was bought by Jason*). They can also replace a noun with a pronoun (*Tina left* to *She left*) or move an adverb (*Holly came today* to *Today Holly came*). Redundant and repetitious words and phrases may also be deleted (*Bill told me and Lori told me* to *Bill and Lori told me*). In each case the deep structure remains the same, while specific language-specific transformations derive alternative surface structures.

The Given-New Contract

Although Chomsky and other linguists focused mainly on describing the structural knowledge we must have to know a language, syntax is also very important psychologically in helping us understand language we hear and read every day. While syntax is not the meaning, it helps to *signal* the meaning and thus help us interpret a given sentence. To take a simple example, the definite article *the* signals that a noun phrase is beginning and one can reasonably expect the next word to be either a noun or a modifying adjective preceding a noun.

Syntax can signal more than just the part of speech that is to follow, however. It can also tell us what information the hearer already knows and what information is new in that sentence. For example, consider (28) and (29).

(28) The ugly toad is on the mushroom.
(29) The toad on the mushroom is ugly.

Both contain the same information, even the same words, but somehow there is a difference. A particular piece of information (that the toad is ugly) is in a different syntactic structure in each sentence. As (28) would normally be used, the hearer and the speaker are both aware of some toad that is ugly (given information) and the speaker is telling the hearer that the toad is on the mushroom (new information). In (29), however, the speaker and hearer know that there is a toad on the mushroom and the new information says that it is ugly.

Part of the unwritten conventions of language is that we have an implicit agreement to put given information in certain syntactic structures of a sentence, for example, in adjectives or prepositional phrases modifying the subject of a sentence, and new information in other forms—in adjectives or phrases following the verb. This allows the listener to pick out what the new information is and link it up with given information already in our memory and repeated in the given part of the sentence. (Clark, 1977; Clark & Haviland, 1977; Haviland & Clark, 1974).

The *given-new* distinction may be further illustrated by looking at appropriate and inappropriate denials of (28) and (29). For example, (30) would be an appropriate denial of (29), but a very awkward and inappropriate response to (28), while the reverse is true for (31).

(30)   No, it's a pretty toad.
(31)   No, it's on the lily pad.

It has long been known that people often do not notice blatantly contradictory information, such as in the old children's riddle "How many pairs of animals did Moses take into the ark?" or "If a plane crashes on a national boundary, where do they bury the survivors?" (Baker, 1985; Erickson & Mattson, 1981). Part of the reason such false information is missed may be due to its given-new status in the sentence. For example, Baker and Wagner (1987) had subjects listen to sentences such as either (32) or (33) below and respond true or false. They were told to respond false if any part of the sentence were false. Subjects correctly identified sentences like (33) false more often than sentences like (32). A second study confirmed that this result occurred independent of the position of the information in the sentence. These findings suggest that one way to manipulate information through language is to place false information in subordinate clauses (given) rather than main clauses (new). People are less likely to notice the false information there.

(32)   Emerald City, the home of the Wizard of Oz, was named after the precious red stone.
(33)   Emerald City, named after the precious red stone, was the home of the Wizard of Oz.

Style

Another manifestation of differences in syntax occurs in the matter of **style**. Certain placements of words and phrases indicate a more formal style than others. Subtle stylistic differences are some of the cues that tip off a teacher that a student paper is plagiarized, because its style is a little too formal to be a typical student composition. Moreover, in formal speaking and writing, people tend to use more complex syntax, involving a greater number of subordinate clauses. In more colloquial speech, shorter, choppier sentences are the rule, if indeed speech is composed of grammatically well-formed sentences at all, which it often is not.

Sometimes the use of an uncommon syntactic transformation is the surest indication of awkward or archaic style. For example, in modern English to transform a declarative (34) into a yes-no question requires the addition of a form of the verb *do* (35).

(34)   Anne likes broccoli.
(35)   Does Anne like broccoli?
(36)   Likes Anne broccoli?
(37)   Think you that the king is mad?

However, in Elizabethan English you could simply invert the subject and verb (36), a form of question common in the time of Shakespeare (37), but no longer used. It is in part the many uses of unfamiliar syntax that makes Shakespeare and his contemporaries difficult for the modern reader. Unfortunately, sometimes contemporary language is also very difficult to understand because of its style. See Box 7–6 for a discussion of a judge's instructions to the jury.

Propositional Structure

At a level more abstract (or deep, if you will) than even the deep structure is the structure of the ideas in the sentence. This is when the division between syntax and semantics becomes murky. Although cognitive psychologists differ as to exactly how to describe and measure these idea-units, most agree that meaningful discourse is composed of semantic units called **propositions**. An example of how a sentence could be broken up into propositions would be (38). Sentence (38) contains five separate simple propositions; we might remember some of these and forget others some time after hearing the sentence.

(38) Brave young Snoopy withstood the cat's sharp blows.
 (a) Snoopy was brave.
 (b) Snoopy was young.
 (c) The blows were sharp.
 (d) The blows came from the cat.
 (e) Snoopy withstood the blows.

As you can see, the propositional level of analysis really involves semantic factors (meaning), as well as syntactic ones. In fact, many psychologists and linguists (Fillmore, 1968; Norman & Rumelhart, 1975; Kintsch, 1974) question the usefulness of talking about a deep-structure level of syntax, preferring to consider the level more abstract than the surface structure as entirely semantic. Arguments for and against these approaches need not concern us here. It is worth noting, however, that when syntax and semantics are carefully considered in their appropriate abstractness, it typically becomes very difficult to separate them completely, as illustrated by our sample propositional analysis (38).

In describing propositions, it is easier to say what they are not than what they are. First of all, they are not analogical, that is, they bear no physical relationship to the referent they represent. They are highly abstract, a fact worth keeping constantly in mind when using graphic or schematic representations of them, which necessarily must represent them as words (see Kintsch, 1974) or some combination of words and graphic representations (Anderson, 1985).

Propositions have several important characteristics. First of all, they are primarily semantically based, that is, a representation of the meaning, although some versions of propositional theory do also contain some structure. Unlike sentences, they are not ambiguous and do not contain the surface structure at all. A proposition coding the idea of John kissing Mary could have had its stimulus source in any one of several spoken or written sentences ("John kissed Mary," "Mary was kissed by John,") or in

---

BOX 7–6   Instructions to the Jury

A current area of considerable concern in forensic psychology is the language in the judge's instructions to the jury prior to deliberation. The custom of the judge instructing the jury arose from the need to inform the jurors and help them apply the law to the case at hand. In the late nineteenth and early twentieth centuries, U.S. state statutes started requiring the courts to reduce all instructions by the judge to writing; this had the effect of a formalization of the instructions and a stratification resulting from their being read verbatim for each such trial. These verbatim instructions were adhered to precisely because these were the instructions that had been upheld on appeal. Any judge who deviated and used another set of instructions ran the risk of having that decision later overturned on a technicality. Now most state and federal courts have those so-called *pattern instructions* available for most crimes. Since they are used for all trials for a particular crime, they are, not surprisingly, broad and abstract and do not allow very well for integration of the specifics of the trial. The instructions seldom use examples, for fear of biasing the jury.

While the use of pattern instructions makes excellent sense from a legal point of view, from an information-processing perspective, the wisdom is considerably more questionable. The legal community generally assumes that the instructions are adequately comprehended; to a cognitive psychologist, this is an empirical question that has not been answered. Frequently the jurors are not allowed to ask any clarifying questions, for fear that the answer given them might in some way bias them in a way that is unfair to one of the parties of the trial or that risks a reversal in the appeals process.

Another problem is that instructions are typically given to a jury *after* they have heard the evidence, just before deliberation begins. Cognitive psychologists would stress the importance of instructions in comprehending the information as it is initially processed and encoded, not after the fact when it must be retrieved and reconstructed. Thus, we have, in pattern instructions and their use, a practical problem of information processing, but one that has not been considered much from that perspective.

In a very interesting and important cognitive study of a judge's instructions to the jury, the lawyer-linguist researcher couple Robert and Veda Charrow (1979) set out to provide some empirical evidence of juror failure to comprehend pattern instructions and to identify some particular linguistic constructions that posed problems. They asked prospective jurors to paraphrase 14 standard civil instructions from the California state judicial system for a highway accident case.

Their results showed that over 60 percent of the ideas in the instructions were either paraphrased inaccurately or completely forgotten. Although ideas from long and short sentences were remembered equally well, certain types of syntactic constructions cause a lot of comprehension difficulty. These included passive constructions, certain prepositional phrases, especially those containing the stylistically awkward expression "as to," and sentences with two or more negations in them. Other constructions causing difficulties included sentences with discontinuous constituents, such as *A proximate cause is a cause which in natural and continuous sequence produces an injury.* The phrase "which produces an injury" is broken up with another phrase, thus making it more difficult to assign a subject of "produces." Another type of phrase that proved difficult was the deletion of optional relative pronouns, as in ". . . questions and facts submitted to you . . . ." In English we can optionally delete the "which are" from this phrase. However, this is often at the cost of some clarity.

Charrow and Charrow examined the claim we sometimes hear that legal language is necessarily complex because the legal concepts are so complex. They did not find support for this, in that jurors' difficulty with the instructions stemmed not from the inherent difficulty of the concepts themselves, but rather from the way the concepts were stated. Every concept was much more understandable if phrased in a way more consistent with our natural language comprehension strategies.

an observation of the event of John kissing Mary. Propositions are not dependent on the form of the input, nor are they typically good avenues to retrieving that exact surface information.

Propositions have some kind of internal organization and, as such, contain both units and relations. Units could be abstract entities like *agent*, *object*, or *instrument*, while relations could be the identity relationship (A is B), possession, or relationships like *acts upon* or *object of*. The internal organization of propositions may be reflected in its different components. For example, an action *hit* may contain elements of agent, object, and instrument, any of which could appear as the surface structure subject of the sentence (for example, "the boy hit the ball," "the ball was hit by the boy," "the bat hit the ball").

Unlike images or some kind of units or concepts alone, propositions often have a truth value (in the case of a statement about something, asserting either a stative relation or an action) or demand a response, in the case of a question or imperative. An image or concept cannot be true or false or demand a response; it is merely a representation. On the other hand, a proposition asserts something, which may in reality be true or false, or requests a response, which may or may not be complied with.

Propositions have developed as a very useful construct in studying linguistic information processing. Memory studies of prose are typically scored for the number of propositions recalled, rather than number of words or sentences. Theoretical models of propositional learning continue to be developed and doubtless will have increasing impact on the study of information processing in the future (see J. R. Anderson, 1976, 1983).

PRAGMATICS

The last major aspect of language to be discussed is its use in a context, or **pragmatics.** Every instance of language is used within some context, even if that context is a total lack of context, a highly unusual situation in the real world. In most cases the contextual appropriateness is assumed; you simply would not say (39) while sitting in class.

(39) My, what a fierce rhinoceros that is!

Occasionally, however, the context lends meaning where it otherwise would not exist at all, as in the case of the deictic words and quantifiers discussed earlier. Other times the context may radically alter the meaning, perhaps totally changing the "speech act" function of the utterance; for example, irony and sarcasm (40), turning a question into a command (41), indicating a metaphorical intent by the speaker (42).

(40) My, what a beautiful day!
      (Context: in a blizzard)
(41) John, are you able to reach the cookies?
      (Context: a hungry speaker out of reach of the cookies and John within reach of them)
(42) The troops marched on into battle for two hours.
      (Context: a harried baby sitter explaining children's rambunctious behavior to their parents upon the latter's return)

Sometimes when scientists study language they easily forget about its typical use in conversation, a continuing dialogue and interplay between two or more people. A conversation may be looked at as a type of game, consisting of a sequence of exchanges involving rule-governed processes (Weiner & Goodenough, 1977). Speakers make different "moves" with their remarks. These moves may be directly dealing with the subject being discussed, or moves that add nothing new to the subject but indicate information about whether the speaker wants to change or to keep the current topic. For example, if in a conversation between two people there is a sequence of two so-called *passing moves*, like *okay, uhhmm*, and *all right*, spoken with falling intonation (not as a question), that usually signals a change in the topic being discussed, as desired by both speakers.

Besides being sensitive to and signaling changes in turns in conversation, people tend to talk differently to others depending on whether or not they perceive them as "experts" or "novices" in the topic being discussed. We assess, supply, and acquire expertise in a conversation. We *assess* how knowledgeable other people are by the wording of their speech. When necessary, we *supply* them with the needed knowledge. We *acquire* that knowledge from others by eliciting information from other people and attending to incidental knowledge cues that they offer in their speech. Isaacs and Clark (1987) studied how people assessed, supplied, and acquired expertise while talking to another person about arranging a series of post-cards of New York City. People familiar with New York referred to and described the scenes differently from those who had never been to New York. Part of what happens in all real conversation is an ongoing assessment of the expertise of the other person and a tailoring of one's speech accordingly.

Beyond the content of the conversation, even the way we address each other can indicate our relative social status or amount of identification with the person (see Box 7–7). Sometimes even the choice of what language to speak in a given situation has social or political implications (see Box 7–8).

BOX 7–7   Formal and Familiar Forms of Language

There are different ways that we address other people to indicate our relationship to them. Many languages have two forms of the second-person pronouns (French *tu-vous*, Spanish *tú-usted*, German *du-Sie*), one to be used with close friends and family members and one to be used with other adults. Modern English only captures such differences through the choice of the use of first name or a title and last name. However, English once did have a familiar second-person pronoun, *thou*, which has now fallen into disuse. Thus, we lose certain distinctions in modern English. For example, in Shakespeare's *Two Gentlemen of Verona* two friends, Proteus and Valentine, address each other with *thou* until one takes the other's girl friend. The indignant friend then begins addressing his former buddy with *you*, a clear mark of distance to Elizabethan playgoers, but a signal likely to be missed by today's audiences.

Whether we use the formal or familiar form of address with another person may depend on how we perceive our relationship on one of two relevant dimensions. The first is power. A person in a position of greater power addresses a person of lesser power with the familiar form, but receives the formal in return. This power may take many forms: teacher-student, parent-child, employer-employee, and so forth.

The second dimension is solidarity, that is, the degree of perceived commonality and shared experience. If this dimension is operating, members of a group with something in common address each other with the familiar form, but address others outside the group with a formal form. These may be members of a family, a class, an office, or whatever. In the modern world, there is a gradual tendency for solidarity to assume more importance in determing forms of address and power to assume somewhat less importance, but both are still important. If they come into conflict, the participants must resolve what forms to use; for example, should all workers in an office address each other with the familiar form or should the bosses expect to be addressed with the formal form?

Formal and familiar forms are subject to dialectal differences. In Spanish, for example, Venezuelan and some Caribbean dialects use *tú* for everyone, regardless of power or solidarity relationships (like the English *you*). On the other hand, European Spanish has, as well as *tú* and *usted*, a special familiar-plural pronoun (*vosotros*), which is not used in Latin America. Even among English-speakers, the British are likely to use titles and last names longer in a relationship than Americans do. Such cultural differences often lead to Americans' perceptions of the British as formal and aloof and Britons' perception of Americans as pushy and impudent.

BOX 7-8   Social Implications of Bilingualism

In spite of the strongly monolingual character of some major nations such as the United States, Japan, Brazil, and Great Britain, bilingualism is actually the rule rather than the exception in most areas of the world. The degree and character of bilingualism varies substantially, however.

It is seldom the case that an individual is exactly equivalent in fluency in all aspects in two languages. For example, many people around the world can read English, which they have studied as an academic language, but they often have almost no facility in speaking or in oral comprehension. Others have a conversational facility in a language, but cannot read or write it.

Although some nations like Switzerland have been happily multilingual for centuries, language can be a divisive force in a country. A good example is Canada, which is officially bilingual, but with a predominance of largely monolingual English-speakers. Predominantly French-speaking Quebec province passed blatantly anti-English laws, and the French influence at the national level is widely resented, especially in western Canada. Similarly, Belgium has had a long history of competition of the Dutch-speaking Flemings and the French-speaking Walloons of the north and south of the country, respectively. Unlike the situation in Canada, however, the Flemings and the Walloons have usually kept closer to a numerical and power balance.

Sometimes a second language may be a source of regional consciousness and political difficulties, especially in cases where speakers perceive that a language is in danger of dying altogether. For example, in Wales there has been a great revival of Welsh over the last two decades. The old Celtic tongue is the first language of a sizable minority (10 to 20 percent) of Welsh, especially in northern Wales, and the whole country has recently seen the introduction of bilingual signs and increased broadcast programming in Welsh. Although its sister tongue Irish is seldom spoken as a first language today, it is sometimes studied by Irish Republican Army prisoners jailed in Northern Ireland; thus it has become a political symbol.

Very frequent in many communities is a situation called *diglossia*, where there is a high-status formal language and a lower-status everyday language, with most people bilingual. This is very typical of immigrant communities of the first or second generation in immigrant societies like the United States, Canada, Brazil, and Australia; typically, in such situations, the original language is lost as the younger generations adopt the host country's language as its vernacular.

Sometimes the diglossia continues for many generations, especially in colonial settings. In colonial Africa, for example, residents learned English, French or Portuguese as the high-status language, but continued to speak their indigenous languages at home. Diglossia has existed relatively unchanged for four centuries in parts of South America, where the everyday language is Quechua or Aymará in much of Peru and Bolivia and Guaraní in most of Paraguay, but where many, if not most, people know Spanish as well. (Baetens Beardsmore, 1982; Grosjean, 1982)

There are implicit rules that we all follow in conversation whether we realize it or not (Grice, 1975). One is to give enough information, but not too much. If a four-year-old asks where he or she came from a response of "Go away" would be too little information, but a 10,000-word treatise on genetics would be too much. Certain conventional expressions carry strong expectations of just how much information to respond with. If someone asks "How are you?" that person really does not want a detailed medical report, and such a response would typically not be appreciated, if even tolerated. Another implicit rule of conversation involves telling the truth, and assuming others are too, unless we have some compelling reason to suspect otherwise, or unless we recognize from the context that some sort of nonliteral conventional use of language is intended.

A speaker can communicate more in a conversation than merely the propositional content. He or she can also communicate information about the speaker's intentions, beliefs, and relations with the listener (Keenan, MacWhinney, & Mayhew, 1977). For example, in response to an idea suggested by another person, you might say (43) or (44).

(43)   Another one of your ridiculous schemes!
(44)   That's a good possibility, though we might want to consider some other factors also.

While the responses are similar in that the speaker is expressing disagreement with the idea, (43) expresses a very different attitude from (44) and would probably lead the conversation in a different direction.

Pragmatic considerations also help to determine if a statement is meant to be taken in some unusual, nonconventional fashion. For example, a statement exactly the opposite of what is appropriate for the context is often the object of *irony*. Thus, if someone says (45) on a cold day after it has snowed all night, he or she is interpreted as being ironic, not psychotic. (Though interestingly enough, if someone labelled mentally ill made the same statement in the same situation, it might be labelled psychotic and not ironic!)

(45)   Can you open the window?

Sometimes *sarcasm* may be used to communicate intentions and opinions of the speaker that have nothing at all to do with its surface, deep, or propositional structure. For example, if a student comes in and says her term paper fell in the mud and washed down a sewer on the way to class, the teacher could respond (46).

(46)   Yes, and I just got trampled by 15 purple elephants in the hall.

This statement has nothing whatever to do with elephants or hallways, but rather communicates to the student that the speaker does not believe the explanation of what happened to the term paper.

Gibbs (1986) tested subjects' comprehension and memory for statements like "You're a fine friend" following a context suggesting either a literal interpretation or one suggesting a sarcastic interpretation. Subjects did not have to first comprehend the literal meaning and then compute the sarcastic one, when that was appropriate. In terms of memory, they remembered the sarcastic version of the same expression better than the literal equivalent. Gibbs (1984, 1986) argued that there may not even be any such thing as literal, context-independent meaning; in real language use, every interpretation must take the context into consideration. In exploring a related issue, Jorgensen, Miller, and Sperber (1984) and Clark and Gerrig (1984) studied the psycholinguistics of irony, proposing two competing theories of how people signify their intention to be ironic with an utterance and how we perceive that speakers and writers have done so.

When is a question not a question? When the context tells you it is a command. For example, suppose I am teaching a class where the room is getting very stuffy and I turn to one of the students near the window and say (45). In terms of surface structure, deep structure, and propositional content, that utterance is a question calling for a yes or no answer. However, a simple *yes* or *no* in the context above would be interpreted as an inappropriate, perhaps even a highly discourteous, response. The context here has told us that what initially appears to be a question is, in fact, an imperative, just as surely as if I had said

(47) Please open the window.

Of course, in some other context, such as my questioning an ailing student about how well he is gaining back his strength in his recently broken arm, such a question could indeed be a yes-no question. Sometimes the context of such expressions can even turn a negative into an affirmative and vice versa. For example, consider the same context as above and someone uttering (48) or (49).

(48) Why not open the window?
(49) Why open the window?

The negative (48) is really an affirmative imperative (*Do open the window*), and the affirmative (49) a negative imperative (*Do not open the window*)! Such is the power of pragmatics.

Along the same line, an apparent question can actually be a statement.

(50) Haven't I been good to you?
(51) Can any group compare to the Beatles?

In many contexts (50), which is an apparent negative question, is, in fact, an affirmative statement (*I have been good to you*) while (51), which is an apparent affirmative question, is a negative declarative (*No group can compare to the Beatles*).

Now that we have examined the phonological, semantic, syntactic, and pragmatic components of language, let us apply these concepts by examining two of the major functions of language—reading and writing.

READING AND WRITING

Writing Systems

Although writing is a newer invention than speech, it is hardly a recent phenomenon, with writing systems going back at least as far as 5000 B.C. in Mesopotamia, Egypt, and the Indus and Yangtze valleys.

There are three different types of writing systems: **logographic, syllabic,** and **alphabetic,** roughly based on whether one written symbol corresponds to a word, a syllable, or a sound. While English and most other languages you are familiar with are alphabetic, it is worth taking a brief look at logographic and syllabic writing systems, because our information-processing systems are also capable of reading in those systems.

A logographic system has one symbol to stand for a word or words. This is the only type of writing system where one symbol represents a semantic unit. Chinese is the most widely used logographic system. Compared to a syllabic or alphabetic system, logographic writing has a very large number of symbols (about 50,000 in Chinese, although only 1000 or so account for about 90 percent of Chinese writing). Obviously the stage of learning to read where one learns the symbols is much more complex in Chinese than in English, although the former is easier in the sense that there is no spelling-sound correlation that must be learned. Another interesting property of logographic systems is illustrated by the fact that all of China, the world's most populous country, uses the same written language of logographic symbols, which are comprehensible anywhere in China. However, there are many spoken languages and dialects (as many as 1800) that are mutually incomprehensible, in spite of the fact that they all use the same written system.

Although the written form of English and other European languages in alphabetic, logographic symbols are not totally outside the realm of our experience. For example, symbols like $+$, $-$, $<$, $>$, $=$, %, &, *, and ™, are logographic symbols and translate directly to meaning, even though in their spoken version, $+$ (for example) might be "plus" in one "dialect," "and" in another, and "added to" in a third.

A syllabic writing system, of which Japanese is a good example, uses one symbol to stand for a syllable. Japanese also uses many logographs borrowed from Chinese and also sometimes transliterations into the Latin alphabet. The Japanese syllabic writing system has about 100 consonant-vowel syllables, which are combined into words.

Alphabetic systems, of which the Latin, Cyrillic, Greek, and Hebrew are examples, have roughly one symbol per sound, although there are many systematic and idiosyncratic exceptions to this rule, such as the many ways of spelling the sound /e/ in English or final consonants not being pronounced in French. An alphabetic symbol has no meaning on its own and is useful only for the way it can combine with other symbols to form words. There have been 200 to 300 alphabets in the world, about half of them in India. The widely used Latin alphabet that we use was originally an adaptation of Greek, which evolved out of ancient Phoenician writing.

There are some significant variations in alphabetic systems. For example, biblical Hebrew represented only the consonants in symbols; vowels were interpreted in as one read. Modern Hebrew, and also Arabic to a large extent, often indicates vowels in writing, but usually only as marks above or below the consonants.

A sort of hybrid system is the Korean *hangul*, which is an alphabetic syllabary. It was invented around 1443 by King Sejong to replace the Chinese logographs, which were ill suited to the polysyllabic and inflected Korean language. The symbols represent particular sounds (19 consonants, 21 vowels), but they are put together into around 2000 syllable blocks (see Fig. 7–1). This system makes reading very easy to learn, and according to Taylor and Taylor (1984), there is virtually no illiteracy or remedial classes in Korea.

Although writing has been around for thousands of years, widespread literacy has not, and for most of human history reading and writing have been the province of the very few. Early Greek and Latin manuscripts were written without spaces between the words; around the eleventh century this innovation appeared in Latin manuscripts. The modern book has its origins in the wooden wax-coated tablets of ancient Greece and Rome. Although paper was known to the ancient Chinese, it was only introduced into Europe by the Arabs in the eighth century and was little used before the twelfth or thirteenth century. With the development of printing in the Renaissance, forms of writing tended to become more standardized, with the most convenient forms gaining ascendancy and acceptance and other forms falling from use. Since that time, spelling has become more standardized and the rate of change in language has decreased. With this background in mind, let us turn to the psychological processes involved in reading and writing.

Eye Movements in Reading

Studies of eye movements have shown that when people read, their eyes move in short jumps and hops, called *saccades*. Most people have a nearly constant rate of saccadic movement, about 3 to 4 movements per second. What differentiates the good from the poor reader or the scanner from the studier is how much information is contained in each saccade. Though most eye movement is forward, there is occasional backward movement; for example, when the reader looks back to check the wording of a prior difficult phrase. Clearly, the more difficult the text, the more such backward saccades we will have and the slower the overall reading rate.

Logographic

Chinese:

你在干什么?　　What are you doing?

我看电视　　I'm watching TV.

Syllabic

Japanese:

カーネーション　　carnation

Alphabetic Syllabary

Korean Hangul:

딸 , 달 , 닭　　egg, moon, hen

Alphabetic

Russian (Cyrillic alphabet):

Мы имеем три книги.　　We have three books.

Hebrew:

באוניברסיטה　　Do you study at the university?

אתה לומד ?

Arabic:

الولد درس　　The boy studied.

Greek:

ἀστραπή　　lightning

Hindi (Devanagari alphabet):

अमेरिकी खाना　　American food

FIGURE 7-1 Examples of different scripts.

Essential Prereading Skills

Before a child can begin to read, he or she must have certain cognitive abilities that adults would take for granted. For example, children have to be able to perceive speech and begin to understand the idea of segmentation in speech and have some rudimentary understanding that there is a correspondence between that string of spoken sounds and the written symbols on the page.

Graphic discrimination is also important. Many preschoolers start scribbling at age two or earlier. They soon progress to drawing, which does not necessarily closely resemble what it purports to represent, but to the child it does represent something. Children aged three to five frequently start copying letters and often do so spontaneously if verbal models are available in the parents. Children must also be able to discriminate writing from pictures before they can begin to read. Even most three-year-olds are able to distinguish writing from nonwriting in sorting tasks (Lavine, 1972). This occurred for children both in Ithaca, New York, and rural Yucatan in Mexico. Written language has several characteristics that pictorial stimuli do not. For one, language is linear, usually left-to-right but occasionally vertical. Further, the units are nonrepetitive and not too systematic in appearance; in fact, if most adults could see (52) or (53), they would quite likely describe them as something other than writing, simply because the repetitiveness is too great to be characteristic of language.

(52)   OOOOOOOOOOOOOOOOOOOOOOOOOOOOOOOOOOOOOOO
(53)   OXOXOXOXOXOXOXOXOXOXOXOXOXOXOXOXOXOXOXOX

Children also learn that words have different numbers of letters, not always five, or two, or whatever. Older preschoolers may start to identify and discriminate certain features of letters that are critical features differentiating similar letters.

Graphic discrimination is good even in preliterate kindergarteners. For example, given a matching task like *G-CQDGO* or *b-hdbfk*, kindergarteners can correctly identify with about 80 percent to 90 percent accuracy which of the five letters is identical with the first (Calfee, Chapman, & Venezky, 1972). Most of the errors youngsters do make are mirror-image transforms (mistaking *d* for *b*, for example). Accuracy with a *bigram* matching task (CQ-OQ OC QC CQ CO) drops to about 40 percent for the same group, with most errors being reversals like QC for CQ.

When children actually do begin to learn to read, there is some controversy today about how to teach members of various minorities. See Box 7–9.

Perception in Reading

Like so much other information processing, reading is a constructive process, not a simple mechanical transmission of written symbols to the mind. As we read, we process information from beyond the immediate focus of our eyes. There is even a measure of how far the eye is ahead of the mouth in oral reading; this is called the *eye-voice span*. Better readers have a longer eye-voice span, and all readers have a longer eye-voice span for easier, as compared to more difficult, prose.

We know from the speed that we read that we could not possibly be processing each individual letter. We know that some letters, and some

┌─────────── BOX 7–9   Bilingual and Bidialectal Education ───────────┐

A major controversy in education is the question of whether it is desirable to teach minority children to read in their own dialect or language or in the prevailing language and dialect of the society, that is, the so-called standard language. This is a complex issue with some strong proponents, especially among minorities, on both sides of the issue. In the U.S. the debate usually centers on Black English dialect or Spanish for the Hispanic population. On the one hand, members of these communities argue that teaching in the majority tongue puts the minority child at a disadvantage, because he or she is not as familiar with that type of speech, and, more seriously, that the very process denies the worth of their own dialect or language, thus relegating it and its speakers to an "inferior" status. On the opposite side, equally vocal spokespersons of the same minority groups argue that to teach the children in anything other than the "standard" language is to deny them forever the tools to "get ahead" in that society, which, for better or worse, will continue to use the majority tongue and require it from those who aspire to rise to higher socioeconomic wrungs of the social ladder. The debate continues.

└──┘

features of letters, are more important than others. Kolers (1972) has done a series of so-called *mutilated word* studies where prose is degraded in various ways and given to subjects to read. Such studies have shown the consonants are more important than vowels; that is, it is easier to construct the missing vowels than missing consonants. Similarly, letters extending above or below the line tend to carry more information than those doing neither. Further, the top halves of letters seem to be more important than the bottom halves, as evidenced from the relative difficulty of reading a text degraded by removing either the top or bottom half of the letters. Eye-fixation studies reveal that eye fixations generally fall to the left of the center of words, suggesting that we are more likely to perceive the first parts of words and construct the last part than the reverse, at least in English.

There is much debate today over the exact relationship between listening and reading. Foss and Hakes (1978) identified three hypotheses that help to clarify this relationship. The *subvocalization* hypothesis argues that, as we read, we are converting the written symbols to subvocal speech. There is limited evidence for such a process sometimes in some people, in that there are occasional movements in the larynx or even the lips that accompany silent reading. In cases where this occurs, evidence suggests that suppressing such activity interferes with comprehension.

However, there is ample evidence that subvocalization does not regularly or necessarily occur, even though it has been observed on occasion. We can read much faster than we could possibly be subvocalizing everything, with comprehension occurring much more rapidly than can the motor response of vocalizing.

In sharp contrast to subvocalization is the *direct access* hypothesis, which says that we go directly from the written symbols to some sort of mental dictionary, with no intermediate step of using a phonological representation. While this is the process that probably occurs regularly in reading logographic languages, as well as logographic symbols (such as $, +, or =), direct access is not a very efficient method for alphabetic languages: each word would have to be a separate logogram and there would be no perceptual way to use the spelling-sound correspondence that exists in such languages. Individuals use the direct-access process in varying degrees. For example, adults who first learned to read using the "whole-word," as opposed to the phonics, method are more likely to use direct access when reading. Thus, they do fine on identifying familiar words, but they have a more difficult time than the phonics-trained readers in reading new words, because they have fewer skills for "sounding them out."

The third hypothesis, *phonological recoding*, argues that written symbols are converted to some sort of underlying sound representation, but not so completely as in subvocalization. Although phonological recoding is probably not absolutely essential, there is ample evidence that it frequently occurs in reading alphabetical writing.

When people proofread, it is more difficult to catch "silent" letters that are incorrect or omitted than it is to catch letters that do represent some sound (Corcoran, 1967; Gough & Cosky, 1977). Similarly, if an incorrect letter would make a sound identical to what the correct letter would make, it is more difficult to catch in proofreading. For example, if someone had intended to write "WORK," it is easiest to catch the error "WXRK," which is unpronounceable in English, hardest to catch "WERK," which is pronounced identically to the correct version, and of intermediate difficulty to catch "WARK," which is pronounceable, but with a different pronunciation from that of the correct version. If direct access occurred with no involvement of the phonological representation, such differences should not occur. Incidentally, the studies obtaining these differences have controlled for physical similarity of the letters and thus have been able to rule that out as the critical factor.

The reading process has been studied extensively in psychology using the tachistoscope (or t-scope), a machine that can present visual stimuli at very fast durations, even a small fraction of a second. Several t-scope studies have shown the importance of phonological recording in reading. For example, on exposures of 30 to 250 milliseconds, pronounceable nonwords (KIV) can be perceived on shorter duration than nonpronounceable nonwords (QKU). While this is perhaps not too surprising, this difference occurs even when the unpronounceable nonword is highly meaningful and the pronounceable nonword is not; for example, BIM is perceived faster than IBM (Gibson, Bishop, Schiff, & Smith, 1964). This argues strongly for the importance of phonological recoding as primary over semantic interpretation, at least at this early perceptual stage.

Another type of evidence for phonological recoding comes from reaction-time studies of classification tasks. For instance, in classifying strings of letters as words or nonwords, the reaction time measured can be a useful yardstick. For certain nonwords, the unpronounceable "SAGM" can be detected as a nonword faster than the pronounceable "MELP," which can in turn be detected faster than "BRANE," which is also pronounceable but, unlike "MELP," has the sound identical to an English word (Rubenstein, Lewis, & Rubenstein, 1971). In classifying pairs of words as words or nonwords, rhyming sets like "set-wet," "handle-candle," and "bribe-tribe" are classified as words faster than sets like "few-sew," "lemon-demon," or "mint-pint," (Meyer, Schvaneveldt, & Ruddy, 1974). Because the direct-access hypothesis would predict no such difference, this again suggests that phonological recoding occurs.

There is also ample evidence for the use of higher-order units in reading. For example, letters can actually be perceived faster in the context of a word than they can by themselves (Reicher, 1969; Wheeler, 1970). For example, if a t-scope flashes one of the following six arrays (54).

(54)   a   N
       b   R
       c   BANK
       d   BARK
       e   ZANK
       f   ZARK

followed by a marker where the N or R had been, subjects can correctly report the letter after shorter t-scope exposures if the letter occurred in the context of a word (c-d) or pronounceable nonword (e-f) than if it had occurred by itself (a-b). While this may seem counterintuitive, since the word array contains four times as much stimulus information as the single-letter array, apparently we do not process each letter as a separate unit. There is something more "cognitively economical" about the pronounceable string in contrast to the individual letter.

In conclusion, then, reading may be viewed as a continual set of processes of constructing and testing hypotheses at several different levels: letter identification, sentence construction, and overall gist. As we have seen in every facet of information processing, top-down and bottom-up processes interact as we actively construct interpretations. Exactly what processes we use will also depend on the purpose and situation in any given instance. Reading aloud is very different from spontaneous speech (see Box 7–10).

Control of Reading Rate

One important way that we control our reading habits is controlling the speed and strategies used in our reading (Anderson, 1985). Surprisingly, many college students and people in general do not do this and thus they try to read novels, textbooks, newspapers, and scientific articles in exactly the same way. Predictably, this often leads to frustration. Sometimes scanning or skimming is sufficient. Scanning (about 10,000 words per minute) is adequate when you need to search for a specific piece of information in a larger text, and that is all you care about; for example, scanning an article to see if there is any mention of Pavlov. There is no need to retain

---

BOX 7–10   Why Lecturers Who Read Are Boring

Why is it always so boring to listen to someone read something aloud, even if it is very well read, where it is much more interesting to hear someone speak spontaneously, even if that speech is more halting and imperfect? Why does it bother us if actors in a play sound like they are reading their lines, rather than speaking them spontaneously? How can we tell the difference, anyway?

There are several ways that oral reading and spontaneous speech systematically differ. Oral reading is generally slower than speech, with speed increasing with the degree of informality. Oral reading contains very few false starts or "filled pauses" (such place-holding interjections as *uh*, *well*, and *um*), while spontaneous speech contains many of both, especially in more informal speech. On the other hand, breathing pauses (places where we stop to breathe) occur almost entirely at major syntactic constituent boundaries in oral reading, but in many different places in spontaneous speech. If someone's breathing pauses are entirely at major syntactic boundaries, that is a strong clue that the person is reading directly from a text, where the constituents are already formed and available to allow for breathing in between.

Oral reading includes many words from one's "passive vocabulary," that is, words that we comprehend but do not ourselves use in speech. Each of us has a large passive vocabulary that we do not use in speaking, even in formal situations.

Oral reading uses relatively flat intonation, while spontaneous speaking shows more variation in pitch and stress, the greater variety being one reason it is more interesting to listen to than oral reading. Enunciation is usually better in oral reading, however; often it is so good that it sounds unnatural.

If you need something to do during the next boring oral presentation you must listen to, try analyzing the language for the characteristics just described.

---

or even process any semantic information except the word "Pavlov." Skimming (about 800 to 1500 words per minute) is used to extract the basic gist of a text without catching details. This would not be an adequate method of reading your psychology text initially, but it might be a useful technique for the very final review before an exam. Many "speed-reading" courses really teach scanning and skimming. Insofar as you could learn to use these skills in ways you have not before, they might be useful. However, to believe you could learn to do all your reading at 10,000 (or even 1000) words per minute and retain everything is unrealistic.

Control of reading rate and purpose is very helpful in professional reading. For instance, many journal articles in my field come across my (RJH) desk, far more than I have time to read even superficially. However, I can scan or skim them (or parts of them), depending on my purpose, and file them away (literally and figuratively) for future reference. If I am interested in seeing if an article deals with pragmatic inferences, I could scan it for the appearance of that term. If I am interested in the procedural details of the study, because I am designing a similar one, I might read part of the method section very carefully and slowly, but scan or skim the rest of the article. Such strategies are necessary skills for a teacher or researcher to gain in order to keep on top of one's field professionally.

Sign Language

One type of reading that is very different from perceiving and interpreting words off a printed page involves interpreting handshapes and position by a person "speaking" sign language. Although many different types of sign language exist, we will focus on American Sign Language (ASL, or Ameslan), where one sign is approximately equivalent to one word and thus has meaning in itself. Today, ASL is the first language of thousands of hearing-impaired people and an acquired second language of many others. In her cognition textbook, Howard (1983) offers an excellent discussion of sign language.

Sign language is not a degenerate or derivative form of spoken language. Historically, ASL is traceable back to French in the early 1800s, whereas British Sign Language is of an altogether different origin. Sign language is not merely a system of gestures and is no more universal than any spoken language. Though there are some signs that physically resemble the thing they signify (for example, sign for drink by making a fist and moving toward mouth), many have no resemblance at all. Historically, ASL has progressed toward signs being less and less iconic in nature. Abstract concepts may be expressed in ASL just as in English, and there is as complex a set of syntactic rules as any language would have. Flexibility, ambiguity, sarcasm, and even wordplay is possible. For example, the sign for "milk" is made by holding both hands at forehead level and squeezing them. The sign for "pasteurized milk" is making the same sign while moving across one's visual field; that is, "past your eyes."

There are four "formational parameters," somewhat analogous to distinctive features, in spoken language. *Hand configuration* refers to the shape of the hand (for example, fingers extended; fist; forefinger pointing). *Place of articulation* refers to where the hand is placed relative to the rest of the body (forehead level; waist level; next to chin). *Orientation* is the direction the hand is pointing (toward self; toward hearer). *Movement* indicates whether or not there is motion, and, if so, in what direction. Two distinct signs may be identical on two or even three of the parameters, only differing in one, just as the word *cat* and *rat* differ in only one phoneme.

In virtually all ways, ASL has the complexity of spoken languages. It is very rich in inflections. For example, making the sign "happy" faster than other signs indicates "very happy." A question may be indicated by leaning forward toward the hearer, holding the final sign longer, or making a quizzical expression on one's face. Making a sign larger than normal shows emphasis, much like abnormally heavy stress in speaking. Past tense is added to a verb by making that verb sign while holding one's hand over the shoulders; future tense is done similarly by holding the hand farther than normal in front of the body.

Even though most of us never learn sign language, we are capable of doing so given the right circumstances, just as we are capable of learning Chinese. There are fewer signs than there are English words, only a few thousand, but the list is ever growing. New or unfamiliar words or proper names may be communicated by fingerspelling, a type of sign language where each letter in English is spelled quickly with the fingers. People can comprehend about the same amount of information (in propositions) per unit time from ASL as from English.

There are also some interesting findings in regard to where signs are processed in the brain. Just as most people perceive spoken language better in the left cerebral hemisphere than in the right, fluent signers are also left-hemisphere dominant for understanding signs; that is, their left hemispheres perceive the signs better than the right. However, both signers and nonsigners are right-hemisphere dominant for perceiving handshapes that are similar to ASL words but not actual words in the language (Virostek & Cutting, 1979), much as visual spatial perception for most people is right-hemisphere dominant.

The Process of Writing

Let us now turn to other major process involving written language, namely, its production. Writing is a critical problem in cognitive psychology, but it has been surprisingly ignored until very recently. Although its oral analogue—speech production—has also been somewhat neglected, writing has been even more so. There is, happily, some evidence that this omission is being corrected (see Frederiksen & Dominic, 1981; Gregg & Steinberg, 1980; Kellogg, 1987; Martlew, 1983; Nystrand, 1986).

Writing as a psychological process may be considered to have three stages: prewriting, drafting, and revising.

Prewriting.   The prewriting stage (also called rehearsing, composing, or planning) deals with the generation, organization, and evaluation of ideas before any text is actually put on paper. This is sometimes conceptualized as the "internal dialogue" in the mind of the writer. Prewriting may involve conscious problem-solving procedures with oneself or others (brainstorming, outlining, notetaking). It may be that exercises to improve one's observational and perceptual skills may be useful in prewriting. People's perception of and memory for very common objects that are seen frequently, but may not be directly attended to often (for example, the design and details of a coin), is surprisingly poor (Nickerson & Adams, 1979). A parallel recommendation is developed in detail by Edwards (1979) in regard to learning to draw.

During the prewriting stage it is necessary always to keep in mind the audience for whom one is writing. Just as we talk very differently to different people on different occasions, so we should write differently for a research paper and a personal letter. Not surprisingly, the prewriting stage is often sadly neglected in the teaching of writing. Many times students are expected to begin immediately to produce prose out of nothing on the blank paper in front of them, with those who cannot easily do so being made to feel inadequate.

Drafting. The second stage of the writing process is drafting, or composition. This involves the actual generation of text, usually in prefinal draft form. The ideas generated and organized in the prewriting stage are here clothed in a surface structure of words and sentences. There are great individual differences in specific strategies for producing this prose. Sometimes it may even be produced initially in parallel with prewriting activites. For example, as I (RJH) write this book, I am initially generating ideas while I write the first draft of these sentences into my computer. The crucial point is not so much whether or not one does prewriting and drafting serially or in parallel, but rather that both are done in some satisfactory way.

Revising. The third stage of writing is the revising, or editing, stage. This is where preliminary drafts are read through and revised to be suitable for the final version of the writing. Several aspects of writing must be monitored during this stage (Anderson, 1985). First of all, does it make sense? Are the ideas expressed good ones, containing truth and no contradictions? Is the writing well organized? In revising, one checks for overall coherence, including whether one's organization decided on in the drafting stage is in fact effective. Also, one examines the draft for so-called connective tissue, that is, appropriate transitions between sections, statements of relationships, overview and summary statements, and headings. This aspect of composition is one of the most sorely neglected in college students' writing, and it is something that could be easily remedied, or at least vastly improved, with a more careful editing job.

Finally, the prose is edited and revised for elements of style, grammar, spelling, and usage. Verbose prose is condensed, inappropriate vocabulary is changed, and spelling and punctuation are corrected. Unfortunately, many students progress through our entire educational system thinking that writing is largely this most superficial aspect of the editing stage. Thus, they are often paralyzed from producing ideas because they are not sure how to spell words or use commas. Such matters, while not unimportant, may be best handled at a much later stage than generation of ideas. Thinking you cannot write because you can't spell well is something like assuming you cannot build a house because you don't know how to lay carpet. There's a lot that can be done before the carpet is laid, just as there's much that can be done in writing before the final spelling is checked. Just as carpet-laying could be subcontracted, so can an editor (often in the form of a friend or colleague) check your writing for mechanical and technical correctness. See Box 7–11 for some examples where spelling errors have led to confusion and embarrassment.

BOX 7–11   Consequential Spelling Mistakes

Signs in laundromat: "No dying in these machines"
                          "Please leave your dog's outside"
Sports report: "There were some scoreless rumors about the star forward"
Ad: "9-inch osculating fan with push-button controls"
Headlines: "Council Members to Open Flies to Public"
                "Statewide Heroine Crackdown to Begin"

Types of Writing

Britton and his colleagues (Britton, Burgess, Martin, MacLeod, & Rosen, 1975) have argued that there are three general categories of writing, although they are not mutually exclusive categories. **Transactional** writing is writing to accomplish something; to inform, persuade, or instruct someone. This can be subdivided into two major subtypes of *informative* and *conative*, basically differentiated by whether there is a behavioral change intended or merely a factual addition to the reader's memory.

The second catgory, **expressive** writing, has as its major purpose of expressing the consciousness of the writer. Expressive writing is typically less structured than transactional writing and may be most clearly exemplified by the personal journal where thoughts are written for the purpose of expressing them, with the writer may be never even intending or desiring anyone else to read them.

BOX 7–12   Using Journal Writing to Teach Psychology

One of the authors (RJH) has used journal writing as a means of teaching psychology. In his introductory psychology classes, students are assigned to keep a personal journal with a minimum of one entry per week, to be turned in and responded to, but not graded. Students are encouraged to apply course concepts to their own lives and experience, but are allowed to write anything they want. Either the instructor or the teaching assistant in charge of the student's weekly recitation section reads and responds in the journals, emphasizing affirming, reassuring, and nonjudgmental responses, as well as answering specific content questions asked. Students responded quite favorably to this experience and felt it had not only helped them understand themselves and the course material better, but also allowed them some opportunity for self-expression. Journals of different sorts have also been successfully applied to upper-level psychology classes. The cognitive processing that is required during writing ensures both a deeper processing of class information and more connections of the new information with knowledge already in long-term memory. Both will help improve memory for the class information. See Harris (1982) for further details.

The third type of writing is **poetic,** which is writing for its own sake, or more specifically, for the aethetic quality of the language itself. This could include much poetry, but also song lyrics, puns, quips, and other verbal humor. Clearly, a given piece of writing could be more than one of the three types Britton and his colleagues describe, but the taxonomy is a useful one to highlight the major emphasis. One interesting application of this taxonomy was the finding from content-analysis studies of writing assigned in elementary and secondary schools, that the bulk (80 percent to 95 percent) of school writing was transactional, with very little being expressive or poetic. Writing can be used to teach in all areas of the curriculum at all levels of education. Box 7–12 explores its use in teaching psychology.

Now that we have examined language in some detail, it is time to return to information processing and memory and examine the processes of comprehension.

SUGGESTED READINGS

The best recent texts on psycholinguistics are Carroll (1986) and Tartter (1986). Both give solid comprehensive views of the field from a research perspective and without strong theoretical bias. A few years older but also worthwhile are the texts by Clark and Clark (1977), Foss and Hakes (1978), and Paivio and Begg (1981), although the unique theoretical perspective of each is very strong.

The reader interested in further detail on Chomsky's transformational grammar could turn to Chomsky's original writings, though these are very difficult. Far easier is John Lyons' paperback *Noam Chomsky* (1970), which, the title notwithstanding, is a highly readable explanation of Chomsky's theory, not a biography.

The best comprehensive text of the psychology of reading is Taylor and Taylor (1984). For a briefer review, see Crowder (1982). Gibson and Levin's (1975) text is also still worthwhile. As for the psychology of writing, the papers in the volumes edited by Whiteman (1981), Nystrand (1986), Gregg and Steinberg (1980), and Frederiksen and Dominic (1981) offer the best insight into current thinking on writing.

For an extraordinarily interesting yet comprehensive review of research on bilingualism, see François Grosjean's *Life with Two Languages* (1982).

8

COMPREHENSION

A common way of thinking about comprehension has been to view the mind as some sort of organic tape recorder, ready to make perfect, or nearly perfect, copies of everything it sees and hears. Something is thought to be understood if that perfect copy is made and is considered to have been not understood, or perhaps forgotten, if no such copy exists. *Meaning* is considered to be an inherent property of the stimulus. Just as a word has letters, or an object has color, so does each word or object contain meaning. Thus, meaning has been most often considered a property of the stimulus.

This chapter will take a somewhat different and more dynamic approach to comprehension, considering meaning not as a property of the stimulus, but rather as an emergent property of the interaction of the stimulus and the mind of the comprehender. Meaning only arises as someone constructs an interpretation of some stimulus, and the meaning that one individual constructs will be somewhat different from what every other person comprehends from that same stimulus. Such a perspective may be termed *interactionist*, in that it stresses the dynamic interaction of the active mind of the comprehender and the external stimulus. In this sense it is different both from a behaviorist position, which stresses the environment, and a nativist position, which claims that the mind develops naturally independent of external stimuli.

This chapter first examines the comprehension of connected discourse, drawing on our study of memory in Chapter 6 and language in Chapter 7. We then proceed to look at schema theory, one of the most popular current approaches to comprehension. Next we will examine the theory and applications of inference-drawing in comprehension. Finally, we shall explore one application in detail, that of misleading advertising, as a practical problem where information-processing psychology, especially the themes discussed in this chapter, can make a significant impact.

THE ROLE OF THEME

Previously we examined the four components of language; now it is time to put these components together and examine connected discourse. Normal comprehension involves parallel processing of linguistic information on the phonological, semantic, syntactic, and pragmatic levels. As well as being guided by the data-driven processes of the language itself, comprehension is also simultaneously guided by the conceptually driven processes of forming hypotheses based on our expectations, prior knowledge, and contextual clues predicting what the speaker (or writer) will be saying.

The Construction of Memory Representations

Just as we cannot discuss memory totally apart from comprehension, it is impossible to discuss comprehension too long without considering memory. What we remember from prose is largely determined by how we understood it to begin with.

Many studies reveal that information in several separate but thematically related sentences is integrated into a single memory representation during the comprehension process. Later it is often difficult to remember the exact input sentences in subsequent memory tasks (see Bransford & Franks, 1971). For example, you can hear (1), but remember that you heard (2). The propositional representation in memory would be identical

(1) a. The house was in the valley.
     b. The house was little.
     c. The valley was green.
     d. The house burned down.
(2) The little house in the green valley burned down.

whether one had heard (1) or (2). Most research has indicated that, after the meaning is comprehended, the surface structure and exact words are largely forgotten. There are, however, some cases where verbatim memory can be substantial (Alba & Hasher, 1983; Keenan and others, 1977; Kintsch & Bates, 1977), especially in situations outside the laboratory.

Theme as an Organizing Top-down Force

One of the most important conceptually driven factors in comprehension is the overall **theme** of the material. A comprehender's expectation of what the passage is about can serve as a guiding force in understanding the material.

The overall theme of a passage can markedly affect most every aspect of comprehension. It is very difficult to understand or remember much from prose such as (3) or (4), which may at first appear to have no theme (Bransford & Johnson, 1972; Dooling & Mullet, 1973; Johnson, Doll, Bransford, & Lapinski, 1974).

> (3) The haystack was important because the cloth ripped.
> (4) With hocked gems financing him, our hero bravely defied all scornful laughter that tried to prevent his scheme. "Your eyes deceive," he had said, "an egg, not a table, typifies this unexplored planet." Now three sturdy sisters sought proof, forging along through calm vastness, yet more often over turbulent peaks and valleys. Days become weeks as many doubters spread fearful rumors about the edge. At last from nowhere welcome winged creatures appeared signifying momentous success.
>
> (Dooling & Lachman, 1971, p. 217)

This effect was also demonstrated pictorially with cartoons (Bower, Karlin, & Dueck, 1975; Bransford & McCarrell, 1974). Subjects who knew that (3) was about a parachute jump and (4) about Christopher Columbus discovering America understood the passages much better and remembered more. Supporting information is remembered better if it is relevant to the overall theme (Bransford & Johnson, 1973; Kozminsky, 1977) or to prior world knowledge (Morris, Stein, & Bransford, 1979); new, but thematically consistent, material is often falsely recognized as having been previously presented (Kennedy, 1973; Sulin & Dooling, 1974).

Prior Knowledge and Point of View

The comprehension of something is dependent on one's *prior knowledge* of the general semantic domain which is the topic of the prose. For example, subjects with a high degree of knowledge of baseball remembered more than "low-knowledge" subjects from a summary of a baseball inning. These "high-knowledge" subjects were better able to integrate the new information with a goal structure in their stored knowledge of the game of baseball (Chiesi, Spilich, & Voss, 1979; Spilich, Vesonder, Chiesi, & Voss, 1979). Teachers would do well to remember that some students have trouble comprehending and remembering assigned reading because they have very little knowledge about that topic already in memory and thus have little previous information with which to connect the new material.

The amount of prior knowledge available can also determine how much attention or cognitive capacity must be allocated to the comprehension process (Britton & Tesser, 1982). For example, a particular array of chess pieces requires an expert to allocate more cognitive capacity than a novice to the task of deciding the next move, because of the much greater amount of knowledge possessed by the expert and activated during the comprehension and decision process.

As another example, a speaker of one language will have different knowledge from a speaker of another language and thus will comprehend a slightly, or perhaps substantially, different meaning from even the most careful and precise translation (Carrell, 1983).

Prior knowledge can also come in the form of a *point of view*, which then helps organize information thematically as it is comprehended. As an example, Pichert and Anderson (1977) and Anderson and Pichert (1978) gave subjects a story to read about two boys playing in a house. One group was told to read the story from the point of view of a burglar considering robbing the place; these subjects tended to remember details about valuable objects, isolation from surrounding houses, and other such details of relevance to a potential burglar. The other group of subjects read the story from the point of view of a real estate agent; these subjects remembered details such as size and number of rooms, condition of the house, and quality of the yard.

In discussing voters' reactions to campaign advertising of candidates George McGovern and Richard Nixon in the 1972 American Presidential election, Patterson and McClure (1976) note strikingly different reactions to the same political advertisement, depending on one's political point of view (5).

(5) a. McGovern had his coat off and his tie was hanging down. It was so relaxed, and he seemed to be really concerned with those workers. (McGovern supporter)

b. McGovern is trying hard to look like one of the boys. You know, roll up the shirt sleeves and loosen the tie. It's just too much for me to take. (Nixon supporter)

Depending on the voter's political outlook, a very different meaning of the same ad was constructed by the two voters in response to the same McGovern TV spot.

SCHEMA THEORY

An important recent development in cognitive psychology has been the growth of **schema theory** (Alba & Hasher, 1983; Brewer & Nakamura, 1984; Casson, 1983; Rumelhart, 1980; Thorndyke, 1984). A fundamental assumption of such an approach is that spoken or written text does not in itself carry meaning; rather, it provides directions for listeners or readers on how to use their own stored knowledge to retrieve and construct the meaning (Adams & Collins, 1979). The goal of schema theory is thus to specify the interface between the comprehender and the text. This involves both data-driven and conceptually-driven processes, with knowledge and input interacting at all levels in the process of reading or listening: word and letter level, syntactic, semantic, and interpretive levels. The original notion of a schema dates back to the cognitive psychologist Sir Frederick Bartlett (1932), the physiologist Sir Henry Head (1920), and more indirectly back to the philosopher Immanuel Kant (1781), who argued that concepts only had meaning insofar as they could relate to knowledge the individual already possessed. Schema theory has also been heavily influenced by computer-science work in artificial intelligence (Abelson, 1981; Schank & Abelson, 1977) and has become an important facet of the cognitive-science approach to studying the mind (Stillings and others, 1987).

What Is a Schema?

A *schema* (plural: schemata) is a very subjective and ill-defined concept, but a central one in contemporary cognitive psychology. Somewhat informally, it may be defined as "a unit of organized knowledge about events, situations, or objects" (Moates & Schumacher, 1980, p. 33) or, more technically, "a data structure for representing generic concepts in memory" (Rumelhart, 1980, p. 34). As such, a schema guides both information acceptance and information retrieval; it affects how we process new information and how we retrieve old information from memory. While the very concept of a schema emphasizes top-down processing, it may be activated either in the context of top-down or bottom-up processing. To illustrate, we may activate and retrieve our knowledge schemata about California either in anticipation of meeting a man we know is from San Diego (top-down) or upon hearing someone say "Joe is from San Diego."

Rumelhart (1980), in an excellent theoretical paper on schemata, described them in terms of four metaphors. First, schemata are like *plays*, which are written with characters, actions, settings, and so forth. However, this information is merely a skeleton for the *instantiation* that will occur when that play is actually produced with particular actors by a particular director on a particular set. Each different production of the same play might be strikingly different, even though the playwright's text would ensure some similarity. The same is true for schemata in each instantiation.

Secondly, schemata are like *theories* in that they guide the construction of an interpretation and become the basis for predictions that are tested and then confirmed or rejected.

Thirdly, schemata are like *procedures*, for example, computer programs; that is, an organization of activities with structural relationships among these activities and other entities. This is especially characteristic of the type of schema called a *script* (discussed below). Finally, a schema is like a *parser*; it breaks down, organizes, and interprets incoming data.

Schemata and Encoding

Although there is a lot of variability in the way that the term "schema" is used, Alba and Hasher (1983) suggest that most schema theorists would agree with four basic principles of how schemata become involved in the encoding process: selection, abstraction, interpretation, and integration.

Selection. The principle of *selection* refers to the fact that, of all the information in a given event or message, only some of it will become incorporated into the memory representation that is constructed. Two factors are relevant in determining the selection of information for encoding. One is simply whether or not an appropriate schema already exists in memory. If no relevant schema is available, both comprehension and memory will be very poor (Bransford & Johnson, 1972; Dooling & Mullet, 1973). Further, if some people have more information available than others, such as a rich network of schemata, they will comprehend and remember more than those with less knowledge, as demonstrated in the baseball studies by Voss and his colleagues.

A second reason that the appropriate schema might not be available would be that it may not be activated from long-term memory, even though it may exist there. For example, a particular schema may be activated by external circumstances, as in the Pichert-Anderson studies where subjects were told to read a story from the point of view of either a realtor or a burglar. The phenomenon of encoding specificity may be reinterpreted as ensuring that the same schemata are available at retrieval that occurred at encoding. When the context has set the theme, this allows you to identify some information as more important—highly related to overall theme. Such information will tend to be processed more deeply and remembered better. Information that appears to be irrelevant or easily reconstructible will likely be forgotten. The accuracy of later recall will largely be a function of both how well the initial information was selected and how accurately it was later reconstructed. See Box 8–1 for two examples of how the choice of a schema greatly affects the meaning that one constructs.

There is some controversy in the research literature about whether the schema information must be present at encoding or whether its introduction at retrieval will suffice to direct memory. Generally, effects have been stronger with schematic information presented at encoding, but its presentation at retrieval has sometimes also been helpful (Alba & Hasher, 1983).

Abstraction. The second principle of encoding is *abstraction*, by which details tend to be lost in a reduction of information into main points, with the schema indicating relative importance of different pieces of information. For example, a friend may give you a lengthy account of last Saturday night's date. Later you may remember only that the couple went to see a movie and went out for pizza later. In this process a lot of detail is lost, which is typical of lengthy recall protocols. Still, however, there is some evidence that sometimes specific information is remembered verbatim.

Interpretation. The third principle, *interpretation*, results from the elaboration during or just after encoding. One major characteristic of schemata is that they have slots or variables where specific information is "filled in" when the schema is instantiated, that is, when it is used to accept or retrieve information about a particular instance. For example, we may use our schema about a California lifestyle to infer how Joe, from San Diego, must

BOX 8–1   Illustrations of a Schema's Effect on the Construction of Meaning

I. Conversation between *A* and *B*:

A: I'd agree with that. But experts sometimes forget.

B: I knew two beginners once. They were in a very large place. Open space all around. Their leader signaled them to raise their bows. They were ready to begin . . .

A: Did they follow through with proper timing?

B. Yes, but they kept missing the mark. I'm glad you didn't hear the terrible noises they were making!

A: Holding the bow the correct way takes years to learn.

B: An additional factor is tension.

A: A loose bow is a sure guarantee of failure.

B. Except when it's being stored—I almost ruined one once by forgetting to loosen it up after I was done using it.

A: And it should be drawn back evenly, with uniform motion.

B. That's not too hard if your bow is well-balanced and not warped. Otherwise there's not much that can be done.

Dubitsky (1980)

II. To start with, here is a set of guidelines:

1. Wait for a sunny day. Depending on where you live, you may want to carry out the procedures all year, although many people start in the spring.

2. Check the oil. Failure to monitor the amount of oil can create serious problems.

3. Do not take more than recommended limits. If you take too much, it's possible everything will become discolored. Color changes can be embarrassing, particularly if you worked hard to make everything look right.

4. One major concern will be bare patches. Sometimes, you'll fail to notice all of them at first. Then, as you proceed, you'll become painfully aware of uncovered sections. They will require special care. And you'll need a good supply of water, although if it starts to rain, you will want to stop immediately.

5. By autumn—again, depending on where you live—you may be tired of the ritual, and happy the season is ended. But generally, after a cold winter, you'll probably be pleased to start again.

(Wittig & Williams, 1984, p. 219)

Depending on which schema is activated and used to process the information, the conversation between *A* and *B* may be seen to be about either archery or playing a stringed instrument. Similarly, the "guidelines" may be either for mowing the grass or suntanning. Depending on which schema is used, the meaning for each individual sentence is entirely different.

spend his time. When we make such inferences, we often are necessarily interpreting beyond the information given. The issue of inference-drawing will be discussed in more detail later in this chapter.

Integration.   The fourth principle of encoding through schemata is *integration*, by which information is combined into relatively holistic representations. Inferences are drawn to relate previously unrelated information. Even the schemata themselves may be integrated, embedded within each other, thus allowing for a hierarchical structure of schematic information. For example, while we have a schema for "face," that it contains two eyes, a nose, and a mouth, we also have subschemata for eyes, noses, and mouths, all subsumed under the most global schema "face." While integration is a principle that operates in everyone, there is some evidence that older people integrate information to an even greater degree than younger adults (Woodruff, 1983). This could be reflected in the fact that more senior professors frequently write theoretical, integrative, professional writing, whereas their younger colleagues frequently are more active in carrying out specific experiments.

Modification of schemata by experience.   Beyond influencing the comprehension and encoding of new information, existing schemata are themselves modified by new experience. This may occur in three different ways: accretion, tuning, and restructuring (Vosniadou & Brewer, 1987). **Accretion** occurs as new information is added to existing schemata without fundamentally changing that knowledge structure (for example, adding information to your "dog schema" that dogs bark). **Tuning** involves changes such as generalizing or reducing the applicability of a schema or altering its default values or minor structural features to better fit the knowledge base it describes (for instance, fine-tune your "dog schema" to include atypical dogs like chihuahuas but exclude doglike creatures like wolves). **Restructuring,** the most radical form of knowledge acquisition involving preexisting frameworks, alters and replaces old schemata with new ones (for example, a young child forming a "dog schema" to encompass previously unrelated instances of the family pet and other canines seen elsewhere and on TV).

The range of schemata.   Clearly, the notion of schema is a very general one, and schemata may be of a great variety. They may be general packets of knowledge about a particular subject area, such as what faces are like, what information is relevant to a realtor, or what the game of baseball is like. It may be a very specific schema, such as what a capital *A* looks like, or very general schemata, such as various literary genres; for instance, what to expect from a mystery story, Western, or television soap opera.

Information may be organized around a motivational schema, that is, a perceived overriding purpose or goal of a character (Owens, Bower, & Black, 1979). It may even be information about oneself, perhaps akin to the traditional personality concept of self (Rogers, 1981; Greenwald, 1981; Markus, 1980); see Box 8–2 for further discussion of this aspect. Finally, a schema may be information about particular actions or classes

---

BOX 8–2   Some Implications of Your Self Schema

Perhaps the richest and most complex schema in our memory is our knowledge and memory about ourselves. That schema is referred to as the personal schema or self-schema. It contains all of the information about ourselves, including our values, our motivations, and those things that have happened to us that we consider personal events.

We have noted that schemata guide and direct both the encoding and retrieval of information from our memory. Our self schema, then, has some very important implications for how we interpret what happens to us and for what we remember about our lives. To give just one example, our self schema is much more rich and complex than our schema for anyone else. As a schema becomes more rich and complex, it should be easier to encode and retrieve information. Thus, we should remember events that we view as "our events" better than events that we view as "someone else's events"— even when those events are of equal importance to us. Thompson (1985a) showed that is exactly what happens. He had some students (recorders) record events (that were public and not embarrassing) for themselves and events for their roommates for a three-week period. The roommates didn't know these events were being recorded. One month after the recording period, both the recorders and the roommates were tested for their memory of the events. In spite of the fact that the recorders selected the events, wrote the description of the events, and knew they were going to be tested for their memory of those events, the roommates remembered the events recorded for them better than the recorders did, impressive testimony to the effectiveness of the self schema in facilitating memory.

---

of actions. It is on this type of action schema, called a script, that we next focus our attention.

Scripts

Schemata about activities or processes are called **scripts.** They have all the properties of schemata already discussed, but are specifically concerned with actions (Abelson, 1981; Bower, Black, & Turner, 1979; Mandler & Murphy, 1983; Pohl, Colonius, & Thuring, 1985; Schank & Abelson, 1977). We have many scripts in our long-term memory for a variety of familiar activities, which may be looked at as complex "action-concepts." A good example is Bower, Black, & Turner's (1979) restaurant script, which contains information about what it's like to go to a restaurant. (see Table 8–1). For example, there are certain roles to be filled (customer, waiter or waitress, cashier), certain "props" (silverware, food, dishes, check, napkins), and certain activities (sitting down, ordering, eating, paying the bill). Not every specific use—instantiation—of this script would provide specific information to fill in all these variables. Still, we would infer that there were dishes, a waiter or waitress, that the customer paid the bill,

TABLE 8–1   Theoretical Restaurant Script[a]

ROLES:	Customer		Cashier
	Waiter/Waitress		Host/Hostess
PROPS:	Table	Check	Plates
	Menu	Money	Silverware
	Food	Tip	Napkins
ENTRY CONDITIONS:	Customer has money		
	Customer hungry		
	Restaurant is open		
RESULTS:	Restaurant has more money		
	Customer has less money		
	Customer is not hungry		

SCENE 1:	Entering
	Customer enters restaurant
	Customer (or Host/Hostess) decides on table
	Customer goes to table
	Customer sits down
SCENE 2:	Ordering
	Customer receives menu
	Customer looks at menu
	Customer orders food
SCENE 3:	Eating
	Waiter/Waitress brings food to customer
	Customer eats food
SCENE 4:	Exiting
	Waiter/Waitress gives check to customer
	Customer pays cashier
	Customer leaves tip
	Customer leaves restaurant

[a] This is a general script. Each scene could be made more specific. This is a script for a general-service, family-type North American restaurant. Script would vary somewhat for fast-food restaurant, nightclub, bar, or for restaurants in other cultures (see Box 8–3).
Source: Adapted from G. H. Bower, J. B. Black, and T. J. Turner. Scripts in memory for text. *Cognitive Psychology*, 1979, *11*, 177–220. Reprinted by permission of Academic Press and the author.

and so forth, even though we may not have been told specifically that these activities occurred.

The way a script operates can perhaps best be illustrated by examining what happens when the stimulus/input information does not fit the apparently appropriate script very well. One especially interesting example of how a script is applied, especially when the incoming data do not precisely "fit," comes from Bransford (1978, p. 184). Assuming that you have a script for eating in a restaurant that is roughly similar to the one most Americans have, how might you process the following story you read or hear someone tell you?

Jim went to the restaurant and asked to be seated in the gallery. He was told that there would be a one-hour wait. Forty minutes later, the applause for his song indicated that he could proceed with the preparation. Twenty guests had ordered his favorite, a cheese soufflé. Jim enjoyed the customers in the main dining area. After two hours, he ordered the specialty of the house—roast pheasant under glass. It was incredible to enjoy such exquisite cuisine and yet still have fifteen dollars. He would surely come back soon.

While all the words make sense in this story, for most people there is a problem. It does not fit the restaurant script that we most naturally retrieve and try to use to process the story. Specifically, it violates information about roles; the customer appears to be entertaining and cooking as well as eating, roles that are generally separate in this script.

Suppose, however, that a new type of restaurant opens, thus introducing a new restaurant "subscript" into your memory, specifically the following (Bransford, 1978, pp. 186–187):

> Assume that Jim went to a very special type of restaurant. The owner allows people who can cook at least one special meal to compete for the honor of preparing their specialty for other customers who desire it. Those who wish to compete sit in the gallery rather than the main dining room (although a central stage is accessible to both). The competition centers on the competitor's entertaining the crowd, by singing, for example, or dancing or playing an instrument. The approval of the crowd is a prerequisite for allowing the person to announce his or her cooking specialty. The rest of the crowd then has the option of ordering it, and the person receives a certain amount of money for each meal prepared. After doing the cooking and serving the meal to the customers, the person can then order from the regular restaurant menu and pay for it out of the money received for cooking. In general, this arrangement benefits the manager as well as the person. The manager obtains relatively inexpensive entertainment, and the person is usually able to make more than enough to pay for an excellent meal.

Now go back and reread the original story; with this new script it may make more sense!

Schemata and scripts are useful concepts beyond the confines of traditional cognitive psychology. To illustrate, social schemata can be very important in processing information about people in social situations (Fiske & Taylor, 1984; Taylor & Crocker, 1981), sex-role stereotyping (Bem, 1981; Markus, Crane, Bernstein, & Saladi, 1982; Payne, Connor, & Colletti, 1987), or responses to mass media (Harris, 1989; Janis, 1980). They also may help shed light on certain kinds of misunderstandings due to cultural differences (Casson, 1983; Harris, Hensley, Lee, & Schoen, 1988; Harris, Schoen, & Hensley, in press). See Boxes 8–3 and 8–4 for further discussion of this latter issue.

The Narrative Schema

One especially important and generalizable example of a schema in Western culture is the **narrative** (story) **schema** identified by Kintsch (1977). The basic unit of the narrative schema is the *episode*, which consists of

---

BOX 8–3   Cultural Knowledge as Scripts

People frequently speak of having to "learn the culture" when they move to another country, or perhaps even a different part of their own country. This knowledge may be conceptualized as scripts about activities in that culture and how to do them. Many times the scripts will be similar to ones we already have from our own culture, but with a few differences in roles, activities, or conditions. Before proceeding further, read the following paragraph:

> Nelson and Sonia sat down at a table on the sidewalk. They were both starving, since it was already almost eleven o'clock. After looking at the menu full of delicious choices, they decided on the lasagna, which they knew to be excellent at that restaurant. It seemed to be an unusually large crowd for such a late hour. Sonia commented that she thought the outside of the building had been repainted since their last meal there some months before. After the waiter had brought the plates, Nelson saw their friends Marcia and Rita a few tables away. He immediately went over and gave the two women a friendly kiss. They had not seen each other for several weeks. As they saw the waiter on his way with their food, Nelson and Sonia returned to their table, just in time to help themselves to some lasagna from the platter. Tasting it, Nelson added some more olive oil and then pronounced it delicious. Sonia thought it had a little too much ham, but she also enjoyed it. The lasagna had been a good choice. Some ragged children came to their table selling roses, but they told them no and turned away. Finally, the waiter chased them away altogether. What a delicious meal, and for a very reasonable cost too. The conversation was also very pleasant. Upon paying the check, Nelson had to break a large bill, but the restaurant changed it easily, and the waiter brought the change to the table. Nelson and Sonia left the restaurant satisfied and happy. They would have to do this more often.

If you live in the United States or Canada, you probably noticed a few details as being strange in this story. However, if you lived in Brazil, it would fit your script of what a restaurant is like. When I (RJH) lived and taught in Brazil and regularly ate at restaurants, I had to learn variations on the restaurant script, such as the fact that you must ask for the check before it is brought, food is always brought on serving dishes to be served by the customers onto individual plates, and that you always pay the waiter and never the cashier. Certain activities, like poor children wandering from table to table selling roses or peanuts, occur frequently in Brazil, but would be very unlikely to occur in North America. Such knowledge of "learning the culture" that an immigrant or long-term visitor must acquire as part of becoming "at home" in the new culture may be characterized as scripts or schemata (Harris, Schoen, & Lee, 1986).

BOX 8–4   The Kyeah Schema (Ahn, Mooney, Brewer, & DeJong, 1987)

New schemata may be learned through exposure to an example (instantiation) or by learning the abstract description of the schema. Some cultures (Korea, India) have a script for a cooperative buying activity called (in Korea) a *kyeah*. American subjects of Ahn and colleagues were exposed either to an Example or an Abstract description of what was presumably a new script for them. The Example version was as follows:

> Tom, Sue, Jane, and Joe were all friends and each wanted to make a large purchase as soon as possible. Tom wanted a VCR, Sue wanted a microwave, Joe wanted a car stereo, and Jane wanted a compact disk player. However, after paying their expenses, they each only had $60 left at the end of every third month. Tom, Sue, Jane, and Joe all got together to solve the problem. They made four slips of paper with the numbers 1, 2, 3, and 4 written on them. They put them in a hat and each drew out one slip. Jane got the slip with the 4 written on it, and said, "Oh darn, I have to wait to get my CD player." Joe got the slip with the 1 written on it and said, "Great, I can get my car stereo right away!" Sue got the number 2, and Tom got number 3. In February, they each contributed the $60 they had left. Joe took the whole $240 and bought a Pioneer car stereo at K's Merchandise. In May, they each contributed their money again. This time, Sue used the $240 to buy a Sharp 600-watt, 1.5 cubic foot microwave at K-mart. In August, all four again contributed $60. Tom took the money and bought a Sanyo Beta VCR with wired remote at Service Merchandise. In November, Jane got the money and bought a Technics CD player at Apple Tree Stereo.

The Abstract version was the following:

> Suppose there are a number of people (let the number be n) each of whom wants to make a large purchase but does not have enough cash on hand. They can cooperate to solve this problem by each donating an equal small amount of money to a common fund on a regular basis. (Let the amount donated by each member be m.) They meet at regular intervals to collect everyone's money. Each time money is collected, one member of the group is given all the money collected ($n \times m$) and then with that money he or she can purchase what he or she wants. In order to be fair, the order in which people are given the money is determined randomly. The first person in the random ordering is therefore able to purchase their desired item immediately instead of having to wait until they save the needed amount of money. Although the last person does not get to buy their item early, this individual is no worse off than they would have been if they waited until they saved the money by themselves. (Ahn, Mooney, Brewer, & DeJong, 1987, pp. 51–52)

In several studies measuring subjects' learning of the schema from a single instance (Example group), college students showed that they had in fact learned the script on the basis of being exposed to just one story.

three parts, the *exposition*, *complication*, and *resolution*. The exposition introduces the characters and setting. The complication occurs when those characters encounter some problem that presents a barrier that must be overcome. Finally, the resolution is the process of overcoming the complication and wrapping up the story.

One major difference between children's and adults' stories is that children's stories more clearly identify the parts of the narrative schema and follow it more closely, whereas adult stories, while still following the same schema, may require the reader to use more inference processes to make use of the schema. For example, fairy tales may start out, "Once upon a time there was . . . ," a very blatant signal that expository material is to follow. In contrast, an adult story might actually begin talking about the problem (complication) and only gradually complete the exposition later. Whereas an adult can make the appropriate inferences to instantiate the schema, the child will have trouble doing so and thus will not fully comprehend (and probably will quickly lose interest in) the story. On the other hand, a children's story will be uninteresting and unchallenging to an adult, because relatively little cognitive effort is required in comprehension; the surface form of the story fits the narrative schema so perfectly that it becomes too predictable. Beyond literature, the narrative schema has many applications in other domains of our experience; watching television, for example (see Box 8–5).

Episodes may have different sorts of structure beyond a simple exposition-complication-resolution format. For example, the complication of a story may contain an entire episode embedded within the larger episode, much as a subordinate clause might be embedded as the subject of a sentence (*What I want to do is to leave*). Another example might be the resolution containing two additional episodes embedded as the last part of the larger episode. In this way the narrative schema offers a sort of syntax for discourse, offering a structural analysis for connected prose, not unlike syntactic analyses of sentences discussed in the last chapter.

Conclusion: What to Call Knowledge Representations

One of the most active areas of current research in cognitive psychology is the development and examination of different types of knowledge structures. This focus on the representation issue has produced an often confusing wealth of terms for these abstract knowledge structures. In an insightful paper designed to sort out and systematize the different terms and distinctions among them, Brewer (1987) suggests two distinctions of primary importance. First is the difference between underlying knowledge structures and the episodic representations formed from these structures during comprehension. Second is a similar distinction, whether the representations are derived from old generic knowledge or constructed at the time of use. This issue reflects back to the issue of taxonomies of memory discussed in Chapter 6.

BOX 8–5   The Narrative Schema on Television

The narrative schema occurs in modern Western society in many manifestations, one of which is in television and other mass entertainment media. Obviously, many television dramas are built around the narrative schema; first there is an introduction of the characters and situation (some of this may be assumed in cases of a series where viewers may be very familiar with the characters already); this is followed by some complication or problem, finally culminating with a resolution of that problem. This is the basic pattern of television dramas and situation comedies, as well as children's stories, fables, and so forth. Sometimes a narrative schema may be intentionally incomplete in order to draw us back to the program. An example would be when a soap opera concludes at the end of the complication, the viewer must tune in the next day to discover the resolution. Our tendency to use the narrative schema is so strong that we are drawn back the next day to complete instantiating the schema.

Beyond television fiction, the narrative schema also applies to a sizeable number of broadcast commercials, as well as print advertising. Frequently the format of ads is one of "problem solving," that is, there is an exposition (Mary is about to do her wash), followed by a complication (her children's clothes are too stained for her detergent to clean), and a resolution (spray on some Scream Spot Remover to get out those tough stains). Such ads have basically the same format as a story where there is a villain who is overcome by a hero, except in this case the villain is usually dirt, stains, inferior taste, or excessive work, and the hero is almost always the product being sold. An advertiser can more easily communicate the message about the product by drawing on this readily available story structure, the narrative schema.

INFERENCE-DRAWING IN COMPREHENSION

Basic Processes

One function of a schema is to guide the **drawing of inferences** from the passage. It is a natural process to draw inferences beyond the material actually presented (Clark, 1977; Harris, 1981; Harris & Monaco, 1978; Rickheit & Strohner, 1985; Singer, 1984). Exactly what inferences will be drawn by a given individual is in part a function of what schemata are initially activated during comprehension. If the reader activates schemata about robberies in response to hearing Pichert and Anderson's story described earlier, very different inferences will be drawn than if the schemata about selling homes are activated. This inferred material has been totally integrated in the constructed memory representations with the information stated directly (Brewer, 1977; Graesser & Clark, 1985; Harris, 1974; Harris & Monaco, 1978; Johnson, Bransford, & Solomon, 1973; Loftus & Palmer, 1974; Marschark & Paivio, 1977; Masson, 1979; Spiro, 1980).

The inferences drawn during comprehension fulfill two general functions (Warren, Nicholas, & Trabasso, 1979). On the one hand, they make connections within the new material and between this new information and knowledge already in memory. This allows for the integration of new material in memory representations of previously learned information and also helps to provide some organization and structure to the information. Secondly, inferences fill in empty "slots" in the overall structure. To illustrate, if a strongly implied instrument of some action is not explicitly mentioned (*Ed hit the nail*), it may be inferred and added to the memory representation (*Ed used a hammer*), just as if it had appeared explicitly (Corbett & Dosher, 1978; Johnson, Bransford, & Solomon, 1973; McKoon & Ratliff, 1981; Singer, 1979, 1981). Although a natural and integral part of the comprehension process, inferences may be drawn even more frequently in response to inadequately developed prose in an attempt to fill the many open slots to make an otherwise elliptical passage comprehensible (Glenn, 1978). The study of inferences drawn in comprehension has been a major recent emphasis in cognitive psychology.

If there is no value for a given variable in the particular instance at hand, then a *default* inference is used to fill in the most typical value which is contained in the stored schema. For example, if we hear "the hungry python caught the mouse," we use our knowledge of pythons and hunger to make the default inference that the snake subsequently consumed the mouse. Such information was not stated in the stimulus input; rather, it was filled in by using a default inference and inferring that, with no evidence to the contrary, the catching was followed by eating. If we had heard "the hungry little girl caught the mouse," a different schema would have been activated. This "small-child" schema would not contain the default inference that, no information to the contrary, little children who catch mice subsequently eat them. Though default inferences are clearly a part of the information-accepting function of schemata, the comprehended information is then stored in memory and remembered as interpreted, which may be inaccurate. For example, in the "python" example above, if a person were subsequently questioned about the fate of the mouse, he or she would probably remember and respond that the mouse had been eaten. In this sense, memory is a by-product of the interpretation during the comprehension process, as it is the residue left after the schemata have done their job of interpreting the new information or reconstructing old information during an attempt to remember.

In some sense, knowledge that we have in any situation is always incomplete and must be "filled in" using inferences (Harris & Monaco, 1978; Harris, 1981). As Collins, Warnock, Aiello, and Miller (1975, p. 414; see also Gentner & Collins, 1981) have said, "People can often extract what they do not know explicitly from some forms of implicit knowledge by plausible, but uncertain inferences." Even very incomplete (or total lack of) knowledge about something can be the basis for an inference, as in answering a question like *Is Malawi a major oil-exporting country?*

Upon finding information (or lack thereof) about Malawi in one's memory, one may find no information about oil. Thus, one may infer that, since there was nothing about that in memory, then probably Malawi is not a major oil-exporting country, since that information would probably be in one's memory if it were true.

For an excellent conceptual article about the role of inferences in comprehension, see Rickheit, Schnotz, & Strohner (1985).

Inferences in Social Cognition

Such inference processes operate more broadly than just in language comprehension settings. For example, we process social information by observing social behaviors and then drawing inferences about those behaviors (Hastie, 1983).

One of the most common types of such social inferences made is that of inferring a causal relationship of events. Owens and colleagues (1979) conducted a causal attribution study about how the inference of a motive for behavior can guide the inferences drawn from a person's actions. Subjects read a story about Jack or Nancy (same story except for names) doing a series of routine actions such as fixing a meal, attending a class, visiting a doctor. Some subjects (the "context subjects") received initial information describing a context that provided a motive for later behavior (Nancy just discovering she was pregnant). On a free-recall task 30 minutes later, the context subjects recalled more episodes and in better order than subjects not receiving the context. They also made more intrusions representing distortions to fit the inferred motive schema (remembering "usual medical procedures" as "pregnancy tests"). Owens and others (1979) concluded that the knowledge of a motive helps integrate episodes into a coherent whole in comprehension.

This tendency to infer causes of observed events is the reason that we so frequently interpret correlated events as causally related. You may remember back to your introductory psychology class where you learned about correlational relationships. At that time you were warned not to assume correlated events are causally related. While it may be obvious that the number of deaths in Bangladesh is not causally related to the consumption of ice cream in Chicago (both are *correlated*, presumably due to seasonal weather patterns in the Northern Hemisphere), it may be more difficult to realize that someone's death after taking an experimental drug may not necessarily be due to the drug.

Many cognitively oriented social psychologists are studying impression formation using memory measures and focusing on cognitive inference processes (Cantor & Mischel, 1977; Hamilton, Katz, & Leirer, 1980; Hastie, 1983; Hastie & Kumar, 1979; Lingle, Geva, Ostrom, Leippe, & Baumgardner, 1979; Rothbart, Evans, & Fulero, 1979; Rothbart, Fulero, Jensen, Howard, & Birrell, 1978; Snyder & Uranowitz, 1978; Woll, Weeks, Fraps, Pendergrass, & Vanderplas, 1980; Woll & Yopp, 1978). The focus of these studies is on how information is combined to form an impression of a person. Though a social process, it is one of information processing as well.

One area where impression formation takes on considerable practical significance is the case where jurors form impressions of witnesses in a courtroom trial. O'Barr (1982; see also Conley, O'Barr, & Lind, 1978; and Erickson, Lind, Johnson, & O'Barr, 1978) has shown that the speech style of a witness may imply much about his or her character, and this, in turn, affects what is encoded into a juror's memory, which later influences a verdict decision. If the speech style implies a relatively "powerless" position, jurors comprehend the witness' message differently than if that witness is inferred to be "powerful," even if the content of the testimony is the same. Similarly, one's accent and its perceived status can influence the outcome of a medical diagnosis (Fielding & Evered, 1980).

Social psychological studies of stereotyping have been reconceptualized in term of schema theory (Hamilton, 1979, 1981). A stereotype that one holds of a certain group will affect how we process information about someone we are told belongs to that group. The cognitive processes that support behavior of prejudice may be looked at in terms of a schema about a group of persons affecting one's information processing at the various levels described earlier.

This may have substantial consequences. One area of great concern recently has been the crime of rape. Traditionally, certain myths have been associated with rape and its victims (for example, "She must have been 'asking for it' "; attractive and provocatively dressed women are more likely to be raped; rape is a crime of unfulfilled sexual desires). These myths may be seen as schemata. Thus, for example, if we hear that someone has been raped, we tend to process and remember selectively, and even distort, information to be consistent with the rape myths (schemata) that we hold (Esper, 1986). Understanding the cognitive processes that contribute to the formation and maintenance of such inaccurate and inappropriate information may be an important first step toward changing people's attitudes about rape and its victims.

In another interesting piece of research, Arkes and Harkness (1980) demonstrated the use of inference in diagnostic procedures. Speech pathology students were given 12 symptoms, eight of which were related to Down's syndrome. After the first four related symptoms were presented, subjects were asked to diagnose the hypothetical patient. In a memory test 12 days later, subjects who had diagnosed the case as Down's syndrome were less able to correctly reject new symptoms related to Down's syndrome than were subjects not making that diagnosis. In other words, the diagnosis had acted as a schema for organizing information and directing inference-drawing during comprehension and for directing reconstruction during retrieval.

For an interesting application of schema theory to the industrial psychology problem of performance appraisal, see Box 8–6.

Thus, inference processes are general cognitive processes that operate naturally in the comprehension of written and spoken language, social interactions, and any situation where information processing occurs. Comprehension involves constructing meanings through the interaction of stimulus information and stored memory representations (knowledge). During these interaction processes, inferences are drawn.

Sometimes what we read does not tie in well to our natural inference-

---
BOX 8–6   Schemas in the Workplace:
Performance Appraisal

Joan Smith has been recently hired as a sales representative for the Acme Brush Company. Often throughout the day Joan sits back at her desk and stares into space for a few minutes and then continues with her normal duties. Her sales during the first month have been typical for a beginning sales rep. At the end of her first month Joan receives the Acme First Month Checkup from each of her supervisors. The checkup is an evaluation based on total sales, as well as general observations of the employee by the supervisor. One supervisor rates Joan's performance as excellent and indicates that she does a good job of planning her time throughout the day. Another supervisor rates Joan's performance as average and indicates that she needs to stop wasting so much time throughout the day.

Why the difference? Each of the supervisors has observed Joan sitting quietly for a few minutes and staring off into space, but they have interpreted this behavior very differently. This simple example illustrates the important role that schemata play in performance evaluation on the job. The first supervisor has a schema for Joan that indicates she is a good worker and therefore the staring into space is interpreted as "planning time." The second supervisor has a "poor worker" schema for Joan and therefore interprets the staring as wasting time.

Schemata play an important role in guiding what behaviors will be encoded by a rater, how the behaviors will be interpreted, and what behaviors will later be recalled by the rater when doing the evaluation. In recent years the field of industrial/organizational psychology has recognized the importance of schemata in the performance-appraisal process. Several models based on cognitive principles have been proposed (J. Cooper, 1981; Feldman, 1981; Ilgen & Feldman, 1983; DeNisi, Cafferty, & Meglino, 1984). DeNisi and others (1984) devised such a cognitive model that recognizes the particularly important role that schemata play in directing a rater's attention and guiding interpretations of employee behavior. (This box by Kirk L. Rogg)

drawing processes; thus, we perceive that text to be difficult or poorly written. Box 8–7 discusses the case of so-called legalese and what really makes it so difficult psychologically. Issues of language comprehensibility have some far-reaching legal and policy-making effects, as explored in Box 8–8. See Charrow (1982) for further discussion of these issues.

Miscomprehension of Advertising

One area where natural inference-drawing processes of language comprehension can lead us to cognitive and even economic difficulty is the realm of advertising, especially ads that may be misleading or deceptive. It is to this problem that we now turn. Each of us sees on the average over 22,000 television commercials per year; we also see and hear many

BOX 8–7   The Miscomprehension of Legal Language

In 1977, U.S. President Jimmy Carter signed an executive order directing federal government agencies to simplify the language used in official documents. Since that time there has been increasing legislation directing insurance companies, government bureaus, and lawyers to write documents in language that everyone can understand.

The issue is basically one of information processing, that is, how people comprehend or fail to comprehend this information in such legal writing. If people are not understanding it, how could that document be written to better communicate its message?

Before examining what is wrong with legal language, it is helpful to look at its purpose. The overriding priority of legal language is conveying information, which is a higher value than aesthetic quality, brevity, or anything else. The language must be explicit, both technically and legally precise, leaving minimal room for the reader to draw inferences other than those clearly intended by the writer. In this sense it is markedly different from artistic writing such as literature, poetry, or even humor, where the reader's imagination is heavily drawn upon. Although the defense of legal language is often made in a defensive manner itself, there is a valid point to the argument. If the information priority is sacrificed, any additional clarity or aesthetic pleasingness is worthless.

Georgetown University linguist Roger Shuy has studied the language of insurance policies to find out exactly what it is that makes such language difficult to comprehend (Shuy, 1981; Shuy & Larkin, 1978).

Shuy makes several recommendations for making legal language more comprehensible. The first is the most general and the most important: Make better use of the natural strategies and expectations that we all bring to the language-comprehension process. To illustrate, we are used to having given information signaled with the definite article "the"; if a contract replaces "the" with "such," this makes the given-new strategy harder to apply.

Much of the insurance contract language examined by Shuy was extremely repetitive, so much so that it was unnatural and thus did not make maximum use of our natural language-comprehension strategies. For example, legal language uses fewer pronouns relative to nouns than does ordinary language. While presumably this is done in order to reduce any possible ambiguity of figuring out who the pronouns refer to, it violates natural conversational rules and thus leads the reader to wonder why these are being violated.

Other types of constructions overused by legal language are passive verbs and the use of nominalized constructions instead of verbs. For example, contracts often use words like "as of the date of signing by the owner" instead of "when the owner signs it" or "at the time of receipt at the home office" instead of "at the time the home office receives it." The more natural way to say such ideas is often the active voice with an active verb. If such constructions can be employed with no accompanying loss in clarity, then it is desirable to do so.

BOX 8–8   The Importance of Readability

Educators have developed readability scales that are used to measure the reading level (difficulty) of textbooks and other prose (see Kintsch & Vipond, 1979). Blumenfeld, Blumenfeld, and Terrell (1978) applied one of these readability scales to the U.S. federal documents explaining the Medicare program to senior citizens, whose average reading level was slightly less than the average high school sophomore. They found that the documents, which are the simplest in a series, required the equivalent of a college sophomore reading level, the same required to understand the King James Version of the Bible!

In the 1970s a landmark case (*Rogers et al.* vs. *U.S. Steel*) entered the courts. This was a class action suit filed on behalf of 600 black steelworkers of a Homestead, Pennsylvania, steel mill alleging discrimination in hiring. The crucial issue was the wording of a waiver from further compensation; the plaintiffs had signed this waiver as a condition to receiving an earlier settlement from the company. Some critical testimony came from linguists and educators who claimed that the readability level of the waiver document was considerably above the level of the plaintiffs. The issue is important because if someone is legally bound to ensure the readability of his or her document for whoever needs to sign it, this forces a new attention to readability.

---

more print and radio ads. The language of advertising raises some interesting information-processing issues (Geis, 1982; Harris, Sturm, Klassen, & Bechtold, 1986; Vestergaard & Schroder, 1985).

One of these is the question of what constitutes deceptive or misleading advertising. The Federal Trade Commission (FTC), the agency of the federal government charged with overseeing advertising practice, defines "false advertising" in its statutes as advertising that is "misleading in a material respect." While this is not a very complete definition, it does contain one interesting and important feature. "In a material respect" means, roughly, in any way which makes a difference. Thus, the door is left open for defining inappropriate advertising by the *effect* it has on the consumer, rather than by the *intent* of the advertiser.

In further exploring these definitional questions, Preston and Richards (1986) made a helpful distinction between **miscomprehension** and **deceptiveness.** Miscomprehension occurs when the meaning conveyed to the hearer is different from the literal content of the message. Deceptiveness, on the other hand, occurs if the conveyed meaning is inconsistent with the facts about the product, regardless of what the ad stated. From an information-processing perspective, the question is much more complex than merely determining the truth or falsity of the ad itself.

If both the literal and conveyed message are true, then there is neither miscomprehension nor deceptiveness. If the literal message is false and is conveyed the same way, there is deceptiveness but no miscomprehension. That is, the hearer constructed a meaning not consistent with reality, but not because he or she misunderstood the ad. For example, if an ad states an incorrect price for a product and we believe it, we have been deceived but have not miscomprehended the ad.

It is also possible to miscomprehend without being deceived. An ad may state a claim that is literally false, but we comprehend it in some nonliteral way that is consistent with reality. For example, the claim that "our cookies are made by elves" is unlikely to be comprehended literally; thus a "miscomprehension" will lead to *not* being deceived. This type of claim is fairly common, for example, in animated television commercials ("a white tornado in every can"). Another type of false nondeceptive ad would be some of the so-called mockups—photographic displays for print or television ads. Because of practicalities of studio photography, certain conventions are often used in some ads (see Box 8–9).

Content in an ad may be either *factual* or *evaluative* (Holbrook, 1978; T.A. Shimp, 1979, 1983). Factual content is tangible, objective, and easily verifiable or falsifiable, often dealing with physical attributes of the product or quantitative dimensions like price. Evaluative content, on the other hand, is much more ambiguous since it involves subjective statements and judgments, claims of nonverifiable psychological benefits, and generally evaluative statements about how wonderful the product is. That latter type of statement is called "puffery" and has been roundly attacked by Ivan Preston (1975, 1977; Rotfeld & Preston, 1981) as being misleading, in spite of being difficult to prove unequivocally false. Puffery and similar types of claims are frequent in the fourth category of ad—the true misleading (deceptive) message.

BOX 8–9 Advertising Mock-ups: False—Yes, Deceptive—Maybe

That cool and sweet ice cream on television might really be mashed potatoes (because ice cream melts too fast under hot studio lights), or that foaming head on that nice cold beer in the magazine might in fact be shampoo (because suds last longer for photographers than do beer heads). Sometimes such acceptable conventions may border on the deceptive. For example, there was a case several years ago where a soup company was censured for putting marbles in the bottom of the soup bowl during photography (Preston, 1975). Although the company argued that this was necessary to buoy up the solid ingredients and keep them all from sinking unseen to the bottom of the bowl while the photographers readied their cameras and lights, the courts ruled that this constituted a misleading implication that the soup contained more solid ingredients than it in fact did. In another famous case, a shaving cream manufacturer used grains of sand on Plexiglas for a mock-up purporting to be a razor shaving sandpaper with its product. While the razor in fact would shave fine sandpaper, fine sandpaper looks like flat paper when photographed. However, if coarse sandpaper was used, the razor wouldn't shave it; hence, the sand grains on Plexiglas solution. Do you consider such a mock-up deceptive?

True-But-Deceptive Ads

The type of advertising claim that is potentially the most damaging is the statement that is literally true but miscomprehended, thus deceiving consumers by inducing them to construct a meaning of the ad that is inconsistent with reality. Such statements may be evaluative or factual statements that imply something beyond themselves. There are several types of language constructions that, though true themselves, may imply something else that is not true. (Harris, Dubitsky, & Bruno, 1983; Schrank, 1977)

First are claims that contain a *hedge* word or phrase that seriously weakens the force of a claim; see examples (6) through (10).

(6) Lavium Pills *may help* relieve tension (then again, they may not).

(7) Spring Fluoride *fights* cavities (but it may fight and lose).

(8) This detergent leaves dishes *virtually* spotless (whatever "virtually" means).

(9) The shampoo *helps control* dandruff *symptoms with regular use.* (What is regular use? Does controlling the symptoms mean controlling the condition? Is helping to control sufficient to control?)

(10) *Nobody can promise you a good return on* your investment, but try us and someday you too *may* be a millionaire (or you may not, and this is no promise anyway).

In all of these cases there is a word or phrase that severely qualifies the basic claim that is made. As such, the statement would be difficult, if not impossible, to prove false. However, if the hedge is not totally understood or remembered, the hearer might receive a much more positive idea of the product.

A second type of true but potentially deceptive claim is the *deleted comparative.* Whenever an adjective or adverb is modified by "more" or an "-er" suffix, it involves a comparison with something else. What this basis for comparison is may or may not be stated, and if it is not, it may or may not be obvious to the inferring reader or listener. Sometimes in ads the basis of the comparison is not stated, and the strength of the claim would vary considerably depending on what that claim was. For example, consider (11).

(11) Snarfo makes you healthier.

If there is anything at all (cyanide capsules?) that is worse to take than Snarfo, then (11) is not false. However, if the consumer infers that Snarfo is being compared to its competitors in the marketplace, miscomprehension may occur and the consumer will be deceived.

A few years ago there was a case where an auto manufacturer claimed that its car was "700 percent quieter." When the FTC asked the manufacturer to produce the research evidence to back up its claim, it produced a study showing that the car was 700 percent quieter on the inside of the car than on the outside! Was that the basis of comparison that you inferred when you first read the claim? If you hear that a car "goes farther on a tank of gas," do you infer that it has better mileage than its competitors (which ones?) or that it has a larger gas tank?

A third category of true but potentially deceptive claims is the *juxtaposed imperative*: (12) and (13). In these cases two imperatives are stated successively. Though no causal relationship of the two is stated, as we have already seen above, it is very easy to infer such a relationship.

(12) Get a beautiful tan this summer. Use Bronzoline.

(13) Help your child get better grades. Buy an Addo computer.

Advertising copy frequently makes use of juxtaposed imperatives to imply a causal relationship, taking advantage of this natural information-processing tendency.

Another way to imply something beyond what is stated is to ask a negative question; for example, (14). Inserting the word "not" into a yes-no question (15) in English changes the question by implying that the questioner believes the answer to be "yes," thus implying that the questioner believes the answer to be "yes," thus implying that to the respondent. Although a lawyer in most cases would not be allowed to ask (16) in the courtroom, advertisers are perfectly free to ask (14).

(14) Isn't quality the most important thing to consider in buying aspirin?

(15) Is quality the most important thing to consider in buying aspirin?

(16) Weren't you in the victim's apartment on the night of the murder?

Another type of true but potentially deceptive claim involves the citing of statistical or other scientific research information. Any evidence of "science" tends to give an ad a greater aura of authority and prestige, but such statistics may often be a very slippery way to imply something very different than what the claim directly states.

One way this may be done is reporting results of a survey only by the absolute number or by the percent, but not both: (17) and (18). Similarly, the number of respondents reporting may be mentioned with no consideration of the number questioned (19). Sometimes the competition in a comparative ad may be inadequately or inappropriately specified (20).

(17) 75 percent of dentists recommended Fizzle Toothpaste (75 percent of how many? Four?)

(18) 5000 doctors recommended Cashprin Aspirin. (5000 out of how many?)

(19) 2000 satisfied customers responding to our survey favored . . . (How many were questioned and didn't respond?)

(20) Czar Scrubitoff Oven Cleaner has 40 percent more cleaning power than another popular brand. (What is cleaning power?) (What was popular about the other brand?)

Results may be reported in piecemeal fashion, with specific comparisons drawn comparing one's product to different competitors, but each on a different dimension. The overall set of comparisons may imply something far beyond what is stated directly. For example, one might infer from (21) that the car was larger on all interior dimensions than any of its competitors, while that is not at all what is stated.

(21)   The Wallaby Medalist has more rear seat headroom than a Nissan Sentra, more leg room than a Ford Escort, a larger trunk than a Toyota Tercel, and more hip room than a Honda Civic.

Sometimes something negative may be implied about the competition without stating it directly, as in examples (22) through (25). All of the statements are unquestionably true, but the implications they carry are considerably more questionable.

(22)   Tipsi-Cola has no cancer-causing artificial sweetener. (But maybe the competition does?)

(23)   S & M Schlock will accompany you to an audit if the IRS questions a tax return we prepare. (Any tax preparer must by law do so.)

(24)   Wouldn't it be terrible to be stuck somewhere with some of those traveler's checks that don't give refunds easily? (But all do give refunds.)

(25)   Slurpo Mushroom Soup—there's no asbestos in our mushrooms! (But beware the other brands.)

Demonstrating deception psychologically.   So far we have discussed several types of advertising claims that may imply more than they state directly and thus possibly deceive while inducing miscomprehension. The psychological question remains to be answered, however. Do people in fact infer the (perhaps false) implications going beyond what is said? Yes, they do, as demonstrated in a research project summarized in Harris, Dubitsky, and Bruno (1983).

The general methodology was to present subjects with a list of about 20 audiotaped commercials 30 seconds long each and later test their memory for the claims put forth in the ads. The crucial test comes from the fact that half of the subjects heard a given commercial state a claim directly (26), while the other half heard the same commercial imply the same claim (27). All subjects later rated the truth of the critical claim (28).

(26)   Do you have tired, aching feet at the end of a long day? You should be wearing the Moon Shoe, with its revolutionary new cushion sole. Be kind to your sore feet. *Moon Shoes will relieve tired, aching feet.*

(27)   Do you have tired, aching feet at the end of a long day? You should be wearing the Moon Shoe, with its revolutionary new cushion sole. Be kind to your sore feet. *Moon Shoes are just right for you.*

(28)   Moon Shoes make your tired, aching feet feel better.

In the baseline condition, subjects make the inferences and believe the claims very strongly regardless of which ad they heard; thus, it does not matter whether the claim is stated directly or merely implied (Harris, 1977a).

BOX 8–10   Other Cognitive Processes in Advertising

Besides the issue of deception in advertising, other problems of information processing of ads are amenable to study using the methods of modern experimental psychology. Some of these issues include how we make purchase decisions, how visual and auditory information interact in television advertising, how repeated presentations of ads affect memory, and how imagery is evoked in comprehending ads.

Three different classes of dependent measures are used in psychological research on advertising (T. A. Shimp, 1983). *Cognitive* measures involve how we interpret the ads. *Attitudinal* measures assess our attitudes or feelings about the product. *Behavioral* measures determine how our behavior changes, with primary focus on buying behavior. The latter is, of course, the "bottom line" in advertising research, but it is also the most difficult of the three types of measures to implement. See Harris, 1983, and Alwitt & Mitchell, 1985, for collections of readings on this topic.

Later extensions of this work tried to train subjects not to draw such unwarranted inferences from radio ads (Bruno & Harris, 1980; Harris, Dubitsky, & Thompson, 1979; Harris, Dubitsky, Connizzo, Letcher, & Ellerman, 1981). This is difficult to do and, although some progress was achieved through small group interactive training, it is very difficult to stop this general information-processing activity from occurring. The most effective training required subjects themselves to generate alternative interpretations besides the obvious implied claim.

Deceptive advertising is not the only advertising issue where information-processing psychology can be of use. See Box 8–10.

CONCLUSION

At the beginning of this chapter we introduced the interactionist perspective on meaning, whereby the meaning is not a property of the stimulus, but rather is something that, emerges from the interaction of the stimulus and the active mind and memory of the hearer/reader. In comprehension, the sounds (listening) or letters (reading) are perceived and recognized and then constructed into words. These words are then decoded to meanings, using information in the mental dictionary and the syntactic structure of the words. In constructing the meaning of a whole sequence of words, one retrieves knowledge schemata from memory and draws inferences based on such knowledge, taking into account pragmatic considerations surrounding the utterance or text. Information of several sorts (phonetic, lexical, syntactic, pragmatic) is processed in parallel during the comprehension process as the meaning is constructed. In this way comprehension involves top-down and bottom-up processing and is a multifaceted set of processes, not an all-or-none operation.

SUGGESTED READINGS

The material in this chapter is usually discussed briefly in chapters on memory or language in cognition texts.

For good integrative discussions of schema theory, see the articles by Rumelhart (1980), Alba and Hasher (1983), Brewer and Nakamura (1984), and Thorndyke (1984).

A highly readable, entertaining, and fact-filled discussion of deceptive advertising, especially in regard to puffery, is Ivan Preston's (1975) *The Great American Blow-up: Puffery in Advertising and Selling*. Michael Geis' (1982) *The Language of Television Advertising* looks at advertising language a bit more generally. Both are highly critical of advertising.

9

THINKING

A panel of psychologists has interviewed and administered personality tests to 30 engineers and 70 lawyers, all successful in their respective fields. On the basis of this information, thumbnail descriptions of the 30 engineers and 70 lawyers have been written. You will find below three descriptions, chosen at random from the 100 available descriptions. For each description, please indicate, on a scale from 0 to 100, what you think the probability is that the person described is an engineer. (Adapted from Kahneman & Tversky, 1973, p. 241).

1. Dick is a 30-year-old man. He is married with no children. A man of high ability and high motivation, he promises to be quite successful in his field. He is well liked by his colleagues. (p. 242)
   Probability Dick is one of the 30 engineers out of the 100 people _____?

2. Jack is a 45-year-old man. He is married and has four children. He is generally conservative, careful, and ambitious. He shows no interest in political and social issues and spends most of his free time on his many hobbies, which include home carpentry, sailing, and mathematical puzzles. (p. 241)
   Probability that Jack is one of the 30 engineers out of the 100 people _____?

3. No information provided on Fred.
   Probability that Fred is one of the 30 engineers out of the 100 people _____?

If you are like the subjects studied by Daniel Kahneman and Amos Tversky, you guessed that the probability that Dick is an engineer is about 50 percent, that Jack is an engineer is about 95 percent, and that Fred is an engineer is about 30 percent.

Only one of these estimates—the last one—is correct. Another group of subjects was told that the initial group of 100 contained 70 engineers and 30 lawyers, and their estimates were identical to yours, except for Fred, who was considered now 70 percent likely to be an engineer. Again, only the estimate concerning Fred is correct.

In the above example, if a person is chosen at random from a group of 30 engineers and 70 lawyers, he or she is much more likely to be a lawyer than an engineer, and so we estimate the chances that Fred is an engineer, correctly, at 30/100, or 30 percent. But as soon as we are given a personality description, we forget about the objective probabilities. The description of Dick is worthless—it could describe any professional person—doctor, lawyer, engineer, politician, scientist, or professor. There is no reason to think Dick is an engineer rather than a lawyer, and so we set down an estimate of 50 percent—equally likely to be a lawyer or an engineer—quite forgetting the population distribution of 30 engineers and 70 lawyers. We ought to treat Dick like Fred and estimate 30 percent, but few of us do.

With Jack we go even further astray. His profile fits the stereotype (schema) of the engineer we have in long-term memory, and we jump to the conclusion that he *must* be an engineer, again ignoring the objective probabilities. Even if the engineer schema is accurate—which it very likely is not—we should not ignore the fact that there are only 30 engineers in the group to begin with, so that *any* randomly sampled profile will probably be a lawyer's. The finding that both groups of subjects—whether told there were 30 of 100 engineers or 70 of 100 engineers—gave the *same* estimate that Jack is an engineer shows that the subjects just ignored the objective probabilities and followed their intuitive personality theory.

We will find that, as this example illustrates, human thinking is an imperfect process, a much more hit-and-miss affair than most of us would care to suppose. We ignore relevant information, rely too much on stereotypes and personal experience, jump to conclusions, resist challenging facts, and even have trouble reasoning according to the rules of logic.

In this chapter we will examine several areas in the psychological study of thinking, including problem solving, reasoning (inductive, deductive, and scientific), and decision making.

PROBLEM SOLVING

When we talk about problem solving, we are considering a very broad topic, which could in some sense include most of the material in this chapter. Hayes (1978) defined a problem as the "gap that separates us from the present state and the goal state." Obviously, this includes a wide variety of situations. Although problem solving has most often been studied by psychologists using little puzzles of some sort (anagrams, cryptarithmetic, or hobbits-orcs problems), the principles of problem solving have broad application beyond puzzles and games to the many problems we face in our daily lives. Our discussion of problem solving will take this broad approach.

The topic of problem solving has been studied in several traditions in psychology. The Gestalt psychologists examined it many years ago, with emphasis on holistic aspects like restructuring the problem and combining elements in new ways. The behaviorist tradition studied problem solving from the perspective of analyzing it into simple processes of learning responses to stimuli and achieving the solution incrementally (see Chapter 3). Finally, the computer-influenced information-processing tradition has dominated recent research, which has been active especially since Newell and Simon's (1972) landmark book, *Human Problem Solving*. It is generally this information-processing approach that is taken in this section, since that best represents current thinking on the topic. We will, however, bring in insights from other traditions as well.

Understanding the Problem

The entire problem situation may be subdivided into (a) **understanding** the problem, and (b) **solving** the problem. Contrary to what might be your first impression, understanding the problem is far from trivial. Many of the barriers to solving a problem stem not from inappropriate strategies in solving but rather from inappropriate conceptualizations of what the problem is all about.

Considering a problem as a sequence of continually changing states from the start to the finish, there are several aspects to understanding the problem. The initial situation (start state) must be understood. What are the "givens" at the start of the problem? These *givens* would include a full description of the context of the problem and all of the parameters under which one must operate in solving the problem. This would include, among other information, a description of the *operators* (moves) available for changing the state of the problem. For example, a description of all the allowable moves of each piece in chess would completely define the operators for that game. In contrast to puzzles and games, many real-world problems do not have the operators so well defined. It may take a depressed person several sessions of counseling just to identify available operators he or she might have to use in order to change that person's life situation and attitude.

Another important aspect of understanding the problem is defining the *goal state*. While this is sometimes very clear, such as in games or many puzzles, often it is ill-defined; this lack of specificity of the goal state becomes part of the difficulty of the problem. For example, if a student has difficulty concentrating in school and feels lethargic and apathetic, he or she may not have a clear goal state for that problem. It is hard to make much progress toward a goal if you do not know what that goal is. Merely knowing that you want to change from the start state is not sufficient. Problem solving must be goal-directed, even though that goal may not always be achieved.

When we construct representations of problems as we understand them, we do so in our working memory and draw heavily on information in our long-term memory, including schemata and scripts (discussed in Chapter 8). The extent and character of our knowledge about that problem area will naturally affect how we understand the problem. For example, if you have considerable mechanical knowledge, you are probably better able to describe the givens and recognize available operators that you have at your disposal to solve the problem of your car dying at the side of the road. A person with little mechanical knowledge could not describe the problem nearly so completely.

Solving the Problem

The actual solution of the problem may be viewed as searching through the "problem space" for a "solution path," a path connecting the start state and the goal state. There may be one or several solution paths; usually the discovery of one good solution path is sufficient. Very often there is a huge number of solution paths for a given problem. For example, a 40-move chess game has around 10^{20} solution paths! Ridding yourself of depression has some unknown number of solution paths.

Algorithms and heuristics. Procedures used in solving problems may be either algorithms or heuristics. **Algorithms** are strategies guaranteed to produce a solution, whereas **heuristics** involve using hunches, good guesses, practical knowledge, and experience.

Algorithms are most useful for well-defined, highly structured problems. For example, we have a division algorithm for solving long-division problems. It is guaranteed to work and in this case is eminently usable. Very often no algorithm exists (for example, you are shy and want to be more popular socially) or the algorithm is so cumbersome that it would make no real sense to use it. For instance, anagrams could be solved by the algorithm of rearranging the letters in all the possible permutations, assuming there is a solution. However, the number of such permutations is huge; the eight-letter anagram THREAGUD has 40,320 possible rearrangements of its eight letters! To start writing these out would be pretty futile. Instead, we draw on our knowledge of English spelling rules to eliminate a large majority of those 40,320 possibilities (words that start out RG or GD need not be considered). Thus, we use heuristics, in this case drawing on our knowledge of the English language. In such a case, heuristics are much more efficient strategies than the available algorithm, though the latter might work better in a computer program.

Sometimes the distinction is made between *well-defined* and *ill-defined* problems. Well-defined problems typically have a clear goal state and often clearly defined operators, such as most games. On the other hand, ill-defined problems are much less structured, and part of the task of the problem solver is to structure the problem. Well-defined problems are often, though not always, amenable to algorithmic solutions, whereas ill-defined problems almost never are. Most of the real problems we face in our jobs and personal lives are ill-defined, at least to a large degree.

In some interesting studies of the solving of very ill-defined problems, Voss and his colleagues (Voss, Greene, Post, & Penner, 1983; Voss, Tyler, & Yengo, 1983) asked subjects to imagine that they were the agriculture minister of the Soviet Union and had to deal with the problem of crop productivity that had been too low for the last several years. In coming up with plans to increase productivity, subjects with more knowledge of the Soviet Union better recognized the need for more information of various sorts. Most subjects, however, approached this very ill-defined problem by recognizing the need to identify causes of low productivity and counteract those causes. They also tended to identify subproblems within the larger problem and to work on solving one subproblem at a time.

Subgoaling.   A good general strategy in problem solving is *subgoaling*, that is, dividing a problem into subproblems to be worked on one at a time. Very often an entire problem can seem forbidding ("I don't know where to begin") and subgoaling can help. For example, I can start writing this book by first making an overall outline, then an outline of a particular chapter, then write a part of the chapter, and so on. Sometimes a counselor can help a client with a personal problem to subgoal that problem; divide the problem of excessive shyness into subproblems of heightened anxiety, a poor self-image, and a lack of social skills in conversation. It is easier to work on each of these one at a time than it is to work generally on being less shy.

If you have a problem of feeling uptight from having too many responsibilities, you could subgoal the problem into particular tasks and work on each separately (your psychology lab due Friday, the chemistry exam Monday, showing your little sister around campus next Saturday). You might also identify particular aspects of your personality to reevaluate (you accept responsibilities too quickly, perhaps from an excessive desire to please others). Such subgoaling can often help move the person off the unproductive dead center of feeling totally immobilized and defeated by the problem ("Where do I begin?").

Restructuring.   Sometimes it may be necessary to restructure the problem in order to solve it. It was this aspect of problem solving that was studied by the Gestalt psychologists, who were interested in holistic approaches to thought. For example, consider the following conversation between a waiter (*W*) and a customer (*C*):

C: DUFNEX?
W: ESVFX.
C: NEM?
W: ESVFM2.
C: DUFT?
W: EST2.
C: LFMNXNT.

The problem is: What was the customer ordering? As long as you do not structure this problem correctly, it is impossible to solve. For example, you may experience *functional fixedness* of being able to think of the letters only as letters spelling words (or perhaps as initials or cryptograms). You have to think of the letters in a new way in order to discover the solution. The inability to see objects in a novel way is a common barrier in problem solution. Restructuring may be necessary to remove the functional fixedness. Such restructuring frequently comes in a moment of insight. There has been a long debate in the psychology of problem solving over whether problem solving occurs incrementally as a result of *trial-and-error* or suddenly in a moment of *insight* (the "aha experience," as the Gestalt psychologists called it). This turned out in many ways to be a false issue, since support for each process was obtained, depending on what task was used. Insight has qualities of dramatic suddenness, at least in terms of conscious experience. It also tends to produce a novel solution that is a complete one, at least to a major subpart of the problem. Sometimes it occurs after a period of incubation, when one goes off and does not work on the problem after a period of intense work on it. Why insight sometimes comes (though certainly not always) after a period of incubation is a matter of some debate. Explanations typically range from arguments that the brain is rested and able to think more productively to claiming that the functional fixedness established in the earlier period of work on the problem has weakened after the rest and thus the problem solver is able to see the problem in a new way. Box 9–1 gives some additional problems where you may experience functional fixedness and need some insight to restructure the problem. The answers to those problems and the answer to what the customer ordered in the preceding example can be found in Box 9–10, at the end of the chapter.

Expertise.   What makes an expert an expert? Some people are obviously much more adept at solving a given kind of problem than other people are. In large part this is due to the greater amount of knowledge about that problem area in their long-term memory. This rich knowledge base allows many more possibilities for reconceptualizing the problem. The Dutch psychologist A. D. DeGroot (1965) studied chess masters and chess novices to determine just how they differed. He found that, while they did not differ in the number of moves they considered on a given turn, the experts considered much better moves than the novices, that is, they were able to use their knowledge of chess and heuristics drawn therefrom to eliminate poor moves from their consideration and only examine the promising ones. The masters had much better memory for chess positions and tended to chunk many pieces together in memory; they would remember not merely one piece and its location but a whole array of pieces and their relationship to each other stored in a unit.

Simon and Gilmartin (1973) estimated that a typical chess master has encoded around 50,000 mental configurations of chess pieces, based on knowledge and experience. Such configurations only included arrangements that realistically occurred or might occur in real chess games, however.

BOX 9–1 Other Examples of Problems Requiring Restructuring

A In days of old, two knights were competing for the hand of the king's daughter. The king, being an ingenious old man, decided to settle the competition in a unique type of horse race. The two knights would be required to race against each other on horseback, but with the unusual stipulation that whosever horse crossed the finish line *last* would be the winner and would get to marry the daughter. How could the knights make sure that this race wouldn't be the slowest race in history?

B In Italy during World War II, American soldiers found standing on the ground small wooden billboards about two feet high. They looked like Figure 9–1. What was the purpose of these boards?

C What is the only English four-letter word ending in -*eny*?

D Given the circle in Figure 9–2, with radius 2, find the length of line *C*.

O
TOTI
EMUL
ESTO

FIGURE 9-1

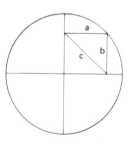

FIGURE 9-2

When chess masters and novices were shown arrays of chess pieces generated at random, masters were no better than novices at reconstructing the pieces on a memory task (Chase & Simon, 1973; De Groot, 1965).

In considering the development of problem-solving expertise in the domains of chess, geometry, physics, and computer programming, Anderson (1985, p. 259) identified four general principles.

1. Experts learn to perceive recurring patterns in the problem and to associate their problem solutions with these patterns. For example, students solving

geometry problems more quickly recognize the applicability of a particular postulate as they acquire increasing expertise (Anderson, 1982).

2. Experts learn to represent the problem in terms of more abstract features, which are more predictive of problem solution. For example, novice computer programmers deal with concepts and problems in terms of a particular computer language, whereas experts represent the concept or problem in more abstract terms not specific to a single computer language. Similarly, novices working physics problems classify problems on the basis of more surface features like rotations or inclined planes, whereas experts classify them on the basis of more abstract principles like "Newton's second law" or "conservation of energy" (Chi, Feltovich, & Glaser, 1981).

3. Experts reorganize their approach to the problem in order to capitalize on features of the domain. For example, Larkin (1981) found that novice subjects tried to work physics problems by working backward, whereas experts used the same procedures in a forward search strategy. This eliminates the need to keep track of subgoals but requires extensive knowledge of the domain in order to know which of the many possible forward inferences are relevant to the eventual solution.

4. Experts develop better memories for information that is involved in the solution of problems. For example, expert computer programmers have stored many patterns of information of the sort that occur in computer programs, much as expert chess players do (McKeithen, Reitman, Reuter, & Hirtle, 1981). Experts also remember such information better than do novices (Anderson, 1983; Jeffries, Turner, Polson, & Atwood, 1981).

Next we will examine a type of problem solving of a more specific and structured sort, *reasoning*.

REASONING

An important component of thinking is **reasoning,** the process of drawing warranted conclusions from evidence or from given premises. There are two kinds of reasoning recognized by philosophers and mathematicians: *inductive* reasoning and *deductive* reasoning. Inductive reasoning involves drawing a general conclusion from a set of data; deductive reasoning involves drawing a conclusion from a given set of initial statements, or premises. We will look at the psychology of these logics in turn, and then consider *scientific reasoning*, which involves both deduction and induction at once.

Inductive Reasoning

A study suggesting that people do not reason inductively as well as they could used a problem familiar to takers of intelligence and aptitude tests: Number series completions. Three numbers, 2, 4, 6, were shown to a subject, who was told they conformed to a simple relational rule, and the subject's task was to discover the rule by generating successive triads of numbers. After generating a triad, the subject (who kept a written list of hypotheses) was told whether the triad fit the rule or not. The subject was instructed to announce the rule when he or she was "highly confident" it was correct. Again, the subject found out if the rule was correct, and if it was not, the subject continued. The following protocol is representative of the results obtained (Wason & Johnson-Laird, 1972, p. 209):

No. 2   Four incorrect announcements. Female. Psychology undergraduate.

Instances		*Hypotheses*
2 4 6 (+)	(Given)	
8 10 12 (+)		Two added each time.
14 16 18 (+)		Even numbers in order of magnitude.
20 22 24 (+)		Same reason.
1 3 5 (+)		Two added to preceding number.

Announcement: *The rule is that by starting with any number two is added each time to form the next number.* (Incorrect)

Instances	*Hypotheses*
2 6 10 (+)	The middle number is the arithmetic mean of the other two.
1 50 99 (+)	Same reason.

Announcement: *The rule is that the middle number is the arithmetic mean of the other two.* (Incorrect)

3 10 17 (+)	Same number, seven, added each time.
0 3 6 (+)	Three added each time.

Announcement: *The rule is that the difference between two numbers next to each other is the same.* (Incorrect)

12 8 4 (−)	The same number is subtracted each time to form the next number.

Announcement: *The rule is adding a number, always the same one, to form the next number.* (Incorrect)

1 4 9 (+)	Any three numbers in order of magnitude.

Announcement: *The rule is any three numbers in order of magnitude.*

The real rule is extremely simple and broad, so that many more specific rules generate triads consistent with it. The only way to solve the problem, unless one stumbles on the right answer immediately, as many children—unused to the usual subtleties of such number series problems—do, is to test one's hypothesis by attempting to *falsify* it by generating triads inconsistent with one's hypothesis.

But this is what Subject 2 (along with most subjects) conspicuously failed to do. Instead, subjects set out to *verify* their hypothesis by generating triads consistent with their rule. But since many rules are consistent with the true rule, a subject can spend quite some time receiving "confirmations" of an incorrect hypothesis. One's mistakes can be discovered much more quickly by seeking falsification rather than verification.

The effect of a single, vivid, confirming piece of evidence can be found in social reasoning. Some politicians have exploited our willingness to believe a compelling anecdote and our resistance to falsifying statistics, tendencies demonstrated in an experiment reported by Nisbett and Ross (1980). Three groups of subjects filled out questionnaires evaluating their attitudes toward welfare recipients. Control subjects were then given correct statistics about people on welfare, including, for example, that the median stay on welfare is two years and that only 10 percent of welfare recipients remain on the rolls for as long as four years. These subjects—who believed initially that the average stay was ten years—were unaffected by the figures, expressing the same generally negative attitudes on a second questionnaire.

Two groups of experimental subjects read a description of a welfare mother that the experimenters had adapted from the *New Yorker* magazine. As described by Nisbett and Ross (1980, p. 57),

> The description painted a vivid picture of social pathology. The central figure was an obese, friendly, emotional, and irresponsible Puerto Rican woman who had been on welfare for many years. Middle-aged now, she had lived with a succession of "husbands," typically also unemployed, and had borne children by each of them. Her home was a nightmare of dirty and dilapidated plastic furniture bought on time at outrageous prices, filthy kitchen appliances, and cockroaches walking about in the daylight. Her children showed little promise of rising above their origins. They attended school off and on and had begun to run afoul of the law in their early teens, with the other children now thoroughly enmeshed in a life of heroin, numbers-running, and welfare.

The experimental subjects were then given information making the woman's case seem either (falsely) typical, or (correctly) atypical.

> In one condition, the woman's very long stay on welfare was characterized as *typical*: "The average length of time on welfare for recipients between the ages of 40 and 55 is 15 years. Furthermore, 90 percent of these people are on the welfare rolls for at least eight years." In the second condition, the woman's length of time on welfare was made to seem atypically high: "The average length of time on welfare for recipients between the ages of 40 and 55 is two years. Furthermore, 90 percent of these people are off the welfare rolls by the end of four years." (Nisbett & Ross, 1980, p. 86)

The effect of the single, vivid case that confirmed entrenched stereotypes (social schemata—see Chapter 8) was dramatic. Whereas the control subjects had stubbornly persisted in beliefs falsified by statistics, the experimental subjects reported *increased* negative attitudes toward welfare recipients on the second form, regardless of whether they had been led to believe the case was typical or not. So not only do we have stereotypes about engineers and "welfare queens," these stereotypes also resist change, and are strengthened by isolated, "confirming" instances. Nor does presenting fair, balanced discussions reflecting both sides of controversial issues help people on each side to understand each other better. See Box 9–2.

Induction is merely learning from experience. What the above experiments seem to show is that we learn from experience in a haphazard, highly selective fashion. Once we form a belief we are loath to give it up, and grasp eagerly for any confirming evidence, no matter how isolated and unusual. Sometimes induction is short-circuited altogether, and real pathology sets in. In Wason's and Johnson-Laird's "2, 4, 6" experiment,

> One subject broke down completely. Our assistant, Martin Katzman, entered the room and informed us, quite politely, that the subject, whom he was

BOX 9–2   Polarizing Opinions
through Balanced Discussions

Nisbett and Ross (1980) describe a study seeming to show that "fair" presentations of both sides of an issue—what every news reporter aims at—is likely to strengthen preexisting opinions, not create an atmosphere of tolerance.

Undergraduates who on a survey reported themselves strongly for or against capital punishment read two articles describing studies either supporting or refuting the deterrent effect of execution. Half the subjects read the confirming study first; half read the falsifying one first. Subjects filled out an attitude questionnaire on capital punishment after reading their first article, and after the second.

As we have come to expect, subjects displayed strong confirmation bias, judging the study that supported them as sound and valid, and dismissing the disconfirming study as sloppy and poorly conducted. Reading a confirming study strengthened their original opinion; reading a disconfirming study had little impact.

The inevitable consequence of these tendencies was polarization of opinion after reading both articles, that is, the "fair," "balanced," total presentation. Since disconfirming evidence had no effect and confirming evidence a strengthening effect, subjects had stronger opinions about capital punishment at the end of the study than at the beginning.

The disturbing conclusion is that presentations of both sides of an issue do not reduce differences between holders of opposing opinions, but widen them. People are not swayed by the balance of the evidence but tend to pick and choose, believing only what conforms to their views and rejecting what does not, all the while growing ever surer that they are correct and that those who differ with them must be fools.[*]

[*] Read Lord, C., Ross, C., & Lepper, M. R. "Biased Assimilation and Attitude Polarization: The Effects of Prior Theories on Subsequently Considered Evidence." *Journal of Personality and Social Psychology*, 1979, *37*, 2089–2109.

testing, was "behaving like a lunatic." And, indeed, he was certainly behaving in a strange way. On the one hand, he would not allow the experimenter to persuade him to break off the task, because "he could do wonderful things with numbers," and on the other hand, he constantly engaged in self-recriminations. What was more disconcerting, however, was that he was apparently unable to stand up, and had to be carried bodily down the stairs, and taken to the Harvard Health Center. (Wason & Johnson-Laird, 1972, p. 235)

Deductive Reasoning

As the philosopher David Hume showed two centuries ago, no inductive generalization is ever certain, because tomorrow's experience may prove it wrong. For certainty and proof we must go to deductive reasoning, where we can deduce conclusions from given propositions in accordance with formal rules, and show that the conclusions must follow from the premises.

For example, if I assert the premise (4)

(4) If a person is 21, then he or she may drink wine

and then am given the information in (5),

(5) Fred is 21

then I may validly deduce the conclusion (6):

(6) Fred may drink wine.

An important thing to bear in mind about deductive reasoning is that following the rules of logic guarantees only that the conclusion is valid, that is, that it really does follow logically from the given premises; there is no guarantee that the conclusion is true: The premises may be false. So the argument—(7), (8), (9)—is just as valid as (4), (5), (6), even though it is absurd:

(7) If Julius Caesar is President, then horses are purple.
(8) Julius Caesar is President.
(9) Therefore, horses are purple.

Although deductive logic cannot assure us that our conclusions are true, it is still an essential component in reasoning. For when we reason,

---

BOX 9–3   Peter Wason's Four-Card Problem

The cards in Figure 9–3 have information on both sides. On one side of a card is a letter, and on the other side is a number.

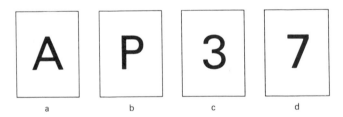

FIGURE 9-3

Here is a rule: **If a card has an "A" on one side, then it has a "3" on the other side.**
Select those cards that you definitely need to turn over to determine whether or not the cards are violating the rule.*

*Instructions from Cox & Griggs, 1982.

we assemble what we know about a problem; in logical terms, we establish a set of premises from which we make inferences. It is important that we reason logically; otherwise, we still may fall into error even with the truest of premises.

Of the various kinds of deductive logic and types of logical rules, we will consider here just one, *reasoning with material implication* (*if . . . then* statements), an important kind of reasoning intensively investigated by several teams of researchers over the last two decades. Sample problems from their experiments are given in Boxes 9–3 and 9–4; the correct answers are found in Box 9–5. Please read these boxes and do the problems before going on to read about the research results.

This basic problem, especially in its original, abstract form (Box 9–3), is especially difficult. Researchers in both Great Britain and America have shown that only about 10 percent of subjects make the correct choices when the problem is presented as in Box 9–3. The most common error is to choose cards *a* and *c* (see Evans, 1982, for a review). Similarly, when subjects are given an abstract rule and asked to draw inferences from it in combination with propositions forming the argument patterns discussed in Box 9–5, they show poor command of logical implication, typically doing *modus ponens* correctly, while rejecting the validity of *modus tollens*, and making the invalid inferences denial of the antecedent and especially affirmation of the consequent (Evans, 1982; Leahey, 1977a, 1977b, Leahey & Wagman, 1974). Such erroneous reasoning has proved most difficult to modify (Wason and Johnson-Laird, 1972; Leahey & Wagman, 1974; Leahey, 1977a).

BOX 9–4   Richard Griggs' Drinking Age Problem

On this task imagine you are a police officer on duty. It is your job to ensure that people conform to certain rules. The cards in Figure 9–4 have information about four people sitting at a table. On one side of a card is a person's age and on the other side of the card is what a person is drinking. Here is a rule:

If a person is drinking beer, then the person must be over 21. Select those cards that you definitely need to turn over to determine whether or not the people are violating the rule.[*]

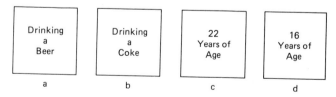

| Drinking a Beer | Drinking a Coke | 22 Years of Age | 16 Years of Age |
| a | b | c | d |

FIGURE 9-4

[*] Instructions from Cox & Griggs, 1982.

BOX 9–5   Answers to the Problems in Boxes 9–3 and 9–4

The correct answer in each case is to turn over only cards *a* and *d*; if you are like most American subjects you almost certainly got Box 9–3 incorrect, and probably got Box 9–4 correct. Remember that you are told to *falsify*— not *verify*—the rule. Turning over a card *a* can do this, since in 9–3 if (say) a 2 is on the other side, the rule is violated, and in 9–4 if the other side says, "Fourteen years of age," the rule is violated. Turning over card *b* can *not* falsify the rule, because it does not satisfy the "if . . ." part of the rule, called the *antecedent*. So no matter what is on the other side, the rule stands unviolated. Card *c* is similarly unhelpful: In 9–4 it does not matter what the 22-year-old is drinking; he can't be violating the drinking law. Similarly, in 9–3 it doesn't matter what is on the other side of the 3; the rule cannot be violated. Finally, card *d* can violate the rule: If the 16-year-old is drinking beer, the rule is violated; if there is an *A* on the other side of the card in 9–3, the rule is violated.

While the two problems differ in content, they both have the same logical structure, and should therefore have the same answer. The formal justification for the correct choices comes from the *truth table* (as logicians call it) for implication, which specifies the conditions under which an implication statement, of whatever content, is to be judged true or false. In logic, an *if . . . then* statement may be represented as $p \supset q$: If *p*, then *q*, which has the following truth table:

p	$p \supset q$	q
T	T	T
T	F	F
F	T	T
F	T	F

That is, the proposition $p \supset q$ (for example, if there is an *A* on the front (*p*), then ($\supset$) there is a *3* on the back (*q*) is *false* when *p* is true (the card has an *A* on front) and *q* is false (there is a 2 on the other side). Otherwise, the proposition is true.

In the two tasks, only cards *a* and *d* can falsify the rule, because only they can give the combination in line 2 of the truth table. Similarly, only two kinds of inferences may be drawn from an implicative proposition. One is called *modus ponens*:

(1) $p \supset q$
(2) *p* is true
(3) therefore, *q* is true.

This is a valid inference, because assuming the premise is true, as one must do in deductive reasoning, if we know that *p* is true, *q* must be true also.

The other valid conclusion is *modus tollens*:

(1) $p \supset q$
(4) q is false (not-q, or $\sim q$)
(5) therefore, p is false (not-p, or $\sim p$).

In *modus tollens* we reason by falsification. Again, assuming the rule is true, given that q is false, it must be the case that p is false.

There are two fallacious forms of reasoning with implication, *denial of the antecedent* and *affirmation of the consequent*. In denial of the antecedent, a person reasons incorrectly:

(1) $p \supset q$
(6) $\sim p$
(7) therefore, $\sim q$.

The truth table shows this to be a fallacy, since if p is false, the rule is always true.

In affirmation of the consequent, one reasons incorrectly

(1) $p \supset q$
(8) q
(9) therefore, p.

Again, inspection of the truth table shows that when q is true, the whole rule is true.

When the problem has been presented in a verbal form, as in Box 9–4, the results have been exceedingly varied. Early results (summarized in Wason & Johnson-Laird, 1972) showed that verbal formulations produced superior performance, even in subjects who could not do the abstract version, suggesting that people understood the logic of implication but just could not bring it to bear on abstract material.

However, these findings could not always be replicated (see Leahey, 1977b), and further research by Richard Griggs and his colleagues (Griggs & Cox, 1982; Cox & Griggs, 1982) and E. Golding (1981) showed why. The verbal formulation yielded improved performance only when the rule and its manner of testing were already familiar to the subjects. So, for example, the drinking age problem (Box 9–4) facilitated performance among American undergraduates familiar—naturally—with alcoholic beverage rules, even though the same subjects did badly with the abstract problem and with concrete versions involving British postal rules or travel between British cities, problems on which British students had done well.

Such results have been explained in several ways, each of which suggests that people do not reason as logically as they suppose, when they reason at all. One factor is the familiar tendency of people to verify a rule, rather than attempt to falsify it, leading them to choose cards a and c, p and q, hoping to find verifying cases, q and p, respectively, on the other sides (Wason & Johnson-Laird, 1972). Evans (1982) has proposed a dual-process theory, claiming that people possess nonrational Type 1 cognitive processes (akin to Freud's primary process) and rational, logical, verbal, Type 2 processes. When a task is especially difficult, as in the abstract four-card problem, Type 2 processes fail and are short-circuited, replaced by the simpler strategies drawn from Type 1 processes; in short, the subjects are not reasoning at all. On top of this subjects do not realize what has happened, and they rationalize their irrational choices by drawing on Type 2 reasoning (Evans & Wason, 1976). Evans' proposal finds support in some interesting recent research (reported in Evans, 1982) showing that subjects reason more logically with their left brain hemisphere than with their right hemisphere, indicating that Type 2 reasoning is controlled by the verbal-rational left hemisphere, while the shortcut strategies of Type 1 processing take place in the right hemisphere, relatively cut off from left-hemisphere verbal report.

On the other hand, Griggs (for example, Griggs & Cox, 1983) has argued that people are not reasoning logically with the verbal material on which they appear to do better. Griggs proposed that superior performance on the concrete tasks is due not to better application of logical abilities, but to sheer familiarity. Specifically, on the familiar, concrete problems people do not figure out—that is, reason out—the correct answers, they already know them from experience and just have to recall them. Florida undergraduates know all about drinking age rules, and can recall the conditions that violate such rules, but do badly on unfamiliar problems concerning British postage and rail travel.

In other words, people seem hardly to reason at all. In abstract tasks, demands are so great that logic is short-circuited and simplified, if nonlogical, strategies are substituted. On familiar tasks, subjects just remember the correct answer; they do not reason logically to a correct conclusion. It appears that only when people can activate what Griggs calls the "detective set strategy"—looking for rule-breaking instances—that logical reasoning occurs at all. And the results reviewed so far indicate that trying to be wrong is something people rarely do.

The conditional reasoning framework is implicit in many situations beyond those where there is an explicit "If . . . then" rule. Box 9–6 gives an example of how advertisers can capitalize on the less-than-logical ways that we reason. The use of implicit conditional reasoning framework is very common in persuasive discourse such as advertising and political rhetoric.

Scientific Reasoning

In practice, inductive and deductive reasoning are rarely practiced alone. In the induction problems we studied, people must draw a generalization from experience, that is, they must use induction, but then they must test the hypothesis by deducing from it predictions about future experience. Similarly, in the four-card problems, subjects had to deduce what would falsify the given premise, and evaluate it against potential evidence.

BOX 9–6   Conditional Reasoning in Advertising

Sometimes the conditional reasoning paradigm is implicitly contained in advertising even when it may not be overtly stated. Consider a claim like "Panacea Capsules relieve headaches." This may be reworded thus: "If you take Panacea Capsules, they will relieve your headache," to put it into the "if *p*, then *q*" form. Consider the four possible logical arguments. Suppose you take Panacea Capsules (*p*); you could then conclude that they would relieve your headache (*q*); this is the *modus ponens* argument. As a second argument, consider that you have a headache that is not relieved (not-*q*); you could conclude that you must not have taken Panacea Capsules (not-*p*). So far both of these arguments have been logically valid (*modus ponens* and *modus tollens*).

Now let us consider the other two possible arguments; first the case where you did not take Panacea Capsules (not-*p*). Like subjects in the reasoning studies discussed earlier, you might conclude not-*q*, that is, that your headache wouldn't be relieved. This is the logically invalid but very frequent fallacy of denying the antecedent, but it may be very useful to advertisers if the consumers make this implied but invalid deduction—that if you don't take their product, you won't get the relief you need.

The last of the four possible arguments is the case where you did experience relief from your headache (*q*). Though you may be tempted to conclude *p*, that you must have taken Panacea Capsules, this, too, is invalid (affirming the consequent fallacy) but potentially useful to advertisers.

Thus, advertisers can draw on natural information-processing tendencies to encourage you to deduce more information than they actually state.

Such interweaving of induction and deduction, prediction and proof, is at the center of science. Moreover, because science prides itself on being rational, logical, and orderly, we should examine scientific reasoning in light of our findings that people are less rational, logical, and orderly than we usually suppose.

Scientists as reasoners.   To start, let us ask if scientists, trained in the rigors of disciplinary methodology, are any better at reasoning than the lay people psychologists study. Kern, Mirels, and Hinshaw (1983) suggest the answer is "not much." They administered several logical problems to university scientists in three fields, including the Wason four-card problem, the results from which are shown in Table 9–1. While the physicists did better than the biologists and psychologists, no group did really well, and performance overall was only marginally better than college-student subjects, even among those scientists with some training in logic.

Mahoney and DeMonbreun (1978) presented Wason's 2, 4, 6 problem to two groups of university scientists (physicists and psychologists) and to a group of conservative Protestant ministers. The results, summarized in Table 9–2, were essentially similar to Wason's findings with college students. Only a minority of subjects adopted a strategy of hypothesis falsification, and very few triads, in fact, resulted in disconfirmation. Many subjects—

TABLE 9–1   Percent of Scientists Giving Correct Responses on the Wason Four-Card Problem, Abstract Version[a]

	FIELD			
	Biologists	Physicists	Psychologists	Trained[b] in Logic
Correctly Identified Cards b *and* c *as Irrelevant*	8%	21%	13%	12%
Correctly Chose Cards a *and* d *as Falsifying*	13%	25%	17%	16%

[a] Table constructed from data reported by Kern, Mirels, and Hinshaw, 1980.
[b] There were too few subjects trained in logic to break down by discipline, and their data are not included in the other cells.

especially the scientists—retested previously refuted hypotheses. The only reliable differences between the scientists and the ministers revealed that the latter more closely fit the conventional image of scientists. The ministers generated lots of triads—that is, collected a lot of data—before advancing an hypothesis, while the scientists based hypotheses on small samples, and seemed to stick to them longer.

One might object that these experiments fail to impugn scientists' reasoning skills since they involve unusual, difficult, and abstract material.

TABLE 9–2   The Relative Performance of Psychologists, Physical Scientists, and Ministers on the Wason 2, 4, 6, Problem[a]

	GROUP PERFORMANCE		
Variable	Psychologists	Physical Scientists	Ministers
Percent who announced the correct hypothesis	47	27	40
Percent who disconfirmed	40	40	33
Percent of trials that were disconfirmatory	9	12	19
Average number of hypotheses generated	3.07	3.33	2.00
Average number of triads generated	7.53	7.60	8.33
Average ratio of triads generated to hypotheses	3.03	2.01	6.22
Average number of triads generated before first hypothesis	1.93	1.07	5.40
Latency in seconds to first hypothesis	35.4	37.7	132.9
Percentage who reconfirmed a previously falsified hypothesis	93	93	53

[a] Adapted from Mahoney and DeMonbreun, Psychology of the Scientist, *Cognitive Therapy & Research*, 1978, 1, 229–238.

Perhaps they would do better on problems in their field, where expertise and methodological sophistication could be brought to bear.

However, the work of Chapman and Chapman (1967, 1969; reported by Nisbett & Ross, 1980), showed scientists committing the same sorts of errors as lay people. The Chapmans studied clinical psychologists' faith in two projective personality tests, the Draw-A-Person (DAP) test, and the Rorschach Inkblot Test. Repeated empirical studies have shown the DAP to be unreliable and invalid, and the Rorschach to be of limited validity. Nevertheless, many practicing clinicians put great faith in the DAP and in discredited forms of Rorschach interpretation. The Chapmans' research indicates that the clinicians' continued faith in the tests is based on well-entrenched "folk" beliefs that resist falsification, and, like the welfare-mother stereotypes, find enough random "confirmations" in their clinical practice to allegedly justify it. For example, the clinicians believe (falsely) that paranoia is expressed in the way a person draws eyes, either under- or over-emphasizing them. The Chapmans found that psychologically naive subjects also believed (falsely) that paranoids would draw emphasized or de-emphasized eyes. Clinical psychologists, then, despite their years of training, are just like anyone else in resisting falsification of their ideas, looking for confirmation, and being swayed by the immediate concrete, isolated, confirming instance against masses of statistical findings.

Perhaps most disturbing is the persistence of incorrect beliefs in areas in which scientists are specifically trained. One folk-belief is the "gambler's fallacy." Suppose we take a coin known to be fair—to have a 50 percent chance of turning up heads or tails (T)—and flip the following sequence: T, T, T, T, T, T, T, T, T; what is the probability the next flip will be heads? Most people commit the gambler's fallacy and think heads is more likely to turn up than 0.50, the correct answer; they think the coin is "due" to turn up heads. To see the fallacy, just realize that nothing has altered the molecular structure of the coin—it's the same coin it was at the start—and, given that it is a fair coin, the probability of heads is still 0.50 on each flip.

Tversky and Kahneman (1981) discovered that the gambler's fallacy persisted among psychologists, who are all trained in statistics and should therefore have been disabused of the mistake. Nevertheless, when questioned on a number of statistical problems, psychologists showed themselves prone to the gambler's fallacy. Most of the problems were too technical to describe here, but one was not. It read:

> The mean IQ of the population of eighth graders in a city is known to be 100. You have selected a random sample of 50 children for a study of educational achievements. The first child tested has an IQ of 150. What do you expect the mean IQ to be for the whole sample? (Tversky & Kahneman, 1981, p. 269)

The correct answer is 101. A score of 150 is *extremely* unlikely: Fewer than 0.07 percent (that's not 7 percent but 7 *one-hundredths* of a percent) of Americans have an IQ of 150 or more. In order to counterbalance the score of 150 you would have to have in the sample an IQ of 50, which is most unlikely to happen; as a result, the whole sample of 30 will likely be a bit unrepresentatively high. Nevertheless, most psychologists, like most people, thought the sample IQ would be 100, because, like the gambler waiting for the coin to turn heads, they thought the 150 would *inevitably* be balanced by a 50. But any given sample hardly ever exactly mirrors the population as a whole—that's why political polls are so unreliable and must be repeated many times.

It seems, then, that scientific sophistication just lets scientists make sophisticated mistakes.

The layman as scientist. Experiments by Doherty, Mynatt, Tweney, and Schiavo (1981), and Mynatt, Doherty, and Tweney (1981) asked student-subjects to pretend to be scientists (archaeologists or physicists), and then placed them in simulated research environments that required the subjects to formulate and test scientific hypotheses. In the physics experiment, some subjects were given indoctrination concerning falsification as the optimum scientific strategy. Regardless of instructions, however, subjects shared a strong tendency to confirm rather than disconfirm their hypotheses, persisted in repeating disconfirmed hypotheses, and especially in the archaeology experiment, were poor at choosing data that could prove *or* disprove their hypotheses.

In social situations—where we conduct "experiments" to find out about strangers—confirmation bias is so strong that it creates self-fulfilling hypotheses. Snyder, Tanke, and Berscheid (1977; reported by Nisbett & Ross, 1980) had male subjects talk over an intercom with an unseen female they had been led to believe was either attractive or unattractive. Another group of subjects listened to tapes made of the female's side of the conversation only and —without seeing her or knowing what the first subject had been told about her appearance—rated her attractiveness. Evidently, the questions and probes used by the conversing males had elicited verbal evidence of attractiveness or unattractiveness, because the second group of males followed the first group's hypotheses. If the women had been labeled "attractive," her verbal behavior made her seem attractive, even to the blind raters in the second part of the experiment. The reverse held for "unattractive" women. So the hypothesis led to questions that created confirming behavior from the questionee, creating a self-fulfilling circle of hypothesis and "evidence."

Conclusion. By now you may want to ask with a reader of Nisbett & Ross (1980): "If we're so dumb, how come we made it to the moon?" One answer—not Nisbett's and Ross'—is that rationality should not be equated with logic (Toulmin, 1972), and that disconfirmation is not really the best way to do science.

Science does work; its success is established. Yet the major result of work in history and philosophy of science over the past few decades has been that scientists are not logical automata; the work we have surveyed in this chapter already supports such a conclusion. Moreover, it seems wise to argue (see Kuhn, 1970) that science succeeds not *despite* its deviations from falsificationist logic but *because* of them (Leahey & Leahey, 1983). In the simulated physics experiment conducted by Mynatt and others (1981), the subject who performed best quickly formulated a partially correct hypothesis and then stuck to it, using disconfirmations to gradually modify the wrong parts. The results described by Mahoney and DeMonbreun suggest that real scientists do likewise.

Ian Mitroff (1981) studied the very scientists who took us to the moon, and his results (dare we say it?) confirm the view that these "good" scientists were illogical. Project scientists singled out three of their colleagues as especially stubborn in defending their ideas, stubborn to the point of infuriating pig-headedness. Yet these same scientists were rated as the three most creative, most brilliant scientists in an already gifted group. Less stubborn, speculative scientists, who cautiously generalized from large amounts of data, were rated as impartial but dull and unimaginative. Speaking of the brilliant but tenacious three, a colleague said:

> The commitment of these guys to their ideas, while absolutely infuriating at times, can be a very good thing too. One should never give up an idea too soon in science—any idea, no matter how outrageous it may be and no matter how beaten down it seems by all the best evidence at the time. I've seen too many totally disproven ideas come back to haunt us. I've learned by now that you never completely prove or disprove anything; you just make it more or less probable with the best of what means you've got at the time. It's true that these guys are a perpetual thorn in the side of the profession and for that reason a perpetual challenge to it too. Their value probably outweighs their disadvantages although I've wondered many times if we might not be better off without them. Each time I reluctantly conclude no. We need them around. They perpetually shake things up with their wild ideas although they drive you mad with the stick-to-itiveness that they have for their ideas. (Mitroff, 1981, pp. 173–174)

The real key to scientific success is not the individual reasoning—logical or not—of the individual scientist, but the collective reasoning—even wisdom—of the scientific community. Scientists function as a group, a tightly knit community, and while each one is often wrong, it is out of the clash of commitments and confirmation biases toward competing viewpoints that success comes. One lunar scientist put it this way:

> Scientist A—Commitment, even extreme commitment such as bias, has a role to play in science and it can serve science well. Part of the business (of science) is to sift the evidence and to come to the right conclusions, and to do this you must have people who argue for both sides of the evidence. This is the only way in which we can straighten the situation out. I wouldn't like scientists to be without bias, since a lot of the sides of the argument would never be presented. We must be emotionally committed to the things we do energetically. No one is able to do anything with liberal energy if there is no emotion connected with it. (Mitroff, 1981, pp. 171–172)

DECISION MAKING

Although a large part of problem solving and reasoning discussed above involves making decisions, there has been a branch of information-processing psychology that has concentrated on studying how people make choices. Much of this work is in a highly mathematical tradition, going back to the seventeenth-century statistician Jacques Bernoulli (1654–1705), who studied probabilities in simple choice situations. Ever since, people have been developing mathematical models of probabilistic decision making, often studying simple tasks like gambling or coin-tossing.

Gambling has been around for thousands of years. There is archaeological evidence of ancient dice in Egyptian tombs from 3000 B.C. The Old Testament speaks of casting lots (Joshua 18:10; Proverbs 16:33), with the results interpreted as the will of God. Ancient Greek amphorae (large jars) show Ajax and Achilles shooting dice.

When we talk about decision making, we can do so in either a **normative** (prescriptive) or **descriptive** sense. That is, we can talk about how people *should* make decisions (normative) or how they actually *do* make decisions (descriptive). While the psychologist's approach to the problem is most often descriptive, nuances of the normative approach creep in frequently, particularly in discussions of particular mathematical models of decision making, which are largely beyond the scope of this book. In recent years the emphasis has been increasingly on a more descriptive approach to decision making, which will be the emphasis in the brief treatment of decision making that follows.

Rationality

When we discuss decision making (or problem solving or reasoning, for that matter), the assumption is usually made that our decisions, if not all of our thought processes, are **rational**. We like to think that thought is rational, but there is some disagreement on what being rational involves. For a review of different approaches to defining and studying rationality, see Jungermann (1983). Many approaches assume some common set of principles of rational thought (see Lee, 1971).

First of all, a rational decision is one that is made *from a set of alternatives* that one has identified and been able to make some choice among. Part of making a good decision is first identifying all the reasonable alternatives to choose from initially. If a highly desirable or likely choice is not even considered, then the final choice may not be the best one.

A rational decision follows the principle of *transitivity*. For example, if, on a given afternoon, you would choose to play tennis rather than golf and choose golf rather than jogging, then you should also choose tennis over jogging, given that choice.

A rational decision is intended to maximize *utility* for the person. Utility is an important concept in decision making; it is the value to a person of a particular consequence. Utility is a psychological, subjective concept. It is related, but not identical, to the concept of *value*. An outcome of the same value may have two different utilities to two different people. For example, bending down to pick up a dollar bill off the sidewalk has the same value to anyone ($1); however, it would have a much greater utility to a poor vagrant than to a millionaire. The higher utility in the one case might lead to the vagrant's deciding to pick it up, while the millionaire might walk on by.

A rational decision is one that has been made based on the relevant, but not the irrelevant, information available to the person. Whenever we make a decision, we consider some information that is relevant, or *diagnostic*, while we ignore (or at least *think* we ignore) other information that is irrelevant (or nondiagnostic). As we shall see later, ignoring nondiagnostic information is not as easy as you might think.

Box 9–7 uses the concept of utility to analyze and use diagnostic information to come to a decision about a personal course of action. You may find this approach useful in your own life.

When we make any kind of decision, the diagnostic information is combined in various ways. Some researchers in decision making focus their studies on what information is combined and how it is combined. Norman Anderson (1981, 1982) uses the term **cognitive algebra** to refer to the mathematical laws that describe how we integrate various pieces of information together to come up with a decision. For example, if Nancy was trying to decide whether to go out with Kevin, she might have an impression of his personality and his appearance. For purposes of research, we could have Nancy quantify these impressions. She could combine these two pieces of information according to an additive (or perhaps an averaging) model if she considered both personality and appearance more or less equally (though this could be changed by introducing weighting factors in the model; for example, weight personality 75 percent and appearance 25 percent).

On the other hand, she could combine the pieces of information multiplicatively. In this case, if Kevin scored high on both personality and appearance, Nancy's total impression of him would be much better than if he were merely moderately high on both. On the other hand, if he was very low on either measure, that would pull her overall impression of him way down, even if he was very high on the second measure (great looks but a zero personality). A multiplicative model fits well with the intuitive notion that someone with personality = 0 is still 0, even if extremely attractive.

Estimating Likelihoods of Occurrence

Some events have objective probabilities of occurrence. For example, the probability of throwing a six on any given toss of a fair die is 1/6. The probability of drawing the six of clubs from a deck of 52 cards is 1/52. The probability as we estimate it is called **subjective probability**, which may or may not be equal, or even close to, the objective probability. Gambling casinos make a lot of money on patrons using subjective probabilities of winning, which are often much greater than the objective probabilities

BOX 9–7 Multiattribute Utility (MAU) Analysis

This is a technique for analyzing a decision with several possible outcomes and several attributes on which to consider each outcome. It also uses the concept of subjective utility.

To understand the MAU approach, let's take a sample problem. Suppose you are trying to decide on what car to purchase. The following discussion will explain the technique through the use of this example. In reality, of course, the development of the example would be different for each individual.

1. The first step is to define the different alternatives (outcomes). Be sure to consider all the alternatives that would be real possibilities. For this example, suppose the cars listed across the top of the table below were the appropriate alternatives, determined through comparative shopping.

2. Next, identify the relevant attributes for making your decision. As with the alternatives, be sure not to leave out an important attribute. These are the criteria on which you expect to make your decision.

3. Third, assign utility values to each alternative X attribute combination on a 9-point evaluation scale, where 1 = bad and 9 = good. These are the values that attribute on that alternative has to you. For example, on the attribute of age, a 1989 Nissan rates a higher utility than an older car, though it rates more poorly on initial cost, because it is more expensive. (Remember that 9 is good and 1 is bad; this is not a cost scale!)

4. Fourth, assign weight values to each attribute based on that attribute's importance to you. *The weights must sum to 100.* In the example below, we chose to weight initial cost and gas mileage much higher than style. The weights, of course, reflect your personal attitudes and values.

5. Next, multiply each utility by the weight value for that attribute. These products appear in the table below.

6. Add the totals of these products for each alternative.

7. Compare the totals for each alternative. The alternative with the highest total should be your best choice. In the example below, that is the 1989 Nissan Sentra.

8. Now try the MAU approach for a decision you face in your own life.

ALTERNATIVES: Utilities/Weighted Utilities for Each Case

ATTRIBUTES	1989 NISSAN SENTRA	1987 FORD TAURUS	1983 PONTIAC TRANS AM	1978 PLYMOUTH FURY	WEIGHT
Age	8/160	5/100	3/60	3/60	20
Initial Cost	2/70	4/140	7/245	8/280	35
Mileage	9/360	5/200	4/160	2/80	40
Style	4/20	5/25	7/35	1/5	5
Sum	610	465	500	425	100

248

that they will do so. Feelings of being "on a streak" or "my luck's got to change" are merely subjective, not objective, probabilities. Many times there are no objective probabilities, and we must rely on subjective estimates. Many real-world decisions are like this.

The Availability Heuristic

It has become increasingly obvious in the study of the psychology of decision making that people do not reason totally as the mathematical laws would predict (Kahneman, Slovic, & Tversky, 1982), just as they do not reason according to laws of formal logic. Rather, they frequently use **heuristics,** or practical strategies, for decision making. Some psychologists at Decision Research in Eugene, Oregon, have studied some of these heuristics extensively, both in the laboratory and the "real world."

One heuristic very widely used is *availability* (Tversky & Kahneman, 1973; Kahneman & Tversky, 1982). In such cases we estimate the likelihood or frequency of occurrence of some event based on the ease with which instances or associations can be brought to mind. Certainly, we always make decisions by retrieving appropriate schemata from long-term memory, but if we interpret our own experience and examples as being more typical than they really are, then we are being biased by the availability heuristic.

For example, when people were asked to say if the letter *K* is more likely to appear in the first or third position in a five-letter word in English, about two-thirds of the subjects responded "first," although, in fact, it is much more common in the third position. It is easier to generate examples of words starting with *K* than those with *K* in the middle, however. Consider how much easier it is to solve a crossword when we know only the first letter (K–) than when we know only a letter in the middle (–K–).

The availability heuristic occurs widely beyond the laboratory, such as its use in interpersonal situations where we draw on availability to make decisions about people in a social context (Ross & Sicoly, 1979; Taylor, 1982). Some of the most available schemata we draw on to interpret the actions of other people often tend to be stereotypes or otherwise inaccurate or biased information. Better understanding of our thought processes in such situations may eventually help us to reduce our dependence upon stereotyped ideas in the perception of others.

Looking at availability more generally, we tend to underestimate the probability of even a very likely event if it has never occurred before, because there is not a readily available instance to use in constructing a scenario. A current and controversial issue in the American Great Plains concerns the rapid depletion of the water table in the once-abundant groundwater of the Ogallala Aquifer that underlies much of the western Great Plains. Scientists warn that unless agriculture reduces its rate of groundwater pumping (primarily through heavy irrigation to nourish thirsty but profitable crops like corn), this rich agricultural region could revert to a desert in the next half century. Though this is a highly probable event if policies do not change, many find the scenario hard to imagine, just as Americans found a projected gasoline scarcity difficult to imagine before 1973. Once the event occurs, however, people may err and over-estimate the probability of its recurrence, as when people move from an area after a very unusual flood that occurred once but would (mathematically) probably not recur in their lifetime. Another example of a perhaps not unlikely but never-before-happened event that people do not take very seriously is the feared excessive accumulation of carbon dioxide in the Earth's atmosphere due to pollution, leading to a calamitous rise in the earth's temperature.

Frequently the mere mention in the media of an occurrence of an event can serve to introduce an available scenario that increases our subjective probability estimations of the likelihood of its occurrence. When Slovic, Fischhoff, & Lichtenstein (1982) studied subjects' perceptions of the likelihood of different causes of death, they found that certain catastrophes were consistently overestimated and others consistently underestimated, and the difference was not particularly related to overall actual frequency (objective probability). For example, people overestimated the likelihood of dying from botulism, tornadoes, floods, venomous bites or stings, and car accidents. A death from such causes is likely to make the front page or the TV evening news. On the other hand, subjects consistently underestimated the probability of dying from asthma, emphysema, diabetes, strokes, and tuberculosis. Some kinds of cancer were overestimated and other kinds underestimated, with differences likely related to media coverage.

Sometimes the media alter our subjective probabilities in a helpful way. For example, when young drivers are shown gory films of auto accidents, they may revise upward their probabilities of having such an accident themselves and thus may drive more carefully. In such a case it might actually be better to overestimate mathematically the likelihood of that event occurring. Thus, the normatively "best" estimate would not be the "best" choice for one's health, just as the most "logical" scientific reasoning discussed earlier in the chapter was not always the "best."

Another way that the availability heuristic manifests itself is in what has sometimes been called *illusory correlation*. People may infer that a causative relationship exists simply because a correlated event with some face validity as a causal agent exists. For example, suppose a hurricane with 100-mph winds is headed for Miami. The government seeds the cloud with silver iodide crystals. Following this, the hurricane gains force to 120-mph winds, slams into Miami Beach, and demolishes several large hotels. The owners try to sue the government for "causing" the destruction by cloudseeding. Who is to say, however, that the hurricane might not have been even worse had the seeding not occurred, or indeed that it had any effect at all? Perhaps the seeding was the cause, but perhaps also the availability heuristic intervened and mentally assigned a convenient cause for a terrible event that people want very much to explain, to keep within the bounds of their rational model of the world.

A similar example may be seen in medical malpractice cases. A man has surgery; his condition deteriorates. Was the deterioration due to the surgery or not? Often courts are called on to make a very difficult decision, in part involving questions of how we process information, particularly

---

BOX 9–8   Medical Decision Making

A very important aspect of medicine involves decision making. Such processes come in at several different points. An individual making a decision whether to seek treatment makes a judgment. A physician or other health professional making a diagnosis and prescribing a treatment makes a judgment. An individual choosing to adhere or not adhere to treatment makes judgments.

Medical decision making has been studied from several perspectives. For example, Zalkind and Shachtman (1980) developed a decision analysis model of a person's decision whether or not to seek a swine flu shot during the influenza scare of the mid-1970s. Arkes and Harkness (1980) showed how a pre-existent mental schema can unduly distort a diagnosis decision. McNeil, Pauker, Sox, and Tversky (1982) examined the choice of surgery or radiation in lung cancer cases. McIntyre, Barnett, Harris, Shanteau, Skowronski, and Klassen (1987) examined the motivational bases of a decision to become or not become an organ donor. Sisson, Schoomaker, and Ross (1976) examined how extra information may actually detract from the quality of clinical decision making. As medicine increasingly takes psychological factors in illness more seriously and psychology increasingly examines biological origins of behavior, the study of cognitive processes in medicine will probably grow substantially in the coming years.

---

our inferring of causal relationships. The psychology of decision making has many applications to medicine (See Box 9–8).

The Anchoring Adjustment Heuristic

Another heuristic is the **anchoring-adjustment heuristic** (Slovic & Lichtenstein, 1971; Tversky & Kahneman, 1974). In these cases we make some initial estimate (*first impression*) and later revise that estimate upward or downward according to new information. However, the bias enters in when we often do not adjust the initial estimate (*anchor*) sufficiently and thus are overly biased by our original estimation. Personality studies show that we often are unduly biased by our first impression of a person. For example, a negative first impression may require many later positive encounters to balance the overall impression. Students sometimes complain that a teacher makes up his or her mind about them early in the semester and labels the student from that point on. For example, students may feel that poor performance on the first exam in a class may forever brand them as "stupid" in that teacher's eyes, even if later test performance is notably better. If the teacher is, in fact, thinking this way, the anchoring-adjustment heuristic is operating. The schema of that person in the teacher's mind would have been formed initially from highly negative information. It thus becomes the prototype from which change must be made.

Another type of example of anchoring-adjustment bias comes from cost and duration estimates for construction projects. For example, it is known that cost overruns and delays are quite frequent in construction. When project costs are figured, they are initially figured at current cost

BOX 9–9   Decision-Making Research
as an Aid in Real Conflict

Can cognitive psychologists have some impact on foreign-policy decision making? Tetlow (1986) suggests that they can. Researchers who have studied social-judgment and decision-making processes may help identify strategies used in foreign-policy decision making and identify points at which error and bias enter.

Assuming a more-or-less rational model of decision making, certain psychological variables leading to deviations from this rational model may be identified. For example, some personality variables irrelevant to the policy issues could affect decisions, as when a relatively authoritarian personality may endorse harder-line measures than a less authoritarian person would do under the same circumstances. Small-group dynamics, such as implicit pressures to conform and encourage group solidarity, may limit the options and views considered and inhibit self-criticism, especially of popular views. Presidents, for example, often must explicitly encourage their staffs to share divergent and unpopular views in meetings, in order to avoid having the tendencies toward conformity and group cohesiveness overshadow the need to hear a variety of policy options.

More germane for our decision here are the cognitive variables affecting decision making. Top-down processes may be used too much relative to bottom-up processes (see chapter 5); for example, a local disturbance somewhere may be quickly identified as "communist aggression" without closely examining the specific facts of the situation. Superficial and simplistic analogies may be drawn from history without adequate recognition of differences of the current and historical situation; for example, looking at events in Nicaragua and quickly reacting "another Cuba!" or "another Vietnam!" Sometimes the political and situational constraints on one's adversaries are not fully recognized and taken into account, partially because of the difficulty of obtaining knowledge of such information. For example, it is difficult to obtain precise knowledge of Soviet economic problems and adequately judge how much they constrain military spending and encourage serious pursuit of arms-control agreements.

Additionally, people tend to be overly confident in the correctness of their own judgments. Also, errors and bias tend to be worse in times of high stress than in less stressful conditions. Identifying such possible sources of bias and error may be the first step toward reducing them. However, the need for such analysis may not be easy to "sell" to the policymakers in question. See Hammond and Grassia (1985) for a discussion of cognitive issues in international conflict and a report of four studies examining cognitive factors in real-world conflict situations.

levels and assuming that construction will proceed as planned. That overall figure is then revised upward to account for projected inflation, allowances for strikes, delivery delays, and other factors. Often, however, this revision is not sufficient; that is, there is too much reliance on the initial estimate.

Hindsight

Another heuristic is **hindsight** or "creeping determinism," as studied extensively by Baruch Fischhoff (1975, 1977; Fischhoff & Beyth, 1975). Fischhoff demonstrated experimentally that people are overly biased by hindsight; that is, how an event came out. When asked to make an estimate of probability of some event occurring from the point of view of someone answering *before* the event occurred, people are unable to ignore their knowledge of the outcome, even when specifically told to do so. The mind's tendency to impose order, structure, and interpretation on events reorganizes information in ways that can distort it.

After an unfortunate event occurs, people often look back and say, "We should have seen that coming." People retrospectively said the Japanese attack on Pearl Harbor in 1941 was predictable. In another type of example, a prisoner on parole commits another crime; people will say the parole officer should have foreseen that. Often people in responsible positions receive the blame after such events occur. No doubt sometimes they are at fault and, indeed, the event should have been anticipated. On the other hand, it is also highly likely that the hindsight bias in information processing is operating in some of these cases, and the unfortunate event really may not have been predictable before it happened. More recent research has tried to identify specific conditions under which such effects occur (see Hasher, Attig, & Alba, 1981). Decision-making psychology may be useful in understanding international conflict in other ways as well (see Box 9–9).

Slovic and Fischhoff (1977) have demonstrated that hindsight operates in interpreting psychological research. For example, we overestimate the likelihood of replicating preliminary results. One disturbing theme found by these researchers has been the way mathematicians and scientists are almost as vulnerable as anyone else to distorted thinking through use of judgment heuristics (cf. results of scientific reasoning studies discussed above).

The Oregon group has frequently been criticized for taking a purely descriptive, atheoretical approach to studying decisions under uncertainty. Others have examined such processes using a more theoretical, model-testing approach. For example, Downing, Sternberg, and Ross (1985) used multiple regression techniques to test several models of making inferences about causality in multicausal situations.

CONCLUSION

As you can see from this chapter, the study of thinking encompasses a wide range of problems and issues, as do your own processes of thinking. There is no comprehensive theory or even theoretical framework that can claim to describe or explain all types of thinking, nor is there likely to be such a theory in the near future. Still, cognitive psychology has managed to shed many important insights on these complex and often mysterious

> ┌──── BOX 9–10   Answers to Problems in Chapter 9 ────┐
>
> To find out what the customer ordered, simply *read the letters*, preferably with a certain intonation pattern:
>
> C: Do you have any eggs?
> W: Yes, we have eggs.
> C: Any ham?
> W: Yes, we have ham too.
> C: Do you have tea?
> W: Yes, tea too.
> C: I'll have ham and eggs and tea.
>
> Answers to Questions in Box 9–1.
>
> A: The knights trade horses.
> B: TO/TIE/MULES/TO (The O is the hole.)
> C: deny
> D: $c = 2$ (c must be equivalent to the other diagonal of the rectangle, which is also a radius of the circle.)

thought processes, processes that caused Shakespeare to write (long before the emergence of cognitive research!) the following description of people:

How noble in reason, how infinite in faculties . . .
In apprehension how like a god . . .
The beauty of the world, the paragon of animals.

SUGGESTED READINGS

Problem solving and reasoning are typically covered in cognition textbooks cited in earlier chapters. Decision making is less often included in such textbooks, though some include material on the heuristics discussed in this chapter, often combined in a chapter on inductive reasoning or development of concepts.

Adams (1976), B. Anderson (1980), Weisberg (1986), and Bransford and Stein (1984) attempt to apply problem-solving research to one's daily life. Beyth-Marom and Lichtenstein (1984) do the same for judgmental biases in decision making.

For an excellent collection of research and conceptual papers on judgment and decision making, see Arkes and Hammond (1986).

10

LEARNING AND BIOLOGY

INTRODUCTION

Two Kinds of Biology

Biology is relevant to the psychology of learning in two ways. First, there must exist physiological mechanisms responsible for the patterns of conditioning, learning, information processing, memory, and thinking described by psychologists. Even if the psychological principles are logically independent of physiology, as radical behaviorists and functionalists argue, they must nevertheless be carried out by biological processes within the living creature. Research into the physiological bases of learning and memory is one of the most exciting and active fields in contemporary science.

Equally exciting, but more controversial, is research connected with the second way biology is relevant to the psychology of learning, namely *sociobiology*. The nervous systems of animals, including human beings, evolved over millions of years, so we can ask why we, and other creatures, possess the brains we do, and why, in consequence, we behave the way we do.

Corresponding to each of these inquiries are two very different kinds of biology, the biology of proximate causes and the biology of ultimate causes. An excellent way to understand the difference is to ask, as a child might, "Why does sugar taste sweet?" (Barash, 1979). To ask why people like sugar seems inane—it tastes sweet. But *why* does it taste sweet? Several kinds of answers can be given. One might give a phenomenological analysis of the pleasures of sweetness. Then one might explain the experience of sweetness in terms of physiological mechanisms in the tongue and brain. For many purposes these answers are sufficient. But we can still ask, "Why do people have a physiology that makes sugar taste sweet?" The only possible answer is evolutionary—that ancestors who tended to like sugary foods, primarily ripe, vitamin-rich fruits, ate them, and this gave them superior energy to continue the struggle for existence, so that they had more off-spring than (say) alkaline-liking rivals. As a result, the gene that expressed itself as "sweetness-liking" so rose in frequency as to become almost universal, driving people to eat not only medically protective apples (an apple a day keeps the doctor away), but also to invent and eat candy bars, to the harm of our teeth.

What makes sociobiology of such potential importance is that it not only addresses the behavior of a species, but also reaches deep into its *mentality*, providing new kinds of answers to questions about mind and behavior. To say I like sugar because it is sweet, or orgasm because it feels good, or to run because it is fun, is to assign the *proximate causes* of my behavior or my likings. That is, in each case I describe the immediate causes of my behavior. I explain what I do or like in terms of what I know makes me do or like them. Physiological explanations also cite proximate causes, describing the physiological underpinnings of tasting sweetness, having an orgasm, or running.

But when we explain psychology and physiology in terms of past evolutionary success, we are moving toward what biologists call *ultimate causation*. Here we describe the evolutionary causes of the proximate causes—why my brain has mechanisms for liking sugar, orgasms, or running. Figure 10–1 (from Alcock, 1979) shows the relation of ultimate to proximate causation, including the developmental connection between genes and the phenotypes that express them, and how these phenotypes—the proximate mechanism of physiology and psychology—lead to behaviors that either succeed or fail in the struggle for existence, affecting the gene-frequencies in the next generation.

Now there is nothing wrong or false about proximate causation. It is perfectly true that you like sugar because it is sweet; the physiologist's explanation of sweetness is equally true. Neither are sham explanations. Ultimate explanation does not destroy the proximate explanations; it just helps us understand where they came from. Some people think that when sociobiologists attribute altruism to the calculus of kin selection it turns the love of a parent for its child into a cynical calculation. Nonsense. Love is no less real because it helps us survive. Love is no more destroyed by ultimate explanation in terms of survival than is Chartres Cathedral destroyed by explaining where the stone that built it was quarried.

Into the Empty Organism: The Search for the Engram

The idea that memories are stored in the brain is very old. Medieval Islamic and, later, Christian physicians believed that the brain was divided into separate compartments, or *ventricles*, each of which was responsible

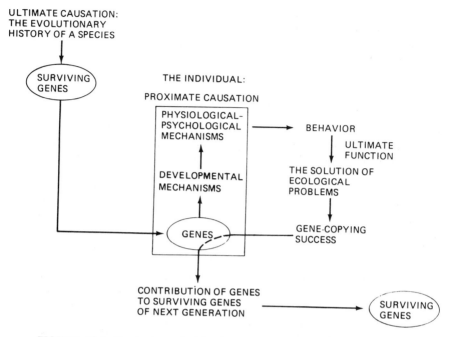

ULTIMATE CAUSATION:
THE EVOLUTIONARY
HISTORY OF A SPECIES

SURVIVING GENES

THE INDIVIDUAL:

PROXIMATE CAUSATION

PHYSIOLOGICAL-
PSYCHOLOGICAL
MECHANISMS → BEHAVIOR

ULTIMATE
FUNCTION

DEVELOPMENTAL
MECHANISMS

THE SOLUTION OF
ECOLOGICAL
PROBLEMS

GENES

GENE-COPYING
SUCCESS

CONTRIBUTION OF GENES
TO SURVIVING GENES
OF NEXT GENERATION → SURVIVING GENES

FIGURE 10-1 Proximate and ultimate causation of behavior. Ultimately an animal has within it certain genes because they have survived to the present. These genes regulate the development of the proximate mechanisms of behavior. These mechanisms make possible certain behavioral responses to environmental events—responses that will determine the number of copies of the individual's genes that are passed to the next generation. The ultimate function of behavior is to meet ecological pressures in such a way that the individual maximizes its gene-copying success.

for a different psychological function. Experiences were thought to be processed from the senses through a series of four to seven ventricles, finally coming to reside in the ventricle for memory. Even Rene Descartes, who thought that soul and body were distinct substances, (the former spiritual and the latter material), believed that memories are stored in the brain, not the soul. In the seventeenth and eighteenth centuries it was discovered that the ventricles of the medieval doctors—who had been forbidden by their religions to dissect the body—did not exist, and the search for the biological basis of learning and memory had to start over again.

Modern neuroscience begins with the research and theories of Franz Joseph Gall (1758–1828). Gall performed the first modern anatomical and comparative studies of human and animal brains, believing that different psychological functions were located in distinct organs of the brain. For example, he located Lust in the cerebellum, Murder just above the ears, and Location and Language behind the eyes. While Gall agreed with the medieval physicians that each psychological function had its distinct organ in the brain, he did not believe that memory was a separate mental power, and he located memories throughout the brain. Gall thought that memories were stored in the organ whose function had been involved with a particular experience. So, for example, memories of sexual experience would be stored with the organ for Lust, while memories for places would be stored in Location.

Unfortunately for the development of neuroscience, Gall's basically correct view of the brain turned into the pseudoscience of *phrenology*. Gall was followed by enthusiasts rather than scientists, and his system became a sort of parlor game of diagnosing people's personalities from the bumps on their skulls, and so phrenology, as it came to be called, fell into disrepute in scientific circles. Gall had been an extreme *localizationalist*, believing that psychological functions could be localized to precisely definable parts of the brain. Partly in reaction to Gall, a rival view arose that maintained that the brain acts as a whole, with psychological functions being distributed throughout the entire brain. The tension between localizationalist and *distributionist* views of mental function has generated controversy and creativity in neuroscience down to the present day.

The distributionist view gained credence from the research of Pierre Jean Marie Flourens (1794–1867), Gall's harshest critic and the leading physiologist of the day. Flourens performed *ablation* experiments, in which he removed (ablated) or destroyed (lesioned) different parts and amounts of animals' brains. He claimed that destruction of parts of the brain resulted in the loss not of specific functions, as phrenology predicted, but of a general capacity for adaptive behavior, suggesting that the brain acts as a whole; thus, as more brain is removed, the stupider the animal becomes. Phrenologists protested, rightly, that Flourens' method was like investigating the functions of an unknown machine by taking an ax to part of it and then observing what the machine does not do. Notwithstanding the crudity of his methods, Flourens' prestige ensured that the distributionist view of brain function would remain dominant for some decades.

The localizationist view began to revive with the clinical findings of Pierre Paul Broca (1824–1880). In his hospital, Broca observed that patients with a certain kind of *aphasia*—difficulty with speech or language—proved, upon autopsy, to have lesions is the left front neocortex of their brains. Broca hypothesized that this area—today called *Broca's area*—was responsible for language, just as the phrenologists had said. In 1870, two German investigators showed that application of mild electrical currents to the brains of living animals resulted in specific muscular responses. As a result of these findings, a sort of "new phrenology" was born. It turned out that Gall had been correct that the brain possessed specialized areas for specific functions, but had been wrong about the sort of functions the brain served. Instead of broad psychological traits such as Lust and Theft, the specialized areas of the brain were responsible for specific sensory or motor functions, such as registering a sound or moving a limb.

However, these discoveries of the late nineteenth century left the physiological basis of learning as mysterious as ever. Was there a brain center for Memory? Were specific memories stored in specific parts of the brain? These questions remained unanswered. As the localizational view gained dominance around the turn of the century, the biologist Richard Semon coined the term "engram" to refer to the trace in the brain storing a particular memory (Squire, 1987). The search for the engram has dominated the physiological study of learning ever since (Thompson & Donegan, 1986).

In the first half of the twentieth century the most diligent searcher for the engram was the psychologist Karl Lashley, a student of John B. Watson's. Lashley had collaborated with Watson on a series of classical conditioning studies—the first ever performed in the United States—and believed that the future of behaviorist psychology lay in the reduction of psychological laws to physiology (Lashley, 1923); hence his ultimately futile search for the engram. Lashley reasoned that if engrams existed at specific sites in the brain—the localizationist hypothesis about learning—then removal of the site of the engram would abolish specific memories. Therefore, Lashley adopted Flourens' ablation method, hoping to remove, and thus find, the engram.

Over years of difficult investigation, Lashely had rats learn mazes, ablating varying amounts and location of brain matter either before or after learning. Lashley's results and conclusions echoed Flourens': The ability to learn was not impaired by lesions to any specific site in the brain, but was gradually lost as greater amounts of brain were removed; similarly, memory for the maze seemed not to reside in any particular part of the brain, but seemed to be gradually erased as more and more brain was removed. In looking back on his search, Lashley ruefully but wryly concluded that, according to his findings, "learning is just not possible. It is difficult to conceive of a mechanism which can satisfy the conditions set for it. Nevertheless, in spite of such evidence against it, learning does sometimes occur" (Lashley, 1950, pp. 477–478). Lashley embraced, as Flourens had, the distributionist, or mass-action, view of the brain, proposing that learning is an activity of the whole brain and that individual memories are stored in the whole brain, not at distinct sites, or engrams. Despite difficulties and controversies over the interpretation of his results (Squire, 1987)—he was, after all, still attacking a delicate mechanism with what amounted to a jackhammer—Lashley's results, when published in 1929, virtually brought to a halt the investigation of the neural substrates of learning and memory (Thompson & Donegan, 1986).

A virtue of the localizationist, engram theory had been that it held out the hope of finding discrete mechanisms of learning and memory, and it pointed the way to investigations searching for them. But Lashley's findings had destroyed the localizationist view. His replacement, *mass action*, seemed to make finding the neural basis of memory a hopeless task, for there seemed to be no place to look for it. However, in 1949, Donald Hebb, a student of Lashley's, revived the field and gave it its modern form with his concept of the *cell assembly*. The cell-assembly concept respected Lashley's findings while reintroducing the localizational hypothesis in modified form. The failing of the old engram view had been its narrowness, essentially claiming that individual memories resided in individual neurons, a hypothesis rendered untenable by Lashley's studies. Hebb proposed instead that the mechanisms of learning, and the sites of memory storage, lay not in isolated neurons but in organized groups, or *assemblies*, of neurons. Moreover, these assemblies need not involve cells adjacent to one another, but might involve connections between cells in different parts of the brain. According to Hebb, then, memories were both distributed, as engrams are not found in single cells, *and* localized, as learning does not involve the whole brain (Thompson & Donegan, 1986; Squire, 1987). Thus, ablation of some piece of brain tissue could not remove a single engram but it might damage part of the circuitries responsible for learning and memory storage, weakening, but not abolishing, learning, as Lashley had found. By proposing that there were mechanisms of learning to be found, Hebb gave new inspiration to the neuropsychology of learning.

The concept of the cell assembly helps show how difficult it is to interpret ablation findings. Any given piece of behavior involves what Richard Thompson (Thompson & Donegan, 1986) calls a *sensory-motor circuit*, beginning with peripheral stimulation and ending with overt motor response. Somewhere in-between is the structure or structures—the cell assemblies—responsible for learning, Thompson's *memory trace circuit*. The memory structures must be *plastic*, capable of modification by experience, and of retaining this modification for a period of time. But finding the central, plastic part of the sensory-motor circuit is difficult, for experiments looking for the memory trace circuit may change behavior by altering structures not involved in learning. For example, ablation may accidentally destroy tissue necessary for making a classically conditioned motor response, but it would be a mistake to think that because the response has disappeared that one has found the memory trace. Ablation experiments are thus no longer the mainstay of researchers on the neural basis of memory.

Research has eliminated some of the logically possible sources of neural plasticity (Squire, 1987). One might think that learning involves growing new neurons in response to experience. However, the brain is incapable of growing new cells, and in fact neurons die unreplaced every day. Moreover, proper development of the brain seems to involve selective pruning of neurons and synapses. Another disproved possibility is that memory was stored in the complex organic molecules found in neural tissue. This hypothesis was popular for a while in the 1960s and led to hopes for learning by taking pills, but the initially exciting findings did not pan out. The remaining possibility is that learning involves changes to the synapses that connect existing neurons. Experience may induce growth of new synapses or changes to the neurochemistry and/or the structure of existing synapses. Thus, the modern "search for the engram" involves, first, locating the plastic structures of the brain that change with learning, and then identifying the cellular mechanisms in these structures that cause learning. Great advances in answering both questions have been made in recent years.

PROXIMATE CAUSES: LEARNING, MEMORY, AND THE BRAIN

Amnesia

Perhaps the most dramatic evidence that learning and memory depend on the brain is organic *amnesia*, when damage to the brain erases old memories and makes it difficult or impossible to form new ones. The study of amnesia, while necessarily less precise than experimental studies of the biology of memory, has nevertheless contributed important information concerning the sites of memory formation in storage. In this section we will focus on the irreversible *amnesic syndrome*; temporary amnesia is treated in Box 10–1. Amnesic syndrome is defined by four symptoms (Butters & Miliotis, 1985; Groves & Rebec, 1988). The first is *anterograde amnesia*, the difficulty or inability to form new memories. Second is *retrograde amnesia*, the loss of some memories prior to the event causing the brain damage responsible for the amnesia. The retrograde amnesia is *graded*, so that the more remote a memory is from the traumatic event the more likely it is to be remembered. The third symptom is *confabulation*: When asked to recall an event lost to memory, amnesics may make up a story instead. Finally, amnesics' difficulties are restricted to memory, for they possess *normal intelligence*.

The most famous and most extensively researched case of amnesic syndrome is the patient H.M. (Cotman & McGaugh, 1980; Squire, 1987). H.M. had suffered from epilepsy from age 16, and in 1953, at age 27, the epilepsy having become uncontrollable by medication, surgery was performed in an effort to relieve the patient's seizures. The operation was successful in controlling the epilepsy, but accidentally and unfortunately it caused total anterograde amnesia. H.M.'s intelligence (IQ 117), personality, and short-term memory (STM) are intact—he has a normal digit span of 6 to 7 items—but he can form no new memories: Even after 25 presentations of a long word list he cannot recall more than the 6 items storable in his STM, and he shows no primacy effect. As H.M. says, "Every day is alone in itself . . . everything looks clear to me, but what happened just before? . . . It's like waking from a dream. I just don't remember" (quoted by Cotman & McGaugh, 1980, p. 334). H.M. cannot even recognize a current photograph of himself, and he needs constant custodial care. We sometimes wish we could forget, but life without memory is horrible.

There is some controversy over the exact nature of the psychological deficit in amnesia: Are amnesics actually unable to form new memories, as appears to be the case, or perhaps do they form memories which they cannot retrieve, as some experimental evidence suggests? For example, amnesics' performance on list learning is improved by providing hints at the time of recall, and when learning new lists amnesics often report words from earlier lists; both results imply that items from the lists have been stored but that retrieval of them is seriously impaired (Cotman & McGaugh, 1980). Additionally, it turns out that amnesics' remote memory is not intact,

BOX 10–1 Temporary Amnesia and Modulation of Memory

The amnesic syndrome involves permanent impairment to the ability to form new memories. Memory loss, including retrograde and anterograde amnesia, can also occur following brain trauma that does not create amnesic syndrome. Figure 10–2 shows the course of such amnesia in one case of severe brain trauma resulting in temporary coma (from Squire, 1987, p. 207).

Note first that the trauma did not result in amnesic syndrome, as new memories were created beginning about five months following the incident. Nevertheless, some permanent loss of memory occurred, specifically retrograde amnesia for the two weeks prior to trauma and for the 3.5 months following recovery from coma.

The most important point from the standpoint of the study of learning and memory is the temporary retrograde amnesia for events lying many years before the brain insult. For example, five months after trauma the patient suffered total retrograde amnesia for all events occurring less than two years before the accident, but gradually memory returned, so that the patient permanently lost memories for events occurring only two weeks or less before brain insult. Findings such as these have led to the concept of *consolidation*, the hypothesis that memory formation is a remarkably gradual process taking weeks or even months. When the process is disrupted, consolidation is slowed, as in the present case for all memories within two years of brain damage, or even blocked entirely, as for the events occurring two weeks or less before injury. The concept of consolidation challenges our common-sense ideas about memory, which suggest that one immediately stores memories the way a VCR does. A better analogy might be to a Polaroid picture that takes not seconds but months to develop. Memories may be laid down when we have experiences, but it takes a long time for the information to be fixed permanently, and it is possible for the fixation process to be altered by damage to the brain mechanisms responsible for it.

The fact that the creation of memories may be affected for good or ill by later events is known as *modulation of memory* (Squire, 1987). Memory formation can be affected not only by brain trauma but also by changes to the brain's chemistry that can accelerate, modify, or retard its progress. For example, one interesting class of memories is *flashbulb memories*, remarkably vivid memories for emotionally significant events. People who were more than 10 or so years old at the time can typically remember where they were when told that John F. Kennedy was assassinated in 1963, when his brother, Robert, was assassinated in 1968, or when the space shuttle *Challenger* blew up in 1986. It has been hypothesized that hormones released by the extreme emotions felt at the time modified the process of memory formation, making it more vivid than other similarly remote events that were less traumatic. On the other hand, we might remember these events well because we often talk about—and thus rehearse—them, or it might be that such memories are vivid but inaccurate.

Whatever the explanation of flashbulb memories may be, it appears that learning takes place not in an instant, but over weeks, and may be controlled by unknown influences science is only beginning to uncover.

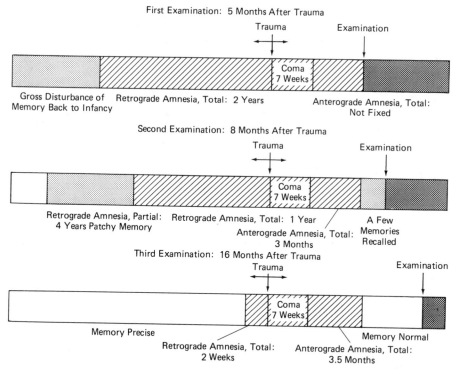

FIGURE 10-2 (From *Memory and Brain* by Larry R. Squire. Copyright © 1987 by Oxford University Press, Inc. Reprinted by permission.)

for when asked about significant events occurring years before testing, amnesics show poorer recall than do normal controls (Gabriel, Sparenborg, & Stolar, 1986).

However, the retrieval-failure theory cannot explain all the facts about amnesia. To begin with, it cannot explain why amnesic's anterograde amnesia is worse than their retrograde amnesia (Gabriel and others, 1986). More revealingly, it fails to explain the graded nature of retrograde amnesia (Gabriel and others, 1986; Squire 1987). If amnesia involved only retrieval failure, all memories should be equally inaccessible, yet the more remote a memory is the more likely it is to be available. Furthermore, if the retrieval failure were said to affect only recent memories, then as memories get older they should become more retrievable. Yet after surgery patient H.M. lost memory for the last few years before surgery, and these memories have never returned more than two decades later (Squire, 1987). So, while amnesia may involve some retrieval difficulties, the major psychological defect is inability, or at least great difficulty, in forming new memories (Squire, 1987).

Cases of amnesia have proven valuable in distinguishing between various forms and processes of memory. The distinction between short-term and long-term memory (LTM) is supported by the amnesic syndrome.

H.M. is typical among amnesics in having a normal digit span, and thus an intact STM, while being unable to lay down memories in LTM. Amnesia also shows that we must distinguish between the site of memory *storage* and the sites of the processes and mechanisms that *create* memories. H.M. can recall remote events, so we know that his permanent memory-storage sites were not damaged by surgery, but he cannot form new memories, so we know that the structures responsible for memory creation were damaged. Moreover, the graded nature of retrograde amnesia suggests that memory consolidation is a drawn out but time-limited process in which some structures of the brain participate in laying down memories in some other part of the brain with which contact is eventually broken off (Squire, 1987).

One remarkable finding with H.M., and confirmed in other cases of amnesia, supports important distinctions between types of long-term memory. H.M. shows essentially normal rates of learning for a variety of motor skills, such as mirror drawing, even though each time he performs the task he says he has never done it before! Amnesics also show normal acquisition of simple Pavlovian responses without memory of the apparatus, although complex Pavlovian phenomena such as latent inhibition and reversal learning are impaired. Such learning without memory even extends to some problem-solving tasks such as the Tower of Hanoi puzzle, in which washers of different sizes making a pyramid shape over the first of three posts must be moved, one at a time and without placing a larger on a smaller, to make the pyramid on the third post, and indicates that there are at least two forms of long-term memory, one of which is spared in the amnesic syndrome. Different theorists have proposed different names for these two forms of permanent memory (Gabriel and others, 1986), but the most useful and widely adopted distinction is Squire's (1987) between declarative and procedural memory, borrowed from philosophy and artificial intelligence (see Chapter 4). Amnesics lack declarative memory, conscious recall of past events, but retain procedural memory, the ability to learn new behaviors. Thus, mirror drawing remains ever new to H.M. even as he gets better and better at it.

Recent research also reveals that amnesics show near normal to normal *priming effects* (Schachter, 1985, 1986a,b, 1987). Usually, memory for a list of words is tested by asking subjects to recall the list or to say whether presented words were on the list or not (recognition). However, if subjects learn a list of words and are later presented even two or three weeks later with a list of word fragments to complete, and are told nothing about any connection between the word fragments and the earlier list, they are more likely than controls to complete the word fragments if the fragments make words that were on the earlier list, and if the fragments have more than one solution, they are more likely than controls to complete the fragment with a word from the earlier list. A related phenomenon occurs when subjects are shown a word and then later are tachistoscopically shown words at extremely brief presentation times, and it is found that the word or words shown to the subject are recognized at much shorter presentation intervals than control words. It appears that mere exposure to a word somehow "primes" that word in memory so that it is much more available than other words for some time.

When amnesics are shown a list of words and then tested on it by the usual means, they do very poorly, showing anterograde amnesia. But if they are simply given word fragments to complete, they show priming for words on the list. This occurs only when they are not told of any connection between the two lists: When they are told that the fragments are hints that will help them remember the earlier list, they again do poorly. The distinction between recognition and priming is dramatically emphasized by research with sufferers from Alzheimer's disease, whose amnesic syndrome grows progressively worse. Alzheimer's subjects show a steady loss in the ability to recognize words from earlier presented lists, but show essentially normal priming (Schachter, 1985). The existence of priming makes possible some learning by amnesics, but within very rigid limits. For example, after extensive drilling, a group of amnesics learned 30 items of computer terminology and retained it over the months of the experiment. They could also learn to write a very simple program. However, their knowledge could only be brought out when test questions were almost exactly the same as the wording of items and definitions at the time of learning. For example, one subject learned to respond "save" to the definition "to store a program," but after having written his simple program and being told to save it, he was unable to do so until prompted with the letter *s*.

As a result of these and other findings, Daniel Schachter (1985, 1987) has distinguished between *explicit* and *implicit* long-term memory. Explicit memory requires conscious awareness of a previous event, and is lost in amnesia; implicit memory does not require conscious awareness and is spared by amnesia. The relation between Schachter's distinction between explicit and implicit memory and between Squire's declarative and procedural knowledge is unclear. In one respect they seem closely related. Implicit memory and procedural knowledge are both unconscious and spared by amnesia, while explicit memory and declarative knowledge are conscious and damaged by amnesia. On the other hand, the two distinctions are not identical. For example, procedural knowledge involves "knowing how": learning how to do things, to respond to stimuli, as in Pavlovian conditioning, while the implicit memory revealed by priming is semantic, not motor. Although future research may reveal deep similarities between Squire's and Schachter's distinctions, at present it is best to conclude that long-term memory may be usefully divided both ways (Squire, 1987).

We have now reviewed the fascinating psychology of amnesia. Can the study of amnesia help us find the brain structures responsible for learning and memory?

Structures

H.M.'s surgery involved the removal of structures from the mediotemporal areas of the brain: two-thirds of the hippocampus, the parahippocampal gyrus, the uncus, and the amygdala (Cotman & McGaugh, 1980). The mediotemporal structures are closely interconnected, appearing to form a functional system within the brain, called the *limbic system*. One case of human amnesia implicates the hippocampus as the most important structure responsible for learning, because unlike H.M., patient R.B. suffered damage only to area CA1 of the hippocampus, yet developed a severe case of the amnesic syndrome (Squire, 1987). Human amnesia can also result from damage to the diencephalic midline of the brain, including the thalamus, hypothalamus, and mammilary bodies, as happens in Korsakoff's syndrome, which follows upon some cases of severe alcoholism.

While cases of amnesia may suggest which structures of the brain are involved in learning, they cannot answer more precise questions about how various structures operate and interact while forming, storing, and retrieving memories. Amnesic's brains may be damaged in ways not always apparent at autopsy, and many amnesics such as H.M., who had suffered epilepsy, and those acquiring amnesia from disease, such as Korsakoff's patients, may have incurred other physiological damage, making identification of memory structures tentative (see Box 10–2). Investigators into the biological bases of learning and memory have therefore tried to develop experimental animal models of human amnesia to pinpoint more precisely the structures involved in learning and memory. The best-developed animal model (Kesner, 1986; Gabriel and others, 1986) has been proposed by Mortimer Mishkin and his associates (see Mishkin & Appenzeller, 1987).

Mishkin has extensively studied the effects of brain lesions on monkeys' ability to learn. Mishkin has mainly used two learning tasks, a simple discrimination task in which a monkey must learn under which of two objects food is to be found, and a complex memory task, delayed nonmatching to sample. In delayed nonmatching to sample, a monkey first finds food under a novel object. After a delay, it is shown a pair of objects, one of which is the same as before and one of which is novel, and it must choose the new object to find food. On each trial new pairs of objects are used and pairs are never repeated. Thus the monkey must learn always to choose the unfamiliar object in any test pair. Mishkin found that removal of the hippocampus alone produced little impairment in learning either task, though this may only be true of animals with no preoperative training (Squire, 1987). Removal of the amygdala alone slowed learning considerably but did not abolish it. Removal of the hippocampus and the amygdala together abolished learning entirely, unless in the delayed nonmatching to sample procedure the test was presented immediately after the sample. Joint hippocampal plus amygdala removal seems to create monkeys with the human amnesic syndrome: intact short-term memory but impaired long-term memory. Mishkin concluded that memory formation can occur via the hippocampus or the amygdala, so that if one is lost the other can take its place, but if both are lost, learning becomes impossible.

Mishkin's results nicely model the mediotemporal amnesia suffered by patient H.M. But damage to the diencephalon also causes amnesia in humans, and Mishkin found learning impairment when the thalamus and mammilary body of monkeys' brains were removed. Moreover, the thalamus and the hypothalamus are connected to the hippocampus and the amygdala,

---

BOX 10–2   Permanent Memory?

Once a memory is completely consolidated, can it be lost? This important question has been much contested in cognitive psychology. While it is obvious that we cannot remember everything we have been exposed to—otherwise we would never get less than 100% on college tests—there are two reasons this might be so. On the one hand, memories might be lost even if after complete consolidation, perhaps because memory traces in the brain simply decay over the years. On the other hand, memories might be permanent, and our loss of them really a loss of ability to retrieve them from storage.

Support for the second point of view seemed to come from serendipitious findings by the neurosurgeon Wilder Penfield in the 1950s. Penfield performed operations on the brains of epilepsy patients in hope of relieving their symptoms. Part of brain surgery—which is always done on awake patients—involves stimulating the brain to discover the precise location of important abilities, so that they will not be damaged by surgery. Penfield reported that in the course of his explorations of the brain, his patients would sometimes seem to relive remote events as if they were being experienced anew. For example, one patient reported hearing music being played, although of course no music was to be heard in the operating room. Penfield and others have argued that these experiences are an accurate reliving of past experience permanently etched in the brain.

However, closer examination of Penfield's findings casts doubt on his interpretation. To begin with, only a tiny minority of Penfield's patients ever reported memorylike experiences. Those who did often reported that they were more like dreams than like real experiences, having either the unreal or fantastic character of dreams or involving experiences the patient could not have had. Moreoever, we should bear in mind that Penfield's patients all suffered from epilepsy, a disorder of the brain, and many of the "recollections" were connected with the patient's epileptic symptoms. For example, one patient's seizures were regularly preceded by a (false) image of a robber approaching him; during surgery he reported the vivid experience of being attacked by robbers in the operating room! It thus seems likely that Penfield's patients were reporting not memories, but artificial experiences created by electrical stimulation of the brain (Squire, 1987). Whether or not memories are permanent remains an open question.

---

and Mishkin discovered that lesions to the fibers connecting the limbic system with the diencephalon, or to the sites in the diencephalon receiving limbic connections, created amnesia too. Similar results also occurred when the connections between the thalamus and the prefrontal cortex were severed, and when the prefrontal cortex was lesioned. Thus the thalamus, hypothalamus, mammilary bodies, and the prefrontal cortex appear to play an important role in memory formation. Nuclei at the base of the forebrain, which produce the neurotransmitter *acetylcholine*, are also implicated in memory formation. Acetylcholine is depleted in Alzheimer's disease, whose victims suffer amnesia. Moreover, animals given a drug that stimulates acetylcholine production learn faster than do normals, whereas the performance of animals given an acetylcholine inhibitor is depressed, and animals with lesions to the basal forebrain exhibit modest learning deficits.

Further research demonstrated the importance of the amygdala in making possible learning across sensory modalities. Mishkin created a delayed nonmatching to sample task in which the stimuli were both visually and tactilely distinct. Thus monkeys could learn the task in the dark by feeling the objects, or in the light by seeing the object. It was then possible to present the sample stimulus in one modality; for example, to touch in the dark, and then present the test in the other modality, in the example visually. The monkey must then associate the appearance of the objects with their feel in order to choose the right object at test, and normal monkeys can do this. But monkeys whose amygdalas had been removed could not.

On the basis of his findings, Mishkin has proposed a structural learning circuit for visual memories (see Fig. 10–3). The circuit begins in the sensory area of the visual cortex, and learning begins when an object is perceived. Connections between the sensory area and the mediotemporal region carry neural impulses to the amygdala and hippocampus. At this point two parallel memory circuits begin, one stemming from the hippocampus and the other from the amygdala. Each circuit connects with the diencephalon, especially to the thalamus and mammilary body. Further connections link the diencephalon to the prefrontal cortex. The mediotemporal structures, the diencephalon, and the prefrontal cortex all connect with the cholinergic system of the basal forebrain, which is rich in connections to the entire cortex, where memories are most likely stored. We know that the structures involved in the memory circuit cannot be the actual storage site of memories, or engrams, if they exist, because the amnesia caused by damage to them is largely anterograde, sparing already processed memories. Mishkin believes that visual memories are stored in the sensory area of the cortex where they began, the learning circuitry acting to fix memories in place rather than process them from structure to structure. The fixing process must take considerable time, given human retrograde amnesia for memories up to two years prior to brain damage.

Squire distinguishes between declarative and procedural memory. The first is lost in amnesia, and involves the limbic system; the latter is retained in amnesia, and involves nonlimbic structures. Mishkin similarly distinguishes memory and habit. *Memory* is like Squire's declarative memory and depends upon the mediotemporal and diencephalic structures discussed so far. *Habit* is like Squire's procedural memory and includes simple classical conditioning. Mishkin believes that the biological basis of habit lies in the striatum, a set of structures in the forebrain. This is a very ancient part of the brain receiving input directly from the senses and sending impulses directly to the motor centers. Thus it is well suited to act as the mediating link between stimulus and response, providing the associative bonding of simple S-R learning.

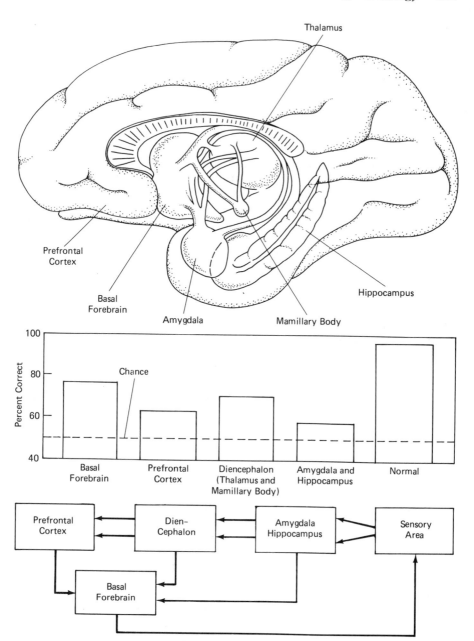

FIGURE 10-3 Mapping the brain's memory system. (From "The Anatomy of Memory," by Mortimer Mishkin & Tim Appenzeller, *Scientific American*. Copyright © 1987 by Scientific American, Inc. All rights reserved)

Circuits

We now move down by one level of the nervous system, from the structures of the brain to the individual neurons of which they are composed, looking for the neural circuits that lay down and store memories. Research in this area, and on the cellular mechanisms of learning that we will describe in the next section, has advanced rapidly in the last few years. For reasons that will become apparent, investigations of learning at the cellular level use very simple animal models—especially invertebrates—and concern simple forms of conditioning. Psychologists hope that, because neurons and synapses are the same in all animals, including humans, the exciting findings from research on invertebrates will prove true of humans too.

The computational approach.   In Chapter 6 we briefly mentioned the new connectionist, or parallel distributed processing (PDP) approach to learning and memory. Advocates of PDP reject the traditional information-processing model of the mind, the computer, and wish to substitute for it a new metaphor, the *brain metaphor*. Until very recently, existing computers were *serial processors* (see Box 10–3), and information-processing models treated the human mind as a similar serial-processing device. However, the brain is in fact a massively interconnected parallel-processing device, with multiple neurons connected to other neurons in a fantastically complex network of interconnections. Connectionists use computers to attempt to stimulate the actual parallel structure of the brain. Instead of flowcharts, PDP theories consist of nodes connected by multiple linkages; learning is modeled as consisting of changes in the strength of the linkages between the nodes. There are input nodes that represent sensory receptors, output nodes that represent behavior, and intermediate, or "hidden," nodes that

---

BOX 10–3   The Connection Machine

Existing computers, from humble PC's to enormous supercomputers, are almost without exception *serial* processors. That is, there is a single processing center—the "central processing unit" or CPU—that carries out computations one at a time in *serial* order. Because CPU's perform their computations incredibly quickly, and because they are linked to large memories, serial-processing computers can accomplish remarkable feats. However, it may be that the physical limits of calculating speed have been reached, for there is a limit to how fast electrons can move from place to place on silicon chips. Furthermore, there are some human abilities that seem effortless and trivial to us, such as recognizing faces, that defeat computers despite years of dedicated effort by computer engineers and programmers.

As a result, some computer designers have turned to the alternative computing architecture, called *parallel processing*. In the early days of computing after World War II, there were some efforts to build parallel processors, but they were abandoned when it turned out to be much easier to design serial rather than parallel-processing machines. In parallel processing there are many processing units, none of which is central, making possible great gains in computing speed. One of the new parallel-processing computers is called The Connection Machine, just now coming to market. Consider the problem of pattern recognition, one of the tasks that traditional computers find most challenging. Imagine a graphic image represented on a computer screen having 256 dots on a side, so that the image is made up of 256 × 256 = 65,536 points of light. Humans can recognize such an image in fractions of a second, but a serial computer may take hours to do the same thing, for it must calculate the value of each point of light one at a time—65,536 separate steps! And the computer is slower than the brain even though neurons conduct signals millions of times more slowly than transistors. The brain's advantage may stem from its being a parallel processor, and The Connection Machine tries to imitate the brain by assigning a single processor to each point of light, making a computation on 65,536 points as fast as a computation on a single point. The Connection Machine can perform several billion computational steps per second, far outstripping conventional computers.

Parallel computers might also be able to model human memory more realistically than serial computers. A serial computer's memory stores information at arbitrary addresses, and when the CPU needs a particular piece of information it looks up the address and extracts the memory stored at the address. However, nothing in the address reveals the content of the store, and any piece of information could be stored at any address, since assignment of information to addresses is arbitrary. Computer memory is thus like postal addresses: Anyone might live at 312 Larkspur Lane, and the address reveals nothing about who lives there. Human memory, however, seems to be organized not by addresses, but by content, as phenomena such as category clustering reveal, making human memory quite different from traditional computer memory.

Parallel processors, however, might be able to remember like human brains, by content. Just as a graphic image can be defined by points lying in two dimensions, so might specific memories be coded along many dimensions. Memory for our friends might be organized along several dimensions: height, weight, hair color, eye color, age, sex, and so on. These dimensions would define a multidimensional space, and each of our friends would be represented as a single point in that space; Alice, for instance, might be tall, thin, blonde, green eyed, 24, female, and so located in memory at the point where all those values intersect. In a parallel-processing computer, each point would have its own processor, and activation of that processor would constitute remembering that person. In such a scheme there would not be the distinction of address and content found in traditional computer memories, since the location of each memory point would be defined by its content, that is, its location in the multidimensional memory space. Perhaps the brain remembers this way, too; if so, the creation of parallel computing may represent an important step toward a better understanding of human learning and memory.

See W. Daniel Hillis (1987, June). "The Connection Machine." *Scientific American* 256: 108–115, and David W. Tank and John J. Hopfield (1987, December). "Collective Computation in Neuronlike Circuits. *Scientific American* 257: 104–115.

interconnect input, output, and hidden units. In their computer simulations, connectionists represent stimuli as activation of the input units and provide reinforcement, or informational feedback, to the system after each response. Feedback modifies the connections between the units, and the connections get modified until the output units are activated in the pattern desired by the simulator. The PDP theorists hope in this manner to simulate the way the brain learns.

For all their concern with the brain, however, connectionists have not proposed models based on known neural circuitry, but have instead constructed hypothetical models of the brain's interconnections, making their models artificial and simplistic (Churchland, 1987). However, one eminent student of the physiological bases of conditioning, Richard Thompson (Gluck & Thompson, 1987), has proposed some simple connectionist circuits for Pavlovian conditioning that are based on neuroscientific findings.

Figure 10–4 represents a PDP model neural circuit capable of Pavlovian conditioning and discrimination. Four neurons constitute this simple cell assembly. At the right is the motor neuron (M.N.), whose axon process to a muscle is not shown. On the left are three sensory neurons, one each for an unconditional stimulus (US), and two possible conditional stimuli (CS1 and CS2). Both CS1 and CS2 possess axon processes that synapse onto the motor neuron's dendrites, but before learning begins these synapses have not been facilitated, so that when CS1 or CS2 is stimulated

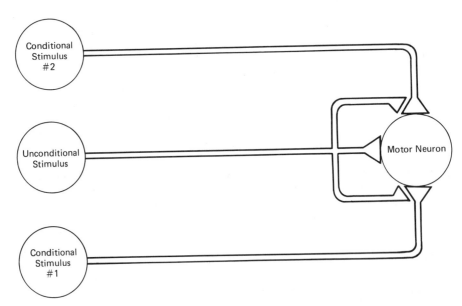

FIGURE 10-4   Pavlovian conditioning and discrimination circuit proposed by Gluck and Thompson (1987). At left are three sensory neurons for conditional and unconditional stimuli; at right is a motor neuron (M.N.). (From Gluck & Thompson, 1987)

to fire a neural spike, little or no response of the motor neuron occurs. Three axon fibers arise from the US, one to the motor neuron, and one each to the synpases of CS1 and CS2 to the motor neuron.

Conditioning begins when a CS neuron, CS1 for example, fires about 0.5 sec before the US neuron fires. The US→M.N. synapse causes the UR to occur, and the activation of the axon end-bulb of the US→CS1+M.N. synapse facilitates the strengthening of the CS1→M.N. synapse. Continued paired firings of CS1 and US gradually strengthens the CS1→M.N. synapse until, as in real Pavlovian conditioning, presentation of CS1 alone causes the M.N. to fire and the UR to occur. Repeated presentation of CS1 alone without the facilitating effect of a US pairing causes habituation, and CS1 loses its ability to evoke the UR. The same process occurs in discrimination learning, except that now CS2 is presented without reinforcement from the US. As a result of habituation, the CS2→M.N. synapse becomes inhibitory, as does an S− in standard Pavlovian conditioning. Gluck and Thompson discuss more complex models incorporating interneurons and more interconnections among the neurons that produce simulated higher-order conditioning and imperfect blocking.

Gluck and Thompson's simple computational models of possible neural circuits responsible for learning provide a convenient introduction to the more complicated and difficult study of the actual learning circuitry of animals.

The Model Systems Approach

We cannot morally or ethically study human neural circuitry at work; nor is it practical to do so, given the human nervous system's size and complexity. However, some marine invertebrates have simple nervous systems made up of large neurons, some large enough to be seen with the naked eye, making it possible to study how each neuron works and how neural connections are modified during learning. Several research programs employ invertebrate subjects (see Davis, 1986, for a review).

Perhaps the most prominent of these research programs is Eric Kandel's investigations of Pavlovian conditioning in the gastropod *Aplysia* (for example, Hawkins & Kandel, 1986), which provided the circuit models simulated by Gluck and Thompson. *Aplysia* is an extremely simple sluglike creature that crawls along the sea floor ingesting water through a siphon projecting from its front. Until Kandel began his work, it was generally believed that *Aplysia* was incapable of even simple learning, and in fact it took Kandel and his associates months of study before they found a behavior they could condition, the gill and siphon withdrawal reflex. If *Aplysia's* siphon is stimulated by a touch, it withdraws siphon and gill into its body to protect them. This reflex proved to be modifiable. If the siphon is repeatedly stimulated with a mild, nonthreatening stimulus, the withdrawal reflex weakens and disappears to that stimulus, demonstrating habituation. The reflex demonstrates sensitization when repeated strong noxious stimulation of *Aplysia's* tail enhances the withdrawal reflex to even the mildest of touches to the siphon. Pavlovian conditioning occurs when a strong shock (US) is applied to the tail one-half second after a weak touch (CS) is applied to the siphon, and after some pairings the withdrawal reflex to the touch is greatly increased. This result is specific to the CS and is not just the result of sensitization to all stimuli, because discrimination learning occurs in *Aplysia*. A touch to another part of the body is unpaired with the shock while the touch to the siphon is paried with the shock, resulting in withdrawal to the siphon CS alone. A learned CR of withdrawal also extinguishes. Gluck and Thompson's conditioning neural circuits represent Kandel's theory of conditioning in *Aplysia*, generalized to all neurons.

Learning circuits get considerably more complex in mammals. Richard Thompson and his colleagues (Thompson & Donegan, 1986) have for some years investigated Pavlovian conditioning in the rabbit, focusing in particular on the nictating membrane response as a UR. This is a defensive response in which a rabbit's inner eyelid (the nictating membrane) closes in response to a threatening stimulus such as a puff of air. Neurologically, conditioning the nictating membrane proves to be quite primitive, as animals whose cerebral cortexes have been completely removed nevertheless learn! Thompson believes that the site of nictating membrane conditioning is the cerebellum, an ancient structure of the brain covering the brain stem.

Although the cerebellum's best-known function is coordination of movement, Thompson and his colleagues believe that it is the site of association formation in Pavlovian conditioning, at least for the responses they have studied. The key association cells are probably the Purkinje cells, because they bring together the inputs from the CS and the US, and also connect to the eyeblink and leg-flexion motor program cell assemblies. Thus this model, along with the invertebrate-based models, support the hypothesis advanced at the beginning of the section on the neural basis of learning that the brain contains from the outset all the circuits involved in learning. Learning does not take place because new neurons are created but because new connections between existing neurons are created or existing ones are modified.

The models of learning circuits that have been proposed to date are interesting and exciting as first steps toward unraveling the mysteries of how the brain learns, but they are first steps. The invertebrate circuits are extraordinarily simple; when we move to mammals with Thompson's model of Pavlovian conditioning in the rabbit, the circuits become much more complex, but still do not involve the cerebral hemispheres. It seems likely that many years, perhaps decades, of research will be required before the first circuits for complex human learning can be proposed. Of perhaps greater immediate importance are recent findings about the processes that take place within neurons as synapses are created and modified. Because all neurons work according to similar chemical and biophysical principles, findings about learning at the cellular level in simple animals may very well apply to all forms of learning, however complex. Human learning circuitry may be incredibly complex, but the processes of association formation may be everywhere the same.

Cells

Everything we have learned so far leads to the conclusion that learning must occur by modifying the connections between neurons—the synapses. Neurons communicate chemically, when the activation of a neuron releases neurotransmitters at its synaptic terminal, which travel across the synaptic cleft to the dendrite of another neuron. There, the neurotransmitter binds onto sites in the dendrite specific to that neurotransmitter, and if enough of the neurotransmitter binds to the dendrite of the receiving neuron, it fires an action potential, releasing neurotransmitters at its terminal, and so on from neuron to neuron throughout some neural circuit. Changes to synapses that occur with learning must involve relatively stable alterations of the functioning either of the presynaptic neuron (the one that sends the transmitter), or to the postsynaptic (receiving) neuron, or perhaps both. Investigating the cellular basis of learning and memory is an intensely active area of research in biology and physiological psychology (Alkon, 1985, 1987; Farley & Alkon, 1985; Davis, 1986; Hawkins & Kandel, 1986; Lynch, 1985, 1986; Woody, 1986) and is likely to soon produce a Nobel Prize for one or more scientists (Allport, 1986). We will present here two examples of research in the field, from Eric Kandel's work with conditioning in *Aplysia*, and from Gary Lynch's studies of long-term potentiation in the mammalian hippocampus.

Kandel and his associates (Hawkins & Kandel, 1986) have proposed cellular biophysical mechanisms for habituation, sensitization, and Pavlovian conditioning in *Aplysia*. Because the models for sensitization and Pavlovian conditioning are quite complex, we will discuss only the model for habituation, to illustrate the general approach of the invertebrate model-systems approach to the problem (see Davis, 1986, for a review).

Kandel's theory of habituation in *Aplysia* proposes that habituation (and also sensitization and conditioning) takes place by means of changes to the presynaptic neuron alone, by inhibiting its production of neurotransmitters at the synaptic site, thus slowing the build-up of transmitter at the binding sites of the postsynaptic dendrites, and in turn slowing the rate of firing of the postsynaptic motor neuron. Inhibition is accomplished by reducing the rate at which calcium (Ca) enters the presynaptic, sensory neuron. Neurons work hard to keep calcium at very low concentration in their intracellular fluid, but when an axon potential travels down a cell's axon, channels in the cell membrane briefly open, permitting calcium to rush into the cell. The calcium in turn triggers the production of the neurotransmitter to be released at the synapse. Repeated stimulation of the sensory presynaptic neuron reduces the permeability of the calcium channels during later action potentials, reducing the influx of calcium, and consequently the production of neurotransmitters, reducing the firing rate of the postsynaptic, response neuron. Sensitization involves more complex processes that facilitate calcium inflows during presynaptic firings, increasing production of neurotransmitter and firing of the postsynaptic neuron. Pavlovian conditioning builds on the cellular mechanisms of sensitization, as US stimulation facilitates the increased permeability of the calcium channels in the sensory neuron. Sensitization and conditioning processes are much more complex than habituation, involving more chemical changes mediating the action of the calcium channels.

We have already found that the hippocampus, although not the site of memory storage, plays an important role in creating memories. Some years ago it was found that when neurons from the mammalian hippocampus are repeatedly stimulated, they become more sensitive to subsequent stimulation, and that this sensitivity is relatively long-lasting, coming to be called *long-term potentiation*. It is possible that long-term potentiation may be part of the mechanism by which the hippocampus participates in learning, and Gary Lynch and his colleagues (Lynch, 1985, 1986) have investigated the cellular mechanism of long-term potentiation.

Again, the critical role if played by calcium, but in this case the locus of change is in the postsynaptic neuron. Lynch's theory is that repeated stimulation by neurotransmitters of the dendrites of a hippocampal nerve cell results in frequent generation of action potentials and therefore production of high levels of calcium in the receiving neuron's intracellular fluid. Calcium in turn activates production of an enzyme called *calpain*. Calpain attacks and breaks down a chemical, *fodrin*, that forms part of the permanent structure of the neuron. Destruction of the fodrin reveals already existing, but previously covered, binding sites for the hippocampal neurotransmitter, *glutamate*. As a result, the postsynaptic neuron becomes much more receptive to glutamate, and fires action potentials more frequently, creating long-term potentiation.

Lynch has supported his hypothesis with experiments in which rats learn to use odors to find the location of food in a radical maze. In these experiments, rats were exposed to pairs of odors, one of which led to reward, the other of which did not. Subsequent trials involved new pairs of odors, and the subjects rapidly learn the principle involved, learning to discriminate new pairs more quickly than the initial pair. Then, Lynch injected leupeptin into the rats' brains. Leupeptin inhibits production of calpain, and should, if Lynch's hypothesis is correct, block long-term potentiation and the learning of new odor discriminations, which is what the investigation found. Leupeptin did not interfere with the rats' ability to remember old odor discriminations, supporting the idea that the hippocampus is involved in the formation of new memories but not the storage and retrieval of old ones.

Significantly, Lynch found that leupeptin did *not* block acquisition of footshock avoidance learning. Learning the principle that one odor leads to reward but another does not appears to be a kind of declarative learning, whereas reflexively avoiding shock is Pavlovian procedural learning. Lynch's results suggest that these two forms of memory not only involve different brain structures, as the behavior of amnesics shows, but also involve different mechanisms at the most basic level of brain function, namely the individual neuron.

Studies of the cellular bases of learning and memory are only a few years old, and no doubt early hypotheses will be revised. Nevertheless, it appears that the first steps toward understanding the proximate causes of learning have been taken.

ULTIMATE CAUSES: LEARNING AND EVOLUTION

Principles of Evolution

Darwinian natural selection. Although everyone has heard of Darwin and Darwin's theory, it is so misunderstood that a review of its basics is called for. The first thing we associate with Darwin is something he did not discover, and which was well on its way to acceptance before Darwin published his *Origin of Species* in 1859. It is the idea of *descent*—the notion that present living forms are the altered descendants of long-extinct predecessors down millions of years of change. What Darwin contributed was a workable *mechanism* for explaining why species should change; why some should go extinct, some remain stable for millenia, and still others undergo alteration toward their present form. Integrated with Mendelian genetics, this Neo-Darwinian theory is the most widely accepted account of the mechanism of evolutionary change, and forms the foundation of sociobiology.

The basic Darwinian concept is simple: species become extinct if they fail in the struggle for existence. They will survive unchanged if they are perfectly suited to their environments. They change (evolve) when some of their members struggle more effectively than others and are therefore able to pass on their genes to more offspring that live longer, while the weak die young and childless and their genes with them. There is no obvious reason to exclude social behavior from the process of natural selection. The ability to find, choose, and keep a mate and to rear offspring with it are abilities needed for the struggle for existence, and so will be subject to selection. When group living confers selective advantage, it will evolve; when the ability to learn quickly and react flexibly to new challenges confers selective advantage, it will evolve.

It is important to realize that natural selection can shape behavior in subtle ways. It is often thought that all evolution does is to promote bloody aggression between individuals. Although evolution may favor aggression, it also constrains it. Moreover, the competition of natural selection may take place in wholly unviolent ways, bringing many behaviors under evolutionary control. The grim view of evolution was stated by Alfred, Lord Tennyson in his poem *In Memoriam* (1850), written even before Darwin's *Origin of Species*. Tennyson coined a phrase that has unfortunately and misleadingly become attached to Darwinian theory:

Who trusted God was love indeed
And love Creation's final law—
Though nature, red in tooth and claw
With ravine, shrieked against his creed—

"Nature red in tooth and claw" is a famous image seemingly borne out by Wallace's description of the struggle for existence. But the struggle is usually quiet, indirect, and involves no bloodshed. All that really counts in evolution is having offspring that live to maturity. *Any* trait or behavior that serves that end, or, more precisely, that aids one in having more successful offspring than anyone else, confers selective advantage.

For example, Bird *A* competes with bird *B* not (necessarily) by attacking it or killing it or depriving it of resources, but in other, more subtle ways. The female (*A*) may attract a stronger, fitter mate, who is better able to help protect and raise her (and his) offspring. *A* may be able to lay more eggs than *B*, have more clutches than *B*, secure a better nest site than *B*. These behaviors need not involve direct competition between *A* and *B*, but they do confer a selective advantage on *A*. She will have more of *her* genes present in the next generation, and that is what evolution is all about—the changing frequencies of genes in the total gene pool.

The concept of fitness.   The concept of **fitness** refers to how successful an individual is in passing his or her genes on to the next generation. Traditionally, as in Wallace's classic passage, the measure of fitness has been the number of offspring, since this is the most obvious and direct way of transmitting one's genes. More recently, however, gene-thinking has expanded the older concept of fitness. In gene-thinking we realize that (to speak metaphorically) it is each gene that seeks to replicate itself, and to increase its frequency in the next generation. Because any individual is genetically related to many people besides one's children, a gene can increase its frequency in the population by changing one's behavior toward one's relatives as a whole. If a gene causes a person to act so as to enhance his or her relatives' fitness, that gene—which is very likely to be present in those relatives—will increase its numbers in the next generation.

Sociobiologists now distinguish the concepts of *individual* fitness and *inclusive fitness.* Individual fitness refers to my genes' level of success in the struggle for existence as measured through my own individual offspring; the more offspring, the higher is the level of individual fitness. Inclusive fitness adds to this a proportion of my fitness measured through my effects on my relatives. To the extent that my genes lead me to help my relatives survive and raise their offspring, I will increase my inclusive fitness. Inclusive fitness *includes* individual fitness, being the measure of my gene's total fitness in the struggle for existence.

Another way of defining inclusive fitness has been suggested by Brown and Brown (1982). We may distinguish between *direct* and *indirect fitness pathways.* An individual receives fitness directly from his or her parent and contributes it directly to his or her children. An individual receives fitness indirectly from others, either from kin-selected behaviors or from reciprocity, and contributes it to others, whether relations (kin selection) or nonrelative (reciprocity). The terms *direct* and *indirect* fitness help us see that inclusive fitness includes effects that may not be based on genetic relatedness, but embrace aid or harm done to nonrelatives as well. So inclusive fitness includes the fitness we inherit from relatives (individual fitness and kin-selected fitness) *and* the fitness we accrue from interactions with nonrelatives.

The concept of inclusive fitness leads to the idea of **kin selection,** already inherent in our discussion so far. A gene whose strategy is to enhance only individual fitness, perhaps by causing an individual to want and raise many offspring, is subject to *individual selection*: Whether it succeeds or fails depends on the life and death of its host survival-machine. A gene whose strategy is to cause me to help my relatives—and thereby to help itself replicate through them—is subject to *kin selection*: Whether it succeeds or fails depends less on my own life or death than on the degree to which my sacrifices aid my kin. The logic of kin selection is central to the sociobiological analysis of altruism.

Levels of selection. Evolution consists, then, of survival of the fittest, but an important question is: "Survival of the fittest *what*? More formally, scientists and philosophers ask what unit is selected by evolution. Evolution may proceed at three levels, the level of the group, of the individual, and of the gene.

Tennyson in his poem *In Memorium* states the case for *group selection*:

> Are God and Nature then at strife,
>   That Nature lends such evil dreams?
>   So careful of the type she seems,
>   So careless of the single life.

The idea of group selection is that, because individuals come and go whereas the species—Tennyson's "type"—endures for generations, evolution acts primarily to preserve the group. Individuals are supposed to behave for the good of the species, sacrificing themselves if necessary so that others may survive. However, it turns out that group selection is extremely rare in evolution, precisely because it is the individual who lives or dies. It is the individual organism who either reproduces or does not, not the species, and individuals act to preserve themselves and their relatives, not strangers who happen to be of the same species. Group selection can occur when selection acts to favor or eliminate entire groups of organisms at a time, but the conditions required to bring it about seldom occur.

Individual selection is, then, the second level at which evolution may occur. There is, however, a third possibility, selection at the level of the gene, which lies behind the gene-thinking we have already discussed. The concept of gene selection is that evolution really operates on an individual's traits and behaviors, rather than the individual itself. Hence, genes that produce favorable traits or favorable behaviors will increase in frequency, whereas those that produce unfavorable traits or behaviors will decrease in frequency. Someone once tried to poke fun at Darwinian evolution by saying that, according to Darwin, a chicken is just an egg's way of making more eggs. Gene-thinkers accept the characterization, viewing individuals primarily as vehicles by which genes struggle to survive.

A lively controversy rages among evolutionary biologists and among philosophers of biology about the various levels of selection (see, for example, Brandon & Burian, 1984), but for our practical purposes only one conclusion is important. Evolution can act at each level: on species, on individuals, on genes. The question then becomes in each case where we have reason to think that a behavior has a genetic basis, to determine how and at what level the behavior was selected.

Constraints on Learning

If evolution shapes behavior, then it ought to shape learning. Specifically, different species should learn in different ways and have different dispositions to learn depending on the demands the natural selection exerted by their ecological situation has placed on them. A nice illustration of how ecology shapes what an animal learns is found in three species of gull. One species nests on open flat ground in close groups, and as a result are able to recognize fine differences between their eggs' size and speckling and the eggs of others that might make their way into their nests. It would reduce fitness to hatch a stranger's egg, and so the gull's powers of visual learning and discrimination are well developed.

Herring gulls, however, nest rather farther apart, so that eggs are unlikely to get mixed up, and herring gulls are poor at recognizing their own eggs. They will even sit on a large, black fake egg in preference to their own small, speckled one. But chicks can run around and get mixed up with one another after birth, so that herring gulls are excellent at learning what their own chicks look like and at recognizing strange chicks.

Finally, kittiwake gulls nest in niches on the faces of cliffs so that neither eggs nor chicks are likely to get mixed up, and the kittiwakes show no sign of recognizing their own eggs or offspring, and may happily tend large, black cormorant chicks substituted for their small white ones (Gould and Gould, 1981; Tinbergen, 1951/1972).

The lesson here is not that some gull species are smarter than others. On the contrary, the gulls suggest that a single dimension of intelligence or ability to learn is not very useful. Although unable to recognize their eggs, herring gulls clearly can learn fine visual discriminations as they must to recognize their own chicks. What biology does is direct the gull's learning in certain ways. Ecologically, it makes sense for herring gulls to learn what their chicks look like but not what their eggs look like, and evolution—the ultimate determiner of behavior—has shaped the herring gull's visual learning appropriately.

The view of biology as shaping and constraining learning is, however, contrary to the received tradition among learning theorists who have generally pursued the goal of a **general process learning theory.**

General process learning theory.   Whatever other issues separated them, the noted learning psychologists believed that there were only one or two kinds of learning, and that the laws of learning were the same for all species. As Skinner (1961b, p. 118) put it, "Pigeon, rat, monkey, which is which? It doesn't matter." The only recognized constraints on what an animal could learn were peripheral: Obviously a dog cannot flap its legs and fly, and a person cannot discriminate a 30,000-Hertz tone from a 32,000-Hertz tone, being unable to hear either one. But apart from that, it was widely held that any stimulus an animal could perceive could be associated by conditioning to any response the animal could make (Seligman & Hager, 1972). The assumption that learning theory was general and not species-specific was particularly important because the real aim of the learning theorists was to explain human behavior, even though they based their ideas on research on animal learning.

However, Skinner's statement of faith in general-process learning theory is seriously mistaken. Behavior from altruism to sex is tuned—often very precisely—by evolutionary pressure to fit organisms into their environmental niches. The ability to learn is an adaptive trait, but clearly it benefits each kind of organism to learn some kinds of things rather than others; it pays the herring gull more to learn how its chicks look than learning how its eggs look. Beginning in 1961 (Breland & Breland, 1961/1972) it gradually became clear to learning psychologists that general-process learning theory was at best a distant hope. (Increasing lines of evidence have emerged, as reviewed by: Bolles, 1975; Domjon, 1980; Garcia, McGowan, & Green, 1972; Rozin & Kalat, 1971, 1972; Shettleworth, 1972; and in Hinde & Stevenson-Hinde, 1973, and Seligman & Hager, 1972).

Without stressing it, we have already touched upon some constraints on learning in earlier chapters. The fact that rats can learn mazes without reinforcement (latent learning) demonstrates that since rats live in underground burrows they are genetically predisposed to learn spatial layouts (Shettleworth, 1972). Autoshaping may be viewed not just as classical instead of operant conditioning, but as revealing an innate connection between food and pecking. Staddon's innate principles of influence implicitly appeal to biology to provide constraints on the kind of behaviors an animal will emit under a given circumstance. But the severest blow to the hopes of general-process learning theory was the "message from Garcia" (Rozin, 1977).

The message from Garcia. John Garcia, for a time a student in Tolman's old laboratory, studied, with a variety of associates, aversion learning based on food. During the course of his research, Garcia discovered phenomena anomalous to the general-process program. Rats allowed to drink a novel-tasting fluid (saccharin-flavored water), and made sick hours later by drug injection or X-irradiation, learned to avoid drinking the flavored water. This violated the usual law of classical conditioning, which holds that the US-CS interval must be very short–about 0.5 second—for learning to occur. Moreover, the aversion was always to the most *recent* novel substance, since rats who drank saccharin water, then familiar tap water, and then got sick, avoided only the saccharin water.

The selectivity of the taste-sickness association is strengthened by further experiments. Rats would learn to avoid foods on the basis of its taste, not its appearance (Domjon, 1980). In an elegant two-factor experiment, Garcia, Clarke, and Hankins (1973) let rats drink saccharin water while

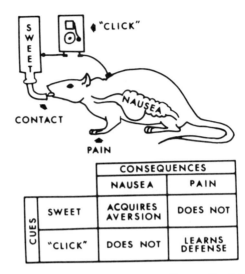

		CONSEQUENCES	
		NAUSEA	PAIN
CUES	SWEET	ACQUIRES AVERSION	DOES NOT
	"CLICK"	DOES NOT	LEARNS DEFENSE

FIGURE 10-5   The cue to consequence paradigm, a fourfold experimental design where two cues, taste or auditory stimuli, are paired with two consequences, illness or pain. Learning is more probable in the cells indicated, and the conditioned responses are qualitatively distinct. (From Garcia, Clarke, & Hankins, 1973)

they heard a click, were shocked, or were later made ill (see Fig. 10–5). The rats learned specifically to associate sweetness with illness and the click with shock. Sickened rats avoided only the food and did not try to run away from the click. Shocked rats tried to avoid the click but drank the sweet water. The obvious conclusion is that sick rats conclude: "It must have been something I ate," and attribute the cause of their distress to the newest food they ate rather than exterior cues or to familiar foods (Domjon, 1980). That this process is genetic is supported by findings that the same phenomena occur in newborn rat pups (Domjon, 1980).

These particular dispositions to learn are well adapted to the rat's ecology (Shettleworth, 1972). Wild rats are omnivores who sample small amounts of new foods and avoid those that make them ill. Long before Garcia, rodent-control experts knew that rats easily become bait-shy, outwitting their hunters. Under these conditions it could be an ill-adapted rat indeed who drank tainted water, later got ill under a bush and learned to avoid the bush (the immediate CS), while returning to drink the water. Evolution has produced rats who adaptively associate taste with illness and external cues with external threats.

Different ecologies produce different food aversions. Wild rats are nocturnal feeders with poor vision, so taste, not food appearance, is their best cue to avoid poison. Quail, on the other hand, are diurnal (daytime) feeders with excellent vision, and they can easily and directly associate a new food's appearance with later illness (Wilcoxon, Dragoin, & Kral, 1972). On the other hand, bluejays, like rats, are scavengers and learn as rats do, in a two-step process: Taste (CS) is averted by illness (US) and then visual cues (CS) are avoided by the aversive taste (US). We must conclude that animals' ecological niches and consequent evolutionary pressures direct the ways animals learn even simple associations (Shettleworth, 1972; Wilson, 1975a; Garcia, Quick, & White, 1984).

Human Evolution

Before turning in the next chapter to sociobiology, we need to review the course of human evolution, focusing on the evolution of humankind's most important trait, intelligence. Figures 10–6, 10–7, and 10–8 summarize the course of human evolution (see Beals, Smith, & Dodd, 1984; Blumenberg, 1983; Cartmill, Pilbeam, & Isaac, 1986; Delson, 1985; Pilbeam, 1984, 1985, 1986a,b; Rensberger, 1986, 1987; B. Schwartz, 1984; Skelton, McHenry, & Drawhorn, 1986; and Smith & Spencer, 1984, for further detail, analysis, and alternative models).

One plausible picture is that the stem creature from which hominids descended was *Australopithecus afarensis*, living about 3.5 million and perhaps as much as 5 million years ago. *Afarensis* gave rise to two distinct lines, the other *Australopethicines*, *africanus*, and *robustus*, which died out about 1 million years ago. The other line began with *Homo habilis* (2 million years) and continued through *Homo erectus* (1.5 million to 1 million years) and finally to *Homo sapiens*. All hominids through *Homo habilis* had small brains, in the case of the *Australopithecines* about the same size as a chimpanzee's, and in *Homo habilis* about 50 percent larger. Around 1.8 million years ago a revolution in brain size occurred when *Homo erectus* appeared, with a brain 2½ times larger than a chimpanzee's; *Homo sapiens'* brain is three times as large (McHenry, 1982). *Homo sapiens* has had three forms, *Homo sapiens neandertalensis*, archaic *Homo sapiens*, and *Homo sapiens sapiens* (ourselves). An important issue involves the origin date of *sapiens sapiens* (Box 10–4). There are a very few apparently *sapiens* forms as early as 300,000 years ago (see the Steinheim skull in Figure 10–6), but some archaeologists dispute these dates and insist that *sapiens sapiens* did not appear until about 40,000 years to 50,000 years ago (Krantz, 1980).

The Evolution of Human Intelligence

What most obviously separates human beings from the other animals is that we study them, not the other way around. Humankind's greatest adaptation is intelligence, which makes us flexible, able to invent and use religion, culture, science, and technology. It is a natural question, then, to inquire into the evolutionary origins of human intelligence. (For background, see Jerison, 1973, 1982; Hahn, Jensen, & Dudek, 1979).

Speculation on the problem is old, and scientists have offered a range of hypotheses, but there seems to be an emerging consensus that the origin and function of intellect is social—to hold society together (Humphrey, 1976; Quiatt & Kelso, 1985). However, the roles of hunting in demanding sophisticated cognition (Jerison, 1982) and diet in changing the chemical functioning of the brain (Blumenberg, 1983) cannot be overlooked. Wilson

YEARS B.C.	GEOLOGICAL PERIODS		CULTURAL TRADITIONS		FOSSIL HOMINIDS
	Europe (Glaciation)	Africa (Pluviation)	Europe	Africa	
15,000	Gamblian III		Magdelenian	Lupemban III	
			Solutrean	Smithfield	
20,000		Aurignacian: Proto. Magdalenian		Solo Man — Rodesoids	
	Gamblian II		Gravettian	Stillbay	Cro-Magnon Combe Capelle
30,000			Perigordian	Lupemban I	
	Würm IV	Gamblian I	Chatelperronian	Proto-stillbay	Florisbad
40,000	Würm III				Classic Chappelle-aux-Saints — Neanderthal
	Würm II	(Drier)	Mousterian	Sangoan	Kanjera (?)
	Würm I				
100,000		Kanjeran		Fauresmith	Progressive — Sapiens
	Riss-wurm Interglacial			Final Acheulean	Sacco Pastore, Enrings-Dorf — ?
200,000		(wetter?)	Micoquian		Fontechevade
	Riss	Mesvinian			Montmaurin
300,000	Interpluvial	Tayacian			Steinheim, Swanscumbe
	Mindel-Riss Interglacial		Acheulean	Acheulean	Rabat, Sidi Abderahman, Homo Erectus (pithecanthropines)
500,000		Clactonian			
	Mindel	Kamasian			
600,000					Kromdram, Swartkrans (Robustus)
	Günz-Mindel Interglacial	Interpluvial	Abbevillian (Chellean)	Chellean	Sterk Fontein, Makapan, Taung — Ternifine, Olduval Bed II, Peking, Heidelberg
1,000,000					
	Günz	Kagerian			AUSTRALOPITHECINES
1,300,000			Pre-chellean? (Eolithic)	Oldowan	
	Villa-Franchian			(Kafuan?)	Zinjanthropus (Africanus), Homo Hablis (?)
2,000,000					
	Pliocene				EARLIEST HOMINIDS (Australopithecus Afarensis In Africa)
13,000,000					Pre- and Proto-Hominids
	Miocene				Early Generalized Anthropoids . . .possibly split between apes and man (Ramapithecus) ((Dryopithecus)
25,000,000					
	Oligocene				Earliest Anthropoid apes (Aegyptopithecus) Earliest monkeys
36,000,000					
	Eocene				Rapid evolution and spread of modern orders of birds, Lemuroids, Tarsioids (Fossil Tarsioid)
60,000,000					
	Palcocene				First Lemuroid Primates; Forerunners of most mammacian orders. (Fossil Lemuroid)
75,000,000					

(PLEISTOCENE marked along left side from ~300,000 to 2,000,000; Levalloisian marked in cultural traditions column)

THE CENOZOIC ERA

Note: This correlation is merely a consensus, and all classifications are fluid.

284

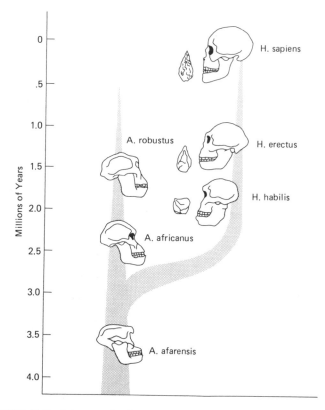

FIGURE 10-7   A human family tree. (From Johanson & Edey, 1981) All the
afarensis fossils can be lumped between 4 and 3 million years,
all the *africanus* ones between 2.7 and 2.2 million years, all
the *robustus* ones between 2.1 and 1 million years, and so on.
Afarensis, the oldest and most primitive hominid known, was
ancestral to all the others. Tools, as the chart indicates, are a
Homo, not an australopithecine, invention.

(1975a) and Dawkins (1976) follow Trivers (1971/1978, 1974/1978) in suggesting that intelligence is required to carry out the sophisticated calculations
of reciprocal altruism, and engage in the "games" of parental investment
strategies and parent-offspring conflict. Alexander (Alexander & Noonan,
1979; Alexander, 1979a, b) argues that intergroup competitiveness created
human intelligence, making adaptive in-group cooperation and altruism,
which in turn depend on foresight and calculation. An older line of thinking
(summarized by Pfeiffer, 1976) traces intelligence to the demands of big-
game hunting with its prizing of male cooperation in the hunt and sexual

FIGURE 10-6   (Facing page) The evolution of *Homo sapiens* as indicated in
the fossil record. (Drawing prepared by, and published with
the permission of, Dr. Robert L. Humphreys, George Washington University)

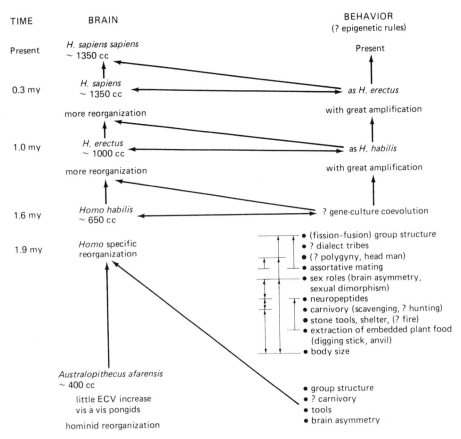

TIME   BRAIN   BEHAVIOR
                                                   (? epigenetic rules)

Present   *H. sapiens sapiens*   Present
           ~ 1350 cc

0.3 my   *H. sapiens*   as *H. erectus*
           ~ 1350 cc

           more reorganization   with great amplification

1.0 my   *H. erectus*   as *H. habilis*
           ~ 1000 cc

           more reorganization   with great amplification

1.6 my   *Homo habilis*   ? gene-culture coevolution
           ~ 650 cc

1.9 my   *Homo* specific   • (fission-fusion) group structure
           reorganization   • ? dialect tribes
                                                       • (? polygyny, head man)
                                                       • assortative mating
                                                       • sex roles (brain asymmetry,
                                                           sexual dimorphism)
                                                       • neuropeptides
                                                       • carnivory (scavenging, ? hunting)
                                                       • stone tools, shelter, (? fire)
                                                       • extraction of embedded plant food
                                                           (digging stick, anvil)
                                                       • body size

           Australopithecus afarensis
           ~ 400 cc
                                                       • group structure
             little ECV increase   • ? carnivory
             vis à vis pongids   • tools
                                                       • brain asymmetry
             hominid reorganization

FIGURE 10-8   (From Blumenberg, 1983)

division of labor. It is also possible that the large human brain resulted from a sudden genetic mutation rather than being the outcome of selection pressures (Blumenberg, 1983). In all cases it is recognized that human intelligence and our upright stance—bipedalism—are intimately related (but see Richards, 1986), because it is through tools that our intelligence works most effectively on the environment, and tool use requires free and skillful hands. The most complete account of bipedalism and the evolution of intelligence is offered by Owen Lovejoy (Lovejoy, 1981; Johanson & Edey, 1981).

The point of departure for Lovejoy's theory is the danger of K-selection: extinction. K-selected species have only a few offspring. Humans are not the most K-selected species. The great apes are, as gorillas, for example, bear about one child every five years. While humans have no doubt hastened the extinction of the apes, their low rate of reproduction would probably have brought them to that fate eventually. K-selection, in other words, can be carried too far. All the forces in early human evolution

---

BOX 10–4.   Eve and the Molecular Clock

The study of evolution used to exclusively involve fossils, the remains of living creatures, and in the case of humans, their tools. However, research in molecular biology—the study of DNA—is now contributing much to understanding human evolution. Molecular genetics has added to the study of human origins in two ways. First, it has become possible to measure the degree to which any two species are genetically related by determining the amount of DNA they share. This makes it possible to classify living species into precise groups, because we no longer need rely on bodily characteristics such as dentition and skull shape, but can directly examine every species' genetic heritage. The second contribution of molecular genetics to the study of evolution is the discovery of a *molecular clock* measuring evolutionary change. It turns out that certain kinds of DNA mutate—change—at a constant rate, making it possible to determine not only how closely two species are related, but also when they diverged from a common ancestor. For example, humans' closest living relative is the chimpanzee, with whom we share over 95 percent of our DNA. Using the molecular clock, it has been calculated that humans and chimps diverged from a common ancestor about 5 million years ago.

The same thing can be done for individual humans, taking DNA samples, comparing them for similarities, and using the molecular clock to calculate when their last common ancestor lived. Recently, such a study was carried out on the human mitochondrial DNA. Mitochondria are organelles in each cell that regulate the metabolism and energy level of the cell. Importantly in the present context, mitochondria are inherited exclusively from one's mother—the DNA does not undergo the mixing of the sexes of the nuclear DNA. Studying mitochondrial DNA, therefore, can reveal the last common *mother* of a group of people. Using a sample of people from all over the world, Rebecca Cann and her associates have calculated that all human beings descended from a single human woman living in Africa about 200,000 years ago. Should these results stand up, there will really have been an Eve. Whether there was an ancient Adam has yet to be determined.

See Rebecca L. Cann (1987, September/October). "In Search of Eve." *The Sciences,* 30–37.

---

were driving us more and more to the extreme of *K*-selection—the need for parental care of children during an extended childhood, which requires increased intelligence and brain development, hence a reduced number of offspring who can only survive within a protective group held together by complex social behaviors, which require intelligence, and so on. Each adaptation was causally linked to each other, being mutually reinforcing, and made us increasingly vulnerable to extreme *K*-selection.

According to Lovejoy, bipedalism is the way out of the *K*-selection trap, for it allows people to avoid the extreme childbearing spacing of the great apes. If women bear one child a year, the benefits of *K*-selection are retained with enough *r*-selection to avoid extinction. To do this, women and children had to move around less, using less energy and being less likely to fall out of trees or be eaten by predators. When movement was necessary, bipedalism was useful, for now a woman could carry her helpless infant.

A problem now arises: How can one woman raise several children at once on a smaller resource-base? They needed help, specifically from males. Males could hunt and bring back meat, which requires bipedalism to carry the meat, supporting offspring from a large area. They would also have to cooperate, and help rear the increased number of chidren.

But why should a man do this? Here Lovejoy proposes a pair-bond theory. Lovejoy points out that human females have not only lost estrus and begun to sexually advertise continuously, they (and men) also become more *individual-looking* than other animals. The sexual symbols of the human female are not just arousing; they are individuating, too. As Lovejoy says, "The development of stimulating systems that are specific to individuals is called epigamic differentiation. I call it being in love." (Quoted in Johansen & Edey, 1981 p. 334) Moreover, epigamic differentiation emphasizes outward differences in male and female appearance, and Lovejoy (1981) thinks that it is this, not polygyny, that has created human sexual dimorphism.

So it is now possible for a man to fall in love with a distinctively individual woman and *want* (proximate mechanisms) to bring her food and help raise *their* offspring. Pair-bonding also reduces intragroup aggression. As women lose estrus they no longer are periodically provocative to all males, who would start fighting over them. (Daniels, 1983). Now each man has his own private gene-receptacle, as it were. Loss of estrus and pair-bonding also gives subordinate males a better chance of reproduction and a stake in the bond. No longer will dominant males be able to sequester fertile females, since no one knows when women are fertile. And women will be able to choose men who, while not fit through ferocity, are willing to invest a lot in her and her children (Alexander & Noonan, 1979). Additionally, loss of estrus accounts for human hypersexuality as opposed to the hyposexuality of other pair-bonding species. Since a woman does not know when her fertile period is, she must be sexy and prepared for intercourse all the time in order to ensure that copulation will occur when she is fertile. Although Lovejoy does not say so, perhaps this is also an adaptive function of the female orgasm—to motivate continuous sexual activity. Finally, Lovejoy's theory may explain the universal human preference for face-to-face copulation: Only thus can one see, appreciate, and be stimulated by the epigamically differentiated features of one's beloved. Humans copulate as individuals, not just as male and female conspecifics.

Once this complex process is underway all the various factors will feed back on themselves and each other, so that the push toward bipedalism, social cooperation, intelligence, self-awareness (Box 10–5), and love (epigamic differentiation) will become self-sustaining. Upright posture made tool use possible, and our socially developed intelligence created sophisticated tools in the beginning of technology. Armed with intelligence, tools, and enough *r*-selection to proliferate, humans quickly spread over the earth's surface and could aim at the stars. Add to this the development

BOX 10–5   Self-Awareness

Within our own minds, humankinds' most striking trait is probably our self-awareness. Indeed, the seventeenth-century philosopher Rene Descartes made self-awareness (*Cogito, ergo sum*," I think, therefore I am") the cornerstone of modern rationalism. Psychologists themselves have debated the importance of human self-awareness. The radical behaviorist B. F. Skinner sees it as no more than a collection of socially learned labels for internal sensations and observations of one's own behavior, while humanistic psychologists, such as Carl Rogers and Abraham Maslow, follow Descartes in seeing self-awareness as the *sine qua non* of the human condition.

In the present context, it is interesting to ask if any other animals possess self-awareness. Descartes thought not; he viewed animals as mere deterministic machines, lacking reflection and consciousness. Gordon Gallup (1977) has used mirrors to investigate the question empirically. Monkeys and apes are known to enjoy looking at mirrors and can even use them as tools to solve visual problems. However, like all animals, they typically respond to a reflection of themselves as an image of a conspecific—they do not perceive them*selves* in the mirror. But since similar self-perception is learned by humans (it does not appear until age two, may never appear in severely retarded persons, and is sometimes lost in schizophrenia) Gallup wondered if perhaps apes and monkeys could learn self-perception.

His first experiment was to place a ten-foot mirror in a cage with wild-born chimpanzees. Initially, they responded to the image as to a conspecific, but after two days their behavior indicated self-recognition. For examples, they groomed parts of the body they could not normally see, they picked their teeth, and they made faces at the mirror. To further test them, Gallup anesthetized the chimps and applied a bright red, odorless, nonsensitive dye over their foreheads. When they awoke, each chimpanzee clearly showed that it knew the dye was on its own face: They examined the spot in the mirror and touched it repeatedly. When the same procedure was performed with chimpanzees who had never experienced mirrors before, they showed no sign of recognizing the red spot as belonging to themselves. Gallup and others have tried these and similar experiments with virtually all species of monkeys and apes, and they have found that only the great apes—our closest living relations—learn self-perception. Despite hundreds of hours of exposure to mirrors, monkeys and the lesser apes (for example, gibbons) continue to see mirror images as just another conspecific.

If we may take self-perception as a reasonable indicator of self-awareness, then, while awareness is not unique to human beings as Descartes supposed, it is limited to a few highest primate species. It also appears that while the great apes may develop self-awareness, they do not do so routinely as humans do. Finally, Gallup's research suggests that as with so much of our nature, the origin of self-awareness is a social phenomenon. Chimpanzees raised in social isolation never learned to perceive themselves in the mirror and never passed the painted forehead test. It seems we must live with others before we can learn to see ourselves.

of culture, and later the discovery of agriculture (Pfeiffer, 1977), and human-kind's enormous success was assured, provided we do not destroy ourselves with our most dangerous tools.

While Lovejoy's proposal is attractive and persuasive, we must remember that like all evolutionary scenarios it is informed speculation, and certain shortcomings should be noted (McHenry, 1982; Langdon, 1985; Quiatt & Kelso, 1985). For example, Lovejoy may be placing the origin of monogamy too early. Most monogamous species show little sexual dimorphism, but present-day humans show modest sexual dimorphism and a modest male preference for modest polygyny. *Australopithecus afarensis*, the species Lovejoy is speculating about, displayed great sexual dimorphism—the males being twice as large as the females—indicating that they were probably strongly polygynous as well. It appears that although *Homo sapiens* is evolving toward monogamy, it is not an ancient trait of our hominid forebears. Similarly, while it is now established that bipedality preceded the development of the human brain, it did so by 2 million years, challenging Lovejoy's thesis that bipedality was an immediate precursor to the explosion of human brain size and intelligence.

CONCLUSION

It should be apparent by now that biology has a lot to tell psychologists of learning. Although underway for only about a decade, much has been learned about the physiological mechanisms responsible for learning and memory. Sometimes these mechanisms support psychological theories of learning and memory, and sometimes they require that psychologists modify their theories. It is also apparent that learning cannot be properly understood divorced from a knowledge of organisms' diverse evolutionary heritages, as the biological mechanisms of learning were produced by natural selection, shaping what and how animals learn. This second insight transcends the studies on the constraints on learning reviewed in this chapter. It seems probable that the entire range of human and animal behavior—from simple learning to complex social behaviors—has been shaped by evolution. The study of the evolutionary background to behavior, especially social behavior, is the controversial enterprise of sociobiology, the subject of Chapter 11.

SUGGESTED READINGS

Understanding the brain is one of the scientific adventure stories of our times, and there are several good popular books on the subject. For those who would like to teach themselves neuroanatomy, see *The Human Brain Coloring Book*, by M. C. Diamond, B. Scheibel, and L. M. Elson (New York: Barnes & Noble, 1985). Do not be put off by the fact that it is a coloring book: It is a serious, adult text designed for and used by universities and medical schools. Richard Restak's

(1984) *The Brain* (Toronto: Bantam Books) is a well-written survey of contemporary brain research, based on the Public Broadcasting series of the same name. The amazing and sometimes tragic quirks of the damaged brain are humanely and humanistically described by clinical neuropsychiatrist Oliver Sacks (1985) in his book *The Man Who Mistook His Wife for a Hat and Other Clinical Tales* (New York: Summit Books). Susan Allport (1986) tells the story of *Explorers of the Black Box: The Search for the Cellular Basis of Memory* (New York: Norton). Her book not only provides a good introduction to the model systems theorists, but is an instructive and revealing study of the human side of science, as we learn about the intense rivalry and competition to be first, which helps drive natural science forward. A good introduction to the study of memory and brain is Squire (1987). For a lively account of human evolution and its investigators, see Cartmill, Pilbeam, and Isaac (1986). The standard work on the evolution of the brain is Jerison (1973); however, it is now becoming out of date. Thus, see Falk (1987) for an update.

11

LEARNING AND SOCIOBIOLOGY

INTRODUCTION

> We are not just rather like animals:
> we *are* animals.

Mary Midgley (1978)

Despite the obvious truth of Mary Midgley's statement, there is no doubt that the sociobiology of *Homo sapiens* is much more controversial than the sociobiology of other species, because acknowledgment of biological roots of human action may be deeply and personally disturbing. A female graduate student and feminist was so enraged after reading Robert Trivers' "Parental Investment and Sexual Selection," for example, that she had herself sterilized (Bingham, 1980).

In addition to working amid controversy, sociobiologists studying human behavior face a more scientific problem: The kinds of data that can be collected on animal behavior are simply unavailable for human beings. The selective breeding experiments of animal behavior genetics are not permissible with humans. Nor are the kind of extended field studies of naturalists possible with our species: No young man or woman about town would tolerate being followed 24 hours a day by a note-taking ethologist; no human family would admit strangers to their most intimate intercourse.

So the sociobiologist is thrown back on analogy, everyday observation, field studies conducted by anthropologists, and speculation. Each of these methods has its drawbacks. Analogy from animals can be useful. Chimpanzees and the other primates are biologically close relatives—very close in the case of the chimpanzee with whom we share 99 percent of our blood factors (Baba, Darga, & Goodman, 1982). So studies of primate societies may be instructive. Although we *are* animals, we are *not* chimpanzees, and extrapolations must be made with care. The same goes for a second kind of animal analogy, from more distant species who are under the same ecological pressures that we are. Bird monogamy may tell us something about human monogamy, but we must be careful in deciding how much.

Everyday observation of ourselves and others is a rich source of human sociobiological data (Box 11–1). Yet our culture is one among many and we must be careful not to take a unique cultural trait as a universal biological condition. Going to other cultures is an important corrective in this connection, but is again of often limited value to sociobiological reasoning. Our knowledge of other cultures comes from anthropologists who collected most of their data before sociobiology came on the scene, and thus had a different set of questions in mind. Hence, important information may be lacking. For example, to test sociobiological hypotheses we would need to know about differential reproduction rates for different members of a studied tribe or village, yet this is the kind of information traditional ethnog-

---

BOX 11–1 A Simple Field Study in Human Sociobiology

Here is an easy-to-carry-out observational study of human beings with results that can be analyzed sociobiologically. This box simply describes what to do; the last box in the chapter discusses the usual results. Please collect your data before looking up the answer.

Go to a place on campus where students are likely to congregate. Then, for about 20 of them—half males and half females—record their sex and how they hold their books, noting particularly which hand is holding the books and whether they are held at the chest or straight at the side. Record your data by making ticks in the following chart:

POSITION OF BOOKS

	Left Hand		Right Hand	
	AT CHEST	STRAIGHT	AT CHEST	STRAIGHT
Male				
Female				

S e x

raphies did not report. Only a few recent ethnographies have been carried out to test sociobiological hypotheses directly.

Although the standard assumption of American psychology has been that people at birth are virtual blank slates, and are, in Skinner's phrase, completely shaped by their environments, evidence has been mounting that many behavior patterns we have taken to be learned do, in fact, possess strong innate components (T. G. R. Bower, 1979; Eibl-Eibesfeldt, 1975; Freedman, 1974; Wells, 1980; Loehlin, Willerman, & Horn, 1988). Cognitive abilities such as attention (Lumsden & Wilson, 1981), intelligence, depth perception, form perception, ability to locate objects in space by eye and ear, integration of sensory modalities and face recognition (T. G. R. Bower, 1974) have been shown to be present at birth or at least as early as they can be tested. There is a universal system of basic color categories that exists even in those cultures that have few basic color terms, and cultures acquire these terms in a sequence that correlates with industrialization and recapitulates children's acquisition of color terms (Lumsden & Wilson, 1981).

On the social side, the development of expressive responses such as smiling, laughing, and crying develop the same way in both normal, blind, and deaf-blind infants and children (Eibl-Eibesfelt, 1975; Freedman, 1974). Cross-cultural analyses reveal universal human patterns of nonverbal expression in such areas as flirting, coyness, eyebrow raising, eating alone, and food-sharing. For example, like chimpanzees and baboons worried about scavengers, humans eating alone—even in civilized restaurants—look up and scan the horizon after every few bites. Food-sharing is used by members of most primitive cultures to foster bonding and allay aggression. A similar if unconscious inclination seems also present in industrialized cultures: Eibl-Eibesfeldt (1975) reports a soldier whose assault on an enemy was forestalled by being reflexively given a piece of bread. So touched was he that he could not kill again. Career interests (Grotevant, Scarr, & Weinberg, 1978) and many personality traits (Loehlin, Willerman, & Horn, 1988) appear to be at least as much heritable as learned.

Abnormal patterns of behavior may also have genetic bases, including schizophrenia, alcoholism, depression, and even criminality (Wilson & Herinstein, 1985). Even lesser disorders such as neuroses may have a biological component. Lumsden and Wilson (1981) suggest that phobias may represent a prepared form of human learning. For example, human fear of snakes is widespread even where wild snakes are never encountered. Chimpanzees also run away from snakes and even hoses in apparent terror. Lemurs, unlike chimpanzees and people, evolved in snake-free regions and find snakes interesting. As Lumsden and Wilson point out, human phobias are most typically evoked by things that would have endangered our early primate ancestors—snakes, spiders, open or closed spaces, heights, thunderstorms—rather than by the real dangers of modern life—guns, knives, electrical sockets, buses.

The most dramatic, if hard to study, evidence for heritability of even the most trivial behaviors comes from studies of twins (see Freedman, 1974), especially the rare and well-publicized (Farber, 1981; Holden, 1980a,

1980b) cases of identical twins reared apart. Striking similarities ranging from dress—one pair of twins reunited only briefly in childhood turned up wearing the same dress—to phobias such as claustrophobia or fear of escalators—turn up among such sets of twins. It is even turning out that separated identical twins may be *more* alike than identical twins reared together, since in the latter case parents and the twins themselves actively try to create distinctive personalities.

While little of this evidence bears directly on the claims of sociobiology, it is nevertheless relevant because it undermines extreme environmentalism. If people are entirely shaped by their environment—by parents, teachers, and culture—then sociobiology could not be true for human beings no matter how true it might be for animals. But evidence of the sort we have briefly reviewed here underscores Midgley's assertion that we *are* animals, possessing partial genetic determination of a wide range of behaviors, attitudes, and personality traits. It in fact appears that the environment, even within families, acts to make people more unlike than alike, causing basically similar relatives to become different (Plomin & Daniels, 1987). Moreover—and this is also a necessary prerequisite for sociobiological analysis (Lumsden & Wilson, 1981)—there is evidence for systematic *variation* in many social traits. For example, compared to European-American children, Chinese-American children are calmer, harder to upset, and less noisy in groups (Freedman, 1974). If evolution is correct, isolated breeding populations ought to show differences in behavior, which seems to be indeed what we find.

THE BIOLOGICAL BASIS OF SOCIAL BEHAVIOR

Sociobiology has been employed to explain social behaviors ranging from group living to parental care (Wilson, 1975a). In this section we will consider sociobiological explanation in four major areas, moving from accounts of animal behavior to human behavior.

Altruism

Helping another at some risk to one's self—**altruism** appears to fly in the face of natural selection. How can there be a gene that puts its bearer, and thus itself, at risk of death? If the organism dies, so do its genes, and so it appears quite impossible for natural selection to have favored altruistic, suicidal genes. The answer lies in gene-thinking: The altruist is the tool of a selfish gene. Three gene-thinking analyses of altruism have been offered, of altruism as kin-selected, of reciprocal altruism and mutualism, and of individually selected "altruism."

Altruism and kin-selection. A number of insect species, including the familiar honeybee and the summer house pest, the paper wasp, have evolved what biologists call *eusociality*, a highly organized social structure including a distinct caste of sterile female workers. Such a caste represents the height of altruism, for these workers give up having offspring of their own and toil "for the good of the hive." Altruism of this order was recognized by Darwin himself as a serious challenge to natural selection, and solution of the problem (Hamilton, 1964/1980; Samuelson,1983; Trivers & Hare, 1976/1980) represented a triumph for gene-thinking.

What was first most suggestive about eusociality was that of the two dozen or so species that display it, all but one (certain termites) are of the order *Hymenoptera*, which possesses a very unusual genetic system called haplodiploidy. In the haplodiploid species the paper wasp (shown in Fig. 11–1), a female mates once with a male and stores his sperm inside her body, and then goes on to found a colony. When she fertilizes an egg and deposits it in the nest, it becomes a female; when she deposits an egg *without* fertilizing it, it becomes a male.

The vast majority of living things are like the female wasp: They are *diploid*, possessing two sets of chromosomes, one set from each parent. For simplicity's sake, only two chromosomes, *A* and *B*, are considered in

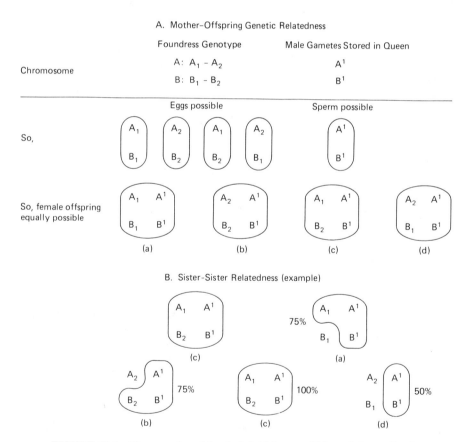

FIGURE 11-1 The genetics of haplodiploid insects. (Adapted from Alcock, 1979)

Figure 11–1. In the female the pairs of *A* chromosomes are called A_1 and A_2, the pairs of *B* chromosomes are B_1 and B_2; thus, the queen carries four chromosomes altogether. Male wasps, however, are *haploid*: Since they develop from an unfertilized egg, they possess only *one* set of chromosomes, not two sets. In Figure 11–1, the male carries only two chromosomes, A' and B'.

When the queen forms an egg from her genotype, taking half the chromosomes, four possible eggs can result, as shown. However, the sperm she carries are all identical—the male must contribute all of his genotype to each sperm, not just half of it as diploid creatures do. This simple fact does odd things to the genetic relatedness of the sisters produced by the queen. Figure 11–1 shows the four possible genotypes that can be formed from each mating of sperm and egg, and then picks one possible female and measures her degree of relatedness to her sisters. In diploid genetic systems, siblings are related by half their genes; however, in the haplodiploid system all sisters begin with the same genes gotten from the haploid father and *add* some degree of relatedness through their mother. As Figure 11–1 shows, each female is on average 75 percent related to her sisters.

These calculations make possible a **kin-selection** explanation of female sterility in eusocial insects. If a sister has her own offspring, she will be related to them by 50 percent of her genes (just as they are related to the queen). But she is related to her sisters by sharing 75 percent of their genes. Therefore, her genes will do better in the struggle for existence—increasing their numbers in the wasp gene pool—by helping the queen produce other sisters who share 75 percent of their genes, than by having their own offspring, who would share only 50 percent of their genes. In this way kin-selection produces selfish altruism. In sacrificing their own individual fitness by "altruistically" remaining sterile and helping their mother run the colony and raise her offspring, worker wasps (and bees) are really acting in the (selfish) interest of their own genes. Selection acts through kin, specifically sisters in this case, rather than through an individual's own offspring.

The kin-selection explanation of altruism can be, and has been, extended to other species including mammals. It may explain why ground squirrels give predator alarm calls when they are near close relatives but not otherwise, why wild turkeys form brother-brother pairs while looking for mates, and why young male Florida scrub jays often help their parents rear more offspring. In general, kin-selection of altruistic behavior may be invoked whenever we wish to explain a behavior that reduces one's own fitness but enhances that of relatives. Whenever the risk to your own genes is outweighed by the benefit to your genes carried by relatives, then kin-selection may take place.

Reciprocal altruism.   Even in the animal world not all altruism is directed at close relatives. Can sociobiology explain the evolution of behavior that immediately benefits neither the individual nor his or her relatives but some total stranger? Perhaps it can (see Trivers, 1971/1980). If one offers aid to another, one likely expects future aid in return. This is **recipro-**

cal altruism: You scratch my back and I will scratch yours. Reciprocal altruism can evolve whenever individuals, at small cost to themselves, can aid another and expect a great genetic return. In baboon troops a male may enlist the aid of another male to defeat a higher status male and steal his mate. Later, the helper is similarly aided by his co-conspirator. Again, sociobiology says that phenotypic altruism is genetically selfish: I will help you only if I can expect to benefit later on.

The evolution of reciprocal altruism may be an engine of cognitive evolution. Imagine a species that cannot recognize its fellows as distinct individuals. An altruist in such a species would blindly aid whoever asked for aid. Quickly a conniving counter-strategy would evolve to prey upon the saintly sucker: Get aid from the altruist but never return it. Only a smart altruist could avoid extinction by the new egotists. He or she would give aid when called upon, but never to one who had earlier cheated by refusing aid. Mathematical models indicate that the smart, reciprocal altruist would soon become the dominant type (Dawkins, 1976). But the strategy of reciprocal altruism necessitates concomitant cognitive evolution. The reciprocal altruist would need to be able to discern individual differences in appearance; be able to remember each individual and associate that individual with acts of helping or cheating; be able to base a behavioral decision on memory and calculation of a risk/benefit ratio. Thus, evolution of one social trait—altruism—may fuel the evolution of cognitive abilities, and as these grow they may in turn feed back on social development. Perhaps intellect originated in just this way; if so, in humans it has ironically expanded to the point of finding reciprocal altruism cynical, and constructed truly nonselfish systems of ethics.

Reciprocal altruism may be seen as a more specific form of a broader class of mutual helping, *mutualism* (Maynard Smith, 1982a; Wrangham, 1982). Mutualism occurs whenever several individuals cooperate for the immediate benefit of all under circumstances in which no individual can exploit a given situation. So, for example, orb weaver spiders, unable alone to throw a web across a stream to catch the many insects flying above, may cooperate with others in the initial spanning of the stream. Then, each spider builds its own nest. Here, unrelated individuals cooperate in order that each spider may enjoy a rich payoff, which is why the behavior has evolved. Since the mutual cooperation occurs at the same time, controls on cheating are unnecessary, so mutualism is simpler than reciprocal altruism. But it remains truly altruistic; although each spider gains an individual reward (each catches its own prey and does not share) it succeeds by aiding and without exploiting its fellows, as occurs with individually selected "altruism."

Beyond the scope of our introduction to sociobiology lies the sophisticated analysis of altruism using *game theory* (see Box 11–2).

Altruism and individual selection.   Finally, it is possible for apparent altruism to be entirely selfish, and to be subject to individual selection. Consider alarm calls in birds. A flock is on the ground eating and a cat stalks up. The first bird to see the cat gives a cry of alarm, and the flock flutters off. The alarm-giver appears to risk calling the cat's attention to itself while "altruistically" warning the flock. But appearances deceive. The caller knows that the flock will take off when it cries (and so the flock benefits), but the caller benefits *even more* because it knows where the predator is and can position itself advantageously in the confusing swarm of birds, and so *increase* its own chances of escape (Alcock, 1979). Altruism in this case is totally selfish: The herd is manipulated by a single member for its own advantage.

Human Altruism

Sociobiologists propose that the forces of natural selection produced human altruism as well as animal altruism. Altruistic behavior can be selected in three ways: through kin-selection, through reciprocal altruism, mutualism or reciprocity, and through individual selection.

While readers of this book live in large, impersonal, modern societies, humans evolved—and most people today still live—under very different conditions in which relationship with an extended community of kin was a major factor in determining social success or failure. Such conditions naturally favor kin-selected altruism. The fitness of any individual gene carrier is greatly enhanced by cooperating with relatives in such matters, say, as negotiating marriage. Conversely, the relative's fitness is also increased because the individual carries some of each relative's genes, which will be increased by the marriage. It pays your genes to help others who carry those genes. The closer blood ties are, the greater altruism is kin-selected, and is simply what we normally call *nepotism*: One's inclusive fitness is enhanced by helping one's relatives. The larger the social organization, the more distant kin ties become, and altruism is less and less kin-selected, but must be based on mutualism and reciprocity—reciprocal altruism.

Studies of traditional cultures support the sociobiological contention that cooperative social interaction is a relatively direct function of degree of genetic relatedness, while conflict splits societies at the weakest links in the chain of relatives. (See van der Berghe & Barash, 1977/1980; Chagnon & Irons, 1979; Chagnon, 1981; Flinn, 1982; and Irons, 1982 for extensive discussions.) To take a simple example, Hames (1979) studied the amount of social interaction between pairs of individuals as a function of their degree of genetic relatedness; this was done among the Ye'kwana of Venezuela's upper Orinoco basin. Hames found a remarkably precise relationship between kinship and amount of interaction, frequency of interaction increasing linearly with degree of relatedness. One's reaction to Hames' finding is likely to be: Well of course, people naturally want to help their relatives, so they live together and must interact more frequently. But remember that sociobiology seeks ultimate causes, to know why sugar tastes sweet and why we "naturally" are fond of our relatives. Hames argues that living together—and, by implication, the desire to live together—is the proximate mechanism by which human kin-selection operates. Only if people live in related groups can they help the genes they share with relatives.

BOX 11–2 Sociobiology and Game Theory

Game theory is a branch of mathematics that has occasionally been applied to psychology; for example, in social psychology's studies of the prisoner's dilemma. Game theory describes the outcomes of interactions between individuals who adopt different strategies in their encounters, and it evaluates the outcomes of each encounter by weighing the relative costs and benefits of adopting each strategy. As is clear already, sociobiology makes extensive use of cost/benefit analysis, and game theory is becoming its most powerful mathematical tool for understanding the strategies genes adopt and the games they play to survive. While the formal refinements of game theory lie well beyond the scope of our book, we will present here a simple and brief analysis of altruism in game theory terms.

Consider a population of organisms, say birds (Dawkins, 1976), who pick lice from each other's heads. We begin with the whole population being *suckers*, who groom any head presented to them—they are completely altruistic. Now imagining we can quantify inclusive fitness, let us assume that the benefit of being groomed is 5 fitness units, and the cost (time lost from foraging or mating while grooming another) is 2 units. Each grooming interaction is beneficial: $5 - 2 = 3$; the *payoff* exceeds the *cost*. However, this happy state of affairs is not an *evolutionarily stable strategy*, or ESS, because a mutant gene may easily arise, creating a new strategy, *cheating*. The *cheat* presents his or her head for grooming and is groomed by suckers, but never grooms in return. The resulting costs and benefits may be summarized in this *payoff matrix*, showing the result of each possible interaction of strategy:

	SUCKER	CHEAT	NET PAYOFF
Sucker	$5 - 2 = 3$	$0 - 2 = -2$	1
Cheat	$5 - 0 = 5$	$0 - 0 = 0$	5

Cheating is a superior strategy, for the cheat gets groomed without ever paying the cost, and the sucker is constantly wasting time grooming cheats. This new pattern is not stable either, because the cheating strategy works too well. Early cheats will flourish among the many suckers, but as cheats multiply (and suckers diminish) the actual payoff of cheating declines, as each cheat finds it hard to get groomed. So the ratio of cheats-to-suckers population may oscillate; pure sucker strategy isn't stable, as a few cheats flourish; pure cheating isn't stable, because then no one gets groomed.

While there may be a stable population ratio of suckers to cheats, this is unlikely, since the optimum strategy, the ESS, is reciprocal altruism; let us call it the *bourgeois* strategy. The bourgeois grooms the heads of those who present themselves—*except* those known to have cheated in the past! We can construct the following payoff matrix, omitting for simplicity's sake the occasional interaction between a new cheat and a bourgeois:

	SUCKER	CHEAT	BOURGEOIS	NET PAYOFF
Sucker	5 − 2 = 3	0 − 2 = −2	5 − 2 = 3	4
Cheat	5 − 0 = 5	0 − 0 = 0	0 − 0 = 0	5
Bourgeois	5 − 2 = 3	0 − 0 = 0	5 − 2 = 3	6

The bourgeois strategy is superior to either cheating or being a sucker, and depending on the actual cost/benefit values, an evolutionarily stable situation should be reached, since no new, superior strategy should arise to displace the bourgeoisie.

Game theory is now being applied to every area of sociobiology—aggressive interactions, altruism, mating strategies, parent-child interactions, population size and so on—and promises to bring mathematical rigor to the field. An introduction to game theory and ESS's may be found in the second edition (not the first) of Barash's *Sociobiology and Behavior* (1982), while the more serious student may see *Evolution and the Theory of Games* by John Maynard Smith (1982b), the pioneer in applying game theory to sociobiology (Maynard Smith, 1982a).

For it is not obvious to reason that we ought to favor our relatives. Selfish egoistic reason would dictate that I ought to treat everyone impersonally as a means to my own gratification: as temporary allies or enemies. Unselfish moral reason would dictate that I ought to treat everyone impersonally as autonomous human beings: each person to be cherished as such and treated equally. But traditional societies—where humans evolved—do not work in these ways. In them people want to help and be helped by their kin, to establish new kin relations as a means to social peace and harmony, and they want to hurt alien kin groups. In these natural preferences we see the hand of natural (kin) selection. People are, by nature, neither egoists nor saints.

This brings us to reciprocal altruism and the problem of mass societies. As the circles of interaction widen from village to tribe and beyond to the nation state and the urban civilization modern Western people live in, ties of kin weaken, and kin-selected altruism becomes irrelevant. Relations with strangers cannot be based on shared genetic interest; they must rest on reciprocal altruism, or reciprocity: I will cooperate with others insofar as I can expect they will cooperate with me.

But, reciprocal altruism encourages cheating, or "negative reciprocity." I take a risk when I help another, and he or she may cheat me by not returning my help. Especially in mass societies when people are likely to interact only once (making it hard to learn who the cheaters are), fraud and deception become serious problems. Just consider commercial transactions. You hand over money at the same time the merchant gives you your purchase: Neither one has to trust the other, for you reciprocate at the same moment. Hence, the merchant's distrust of checks—he or she has learned by experience that, like the empty balloon with which the male hanging fly woos his mate (see below), some people's checks signify nothing of value. Thus, the consumer's distrust of mail-order business, since one entrusts one's money to strangers with no guarantee it will buy anything. In urban societies, altruism may even become maladaptive (Mac-Donald, 1984).

But reciprocity is the only social cement that holds urban society together. Cultural evolution in Western civilization has produced complex mechanisms for enforcing reciprocity: government, police, the law. In the absence of kin ties we bind ourselves with the impersonal ties of rules and regulations. Biological evolution has given us a conscience and guilt (Trivers, 1971/1980). Guilt motivates a cheater to make amends, and restores his or her position in society. A cheater with no guilt, on the other hand, would be ostracized by society; unrepentant cheaters' genes will die with them. The guilty cheater returns and may prosper; his or her guilt-feeling genes survive him or her.

As in the other animals, then, human altruism may be evolved by kin-selection and by the evolution of reciprocal altruism. It may also be produced by pure individual selection (Moore, 1984). Outspoken biologist Michael Ghiselin (1974) has gone farthest in favoring individual selection, arguing that kin-selection is not operative, even among the hymenoptera, and that reciprocal altruism is a sham. For him, helping others is only an indirect way of helping one's self, and will not happen except when it is in one's own interest.

Besides the theoretical arguments that altruism can be an innate human trait, there is now direct evidence that it is (Pines, 1979). Some infants as young as one year of age, before any appreciable degree of social learning can take place, attempt to console or even help people who are crying or in pain. Differences in altruism at one year persisted in a follow-up study five years later: One-year-old altruists became six-year-old altruists. There was also evidence of parental correlates of baby altruism. Parents who forcefully and emotionally explained how their child had hurt someone had more altruistic children, as did parents who were themselves altruists. It is unclear however, if these parental behaviors caused the children to be altruistic, or if they simply reinforced a predisposition toward altruism shared by parent and child alike. The early appearance of altruistic behavior, individual differences in altruism, and its temporal stability, all point to some genetic basis for this important human trait, based perhaps on a genetic propensity to become affectionate with those who raise us and with whom we are raised (MacDonald, 1984), and to like those whom we resemble (Glassman, Packel, & Brown, 1981).

Aggression

We cannot ignore the fact that aggression is part of animal living—nature *is* sometimes red in tooth and claw. Contrary to the writings of cynical misanthropes, it turns out that animals are at least as guilty of murder, cannibalism, and killing more than they need to eat as are human beings. Nonetheless, most animal aggression is controlled, seldom resulting in death or serious injury to either combatant. Two questions pose themselves: Why do animals fight at all? And why is their aggression so seldom lethal?

Why aggression occurs has a simple sociobiological answer—sometimes it benefits an individual's inclusive fitness. Aggression can enhance fitness in many ways. It is usually males who are aggressive, and their fitness may be improved by fighting for a territory to control and to live off, for one or more females to mate, or for high status in a dominance hierarchy and the access to females that this ensures. Excluding parental discipline and predator-prey aggression most aggression is a form of competition for resources, typically either for scarce natural resources or for a limited supply of females.

Thus success at aggressive competition enhances fitness. The successful aggressor with a good territory and many mates will pass his genes on into the next generation in greater numbers than the vanquished will. If this be so, why is aggression restrained at all? Surely the best strategy would be for a male to kill all his rivals, ensuring that their genes have no hope of survival.

The answer to this apparent puzzle is that aggression always entails *risks*. As with altruism, sociobiology holds that an organism acts as if it calculates the ratio between the benefits of aggression against its costs. To enter an all-out fight to the death is to risk losing everything; even should one win, one might be so damaged that later fitness is reduced. A drive for lethal aggression would be so detrimental to its holders that a gene for it cannot evolve. Moreover, even losers in aggressive interchanges benefit from controlled aggression. If one dies, one's genes die too. But if one loses nonfatally, one can hope to be more successful later.

Aggression exists in nature, therefore, in a kind of compromised state. Aggressiveness enhances fitness, so it has evolved; at the same time too much aggressiveness reduces fitness, so constraints on aggression have evolved. The result is the evolution of a set of behavioral mechanisms that give individuals of many species the capacity to fight, but which limit the aggression to the establishment of competitive superiority—for a territory or for females—without resulting in the death of the loser. In the animal world, nature is red in tooth and claw, but within certain evolutionary constrained boundaries.

Human Aggression

Ever since Cain slew Abel, aggression has been the dark side of human nature. The men of Homer's *Iliad* seem to enjoy killing and worship the glory to be won in war. The seventeenth-century political philosopher Thomas Hobbes observed that without society—and a strong ruler—human life would be solitary, nasty, brutish, and short. This view of human aggression as an impulse barely checked by repressive civilization was shared after World War I by Sigmund Freud, who had previously rejected it.

And, of course, the background to all philosophical and scientific speculation—and no one has gone much beyond speculation—on human aggression is our species' history of murder, torture, war, and genocide.

In the modern era, but before sociobiology, proponents of theories
of human aggression have divided into two quarrelsome camps. On one
side was the ethological neo-Freudian view whose scientific spokesman
was Konrad Lorenz (1966) and whose able publicist was author and screen-
writer Robert Ardrey (1966). Like Freud, Lorenz claimed that aggression
was a distinct innate *drive*, a *need* to be aggressive that constantly seeks
expression. Unlike Freud, in the ethological perspective the aggressive
drive was only a "so-called evil" (the subtitle of Lorenz' book in German),
since aggression was recognized to have the adaptive properties discussed
earlier. For Lorenz, the problem of human aggression was that the drive
was no longer under the control of the mechanisms that in animals constrain
it short of murder, a problem multiplied many times by humankind's inven-
tive technology of death. The solution to the problem of aggression was
to rechannel aggressiveness into moral equivalents of war—activities that,
like space exploration, provide the thrills, glory, heroism, and solidarity
of war within a socially constructive context. For Lorenz and his followers,
then, aggressiveness was an ineradicable part of human nature, a drive
that could not be escaped but could be redirected.

The other side viewed aggression as alien to the human condition
(Montague, 1968), a view represented in psychology by the social learning
tradition (for example, Bandura & Walters, 1963). Like Lorenz' view, this
camp developed in part from psychoanalysis, following Freud's earlier idea
that aggression was not an autonomous drive but derived from frustration
of other drives such as sex or hunger and from infantile oral-aggressive
sexuality. So the Montague camp argued against Lorenz that aggression
was a product of culture and not of biology. Through imitation of observed
aggression, especially when it was seen to pay off, and reinforcement of
aggressive acts, a child was molded by its environment into an aggressive
adult. According to these environmentalists, aggression was nothing more
than a set of learned skills that could be unlearned by an adult and, of
course, not taught to children. A pacific utopia is to be achieved not by
redirecting aggression but by refusing to model it and refusing to let it
pay; aggression could go the way of the bustle.

The sociobiological view is, in effect, a compromise between Lorenz'
adaptive aggressive drive and social learning's set of learned skills. Rejecting
any notion that aggression is an instinctive drive, sociobiology holds that
aggression results instead from *competition*. Whenever resources are in limited supply—be they food, space, or mates—aggression becomes an adaptive
response. Thus, for the sociobiologist, aggression is an innate set of skills,
or an innate disposition to *learn* aggressive skills, which evolved because
it has been adaptive in the past. Sociobiology shares with Lorenz the insight
that aggression is not a purely gratuitous evil, but shares with the social
learners the insight that aggression is a capacity, not a drive, whose learning
and manifestation depend on environmental circumstances.

Some anthropological evidence indicates that human aggression occurs for the same reasons as aggression between animals. To begin with, aggression may stem from efforts to establish dominance. People, especially males, struggle to establish power over others in our numerous hierarchical organizations. Status displays, such as joining the country club or buying a Rolls-Royce, are peaceful ways of showing one's superior dominance position. As in animals, human aggression sometimes—but all too rarely—is channeled into ritualized mock combat, as in medieval jousts, when one knight established his superiority over his rivals.

Human aggression and warfare are also caused by resource competition. The Munducurú of Brazil fight frequent wars with their neighbors, wars that appeared quite senseless until fitted to a sociobiological model (Durham, 1976). As were human beings for most of their evolutionary history, the Munducurú are hunter-gatherers who rely on hunting as their primary source of high quality protein. The mere existence of other tribes—in Munducurú the word for *enemy* means all who are not Munducurú—threatens their supply of game. So their propensity for war is adaptive for each and every individual of their tribe by helping assure a plentiful supply of protein. The individual fitness of the best warriors is directly increased through increase in social status and lavish gifts. The most outstanding warrior in a particular battle is by no sociobiological accident called "mother of the peccary": one who increases valued game by killing those who might diminish it. Where women are a scarce resource, as in periods of rapid geographical and population expansion (for example, among the Yanamamö of Brazil and Venezuela) men fight for opportunities to take wives. In short, where some resource is in short supply, aggression occurs, even among groups that are otherwise quite pacific (Eibl-Eibesfeldt, 1975); Western children's fights over toys are regulated by the same factors as among the Munducurú (Weigel, 1984).

Factors that tend to inhibit aggression are also explicable in sociobiological terms. Medieval rulers arranged marriages to make alliances with each other, reducing the likelihood of war between them, a practice pursued by many primitive groups as well. One is less likely to kill kin than to kill strangers, for kin carry one's genes, and their murder would harm one's own inclusive fitness. Reciprocal altruism, too, can check forces pushing toward aggression. Where people and groups of people can cooperate to increase their fitness over what each alone could achieve through aggression, aggression will no longer pay and would be shunned.

Apart from these general tendencies that humans share with other animals, tendencies that lead us at once toward and away from fighting, sociobiologists have considered the unique problem of human aggression. First, however, it should be pointed out that there may not be a special problem of human aggressiveness, despite Lorenz. Human technology makes humans uniquely *efficient* killers, but it does not follow that we are the most aggressive—even if we are the most dangerous—species on earth. Wilson (1975a) has catalogued among animals brutalities extending to cannibalism. As Wilson (p. 107) observes, "If hamadryas baboons had nuclear weapons they would destroy the world in a week. And alongside ants, which conduct assassinations, skirmishes, and pitched battles as routine business, men are all but tranquilized pacifists."

Nevertheless, human aggression does possess certain unique features. The naked (human) ape is an ill-equipped killer. Our teeth and our claws, or fingernails, are poor offensive weapons set alongside the natural equipment of the lion or wolf. Unfortunately, as Lorenz originally suggested, this means during our early evolution in the pretechnological past it was so unlikely that a man could kill another that we lack the reflexive aggression-inhibiting responses possessed by lions and wolves. So give a human a weapon, and death can follow all too readily. It is not surprising, then, that while ritual aggression is common in the rest of the animal kingdom, knightly mock combat occurs but seldom. Human intelligence and our capacity for morality (or at least for moralizing) create the unique human capacity for moralistic aggression (Trivers, 1971/1980). Human history is replete with crusades, massacres, and orgies of execution in the name of a higher moral power, be it God, Allah, the State, or Reason. The suggestion here is not that moral reasons are just rationalizations for innate bloodthirsty behavior. Quite the contrary. Sociobiology says that we are driven not to kill but to be moral, to cooperate with our in-group. Morality is a human imperative that makes us *want* to kill the immoral, the out-group. Morality *causes* aggression; it does not rationalize it.

The main evolutionary roots of human aggression can be traced to our long period spent as technologically primitive hunter-gatherers. Since most of our evolution occurred in this stage, sociobiologists look there for the ecological pressures that created human nature. As humans moved from the trees to the plains, they began to hunt game and to be exposed to predators who hunted them. Given the poor fighting equipment of the individual human, survival became possible only by cohesive group living and the ability of human beings to cooperate. Now while cooperation is one of our most admirable traits, it also made warfare possible and intensified the human capacity for certain forms of aggression. *Groups* now competed for resources and resource-rich territory, creating warrior groups and warfare. Sex-based division of labor also occurred, with consequences to be explored later.

Cooperativeness and the tendency to form dominance hierarchies created in people tendencies toward social compliance and obedience toward superiors. The shocking dangers of compliance and obedience have been amply demonstrated by Stanley Milgram's (1974) classic experiments. Milgram has shown that while no one thinks he or she would deliberately injure another person just because a researcher tells that person to, a great many people will, in fact, do so. When told to administer intense electric shocks to a "learner" for failing to learn a paired-associate list, most subjects did so, despite screams of pain from the learner (really a confederate of Milgram's) in the next room. Even when the "learner" was in the same room with the "teacher," and the real subject, (the "teacher") could *see* the agony he was (apparently) inflicting, 40 percent of the subjects nevertheless delivered the maximum shock (450 volts) as ordered; 30 percent did so when they had to hold the "learner" to the shock-delivering electrode.

We see, then, that while the human capacity for aggression is in most ways similar to aggression in the rest of the animal kingdom, special features of our evolutionary ecology have affected how that capacity is directed and used. If this sociobiological analysis is correct, we may be relieved that there is no inherent aggressive drive ineluctably pressing for release, but we must be wary of the human propensities to kill in the name of morality and to kill simply because one has been told to kill. It is because of these propensities to cooperate and obey—not because of aggressive capacity per se—that human history is so often blood-red, from the butchery of the Hundred Years' War to the reign of terror during the French Revolution, to the nightmare of Auschwitz, to the misdirected revenge at My Lai, to the tribal genocide in Idi Amin's Uganda.

Sexual Behavior

Sex is the essence of individual fitness. Therefore, we must expect the struggle for existence to have strongly shaped the way animals attract mates and reproduce.

The first significant fact about evolution and sexual behavior is that the struggle for existence—or more precisely in this context, the struggle to mate—has fallen much harder on males than females. Studies and experiments on many species from insects to apes have shown that every female has opportunities to mate and produce offspring, but that only some males get such opportunities. In the vast majority of animal species, females represent a limited resource for which males compete. Therefore, male sexual behavior, being under evolutionary pressure, has been more strongly shaped than female behavior.

Once sex itself appeared on earth millions of years ago—for reasons that are still unclear—the basic fact underlying male-female differences emerged. This is the fact that the *parental investment* (Trivers, 1972/1978) of each parent in its offspring is quite radically different. The male gametes (sperm) are small, biologically cheap to produce, highly mobile, and can be made continuously in huge numbers; the sperm in one male human ejaculate are enough to fertilize every woman in North America. The female gamete, or egg, on the other hand, is larger and biologically more expensive to make, since it contains both genetic material and nourishment for the developing organism. The egg is also incapable of movement, and is produced in smaller quantities only at certain periods of the female biological cycle.

Additionally, in mammals the female must bear and nurse her young, a task spared the male. We see, then, that the biological investment of male and female parents in their offspring is vastly different. A male can sire many offspring in many females quickly and cheaply, while a female must invest, especially if a mammal, a great deal of energy and time in each of her young. We can add to this basic difference a further, related fact, that a female knows with certainty that its offspring are her own and must carry her genes, while a male can never know with certainty that "his" offspring truly carry his genes.

Putting all these considerations together we should expect to find—and do find—that evolution has produced very different strategies by which males and females go about the business of reproducing. The most dramatic illustration of this difference, at least in animals, is called the *Coolidge effect*, from the following story (Berment, 1976, pp. 76–77):

> One day the President and Mrs. Coolidge were visiting a government farm. Soon after their arrival they were taken off on separate tours. When Mrs. Coolidge passed the chicken pens she paused to ask the man in charge if the rooster copulates more than once each day. "Dozens of times" was the reply. "Please tell that to the President," Mrs. Coolidge requested. When the President passed the pens and was told about the rooster, he asked, "Same hen every time?" "Oh, no, Mr. President, a different one each time." The President nodded slowly, then said, "Tell that to Mrs. Coolidge."

In a great many mammals, a male will mount a given female only a few times and then lose interest. But if a new female is introduced he mounts her just as enthusiastically as the first. This pattern can be repeated over and over. Males are also remarkably hard to fool into re-mating with an already inseminated female: They have sex indiscriminately but are nonetheless discriminating about the condition of their partners (Symons, 1979). The Coolidge effect is almost absent in females.

This makes a great deal of evolutionary sense given the basic difference between egg and sperm. Once fertilized, a female has nothing to gain by further copulation with any male at all; her genes are now developing (along with the father's) into a new member of the species. For her, further sexual activity is pointless at best and risky at worst. On the male side, further copulation with a female he has just fertilized is pointless for the same reason, and he should lose interest in her; further copulation just wastes time, effort, and sperm, thereby reducing fitness. But it would pay to have sex with new, unfertilized females. Sperm are cheap and continuously produced, so further opportunities for sex with new females should be seized to increase individual fitness by impregnating them. So it is genetically profitable for males, but not for females, to desire and perform sex with many partners. The reproductive strategies of male and female thus share their mentalities and desires in different directions.

All these differences create two different kinds of selection pressure on the further evolution of sexuality. First, females become for males a desirable resource to control. If a male can collect many females—which he is likely to desire—and impregnate them himself to the exclusion of other males—which he is capable of doing—then his individual fitness will be enhanced and the fitness of others harmed. He will gain in the struggle for existence. Males will therefore compete for possession of females, creating *intrasexual selection*: Males who successfully compete will be selected and their fitness enhanced.

For a female the situation is rather different. A male can have profligate sex with many females whose own fitness may be high or low. But this is of small moment, for *some* of his sperm will impregnate *some* fit females, and so his genes will survive. But a female is putting up a large investment when she copulates, a large investment of biological matter (her eggs) and time and effort in bearing, nursing, and raising the offspring. Should she mate with an unfit male her fitness will be correspondingly harmed. So in the struggle for existence it pays for females to be choosy, to mate only with the fittest available male in order to protect her large (and his small) investment. And females can be choosy because they are a scarce resource. The criteria for their choices create a selection pressure, called by Darwin *sexual selection*, but now called *epigamic selection*. Genes carried by male survival machines that meet female criteria will prosper, while those carried by losers will go extinct. Male appearance and behavior will thus be pushed in the direction of pleasing the female.

In this way is born the strategem and counter-strategem of the war between the sexes. Females set criteria for male fitness, and males try to meet them or deceive females into *thinking* they met them. Females see through the ruses and set new tests; new, craftier deceptions evolve, and so on through an endless and fascinating cycle.

Intrasexual selection. Competition among males (and in a *very* few species, females) has resulted in a number of adaptations that serve each competitor, summarized in Table 11–1 (from Alcock, 1979).

The first set of adaptations help a male compete for access to females. First (A), males, much more than females, are easily aroused and sexually promiscuous; males need not be choosy and need to be ready to seize every opportunity, while females must be more cautious. Second (B), in many group-living species the males fight one another, generally without bloodshed, to establish a *dominance hierarchy*, which runs from the dominant "alpha" male who can defeat everyone else, to a lowest ranking male who defers to everyone else. Dominance expresses itself in reproductive success in the ways listed in Table 11–1:

1. A dominant male may be able to keep away all other males from a female who is receptive (that is, in estrus, or "heat").
2. He may gather unto himself a harem of females for his exclusive use.
3. In social species without harems the dominant male(s) typically have first or exclusive access to the females.
4. In some species, typically birds, dominant males establish territories that are attractive to females because of bountiful resources or some other feature.
5. Dominant males are more attractive to females than the territories of lesser males, and the attracted female(s) will then mate only with him.

In all these ways males' struggle for dominance aids their reproductive success and therefore increases their individual fitness.

Third (C), subordinate males have strategies open to them that give their genes a chance at survival. As we mentioned earlier in discussing aggression, submitting now in a dominance fight leaves open the possibility

TABLE 11-1   Results of Intrasexual Selection on the Evolution of Male Behavior

ADAPTATIONS THAT PLAY A ROLE IN THE COMPETITION TO SECURE COPULATIONS

A.   A low threshold for mating attempts
B.   Dominance behavior (the monopolization of females): the exclusion of other males from:
1.   The vicinity of a female that is or will become receptive
2.   A harem of females
3.   Positions of high status in multimale groups
4.   Areas with useful resources attractive to females
5.   Display sites attractive to females
C.   Subordinate behavior (coping with dominant males)
1.   Submissive behavior and the (temporary) postponement of attempts to reproduce
2.   Courtship of females only when dominant males are absent or occupied
3.   Sneak copulations
4.   Rape

ADAPTATIONS THAT HELP A MALE ENSURE THAT HIS SPERM WILL BE USED BY FEMALES HE HAS INSEMINATED

A.   Guarding behavior
1.   Temporary guarding of a recently inseminated female
2.   Prolonged protection of a female or harem against other males
B.   Behavior that reduces the likelihood that an unguarded female will copulate again
1.   The insertion of mating plugs in females after copulation
2.   The use of biochemical or behavioral signals to active mechanisms within the female that reduce her receptivity

ADAPTATIONS THAT LOWER THE REPRODUCTIVE SUCCESS OF COMPETITORS

A.   Sexual interference
1.   Interruption of another male's courtship
2.   Female mimicry by males that induces other males to waste time, energy, or sperm
B.   Attempts to injure competitors
1.   Assault on other males, including homosexual rape
2.   Assault on mates or offspring of other males

of later success as practice perfects competitive abilities and dominant males weaken or die. Or males may try to court (2) or secretly copulate (3) with females when a dominant male is absent or occupied. Finally, there is the possibility of rape, which, contrary to general opinion, is by no means confined to humans (Shields & Shields, 1983).

The second set of male adaptations produced by intrasexual selection has evolved to help a male be sure it is his sperm that fertilize a female's egg, since in many species it is not the first male's whose sperm succeeds, but rather the last male's. Even when this is not the case, it is in a male's interest to increase his certainty of paternity. To accomplish these ends, males can guard their mates (A) either just long enough to ensure insemination (1) or more permanently through monogamous union or harem keeping (2). Other behaviors may be used to keep females from mating again (B). In some species, including the familiar rat, a male inserts a plug in the female after copulation that at once retains his own sperm and excludes others (1). In some species a male may use chemical or behavioral signals that automatically reduce a female's receptivity after mating (2). It appears that male lions do this by gently biting the neck of their mate during copulation, signaling her that she is inseminated.

Finally, there are adaptations that directly lower other males' reproductive success. Males can interfere with other males' courtship or copulations (A,1), perhaps by attacking them *in flagrante*. In a few species, for example, the salamander *Plethodon jordani*, males pretend to be females and induce other males to waste time, effort, and sperm (A,2) to the detriment of their fitness. And, of course, males can turn red in tooth and claw and try to injure each other or each other's mates (B,2), or to kill the offspring of other males, as langurs and lions do. Homosexual rape may be included here (B,1), which takes a particularly bizarre form in an insect species wherein a male may rape another male, depositing his sperm in his victim's genitals, seeing to it that if the victim later mates with a female it will be the rapist's semen and genes that survive, not the poor victim's!

We can summarize the effects of intrasexual selection by saying that most of the evolutionary pressures favor males who are aggressive with each other and their mates, are easily aroused and sexually promiscuous, and who jealously watch over their mates. The sole countervailing pressure is the advantage of monogamy in heightening certainty of paternity. Whether and in what ways these pressures have affected male human sexuality will be explored later in this chapter.

Sexual or epigamic selection. Because of the differences between egg and sperm, female behavior has been very differently affected by evolution. A female must exercise great care in selection of a mate; she must be cautious, willing to test out possible suitors before committing her eggs to his sperm. Table 11–2, based on Trivers (1972/1978) and Alcock (1979), summarizes criteria suggested by sociobiologists, especially Trivers, that females can use in choosing a mate.

The first set of criteria (I) are used by all females but especially those of the many species in which the male does nothing to help raise his offspring. The most basic question is whether a given male can, in fact, fertilize the female's eggs (A), as indicated by the four listed criteria. Doing this is not always as obvious as it seems. Many insects resemble each other, especially if they are related species or members of a species that practices mimicry. Usually, the male's courtship behavior, which is often highly elaborate and ritualized, indicates *yes* answers to all these questions, so the female can then choose among qualified males. Thus, the fact of female choice becomes a pressure on *male* behavior: Male courtship rituals have evolved

TABLE 11–2   Criteria Used by Females on Choosing Mates

I.   Criteria used by females of all species, but especially those where males offer little parental care.

   A.   Can he fertilize my eggs?
      1.   Is he of the correct species?
      2.   Is he of the correct sex?
      3.   Is he mature?
      4.   Is he sexually competent?

   B.   What is the quality of his genes?
      1.   Does he show high survival ability?
      2.   Can he dominate other males?
         (a) as shown by high dominance ranking
         (b) by fighting well when I incite him

II.   Criteria used by females of species whose males offer parental care.

   A.   What will be the quality of his care?
      1.   Is he able to control needed resources?
      2.   Is he willing to share these resources?
      3.   Is he willing to protect me and my offspring?

Adapted from Trivers (1972) and Alcock (1979)

precisely because of the need to convince females that a male is ready, willing, and able to perform his role.

   Next, in order not to waste her precious eggs on an unfit mate, the female must assess her suitor's individual fitness (B). She can ask if he possesses (and thereby his genes ought to possess) high survival ability (B,1). The most obvious measure of fitness is age: A young male is untested while an older male has, by definition, survived. So a female should prefer an older to a younger suitor. Gene quality may also be measured through dominance (B,2). Dominance hierarchies, in those species that have them, provide a direct measure of fitness. Lacking a hierarchy, females might get males to fight each other and pick the winner.

   Additional criteria come into play if a female can choose a mate who will invest in his offspring (II). Now she must weigh the quality of his parental care. Can he control resources (A,1) needed by her and her offspring? In territorial species females will prefer males having environmentally rich territories. Will he share resources (A,2)? In many species males give females valuable presents, especially food, to induce them to mate. Finally, can he protect me and my offspring (A,3)? Often these criteria boil down to assessing general genetic fitness, as above.

   Two important observations need to be made about this last class of criteria. First, to the degree that males invest in caring for their offspring they risk lowering their fitness by giving up possible copulations with other females. Therefore, to the extent they invest in offspring they must act like females and be choosy about their mates. If, for example, a species is really monogamous, the male has just as much invested—everything—in his offspring as his mate. Both he and she must be equally careful in choosing a partner for life, or even for a breeding season. In a very few species such as doves and giant water bugs this process has gone so far that males invest more in offspring than females do, and the usual roles are reversed, males being cautious and sexually reserved while the females are aggressive and promiscuous. Such apparent exceptions to the general run of things in fact support Trivers' sociobiological analysis: Sexual behavior depends on the degree of biological investment in offspring. To the degree an individual's investment is large and lasting, the usual "female" strategy will be adopted; to the degree that investment is small and fleeting, the usual "male" strategy will be adopted.

The second observation about this last class of female criteria is that it gives rise to the strategem and counter-strategem of the war of the sexes, for males may pretend to be more fit than they are. They may share resources only long enough to copulate and then abandon the female; especially if the female can rear her young alone, this becomes an important male option for it frees him to increase his fitness with other females. Fortunately for females, if they *all* require long courtship and monogomous mating, abandonment will not pay, for lengthy courtship reduces male fitness, and monogamy reduces the population of available females. Under these circumstances, deception may arise, as males pretend to be more willing to invest than they are, and females attempt to see through the deceptions, which only calls forth more male cunning—and so on.

Deception is well illustrated by the hanging fly, whose species exhibit a gradation from male sincerity to flattery to fraud. In one species, the male brings a present of food, a blowfly he has caught. She feeds on it during copulation, which enhances her fitness and keeps him from being eaten in the way male praying mantises are. In another (more advanced?) species the male makes the present more attractive by wrapping it in a balloon of silvery webbing. The female unwraps the present, which gives the male a little longer, and feeds. In another species she opens the wrapping and finds a fly already sucked dry—too late, for the male is gone. Finally, in the highest (?) species, the female unwraps her balloon to find . . . nothing!

Mating systems. All these varied factors that play a part in evolving sexuality have resulted in a variety of stable mating systems; the ecology of male investment that gives rise to these systems are summarized in Table 11–3. What Table 11–3 shows—its content speaks for itself—is the powerful synthesizing power of sociobiology. It allows us to give a useful classification of a complex and varied set of behaviors (mating arrangements) and account for the classification on a few quantifiable principles, primarily the degree of male investment in offspring. Even the unusual case of polyandry fits neatly in place, not as an exception, but as the logical outcome of more male than female investment. Examples are given of each mating system. Where do people fit in?

TABLE 11–3 The Ecology of Mating Systems. Different Mating Systems Reflect Ecological Factors That Determine How Much a Male Can Help His Mate Produce and Rear Offspring and How Much Males of a Species Vary in Their Ability to Assist Their Mates. (From Alcock, 1979)

MALE ABILITY TO PROVIDE USEFUL SERVICES TO MATE		FEMALE CHOICE	MATING SYSTEM
	Most males offer same medium-to-high assistance	Females prefer unmated males	Monogamy robins, foxes
Males can monopolize useful resources or provide parental care	Some males offer much more than others	Females prefer superior helpers	Parental investment polygyny redwing blackbird, impala
Ecology of species	Male's parental ability exceeds that of female	Females invest in egg production only, mating with several males	Polyandry stickleback fish, tinamou
Males cannot provide useful assistance to females	Males compete to demonstrate genetic quality to females or to monopolize group of females	Females choose the competitively superior male	Pure dominance polygyny manakins, elephants

Human Sexuality[†]

When sociobiologists enter the field of human sexuality, they find well-trodden ground. Because it is such a consuming interest of human beings, sexuality has touched and been touched by every human endeavor and institution from literature to religion to science. Social scientific studies on sex and sex roles numbered at least 10,000 by 1975 (Heilbrun, 1981). So virtually anything sociobiologists might propose would be controversial.

[†] In addition to the standard sociobiological works cited in the animal section, the present account of sexuality draws especially on Symons (1979), Daly and Wilson (1978), and van den Berghe (1979). For views contrary to Symons, see Hrdy (1981). Hrdy (1979) reviewed Symons' book, and Symons (1983) reviewed Hrdy's.

We can here only scout around this fearsome territory, beginning by recalling the typical patterns of sexuality found in other animals. We have found that the parental investment of males in most species is much less than that of females. Consequently, natural selection has produced males who are aggressive with each other and toward prospective mates, who are easily aroused and sexually promiscuous, and who watch jealously over their mates. Additionally, males are high-variance gambles in the struggle for existence: Many males do not mate at all and are evolutionary failures, while some males are spectacularly successful, siring large numbers of offspring. Females, on the other hand, have been selected to be unaggressive, sexually reserved, and choosy about their mates. Females are safe but low-paying evolutionary investments: Every female can find a mate, but the number of offspring she may have is small compared to males. We will now consider whether this common pattern fits human beings.

Aggressiveness. One of the few generally acknowledged sex differences is that males are inherently more aggressive than females (Maccoby & Jacklin, 1974). The general division of labor in cultures around the world reflects this fact: Men hunt, make weapons, and go to war, while women gather and prepare food. In our own society, violent crime is committed almost exclusively by impoverished young males, those old enough to seek mates but who find themselves denied the usual signs of fitness awarded by our society, namely, education, wealth, status, and prospects for advancement. Among the middle class, competition for women is nonviolent and indirect; among the poor and disenfranchised, nature turns red in tooth and claw, and male youths seek female attention through toughness, *machismo*, and dominance within a male gang (Alexander, 1979a).

Viewed sociobiologically, the human pattern makes sense. The young male must fight to become a man, whether through actual physical competition with others, through indirect status-competition, or through the ritualized torture of initiation rites unknown to females (Barash, 1979). Only through competition can males earn females, thus ensuring their fitness, while females need but choose the successful competitor. Unfortunately, as among animals, human males may turn to rape as an adaptive strategy, especially when the cost is low (Shields & Shields, 1983; Thornhill & Thornhill, 1983).

The proximate mechanism of male aggressiveness is the male hormone testosterone, produced by the testes. Testosterone creates the male pattern, an energy-consuming, active, and aggression-prone way of life; female animals injected with testosterone become more active and aggressive. But testosterone also contributes to characteristic male vulnerability. By driving the male toward activity and aggression—the basic male fitness strategy—it makes him more likely to be killed (Daly & Wilson, 1978). Males also tend to suffer higher rates of embryonic, fetal, and infantile mortality, and to senesce more rapidly than females (Alexander, Hoogland, Howard, Noonan, & Sherman, 1979).

Contrary to popular beliefs, cultural sex-typing falls more heavily on males than on females, for sexual stereotypes are more rigidly imposed on males. Even contemporary American couples consciously trying to raise their children apart from sexist stereotypes find it easier to do so for girls. The girl playing with a fire truck is applauded: but the boy playing with dolls is often not (Katchadourian, 1979).

Cultural expectation reflects and magnifies the underlying biological reality that males are risk-taking, aggressive people who must struggle for success, for biological fitness. Girls will become women and find mates as a matter of course, so culture need not teach any particular role. These differences are evident even when we determinedly try to change. Contemporary sexual liberation has usually meant women becoming free to act like men—seeking places in business, industry, and the professions, where aggressiveness and risk-taking pay—rather than the other way around. The househusband is much more a curiosity than the female stockbroker.

Sexual arousability. Observation of the contemporary American scene also suggests that human males are, like most males, easily aroused sexually, while human females, like most females, are not. Pornography—manufactured sexual stimulation—is a huge business run by men for men. Sales of everything from *Playboy* to hardcore pornographic magazines run to about $2 billion a year, and are made for men, whether heterosexual or homosexual, while attempts to sell pornography to women of any orientation have proved unsuccessful. There is evidence that the modest success of the one magazine that aims pictures of naked men at women partly results from sales to homosexual men, while lesbians find magazines such as *Playboy* rather silly and puzzle that men enjoy them (Symons, 1979). So the bull market for arousal thrives on men, no women.

Some recent research has suggested that women can be aroused by sexually explicit materials at least as much as men, at least in experimental settings in which subjects view or read erotica and have their arousal measured through self-report or physical monitoring. These results have been taken to cast doubt on traditional stereotypes of the "turned-on" man and "frigid" woman. However, a closer look reveals features that support sociobiological hypotheses.

To begin with, close analysis of one such experiment (Heiman, 1975, reanalyzed by Symons, 1979), showed that men responded more strongly than women to tapes depicting sexual activity. Moreover, men, but not women, responded (at least initially) about as strongly to control tapes—a discussion between a male and female student about choice of college major—as to any explicit tape. Males are clearly more easily and strongly aroused by *any* situation in which sex *might* play a part. Women often complain that on dates any word or gesture meant as general friendliness is taken as expressing sexual interest, a real-life finding well grounded in sociobiology.

Analysis of these studies also shows that the proximate psychological mechanisms of sexual arousal are entirely different in males and females (Money & Erhardt, 1972; Symons, 1979). A man responds directly to the image of the woman photographed or described, and fantasizes about having sex with her. A woman, if aroused at all, is aroused by identifying with a photograph of a naked woman, and imagines herself to be similarly desirable. In erotica with male-female interaction, she is likely again to identify with the woman to learn ways in which she can be arousing and sexually skilled herself. So sexual arousal from erotic literature is possible for both men and women, but the thoughts that connect erotic depiction to actual arousal are not the same in men and women.

Men and women also respond differently to first appearances (Hill, Nocks, & Gardner, 1987). Males distinguish between a female's sexual attractiveness and her potential as a marriage partner. When shown pictures of women varying in both sexiness of dress and socioeconomic status display, men rated low status but sexily dressed women as desirable sex partners but as undesirable mates. High-status women were regarded favorably as potential wives regardless of sexiness of appearance. Women evaluating male models, in contrast, preferred high-status, unsexily dressed men both as potential sex partners and as husbands. In fact, women seemed to a degree turned off by male displays emphasizing the body.

Finally, we must remember that only men *seek* arousal through pornography. This is not a cultural artifact created by sleazy adult bookstores that socially inhibited women fear to enter. Kenrick, Stringfield, Wagenhals, Dahl, & Ransdell (1980) called male and female college students and asked if they would volunteer to participate in experiments involving seeing geometric figures, soft-core "loving" erotica, or hard-core "lustful" erotica. Women were less likely than men in every case to volunteer for the erotic experiment, and, when they did choose erotica, they preferred the soft-core description. As the marketplace indicates, men seek arousal while women do not.

All of this suggests that we must make an important distinction between *appetitive* sexuality, or an actual sex drive, and sexual *responsiveness*. Once they are in a sexual situation, women are at least as sexually responsive as men, and perhaps even more so, given the female ability to have multiple orgasms (Hrdy, 1979). Nevertheless, women seem not to have the driven sexual appetite of men; they do not seek out arousal through pornography. There are cultures in which the female orgasm is unknown, indicating that women do not have a drive to seek sexual outlet as men do (Symons, 1979). Again, the proximate mechanism seems to be testosterone. Women who for medical reasons have high levels of this hormone show characteristically male patterns of sexuality, becoming much more sexually aggressive. When treated, such women express relief at being able to return to "normal"—that is, nondriven, sexuality (Money & Erhardt, 1972; Symons, 1979).

Promiscuity. We come naturally, then, to promiscuity, a characteristic male trait in nonhuman animals. There is good evidence that men—whose minimum parental investment is so much less than women's—seek sexual variety. They fantasize about sex with many different women through pornography: No erotic publication contains pictures of just one woman. While adultery rates for men and women may be equalizing, men still have more partners than women do, and they are more likely to have one-night stands; the roving male seeks sex, the female is looking for a better partner. The Coolidge effect appears to apply to humans. The frequency of intercourse falls off after a couple is married, and wives are often puzzled by male adultery when they are always available to their husbands. Sexual autobiographies suggest that males are readily re-aroused by a new woman shortly after intercourse with another, who may instantaneously be transformed from alluring to repulsive (Symons, 1979). "Swinging" is largely a male-instigated practice, and most frequently involves adding a new woman to a married couple, sometimes a merger of couples, and almost never the addition of a new man (van den Berghe, 1979).

Patterns of homosexual conduct reinforce our picture of this pattern. Indeed, Symons (1979) has suggested that homosexuals represent the "acid test" of theories of sexuality, for in a homosexual encounter male and female strategies will be directly revealed, there being no need to compromise with or manipulate the other sex's strategy. Male homosexuals are quite promiscuous, and even though they desire permanent, stable relationships, they find them difficult to maintain, and often institutionalize sex with another partner outside the relationship. Male homosexuals seek out quick, anonymous, orgasmic encounters, even finding many in one night with multiple partners. The lesbian pattern is quite different. Relationships between couples are more stable and more frequent, there is little compulsive seeking of new partners, and lesbian sex is more extended and does not center on the orgasm (Symons, 1979).

Promiscuity—or rather a tendency toward it—seems to characterize human male sexuality.

Jealousy.   Although jealousy is clearly an emotion experienced by both men and women, the evidence is that it is a more powerful emotion in men (Daly, Wilson, & Weghorst, 1982). The enraged husband slaying his wife and her lover (and getting off) is well known; the reverse is not. This pattern—the classic double-standard—is found in almost all cultures (Symons, 1979; Daly, Wilson, & Weghorst, 1982). That males should be especially jealous makes good biological sense. Men can never be certain of paternity, and adultery by their wives (who they know in their hearts can find willing partners) reduces their fitness. So evolution has produced men who feel sexual jealousy and become outraged by their wives' affairs, even while they themselves aim to seduce their neighbor's wife. Male sexual jealousy is perhaps the leading cause of familial assault and murder (Daly, Wilson, & Weghorst, 1982). Women, on the other hand, are certain of maternity, and their fitness is not harmed by any purely sexual liaisons their husbands might have. The natural female fear is being abandoned for another woman, losing valuable male investment in child-rearing. Therefore, jealousy has a different, more biologically remote basis in women, and is less purely sexual.

Male uncertainty of paternity and sexual jealousy also leads to attempts by men to control female reproduction, just as male animals do. There are practices designed to isolate women from men who are neither husbands nor fathers; they help increase male certainty of paternity and thus have a biological basis not always apparent to the culture, which often views them as "protection" of women. Some such practices are:

Chinese footbinding. From an early age Chinese girls' feet were tightly bound, preventing proper growth of the foot, resulting in tiny, misshapen feet. Chinese men thought of this as a technique for enhancing women's sexual attractiveness, but it kept women literally hobbled and mostly at home. (Dickemann, 1982).

Claustration and veiling (*Purdah*). This practice involves the isolation of women from men other than kin or husband, and the covering of their bodies when they do go abroad. The Koran explains this as a means by which women "may be recognized and not annoyed" (Dickemann, 1982), but it serves men's reproductive control of women.

Surgical procedures such as sewing up of the vagina (until the husband wants access) or castration of the clitoris. The former is usually recognized as a means of reproductive control, while the latter may be explained, as in the nineteenth century, as a way to prevent masturbation. (Barker-Benfield, 1976).

What all of these practices really accomplish is control of women's reproduction in the interest of male genes.

Female choice. So far we have catalogued differences between men and women on arousability, sex drive, promiscuity, jealousy, and probable degree of reproductive success, focusing on the consequences of minimum male parental investment. Now we look at the consequences of human female parental investment. In our species it is especially large. A woman produces a single protein-rich egg once a month for about 35 years and can have *at most* 20 or so children regardless of how many partners she has. (This is in stark contrast to the male whose cheap sperm may father hundreds of children in many women.) She must then bear the child for nine increasingly difficult months, followed by several more months of nursing. The child who is born is singularly helpless, needing prolonged care, supervision, and education. Child-rearing would be easier with continuing male interest after marriage.

It is therefore of paramount importance in our species—as in other slowly reproducing species—for females to be choosy about their mates. While modern contraception distinguishes choice of sexual partner from choice of father for one's children, people did not evolve with contraceptives.

The criteria for women's choices adduced by sociobiologists are human versions of most of the criteria used by females of other animal species in which males may offer care of offspring. First, it is a cultural universal that close relatives are not suitable mates—Freud's famous incest taboo. There is a good biological basis for it, since it prevents incestuous inbreeding that would likely result in combining recessive lethal genes, reducing fitness of offspring (van den Berghe, 1983). A woman must gauge the willingness of a man to provide parental investment, which may be indicated by his behavior toward her and his general reputation—a uniquely human possession. As with many other animals, it is quite common in all cultures for a man to woo a woman with gifts, especially meat from the hunt in traditional cultures. Such behavior shows, at least on the surface, a willingness to share resources. Of course, human females—like hanging fly females—may find male gifts deceiving. Finally, not only must a man be willing to share resources, but he must also possess resources to share, and a woman must estimate these by judging the quality of his gifts, his wealth, his status, and his intelligence, or as our Victorian ancestors might have called it—his "prospects." Cross-cultural research has confirmed that the sorts of traits listed by Alcock are in fact those used by women and/or their relatives in the choice of a husband. Physical appearance counts for relatively little (Hill, Nocks, & Gardner, 1987).

Given the importance of female choice to their individual fitness, we can readily see that it is most adaptive for women to be less arousable than men and to largely lack appetitive sexuality. A woman driven by constant stimulation and an autonomous sex urge would be relatively unable to test and evaluate men's fitness. Women find it relatively easy to control their sexual desires with strangers, and this is of great adaptive value. Males, on the other hand, benefit—in ultimate terms—from their constant sexual stimulability and sex drive, for it makes it possible for them to search for and seize opportunities to mate, and so enhace their fitness. Of course, this does not justify their doing so, but it does mean that the tendency is an inherent part of male human nature and must be controlled, not wished away.

What about male choice? From what we have learned about male sexuality, we would expect their criteria to be simple physical attractiveness, which research and cross-cultural studies strongly support. Precisely because men are primed for quick physical arousal, they will judge a woman by her looks, by how arousing she is. Because his minimal parental investment is so low—simple insemination—a man is not likely to evaluate a woman on any deeper criteria. The basic male strategy is the high-risk one: impregnate many women (which he desires to do) and his genes are bound to survive.

The sociobiological result of these differences between men and women is the war between the sexes. A woman evaluates the fitness of a man and tries to get him to invest in her to show whether he will invest in offspring after birth. A man wishes to impress females, trying to act fitter than he is, and to invest just enough in a woman to seduce her but without committing himself and without giving up opportunities to enhance his fitness with other women. Popular songs are full of the battles between the sperm and the egg—the man who professes his love as a tactic of seduction versus the woman who hopes to turn the tactic into a reality.

Changing cultural environment may change the rules of the game. In a strongly monogamous environment, men will act more like women. A long courtship followed by a permanent marriage multiplies the male's actual parental investment many times over his minimal one. So men will be choosy not about whom they bed but whom they wed. They will look for maternal and perhaps economic qualities that will ensure their off-spring's fitness. In our culture, to cite another example, men have tradition-ally sought female approbation through swaggering machismo—advertising their fitness by (at least apparent) toughness. But as the satirists on the TV show *Saturday Night Live* (October 10, 1981) suggest, machismo may now be a losing strategy, and the man who wants to attract the new woman would do well to imitate the sensitivity and emotional vulnerability of Alan Alda. On the other hand, the new (since the first edition of this text) popularity of male "hunks" and unpopularity of "wimps" with women suggests the pendulum is swinging back to machismo, to men's confusion.

Sociobiology offers a picture of human sexuality that conforms to the more firmly established sociobiology of nonhuman creatures, that makes sense of our own observation of our everyday lives, and is reasonably supported by cross-cultural data and research results from social psychology. Many may find it an unpleasant picture, preferring to think of differences in sexuality as cultural products, especially of our own "sexist" society. The account is also disturbing in its suggestion that in such an intimate arena men and women are so different that they almost cannot communi-cate, cannot intuitively understand one another. Nevertheless, if we share our sexuality with the animals, sociobiology likely describes our condition. It will take the resources of humankind's master trait—intelligence—to bridge the gap between man and woman through art, poetry, writing, science, and a determined effort to understand and respect those with whom we share our lives.

Parental Care

Once mating has occurred and young are born, what happens? In many species the young are left entirely on their own, to fend for themselves or die. This lack of parental care usually occurs in species living in unstable, unpredictable environments, which produces *r-selection*. Species subject to *r*-selection generally adopt a strategy of producing a huge number of off-spring all at once (and sometimes only once), and completely neglecting them. Although most will die, enough offspring—the toughest and lucki-est—will survive to reproduce.

Degrees of parental care evolve under *K-selection*, which occurs in stable, predictable environments. *K*-selection leads to larger size and longer life, giving parents the capability of extended child care. It leads to smaller brood sizes as animals reproduce many times in a longer life, giving parents a greater investment in each child than under *r*-selection. *K*-selection, there-fore, is likely to lead to increased parental care. It may be helped along by a dangerous environment requiring parental protection, and also by the evolution of offspring who are helpless long after birth and who thereby need parental care if they (the holders of the parents' genes) are to survive at all. In humans, *K* and *r* may be regarded as different reproductive strategies associated with different personality traits and different socioeco-nomic levels (Rushton, 1985).

Once parental care has evolved, however, it is usually the female who bears the burden of child-rearing. Only in the most strictly monogamous species (a small minority) is child care about equally shared. Otherwise, the male does much less, because his investment is much less. Females *always* have a high investment in their offspring, as we have seen, and for them parental care always pays. Males, however, typically have a lower degree of investment and so typically care less to begin with; furthermore, they are less certain a given child is theirs, taking some of the edge off the desire to care for what may be an imposter. Moreover, in nonmonogamous species, the male's (or females' under polyandry) fitness is better served by begetting more offspring with more females, as in a harem, than by caring extensively for one mate's small brood. Thus, many animal families resemble the lion's pride. The females possess the territory (passed by inheritance through a group of sisters), care for the young, and do all the hunting (although the male of the pride gets to eat first). The male's role is merely looking regal, protecting the pride from occasional harm, and begetting offspring.

Sociobiological analysis can be extended to parent-offspring interactions, as Trivers (1974) has done with his parental investment concept. Attachment—the bond between parent and child—is a much studied phenomenon of human and animal behavior. It must have biological roots because it is so fitness-enhancing. Emotional attachment is the proximate motivator of parental care, and has evolved to protect the parents' investment in their offspring and, of course, the offspring's investment in itself.

Given this, we might expect parent-offspring behavior to be harmonious, which every parent knows is not true. Trivers' analysis suggests why. Certainly a parent has an investment in his or her offspring, for it carries his or her genes—but only 50 percent. A child, on the other hand, has a 100 percent investment in itself. This differential investment means there will be times when the parents' genetic interest and the child's are not identical.

Trivers' analysis suggests a further point, increasingly (and independently) recognized by developmental psychologists, that contrary to the usual view, the parent-child relationship is not a one-way affair in which the parent molds a passively dependent child. Parents and child differ in their investments in each other and themselves rendering conflict inevitable. Although it appears that the parents have all the power, children are not without resources. Consider the *attachment bond*. Every human parent knows the ineffable joy of an infant's smile, which can wash away anger and resentment; of course that smile is sweet—for the same reason sugar is sweet. A child can manipulate a parent with that smile and through attachment. Many a parent has been gulled into doing something against his or her better judgment by the cute demeanor and innocent smile of his or her three-year-old! Just as deception and a war of strategem and counterstrategem occurs between the sexes, so does it occur between parent and child.

Families, Parents, and Children

There are two features of *Homo sapiens'* sexuality—specifically, women's sexuality—that, while not entirely unique among animals, have been carried to a high pitch among our species. Women are unusual in experiencing orgasms, and in concealing ovulation, that is, not entering a period known generally as "heat" (technically **estrus**) when they advertise fertility and sexual availability. There is a lively controversy within sociobiology about the significance and possible adaptive value, if any, of these female traits.

The most popular hypothesis, possessing roots in ethology, is the theory that both female orgasm and loss of estrus are adaptations creating a male-female pair-bond, which in turn creates the basic nuclear family (see Wilson, 1978; Barash, 1979; van den Berghe, 1979). According to this reasoning, loss of estrus makes a woman continuously sexually available to a male partner, who then has less need to look elsewhere for sexual satisfaction, creating a bond between him and her. The bond is reciprocated by the woman's deriving pleasure from sex with her partner. Thus is created—so the pair-bond story goes—the intimate loving attachment between husband and wife that is the rock of the nuclear family, enhancing the fitness of both mother and father.

Consoling as this idea may be, there are good reasons to think it fable rather than fact (Symons, 1979; Hrdy, 1979, 1981). As Wilson pointed out in his book *Sociobiology*—notwithstanding his later belief in the pair-bond theory—sex is a divisive, not a solidifying, force in animal or human society. In the animal world, monogamous species are *hyposexual*—engaging in little sexual activity—a characterization that hardly fits *Homo sapiens*. Primates copulate throughout the sexual cycle and have not developed monogamy (Daniels, 1983). In the vast majority of societies, marriages are arranged on calculations of gain to the partners and (especially the man's) kin group, not on grounds of mutual satisfaction. Finally, in most cultures couples stay together despite quarrels over sexuality (mutual recriminations concerning adultery and abandonment) and when marriages become happy they do so late in life, when sexual fires are dampened. In the general run of human experience, then, it appears that marriage—the pair-bond—is not built on sexuality but endures when it does in spite of sexuality. Human sexuality seems instead to be an adaptation to a cultural environment in which marriage is ubiquitous, the man seeking outside opportunities to increase his fitness and the woman seeking to increase her husband's parental investment.

Unfortunately, although the pair-bond theory may be challenged, sociobiologists do not agree on the origins of the family, the adaptiveness of women's concealment of ovulation, or their ability to have orgasms. Symons (1979) argues that female orgasm is a physiological accident rather than an adaptation, pointing to the fact that unlike the male orgasm it is not necessary to procreation, hence plays no role in fitness and cannot have been selected. In some societies female orgasm is unknown; in most it is highly variable between and within women; and in those societies in which it is expected as normal, it only comes about from men being carefully trained in the arts of love.

On the other hand, Alexander (1979b) thinks that orgasm, through its outward manifestations, is an adaptive signal from the woman to her lover that she finds him sexually satisfying and is unlikely to cuckold him, reassuring his feeling of paternity; Hrdy (1979, 1981) suggests that the capacity to have orgasm makes a woman have many lovers, all of whom may invest in her offspring.

With regard to concealment of ovulation, sociobiological theories are even more at odds. The problem is simple but intractable: When women ceased to go into estrus did they thereby stop advertising their sexual availability, or did they begin to *continuously* advertise their availability? Alexander (Alexander & Noonan, 1979; Alexander, 1979b) adopts the former line of reasoning. He argues that by concealing ovulation women enticed men into an extended consortship, for since neither he nor his mate knew when she was fertile, he would have to remain with her to keep inseminating her and guarding against insemination by other males. At the same time, by no longer going into estrus, the woman reassured her mate's sense of paternity by making her less likely to seek or attract adulterous partners during "heat." One might call Alexander's theory the Machiavellian pair-bond based on uncertainty and manipulation.

Symons (1979) and Hrdy (1979), on the other hand, think that women continuously advertise their sexuality, *reducing* their mate's certainty of paternity, since she is always available for sex with another male. Symons offers two scenarios by which loss of estrus might be adaptive and have evolved. In the first, continuously advertising women would be more success-ful than estrus women in obtaining meat from males to exchange for sex. In the second, continuous availability is adaptive by allowing a woman to be fertilized by presumably fitter males other than her husband. Hrdy (1979) suggests additionally that loss of estrus made it easier for a woman to manipulate men's uncertainty about paternity, entangling them in a web of parental investment, serving her own genetic fitness.

Finally, Daniels (1983) suggests that loss of estrus promotes general social solidarity. Open estrus would constantly incite men to competition not cooperation, and would divert female attention from social tasks such as child-rearing and food gathering.

Whatever the origin of the human family, it is a cross-cultural univer-sal, although it may take on very different forms in different cultures.

Surveys of the world's cultures find that polygyny in some form is the most common marital arrangement (when polygyny is "usual," most men have or want to have two or three wives; when it is "occasional," a few high-status men secure a large number of wives, leaving few women for other men to marry). Monogamy is uncommon, and was quite rare until the coming of religions that impose it as a moral requirement. Polyan-dry is practically unknown; as among other species it occurs only in rare ecological situations and is viewed by its participants as making the best of a bad deal (van den Berghe, 1979). Humans also display the sexual dimorphism of a mildly polygynous species: Generally speaking, the greater the difference in bodily size between males and females of a given species, the greater is their degree of polygyny, and among humans, men are on average slightly larger than women (Alexander, Hoogland, Howard, Noonan, & Sherman, 1979). If we use data on sexual dimorphism we can calculate that on average men should want about two or three wives, as is the case with "usual" polygynous societies, and in the nominally "monogamous" ones that allow a man to keep concubines. These data, taken together with human hypersexuality, indicate that as far as nature is concerned, human beings are polygynous, not monogamous.

One should remember that this represents the ideal state of affairs for men only, since they, but not women, can increase their fitness by holding many mates, at once gaining women to impregnate and keeping other men from finding wives. Women, on the other hand, are hurt by polygyny, since female fitness declines in polygynous marriages among all species (Daly & Wilson, 1978). Emotionally, too, women prefer monogamy, since in general women see sex as part of a deep, intimate, and loving relationship with another person, not as an end in itself or as superficial recreation (Symons, 1979). Therefore, if we apply human intelligence to the question of marriage systems we may freely disagree with natural selection's production of natural human polygyny, and say that monogamous union based on love, respect, and personal intimacy is the ideal for which we should aim.

At the same time, evidence from utopian experiments indicates that it would be unwise to depart too far from the form of the family as it has naturally evolved. During the heyday of the U.S. counterculture of the 1960s and early 1970s, various communitarian "families" were established, few of which survive today. Study of their children reveals a dismal record: children neglected, deprived and emotionally stunted, incapable of prolonged attention or making friends (Barash, 1979). A more formal and determined experiment in communal living was undertaken in Israel's kibbutzes. The dedicated, socialist, kibbutzim aimed to abolish sexual discrimination and to replace the nuclear family with the crèche, a child being raised and living with his or her peers and not with the natural parents. Nevertheless, the division of labor within kibbutzes reflected traditional practices; men predominatng in primary production jobs and in holding leadership posts, women predominantly in the service occupations and running the children's houses (van den Berghe, 1979). Furthermore, primarily in response to complaints by women, the kibbutzes are returning to more traditional modes of family life and sex-roles (Beit-Hallahmi & Rabin, 1977). In common with animals, higher-status humans have more offspring than lower-status ones, though this finding is controversial. (Faux & Miller, 1984; Essock-Vitale, 1984; Mealey, 1985; Vining, 1986, and following commentary).

Within the family, parent-offspring conflict—even child abuse (Box 11–3)—can be expected to occur. The rudiments of parent-offspring conflict were covered earlier. Those simpler forms of conflict should apply to hu-

---

BOX 11–3   Child Abuse and Evolution

Most sociobiological theories about families attempt to understand why families work—why parents and children love each other, how children are socialized, how parent-offspring conflict is mediated. But as we know all too well today, families don't always work; child abuse and neglect are tragically commonplace even among animals. Can sociobiology shed any light on abnormal family patterns? Daly and Wilson (1982) think it can, that patterns of abuse and neglect can be explained in terms of biologically likely variables.

For example, degree of paternal investment in offspring after birth, throughout the animal kingdom, is a function of confidence of paternity. The more a species' behavior or ecology makes it possible for a male to be sure a female's offspring are his, the more likely is he to help raise them. From the standpoint of fitness, this is quite sensible, since raising offspring not your own would injure your own fitness and increase that of someone else. Daly and Wilson present data showing that abuse and neglect are more common between step-parents and children than in intact families, and is more likely perpetrated by men than women. Other factors that vary with child abuse and neglect also are compatible with sociobiological reasoning: Neglect and abuse are more likely when resources are scarce or when the child is abnormal, cases in which a parent may estimate that the reproductive capacity of the child as an adult will be low, making awaiting new times or a new child a reproductively more attractive option. Finally, factors that disrupt mother-child bonding—the proximate cause of maternal love—are likely to lead to later neglect or abuse. Such factors include prematurity or congenital disease, indicators of poor reproductive potential.

Observe that in each case, parents' behavior is adaptive or at least not maladaptive for them. The father who suspects a child is not his own is likely to abandon it and its mother for reproductive success elsewhere. A child whose life is at risk due to malnutrition, disease, prematurity, or defect is a poor reproductive investment. Morally, child abuse and neglect are abhorrent, and we all must strive to eliminate these ills. But to do so, we should first understand them, see that there are explicable causes to bring about abuse and neglect, in order to act effectively. Shrinking back in horror and condemnation is unlikely to lead to effective action. For example, an important proximate cause of mother-infant bonding appears to be very early contact—in the first hours after birth—between mother and child. Hospitals should encourage such contact, especially in the case of children born prematurely, who are often kept for days away from mother in an incubator. Similarly, presence at birth of the father may stimulate father-child bonding. We may think such measures trivially obvious—such conclusions are just "natural." The perspective of evolutionary biology lets us see why they *are* natural.

---

mans as to other species. But human intelligence increases the sophistication of the conflict. For example, conflict should arise between parents and children over altruism between siblings. A pair of siblings share 50 percent of their genes, which motivates kin-selected altruism between them. But a given child has a 100 percent genetic investment in one's self and will be altruistic only when the benefit to one's brother or sister is at least twice the cost to one's self. But parents are equally (50 percent investment) interested in all their children and will encourage sibling altruism whenever costs and benefits between them are equal. Conflict is inevitable: Parents will emphasize precise sharing and "fairness," treating each sibing equally, while each individual child will want something more than his or her exact fair share (Trivers, 1974/1980). Socialization plays an important proximate role for the parent. Parents and cultures value honesty, fairness, openness, generosity, self-denial, and sharing, and when parents teach these values they are passing their culture on to their children and their children are becoming members of the culture. At the same time, however, the parents are furthering their genetic investment in all their children, because mutual aid and support ensure that all the children will be able to reproduce.

CONCLUSION

Genetics or Learning?

It is on the issue of genetic determinism that sociobiology conflicts with the psychology of learning. Psychologists assumed for many years that animals, including people, are behaviorally a sort of putty to be shaped—Skinner's term—by the environment acting through reinforcement and punishment. However, sociobiology seems to suggest—especially if we read genetic determinism into it—that learning does not accomplish very much, that males grow into men and females into women. We do not just learn these things from the culture that labels us and shapes us because of our socially irrelevant genitalia, as most psychologists believe (see Bem, 1981).

But no sociobiologist, even Dawkins, denies the role of the environment, culture, and learning in determining human behavior. They insist, as all modern geneticists do, that development is not an either-learning-or-genes proposition, but is instead a complex interaction between genetic givens and cultural shaping.

For example, Alexander (1979a) maintains that social learning is a proximate mechanism serving adaptive ends. We may illustrate this with the incest taboo. In both animals and humans, close inbreeding is genetically dangerous, and that therefore we ought to have evolved to innately avoid sex and marriage with close relatives. In human beings, social learning may be the proximate mechanism that prevents brother-sister incest.

In traditional Israeli kibbutzes, groups of similar-aged but unrelated children are reared together collectively. Now although it is certainly in the interest of the kibbutz to get these children to marry one another as adults, and there is pressure for them to do so, marriages between such children simply *do not occur*, nor does sex between adolescent age-mates seem to occur. Similarly, in some areas of old China (and sometimes in Taiwan today) there was a practice of contracting marriage between an infant boy and girl, and bringing the girl to grow up with the boy's family. But when the children reached marriage age they usually resisted carrying out the marriage contract.

Clearly this is a form of learning. It appears that boys and girls who grow up together on an intimate, everyday, familial basis *learn* to not feel sexual desire for each other later on. Such learning under normal family circumstances would keep brother-sister incest from happening, and so it is a useful proximate mechanism serving the ultimate end of outbreeding. In both the kibbutz and the Chinese family, the learning misfires, but in so doing reveals itself to us.

So incest avoidance is both genetic *and* learned. Our species is so constructed by evolution to avoid close inbreeding (ultimate cause) by having its members learn (proximate cause) to inhibit sexual desire toward intimate age-mates (van den Berghe, 1983). The species was shaped by evolution, but the particular individual learns to avoid sex with certain other particular individuals. This situation reminds us of the constraints on animal learning recently discovered by psychologists, discussed in Chapter 4. Biology makes certain kinds of learning easier than others, and now we see evidence of the same thing in people. The "whisperings within" may constrain learning, but they do not substitute robotic preprogramming for the flexible and adaptive patterns of learning.

In people, of course, flexibility and learning are most highly developed, as all sociobiologists recognize. The vast majority of human adaptation is cultural; there are no genes for building airplanes, telephones, or computers, or for writing books and attending classes. What we have evolved is an enormous capacity to be flexibly clever. We adapt by what we make, rather than by changing our bodies, and by turning our cleverness on the world itself, making it serve our ends rather than we serve its ends.

Uniquely Human: Co-evolution

Sociobiologists and sympathetic social scientists are coming to recognize that understanding human beings requires attention both to cultural factors (which classic animal-based sociobiology naturally overlooked) and biological factors (which traditional psychology overlooked) if it is to be at all adequate. Recently, the notion of cultural-biological co-evolution has been proposed by various authors (Axelrod, 1987; Ball, 1984; Cavalli-Sforza; Feldman, Chen, & Dornbusch, 1982; Durham, 1978, 1982; Flinn & Alexander, 1982; Lumsden & Wilson, 1981, Rindos, 1985, 1986a, b; Ruse, 1979; for criticism of the approach, see Hallpike, 1985, and Kitcher, 1985).

Co-evolutionary theory recognizes that natural selection has produced in human beings a creature whose nature is much less constrained by the genes than is that of other animals. Human beings' abilities to learn, to speak, and to build culture have evolved because they have worked in the struggle for existence. Therefore, while *natural* selection has evolved an open and flexible human nature (within broad limits), it has thereby created a new selection pressure, *cultural selection*, which acts on cultural

---

BOX 11–4   Results of the Field Study

Perhaps the most important emotional attachment in life is between mother and infant. One component of this emotional bond seems to be based on the mother's heartbeat, since infants can be soothed by recording of the human heart beating at a normal rate, but are disturbed by recordings of a faster heartbeat.

As discussed by Lumsden and Wilson (1981) women unconsciously enhance this effect by holding infants to the left side, near the heart. Studies of mothers carrying infants found that 78 percent of left-handed mothers, and 83 percent of right-handed mothers carried their babies on the left near the heart. These findings have been replicated in non-Western cultures. Men, on the other hand, carry their infants equally on the right and the left. Interesting confirmation of these biases come from Western (Grüsser, 1983) and non-Western art, in which women are shown holding babies on the left while men hold them to either side.

Book-carrying is a possible analogue to baby-carrying, and a study found that 82 percent of male students carried their books held straight along the right side, while 79 percent of female students carried them pressed to the left side by the forearm or clasped to their chest. We hope you got similar results in your study.

A strong mother-infant bond is assuredly adaptive to the genes of both mother and child. For her genes to thrive, the mother (as the primary caretaker) must be emotionally moved to care for a helpless infant who is often troublesome and at times hard even to like. The infant, too, must learn to love its mother, to seek her care and protection if it is to survive.

How the infant is held appears to be one of the many proximate mechanisms that enhance the mutual love of mother and infant child, love which is itself a proximate mechanism ensuring survival of the genes in the next generation. In its turn, the genes have created a bias in women to hold their infants in the optimal way, and the circuit of ultimate and proximate causation is closed.

---

practices, ideas, and institutions. Any given human trait is the joint product of natural selection, which gives us our genetic dispositions, and cultural selection, which gives us our individual ideas and dispositions (Boyd & Richerson, 1985).

Ruse (1979) offers an informative example of this in the case of sexuality. The fact that a male is sexually aroused by the female form is an obvious (and obviously adaptive) biological disposition. Yet a contemporary Western male will be (if he is typical) especially aroused by large breasts (which may be habitually uncovered in another culture) but unmoved by the bare female ankle (which may have driven his Victorian great-grandfather to feverish lust). Biology and culture meet to determine the concrete mind of the individual in society.

Co-evolution, however, is more than a simple juxtaposing of biological and social sciences, for it emphasizes the pervasiveness of selection. Natural selection favors genes that promote survival; cultural selection favors ideas, practices, and institutions that promote survival. In either case, the scientist must ask questions new to the social sciences: Whom does culture benefit and how? Cultures that violate selection too wantonly cannot survive. The Shakers refused, on moral grounds, to reproduce, so their moral ideas went extinct. In both the biological and cultural realms, co-evolutionary theory focuses our attention on selection, on how human traits, whatever their source, help or hinder our ability to survive and grow.

Finally, co-evolutionary theory points out that cultural and natural evolution must interact in important ways so that we can never again consider each in isolation. Cultural evolution must ultimately serve reproduction and survival, or the culture will become extinct. Cultural change cannot wander too far from the underlying biological imperatives of human nature. At the same time, once culture is created it imposes new selection pressures on biological evolution. Culture is the most important part of the environment in which humans develop, mate, and raise children. Therefore, cultural pressures for or against aggression, for or against altruism, for or against traditional sex roles, will act on the underlying genotypes and change their relative frequencies. So not only can *Homo sapiens* construct their own social nature, but their own nature as an animal.

Sociobiology as Science and as Interpretation

Two important points about the scientific power of sociobiology should be recalled. First, despite the fact that it is quite sensitive to species differences in behavior, the hard-core principles of sociobiology are held to be universal. For example, Triver's theory of parental investment is asserted as applying to all sexually reproducing species, and his hard-core theory leads to specific hypotheses that modify the basic principles of parental investment according to the ecology of each species. Hence, all the diverse mating patterns observed in the wild are explained by combining the concept of parental investment with the ecological circumstances in which animals find themselves. Right or wrong, this theory is an outstanding example of scientific thinking, the precise application of a few general principles to an initially bewildering array of observations.

The other important point to bear in mind is that sociobiology is, at least potentially, not only a theory about behavior. For sociobiology may be able to explain the ultimate causes of a species' *mentality*. This is not readily apparent in talking about animals to whom we ordinarily feel uncomfortable attributing mental states such as wants and desires. However, when we talk about human beings in sociobiological terms, our discussion soon embraces mental life. The Coolidge Effect only leads us to attribute a *disposition* to enjoy female variety to male animals, but when we turn to male humans we may want to say men *desire* female variety. Such attributions of mentality strike us as uncomfortably presumptuous. We do not like to be told that our most intimate likes and dislikes, desires and schemes, have a merely genetic ultimate causation. Controversy boils to white heat when sociobiologists' claims of what constitutes "natural" mentality run counter to cultural orthodoxies. You should remember, however—and bear it in mind during any discussion about the biological basis of behavior—not to confuse the natural with the good. Polio is natural; vaccination is unnatural.

Finally, at its present stage of development, *human* sociobiology should not be regarded as science, but as interpretation. As with the experimental analysis of behavior, the scientific status of sociobiology's animal studies is secure, as even sociobiology critic Philip Kitcher (1985, 1987) concedes, but its application to human behavior remains mostly a matter of plausible interpretation. Applied to human affairs, sociobiology offers new and revealing perspectives, even when its specific hypotheses prove incorrect. Moreover, as with much of psychology, limitations on method may prevent human sociobiology from ever achieving the precision of its animal counterpart. Sociobiology should be valued for its novel insights, and these should not be discarded because of a fetish for methodological purity.

SUGGESTED READINGS

The ambitious reader may want to tackle E. O. Wilson's original *Sociobiology* (Harvard University Press, 1975), which is surprisingly readable, especially in its abridged paperback edition, from which the more fearsome mathematics was pruned. Two other lively secondary primers are available—Richard Dawkins' *The Selfish Gene* (Oxford University Press, 1976), which is the most aggressive sociobiology work, and David Barash's *Sociobiology and Behavior* (Elesevier, 1977, 2nd ed., 1982), which is written with clarity and grace. Finally, students of animal behavior should read John Alcock's *Animal Behavior: An Evolutionary Approach* (Sinauer Associates, 1979), a truly excellent book on which this chapter relied for much of the data on animal behavior. Alcock does a superb job summarizing data and theory for all areas of animal behavior, not just sociobiology. An excellent introduction to human sociobiology is Barash's *The Whisperings Within* (Penguin, 1979). The most thorough presentation of co-evolution—they call it "dual inheritance"—is Boyd and Richerson, 1985.

12

THE ORIGIN AND DEVELOPMENT OF LANGUAGE

INTRODUCTION

Whatever else may be unique about the human species, there is no doubt that our most important single possession is language. Language makes human culture possible, creating the co-evolution of biology and society that is uniquely human. We can express and explore ideas and feelings in ways unknown to the animal world. With language we can communicate, entertain, and rhapsodize. Without language we would surely not be human.

But important as language is, is it *special*? Is human language a particular and unique species-specific human trait—as is the opposable thumb—or is language a consequence of other, more general learning and cognitive abilities, and therefore unique to humans (if it is unique) only because our conceptual powers are so highly developed? This question, which is very old but still controversial, will occupy us in this chapter.

Behaviorism and Language

The shared attitude of the behaviorists (see Mowrer, 1954; Skinner, 1957; Osgood, 1963/1967) was that "we neither wish nor require any special theory for language" (Osgood, 1963/1967, p. 110). Language was viewed as just another (albeit complex) behavior to be explained by behavior theoretic principles, and its acquisition was explained as processes of classical and/or operant conditioning. For example, Mowrer (1954) described semantics in terms of classical conditioning. Word meanings are acquired as CS's paired with the objects or actions they designate (US's) with the result that some component of one's reactions to objects and actions come to be elicited by words; this component is the word's "meaning." B. F. Skinner, on the other hand, described language learning as a process of operant conditioning, as we saw in Chapter 4. According to him, concepts are operant response classes learned under stimulus control through differential reinforcement by the language community.

What we have already learned about language in earlier chapters suggests that behaviorist accounts of language are implausible at best (Chomsky, 1959). Interestingly, though, whatever their other differences with behaviorists, cognitive psychologists by and large agree that language is not special, but is just an expression of complex information-processing abilities. In this they differ from the followers of Noam Chomsky, the major modern proponent of the idea that language is a unique, species-specific human adaptive organ.

Could Language Be Innate?

Chomsky's thesis. Noam Chomsky calls himself a Cartesian linguist (Chomsky, 1965b) for believing in language's uniqueness to human beings and its creative power. René Descartes (1596–1650) followed the older rationalist philosophical tradition of Plato in maintaining that some of our ideas are **innate.** For example, Descartes held that one's idea of God is innate for we know about God without ever having met God. Similarly, many mathematical truths are known without being based on experience. If $A = B$ and $B = C$, we know immediately that $A = C$, and this is an abstract truth not derived from experience. It is an unlearned, *innate* truth. Of course Descartes, like Plato before him, did not think that little babies can do math. Rationalists allow a role for experience as an activator of innate ideas, a concept quite in keeping with modern genetic thinking.

Unlike Plato, Descartes—and Chomsky—assigned a special role to language. Descartes argued that only human beings think, have ideas to express, and so only human beings have language, which is the expression of thought. Language is therefore specific to the human species, because animals do not think. A later Cartesian, Julien Offroy de la Mettrie (1709–1751), however, proposed that at least some animals could think and therefore could learn language. Specifically, he suggested teaching language to an ape, making him a "perfect little gentleman." La Mettrie's research proposal was finally carried out some two centuries later, as we shall see.

While Chomsky's proposal that language is innate is in the Cartesian tradition (but see Aarslef, 1982), he views language as even more special than Descartes did. Descartes viewed language as the expression of cognitive processes unique to humans, thereby making language unique to humans. But as la Mettrie's argument shows, if animals can think, however simply, they can possess language, however simple. Chomsky goes further, proposing that language has the general properties of an organ of the body

(Chomsky, 1976, in following discussion). For Chomsky, then, language is something very special indeed—the function of an innate language faculty—and not the result of anything else, of learning or cognition, or thinking. For Chomsky, language is an evolved species-specific organ. What argument and evidence does Chomsky offer to support his extreme view?

Chomsky's major contribution to linguistics is his powerful analysis of syntax, transformational grammar. There are several insights from the study of syntax that he brings to bear on formulating the problem of language acquisition.

To begin with, as we learned in Chapter 7, language possesses an invisible structure—**syntax**—that is not given by spoken words themselves, but must be applied by the listener. The hidden syntactic structure of language is important to defining the language acquisition problem in two ways. First, since as adults we use syntax to understand sentences, we must have acquired these rules somehow as children. In our society we tend to think we were taught them directly; we all remember grammar drills at school and being corrected for certain grammatical errors ("Me and Jimmy went . . ."). However, in preliterate cultures, grammar is not taught. Natives do not know the rules of their own language; it takes an anthropologist months or years to work out the rules. Moreover, even in our own culture children begin to speak in sentences before they go to school and before anyone fusses over their grammar.

The second way that syntax defines the language acquisition problem is more important for Chomsky's thesis. It is the fact that the syntactic structure of the sentences a child hears is not *in the words themselves*. Grammar is an invisible organizer of words into sentences, and somehow children must figure out their language's syntax without direct exposure to it. This suggests that chldren already know something about grammar, furnishing a basis for constructing the rules of their individual grammar.

So far, we have only discussed the surface structure of sentences. But underneath the surface structure of each sentence lies its more remote deep structure, and these deep-structure rules must also be learned. Since deep-structure rules are far removed from the words of sentences, learning them is an especially difficult task, thus reinforcing the notion that the child brings to the task of language acquisition more than just an ability to make associations, possessing some innate faculty for constructing linguistic rules.

In tackling this formidable task, the child faces two additional problems also faced by an anthropologist trying to unravel a novel language. First, it is generally the case that given any finite set of sentences that a child has heard—or an anthropologist has recorded—up to a given moment, more than one grammar can be written to describe their structures. The anthropologist's problem (and the child's) is to decide which grammar is correct. It would help if certain universal features of all human languages existed to help rule out certain grammars as simply impossible. Such universals do, in fact exist—the agent/object distinction, for example—and Chomsky argues that they reflect innately invariant properties of the language faculty, and place constraints on the kinds of grammars the child will construct. Since all speakers of a given language appear to have learned the same rules, even though many rules may be consistent with the data, Chomsky believes that a universal language faculty is at work. At this juncture it should be pointed out that Chomsky does not think that the Chinese child comes prepared to learn Chinese, the French child to learn French, and so on; obviously, this is false. Rather, Chomsky claims that human children come prepared to learn a human language, and the language faculty already knows, in a sense, what human languages are like, setting out of bounds other plausible, but nonhuman syntactic systems.

The second problem shared by both anthropologist and child is that actual speech, what one can listen to and record, is influenced by factors irrelevant to the grammar of the language. An analogy may be made to hearing a symphony. If a musician records each note as it is played in performance (and does not have the score) what he or she writes down will not be the symphony itself. The performers may be tired, may be unfamiliar with the conductor, may be playing from memory, or may have varying degrees of talent. All these factors, which are irrelevant to the symphony, will lead to mistakes, so that the performance is not a true representation of the symphony, but a distortion of it. And mistakes are inevitable.

In language the situation is similar. Anyone who has read unedited speech, or listened carefully to it, knows that speech is influenced by many extra linguistic factors: memory, change in the point one wanted to make, false starts, hesitations, and so on. Although speakers know the rules of their language, their actual performance—like musicians—is a distorted embodiment of them. So the anthropologist and child must somehow ignore or correct the errors. Indeed, they must first figure out what is error and what is correct syntax before they can uncover both the surface and deep structures of the language they are confronting. Again, this learning would be greatly facilitated by some preexisting knowledge of human language to be applied to one's specific situation. And the child—who learns most of his or her syntax between ages two and five—does not have the anthropologist's professional training, so that the child's preexisting knowledge must be innate.

Chomsky calls the difference between people's knowledge of their grammar and their actual use of it the **competence/performance distinction,** and we may now formulate the problem of language acquisition as Chomsky sees it.

The problem is to account for the acquisition by a child of linguistic competence in his or her native tongue. Acquisition of language is based on limited exposure to primary linguistic input flawed by deficiencies in adult performance, from which a child between the ages of two and five must nevertheless correctly abstract surface and deep-structure rules without direct teaching. The magnitude of the problem suggests that children are born with a language faculty, or, in more modern terms, *a language acquisition device* (LAD), richly furnished with knowledge of human language in general. This LAD constrains and makes manageable the child's task. Children do not begin to acquire language before 15 months of age or so, and acquisition of a second language in adolescence or adulthood is a markedly different and more difficult process. These facts indicate that there is a critical period in which the LAD is active and during which language acquisition must take place. All of this adds up to the proposal that language is a species-specific human faculty rooted in our biological ancestry.

Criticisms of Chomsky's thesis. Complaints and criticisms concerning Chomsky's proposal have been numerous and varied, ranging from philosophers who find it unintelligible to psychologists who find it intelligible and interesting, but who cannot reconcile it with the data. The usual alternative offered to Chomsky's rationalism is an empiricist cognitive hypothesis (see Bever, 1970; Eliot, 1981). Behaviorism finds few defenders, but empiricism is common to it and the cognitive approach. What these scientists offer is the view (specifics, of course, vary) that a child possesses certain general cognitive abilities related to perception, learning, reasoning, and so on, that the child can *also* apply to learning language. What is learned on this account is thus neither competence (linguistic grammar) nor even mental grammar, but rather the application of information-processing abilities to the domain of language. Psychologically speaking, then, there is no such thing as grammar at all, only the processing of linguistic information.

One proposal for testing these hypotheses has special relevance to the nativist approach to language acquisition: teaching language to apes. Following la Mettrie's research proposal of 1748, the idea is that apes have cognitive abilities and even some form of self-awareness (see Chapter 11), but do not naturally have language. Therefore, if apes could be taught language it would show that general information-processing skills can underlie language acquisition even in humans.

Before examining the fascinating but problematical results of these studies, we should put the entire issue in a biological context by examining the possible evolution of language and communication.

ANIMAL COMMUNICATION

One important question that Chomsky tends to ignore in his rationalist emphasis on human uniqueness is what continuities, if any, exist between human language and animal communication systems. This question is nevertheless important for a biological approach to human language.

Patterns of Animal Communication

Defining communication. Defining communication is surprisingly difficult. Clearly, as I write this I am communicating—I hope!—with the reader. What if I sneeze? Someone who hears me may find out that I have a cold. But have I *communicated* with that person? Or suppose I sneeze deliberately in my wife's presence to let her know I have a cold and so elicit her sympathy; this would seem to be communication, for it is intentional, even if I have not used language. Finally, however, a psychoanalyst might claim an "accidental" sneeze near my wife is really an unconscious but real communication, a reaching out for sympathy that my conscious mind, not wanting to feel dependent, rejects. Much of our nonverbal communication is just like this: unconscious and often beyond our willful control—except, of course, for the actor or poker player.

We should recognize a continuum of communication from verbal language used purposefully to unconscious, nonverbal communication. In the case of animals, defining communication is especially problematic because we can assess intention only with difficulty, and are reluctant to attribute intentions to lightning bugs, for example, who not only communicate, but even lie (see Box 12–1).

Green and Marler (1979) have proposed a useful definition of animal communication. To count as communication, a signal or set of signals must meet three criteria. First, the signals must be *nonconstant*, that is, emitted only on some occasions. This rules out signals such as coloration or shape, which convey information such as species identity, but are not communication in any useful sense. Second, the signals must be *specialized* to serve a communicative function. Third, there must be *internal processing*, the encoding and decoding of signals. Green's and Marler's criteria seem to formalize our intuitive notion of communication while allowing room for doubtful cases such as the unconscious sneeze.

Functions of communication. However we define it, communication serves many important functions in animal life, for species ranging from the slime mold—who reproduce in hard times by emitting a pheromone that gathers a crowd of fellows who temporarily form themselves into a large fruiting body (Gould, 1982)—to human beings. Table 12–1 lists the functions of communication adduced by Wilson (1980) with some examples. One can see that communication is involved in every aspect of animals' lives from birth to death, serving many functions essential to survival. Animal communication must, therefore, have a strong innate component.

Evolution of communication Because communication is so important to individual and group survival, signaling and receiving systems and behaviors are under strong selective pressure (Green & Marler, 1979). On the sending side, an individual must be able to send appropriate and perceivable messages so that natural selection acts on the morphology, behavior, and even cognitive abilities of organisms. For example, signals designed to attract a mate must be locatable, so that the prospective mate can find the signaller. On the other hand, an alarm call should be hard to locate so as not to attract a predator's attention. Thus, selection tends to develop the ability to produce distinctive kinds of calls, and the ability to use each appropriately.

On the receiving side, selection favors sensory abilities and acuities involved in communication. Thus, any animal's most acute range of sensory discrimination generally coincides with the range of signals. In both cases

BOX 12–1   Do Animals Lie?

One thing we learn from sociobiology is to analyze the costs and benefits of different classes of behavior. And nothing costs less than sending a message: Talk is cheap. Since there are obvious benefits to be gained from lying, we might expect to find many cases of deceitful communication in nature, and our expectations are amply confirmed (Barash, 1982). For example, monarch butterflies feed on milkweed plants, which contain a toxin not digested but stored within the butterfly. Birds who eat monarchs get violently ill and, in an example of conditioned food aversion (Chapter 4), avoid eating monarchs thereafter. The distinctive coloring of the monarch signals danger, an honest communication adaptive to both predator and butterfly. But then there is the viceroy butterfly that does not eat milkweed and contains no toxin, but has evolved to look like the monarch. It sends a false message of danger, and since this message is heeded by wary predators, natural selection has favored the viceroy's deceitful coloration. Such mimicry is fairly common among insects, and it was partly his consideration of mimicry in Amazonian insects that put A. R. Wallace onto the theory of evolution.

A particularly interesting form of deceit occurs among fireflies (Gould, 1982). Fireflies' flashing lights serve two adaptive functions. Like monarch butterflies, fireflies contain toxic cardiac glycerides (although they make their own) and the flashing warns predators that they are poisonous. More importantly, firefly males and females locate each other for mating by exchanging coded signals, and each of the many firefly species has its own characteristic code. Females remain stationary as the males fly around flashing. Females—sensing a species' correct flashing pattern in the air—return the males' signals, and the distinctive timing of the return flash lets the male know of an appropriate conspecific female. He lands near her, and perhaps using smell and shape as a final test that she is the correct species, copulates with her.

Females of the species *photuris versicolor* have learned to lie to their own benefit. After mating with a conspecific male, preparing to bear and hatch offspring, the *photuris* female begins to attract males of other species by mimicing the code of their females. The unwitting male firefly is lured to *photuris* by her deceptive signal and approaches, learning too late that he is going to be a meal, not a mate. *Photuris* females in this way gain an excellent source of protein for very little work: Talk is cheap.

By the way, you can perform the same trick yourself with a penlight (Gould, 1982). Try various delay times between the offset of a flying (and therefore male) firefly and when you turn on your penlight in return. Some trial and error will give you the right latency, and then you can lure in the male. Of course, you won't smell right and so he won't try to mate with you, or the flashlight.

Fortunately, deceit is not rampant in nature because false signals often exact costs—the liar is found out and his or her fitness reduced. Moreover, natural selection has evolved various reliability signs into many messages (Barash, 1982). For example, the loudness and the low pitch of aggressive roaring among many males—including species as different as Fowler's toad and red deer—correlate well with fighting ability, since a strong male is large and well-muscled. Such correlations help establish truth-in-advertising in the wild kingdom.

the physical environment—and changes in environment produce evolution—is important, for signals must survive and be received despite noise, obstacles, aquatic thermoclines, and other hazards. So each species' characteristic mode and manner of signalling—chemical, visual, auditory, tactile, or electric—will evolve in accordance with its environment and way of life (Wilson, 1980).

The most important process involved in the evolution of communica-

TABLE 12-1 Functions of Communication

Function	Description and Examples
FACILITATION AND IMITATION	Behaviors that facilitate group living and cooperation. *Example*: *Kinopsis* in large-eyed ants, wherein an ant in rapid motion, probably toward prey, attracts other ants.
CONTACT	Signals that maintain contact between members of a group. *Example*: Under condition of poor visibility (e.g., dense vegetation) South American tapirs emit a short squeal to stay in touch with their herd.
INDIVIDUAL AND CLASS RECOGNITION	Signals that identify a particular individual and/or his or her (or its) class. *Example*: Pheremones emitted by queens in ant, termite, and bee nests cause workers to act in special ways toward her.
STATUS SIGNALING	Signals that communicate the rank of an individual in a status hierarchy. *Example*: Dominant rhesus monkeys walk with head and tail erect, low-ranking males with tail and head drooping.
BEGGING AND OFFERING OF FOOD	Signals that indicate readiness to share food or that elicit sharing. *Example*: Open mouth gape of baby bird in nest triggers parent placing food in mouth.
GROOMING	While it may also serve hygienic functions, *allogrooming*—the grooming of others—can be a social signal. *Example*: Grooming among primates forestalls aggression and reinforces status hierarchies.
ALARM	Signals indicating danger and mobilizing some response *Example*: Alarm calls in birds and ground squirrels.
DISTRESS	Signals indicating that the sender is in trouble. *Example*: Leaf-cutting ants summon help when caught in a cave-in by *stridulating*, emitting a squeak by scraping carapace segments together. And, of course, babies cry.
ASSEMBLY AND RECRUITMENT	Signals drawing conspecifics closer together and/or recruiting them for a purpose. *Example*: Wolves howl to gather a pack scattered over a patrolled territory.

TABLE 12–1   *(Continued)*

Function	*Description and Examples*
LEADERSHIP	Signals that organize a group behind a leader. *Example*: the "swing step" of a dominant male hamadryas baboon, which induces troop to fall in behind him.
SYNCHRONIZATION OF HATCHING	Signals inducing a clutch of precocial birds to hatch together. *Example*: click vocalization by chicks in the egg that are most persistent nearest to hatching.
PLAY INVITATION	Signals initiating play. *Example*: the relaxed open-mouth display of the crab-eating monkey.
THREAT, SUBMISSION AND APPEASEMENT	Signals occurring in connection with aggression. *Example*: the fluffing-up of a cat's fur in the presence of an enemy.
NEST RELIEF CEREMONY	A ceremony occurring between parent birds as they take turns foraging and guarding. *Example*: The male nightjar approaches the nest with a distinctive call returned by the female.
SEXUAL BEHAVIOR	Signals associated with sexual activity, such as courtship rituals. *Example*: See Chapter 11.
CASTE INHIBITION	*Example*: Queens of advanced social insects emit pheromones inhibiting the development of immature stages into new queens.

tion is what ethologists call **ritualization** (Wilson, 1980; Hinde, 1974). Ritualization transforms preexisting behaviors unrelated to communication into stereotyped, patterned behaviors that can serve as distinct signals. The process is also called **semanticization** (Wilson, 1980) because the essential change taking place during ritualization is that the behavior acquires *meaning*, and is no longer just a behavior occurring because of some external or internal cause. A ritualized behavior becomes a signal that affects another's behavior rather than one's own.

Two Examples: Honeybees and Birds

Nature offers two highly developed forms of communication that approach human language in many respects. One is the **language of the honeybees,** one of the most famous discoveries of ethology, and the other is **birdsong,** long beloved but only recently the object of scientific scrutiny.

The language of the honeybees. That bees can communicate to each other the location of pollen had long been suspected. Aristotle thought that a bee who finds a trove of pollen returns to the hive and recruits her fellows into following her to the pollen site. Early comparative psychology quickly disproved Aristotle's theory. Discoverer bees were marked when they discovered pollen, allowed to return to the hive but captured upon reemergence. Nevertheless, the other workers made straight for the newly found pollen (Gould, 1982). It remained for German ethologist Karl von Frisch to unravel the mystery, showing that bees communicate the location of pollen through a language of dance.

When the bee returns to the hive, she announces her find by dancing in a figure-eight pattern with a waggle in the middle during which the bee shakes rapidly back and forth and gives off a buzzing sound by vibrating her wings (Fig. 12–1). Other workers gather around her, touching her,

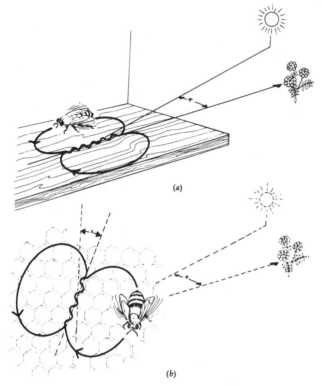

(a)

(b)

FIGURE 12-1   The waggle dance of the honeybee. As the bee passes through the straight run she vibrates ("waggles") her body laterally, with the greatest movement occurring in the tip of the abdomen and the least in the head. At the conclusion of the straight run, she circles back to about the starting position, as a rule alternately to the left and right. The follower bees acquire the information about the food find during the straight run. In the examples shown here the run indicates a food find 20% to the right of the sun as the bee leaves the nest. If the bee performs the dance outside the hive (a), the straight run of the dance points directly toward the food source. If she performs a dance inside the hive (b), she orients herself by gravity, and the point directly overhead takes the place of the sun. The angle x (=20%) is the same for both dances. (From Curtis, 1968)

and soon begin to take off for the new food source, locating it with remarkable accuracy. It is the waggle part of the dance that communicates the location of food. The length of the waggle portion and the rapidity of waggling are graded signals indicating distance to the food site, while the angle of the dance with respect to the sun (if outside) or the gravitational vertical (if within the hive) indicates the direction with respect to the sun along which the food will be found. There are different dialects of honeybee language, so that different species code distance differently into their waggling (Gould, 1982).

Considering the simplicity of the bee's nervous system, all of this is a remarkable—and clearly quite adaptive—achievement. How much it resembles human language is open to debate, however. There is symbolism in that the waggling run represents time (specifically, the effort needed to make the flight; Gould, 1982) and direction to the food, while the quality and the quantity of food are indicated by whether or not dancing occurs at all. The symbolism is abstract in that the object "talked about" is not present, and partly, arbitrary (like human words) in that distance is marked by dialect-specific waggle-lengths and speeds. Finally, there is some creativity in that a dancer can "say" new things, reporting unique locations.

On the other hand, honeybee language is quite restricted compared to human language (Wilson, 1980). Most importantly, bees can only communicate about one thing: food location. Bees cannot break out of this rigid context and use language in a truly creative way. Their language is *too* preprogrammed and innate to admit any flexibility and creativity. Nonetheless, we should respect the language of the bees as a wonderful example of the subtleties of natural selection.

Birdsong learning.   Another remarkable achievement of evolution is *birdsong*, which serves many functions in most bird species: courtship, mate location, establishment of territory, alarms. While lovers of nature and bird enthusiasts have long appreciated birdsong as an art, it is only since World War II that birdsong has been studied scientifically. Research on how birds learn to sing may provide a model for discussing human language acquisition, for we may do experiments on birds that we may not morally perform on children. W. H. Thorpe and then Peter Marler (see, Marler, 1970; Marler & Peters, 1981) conducted brilliant sets of research showing that birdsong (at least in the species studied by them) is both innate *and* learned.

Many experiments have been performed by Thorpe, Marler, and others, but the basic results are summarized in Figure 12–2, from Gould (1982). After hatching, baby birds are reared in isolation, and during the critical period for song-learning, the youngsters are either played tapes of birdsong, or hear nothing. In Case A, the babies heard both their own species' (the white-crowned sparrow) song and that of a related species, the song-sparrow, whose songs are within their vocal capabilities. Then, for many weeks the birds heard nothing (research has shown that exposure after 50 days or so has no effect) and were silent. Then, after 100 days,

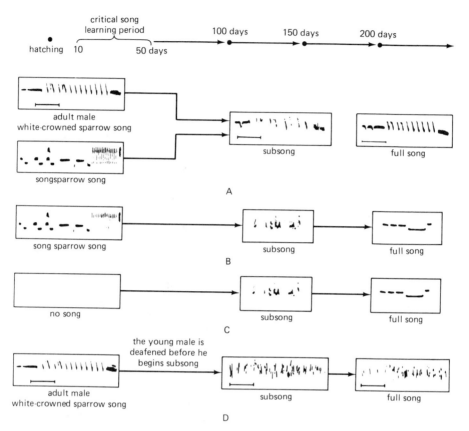

FIGURE 12-2 White-crowned sparrows learn their species' song during a critical period from 10 to 50 days of age. At about 150 days they begin to vocalize and practice making syllable sounds. By 200 days they have developed a stable song which closely matches the song heard during the critical period. The song learning is selective, so that if offered a choice, birds will learn only their own species' song (A); and if offered the wrong song (B) or no song at all (C), the bird will learn nothing and sing only a simple tune. If deafened before he begins to practice (D) the bird will never sing anything melodic while if deafened after the song "crystallizes," subsequent singing is perfect. These visual displays of the songs were made with a sound spectograph, a device which represents frequency on the vertical axis, time on the horizontal axis, and indicates intensity by the darkness of the trace. (Reproduced from *Ethology*, The Mechanisms and Evolution of Behavior, by James L. Gould, by permission of W. W. Norton & Co. Copyright © 1982 by James L. Gould)

the birds break out into their subsong, a sort of practice period preceding appearance of the full song. Case A is analogous to the situation in the wild in that more than one sound is heard, and development is normal.

In Case B only the song-sparrow song is played during the critical period, and we see that the subsong is abnormal, and the full song, while structured, does not resemble the normal song. This case rules out simple imitation as the basis of song-learning, since the white-crowned sparrows do not learn the song-sparrow song.

Case C represents total acoustic isolation, the results of which are identical with hearing the wrong song. Therefore, song-singing is not the result of simple maturation, in which an innate program simply expresses itself at maturity, as in bees.

Finally, Case D reveals the importance of practice and feedback during the subsong phase. Here, the young bird is exposed to the correct song, but is deafened prior to beginning subsong. In this case both subsong and full song are disorganized peeps.

These findings beautifully illustrate the complex and subtle interplay between the innate and the experienced at the base of all learning. Any simply maturational model of birdsong development is untenable. Equally untenable is any behaviorist reinforcement theory, since there is no reinforcement during initial exposure or subsong phases. Nor are the constraints on song learning merely peripheral, being set only by what the bird can hear or the notes it can utter, since songs of physically similar birds of different species are unlearnable.

There must be in species such as the sparrow central constraints on learning. As in humans, bird language is a specialized function of the left hemisphere of the brain, and it is there that natural selection has acted to constrain birdsong learning. It appears that the songbird is born with a template active only during a critical period early in the baby bird's life (Marler, 1970). The template contains a sort of model of the appropriate song of the species. The model is not specified in precise detail, because songbirds develop dialects peculiar to different geographic regions, and young birds can learn any dialect of their song. The template acts as a filter, directing the brain's attention to the biologically important sounds in the helpless infant's environment: its species' song. Sounds of passing 747's, of owls, robins, and other kinds of sparrows are models which, if followed, would lead to an adult male unable to attract a mate. (Females do not sing unless injected with testosterone; their knowledge of the song is adaptive in causing recognition of a true conspecific.) The template thus becomes a model of the correct song against which the adolescent bird can later check his vocalizing during the subsong phase. Feedback checked against the model leads to adjustments and the emergence of full song.

Marler has proposed that birdsong learning is a model for human language acquisition. In a later section we will review evidence bearing on his hypothesis.

CAN CHIMPS READ?

To propose an analogy between songbirds and humans is to do one form of human sociobiology, in approaching humans via a perhaps distant species that, nevertheless, is similar ecologically and functionally. Like human babies, altricial (helpless at birth) bird nestlings are helpless but must anyway learn a sophisticated signalling system essential to later reproductive success. The other kind of analogy one can draw is between humans and their most closely related relatives—primates—especially chimpanzees and gorillas. This is the strategy of the various research teams engaged in teaching language to apes. Their work has proven quite popular, turning up in prime-time TV documentaries and morning news shows. It has also generated heated controversy; the latest claim—by a former believer—is that the apes have only learned a few cute tricks, not language at all, making monkeys out of the investigators.

Ape Language Projects

Early attempts to teach apes language* failed. Best known was the charming endeavor by a married pair of psychologists to teach a chimpanzee language by raising it with their own child. This attempt was bound to fail if only because chimps' vocal apparatus is ill suited to language. La Mettrie's challenge to Descartes was not carried out until the 1960s in response to Chomsky's revived Cartesian linguistics. The spirit in which la Mettrie's hypothesis was revived is nicely captured by the title of the first modern project report on ape language (Premack, 1965a): "Preparations for Discussing Behaviorism with a Chimpanzee." Interestingly, this project failed because the artificial language Premack devised to get around the vocalization problem involved emitting sounds with a joystick-controlled soundbox, and was too difficult for Premack's assistants to learn, much less the chimps!

There is no doubt that monkeys and apes communicate in the wild, both vocally and nonvocally, often sending fairly elaborate messages. For example, the alarm calls of the vervet monkey, a small monkey relatively

---

*The literature on ape language is vast. There are at least four popular books on the subject, Eugene Linden's *Apes, Men, and Language* (1974; rev. ed. 1981); Ann J. Premack's *Why Chimps Can Read* (1976), which inspired the title for this section of your text; Herbert S. Terrace's *Nim: A Chimpanzee Who Learned Sign Language* (1979a); and Francine Patterson's and Eugene Linden's *The Education of Koko* (1982). Linden's books must be read with care, because he oversimplifies Western intellectual history and reads portentous significance into the ape projects.

Scholarly reviews of the projects, sometimes including accounts of earlier twentieth-century work, include Rumbaugh (1980); Fouts and Rigby (1980); Hill (1980); Ristau and Robbins (1982).

Descriptions of the projects by the investigators themselves include Premack (1976); Savage-Rumbaugh, Rumbaugh, and Boysen (1979/1980a); Savage-Rumbaugh and Rumbaugh (1980b); Gardner and Gardner (1969/1972, 1978/1980a, 1980b); Terrace, Petitto, Sanders, and Bever (1980); Patterson (1980), Savage-Rumbaugh (1986).

distant from *Homo sapiens*, are remarkably sophisticated. The calls can designate different predators, and can distinguish moving from nonmoving predators. Vervet monkeys are therefore able to convey a lot about the location and type of predator, with ensuing behavior adaptively nuanced as a result.

Several research teams are investigating the acquisition of language by great apes, primarily chimpanzees. Since it is clear chimpanzees and gorillas cannot acquire vocal language, researchers have had to devise nonvocal languages to teach to their subjects. David Premack, after the failure of his soundbox analogue to vocal language, turned to a visual "language" in which chimp and human communicate by placing plastic tokens (roughly equivalent to words) on a board following specified grammatical rules. At the Yerkes Primate Research Center, Georgia, E. S. Savage-Rumbaugh and Duane Rumbaugh use an artificial language called *Yerkish*, in which a chimp "talks" with a computer by pressing symbolic keys—lexigrams—(roughly equal to words) following rules of syntax. The system allows the computer both to "talk" to the chimp, and to provide human-chimp and chimp-chimp interaction.

The best-known projects, however, follow up an old suggestion made by the great primate psychologist Robert Yerkes in the 1920s, using the American sign language of the deaf (Ameslan or ASL) as the medium of communication. The pioneer project was carried out by Beatrice and Allan Gardner at the University of Nevada at Reno with a chimp named Washoe. Work with Washoe and others was carried on by Roger Fouts in Kansas, while, in New York, Herbert Terrace and his associates taught ASL to Neam Chimsky (!) or Nim; Francine Patterson in California taught it to a gorilla, Koko. It should be pointed out that in addition to skill and patience, these projects require real courage. Chimps grow up to weigh nearly as much as a large man, are three times as strong, and can—even inadvertently—do real harm to people and property. Many of the projects can only last a few years, until the chimp reaches puberty and becomes a potential danger.

Whatever method was used, the findings of the ape-language projects establish beyond doubt that apes can express themselves symbolically. They can make requests, convey their feelings, and discuss the past. Other experiments have shown that apes can invent new sign or lexigram strings, can name objects, and can communicate about things such as a tool needed to get a piece of food. However, the exact significance of these findings remains unclear and controversial. Have any of the apes learned *language*, not just a new communication system? Can these projects tell us anything about the evolution of human language? How similar is an ape's acquisition of signing (or lexigram use) to the acquisition of language by children?

Controversy

Is it language?   From their inception, the ape-language projects provoked controversy, primarily over the issue of whether or not what apes acquired was language (it was clearly communication) and, consequently, whether their learning processes were the same as a child's learning language. Roger Brown (1970), a pioneer in the study of human language acquisition (see R. Brown, 1973) argued that the Gardner's Washoe did not seem to possess syntax. That is, she constructed utterances out of random aggregations of signs rather than showing any following of word (sign) order rules, namely, syntax. This implied the important conclusion that Washoe did not have semantic intentions while signing, but instead just emitted behaviors until reinforcement was forthcoming. Later, Brown (1973) modified his view, conceding that Washoe did have semantic intentions, without word order, because of his finding that children learning languages that are less strict about word order than English speak intentionally without exhibiting regular syntax.

Using data from Nim, Terrace and colleagues (1980) directly investigated the question of rule-governed combination of signs, and finding that while Nim assembled multisign utterances, there was no evidence there of regular sign-order. They concluded that Nim was just a random sign-generator, emitting signs until they had some desired effect. Similarly, the Yerkes group has tempered earlier claims that its chimps showed syntactic structure in their utterances (Ristau & Robbins, 1982). Because their computer language requires linear symbol-by-symbol production, it should be ideal for eliciting syntax in apes; in fact, it might produce syntax as an artifact of the experiment. So if there is poor evidence of grammar acquisition in Yerkish, it seems syntax is difficult, perhaps impossible, for chimps to acquire.

The issue of grammar is quite important, for it is syntax that gives human language its infinite expressive and productive powers. Without syntax, only the most rudimentary thoughts or desires can be expressed, and communication must remain tied to an immediate concrete context. With syntax, nuances of expression become possible, and intellect is freed from the immediate and concrete and can soar to the distant and imaginary.

Is it problem solving? It was not about chimps learning sign language that it was first said "that an animal can think in human ways and can express human ideas in human language" (Hediger, 1981, p. 1). The animal in question was Clever Hans, a horse, who early in the twentieth century fooled many people, including a panel of eminent scientists, and his owner himself, into believing he could do mathematics, think, and understand spoken and written language. It took the clever research of a young psychologist, Oskar Pfungst, to show that in apparently teaching Hans arithmetic and language, his owner had really taught him to attend to subtle, unconscious, nonverbal cues given off by his questioner. Clever Hans should remind us that a very plausible imitation of language is not language itself (Heil, 1982).

Accusations that the linguistic apes were in effect simian Clever Hanses have been raised by Terrace (Terrace, 1979a, 1979b, 1979c, 1982; Terrace, Petitto, Sanders, & Bever, 1979), who argues that the apes did not really learn language, but only to gesture (or arrange plastic tokens, or push computer lexigrams) to satisfy their masters and get things they want.

Sebeok and Umiker-Sebeok (1979, 1980; Sebeok, 1980) also make this claim. This new aspect to the ape language controversy has engendered a bitter debate between skeptics and most of the project directors (Benderly, 1980). Indeed, at a conference devoted to the Clever Hans phenomenon with respect to the ape language projects (Sebeok & Rosenthal, 1981) the phrase "witch hunt" was used by Duane Rumbaugh (1981; see also Linden, 1981).

Unfortunately, evaluating claims of deceptive communication is difficult because of the methodological deficiencies of the various studies (Ristau & Robbins, 1982). In general, the data base from all the projects—save Nim's—is very poor. The Gardners' data (1969/1972) consist of diaries, and one study showed serious errors in recording the apes' signing. The Yerkes project only recorded what the apes punched on their keyboard, but not the possibly cuing activities of the trainers. Sarah, the Premack chimp, was drilled in such a way that she could have functioned by rote-learning of symbol sequences rather than language-rule learning. Most of the famous and persuasive creative utterances of the chimps are merely anecdotal, and open to other interpretations than those given by the investigators, who, of course, wanted the apes to have language. The best-known of these events was Washoe's signing "water bird" upon seeing a swan on a river. Advocates of chimp language (for example, Linden, 1981; Lieberman, 1984) see this as creative naming—calling the swan a "waterbird." Skeptics see it as two separate signs under distinct stimulus control, "water" (water was present) and "bird."

The only project with adequate records was Terrace's Nim project, where extensive videotapes were made. Terrace for a long time believed Nim had learned language until he started studying the videotapes after the project ended. Among other things, he detected the Clever Hans phenomena, specifically cuing in the form of signs that Nim could imitate. Apparently, Nim's trainers were unaware of their cuing, for they expressed surprise on seeing the tapes.

The best conclusion to be drawn from attempts to teach language to chimpanzees and gorillas is skepticism (Ristau & Robbins, 1982). While it is clear that chimps and gorillas can learn to communicate with sign language and to use signs or lexigrams to represent objects, they do so only after a great deal of intensive and systematic training (Savage-Rumbaugh, McDonald, Sevcik, Hopkins, & Robert, 1986) very different from what human infants experience. Although the subjects of these experiments may have learned language, significant differences exist between apes' acquisition of communicative competence and children's acquisition of language. However, light may be shed on the traditional ape-language projects by a new line of research using the rarest of the great apes, pygmy chimpanzees (*Pan paniscus*) (Savage-Rumbaugh and others, 1986). Pygmy chimps are brighter and socially more like us than are ordinary chimps (*Pan troglodytes*). Among pygmy chimpanzees, in contrast to ordinary chimpanzees, male–female bonds are strong and fathers help rear offspring. Moreover, pygmy chimps in the wild possess a much larger repertoire of vocal and gestural symbols than do *Pan troglodytes*. They are, perhaps, much better candidates for language learning than gorillas and *Pan troglodytes*. The most important subjects of Savage-Rumbaugh's study are two young offspring of a female pygmy chimpanzee who was taught Yerkish. They acquired Yerkish spontaneously, simply by being exposed to its use between their mother and her trainers. Continuing to work with—but not instruct or reward—these youngsters, Savage-Rumbaugh and her associates found that Kanzi and Mulika were active learners, rapidly mastering Yerkish and able to apply it in novel contexts, such as guiding a blind researcher around an enclosed forest. Unlike the chimps who had learned Yerkish, Kanzi and Mulika began to understand the English vocal names for the lexigrams, although of course they could not learn to speak. Most significantly, unlike the Yerkish chimpanzees and unlike Nim, who just signed to get something for themselves, the pygmy chimpanzees came to use Yerkish unselfishly. They often used Yerkish to request that the experimenters do something for the other, or for another person. Although the investigators conclude that pygmy chimpanzees master Yerkish in a completely different manner from ordinary chimpanzees, and draw parallels between human language acquisition and their subjects' Yerkish acquisition, Savage-Rumbaugh and colleagues shy away from claiming that Kanzi and Mulika have learned human language. Perhaps *Pan paniscus* represents a grade of hominization between *Pan troglodytes* and *Homo sapiens*. If so, further research may help establish how much of human language depends on sophisticated cognition, and how much on language-specific, innate neural mechanisms.

Conclusion

Chomsky's remarks (1979, 1980a) on the linguistic apes raise the crucial issue: What is language and what is *human* language? For it is not clear that even if the various apes do in fact acquire language that they have acquired human language.

Confounding the two runs all the way through our interpretation of what the apes are doing. Consider interpreting two- and three-word sentences—assuming even that they are sentences—such as "water bird." Children, too, pass through a two-word stage, and we assume that their utterances are simple language. Defenders of the linguistic capacity of apes have said that skeptics apply a double standard, requiring more of the ape than of the child to call these utterances "language." Chomsky's analysis suggests the double standard is not misplaced: We call the children's two-word sentences language in view of what they later will achieve, not by virtue of their present linguistic sophistication, which indeed is no greater than the apes'. Terrace's data support Chomsky's argument, since he found the mean length of Nim's utterances got stuck at three or four words, while children's—even of comparable stages of linguistic experience—continued to grow.

Chomsky points out that no matter how sophisticated chimp or gorilla language may be, there is (at present) no strong reason to see it as incipient human language. It is more likely to be a separate cognitive activity not closely related to normal human language. Chomsky (1979) cites studies in which patients with damage to the language centers of their brains are able to acquire symbol-systems akin to the apes, and whose use of these systems seems much like the use of signing and symbols by the apes. If Chomsky's parallel is valid, it means that the ape-language projects may tell us much about ape mentality, but can offer us little insight into human language. The interesting results obtained with pygmy chimpanzees by by Savage-Rumbaugh and others (1986) are too preliminary to settle the ape-language controversy.

HUMAN LANGUAGE

Evolution of Language

The evolution of language is a venerable field of human speculation (Aarsleff, 1976) that has again become active (Harnad, Steklis, & Lancaster, 1976). Chomsky's nativist thesis, the ape-language projects, improved knowledge of the human evolutionary tree (Johanson & Edey, 1981), including studies in paleoneurology, and sociobiology have all come together to revive theories of language origins. We must remember as we proceed, however, that informed speculation is the best we can achieve. Behavior does not fossilize: All we can do is to infer cognitive and linguistic capacities from fossil skeletons, remains of tools, campsites, and art, seasoned with judicious cross-species comparisons. It is most unlikely that any final answers can be forthcoming. Before continuing, the reader may wish to review the material on human evolution in Chapter 10.

The first reasonable question to ask is when language appeared in human evolution. Evidence from hominid fossils is equivocal on this question. Lieberman (1975, 1984) has proposed reconstructions of hominid skulls indicating that *only* Homo sapiens sapiens could speak, ruling out even the Neandertals from having vocal language; however, his reconstructions are not universally accepted (Harnad and others, 1976). Paleoneurologists have been trying to infer the size and structure of the brain of ancient hominids in order to see if they had brains capable of language, but they cannot reach agreement. Holloway (1976) believes australopithecines had small brains of nevertheless human structure, and suggests they may have had language.

Jerison (1976), on the other hand, is skeptical of the possibility of inferring brain structure from fossil skulls, and on the basis of computations of brain size in relation to body weight argues that australopithecines did not have language, that *Homo erectus* probably did not, and that all *sapiens* forms (including Neandertal) did. More recent finds and analyses tend to support Jerison's conclusions (McHenry, 1982).

Evidence from artifacts—tools, engraved bones and so on—generally supports a date of about 40,000 years B.P. for the final development of language. As with the chimps, the very simple stone tools made by *Homo habilis* probably do not require or imply language, and these tools did not change much for hundreds of thousands of years. However, they do increase greatly in sophistication at about 40,000 years B.P. (Isaac, 1976), and at about the same time and a little earlier there is evidence of symbolic abilities in engraved bones (Marshack, 1972, 1976). Evidence from glottochronology coincides with these dates (Miller, 1981). *Glottochronology*, the study of how languages change, has found that for historical periods languages all change at a fairly steady rate. If this rate is used to extrapolate back in time, vocal language—the first language spoken by human beings—cannot have begun later than 10,000 years B.P. or earlier than 100,000 years, so that the date of 40,000 to 50,000 years B.P. looks like a fair compromise.

So far we have considered only vocal language, but we now come to an important question: Did vocal language develop suddenly, perhaps as a mutation (Myers, 1976), or did it slowly evolve out of some other communication system, whether simianlike cries (Jaynes, 1976b; Marler, 1976) or a preceding gestural language that later shifted to the vocal-auditory channel (Hewes, 1975, 1976, Lamendella, 1976; Steklis & Harnad, 1976; Parker & Gibson, 1979)?

We have already noted that monkeys possess vocal signals such as alarm calls, and there is now evidence that these signals are truly symbolic (Ristau & Robbins, 1982; Snowden, 1983). Vervet monkeys have calls that separately name each major predator they encounter; squirrel monkeys use certain friendly calls only between closely affiliated females; while titi monkeys utter syntactically organized call sequences. One might then hypothesize that such prehominid calls were the raw material out of which natural selection fashioned human language.

However, the problem with this hypothesis is that the neural substrates of human language and monkey calling are different. Human language is controlled primarily by the left frontal neocortex, while monkey calling is controlled by much older brain systems, particularly the limbic system (Malmi, 1976). Moreover, monkeys show little (Snowden, 1983) or no (Warren & Nonneman, 1976) cerebral lateralization for vocal functions. It is interesting to observe in this context that aphasics—people who have lost language due to damage to the language centers of the cortex—are most likely to retain simple, emotionally charged utterances such as curses (Robinson, 1976), suggesting that their intact limbic system controls monkeylike cries that are not really language any more.

Additionally, the ontogeny of monkey calls is quite different from human language (Snowden, 1983) or even birdsong, it being much more preprogrammed than either. Isolated and deafened monkeys develop mostly normal calls, unlike humans or songbirds. At best, their innate cries are refined by experience to apply to a precisely delimited group of objects, suggesting a process of simple stimulus discrimination learning based on built-in vocalizations.

These considerations do not, of course, completely rule out the possibility that evolution gradually shifted the control of vocalization from the limbic system to the cortex—*encephalization*, as suggested by Jaynes

(1976a,b)—but they do point out a large gap between animal and human vocal communicaton that seems hard for evolution to bridge (Myers, 1976). A popular alternative theory is to seek antecedents of vocal language in gestural language.

Seeking the origin of vocal language in a preceding language of gestures goes back in psychology to psychology's founder, Wilhelm Wundt (Wundt, 1973), and has been revived by the efforts to teach sign language to apes (Hewes, 1975). If human vocal language did not evolve from existing prehominid calls, perhaps it is a specialization of the cognitive abilities that the signing apes use in today's research.

Again, the hypothesis faces difficulties. As we have seen, there is some question about whether or not the signing apes have language or are just gesturing until they get what they want. The gesture-language hypotheses also face a problem similar to the encephalization problem of the vocal theorists. Once gesture language arose, why did a shift take place to spoken language? It is easy to see that vocal language is superior—we can talk, but not sign, in the dark and around corners—but evolution is conservative and not teleological. Vocal language may be better, but gesture language may have been good enough for reproductive survival, which is all that counts in evolution. Moreover, why has gesture language so atrophied in humans if it was once so important? Why do not our monkey and ape relatives show evidence of gesture language?

However language appeared—perhaps throwing rocks had something to do with it (Box 12–2)—there is no doubt that once in existence it has had a powerful effect on the evolution of *Homo sapiens.* Language creates culture, and culture-change, directed and Lamarckian, begins to replace pure evolution as the major mode of human adaptation (Lumsden & Wilson, 1983). Krantz (1980) and Washburn (1981) have reviewed evidence suggesting that language was the major selective factor in the final emergence of *Homo sapiens sapiens* out of *Homo erectus* types, including the Neandertals. Lieberman (1984), adopting the hypothesis that Neandertals and *Homo sapiens sapiens* evolved separately, proposes that language was the critical skill allowing *Homo sapiens sapiens* to supplant Neandertal. Around 40,000 years B.P., many changes appear in human life: More complex tools and more types of tools are manufactured; tools become specialized to particular jobs; the first projectile points (spear and arrow tips) appear in addition to hand tools; use of fire becomes an everyday activity not confined to cold periods; the pace of technological change accelerates; population increases and expands geographically. All these changes are associated with the fossil remains of *Homo sapiens sapiens.* Krantz argues that around 40,000 years ago vocal language—and therefore the human culture it creates— appeared, favoring those anatomical forms (that is, *sapiens sapiens*) that could learn and use vocal language. The result was relatively rapid evolution, over only about 10,000 years, of *Homo erectus* into *Homo sapiens sapiens,* a change marked by the developments reviewed above. Once the evolution of *Homo sapiens sapiens* was complete, language acquisition became an essential task for every human child.

BOX 12–2   Just a Stone's Throw to Language?

William Calvin (1982) has recently proposed an unusual basis for the evolution of the large human brain and human language: throwing stones. Apes throw stones with both hands only a short distance and with little accuracy. Humans— especially young males—love to throw things, can do so with great speed and accuracy, over a fair distance, and even invent games that turn on throwing skills. When we find something that a species loves to do and does well, we should suspect that evolution—ultimate causation—has been at work.

Calvin proposes that one-handed stone throwing was an efficient hunting technique for our omnivorous ancestors. While one cannot bring down big game with a rock, it ought to be possible to hunt smaller animals with rocks, later aided by spears, spear throwers, and slings. Once begun, skill in throwing would be quickly selected for, with important consequences for brain development. Stone throwing would tend to enlarge the brain, for accurate throwing requires complex and finely controlled patterns of muscle movement and eye-arm-hand coordination. Since accurate throwing is done with one hand, hemispheric specialization would be favored, and we find that it is males who have the more lateralized brains today. So stone throwing could help create the large, specialized brain of modern *Homo sapiens*, and because throwing is an infinitely improvable skill—faster and more precise throws are always better—it would set off an autocatalytic effect of continuing pressure toward larger, more specialized brains.

Certain broader benefits would accrue as well. The skill of stone throwing would open new niches for exploitation, and would also improve the motor skills needed to make better stone tools. Finally, with respect to language, the neural organization needed for good throwing would require precise sequencing of complex neural firing patterns, precisely what is needed in human language function. Most people are right-handed, the side controlled by the left, linguistic hemisphere. According to Calvin, this is no accident, but arose because we evolved throwing skills in the left hemisphere, whose neural circuitry could then be adapted to the sequential skill of language.

Evolution is normally very slow. One of the puzzles of human evolution is our (relatively) rapid change from ape to human. If Calvin's hypothesis contains any truth it could partially solve this puzzle, because throwing is a single and highly adaptive skill that ramifies in many ways, all of which would push our ancient ancestors in the direction of *Homo sapiens sapiens*.[*]

[*] See William H. Calvin. *The Throwing Madonna: From Nervous Cells to Hominid Brains.* New York: McGraw-Hill, 1983.

Acquisition of Language

The three major approaches to explaining language acquisition[*] in children are biological, cognitive, and behavioral. The last was largely eliminated as a general explanation by some of the first studies of child language acquisition inspired by Chomsky's revival of the issue.

The behaviorist treats language just like any other behavior, possessing no special properties or biological specialization (Skinner, 1957). Therefore, the behaviorist would expect language—verbal behavior—to be shaped by reinforcement contingencies, perhaps supported by imitation of adult forms. However, both these processes can be ruled out as the sole determiners of language acquisition and use—children use language to get what they want, and can only talk about what they have heard about—but they seem to play little role in acquiring syntax.

Studies of parent-child interaction have shown that, aside from a few pet language peeves we all remember, such as "ain't," parents pay more attention to—that is, reinforce or punish—the content of what their children say than to its grammatical form. Moskowitz (1978) reports a charming example of this. A mother hearing her son, Stevie, say, "Tommy fall my truck down," quickly turned to Tommy and asked, "Did you fall Stevie's truck down?" The mother was clearly more concerned about the truth of Stevie's claim, and the moral issues it raised, than with its syntactic correctness. Since this is generally true, it follows, as Brown (1973) points out, that if the contingencies of reinforcement shaped language, we should

---

[*] Back when psychology was the "Science of Mental Life," language acquisition (like language evolution) was an important topic. Although formal studies were not done, many eminent scientists—including Charles Darwin and Wilhelm Wundt—kept "baby diaries"—records of their own children's language acquisition—and they discovered some of the phenomena later recovered by modern research. Extracts from several such diaries (along with some of the pioneering modern studies) may be found in Bar-Adon and Leopold (1971). During the behaviorist era, developmental psycholinguistics lay fallow; the only studies were of vocabulary acquisition, it being assumed that words were the behavioral units of language being learned as classical or operant responses.

Chomsky's nativistic thesis reawakened interest in children's language, and modern developmental psycholinguistics began. It has remained a growth industry ever since. There is so much data available it defies easy summary, and the problem is compounded by the current tendency, evident in the 1983 Annual Review by Eve Clark, for psychologists to narrow their research focus to small puzzles, a tendency no doubt inspired by the information-processing approach.

Given these difficulties and our own major concern with theoretical explanation, this section will not attempt to review research findings. The interested reader may find useful summaries in several book-length treatments. McNeil (1970) was the first synthetic treatment and represents a strong nativist approach. Comprehensive, relatively atheoretical treatments include Dale (1976); Bloom and Lahey (1978), which includes chapters on abnormal language development; and de Villiers and de Villiers (1978). Eliot (1981) is a brief summary from a cognitivist perspective. The chapters in Fletcher and Gorman (1986) provide thorough discussions of current research and theory; the editors find no major theoretical advances since the first edition of their text. Atkinson (1982) provides a broad consideration and evaluation of major approaches to exploring language acquisition. Miller and Gildea (1987) discuss acquisition of words by elementary school children.

find ungrammatical but truth-telling adults. Obviously, though, what develops is people who lie with good grammar.

Imitation, too, has been found to be a less important process in language acquisition than most people and psychologists have believed. Bloom, Hood, and Lightbown (1974) showed that there is considerable difference between children in whether or not they imitated utterances they had heard. Some children imitate very little, yet learn language as quickly as their peers who imitate a great deal. More generally, imitation is ruled out by the fact that as children construct their grammatical rules—which, of course, should not exist according to behaviorist theory—they use rules at first that differ from adult rules, and to create utterances that they cannot have heard.

The phenomenon of over-regularization offers a nice example establishing that language is rule-learning, because it requires invoking cognitive structures underlying behavior, and cannot be due to imitation. Language is based on rules, but the rules have exceptions, and children must learn what they are. For example, most verbs in English convert to the past tense by adding the morpheme /-ed/. However, there are many common exceptions to this rule, such as *fall-fell* or *go-went*. As they learn language, children typically first learn both the regular and irregular verbs correctly, and can say, "I went home." Then, however, they formulate the general rule but over-apply it: "I goed home." Now they cannot be imitating *goed*, nor has it been shaped by reinforcement. Instead, the child has induced a general rule and over-generalized it, losing the correct, reinforced form and suddenly emitting a new, deviant form in its place. Later, perhaps after a phase of saying "I wented home," the child learns the exceptions and returns to the correct form, "I went home." (Moskowitz, 1978.)

So it is clear that language acquisition cannot be explained behaviorally. We must invoke inner processes to explain language, and changes in those processes to explain language acquisition. The usual behavioral forces of selective reinforcement and imitation are inadequate to explain language learning. What remains is to try to sort out how much of language acquisition is a unique, species-specific process, and how much is a consequence of broader human intellectual sophistication.

The leading exponent of the view that language is a species-specific biological capacity of *Homo sapiens*, and that much of language acquisition is simply maturation, was Eric Lenneberg (1964, 1965, 1967, 1969/1972). We may list some of the more important reasons Lenneberg adduced in support of his thesis:

1. Humans possess many anatomical specializations related to language use from the shape and placement of the larynx to specialization of language functions in the left hemisphere of the brain. (See Marshall, 1980, for a more recent review.)

2. Damage to certain parts of the brain (in the left hemisphere only) lead to damaged or lost linguistic abilities. Moreover, time of damage during childhood is related to clinical outcome. Damage to the left hemisphere during the first few years of life can be overcome; after puberty it cannot be. Recent

research shows Lenneberg to have conceded too much to the environment. Woods (1980) provides evidence of very early left hemisphere specialization for language. Dennis (1980) has found that infants who have their right hemispheres removed at birth develop normal language, while those who lose their left hemispheres have only imperfect (though usable) language all their lives.

3. Language cannot be suppressed. Studies of completely untutored deaf children found that they spontaneously invent sign language to use with each other: Teaching signing to chimps is hard work, but children learn language by themselves (Miller, 1981). On the other hand, language learning cannot be speeded up by more than a few days, as training studies have shown (Moskowitz, 1978).

4. The time of onset and early steps of language learning are universal around the world.

5. The early sequence of language acquisition is closely correlated with motor development, which is known to be due entirely to maturation. Just as children kept swaddled begin to walk at the same time as unswaddled children. Lenneberg reports a baby at the babbling stage who was tracheostomized for six months, and who picked up babbling not where she left off but where she should have been when the tracheostomy was reversed.

6. Language cannot be taught to any other species. Although this claim is controversial, it is not clearly false.

7. Linguistic universals do exist.

8. Certain forms of aphasia (disordered language) are inheritable.

9. Timing of speech onset and onset of speech deficits (if any) are more similar between identical than between fraternal twins.

10. So-called wolf-children denied access to speech until adolescence cannot learn language despite intensive tutoring (Jeffrey, 1980), while similar children discovered at an earlier age can learn language.

11. Language is present in all cultures.

To Lenneberg's list we can add some further considerations:

12. There is a clear difference between learning a second language in adulthood and first language learning. We learn our primary language without thinking: most of us struggle through language classes with great difficulty, despite adult cognitive skills and careful instruction. Vocabulary learning provides a dramatic contrast. The adult language learner struggles to master a few new words a week. Without trying, the average six-year-old learns 22 new words a day! As Miller (1981) puts it: "Their minds are like little vacuum pumps designed by nature to suck up words." (p. 119)

13. Both children and adults suffering from aphasia can learn Premack's token "language," indicating that the problem-solving, but not linguistic, parts of their brains are intact (Cromer, 1981).

14. Neonates (12 hours old) show "interactional synchrony" with spoken language (Condon & Sander, 1974; Bower, 1977). When they hear human language—any human language—but not when they hear other sounds, they move their bodies in a regular rhythmic fashion following the sound pattern of what they hear. Speech is clearly a special sound to even the youngest human.

15. Human speech perception is categorical (Chapter 5), and there is evidence that these categories are innate. Eimas, Siqueland, Jusczyk, and Vigorito (1971) and Miller and Eimas (1983) showed that prelinguistic infants show the same kind of categorical perception, and they proposed that infants have innate human speech detectors. Subsequent research has shown that some other (but not all) distinctive features are recognized by infants including features not used in their natural language (see Blumenstein, 1980, for a review). On the other hand, nonhuman species perceive categorically, too (Eilers, 1980): Chinchillas, like adult and infant humans, categorically perceive (*ba*) and (*pa*). So the species-specificity of this ability is unclear. Evolution may have incorporated pre-existing perceptual abilities into the human language system.

Taken together, these considerations suggest that human language acquisition is a biologically based, genetically constrained and directed form of learning that takes place during a fixed critical period ending at adolescence. The analogy to birdsong is striking. In both cases language does not simply mature, but requires input and practice that must occur in a certain period of time. In both cases there is a range of languages (or dialects) that may be learned, but certain kinds of languages may not be learned. In both, there is cerebral (left hemisphere) specialization of language function.

The cognitivist counter-proposal is based essentially on negative reasoning: It is not *necessary* to postulate specifically linguistic innate processes and structures (see Atkinson, 1982, for a review). With regard to neurology, it is claimed that hemispheric specialization is really for two broad types of cognitive abilities, linear (left hemisphere) and holistic (right hemisphere) so that language winds up in the left hemisphere by virtue of being a linear processing task (Bever, 1980). With regard to the work on categorical speech perception in infants, the cognitivists maintain that since not all distinctive features are innate, and those that are not species-specific, there is no linguistic specialization at work (Aslin & Pisoni, 1980). This, by the way, is an objection of limited force, since as Gould (1982) points out, evolution is a great opportunist, and in building language it took advantage of older, preexisting abilities. In general, communication systems show a careful tuning between already present sensory abilities and characteristics of the message (Wilson, 1980).

Although the cognitivist hypothesis is the favorite among current psychologists (Moskowitz, 1978; Elkind, 1981), a careful review of their claims (Cromer, 1981) shows it to be flawed. The general problem with the cognitivist approach is oversimplification. It assumes that once a cognitive strategy or concept is acquired it is immediately translated into language. But Cromer argues that the translation is not a trivial automatic affair, and is likely to involve specifically linguistic processes, perhaps innate ones. In any event, despite its popularity with psychologists, there is no cognitive theory of language learning as detailed as the nativist hypothesis (Campbell, 1986).

On the empirical side, evidence indicates that cognitive and linguistic development can be almost completely decoupled, suggesting separate developmental paths. Cromer cites a study with two subjects in whom such decoupling took place in opposite ways. One subject was a 20-year-old female deprived of language until 12, and who despite intensive instruction had still not acquired language beyond a two-year-old level; nevertheless, her general cognitive ability was much higher, at Piaget's level of concrete operations (7 to 12 years old). Another subject—a child—did poorly on cognitive tests, but spoke using highly complex syntactic constructions. The content of his speech—clearly depending on thinking—was often nonsense, but his grammatical skills were high. In this connection we may again mention the ape language projects, because chimpanzees have (relatively) sophisticated intelligence, but acquire only rudimentary language at best.

One of the major findings making the cognitivist hypothesis attractive has been the discovery of baby talk, called *child-directed speech* (Snow, 1986), or "motherese." Chomsky alleged that children heard only fragmentary, ill-formed utterances, from which only an innate language faculty could extract linguistic competence. However, studies (see Snow, 1972/1978) of parental speech to children showed that it differed from speech to adults, and was in general well formed and framed in short sentences. From this, advocates of cognitivism concluded that children were getting a sort of tutorial in language, and that Chomsky's nativism was unnecessary.

However, Cromer uses a careful study of motherese (Newport, Gleitman, & Gleitman, 1977) to undermine the cognitivist claim. One problem with the idea that motherese is used to teach children language is that baby talk, motherese, could have other functions than teaching: to express affection (it is used between lovers), to facilitate communication (it is used with foreigners), or to assert power (nurses use it with patients). Against the tutorial view Newport and others (1977) found that while motherese sentences are short, they are syntactically complex, by some measures more complex than speech between adults. Moreover, the "lessons" seem ill designed to teach syntax. For example, the canonical form of English sentences is a declarative sentence in subject-verb-object word order: 87 percent of adult-adult sentences are of this type; but only 30 percent of sentences directed to children are, there being many more commands and questions. In investigating the influence of motherese or subsequent child speech, Newport and others (1977) found that motherese affected the acquisition *only* of English-language specific structures, and had no impact on the rate of acquisition of more universal aspects of language.

More recent studies of child-directed speech have focused on its semantic properties. Early views of motherese assumed that mothers were giving their babies lessons in syntax, overlooking the fact that mothers were really trying simply to communicate with their children, to convey and understand information, not to teach grammar (Snow, 1986). Therefore, utterances to children are simple because the ideas being dealt with are simple, not because the parents' sentences are designed to teach language. The shift in researchers' focus from syntax to semantics revealed that how parents speak to their children may speed up language acquisition. In particular, when parents talk at length about what their child is doing—even when

---

BOX 12–3   Learnability Theory

A promising line of investigation of language acquisition has been begun by Kenneth Wexler and Peter Cullicover (1980), called **learnability theory**. Wexler and Cullicover point out that there is a necessary tradeoff between the kinds and power of learning mechanisms invoked to explain language acquisition on the one hand, and constraints on the forms of possible human grammars on the other. Very general—and therefore linguistically weak—learning mechanisms will only be able to learn a small class of highly constrained grammers; that is, specific universal constraints on kinds of human language grammars will have to be innate. On the other hand, if a broad variety of relatively unconstrained grammars exist to be learned, much more (innately) powerful learning mechanisms will have to be invoked.

Earlier work (see Atkinson, 1982, 1986 for simplified accounts) had proved that even implausibly powerful cognitive mechanisms could not, *in principle*, learn the accepted grammars of human language, or even simplified versions thereof. What Wexler and Cullicover have done is to prove that if language is to be learned at all—as it clearly is—there must exist specific linguistic constraints (innate universals) on the form of possible grammars, and these two researchers offer specific (highly technical) hypotheses as to what these might be.

Wexler and Cullicover have opened a new path to studying language acquisition by focusing our attention on exactly what the child must learn. Once we better understand the dimensions of the task, and the kinds of principles that must be innate, we will be in a much better position to learn from what children and their parents say to one another.

---

an infant is too young to respond linguistically—the rate of language learning is accelerated. These findings are especially important to the newest form of linguistic nativism, *learnability theory* (Box 12–3). Learnability theory assumes that children learn syntax by decoding the meaning of what parents say without using syntax, and then matching the meanings with the syntactic structures that express them. Genes provide hypotheses about syntax that simplify the process of matching meanings to grammatical structures, but semantics leads syntax because figuring out what parents are saying makes it possible for a child to figure out how his or her parents are saying it (Snow, 1986).

CONCLUSION: THE BIOLOGICAL BASIS OF LANGUAGE

Let us reflect once again on the difference between child and chimp. The child learns language naturally, with little or no tutoring and with little visible effort. The chimp is carefully taught by a team of intelligent, dedicated researchers who want very much to succeed and who work as hard as possible to give their subjects language. Yet the chimp—despite such heroic efforts—acquires no more than the simplest language, and perhaps not even that.

Whatever else may be innate, it is quite clear that human children have a powerful *drive* to learn language (Gould, 1982). Even if all the mechanisms of language acquisition should turn out to be those of general intelligence—which, as we have seen is by no means clear—evolution has provided at least this much: To learn human language is one of a child's deepest needs.

Given the evidence we have reviewed in this chapter, concerning the evolution of communication in animals, the mixed results of the ape-language projects, the speculations on human language evolution, and the findings on child-language acquisition, we can reach a stronger conclusion. We humans swim in a sea of language. It is the key to much of our adaptive success, providing the basis for educating the long-helpless, K-selected infant, for socializing our children, for cooperation, for binding ourselves together in groups and for expressing love for our epigamically differentiated loved ones. Without language we would not be human, and so it is unlikely that evolution—natural selection—did not produce a human language faculty.

SUGGESTED READINGS

The full range of mammalian communication systems from hedgehogs to humans is presented in Roger Peters' *Mammalian Communication* (1980). A good place for the student interested in Chomsky's work to start is with his *Language and Mind* (1968; enlarged ed., 1972). As a previous footnote in this chapter explained, there are many popular books on the ape-language studies; Herbert Terrace's *Nim* is recently out in a mass-market paperback. There is no easy work on language evolution, but chapters in George Miller's *Language and Speech* (1981) provide an introduction, and *Origins and Evolution of Language and Speech* (Harnad and others, 1976), the proceedings of a conference on the subject, provides a bewildering variety of approaches and speculations. On child-language acquisition the standard reference seems to have become Jill and Peter de Villier's *Language Acquisition* (1978), though other works are listed in the footnote on page 354.

13

DEVELOPMENT, LEARNING, AND COGNITION

INTRODUCTION

Defining Development

That human development is teleological—directed to a final end, mature adulthood—is a commonplace idea reaching back to Aristotle. He envisioned the development of any living being as the unfolding of a preexisting plan of development (called an *entelechy*) that brought an organism from seed to mature plant, from egg to adult bird, from embryo to mature animal, from fetus to mature human being. While this view may be challenged, as we will see in this chapter, it is undeniably comfortable and appealing.

In nineteenth-century Europe—the birthplace of much of psychology—the teleological view of development was particularly strong, and had been extended to include the history of human society. So it was widely believed that just as a human being passes from the simple and primitive thoughts and feelings of infancy to the sophisticated thinking and nuanced emotion of adulthood, so did human societies progress from simple and primitive tribalism to the sophistication of the Western nation-state; usually, it was hoped that one stage yet remained: achievement of a harmonious brotherhood of all people under a peaceful world government. Karl Marx's theory of history is the best-known example of such historicism today; Marx envisioned history as an inevitable progression, beyond the possibility of human intervention, through a series of stages from barbarism to feudalism to capitalism and finally to world socialism, at which point history ends. For Marx the autonomous force underlying historical development was economic change, specifically changes in who owns the means of production characteristic of each stage. Moreover, each system of ownership (save socialism) possesses internal contradictions that ensure its eventual overthrow and replacement by a superior one. History, according to Marx, is the inevitable progress of humankind to economic and social maturity as the logic of economic change unfolds.

Historicism did much to reinforce and preserve the teleological concept of human development, and it is therefore not surprising that shortly after psychology began there appeared in Europe historicist-developmentalist theories of human development. For example, there are interesting parallels between Marx's theory of history and Piaget's and Kohlberg's theories of cognitive and moral development. They propose that cognition and morality develop through fixed sequences of stages such that each stage (save the last) contains inconsistencies that bring about its overthrow and replacement by a more adequate one. Human development is therefore the inevitable progress of a child to cognitive and moral maturity as the logic of development unfolds.

Heinz Werner and Orthogenesis

The theorist who most emphatically distinguished between mere change and true development, and who applied the concept of development to everything from perception to history was Heinz Werner (1890–1964). Werner was educated in Germany, steeped in the German historical-developmental tradition, before fleeing the Nazis and settling in the United States. Werner studied the processes of development from an organismic-teleological perspective as manifested in children and adults, primitives, and moderns, and in psychotics and normals (Baldwin, 1980; Langer, 1970; Werner, 1978).

Werner carefully distinguished development from change or growth. Not all change is development, for change may be regressive. Nor is all growth development; a savings account "grows" as interest is added, but this does not constitute development because no qualitative improvement takes place. Werner (1978) borrowed the term **orthogenesis** from embryology to define development:

> It is an orthogenetic principle which states that whenever development occurs it proceeds from a state of relative globality and lack of differentiation to a state of increasing differentiation, articulation, and hierarchic integration. (Werner, 1957, p. 126)

The principle naturally fits embryogenesis. What begins as a single nonspecialized cell gradually develops into an organism, a collection of specialized cells (differentiation) structurally organized (articulation) into an efficient system under central control (hierarchic integration). Werner thought that the same functional principles of development characterized not only the development of the embryo, but the evolutionary history of a species (phylogenesis), the long-term development of a person (orthogenesis), the short-term development of thinking, emotion, and perception (microgenesis), the development of societies (ethnogenesis), and the development of psychopathology (pathogenesis). Although the material basis (what develops) in each case is different, Werner believed the orthogenetic principles of development—the teleological drive to differentiation, articulation, and integration—could be found in each case (Langer, 1970).

COGNITIVE DEVELOPMENT

There are two areas where the development *vs.* learning controversy has been most hotly debated. One of them is cognitive development, where the leading developmentalist theory is Jean Piaget's genetic epistemology, which has been attacked by non-developmentalists of all theoretical persuasions.

Genetic Epistemology

Piaget as philosopher.   Jean Piaget was one of the towering psychological theorists of the twentieth century, yet his ideas are often misunderstood and misrepresented. One reason for this is that Piaget represents the European developmentalist tradition alluded to already. Specifically, he belongs in what Blumenthal (1980), following Brett (1912) calls the Leibnizian (European) tradition in philosophy. Gottfried Leibniz (1646–1716) described the mind as an active entity, developing itself through inner-directed principles toward ever-greater perfection. The Leibnizian tradition stands in contrast to the English empiricist tradition that depicts the mind as passive, building up knowledge by receiving and copying sense impressions as if it were clay to be molded (compare Skinner's term "shaping"). Because Americans are raised in the empiricist tradition, it is hardly surprising that Piaget's theory may strike us as odd and hard to understand.

The other main reason for misunderstanding Piaget is less often acknowledged: In an important sense Piaget—despite collecting data and theorizing about cognition—was not a psychologist at all. He called what he did **genetic epistemology,** the study of the origins (genesis) of knowledge (epistemology), specifically in child development. But the term *epistemology* needs closer attention, because it was Piaget's concerns as an epistemologist that led to his developmentalism.

Epistemology is the branch of philosophy concerned with knowledge— what it is and how we acquire it. Naively, we think that knowledge is true belief; I can say I *know* that George Washington was the first President because it is true. But this cannot be all that knowledge is. On an American history test you might be asked, "Who was the third President?," and be unable to remember. So you recall the name of the only President after

Washington and before Lincoln you can remember, namely, Jefferson, and write that down. The answer happens to be correct, but we would not say that you knew Jefferson was the third President even though you expressed the true belief that he was. Philosophers concede that knowledge is more than simply true belief, but what that "more" is remains elusive. Some have even given up the quest altogether and asserted that there is no knowledge, only workable beliefs that may nevertheless eventually be proven wrong. This was the view of the Scottish philosopher David Hume and the American philosopher and psychologist William James, so it is part of Americans' intellectual heritage.

Piaget, however, is among those philosophers who have not given up the quest, and he proposes his genetic epistemology as an answer to this central problem of epistemology. One old candidate (going back to Plato) for what is needed to make true belief knowledge is *provable certainty*. To count as knowledge, something must have the character of a mathematical or logical theorem—it can be proven true by deductive logic (see Chapter 9).

Manifestly, any generalization from experience cannot have this characteristic of provable certainty, as David Hume showed in the eighteenth century. No matter how confident I may be that all swans are white from having examined 2000 of them, I must realize that I could be wrong, that the 2001*st* swan may be some other color. Therefore, while experience may yield up true beliefs, it cannot yield up knowledge.

Another move in the search for knowledge was tried by many thinkers from Plato down to the present. It is to claim that human knowledge is *innate*. So, for example, the eighteenth-century Scottish philosopher Thomas Reid (1710–1796) held that humans possess God-given beliefs and cognitive processes, which, since God made us in His image, cannot be mistaken. These, therefore, constitute knowledge.

However, in light of modern evolutionary theory such a comfortable nativism is no longer convincing. Whatever human propensities and abilities may be innate, they were selected by the nondirective happenstances of natural and sexual selection. They are not necessarily true; had our ancient ecology been different, our human nature would be different. In a sense, innate ideas are not very different from ideas drawn from experience—useful, but the product of whatever experience our ancestors had and therefore not certain, not knowledge.

Now none of this need bother a psychologist; he or she can study what's innate and what's learned without caring whether our beliefs are ultimately true or not. In this the psychologist would resemble Hume or James. But Piaget, even as a teenager, wanted certainty, and his genetic epistemology is in his view a third way to knowledge through development rather than through learning or heredity.

Piaget proposes that cognitive development unfolds in much the way a logical argument unfolds, step by step in a logically necessary sequence of stages and substages. The child's cognitive structures might be regarded at any moment as a set of logical premises. Experience provides information that chldren can use to make deductions from their premises, resulting in a new set of premises or logical structures, from which further deductions are made in the light of experience, and so on until an adequate set of structures is achieved that can deal effectively and creatively with the environment.

If Piaget is correct, then the making of deduction after deduction from given cognitive structures, or premises, has the character of a logical argument, moving step by step to a provably certain conclusion. In short, cognitive development is the construction of knowledge. We see, then, that it is his epistemological concerns that led Piaget to postulate autonomous developmental forces beside maturation (nativism) and experience (empiricism), and it is these concerns, together with his inheritance of the Leibnizian tradition, that can make him so hard to understand.

The process of development   Piaget's area of earliest interest and university training was biology, so he brought a strong biological, adaptationist influence to developmental psychology, in addition to his philosophical aims.* In fact, his goal was to make epistemology a science along biological lines. He viewed intelligence—cognitive structures and processes—as an organ of biological adaptation like the hand or the eye. The only unique thing about intelligence as an adaptation is that it is mental and behavioral rather than morphological. Intelligence, especially human intelligence, is the most powerful organ of adaptation there is, and we reflected on its evolutionary origins in Chapter 10. Piaget is concerned with the evolution of intelligence in the individual child as he or she attains mature cognition, perfect adaptation to the environment, and certain knowledge.

Piaget draws a sharp and significant distinction between physical (or *empirical*) and *logico-mathematical* knowledge, which correspond to *learning* and *development* respectively (see Fig. 13–1). Empirical knowledge has to do with facts—knowledge of the outside world—and how we represent them internally, which Piaget calls *figurativity*. Logico-mathematical knowledge has to do with our actions on the world or its internal representations, which Piaget calls *operativity* in an unconscious echo of Skinner's coinage "operant." Both Piaget and Skinner thereby emphasize an organism's activity and study how it operates on the world it lives in.

The source of empirical knowledge is experienced objects. As we perceive and interact with the objects in our environment we learn about them through *perception* and the cognitive process of **empirical abstraction,** which gives rise to concepts. For example, a child meets many small furry animals and must learn to group them into distinct conceptual categories

---

*The following discussion of Piaget's theory is based primarily on the following sources: Piaget (1963, 1965, 1967a, 1967b, 1969, 1970a, 1970b, 1971a, 1971b, 1971c, 1972, 1973, 1976); Piaget and Inhelder (1969a, 1969b, 1969c, 1971, 1973); Inhelder and Piaget (1958). Secondary sources consulted include Elkind and Flavell (1969); Baldwin (1980), Furth (1969). An interesting attempt to picture Piaget as a learning theorist is Gallagher and Reid (1981). A good single source for reading Piaget is Gruber and Voneche (1977), which contains extracts from Piaget's leading work over his entire lifetime, together with thoughtful and insightful commentary.

PROCESSES OF TRANSFORMATION

TYPE OF CHANGE	TYPE OF KNOWLEDGE	SOURCE	TYPE OF ABSTRACTION	BEHAVIORAL BASIS	MENTALIZATION PROCESS	MENTAL UNITS	PROCESS OF CHANGE
Learning	Empirical Field of Figurativity	Objects	Empirical	Perception	Internalization	Schemas (Representations, Concepts)	Learning
Development	Logico-mathematical Field of Operativity	Actions	Reflective	Schemes (Abstracted actions)	Interiorization	Operations (Mental actions)	Assimilation Accommodation Equilibration

FIGURE 13-1 Processes and units of learning and development in Piaget's theory. Terms *internalization* and *interiorization* are Furth's (1969) clarifications of Piaget's French usage.

such as dog, cat, and gerbil. Each class will have features in common with the others—dogs, cats, and gerbils are all furry; all of them eat, drink, and move; many are brown. Other features distinguish each class from the others. Dogs chase cats and cats chase gerbils; dogs bark, cats meow, and gerbils (occasionally) squeak. What the child does is to abstract from each particular animal the features that define its class, and so builds up a concept of DOG, of CAT, of GERBIL. This process Piaget calls *empirical* (sometimes *physical*) *abstraction*, because it is an abstraction from the perceived physical world. The child is also able to represent the world internally, both as memory of his particular experiences (for example, an image of a pet gerbil) and as concepts representing general classes (what gerbils are). Developing representations is an *internalization* of one's experience, and the representations themselves are called *schemas*. This represents *learning* for Piaget.

Now while this kind of knowledge is important, useful, and adaptive, it is less important than logico-mathematical knowledge to Piaget. To begin with, it falls short of the universality Piaget seeks in true knowledge. Indian children learn about *dacoits*, *dhotis*, and Krishna, while American children learn about muggers, suits, and Jehova: Empirical knowledge—facts—are culture-specific and particular. More importantly, facts are meaningless and unlearnable without actions and cognitive processes, and these change over time while objects do not. To an infant, a gerbil is an interesting moving object; to a six-year-old it is a beloved pet coming from a mysterious place called Mongolia; to a biology student a gerbil is a member of the class of rodents along with mice and rats, with certain unique properties resulting from its evolution in a specific ecological niche. So Piaget rejects the copy theory; concepts and schemas are not simply given by experience impressing itself on a child, but depend on the child's preexisting and changing cognitive structures. Piaget's work has concentrated on these cognitive structures that he believes are human universals that pass through an invariant sequence of development.

Cognitive structures comprise human logico-mathematical knowledge and are rooted in action rather than the perception of objects. Piaget tells a story about a mathematician friend of his who, as a child, had a great insight one day playing with pebbles. The boy found that if he lined up ten pebbles in a row, he had ten; if he changed the line to a circle, still ten; to a square, still ten. He discovered what Piaget calls *conservation of number*, that no matter how a group of objects is arranged, their number remains the same. This piece of knowledge is logico-mathematical knowledge, and it is far more general and certain than empirical knowledge, for it is capable of proof and applies to pebbles, rocks, bricks, children, *dacoits*, U.S. Senators, and stars.

Naturally, the boy was gaining empirical knowledge about the pebbles, too. He had schemas (images) of the pebbles he was using, and doubtless had a schema (concept) of the PEBBLE, abstracting away the features common to all pebbles. But the generalization about conservation of number did not derive from the pebbles, since the same insight could have come from playing with leaves, Lego pieces, toy soldiers or pieces of candy.

Piaget maintains that logico-mathematical knowledge is an abstraction, called **reflective abstraction,** from a child's actions. The young mathematician could have arranged pebbles, leaves, Lego pieces the same way, and what would be the same in each case, and therefore abstractable as a generalization, is the acts of arranging and counting, getting the same number in each configuration. Again, observe that the actions, like conservation of number, are quite general, applying to any countable objects, and operative on the world. Logico-mathematical knowledge is operative knowledge and constitutes an organ of adaptation, because it is able to deal effectively with virtually every concrete situation and is not limited to any given context or culture.

Reflective abstraction creates two units of operative intelligence corresponding to sensori-motor, or behavioral, and mental intelligence, respectively; these units are the *scheme* and the *operation.* Schemes are sensorimotor ways of knowing the world by direct perception or action. Attentive looking or grasping qualify as schemes. Schemes are rather like Skinnerian operants, in that they are defined by their consequences or purposes, not by their topography. Thus, schemes, like operants, are not specific muscle movements but are purposive actions. Piaget (1963) describes an incident involving his infant daughter, Jacqueline, that illustrates how schemes are to be understood. Piaget arranged a mobile over her crib and tied one end of a string to the mobile and taped the other end to her right arm. Like all infants, Jacqueline would wiggle; she discovered that her wiggling would jerk the mobile about, which she found fascinating. After a great deal of trial and error she learned to move the mobile just by pulling on the string with her right arm. Piaget then taped the string to the left arm. If Jacqueline had acquired only a specific muscular response, she would have had to relearn it with her left arm. However, she immediately began to use her left arm to work the mobile, showing that she had learned something more general and goal-defined, namely, a scheme.

Schemes provide the original behavioral foundations of later mental actions. Schemes operate on immediately given physical objects; objects are internalized into mental schemas, and as such they are subject to mental action by *interiorized* schemes, called *operations.* For example, infants "classify" objects by what can be done to them—that is, what schemes apply to them. Some objects can be sucked on, others hit, some picked up, and so on. This constitutes a primitive, sensory-motor sort of classification of objects into overlapping classes. Piaget believes that this sensory-motor "classification" becomes interiorized and more general, providing the cognitive structures underlying classification of objects under conceptual heads in later childhood and adulthood. As he does with all thought, Piaget thus views classification as action—mental action—whereby objects are actively sorted into groups; classes are not given by nature and imposed on a passive organism.

The adaptive virtue of operations as opposed to schemes—and therefore the source of the evolutionary advantage—is that they make possible mental trial-and-error learning, enhancing adaptive coping. At the sensorimotor level one can only act and then discover—perhaps to one's great, even fatal cost—that the act was unwise. Operations encourage prudence, because one can try out a line of action (operations) on one's mental world (schemas), estimating its likelihood of success or failure. Piaget calls this the *precorrection of errors* made possible by operational thought.

Individual schemes and operations develop because of two processes, **assimilation** and **accommodation**. Assimilation and accommodation come into play when a child (or adult) encounters a new object or situation requiring adaptive mastery. Piagetian organisms, being active learners, seek out new learning opportunities, boldly going where they have not been before. *Assimilation* refers to the organism bringing a new object, concept, or situation within the competence of its schemes or operations. An infant coming across a keyring for the first time (infants find them fascinating) fumbles with it for a while until it can securely grasp it, rattle it, and pass it from hand to hand (all schemes). This process may take days, and to the Piagetian-informed parent is fascinating to watch. When all these things can be done smoothly and competently, the object is assimilated to the schemes and will soon become boring.

At a more mature level, you fumbled with the concept "parental investment" until you mastered it (we hope), thereby assimilating it to your operations. Neither you nor the baby was unchanged during all of this. The infant's schemes were tested and refined by the encounter with the keyring, improving its adaptive fit to the environment and better equipping it for future challenges. Encountering "parental investment" tested and refined your intellectual operations, improving your adaptive fit to your academic environment, and better equipping you for future challenges whether in psychology or in marriage. A change to schemes and operations taking place during an adaptive learning encounter Piaget calls *accommodation*, which always takes place alongside assimilation. In fact, Piaget maintains that while we can conceptually separate them, assimilation and accommodation are inextricably intertwined in the actual development of infant, child, and adult.

There is one final development process, shown in Figure 13–1, **equilibration.** Equilibration is the master *developmental* process, lying behind assimilation and accommodation and being responsible for transitions between Piaget's well-known stages of cognitive development. As for theorists of evolution, so with development for Piaget: He needs to find a motor to move it forward. In evolution, the orthodox motor (Chapter 10) of the neo-Darwinians is the struggle for existence and natural selection. In development, the common alternatives are maturation, espoused by nativists (Piaget calls them *preformationists*) or the environment, which simply shapes the organism through learning, according to empiricists and behaviorists.

We have seen that for Skinner the process of learning is the same as the process of evolution, selection by the environment among random variations emitted by organisms. Piaget agrees that evolution and development (not learning) are based on the same process, but seeks, as usual, a *via media* between learning and maturation, proposing a basic process quite different from Skinner's: *equilibration* (Piaget, 1971a, 1978). Equilibration refers to what Piaget also calls the *auto-regulation* of behavior and behavior change. He maintains with Lamarck that organisms do not just respond passively to a selecting environment, but actively strive to improve their adaptation. They seek not just an adequate level of adaptation, but the best adaptation possible (Flanagan, 1983). Auto-regulation (a term Piaget in his last works preferred to equilibration; Furth, 1969/1981) captures what Piaget means—organisms regulate their own behavior, their own adaptive fit; it is not blindly imposed on them by either environment (as empiricists argue) or genes (as maturationists say).

Cognitive development is driven by equilibration: assimilation and accommodation, reflective abstraction, and interiorization are all processes that alter the child's understanding, schemes, and operations in search of superior logico-mathematical knowledge, which uses the facts and concepts gleaned from experience. Therefore, equilibration and its various processes of logico-mathematical development are far more important than learning in accounting for intellectual development; from first to last it is equilibration that shapes perception, concept formation, and behavior. Auto-regulation is also responsible for the general restructuring of logico-mathematical knowledge that occurs three times in a child's life. Piaget believes that logico-mathematical knowledge can be described as a set of logical structures of schemes and/or operations, and that these structures are assembled in distinct ways at different points in cognitive development, moving from immediate, context-bound knowledge to abstract, context-free creative knowledge. Each structured ensemble of logico-mathematical structures defines a distinct *stage* in cognitive development.

Stages of development. Thinking of development in terms of *stages*, is quite common, occurring in all the developmentalists surveyed in this chapter. The intuitive appeal of stages is evident in our common-sense usage: We divide life into infancy, childhood, adolescence, adulthood, and old age. However, we mean by these things no more than convenient descriptions—"the terrible twos"—and do not take them to be real entities in any fundamental sense. But Piaget does; his stages are proposed as psychological realities, not convenient sketches of age-typical behavior. See Table 13–1. You may investigate stages of development by doing the simple experiment described in Box 13–1.

TABLE 13–1   Piaget's Stages of Intellectual Development

I.   SENSORI-MOTOR INTELLIGENCE (0 TO 24 MOS.)

Adaptation is "practical," oriented to the here and now, based on behavioral schemes only—few if any mental representations present. Interiorization, coordination, and enriching of sensorimotor schemes provide basis for operational thought. Six substages:

1   *Modification of innate reflexes* (0 to 1 mos.)   Initially fixed S-R reflexes become adaptive schemes as they assimilate objects and accommodate reality.

2   *Acquisition of new habits* (1 to 4 mos.)   First new schemes, *primary circular*

TABLE 13–1 (*Continued*)

reactions, learned. Child discovers some behavior centering on its own body that has interesting effects (for example sucking a thumb) and it learns to reinstate it.

3 *Secondary circular reactions* (4 to 10 mos). Reinstatement of interesting effect taking place in outside world (for example, Jacqueline and the mobile). First signs of *object concept*; for example, child will now continue to track the trajectory of a previously visible, now occluded, object.

4 *Coordination of secondary schemes* (4 to 12 mos.) First indication of true intentional intelligence and first step toward general knowledge. Infant can now detach an old scheme from its familiar context (for example, hitting things to see them move or hear them make noise) and use it as a means to a more remote end (for example, striking an obstacle to the grasping of an interesting object). Object concept much more developed: Child will now search for a vanished object, showing it now knows that objects continue to exist even when they cannot be sensed.

5 *Tertiary circular reactions* (12 to 18 mos.) Secondary circular reactions with systematic variation to explore the effect of behavior on the world instead of just repeating an old effect, as before. New schemes invented on the spot to solve problems instead of use of older scheme in new context.

6 *Beginnings of thought* (18 to 24 mos.) Transition to next major stage as semiotic function—the ability to represent mentally—begins to appear, insightful problem solution—the result of the precorrection of errors—now possible as solutions are first tried mentally before being translated into behavior. Full development of the object concept as child can now infer location of a hidden object from witnessing a series of both visible and invisible displacements.

II PREOPERATIONAL INTELLIGENCE (2 TO 7 YRS.)

With the acquisition of the semiotic function (marked by appearance of delayed imitation, symbolic play (pretending), drawing, mental images, and above all by language acquisition) real thinking, the manipulation of a mental world begins. During this period, schemes are interiorized into operations as concrete operational intelligence is constructed. Two substages.

A *Preconceptual* (2 to 4 yrs.) Interiorization of schemes just beginning, so that a child can do many things in reality but not with representations. For example, a four-year-old may be able to navigate a path between its house and nursery school, but be unable to tell anyone else how to do it, even with the aid of a realistic map on which are set the principle landmarks.

B *Intuitive*, or *Functional* (5 to 7 yrs.) Operations beginning to appear but are not yet integrated and coordinated into an overall logical structure. Child intuitively understands certain functional relations but fails tests of deeper understanding. For example, shown a nail driven into a board with a string running around it at right angles such as this:

The child understands that if one pulls on the end of string at A, the distance B-C will shorten and vice-versa, i.e., that lengths A-C and B-C are functionally (in-

TABLE 13–1   (*Continued*)

versely) related. But this understanding is not fully coordinated, for the child will deny that the total length of the string A-C is unchanged by moving the string around the nail. Child does not yet *conserve* length.

III   CONCRETE OPERATIONAL INTELLIGENCE (7 TO 12 YRS.)

Appearance of logically integrated thought. The logic at this stage is the logic of classes, similar to formal syllogistic logic. That is, the child can reason about logically defined classes defined over *objects* (hence, *concrete* operational), and can represent (and internally manipulate) concrete, familiar, objects competently and adaptively, so errors are precorrected. Two substages.

A   (8 to 9 yrs.)   Operations coordinated into a logical system. Onset best marked by the first appearance of the *conservations*, the knowledge that physical quantities do not change despite changes in appearance. An example is conservation of amount, or continuous quantity. A child is shown two identical glasses filled with identical amounts of water, A_1 and A_2, and an empty vessel B, much narrower but taller than A. The water in A_2 is poured into B, and the child is asked if there is still the same amount in A_1 and B. At IIA, the child denies this, claiming B has more because it's taller. At IIB the child may answer correctly but be unable to justify its response, even though it does conserve the water's identity, recognizing that the water in B is the same water that was in A_2; it was merely poured. At IIIA, the child can justify its response.

B   (10 to 12 yrs.)   Continuation of the consolidation of concrete operations into an equilibrated system; more conservations mastered. Limitations to concrete logic can be seen. Most importantly, the child cannot think *hypothetically* about all the things that might be done in a given situation so that they might be explored systematically. For example, given a set of clear liquid chemicals and told that some combination of them will produce a yellow color, the child proceeds haphazardly, combining pairs of chemicals at random (never trying three), so that even if the solution is achieved, it likely cannot be explained or repeated. Possibility is still subordinate to reality.

IV   FORMAL OPERATIONAL INTELLIGENCE (12 YRS. ON)

Operations become yet more abstract and formal, dealing not with objects at all but with formally stated relations or hypotheses. The logic of this stage is *propositional* logic, in which what is understood and manipulated are not classes of objects (concepts) but whole statements or propositions. The power of this stage is that in language—propositions—one can state anything, whether true or false, real or imaginary, so that reality becomes just an instantiation of one among many possible worlds. Einstein's elevator (Box 13–2) is an excellent example of formal thinking at its best. Adolescents' involvement with novel political systems, utopias, and their identity crises are partly the outcome of formal operational thinking, as the teenager is both exhillarated and confused by what he or she and society may be, and angry and resentful of what he or she and society are. Reality becomes subordinate to possibility, and the imagined possible gleams like utopia from the future. But remember, u-topia means "no-where."

Substages are not clearly marked, but around 12 years the child shows the ability

TABLE 13–1   (*Continued*)

to think hypothetically. In the chemical combination task the subject of formal operations will work systematically through all possible combinations, keeping records of what was done as all possibilities are exhausted. He or she will be able to explain his or her strategy and repeat the solution if asked. There is now a great deal of evidence, some of it reviewed in the chapter (9) on Thinking, that for most (perhaps all) people, formal operational thinking remains more an occasionally reached ideal than an everyday actuality, manifesting itself only in familiar domains, but not everyday in every decision. This may be just as well, since weighing all possible *pros* and *cons* of every decision is probably not adaptive. It is said that the great philosopher Immanuel Kant—a formal operational reasoner, surely— took so long to weigh the *pros* and *cons* of marriage that by the time he decided to propose, his intended was already wed!

One final note on Piaget's stages. The ages given are approximations only, and are not to be taken as norms in any sense. There will be wide individual variation from child to child in the speed with which the stages are traversed. What matters to Piaget is the invariant sequence of the stages, not their age of acquisition.

BOX 13–1   Tilting a Bottle: Procedure

One interesting pencil-and-paper Piagetian task that is easily done is his water-level problem.

Draw a picture of a table from a side view, with a glass on it, as shown in Figure 13–2.

FIGURE 13-2

Now draw a bottle or pitcher pouring water into the glass, and be sure to show some water remaining in the bottle or pitcher. Collect as many as possible such drawings from friends and classmates before reading Box 13– 3, which discusses the usual results.

BOX 13–2   Einstein's Elevator

When formal operations are achieved anything becomes possible in thought. Piaget emphasizes that the great power of formal operational thought lies in how it subordinates reality to possibility. While most of us may make little use of this power, merely imagining pleasant things that cannot be, in a genius with scientific discipline it may build possible worlds that turn out, however unlikely to common sense, to be our world. The finest example is the vivid imagination of Albert Einstein. Einstein obtained many of his insights through *Gedankenexperimenten* (thought-experiments): imaginary worlds created in his mind rigorously manipulated to produce deep insights into the nature of reality.

In one of his famous thought-experiments, Einstein imagined an elevator in empty space, drawn upward by an imaginary genie pulling a rope of infinite length at a constant acceleration producing a downward force of 1_g (i.e., 1 gravity, equal to the force of gravity at the earth's surface).

A person standing in Einstein's elevator would be unable to tell if he or she were at rest in the earth's surface or under 1_g acceleration in empty space. Reasoning that if two forces have the same observable effects they are really the same force, Einstein concluded that gravity and the force exerted by acceleration were the same, and he derived a stunning prediction from his imaginary elevator.

The elevator is moving through space at a constant acceleration. Imagine now a hole cut in the side of the elevator through which we shine a beam of light. Because the elevator is moving, what happens, as seen by the person shooting the beam of light at time 1 (t_1) is shown in Figure 13–3.

That is, the person sees a straight beam of light enter the elevator and strike the other side at a point some distance down from the point opposite the entry hole. It is just as if someone threw a ball into the open front driver's window of a moving car—it wouldn't pass out the passenger's window, but land in the back seat.

However, the elevator's passenger sees what is shown in Figure 13–4. Relative to his or her perspective the light has taken a curved path, as the thrown ball would to the car's occupants.

Now, if accelerational force and gravity are the same force, and since light bends for a viewer influenced by accelerational force, it should also bend in the presence of gravity. Of course the bending in our illustrations is

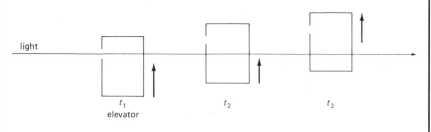

FIGURE 13-3

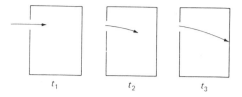

FIGURE 13-4

much exaggerated—light is very fast—but Einstein's proposition can be tested by looking at light rays from distant stars as they pass near the Sun and through its strong gravitational field. Such observations have been made, and they accord well with Einstein's precise mathematical predictions.

Even without the mathematics, we can appreciate—and marvel at—Einstein's disciplined but playful use of formal operational thought. In accord with simple assumptions, he imagined a conceptually possible (if practically impossible), little universe from which he drew a strong, counterintuitive proposition that was brought back to the actual world and proved. Einstein himself always explained his mind in terms of visualizing possible worlds, not in terms of mathematical equations; they came later and tidied up and made rigorous insights achieved in thought-experiments.[*]

[*]Read Albert Einstein and Leopold Infeld, *The Evolution of Physics*. New York: Simon & Schuster, 1954.

BOX 13–3 Tilting a Bottle: Results

When Piaget asked children to do a task similar to that described in Box 13–2, he reported results as shown in Figure 13–5.

Interestingly, however, when groups of adults are given this problem (having been a subject once, one of us (THL) has done this as a class demonostration for years) few of them get it right. Although no one gives the preschooler's response (Stage I), their responses cover Piaget's entire range of drawings, the most common being the IIB drawing and the IIB–IIIA drawings.

Piaget interpreted his results as reflecting *decentration*, the increasing ability of children to consider an ever larger frame of reference for their activities. The young child of five focuses (*centers*) narrowly on the bottle itself, defines the frame of reference for water level as the sides of the bottle, and maintains the familiar right-angle relationship of water surface and bottle side of a bottle standing up, even when the child is drawing a tilted bottle. This centration only gradually breaks up through intermediate stages, as the child realizes that something happens to the water's surface, but cannot yet grasp the correct frame of reference. That frame of reference is the surface of the earth: Water responds to gravity and so maintains a surface parallel to the ground whatever the orientation of the bottle.

If your results are typical, you caught many subjects' cognitive processes napping. Clearly a moment's reflection would reveal the absurdity of one's

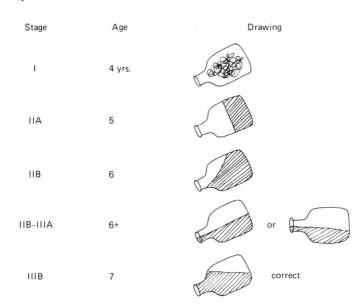

Stage	Age	Drawing	
I	4 yrs.		
IIA	5		
IIB	6		
IIB-IIIA	6+		or
IIIB	7		correct

FIGURE 13-5   From Piaget and Inhelder (1948/1967).

response to an adult who drew a Stage II drawing, but it appears that when they are not careful, people lapse back into earlier forms of thought. Such findings suggest again that real-world reasoning is a mixed bag of hunches, fancies, and misconceptions tainting a larger set of correct information processed in a rather haphazard fashion.[*]

[*] Read Jean Piaget and Bärbel Inhelder, *The Child's Conception of Space*, New York: Norton, 1967 (Originally published 1948.)

Piaget has offered various criteria for defining true stages, and they have been usefully assembled by Pinard and Laurendeau (1969), Brainerd (1978a,b), and Flanagan (1983):

1. Each stage must be *qualitatively different and more complex* from the previous stage. Piaget maintains that the growth of knowledge is more than the slow accumulation of facts and skills, but that the *way* children think at a given stage is qualitatively different from other stages. So at IIB there is a logic of functions, at IIIB a logic of classes, and at IV a logic of propositions.

2. Each stage is *more adequate*, that is, more adaptive, than the previous one.

3. The stages must follow each other in an ordered sequence such that
   a   the sequence is *culturally universal*
   b   it occurs in the *same order* for everyone
   c   all normal children *reach the last stage*
   d   there is *never regression* from a higher to a lower stage.

4. Each stage subsumes and integrates the abilities of the previous stage. The stages thus form a *hierarchy* such that formal operations includes and reintegrates concrete operations, which includes and reintegrates functional and sensori-motor structures. Abilities from earlier stages are not lost or erased, therefore, but take a new place in the higher form of intelligence.

5. Each stage's schemes and operations form a *structured whole*. The schemes and operations do not exist simply as a collection of loosely connected parts but are integrated into a larger, overall structure, that is, the logic of classes or the logic of propositions.

Taken together, Piaget's claims assert that the development of intelligence is not a continuous process of growth, but is marked by leaps from one mode of knowing to a distinct, more adequate one, and that these leaps are made by all individuals in all cultures without backward steps. While development is thus not continuous, it is cumulative, since the structures of earlier stages are not abolished by later ones, but are restructured into a new and more adaptive way of knowing.

Criticisms of Genetic Epistemology

Piaget's genetic epistemology has naturally attracted a great deal of criticism, ranging from accusations of poor design and sloppy methodology (Gruen, 1966) to findings that his formulation of symbolic logic is inadequate (Parsons, 1960). Here, we will focus on attacks on Piaget's stage concept of development. Followers of Piaget have termed it a "key" part of the overall theory (Pinard & Laurendeau, 1969), and stage-thinking is characteristic of developmentalists generally. The central developmental force of equilibration is closely tied to the stages, for stage transitions come about because of equilibration, not learning. The postulation of real, explanatory stages is therefore perhaps the major issue that separates developmentalists from nondevelopmentalists.

Beginning with the simpler and more testable criteria, those concerning the ordered sequence of stages, we find that the empirical evidence is mixed. Criteria 3a and 3b from the list of criteria defining a true stage theory say the stage sequence must be culturally universal, and most cross-cultural Piagetian research indicates that children do pass through the stages up through concrete operations in the same sequence, with the speed of acquisition varying from culture to culture, usually as a function of degree of Westernization (Dasen, 1972). However, reaching the stage of formal operations is *not* a cross-culturally universal achievement, and the findings we discussed in Chapter 9 (Thinking) suggest that formal operations are not routinely used even by scientists. Therefore, criterion 3c is not met, formal operations remaining an ideal to be aimed at, rather than a realistically achievable goal. Criterion 3d states there must be no regression from a higher stage to a lower. Temporary regression has been observed by Inhelder, Sinclair, and Bovet (1974) in experiments challenging the thought of early concrete operational children, by replicators of Piaget's memory studies (Liben, 1977), and suggested by a cross-sectional study of acquisition of conservation of liquid problems (Leahey, 1977c). While permanent regression would be a serious blow to Piaget's theory, temporary regressions may be only a sign of confused thought during the restructuring of cognitive structures taking place at stage transitions. On the other hand, an information-processing perspective could see temporary regressions as similar to overgeneralization phenomena in language acquisition when learning a new rule leads to apparent loss of mastery of irregular forms. So regression could be the result of an incremental learning process and not a mark of stage boundaries. On the whole, data regarding criterion 3 is equivocal, offering neither clear support nor disproof of Piaget's stage hypothesis.

Criterion 2 claims that each stage is more adequate than the previous one. This criterion is more philosophical than empirical, and seems uncontroversial (Flanagan, 1983). Piaget's stages are so constituted that if they are real, clearly formal operations are more adequate—more adaptive—than concrete operations, which in turn is better than preoperational thinking, which in turn, is an advance over sensory-motor intelligence.

The remaining criteria—that the stages are *qualitatively different* (1), that they form a *hierarchy* (4), and that each stage's structures form a *structured whole* (5)—are much more difficult to test and have been the subject of much controversy (Brainerd, 1978b, and subsequent commentary). Most observers agree that taken together, these criteria suggest that stages should appear relatively abruptly, as equilibration restructures thinking according to a new logic now applied to all experience. Three lines of research have been brought to bear on this empirical prediction: training studies, studies modifying the content of the standard Piagetian tasks, and studies of horizontal *decalages*, differences in the ages at which the same children master closely related cognitive tasks.

When Piaget attracted the attention of American psychologists during the cognitive revolution of the 1960s, they asked him a question that had not arisen during decades of research in Europe. The "American question," as Piaget called it, was: "How can we make the stages go faster?" Besides illustrating the American character, this question raises important issues about the unity of the stages (criterion 5) and the reality of equilibration. For if mastery of some Piagetian task (for example, conservation of liquid) can be taught, it would undermine the concept of stages as structured wholes—only a single task is mastered—and support a learning as opposed to an equilibration account of development. Success in training would also suggest that various cognitive skills are learned piecemeal rather than appearing as part of an overall stage change.

For both practical and theoretical reasons, therefore, studies attempting to train children on Piagetian tasks became very popular (Brainerd & Allen, 1971) and were even carried out at Geneva by Inhelder and her colleagues (Inhelder and others, 1974). Overall, the studies show that a wide variety of techniques can be used to turn preoperational into operational reasoners for some skill area in a short period of time. However, interpreting these findings is difficult, since the results may be assimilated to Piagetian theory, and because there may be differences between trained and untrained children despite superficial similarities (Cromer, 1981).

Consider the classic training experiment by Smedslund (1961/1968), who trained children on *conservation of weight*. In the standard Piagetian form, a child is shown two identical balls of clay that the child acknowledges to be of the same weight. Then one ball is transformed, typically by rolling it into a sausage, and the question is repeated. The preoperational subject will now deny equality of weight, usually claiming that the sausage shape is lighter because longer, even when the child can pick up the pieces. The concrete operational child conserves weight, pointing out that the experimenter only altered the appearance of the clay, not its weight.

Smedslund pretested children on the standard task and then put the nonconservers through a training phase in which he used a balance to demonstrate several times that weight is unaffected by shape, the two pieces of clay remaining equal in weight before and after transformation. The nonconservers came to say that weight remains unchanged in the standard task. Smedslund now repeated the standard task with all subjects, except he secretly removed some clay during the transformation and used the balance to show a difference in weight. Smedslund found that trained conservers quickly reverted to nonconservation, concluding that sometimes weight *does* change when shape is changed. Natural conservers, on the other hand, stood their ground, insisting that weight *must* remain the same and that the experimenter must have somehow cheated.

Smedslund's results suggest that even if a training program appears to be successful, it may have had only a surface effect, engaging a child's verbal agreement but leaving untouched the deeper cognitive processes that change with development. Inhelder and co-workers (1974) argue, and provide data to show, that training can be successful only when, first the child is nearing stage transition anyway, and second, when it induces cognitive conflict by challenging the child's preoperational understanding. By creating disequilibrium, equilibration is brought into play, and the child is accelerated into operational structures. Therefore, the successful training studies can be explained as the creation of superficial verbal change or acceleration of a deeper change already underway.

Another empirical difficulty for the unified stage hypothesis is that different methods of assessment from those of Piaget's often find Piagetian concepts at much earlier ages than the standard tasks. For example, Gelman (1972) used conjuring techniques to violate conservation rules. Gelman found that very young children who failed ordinary number conservation tasks could detect when one penny was secretly removed from a small collection of coins (three or four), causing them to unfairly lose a game played with the experimenter, which indicates a sense of number conservation with small, but not large, arrays. There is now a large amount of data demonstrating similar effects for many Piagetian concepts (Gelman, 1978, 1983). Critics take such findings to indicate that concrete operational cognitive abilities are present very early in a child's life and grow slowly and incrementally, Piaget's apparently discrete stages being artifacts of his particular measurement tasks (Gelman, 1978; Donaldson, 1978). While these studies showed that some abilities appear much earlier than Piaget thought, other investigators found that adults do not understand some things they should (see Box 13–4).

BOX 13–4   Intuitive Physics

As children, most of us tied something heavy to a string, twirled it around our heads, and then let it go. How much do we actually *understand* about such a familiar bit of physics? Even if we learn to hit a target with our primitive sling, do we grasp the principles underlying our behavior? Figure 13–6 shows a man twirling a ball on a string and releasing it when the ball is at the point of the filled-in circle. Which path shown will the ball subsequently take, Path 1 (left) or Path 2 (right)?

Michael McCloskey (1983) asked college students this and other questions testing their intuitive knowledge of physics, specifically concerning the laws of objects in motion. Fifty-one percent correctly chose Path 1; 30 percent incorrectly chose Path 2, and 19 percent made other errors. Path 1 is correct because according to Newton's laws of motion an object once set in motion will continue in a straight line unless acted on by an outside force. As long as it is held, the string acts as such a force and the ball moves in a circle. When the string is released its constraining force vanishes and the ball moves in a straight line. Path 2 would be expected from medieval impetus theory, which held that the circular motion would persist after the string was released, resulting in a curved trajectory. In other experiments, McCloskey found that many, sometimes most, of his well-educated subjects' intuitive physics was closer to medieval natural philosophy than to modern physics. Even having passed physics courses did little to alter students' folk beliefs.

Such findings pose a special problem for Piagetian theory, especially its account of formal operations. For here are familiar situations (every child has spun objects on a string, thrown and caught balls, and dropped objects while moving, providing rich opportunities for accommodation, assimilation, and reflective abstraction), yet conscious understanding of such activities is

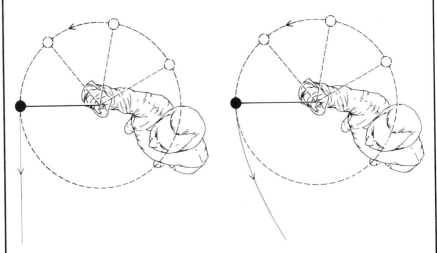

FIGURE 13-6   (From "Intuitive Physics," by Michael McCloskey, *Scientific American*. Copyright © 1983 by Scientific American, Inc. All rights reserved)

weak. They may be done—sensori-motorically—very well, even brilliantly as by sports stars, yet they are reflectively known very poorly.

In Piagetian terms, McCloskey's results provide further evidence that formal operations are not a universal achievement. Piaget has always held that at earlier stages consciousness knows only the products of cognitive operations, not the operations themselves. Here we see how hard it is for people to understand what they may do very well, and conscious understanding is a formal operational achievement.

More broadly, we again are reminded of the surprising gulf between behavior and insight. Much of what we do is learned effortlessly and without tuition. Yet being able to explain what we do, to understand it consciously, requires great effort, the insights of genius and deliberate education. And it is disappointing to the professor and scientist to find that years of education leave many young people back in the Middle Ages, behind Newton and far behind Einstein.[*]

[*]Read Michael McCloskey, "Intuitive Physics." *Scientific American*, April 1983, 248 (4) 122–130.

This problem is linked to the broader and most serious one of what Genevans call *horizontal decalages*, or differences in the age of acquisition of behaviors supposedly depending on the same operational structures. A well-established *decalage* involves the conservations, all of which depend on concrete operational structures, according to Piaget. Table 13–2 shows the sequence of acquisition—stretching over at least five years—for several physical quantity conservations. Observe that all the tasks have the same structure: two quantities are established as equal, the shape of one is changed, and the subject asked if the quantity is still the same. Conservation of substance and weight are especially similar, yet appear about three years apart. Even slight changes in the material used can change the child's response from nonconservation to conservation (Uzgiris, 1964/1968).

The existence of *decalages* such as these suggests that cognitive development is not a very stagelike affair, proceeding, instead, in an incremental, but still orderly, way. Many critics of Piaget's stage concept have simply concluded that his stages should be taken as descriptive only, and that equilibration is an unnecessary and seemingly mysterious force (Brainerd, 1974a, 1974b, 1978a, 1978b; Flavell, 1971, 1977; Flavell & Wohlwill, 1969; Toulmin, 1971; Macnamara, 1976). Some neo-Piagetians have backed away from the stage hypothesis, asserting that while invariant sequence in the acquisition is an important part of Piaget's theory, the existence of large comprehensive stages is not (Gruber & Voneche, 1977), or have moved toward an information-processing view of cognitive development (Cellerier, 1971; Inhelder, 1972). Whatever the fate of Piaget's stages, however, the general question of the existence of stages is not resolved as yet (Flavell, 1982; Cairns & Valsiner, 1984). Simply because one stage theory is mistaken, it does not follow that there are no stages to be found.

TABLE 13–2   *Decalage* in the Development of Physical Quantity Conservation Problems

APPROXIMATE AGE REQUIRED	TASK DESCRIPTION
1 6	*Conservation of discontinuous quantity* Child fills two identical vessels with the same number of discrete objects, such as marbles; experimenter pours contents of one glass into a differently shaped one and asks if contents still same in amount.
2 6½	*Conservation of substance* Child shown two identical balls of clay that he or she acknowledges to be the same in amount (or they are adjusted); experimenter transforms one ball into a sausage and asks if there is still just as much clay in each piece.
3 7	*Conservation of continuous quantity* Same as (1) except begin with vessels identically filled with a liquid.
4 9 to 10	*Conservation of weight* Same as (2) except questions concern weight of clay pieces.
5 10 to 11 (some data indicate concept not present in all college freshmen)	*Conservation of volume.* Begin with identical glasses of liquid and balls of clay. First ball placed in a glass; liquid level rises. Second ball deformed; subject asked (1) if deformed piece placed in glass how high will liquid rise? and (2) do the two pieces take up same amount of space?

Alternatives to Genetic Epistemology

Radical behaviorism.   The radical behaviorist approach to cognitive development is a straightforward application of the principles of operant learning reviewed in Chapter 4 (see Bijou & Baer, 1968; Bijou, 1976). No special principles of development are invoked; no explanatory stages are postulated. The child is viewed as an organism emitting responses that are shaped by reinforcement contingencies into the behaviors characteristic of the adult in the child's culture. From the standpoint of the experimental analysis of behavior, developmental psychology scarcely exists, since the developmental psychologist is simply a behavior analyst who has chosen to study children instead of animals or adults.

Information processing.   Since the early 1970s—Farnham-Diggory (1972) provides a useful starting point—information-processing concepts have been applied to cognitive development as cognitive science extended its influence over human experimental psychology. While as yet there is no generally accepted theory of development from this perspective, two lines of research have been pursued by cognitive scientists: writing information-processing accounts of Piagetian problems and studying the development of standard information-processing topics such as memory (Kail, 1984; Brainerd & Pressley, 1987).

As an example of the former approach (rethinking Piaget) we may take the work of Klahr and Wallace (1973, 1976; Klahr, 1984; Klahr, Langley, & Neches, 1987; Wallace, Klahr, & Bluff, 1987) on the development of conservation. They view conservation as the induction of general rules—statements of conservations—reflecting what is learned about the invariance of physical properties despite apparent transformations.

Klahr and Wallace endow the young information processor with three **quantification operators** whose operations provide the data base for learning conservation rules. The first operator to appear is *subitizing*, an innate quantifier which applies only to very small arrays of discrete objects, never more than four. Subjects presented with such small displays just see without counting that there are 1, 2, 3, or 4 objects, even with very brief display times. The next quantification operator is *counting*, dependent on social learning, applicable in principle to any array of discrete objects, but under time limitation abandoned in favor of the third operator, *estimation*: No one tries to count the beans in a jar of jelly beans. Estimation also applies to continuous quantities, such as liquid amount, which cannot be quantified by subitizing or counting.

In each of its domains, conservation rule learning develops in the folllowing manner. The child quantifies an array (for example, two rows of six jelly beans each, by counting), sees one altered, as in the usual Piagetian task, and quantifies again, getting the same result. Eventually, repeated experience leads to rule induction: Number (or whatever attribute is at issue) remains invariant despite changes in appearance. The motivation for forming conservation rules is *economy of processing*. Simply knowing that a property is conserved eliminates the need for constant quantifications and comparisons.

The rule-learning approach easily explains some of the data—particularly the *decalages*—so troublesome for Piaget. Since development is seen as gradual (the slow accumulation of conservation rules) there is no reason to be troubled by an absence of sharp stage boundaries. Moreover, the observed *decalages* fit well with the theory. Subitizing is the most primitive quantification operator, possessed before counting is taught, and we found that very young children conserve small arrays but not larger ones. At the other extreme, a quantity like *volume* is very hard to estimate and is the last conservation learned, while more tangible, estimatable quantities such as *weight* form a middle ground between number and volume.

The second kind of research done in cognitive development by information processors is to watch children doing the same thing researchers get adults to do: remember, pay attention, comprehend, and so on (Cairns & Valsiner, 1984). The picture that emerges is rather undevelopmental: Children are incompetent adults. That is, they possess (to use the computer metaphor quite strongly) all the wiring of the adult computer, but have yet to learn the control strategies to use it efficiently. To take a simple example, young (preoperational) children have short memory spans, about three or four items, because they have not learned to rehearse. If they are taught how, their memory spans leap up to the usual adult level—six or seven items. The short-term storage capacity of the adult was there, but was not being used (Hagen, 1972).

Nevertheless, even without stages and equilibration to worry about, the greatest challenge facing the cognitive scientist studying development is explaining how the processor changes (Sternberg, 1984). It is easy to write a simulation of the age 4 nonconserver and of the age 10 conserver; it is very much harder to get model 1 to change by itself into model 2, as the developing child does.

A sketch of an answer—it is no more than a sketch—has been essayed by Kail and Bisanz (1982). As we learned in earlier chapters, the major bottleneck in human information processing is the limited amount of attentional resources we have to allocate to different tasks. In the view of Kail and Bisanz, cognitive development is driven by dealing with this bottleneck, through maturational growth in total amount of resources (as the brain matures), or through increased availability of resources within an unchanging capacity as mental processes that were once conscious become unconscious and automatic—*automatized*—reducing their demand for attention.

Increased availability of attentional resources both facilitates and is made possible by **knowledge modification processes.** These are the agents of cognitive development, and they consist of two main operations; first, adding or deleting memory nodes and connections (representations) in LTM, or control processes; and second, strengthening or weakening connections in LTM. Change is abetted by the *performance monitors* that detect *inconsistencies* to be eliminated, such as believing whales are fishes while knowing they are warm blooded and nurse live-born young, or *regularities* that can be more simply handled, (as when a conservation rule is induced based on observed regularities in quantification operations), in the Klahr and Wallace model of conservation. Information-processing theories of cognitive development invoking similar mechanisms are offered by the authors collected by Sternberg (1984).

Cognitive schema theory has been applied to cognitive development by Vosniadou and Brewer (1987). Following Carey (1985), they distinguish between *global restructuring* of thought and *domain-specific restructuring* of thought. Piaget's theory of development through qualitatively different stages involves global restructuring, when the mode of thought of a new stage supplants the mode of thought of the previous stage. We have reviewed evidence that casts doubt on the stage concept, and like other information-processing theorists, Vosniadou and Brewer argue that development proceeds through restructuring of thought limited to specific content areas. In their view, development proceeds piecemeal, as children master different tasks and domains through experience and teaching.

As examples of domain-specific restructuring, Vosniadou and Brewer cite studies of the *novice-expert shift* carried out with adults. Cognitive scientists have studied in a variety of fields from chess to physics the differences between novices and experts. Two kinds of change seem to take place as one acquires expertise. *Weak restructuring* is the accumulation of knowledge in an area; *radical restructuring* involves the creation of new schemas to organize knowledge. Thus, experts are different from novices not only in how much they know about their field, but also in how they think about and perceive it. As information-processing theorists, Vosniadou and Brewer do not distinguish between child mind and adult mind, suggesting that cognitive development proceeds through the same kinds of domain-specific restructurings, both weak and radical, that characterize the novice-expert shift. In short, children are novices at everything, and become experts at adult life through episodes of domain-specific restructuring. Vosniadou and Brewer advocate teaching through analogy—application of familiar schemes to new domains, and Socratic dialogue—helping the child find and resolve inconsistencies in his or her understanding of a topic—as the best ways of fostering radical restructuring.

To what extent are information-processing theories of cognitive development truly developmentalist? Klahr (1984) argues that information-processing theories that posit self-modifying mechanisms of cognitive change, such as his, Kail and Bisanz's (1982), and Vosniadou and Brewer's, capture "the essence of development" and are not simply theories of learning. He points out that such models involve internally based mechanisms that produce spontaneous change not caused by reinforcement, and that the changes produced are qualitative and structural, not just quantitative and local. Thus Klahr's own theory of conservation acquisition posits an internal mechanism that monitors past and present quantitative transformations looking for consistencies that can be used to formulate conservation rules going beyond the currently given information.

Against Klahr's position, however, stand two important differences between information-processing theories and traditional developmentalist theories such as Piaget's. As we have seen, information-processing theories propose that cognitive change is domain-specific, not global, denying the existence of the stages that are the hallmark of developmentalist theorizing. More important, developmentalist theories are heirs to historicism, holding that development is guided toward a final goal by an autonomous process pressing thought to progress to the best possible cognitive adaptation. Information-processing theories are not teleological, seeking at best only adequate, not ideal, adaptation. Lacking a teleological drive for perfection, information-processing models are driven more by experience and teaching than are developmentalist models. Klahr is no doubt correct in asserting that self-modifying information-processing theories are more developmental than behaviorist-conditioning theories, but they are still much less developmental than Piaget's.

PERSONAL AND MORAL DEVELOPMENT

Although several of the most important developmentalist theories—Freud's, Erikson's, and Kohlberg's—fall somewhat outside the range of learning and cognition, they merit some attention precisely because they challenge standard notions of behavioral and cognitive learning. And, of course, we must remember that much of what a person learns in the course of development has to do with feelings, attitudes, and values, problems that ultimately even information-processing psychology will have to cope with.

Personality Development: Psychoanalysis

Sigmund Freud and biogenesis.[†]   Freud proposed a theory of development based on a concept that we know today to be false. It was, however, extremely popular in Freud's time, and some people still unwittingly believe it: Ernst Haeckel's biogenetic law. Haeckel was the leading nineteenth-century exponent of evolutionary theory in Germany, and his biogenetic law is based on Lamarck's theory of evolution in which species improve over time by accumulating favorably acquired traits learned by each generation. The biogenetic law stated that, "Ontogeny [the development of an individual] is a short and quick repetition, or recapitulation of Phylogeny [the evolution of a species] . . ." (quoted by Flanagan, 1981). Haeckel's law is (falsely) appealing because embryos do seem to pass through stages in which they resemble "lower" evolutionary forms. So a developing human embryo goes through a phase when it resembles a fish, then a lizard, then a lower mammal, and at the earliest stages of embryonic development different mammals resemble each other very closely, reflecting shared common ancestors, and resemble each other less at later stages of development, reflecting their ancestor's branching off the evolutionary tree (Sulloway, 1979). Haeckel also proposed that the units of heredity carry "unconscious memories" of the experiences of past ancestors; Freud took up this idea, turning it into a general theory of personality development that is very biological and maturational in character.

As is well known, Freud proposed a stage theory of human development (see Fig. 13–7), and he viewed the stages as the biogenetic unfolding of the past phylogenetic history of the human species. Freud is quite explicit on this. Speaking of the first (oral) stage of development and the attachment to the mother brought about by the infant's gratification at mother's breast,

---

[†] The importance of childhood and concepts of development are so important to psychoanalysis that they lie explicitly or implicitly in almost every line Freud wrote, but he never sat down and wrote on development per se. Certain works are, nevertheless, somewhat more developmental in their concerns than others, and these are: *Three Essays on the Theory of Sexuality, The Ego and the Id*, "Some Psychological Consequences of the Anatomical Distinction Between the Sexes," *A General Introduction to Psychoanalysis* (Chapters 20 to 23), *Civilization and Its Discontents* (Chapter 8), and *Outline of Psychoanalysis* (Chapters 3, 5, 7). Sigmund's daughter, Anna, became a great psychoanalyst in her own right, and prepared a work. *Psychoanalysis for Teachers and Parents*, which provides the sort of child-rearing tutoring her father seldom offered. She was also the major force behind the development of child analysis, and every year a new volume in the series *The Psychoanalytic Study of the Child* appears, containing papers on various aspects of developmental psychoanalysis.

Useful secondary sources include Rapaport (1960) and Talbott (1982), who review the analytic and neoanalytic approach to development, and Loevinger and Knoll (1983), who review the most recent data.

Finally, one should consult Frank Sulloway's (1979) tremendous *Freud: Biologist of the Mind* for a detailed study of Freud as a Lamarckian, biological developmentalist.

FIGURE 13–7 Three Stage Theories

APPROXIMATE AGE	ERIKSON			FREUD	PIAGET
	ZONE AND MODE	CRISIS	INSTITUTION		
Infancy 0–2	Oral-sensory	Basic trust vs. mistrust	Religion	Oral	Sensory-motor
Early childhood 2–3	Muscular-anal	Autonomy vs. shame and doubt	Law	Anal	Preoperational
Middle childhood 3–6	Locomotor-genital	Initiative vs. guilt	Economics	Phallic	
Late childhood 6–12	Latency	Industry vs. Inferiority	Technology	Latency	Concrete operational
Adolescence 12–18	Puberty and Adolescence	Identity vs. role confusion	Ideology and Aristocracy	Genital	Formal operational
Youth 18–25	Young adulthood	Intimacy vs. isolation	[Courtship]		
Adult & middle-age 25–65	Adulthood	Generativity vs. stagnation	[Education]		
65–	Maturity	Ego integrity vs. despair	[?]		

he wrote, "In all this the phylogenetic foundation has so much the upper hand over personal accidental experiences that it makes no difference whether a child has really sucked at the breast or has been brought up on the bottle . . . In both cases the child's development takes the same path . . ." (Freud, 1949, pp. 45–46).

Freud thought of sexuality not as a single instinct aiming at reproduction, but as a collection of component instincts rooted in different erotogenic zones that must pass through a complex developmental sequence before they fuse—at least in the normal human—into adult reproductive sexuality. Freud believed that a biological timetable, repeating the phylogeny of the past, activated each erotogenic zone in a fixed, universal sequence, and he defined each stage around the erotogenic zone dominant at that period. Each stage recreates in the individual a mode of life from the distant evolutionary past. For example, the oral stage recreates the mode of life of simple asexual organisms that feed by constant ingestion of food into an opening designed for the purpose, a sort of mouth.

The first two stages of development are the **oral** and the **anal,** and are referred to as the pregenital phases in which development is the same for males and females. Sexuality—by which Freud meant the getting of any sort of physical pleasure—is centered first on the oral erotogenic zone, the mouth, and then the anal erotogenic zone, the anus, as the child gets pleasure from sucking and biting (especially the mother's nipple and one's own fingers) and then withholding and releasing feces. Sexuality is also said to be narcissistic, as the child gratifies itself and no other. During these phases the child develops a deep primary attachment to its mother as the one who feeds, pleases, and consoles.

The next stage is the **phallic** stage, Freud's most controversial, in which the development of boys and girls takes different paths. The boy's path is the less troublesome one, though not lacking for conflict from both innate moral factors and social demands. Biogenetic development activates the penis as the dominant erotogenic zone, and, in a still narcissistic way, the boy begins to masturbate. At the same time the first stirrings of genital sexuality appear, and sexual desire is aroused toward mother, already loved as caretaker and comforter. Any such union would be incestuous, and innate factors and society's incest taboo engender feelings of guilt in the young child. According to Freud, the imagined punishment is loss of his penis, castration, reinforced by discovering that girls do not—as the boy had egocentrically assumed—have penises, and perhaps by actual parental threats of castration, probably made to discourage masturbation. The tremendous resulting *castration anxiety* smashes the Oedipus complex— the boy's desire for his mother and fear and hatred of the father as a rival for her—bringing on latency, which is also a biogenetic recapitulation of the ice age, during which sexuality dampens down.

At puberty, biological development reawakens sexuality in the genital stage, and all the component instincts come together under command of reproductive sexuality, which seeks out a new partner for love, affection, and child rearing. In abnormal individuals, in whom the Oedipus complex is repressed instead of smashed, puberty brings on either abnormal sexual behavior, such as homosexuality or fetishisms, neurosis, or a narcissistic inability to love another.

The developmental path of females is less certain and is strewn with obstacles. The chief problem they face is that unlike boys they must abandon their initial attachment to mother and redirect it to father. Since adult choice of a partner to an extent repeats the choice of childhood, the turning of the young girl from mother to father is crucial to the development of her sexuality, and it greatly complicates her sexual development.

Castration anxiety—what destroys the male Oedipus complex—is the event that triggers it in the female. When she discovers that her clitoris—activated by maturation—is a poor imitation of a male's penis, she is at once overwhelmed by **penis envy,** desiring to have one and coveting it in all boys. She feels that she herself has been castrated and, blaming her mother for her mutilation, transfers her affections to her father, which take on a sexual tone with her first genital sexuality. But her desire and love are tinged with envy of her father's possession of a penis, so she feels inferior to him in a way a boy never does toward his mother during his Oedipal phase.

Observe now that there is no force to smash a girl's Oedipus complex; it can only be repressed, with unfortunate implications for her adult personality. Freud claims that a woman is more likely to become neurotic than a man, and can find true happiness only in submission to a patriarchal husband, reliving her Oedipal fantasies. Latency is entered more slowly, as ontogeny recapitulates phylogeny, and incest taboos repress her incestuous desires.

One more difficult transition lies ahead, however. At puberty, genital sexuality reawakens, but the girl must renounce her clitoral sexuality, as it is an imitation of male genital sexuality, and find sexual satisfaction in her vagina. Indeed, Freud (1962) went so far as to say that sexual drive— *libido*—is inherently masculine, so that any woman who retains her clitoris as her adult sexual zone is necessarily abnormal. If she can achieve this second transformation of her sexual life, penis envy will become a desire to bear a child, particularly a male child, fulfilling indirectly her old longing.

For both men and women, the Oedipal period is the most important one. Difficulties at this stage lead later to full-blown neuroses, psychoses, or sexual aberrations—true mental illnesses. Difficulties at pregenital stages lead only to less severe character disorders such as narcissism. The stage is also crucial to the formation of a person's internal moral agent, the **super-ego.** Especially in the boy, the Oedipus complex strengthens identification with the same-sex parent—he wants to be like his father because his father already possesses mother and because he fears him as the enforcer of moral law. A girl's relations with each parent are a good deal more ambivalent—and the child *introjects*, or takes into itself the values of the parent. Again, Freud also offered a Lamarckian explanation of morality, arguing that the superego is a residue of moral prohibitions—especially that against incest—laid down in the ancestral past:

One gets an impression from civilized children that the constructions of these (moral) dams is a product of education, and no doubt education has much to do with it. But in reality this development is organically determined and fixed by heredity, and it can occasionally occur without any help at all from education. (Freud, 1962, pp. 43–44).

Erik Erikson and epigenesis. Freud had many followers, and one of them, Erik Erikson, turned Freud's theory of psychosexual development into a broader perspective on *psychosocial* development (Erikson, 1963). Like Piaget, Erikson describes his theory as one of **epigenesis,** although following Freud he takes a stronger biological position than Piaget:

> [T]his evolutionary principle of epigenesis . . . governs the unfolding before birth of the organic basis for all behavior and continues after birth to govern the unfolding of an individual's social potentialities in the successive encounters of impulse systems and cultural realities. (Erikson, 1939, pp. 131–132; quoted in Rapaport, 1960, p. 217).

While Lamarckianism and biogenesis have had to be abandoned, Erikson retains Freud's belief that development is an unfolding of given potential, which qualifies him as a true developmentalist.

Erikson's proposed stage sequence is also given in Figure 13–7, and will be briefly summarized. The first five stages—of childhood—build closely on Freud's foundations, but the remaining stages break new ground in proposing for the first time that development does not stop a puberty, a recognition at long last fully realized in the new field of life-span developmental psychology. Erikson defines his stages (at least the first five) around erotogenic zones, and their major modes of functioning are an addition to Freud's narrower perspective (Rapaport, 1960). Associated with each stage is a crisis, the happy resolution of which leads to a personality strength, and the unhappy resolution of which leads to a weakness. Finally, reflecting Erikson's larger social concerns, each strength-weakness pair has associated with it a societal institution that embodies and expresses it in adult life.

Conclusions. While both Freud's and Erikson's theories of development have their attractions and have exerted undeniable influence on psychology and society, neither is entirely satisfactory. Freud's account of development is, of course, seriously undermined by the fact that Lamarckianism and biogenesis are wrong. Yet without ontogeny recapitulating phylogeny there is nothing to make development go. Erikson, while avoiding the explicit mistake of citing biogenesis, winds up with a mysterious epigenesis, or "unfolding," of innate potential. Certainly the claim for a biological basis for development weakens after the locomotor-genital stage, and as individual circumstance and cultural influence become more important determinants of development than does biology. Finally, while Freud's theory is impressive (if wrong) by being quite detailed, Erikson seems to get by with liberal sentiments and scientific hand wavings, offering a vision of development, not a theory of it (Roazen, 1976).

Moral Development: Lawrence Kohlberg

One of Freud's legacies to psychology was his treatment of morality as part of emotional and personality development. His focus on the feelings associated with morality, especially shame and guilt, has continued to be the focus of even anti–Freudian developmental psychologists. But as almost any philosopher of ethics would remind us, morality has a strong intellectual element, at the very least in weighing moral ends and calculating the best means to them. Influenced more by Piaget than Freud, Lawrence Kohlberg has redressed the imbalance by offering a cognitive developmental view of moral development.

One of Piaget's methods for investigating children's levels of moral understanding was to present them with a little moral anecdote and then ask the child questions about it. So the child might be told that while helping her parents prepare for a party, Sarah inadvertently broke a dozen records, while in a contrasting case Becky broke one record while playing in a closet she knew was forbidden to her. Subjects are asked which child had done the naughtier deed, which should be punished more, and why? Up until about age nine, children, in Piaget's terms, are **moral realists,** weighing right and wrong solely in relation to the objective damage done. So in the story above, Sarah is more in the wrong and more to be punished because she broke more records than Becky. After about age nine, children become **moral relativists,** judging actions more in relation to the virtue of the intent behind them. The moral relativist reverses the judgment of the moral realist, recognizing that Sarah was trying to be helpful, breaking the records out of clumsiness only, and condemning Becky's willful flouting of a clear rule, however slight the actual damage.

Beginning in 1958, Kohlberg (1958, 1971, 1969/1976; Kohlberg & Kramer, 1969; Rosen, 1980) has developed the Piagetian cognitive-developmental approach to morality into a comprehensive theory of moral development, including the assessment of stage of moral reasoning, a theory of stage-change, and plans for improving individuals' moral judgments.

Kohlberg's assessment instrument is a more structured form of Piaget's clinical method. A child (or adult) is presented with a series of dilemmas turning on a moral issue (for example, is it right for a poor man to steal a rapaciously priced drug in order to save his dying wife?) and has to choose and defend a particular course of action, or condemn its opposite. These dilemmas are meant to measure a person's moral *reasoning* only, and not his likely moral *behavior.* Indeed, the same style of moral reasoning may yield different prescriptions for moral action.

What has emerged from Kohlberg's research is a multistage theory of the development of moral reasoning rather more complex than Piaget's. Kohlberg has proposed somewhat different stage sequences in different publications over the years, and Table 13–3 shows every stage ever proposed, whether or not Kohlberg is presently committed to it. There are three *levels* of morality, divided into two or three substages each. Empirically, the preconventional levels are found in childhood, the conventional levels in most adults, and postconventional levels in a few superior men and

TABLE 13–3   Definition of Moral Stages

I.   PRECONVENTIONAL LEVEL

At this level the child is responsive to cultural rules and labels of good and bad, right or wrong, but interprets these labels in terms of either the physical or the hedonistic consequences of action (punishment, reward, exchange of favors), or in terms of the physical power of those who enunciate the rules and labels. The level is divided into the following two stages:

STAGE 1: *The punishment and obedience orientation.* The physical consequences of action determine its goodness or badness regardless of the human meaning or value of these consequences. Avoidance of punishment and unquestioning deference to power are valued in their own right, not in terms of respect for underlying moral order supported by punishment and authority (the latter being Stage 4).

STAGE 2: *The instrumental relativist orientation.* Right action consists of that which instrumentally satisfies one's own needs and occasionally the needs of others. Human relations are viewed in terms like those of the market place. Elements of fairness, of reciprocity, and of equal sharing are present, but they are always interpreted in a physical, pragmatic way. Reciprocity is a matter of "you scratch my back and I'll scratch yours," not of loyalty, gratitude, or justice.

II.   CONVENTIONAL LEVEL

At this level, maintaining the expectations of the individual's family, group, or nation is perceived as valuable in its own right, regardless of immediate and obvious consequences. The attitude is not only one of *conformity* to personal expectations and social order, but of loyalty to it, of actively *maintaining*, supporting, and justifying the order, and of identifying with the persons or group involved in it. At this level, there are the following three stages:

STAGE 3: *The interpersonal concordance of "good boy–nice girl" orientation.* Good behavior is that which pleases or helps others and is approved by them. There is much conformity to stereotypical images of what is majority or "natural" behavior. Behavior is frequently judged by intention—"he means well" becomes important for the first time. One earns approval by being "nice."

STAGE 4: *The "law and order" orientation.* There is orientation toward authority, fixed rules, and the maintenance of the social order. Right behavior consists of doing one's duty, showing respect for authority, and maintaining the given social order for its own sake.

STAGE 4½: *Ethical egoistic orientation.* Apparent Stage 2 reasoning by previously conventional Stage 4 person. Argues that all moral judgments are relative, that there are no moral absolutes, and that moral judgments are primarily emotional, not rational. Moral terms such as "duty" are dismissed as meaningless. Represents breaking up of conventional morality in preparation for Stage 5.

TABLE 13–3   (*Continued*)

III. POSTCONVENTIONAL, AUTONOMOUS, OR PRINCIPLED LEVEL

At this level, there is a clear effort to define moral values and principles that have validity and application apart from the authority of the groups or persons holding these principles, and apart from the individual's own identification with these groups. This level again has three stages:

STAGE 5: *The social-contract legalistic orientation*, generally with utilitarian overtones. Right action tends to be defined in terms of general individual rights and standards, which have been critically examined and agreed upon by the whole society. There is a clear awareness of the relativism of personal values and opinions and a corresponding emphasis upon procedural rules for reaching consensus. Aside from what is constitutionally and democratically agreed upon, the right is a matter of personal "values" and "opinion." The result is an emphasis upon the "legal point of view," but with an emphasis upon the possibility of changing law in terms of rational considerations of social utility (rather than freezing it in terms of Stage 4 "law and order"). Outside the legal realm, free agreement and contract is the binding element of obligation. This is the "official" morality of the American government and Constitution.

[STAGE 6: *The universal ethical principle orientation*. Right is defined by the decision of conscience in accord with self-chosen ethical principles appealing to logical comprehensiveness, universality, and consistency. These principles are abstract and ethical (the Golden Rule, the categorical imperative); they are not concrete moral rules like the Ten Commandments. At heart, these are universal principles of *justice*, of the *reciprocity* and *equality* of human *rights*, and of respect for the dignity of human beings as *individual persons*. The Declaration of Independence is at Stage 6.]

[STAGE 7: *The cosmic-transcendental orientation*. Shift from humanistic reasoning of previous stages to religious, transcendental intuition. Right and wrong not defined in terms of human need or dignity, but in terms of an infinite, trans-human perspective of absolute right and wrong.]

Source: Kohlberg (1971) except for descriptions of Stage 4½ and 7, which are based primarily on Kohlberg & Kramer (1969) and Rosen (1980). Stages in brackets (6 and 7) are hypothetical only, since no one studied by Kohlberg has achieved them. See text for discussion.

women. The table speaks pretty well for itself, so we will comment only upon certain difficult points.

Positing a Stage 4½ (sometimes called 4B) was an awkward step forced on Kohlberg by the depth of his commitment to the cognitive-developmental research program. One of the central assumptions of Piaget's stage theory was that cognitive development proceeds universally through a fixed series of stages showing no regression from an attained higher stage to a lower one. (Having just read Freud's theory, the alert reader may detect a whiff of the biogenetic law.) However, in following Kohlberg's initial adolescent sample (Kohlberg, 1958) into their thirties, Kohlberg and Kramer (1969/

1976) found evidence that many subjects who had initially tested as solid Stage 4 or even Stage 5 now seemed to reason at Stage 2!

Now common sense would fully expect this, for it often happens that youthful idealism, nurtured in the hothouse of high school, gives way to a more practical outlook upon contact with adult life. Jerry Rubin, Yippee leader and one of the noisiest of the Chicago 7, for example, wound up working on Wall Street. It is, however, entirely at odds with the cognitive-developmental paradigm. Unwilling to abandon the fixed-stage concept, Kohlberg denied that any of his subjects regressed, undergoing instead what he is pleased to call *retrogression* (Kohlberg & Kramer, 1969/1976).

Kohlberg argues that the subjects he tested had never really achieved Stage 4 or Stage 5 to begin with, and that their seeming to do so was a failing of the initial test instrument, not cognitive-developmental theory. Kohlberg's most recent scoring system has been revised to correct those alleged errors. Stage 4½ represents a transitional stage between conventional and postconventional thinking, resulting from the breaking up of rigid, social-oriented conventional morality preparatory to the individual-rights centered philosophy of Stage 5. But in the meantime, there is an apparent return to egoism and a questioning of all absolutes. Kohlberg defends his view by pointing out that unlike real Stage 2 subjects, the Stage 4½ subjects still understand Stages 3 and 4, and can reason at those levels if asked to do so.

Kohlberg's rethinking of his scoring procedures has also had the startling effect—to anyone who has read about the theory before—of eliminating Stage 6. It remains an ideal to be aimed at, and perhaps has been achieved by great minds such as Thomas Jefferson, author of the Declaration of Independence (and a slave-owner), but it no longer is the achievement of any of Kohlberg's subjects (Levine, Kohlberg, & Hewer, 1985).

Even more remote, therefore, is Stage 7, once proposed in a paper on moral development in the elderly (Rosen, 1980). In Stages 1 through 5, right and wrong can be grounded in secular, purely human terms, ranging from simple pain and pleasure through social rules to the notion of the freely chosen contract. However, Stage 6 posits rules that transcend human experience, social rules, or contracts, which may be used to strike the latter. It appears difficult to justify such principles without appealing to some moral dimension outside human life and society, a more cosmic perspective, and it is this that is found at Stage 7.

Finally, with regard to the facilitation of moral development, Kohlberg has advanced an equilibration account of moral development and its improvement. Various studies by Kohlberg and others (see Turiel, 1973) have found that if presented with an array of answers to a moral dilemma, subjects typically choose as the best answer that from one stage beyond their own stage. If, as cognitive developmental theory maintains, development is a process of successive equilibrations in resolution of cognitive conflict, this finding suggests that the best way to foster moral development is quite simple: promote discussions of moral issues. Any sufficiently heterogeneous group (a high school class, for example) will have members at almost all levels (save the first and the last), so that a person at Stage X

will give arguments of that stage that will help another at Stage $X - 1$ move up, and will be exposed to arguments at Stage $X + 1$, advancing his or her own development.

Kohlberg's theory is well known, influential, and controversial (Modgil & Modgil, 1986). Texts in introductory or developmental psychology discuss it at least briefly. Questions on teacher competence exams concerning ways to foster morality are based on the theory. Nevertheless, Kohlberg's work has serious deficiencies and some vocal detractors (for reviews see Kurtines & Greif, 1974; Flanagan, 1983; reply in Levine, Kohlberg, & Hewer, 1985).

To begin with, as a cognitive-developmental theory closely modeled on Piaget's, it faces all the difficulties of the latter, such as the problem of *decalage*. A subject's responses to Kohlberg's instrument may scatter over three or more stages, making it hard to determine the subject's "dominant" stage (Kurtines & Greif, 1974). A student of Kohlberg's, James Rest (Rest, 1986) has responded to such criticisms by creating a more structured assessment instrument, the Defining Issues Test. Rest is also less committed to stages than is Kohlberg.

Two special problems within the cognitive-developmental framework arise for Kohlberg's theory as compared with Piaget's. First, Kohlberg runs up against the intuitive and reasonable idea that development of reasoning about morals is different from development of reasoning about physical concepts (Flanagan, 1982a, 1982b). Every child everywhere grows up in the same physical universe—the laws of motion, matter, and mathematics are indifferent to a culture's beliefs. But not every child grows up in the same moral world. Each culture and subculture has its own values, religious beliefs, notions of justice, and procedures for righting wrongs; there is no underlying physical reality common to everyone in this domain. So our astonishment at Kohlberg's claim of universality and the data he offers to support it may be so great to make us doubt his test and his theory rather than doubt our belief that human cultures are morally heterogeneous (Reid, 1984).

The other problem faced by Kohlberg more than by Piaget is his claim that the final stage in his hierarchy is the most adequate. Whether or not Piaget has correctly described the most adequate form of scientific reasoning with his model of formal operations, at least it is easy to decide what kind of reasoning is more adequate when dealing with physical concepts: Which level of reasoning gives the better scientific answers, concrete or formal operations? Clearly, formal operations are more scientifically adequate, Kohlberg, however, has to claim that Stage 6 (or the newly combined Stage 5–6) is the most *morally* adequate stage.

That is, unlike the sociobiologist often wrongly accused of it, Kohlberg is trying, in his own words, "to commit the naturalistic fallacy and get away with it" (Kohlberg, 1971 p. 151). The incoherence of moving from "is" to "ought" is easily found in Kohlberg's theory. For years he argued that Stage 6 was clearly the highest form of morality but now says that almost no one reaches that stage, so now there is no "is" on which to base the "ought." And what about Stage 7? Furthermore, how can we assess any claim that the last stage is morally best? Kohlberg likes to point to a convergence between his Stage 6 and philosopher John Rawls' book *A Theory of Justice*. This, however, is just an appeal to authority that settles nothing. Another well-regarded Harvard philosopher is Robert Nozick, whose ethical theory *Anarchy, State, and Utopia* is libertarian, and looks like Stage 2. Recently, Kohlberg (Levine, Kohlberg, & Hewer, 1985) seems to have conceded that his theory contains hidden ethical assumptions, and that it is not a scientific theory in the usual sense.

Difficulties of claiming moral superiority for a given stage are pointed out by two arguments having a rather sociobiological air about them (unintended by their proponents). Consider the following moral problem. A mother is on the shore watching her child and a stranger's child rowing a boat out on the lake. Suddenly, the boat capsizes and the helpless children are flipped into the water. The mother can save only *one* child. She swims out and saves the stranger's child, justifying her action with the clear Stage 6 assertion that all human lives are of equal value, so she flipped a coin saying, "Heads my child, tails the other child." Tails came up and she saved the other child. (Flanagan, 1983). How do we feel about the mother and her actions? Flanagan and the people he has queried on this problem felt strongly that the mother did the wrong thing and that they would feel very strange around such a person.

What our example reveals is an important limitation on Kohlberg's theory; there is more to morality than the impersonal equal distribution of justice. In particular, it suggests that Kohlberg's highest stages represent the best way to administer justice in a particular social world, specifically our own modern, industrialized, impersonal West (Flanagan, 1983). In Chapter Eleven we saw how modern society is quite unlike the societies that shaped human evolution and in which most people still live. In those societies, kinship still plays the most important role in regulating human affairs, and certain contemporary problems can be traced to the breakdown of kin ties. Our example reveals that kinship still plays a role in our concepts of right and wrong. Stages 5 and 6 describe right and wrong in a society of strangers—but not all human beings are unrelated strangers.

The second sociobiological-sounding difficulty concerns the consistent finding that women always score lower than men on Kohlberg's scale. Now while Freud would have expected this finding, it seems extraordinarily unlikely that women are really less moral than men. One of Kohlberg's own students, Carol Gilligan (1977, 1979, 1982), has argued that Kohlberg's scale—based on the initial testing and continued following of 84 males— is sex-biased. She argues that men's concepts of morality focus on stern, abstract principles of justice rationally arrived at, whereas women are more attuned to personal relationships, to feelings, and to the unique context of particuar moral problems. Gilligan states:

> Whereas the rights conception of morality that informs Kohlberg's principled level (Stages Five and Six) is geared to arriving at an objectively fair or just resolution to the moral dilemmas to which "all rational men can agree," the responsibility conception focuses instead on the limitations of any particular

resolution and describes the conflicts that remain . . . . a woman in her thirties
. . . says that her guiding principle in making moral decisions has to do
with "responsibility and caring about yourself and others, not just a principle
that once you take hold of, you settle (the moral problem)." The principle
put into practice is still going to leave you with conflict. (Gilligan, 1977, p.
482).

We can detect in this contrast of male and female moral styles the
same sorts of sex differences surveyed in Chapter 11. From the earliest
days, girls are more alert to emotional expression and nuances of feeling
than are boys, and in women and men this carries through to a wide
range of differences, including, we now find, differing conceptions of morality and justice. We should not conclude that women are less (or more)
moral than men but that, to borrow Gilligan's phrase, they speak "in a
different voice" about moral issues. If it is correct that much of human
violence is instigated or at least abetted by moral imperialism—crusades
against those labeled "evil"—as Alexander suggested (Chapter 11), then a
voice of compassion and feeling is one that is well heeded. Impersonal
abstract justice easily becomes persecution; morality erected on intimate
personal ties does not.

Of the various deficiencies that mark Kohlberg's cognitive-developmental theory of moral development, the one that troubles most psychologists is its indifference to behavior. What practical good is high moral
reasoning if it does little to reduce crime and war? Concern with moral
behavior and its causes has characterized the major alternative to both
psychoanalysis and cognitive-developmentalism, namely, social learning
theory.

Alternative: Social-Learning Theory

In sharp contrast to Kohlberg's developmentalism, **social-learning
theory** views personality and morality as learned, part of the overall socialization of children. Social-learning theory began some decades ago as an
attempt to marry what were then seen as the artful insights of psychoanalysis
with the scientific rigor of behaviorism (Dollard, Doob, Miller, Mowrer, &
Sears, 1939; Dollard & Miller, 1950; Miller & Dollard, 1941; Whiting &
Child, 1953). Over the years social-learning theory has changed, moving
away from its Freudian roots and becoming, along with the rest of psychology, more cognitive (Mischel & Mischel, 1976; Bandura, 1982). Nevertheless, despite these changes and despite often strong disagreement among
its proponents on theoretical details (Graham, 1972), the social-learning
perspective maintains its emphasis on moral behavior and learning. In
this section we will focus on the living and lively controversy (Wren, 1982,
and following papers) between social-learning and cognitive developmental
theories of morality.

Two aspects of the psychoanalytic approach to moral socialization
have been retained down to the present and, more specifically, distinguish
it from Kohlberg's approach. One of these is paying more attention to
the affective side of morality—feelings of anxiety, shame, and guilt—than

to the cognitive (although recent work by Bandura, 1974, 1978, 1982 certainly does not neglect cognition). The other is attentiveness to parental and social role models as sources of moral values and behavior.

From a dynamic psychoanalytic perspective, conscience is built on feelings of shame, guilt, and moral rightness that are internalizations of parental punishment and reward. This accords well with any behavioral perspective, which holds that, because moral behavior *is* behavior, it must follow the usual laws of punishment and reinforcement. Morality, therefore, consists in learning to inhibit actions that are punished, and to perform those that are rewarded. So, for example, Aronfreed (1976) reports that children punished for choosing the more attractive of a series of toys quickly learn not to choose them. Furthermore in keeping with the standard laws of learning, this inhibition, or resistance to temptation, generalizes best to a test situation when the child is alone, if the punishment is delivered immediately after the "wrong" choice, rather than delayed. An inner moral agent—a conscience—is formed as the child internalizes moral rules and learns to regulate its own behavior rather than having to receive actual rewards and punishments (Aronfreed, 1976; Mischel & Mischel, 1976). That both *cognition* and *affect* are part of internal moral regulation is indicated by Aronfreed's (1976) further finding that punishment delivered with a plausible rationale was more effective in inducing later resistance to temptation than punishment alone.

Freud and the other psychoanalysts placed great stress on *identification* as a source of morality. Children identify with their parents first because they depend on them to meet their needs (anaclitic identification) and then because they fear them as punishing agents (identification with the aggressor); the latter is especially strong in boys' Oedipal period. Identification leads to imitation of the parents and the adoption (introjection) of the parents' values.

While learning theorists play down the role of identification in socialization and speak of *imitation* as a direct behavioral copying of a model (Bandura, 1967), and while they disagree over whether imitation is a spontaneously occurring natural process relatively independent of reinforcement (Bandura, 1974), or is itself something that must be learned through shaping (Gewirtz & Stingle, 1968), they all agree with Freud that parents and others provide models of moral behavior from which their children learn right and wrong (Miller & Dollard, 1941; Bandura & Walters, 1963; Bandura, 1967; Rushton, 1982a, 1982b).

Liebert & Poulos (1976) illustrates how most social-learning theorists regard the process of imitation, modeling, or observational learning, as it is variously called. The first of the three stages in modeling is simply *exposure* to the model, seeing some behavior occur. The second stage, *acquisition*, may or may not take place in a given instance. According to more cognitively oriented learning theorists (see Bandura, 1974), acquisition depends on having paid attention to the model and on constructing an internal representation of the behavior that serves as a template for later imitation.

If the template is acquired, then it may or may not affect behavior. This is the phase of *acceptance*. Various factors may lead to nonimitation, such as the degree of identification (or lack thereof) the child feels with the actor (Eron, 1982). If imitation does occur, it may be *imitative* or *counter-imitative*. Imitative effects include *direct imitation* of the modeled behavior or *disinhibition* of similar behaviors. Counter-imitative effects include *direct counter-imitation* and *inhibition* of similar behaviors. Again, various factors determine whether an actor's behavior is imitated or counter-imitated, but the most important seems to be the consequences following that behavior. If the actor is rewarded, imitation is more likely; if punished, counter-imitation is more likely; but the effect is weaker (Bandura & Walters, 1963; Liebert & Poulos, 1976).

One particularly interesting source of models intensively studied by social-learning theorists is one Freud did not have to worry about: the mass media, especially television (Liebert & Poulos, 1976; Roberts & Bachen, 1981; Eron, 1982). Television and movies provide a wide range of possible models to imitate for good or ill from characters such as Hawkeye and Captain Kirk to J. R. Ewing and Darth Vader. Social-learning theorists have investigated whether films as well as parents *can* influence behavior, and whether what children actually see on television *does* influence their behavior.

Beginning with the work of Bandura and his colleagues around 1960 (see Bandura, Ross, & Ross, 1961), the answer to the first question is quite clear. Laboratory experiments soon showed that viewing films or video can have dramatic impact on children's behavior. If children see an adult or another child being aggressive, especially if the actor is rewarded or not punished, children will later act aggressively in remarkably similar ways (Bandura, 1967).

While the results are not as dramatically unequivocal, it also appears that children's behavior is, in fact, affected by their exposure to real television, which is many hours each day. Most field research has focused on television violence, asking if it leads to increased levels of aggression or toleration for aggression in children (Eron, 1982) or even adults (Roberts & Bachen, 1981). The consensus of researchers is that it does (APA *Monitor*, 1983). Of particular concern is the self-reinforcing nature of aggressiveness and television watching: Children proven to be aggressive watch more violent television (Eron, 1982).

Social-learning theory's stress on morality as learned and on understanding the determinants of moral learning and behavior naturally leads it to be much more relativistic than Kohlberg's theory at all levels—cultural, familial, and situational. Kohlberg's theory posits a universal sequence of stages of moral development cutting across cultures and families, and it maintains that people should be reasonably consistent, showing judgment and behavior consistent with their stage of moral development across the situations they find themselves in.

By contrast, social-learning theorists view morality as relative. Different cultures have different values and practices, so that people in different cultures espouse different moralities (Whiting & Child, 1953; Garbarino & Bronfenbrenner, 1976). Because parents have different child-rearing practices, different effects on moral learning should occur. For example, parents who use love-withdrawal rather than physical punishment as a discipline technique produce more moral children (Hoffman & Saltzstein, 1967; Hoffman, 1976, 1979), and this is particularly true of those who are authoritative—firm, but giving explanations of their actions—as opposed to authoritarian or permissive parents (Baumrind, 1971).

Finally, because social-learning theory focuses on the environmental determinants of behavior, social-learning theorists expect moral behavior to be situation-specific rather than consistent across situations. An especially distressing example of the situational specificity of morality is an experiment by Haney, Banks, and Zimbardo (1973). They built a simulated prison in the basement of the psychology department at Stanford University, and chose a group of male students to be either "prisoners" or "guards" for several weeks in this pretend prison. The subjects were screened for emotional stability and assigned randomly as "prisoners" or "guards." The researchers were shocked to discover that very quickly the "guards" became guards—brutal, domineering, and inhumane—and the "prisoners" became prisoners—fearful yet hostile, prepared to riot and rebel, or to go into depressive withdrawal. So vicious did the situation become that the experiment was ended very early. This study and others (see Milgram, 1974) seem to show that morality—indeed, perhaps personality—is not a permanent, enduring part of an individual, but a momentary product of his or her surroundings.

In the social-learning view, then, actual moral behavior and reasoning are relative indeed. They are relative to the culture in which you grow up, the family that raises you, and the circumstances in which you find yourself. Philosophically, right and wrong may be universal—indifferent to culture, family, and circumstance—but psychologically they are not. Kohlberg perhaps catches people's understanding that morality ought to be universal, applicable to all men and women everywhere. Every stage offers some general, universal guide to right behavior, though in each case the guide is grounded differently. Yet in the actual world we fall short, as social-learning theory demonstrates; morality, in fact, is relative. Kohlberg and social-learning theory fall on the two sides of the is–ought dichotomy, Kohlberg studying what people *think* ought to be right and wrong, social-learning theory studying people *being* right and wrong.

BIOLOGY OF DEVELOPMENT

Proximate Causes

Along with the rest of the body, the nervous system continues to develop after birth. Neuropsychologists have studied how the nervous system changes by using two main experimental paradigms: depriving young animals of visual experience during early stages of visual development, and rearing animals in varying conditions of environmental richness. In both cases, investigators try to assess the effects of experience on the structures of the nervous system (see Black & Greenough, 1986, for a review.)

Mammals reared in the dark show abnormal visually guided behavior. For example, one test of depth perception is the visual cliff, which invites animals placed on the top of a laboratory cliff to step off into space, the animal being protected from harm by a layer of glass. Normally reared kittens refuse to step over the cliff, but kittens reared since birth in the dark go right ahead. In a study of more specific deprivation, kittens were reared in a contrived environment that keeps them from seeing vertical lines. The kittens developed into cats who walked into table legs and who didn't play with strings dangled in front of them, but could jump onto chair seats and tables, suggesting that they simply did not see vertical lines. Kittens reared in environments without horizontal lines show reverse defects.

Not surprisingly, visual deprivation causes quantitative and structural changes in the brain. Neurons in the visual cortex of visually deprived cats have fewer dendritic branches and fewer synapses per neuron than in normal cats. The orientation of dendrites in Layer III pyramidal cells of the visual cortex was differentially affected in the kittens raised in oppositely striped environments. Dendrites were oriented in one direction only, perpendicular to the lines to which the kittens were exposed, so that the kittens in each group had oppositely oriented dendrites.

A number of studies have examined the effects of rearing rats alone in normal laboratory cages (deprived condition), in groups in normal laboratory cages (deprived-social condition), and in groups living in large cages with toys that are changed every day (enriched condition). Profound behavioral differences result from differential rearing: Enriched-condition animals are superior at learning mazes under almost all conditions, with deprived-social rats showing only modest superiority to deprived rats. Behavioral differences are mirrored in changes to the rats' brains. Compared to either group of deprived rats, the brains of enriched-condition rats are heavier, possess more dendrites and have larger dendritic fields, have larger cell bodies, possess more glial cells, and have more synapses per neuron. Differences between deprived and deprived-social rats' brains have been found to be small to nonexistent. These effects are not dependent on age, but can occur when animals are differentially raised beginning in adolescence. Finally, active use of the enriched environment is necessary to cause changes to the brain; rats raised as a group in a small cage inside an enriched environment had brains identical to those of deprived rats.

It is clear that the mammalian nervous system does not simply mature independently of experience, but is affected by the kind of environment in which the growing young animal lives. Black and Greenough (1986) propose that there are two kinds of neural plasticity underlying nervous systems' response to the environment, namely, *experience-expectant plasticity* and *experience-dependent plasticity*. Because many features of the world are stable from generation to generation, organisms have evolved to expect certain kinds of experiences to be reliably available, providing input to activate preadapted parts of the brain. For example, in any normal environment visual lines of all orientation are found, and different pyramidal cells of the cat's visual cortex have evolved to be activated by and attuned to these different kinds of visual input. This is experience-expectant plasticity: Parts of the nervous system expect and are sensitive to standard, expectable, environmental events. On the other hand, an animal's brain must be able to master novel problems and be appropriately changed by unique and unfamiliar aspects of the particular environment in which an individual organism happens to be born. Such neural plasticity is what we usually call learning, but is what Black and Greenough dub experience-dependent plasticity.

Black and Greenough propose that different mechanisms of neural change underlie the two types of plasticity. With regard to experience-expectant plasticity, studies of the maturation of mammalian nervous systems (including the human) have shown that the number of dendrites and synapses in many parts of the brain peak sometime in childhood and then fall off in number as the organism enters adulthood. Connections in the nervous system seem thus to be at first overproduced and then weeded out as development proceeds. The nervous system appears to prepare for expected experience by proliferating neural interconnections from which experience, acting like natural selection in evolution, eliminates unneeded connections and preserves useful ones. The mechanisms of experience-dependent plasticity are the neural mechanisms of learning we discussed in Chapter 10.

Ultimate Causes

With the exception of Freud, whose Lamarckian biogenesis is now known to be incorrect, the theorists we have surveyed, whether developmentalist or learning, share a general hostility to biological, nativistic explanations of learning and development. However, their rejection of biology rests on a familiar misconception of genetics, namely, the belief that if a behavior, trait, or developmental sequence is innate, it is rigid, inflexible and uninfluenced by the environment. Piaget, for example, labels nativism "preformationism" and claims, with regard to Chomsky's linguistic nativism, that if Chomsky were correct, children would talk at birth.

However, as we learned in Chapters 10 and 11, such a characterization of nativism is a caricature. Modern biology and genetics recognize that genes and environment interact—that behavior can be both innate *and* learned at the same time. What genes provide is a direction for development, not a mechanical series of steps. The evolutionary biologist C. H. Waddington (see, for example, 1968) calls the direction-giving of the genes **canalization**. Canalization keeps development on a normal course, responding to environmental challenges—assuming an environment within a broad normal range.

One of the problems learning theory faces is that people are everywhere much the same, within limits, indicating that learning neglects some unifying force behind development. Developmentalists, of course, postulate a unifying, direction-giving force, such as Werner's orthogenesis or Piaget's equilibration. Unfortunately for developmentalists, such forces seem rather mysterious and metaphysical to most psychologists, who remain committed to some learning theory, today usually of a cognitive sort.

Both biology and the concept of canalization provide a new way to look at development, a way that recognizes the role of learning and experience, but explains the direction of development without positing any unusual causal force. Some psychologists began to take a biological approach to development at about the same time Wilson was propounding *Sociobiology* (Chevalier-Skolnikoff & Poirier, 1977; Fishbein, 1976; Freedman, 1974; Hinde, 1974; Scarr-Salapatek, 1976; P. Smith, 1974), and the approach is gaining acceptance as a force in developmental psychology (Siegler, 1983; Bateson, 1985; Butterworth, Rutkowska, & Scaife, 1985). A useful example of the evolutionary-biological approach to development is the neobiogenetic account of Piaget's stages of cognitive development (Parker & Gibson, 1979; Parker, 1985; Gibson, 1985).

Parker and Gibson integrate Piaget's stages of development with comparative studies of intelligence in our simian relatives and the likely course of evolution of the early hominids, our distant ancestors. Studies of the behavioral abilities of our animal relatives suggest that, in Piagetian terms, as we move from simple simians through the monkeys and to our closest relatives, the great apes (chimpanzees and gorillas), higher levels of sensory-motor intelligence are obtained, until with the apes, early preoperational, representational intelligence is achieved. It is the symbolic capacity of the apes that has made it possible for some of them to learn to communicate, as we saw in the last chapter. Parker and Gibson argue that the evolution of early human ancestors reflects a similar increase in cognitive capacity, ultimately moving past the achievements of the apes to human preoperational intelligence marked by the distinctive human traits of tool manufacture, the building of shelters, and throwing stones as a hunting tactic. If Parker's and Gibson's proposed evolutionary sequence is correct, then a new biogenesis without Haeckel's obsolete biogenetic law may be proposed: that human cognitive development—ontogenesis—recapitulates the phylogeny of human evolution.

CONCLUSION: CONSTRAINTS ON DEVELOPMENT

Piaget began to study development when, as a young man, he administered intelligence tests to children. He observed that children of about the same age who missed the same item nevertheless give similar or identical wrong answers. This is surprising, because although there is only one right answer to a question, there are many wrong answers, yet children only gave one. The same remarkable point emerges from Piaget's studies of development, which elaborated and explored his youthful finding. Consider conservation of amount, for example: Before Piaget no one had even noticed that young children believe that the amount of water changes when you pour it; of course, children have never been instructed about conservation, yet all children in all cultures move through the identical sequence of conservation acquisition. It appears that cognitive development proceeds the same way everywhere on the globe, independent of teaching and culture. Although no two children are exactly alike, general process of development appears to be uniform. Contrary to behaviorists, it seems clear that children are not simply shaped by reinforcement contingencies, which led Piaget to propose his teleological equilibration model of development through stages.

But teleology is suspect among scientists, and we have seen that Piaget's claim of qualitiatively different stages of thought is shaky and is being abandoned in favor of information-processing theories of cognitive development. Yet information-processing psychologists must face Piaget's great insight that development is remarkably uniform and individual differences narrow. Biological thinking has supplied an answer to similar phenomena in other areas. Language acquisition appears to move along similar lines in all children, and it is plausible to suppose that this is so because of innate constraints on the kinds of languages humans can learn and be exposed to. Similarly, learning psychologists have come to recognize that what and how an animal learns is constrained by the genetic legacy of its environmentl history. Perhaps the concept of biological constraints can be fruitfully applied to development, seeing it as a process or set of processes operating within biologically given constraints, such that development is guided—without stages and without a Lamarckian goal—within a range of possible individual differences. Frank Keil (1981, 1984) has proposed just such an approach to cognitive development.

Keil offers a quotation from the American philosopher Charles Sanders Peirce (1839–1914), who first proposed the constraints approach, nicely summarizing its basic argument:

> Suppose a being from some remote part of the universe, where the conditions of existence are inconceivably different from ours, to be presented with a United States Census Report which is for us a mine of valuable inductions, so vast as almost to give that epithet a new signification. He begins, perhaps, by comparing the ratio of indebtedness to deaths by consumption in counties whose names begin with different letters of the alphabet. It is safe to say that he would find the ratio everywhere the same, and thus his inquiry would lead to nothing. The stranger to this planet might go on for some time asking inductive questions that the Census would faithfully answer without learning anything except that certain conditions were independent of others. . . . Nature is a far vaster and less clearly arranged repertoire of facts than a Census report; and if men had not come to it with special aptitudes for guessing right, it may well be doubted whether in the ten or twenty thousand years that they may have existed their greatest mind would have attained the amount of knowledge which is actually possessed by the lowest idiot. But, in point of fact, not man merely, but all animals derive by inheritance (presumably by natural selection) . . . classes of ideas which adapt them to their environment.
>
> Side by side, then, with the well established proposition that all knowledge is based on experience, and that science is only advanced by the experimental verifications of theories, we have to place this other equally important truth, that all human knowledge, up to the highest flights of science, is but the development of our inborn animal instincts. (Keil, 1981, p. 199)

There is nothing very mysterious about Keil's argument that cognitive ontogeny is subject to innate constraints, for it, along with the language-learning constraints theory of Chomsky and Wexler and Cullicover, is simply an extension of well-established views in sociobiology and animal learning applied to human beings. In Chapter 10 we saw that animal learning is constrained—some things are easy for a given species to learn, others difficult. It is important to see that the idea of modern nativism departs from the stereotypical view of innate behaviors as rigidly preprogrammed. Conditioned nausea is both learned, as experience is needed to learn what causes illness, and innate, as rats, by virtue of their evolution, learn to avoid poisonous foods by taste cues, while birds, by virtue of their evolution, learn to avoid them by visual cues.

Richard Coss' (1985) investigations of the evolution and learning of ground squirrel anti-snake behaviors provide a good example of how evolution constrains development, and how experience affects the course of evolution. Ground squirrels living in many parts of North America are subject to predation by gopher snakes and rattlesnakes, the latter being more dangerous because they are poisonous as well as carnivorous. Ground squirrels in snake-infested habitats respond with alarm calls, tail waving, and a variety of harassing attacks, including throwing dirt and sticks at the predator. However, in some areas either rattlesnakes, gopher snakes, or both are no longer threats to squirrels, and Coss has studied how evolving in different habitats for different amounts of time has affected ground-squirrel behavior.

In one experiment, Coss compared the anti-snake behaviors of two groups of snakes, one caught in a habitat infested with both rattlesnakes and gopher snakes and the other group caught from an area free of rattlers but not of gopher snakes. Squirrels from the latter area were much bolder in approaching the three kinds of snakes to which they were exposed, rattlers, gopher snakes, and garter snakes, reflecting the greater threat of rattlers. That these differences were primarily hereditary was shown by exposing a garter snake to laboratory-reared pups born from each. Pups from the population predated by both rattlers and gopher snakes were much more cautious in approaching the test snake than were pups from the rattler-free population.

An additional study shed more light on the evolution—specifically, the loss—of anti-snake behavior. Three groups were studied: The first group was caught in Folsom State Park, where rattlesnakes are common but gopher snakes are quite rare. A second was trapped at Lake Tahoe, free of both kinds of snake. The third group came from the Sacramento delta, where there are no rattlers, but some gopher snakes. Using molecular clock techniques (see Chapter 10), it was determined that the first two groups had been isolated for about 35,000 years, the third for about 85,000 years. After living for nine months in laboratory enclosures simulating wild conditions, each group was exposed over several trials to either rattlesnakes or gopher snakes. Persistence of genetic knowledge over thousands of years was revealed by the Lake Tahoe squirrels, who reacted to both kinds of snakes in typical ways, including jumping back after approaching a rattler in order to avoid its venomous strike. Thus, ground squirrels' innate knowledge of rattlesnakes included not just response to it as a threat, but knowledge of what rattlers *do*. Experience can modify genetic patterns, however, as shown by the Folsom squirrels, whose experience with rattlesnakes in the wild had made them wary, approaching snakes cautiously and soon avoiding them altogether. The behavior of the Delta population revealed anti-snake behavior in the process of being lost. Some of the animals behaved toward snake threats in the same excited way as the Folsom group, whereas others engaged in anti-snake tactics only sluggishly, and seemed to habituate to the snake's presence, ceasing to regard it as a threat. It appears that genetic knowledge of snakes persists at least 35,000 years, but begins to be lost after 85,000 years.

Follow-up research was conducted with other groups of ground squirrels. Arctic ground squirrels have lived without snake predation for 3 million years. When tested, they responded to rattlesnakes as interesting novel objects despite numerous strikes and rattled warnings, suggesting that innate knowledge of snakes as threats can persist for perhaps 100,000 years, but not 3 million. In a related experiment, two groups of pups from two ground-squirrel groups were tested. One group came from a population exposed only to gopher snakes, the second to both types of snakes; the populations had diverged about 3000 years ago. Pups from the second group distinguished between the two species of snake, regarding rattlers as the greater menace. The first group was vigilant about both kinds of snakes, but did not treat the rattlesnakes differently from the gopher snakes. Because these were lab-reared, snake-inexperienced pups, it appears that knowledge about snakes can begin to be affected differentially by evolution in fewer than 3000 years, a remarkably brief span of time on the evolutionary time scale.

Coss concludes that "learning is part of a continuum of adjustment over phylogenetic [evolutionary], ontogenetic [developmental], and proximate [immediate response] time scales." An organism's adjustment to—knowledge of—its environment is based first of all on its genetic heritage, which is shaped by evolution over thousands of years to its subspecies' habitat. Thus, even as pups without experience of snakes, different subspecies of ground squirrels react differently to snakes. The individual's genetic base guides development, combining innate knowledge with individual experience to produce an adult whose behavior is well tuned to its own surroundings. Hence, adults in snake-infested areas, equipped with antisnake behavior by their genes, have learned to be wary of snakes, attacking them less vigorously than inexperienced pups. Finally, the developed organism must constantly monitor its immediate, short-term environment for challenges and opportunities. Thus, mature ground squirrels when they encounter a snake muster their genetic resources and learned caution to treat it as the serious threat it is.

A human case discussed in Chapter 11 may be usefully recalled now, the case of incest taboos. Freud, in his Lamarckian biogenetic way, viewed the incest taboo in a child as a racial memory from the ancient past. Social-learning theorists reject all nativism; they argue that incest avoidance is a learned behavior based on direct punishment of incipient incestuous acts and modeling (negative imitation) when others are seen to be punished for incest. In a modern biological account, both views are partly correct. As we learned in Chapter 11, avoidance of inbreeding is a widespread animal behavior firmly based on consideration of fitness. So there is a likely genetic basis for incest avoidance, but not Freud's Lamarckian one. At the same time we found that incest avoidance is a learned phenomenon— we must *learn* with whom sexual relations must *not* take place. More specifically, it appears that humans are prepared to learn not to feel lust for the constant age-mates of childhood.

If outmoded ideas about evolution and genetics can be discarded, developmentalists and cognitive-learning theorists may be reconciled. Like the defensive behaviors of ground squirrels, human knowledge, personality, and even morality are both innate *and* learned; they develop through universal patterns set by genetic constraints within which learning acts to produce each individual's path of development.

SUGGESTED READINGS

The best general survey of theories of development is Alfred Baldwin's *Theories of Child Development*, 2nd ed., 1980. Baldwin is weak on the information-processing view that now dominates cognitive development, but a fine survey is provided by Siegler (1986); Siegler was one of the first to apply information-processing to children's thinking. On the intersection of evolution and development, see Butterworth, Rutkowska, and Scaife (1985).

REFERENCES

AARSLEFF, H. (1976). An outline of language origin theories since the Renaissance. In Harnad, Stelkis, & Lancaster.

AARSLEFF, H. (1982). The history of linguistics and professor Chomsky. In H. Aarsleff, *From Locke to Saussure*. Minneapolis: University of Minnesota Press.

ABELSON, R. P. (1981). Psychological status of the script concept. *American Psychologist, 36,* 715–729.

ADAMS. J. L. (1976). *Conceptual blockbusting.* San Francisco: San Francisco Book Company.

ADAMS, M. J., & COLLINS, A. (1979). A schema-theoretic view of reading. In R. O. Freedle (Ed.), *New directions in discourse processing.* Norwood, NJ: Ablex.

AHN, W.-K., MOONEY, R. J., BREWER, W. F., & DEJONG, G. F. (1987). Schema acquisition from one example: Psychological evidence for explanation-based learning. In *Proceedings of the Ninth Annual Conference of the Cognitive Science Society*, pp. 50–57, Hillsdale NJ: Lawrence Erlbaum Associates.

ALBA, J. W., & HASHER, L. (1983). Is memory schematic? *Psychological Bulletin, 93,* 203–231.

ALCOCK, J. (1979). *Animal behavior* (2nd ed.). Sunderland, MA: Sinauer Associates.

ALESANDRINI, K. L. (1983). Strategies that influence memory for advertising communications. In R. J. Harris (Ed.), *Information processing research in advertising.* Hillsdale, NJ: Lawrence Erlbaum Associates.

ALEXANDER, R. D. (1979a). *Darwinism and human affairs.* Seattle: University of Washington Press.

ALEXANDER, R. D. (1979b). Sexuality and sociality in humans and other primates. In Katchadourian.

ALEXANDER, R. D. (1987). *The biology of moral systems.* Hawthorne, NY: Aldine.

ALEXANDER. R. D., HOOGLAND, J. L., HOWARD, R. D., NOONAN, K. M., & SHERMAN, P. W. (1979). Sexual dimorphisms and breeding systems in pinnipeds, ungulates, primates, and humans. In Chagnon & Irons.

ALEXANDER, R. D., and NOONAN, K. M. (1979). Concealment of ovulation, parental care, and human social evolution. In Chagnon & Irons.

ALEXANDER, R. D., & TINKLE, D. (Eds.) (1982). *Natural selection and social behavior.* New York: Chiron Press.

ALKON, D. L., (1985). Conditioning-induced changes of Hermissenda channels: Relevance to mammalian brain function. In Weinberger and others (1985).

ALKON, D. L. (1987). *Memory traces in the brain.* Cambridge: Cambridge University Press.

ALKON, D. L., & FARLEY, J. (Eds.). (1984). *Primary neural substrates of learning and behavior change.* New York: Cambridge University Press.

ALLOY, L. B., & ABRAMSON, L. Y. (1982). Learned helplessness, depression, and the illusion of control. *Journal of Personality and Social Psychology, 42,* 1114–1126.

ALLPORT, SUSAN. (1986). *Explorers of the black box: The search for the cellular basis of memory.* New York: Norton.

ALWITT, L. F., & MITCHELL, A. A. (Eds.) (1985). *Psychological processes and advertising effects: Theory, research, and application.* Hillsdale NJ: Lawrence Erlbaum Associates.

AMAN, R. (1982). Interlingual taboos in advertising: How not to name your product. In H. DiPietro (Ed.), *Linguistics and the professions.* Norwood, NJ: Ablex.

AMERICAN PSYCHIATRIC ASSOCIATION. (1980). *Diagnostic and statistical manual of neural disorders* (3rd ed.). Washington, DC: American Psychiatric Association.

AMSEL, A. (1958). The role of frustrative nonreward in noncontinuous reward situations. *Psychological Bulletin, 55,* 102–119.

AMSEL, A. (1962). Frustrative nonreward in partial reinforcement and discrimination learning. *Psychological Review, 69,* 306–328.

AMSEL, A. (1967). Partial reinforcement effects on vigor and persistence. In K. W. Spence & J. T. Spence (Eds.), *The psychology of learning and motivation* (Vol. 1). New York: Academic Press.

ANDERSON, B. F. (1980). *The complete thinker.* Englewood Cliffs, NJ: Prentice-Hall.

ANDERSON, J. R. (1976). *Language, memory, and thought.* Hillsdale, NJ: Lawrence Erlbaum Associates.

ANDERSON, J. R. (1982). Acquisition of cognitive skill. *Psychological Review, 89,* 369–406.

ANDERSON, J. R. (1983). *The architecture of cognition.* Cambridge MA: Harvard University Press.

ANDERSON, J. R. (1984). Spreading activation. In J. R. Anderson and S. M. Rosslyn (Eds.), *Tutorials in learning and memory.* San Francisco: W. H. Freeman. Pp. 61–90.

ANDERSON, J. R. (1985). *Cognitive psychology and its implications* (2nd ed.). New York: W. H. Freeman.

ANDERSON, J. R., & BOWER, G. H. (1973). *Human associative memory.* Washington, DC: Winston.

ANDERSON, N. H. (1981). *Foundations of information integration theory.* New York: Academic Press.

ANDERSON, N. H. (1982). *Methods of information integration theory.* New York: Academic Press.

ANDERSON, R. C., & ORTONY, A. (1975). On putting apples into bottles—a problem of polysemy. *Cognitive Psychology, 7,* 167–180.

ANDERSON, R. C., & PICHERT, J. W. (1978). Recall of previously unrecallable information following a shift in perspective. *Journal of Verbal Learning and Verbal Behavior, 17,* 1–12.

APA (1983). *Monitor.* Caution: TV on. Letter from 43 psychologists and communications researchers. APA *Monitor,* May *14*(5), p. 4.

D'AQUILI, E. G. (1978). The neurobiological bases of myth and concepts of deity. *Zygon, 13,* 257–275.

ARDREY, R. (1966). *The territorial imperative.* New York: Atheneum.

ARKES, H. R., & HAMMOND, K. R. (Eds.). (1986). *Judgment and decision making: An interdisciplinary reader.* Cambridge: Cambridge University Press.

ARKES, H. R., & HARKNESS, A. R. (1980). The effect of making a diagnosis on subsequent recognition of symptoms. *Journal of Experimental Psychology: Human Learning and Memory, 6,* 568–575.

ARONFREED, J. (1976). Moral development from the standpoint of a general psychological theory. In Lickona.

ASLIN, R. N., & PISONI, D. B. (1980). Some developmental processes in speech perception. In Yeni-Komshian and others.

ATKINSON, M. (1982). *Explanations in the study of child language development*. Cambridge: Cambridge University Press.

ATKINSON, M. (1986). Learnability. In Fletcher & Garman (1986).

ATKINSON, R. C. (1975). Mnemotechnics in second-language learning. *American Psychologist*, *30*, 821–828.

ATKINSON, R. C., & RAUGH, M. R. (1975). An application of the mnemonic keyword method to the acquisition of Russian vocabulary. *Journal of Experimental Psychology: Human learning and memory*, *104*, 126–133.

ATKINSON, R. C., & SHIFFRIN, R. M. (1968). Human memory: A proposed system and its control processes. In K. Spence and J. Spence (Eds.), *The psychology of learning and motivation* (Vol. 2). New York: Academic Press.

AXELROD, R. (1987). Laws of life: How standards evolve. *The Sciences* (March/April): 44–51.

AZRIN, N. H., HOLZ, W., ULRICH, R., & GOLDIAMOND, I. (1961). The control of the content of conversation through reinforcement. *Journal of the Experimental Analysis of Behavior*, *4*, 25–30.

BABA, M. L., DARGA, L., & GOODMAN, M. (1982). Recent advances in molecular evolution of the primates. In A. Chiarelli & R. Corruccini (Eds.), *Advanced views in primate biology*. Berlin: Springer-Verlag.

BADDELEY, A. D. (1978). The trouble with levels: A reexamination of Craik and Lockhart's framework for memory research. *Psychological Review*, *85*, 139–152.

BADDELEY, A. D. (1982). Domains of recollection. *Psychological Review*, *89*, 708–729.

BAETENS BEARDSMORE, H. (1982). *Bilingualism: Basic principles*. Clevedon, UK: Tieto.

BAKER, L. (1985). Differences in the standards used by college students for evaluating their comprehension of expository prose. *Reading Research Quarterly*, *20*, 297–313.

BAKER, L., & WAGNER, J. L. (1987). Evaluating information for truthfulness: The effects of logical subordination. *Memory and Cognition*, *15*, 247–255.

BALDWIN, A. (1980). *Theories of child development* (2nd ed.). New York: John Wiley.

BALL, J. A. (1984). Memes as replicators. *Ethology and Sociobiology*, *5*, 145–161.

BANDURA, A. (1967). The role of modeling processes in personality development. In W. Hartup (Ed.), *The young child: Reviews of research*. Washington, DC: National Association for Education of Young Children.

BANDURA, A. (1974). Behavior theory and the models of man. *American Psychologist*, *29*, 859–869.

BANDURA, A. (1978). The self-system in reciprocal determinism. *American Psychologist*, *33*, 344–358.

BANDURA, A. (1982). Self-efficacy mechanism in human agency. *American Psychologist*, *37*, 122–147.

BANDURA, A., ROSS, D., & ROSS, S. (1961). Transmission of aggression through imitation of aggressive models. *Journal of Abnormal and Social Psychology*, *63*, 575–582.

BANDURA, A., & WALTERS, R. (1963). *Social learning and personality development*. New York: Holt, Rinehart & Winston.

BAR-ADON, A., & LEOPOLD, W. F. (Eds.). (1971). *Child language: A book of readings*. Englewood Cliffs, NJ: Prentice-Hall.

BARASH, D. (1979). *The whisperings within*. New York: Penguin.

BARASH, D. P. (1977). *Sociobiology and behavior* (1st ed.). New York: Elsevier.

BARASH, D. P. (1982). *Sociobiology and behavior* (2nd ed.). New York: Elsevier.

BARCLAY, J. R., BRANSFORD, J. D., FRANKS, J. J., McCARRELL, N. S., & NITSCH, K. (1974). Comprehension and semantic flexibility. *Journal of Verbal Learning and Verbal Behavior*, *13*, 471–481.

BARKER-BENFIELD, G. J. (1976). *The horrors of the half-known life*. New York: Harper Colophon.

BARLOW, G. W., & SILVERBERG, J. (Eds.) (1980). *Sociobiology: Beyond nature/nurture?* Boulder, CO: Westview Press (AAAS Selected Symposium 35.)

BARON, A., KAUFMAN, A., & STAUBER, K. (1969). Effects of instructions and reinforcement-feedback on human operant behavior maintained by fixed-internal reinforcement. *Journal of the Experimental Analysis of Behavior*, *12*, 701–712.

BARSALOU, L. S. (1983). Ad hoc categories. *Memory and Cognition*, *11*, 211–227.

BARTLETT, F. C. (1932). *Remembering: A study in experimental and social psychology*. London: Cambridge University Press.

BARTLETT, J. C., BURLESON, G., & SANTROCK, J. W. (1982). Emotional mood and memory in young children. *Journal of Experimental Child Psychology, 34*, 59–76.

BARTLETT, J. C., & SANTROCK, J. W. (1979). Affect-dependent episodic memory in young children. *Child Development, 50*, 513–518.

BASTIAN, J., EIMAS, P. D., & LIBERMAN, A. M. (1961). Identification and discrimination of a phonemic contrast induced by silent interval. *Journal of the Acoustical Society of America, 33*, 842.

BATESON, P. (1985). Problems and possibilities of fusing developmental and evolutionary thought. In Butterworth and others (1985).

BATTAN, J. F. (1983). The "new narcissism" in 20th-century America: The shadow and substance of social change. *Journal of Social History, 17*, 199–220.

BAUMRIND, D. (1971). Harmonious parents and their preschool children. *Developmental psychology, 4*, 63–72.

BEALS, K. L., SMITH, C. L., & DODD, S. M. (1984). Brain size, cranial morphology, climate, and time machines. *Current Anthropology, 25*, 301–320.

BECK, B. (April 10, 1983). Tools and intelligence. Paper presented at the Second National Zoological Park Symposium, Animal Intelligence, Washington, DC.

BEGG, I., & PAIVIO, A. (1969). Concreteness and imagery in sentence meaning. *Journal of Verbal Learning and Verbal Behavior, 8*, 821–827.

BEILIN, H. (1980). Piaget's theory: Refinement, rejection, or revision? In R. H. Kluwe & H. Spada (Eds.), *Developmental models of thinking*. New York: Academic Press.

BEIT-HALLAHMI, B., & RABIN, A. (1977). The kibbutz as a social experiment and as child-rearing laboratory. *American Psychologist, 32*, 532–541.

BENDERLY, B. L. (July-August 1980). The great ape debate. *Science 80, 1*(5), 60–65.

BERLIN, B., & KAY, P. (1969). *Basic color terms: Their universality and evolution*. Berkeley: University of California Press.

BERMANT, G. (1976). Sexual behavior: Hard times with the Coolidge Effect. In M. Siegel & H. Zigler (Eds.), *Psychological research: The inside story*. New York: Harper & Row.

BERNE, E. (1964). *Games people play*. New York: Grove Press.

BEST, J. B. (1986). *Cognitive psychology*. St. Paul, MN: West.

BETHELL, T. (December 1980). Burning Darwin to save Marx. *Harper's, 257* (1543), 31–38, 91–92.

BEVER, T. G. (1970). The cognitive basis for linguistic structures. In Hayes.

BEVER, T. G. (1980). Broca and Lashley were right: Cerebral dominance is an accident of growth. In Caplan.

BEYTH-MAROM, R., & LICHTENSTEIN, S. (1984). *An elementary approach to thinking under uncertainty*. Hillsdale, NJ: Lawrence Erlbaum.

BIJOU, S. (1976). *Child development: The basic stage of early childhood*. Englewood Cliffs, NJ: Prentice-Hall.

BIJOU, S., & BAER, D. M. (1968). *Child development: Readings in behavior analysis*. New York: Appleton-Century-Crofts.

BINGHAM, R. (March/April 1980). Trivers in Jamaica. *Science 80, 1* (3), 56–67.

BLACK, A., COTT, A., & PAVLOSKI, R. (1977). The operant learning theory approach to biofeedback training. In G. Schwartz & J. Beatty (Eds.), *Biofeedback: theory and research*. New York: Academic Press.

BLACK, J. E., & GREENOUGH, W. T. (1986). Developmental approaches to the memory process. In Martinez & Kesner (1986).

BLANCHARD, E., & EPSTEIN, L. (1978). *A biofeedback primer*. Reading, MA: Addison-Wesley.

BLOCK, N. (Ed.). (1981). *Imagery*. Cambridge, MA: MIT Press.

BLODGETT, H. S. (1929). The effect of the introduction of reward upon the maze performance of rats. *University of California Publications in Psychology, 4*, 113–134.

BLOOM, L. (Ed.). (1978). *Readings in language development*. New York: John Wiley.

BLOOM, L., HOOD, L., & LIGHTBOWN, P. (1974). Imitation in language development: If, when, and why. *Cognitive Psychology, 6*, 380–420. Reprinted in Bloom (1978).

BLOOM, L., & LAHEY, M. (1978). *Language development and language disorders*. New York: John Wiley.

BLUMENBERG, B. (1983). The evolution of the advanced hominid brain. *Current Anthropology, 24*, 589–623.

BLUMENFELD, W. S., BLUMENFELD, E. R., & TERRELL, S. A. (1978, August). Readability of source and explanatory materials associated with the Medicare program. Paper presented at meeting of the American Psychological Association, Toronto.

BLUMENSTEIN, S. E. (1980). Speech perception: An overview. In Yeni-Komshian and others.

BLUMENTHAL, A. (1980). Wilhelm Wundt and early American psychology: A clash of cultures. In R. W. Rieber (Ed.), *Wilhelm Wundt and the making of a scientific psychology*. New York: Plenum.

BOLLES, R. C. (1971). Species-specific defense reactions. In R. F. Brush (Ed.), *Aversive learning and conditioning*. New York: Academic Press.

BOLLES, R. C. (1975). Learning, motivation and cognition. In W. K. Estes (Ed.), *Handbook of learning and cognitive processes* (Vol. 1). Hillsdale, NJ.: Lawrence Erlbaum Associates.

BOURNE, L. E. JR., DOMINOWSKI, R. L., LOFTUS, E. F., & HEALY, A. F. (1986). *Cognitive Processes*. (2nd ed.). Englewood Cliffs, NJ: Prentice-Hall.

BOWER, G. H. (1981). Mood and memory. *American Psychologist, 36*, 129–148.

BOWER, G. H., BLACK, J. B., & TURNER, T. J. (1979). Scripts in memory for text. *Cognitive psychology, 11*, 177–220.

BOWER, G. H., KARLIN, M. B., & DUECK, A. (1975). Comprehension and memory for pictures. *Memory and Cognition, 3*, 216–220.

BOWER, G. H., MONTEIRO, K. P., & GILLIGAN, S. G. (1978). Emotional mood as a context for learning and recall. *Journal of Verbal Learning and Verbal Behavior, 17*, 573–587.

BOWER, T. G. R. (1974). *Development in infancy*. San Francisco: W. H. Freeman.

BOWER, T. G. R. (1977). *A primer of infant development*. San Francisco: W. H. Freeman.

BOWER, T. G. R. (1979). *Human development*. San Francisco: W. H. Freeman.

BOYD, R., & RICHERSON, P. J. (1985). Culture and the evolutionary process. Chicago: University of Chicago Press.

BRAINERD, C. J. (1974a). Neo-Piagetian training experiments revisited: Is there any support for the cognitive-developmental stage hypotheses? *Cognition, 2*, 349–376.

BRAINERD, C. J. (1974b, June). Structures of the whole: Is there any glue to hold the concrete-operational 'stage' together? Paper presented at the annual meeting of the Canadian Psychological Association, Windsor, Ontario.

BRAINERD, C. J. (1978a). *Piaget's theory of intelligence*. Englewood Cliffs, NJ: Prentice-Hall.

BRAINERD, C. J. (1978b). The stage question in cognitive developmental theory. *Behavioral and brain sciences, 1*, 173–213.

BRAINERD, C. J., & ALLEN, T. W. (1971). Experimental inductions of the conservation of 'first order' quantitative invariants. *Psychological Bulletin, 75*, 125–144.

BRAINERD, C., & PRESSLEY, M. (EDS.). (1987). *Basic processes in memory development*. New York: Springer.

BRANDON, R. N. & BURIAN, R. (Eds.) (1984). *Genes, organisms and populations: Controversies over the units of selection*. Cambridge: MIT Press.

BRANSFORD, J. D. (1978). *Human cognition*. Belmont, CA: Wadsworth.

BRANSFORD, J. D., & FRANKS, J. J. (1971). The abstraction of linguistic ideas. *Cognitive psychology, 2*, 331–350.

BRANSFORD, J. D., & JOHNSON, M. K. (1972). Contextual prerequisites for understanding: Some investigations of comprehension and recall. *Journal of Verbal Learning and Verbal Behavior, 11*, 717–726.

BRANSFORD, J. D., & JOHNSON, M. K. (1973). Considerations of some problems of comprehension. In W. Chase (Ed.), *Visual information processing*. New York: Academic Press.

BRANSFORD, J. D., & MCCARRELL, N. S. (1974). A cognitive approach to comprehension: Some thoughts about understanding what it means to comprehend. In W. B. Weimer, & D. S. Palermo (Eds.), *Cognition and the symbolic processes*. Hillsdale, NJ: Lawrence Erlbaum Associates.

BRANSFORD, J. D., & STEIN, B. S. (1984). *The ideal problem solver*. New York: W. H. Freeman.

BRELAND, K., & BRELAND, M. (1961/1972). The misbehavior of organisms. In Seligman & Hager.

BRETT, G. S. (1912). *A history of psychology* (Vol. 2). London: Allen.

BREWER, W. F. (1974). There is no convincing evidence for operant or classical conditioning in adult humans. In W. Weimer and D. Palermo (Eds), *Cognition and the symbolic processes*. Hillsdale, NJ: Lawrence Erlbaum Associates.

BREWER, W. F. (1977). Memory for the pragmatic implications of sentences. *Memory and Cognition, 5*, 673–678.

BREWER, W. F. (1986). What is autobiographical memory? In D. C. Rubin (Ed.), *Autobiographical memory*. Cambridge: Cambridge University Press. Pp. 25–49.

BREWER, W. F. (1987). Schemas versus mental models in human memory. In P. Morris (Ed.), *Modelling cognition: Proceedings of the International Workshop on Modelling Cognition*. New York: John Wiley.

BREWER, W. F., & HARRIS, R. J. (1974). Memory for deictic elements in sentences. *Journal of Verbal Learning and Verbal Behavior, 13*, 321–327.

BREWER, W. F., & NAKAMURA, G. V. (1984). The nature and functions of schemas. In R. S. Wyer & T. K. Srull (Eds.), *Handbook of social cognition*. Hillsdale, NJ: Lawrence Erlbaum Associates.

BRIGHAM, J. C., MAAS, A., SNYDER, L. D., & SPAULDING, K. (1982). Accuracy of eyewitness identification in a field study. *Journal of Personality and Social Psychology, 42*, 673–681.

BRITTON, B. K., & TESSER, A. (1982). Effects of prior knowledge on use of cognitive capacity in three complex cognitive tasks. *Journal of Verbal Learning and Verbal Behavior, 21*, 421–436.

BRITTON, J., BURGESS, T., MARTIN, N., MACLEOD, A., & ROSEN, H. (1975). *The development of writing abilities (11–18)*. London: Macmillan Education.

BROADBENT, D. (1958). *Perception and communication*. New York: Pergamon Press.

BROADBENT, D. (1982). Task combination and selective intake of information. *Acta Psychologica, 50*, 253–290.

BROWN, J. A. (1958). Some tests of the decay theory of immediate memory. *Quarterly Journal of Experimental Psychology, 10*, 12–21.

BROWN, J. L., & BROWN, E. R. (1981). Kin selection and individual selection in babblers. In Alexander & Tinkle.

BROWN, P. C., & JENKINS, H. M. (1968). Autoshaping of the pigeon's key peck. *Journal of the Experimental Analysis of Behavior, 11*, 1–8.

BROWN, R. (1970). The first sentences of child and chimpanzee. In *Psycholinguistics: Selected papers*. New York: Free Press. Reprinted in T. A. Sebeok & J. Umiker-Sebeok (1980).

BROWN, R. (1973). *A first language*. Cambridge, MA: Harvard University Press.

BRUNO, K. J., & HARRIS, R. J. (1980). The effect of repetition on the discrimination of asserted and implied claims in advertising. *Applied Psycholinguistics, 1*, 307–321.

BRYANT, P. (1974). *Perception and understanding in young children*. New York: Basic Books.

BUCKHOUT, R. (1974). Eyewitness testimony. *Scientific American, 231(6)*, 23–31.

BUTTERS, N., & MILIOTIS, P. (1985). In K. Heilman & E. Valenstein (Eds.), *Clinical neuropsychology*. New York: Oxford University Press.

BUTTERWORTH, G., RUTKOWSKA, J., & SCAIFE, M. (Eds.). (1985). *Evolution and developmental psychology*. New York: St. Martin's Press.

CAIRNS, R. B. & VALSINER, J. (1984). Child psychology. *Annual Review of Psychology, 35*, 553–577.

CALFEE, R. C., CHAPMAN, R. S., & VENEZKY, R. L. (1972). How a child needs to think to learn to read. In L. W. Gregg (Ed.), *Cognition in learning and memory*. New York: John Wiley.

CALKINS, M. W. (1894). Association. *Psychological Review, 1*, 476–483.

CALVIN, W. H. (1982). Did throwing stones shape hominid brain evolution? *Ethology and Scoiobiology, 3* 115–124.

CAMPBELL, R. N. (1986). Language acquisition and cognition. In Fletcher & Garman (1986).

CANTOR, N., & MISCHEL, W. (1977). Traits as prototypes: Effects on recognition memory. *Journal of Personality and Social Psychology, 35*, 38–48.

CAPALDI, E. J. (1966). Partial reinforcement: An hypothesis of sequential effects. *Psychological Review, 73*, 459–477.

CAPALDI, E. J. (1971). Memory and learning: A sequential viewpoint. In W. Honig & P. James (Eds.), *Animal memory*. New York: Academic Press.

CAPLAN, A. L. (1978). *The sociobiology debate*. New York: Harper Colophon.

CAPLAN, D. (Ed.). (1980). *Biological studies of mental processes*. Cambridge, MA: MIT Press.

CAREY, S. (1985). *Conceptual change in childhood*. Cambridge, MA: MIT Press.

CARRELL, P. L. (1983). Background knowledge in second language comprehension. *Language Learning and Communication, 2*, 25–33.

CARROLL, D. W. (1986). *Psychology of language*. Monterey CA: Brooks/Cole.

CARTMILL, PILBEAM, D., & ISAAC, G. (1986). One hundred years of paleoanthropology. *American Scientist, 74*, 410–422.

CASSON, R. W. (1983). Schemata in cognitive anthropology. *Annual Review of Anthropology, 12*, 429–462.

CAVALLI-SFORZA, L., FELDMAN, M., CHEN, K., & DORNBUSCH, S. (1982). Theory and observation in cultural transmission. *Science, 218*, 19–27.

CAVANAUGH, J. C., & PERLMUTTER, M. (1982). Metamemory: A critical examination. *Child Development, 53*, 11–28.

CELLERIER, G. (1972). Information processing tendencies in recent experiments in cognitive learning—theoretical implication. In Farnham-Diggory.

CHAGNON, N. A. (1980)). Kin-selection theory, kinship, marriage and fitness among the Yanomamö Indians. In Barlow & Silverberg.

CHAGNON, N. A. (1981). Terminological kinship, genealogical relatedness and village fissioning among the Yanomamö Indians. In Alexander & Tinkle.

CHAGNON, N. A., & IRONS, W. (Eds.) (1979). *Evolutionary biology and human social behavior*. North Scituate, MA: Duxbury Press.

CHANG, T. M. (1986). Semantic memory: Facts and models. *Psychological Bulletin, 99*, 199–220.

CHAPMAN, L. J., & CHAPMAN, J. P. (1967). Genesis of popular, but erroneous diagnostic observations. *Journal of Abnormal Psychology, 72*, 193–204.

CHAPMAN, L. J., & CHAPMAN, J. P. (1969). Illusory correlation as an obstacle to the use of valid diagnostic signs. *Journal of Abnormal Psychology, 74*, 271–280.

CHARROW, R. P., & CHARROW, V. R. (1979). Making legal language understandable: A psycholinguistic study of jury instructions. *Columbia Law Review, 79*, 1306–1374.

CHARROW, V. R. (1982). Linguistic theory and the study of legal and bureaucratic language. In L. K. Obler & L. Menn (Eds.), *Exceptional language and linguistics*. New York: Academic Press.

CHASE, W. G., & SIMON, H. A. (1973). The mind's eye in chess. In W. G. Chase (Ed.), *Visual information processing*. New York: Academic Press.

CHERRY, E. C. (1953). Some experiments on the recognition of speech with one and two ears. *Journal of the Acoustical Society of America, 25*, 975–979.

CHEVALIER-SKOLNIKOFF, S., & POIRIER, F. (Eds.). (1977). *Primate bio-social development*. New York: Garland.

CHI, M. T. H., FELTOVICH, P. J., & GLASER, R. (1981). Categorization and representation of physics problems by experts and novices. *Cognitive Science, 5*, 121–152.

CHIESI, H. L., SPILICH, G. J., & VOSS, J. F. (1979). Acquisition of domain-related information in relation to high and low domain knowledge. *Journal of Verbal Learning and Verbal Behavior, 18*, 257–273.

CHOMSKY, N. (1957). *Syntactic structures*. The Hague: Mouton.

CHOMSKY, N. (1959). Review of Skinner's *Verbal Behavior*. *Language, 35*, 26–58. Reprinted in Jakobovits & Miron, (1967).

CHOMSKY, N. (1965a). *Aspects of the theory of syntax*. Cambridge, MA: MIT Press.

CHOMSKY, N. (1965b). *Cartesian linguistics*. Cambridge, MA: MIT Press.

CHOMSKY, N. (1972). *Language and mind* (Enlarged ed.). New York: Harcourt Brace Jovanovich.

CHOMSKY, N. (1976). On the nature of language. In S. R. Harnad, H. D. Steklis, & J. Lancaster.

CHOMSKY, N. (1979). Human language and other semiotic systems. *Semiotica, 31*–44. Reprinted in Sebeok & Umiker-Sebeok, 1980(a).

CHOMSKY, N. (1980b). *Rules and representations*. New York: Columbia University Press.

CHURCHLAND, P. S. (1987). Epistemology in the age of neuroscience. Paper presented at a conference on The Brain: Philosophy, Psychology, and Artificial Intelligence. University of Pittsburgh, Pittsburgh, PA, May 6.

CLARK, D. M., & TEASDALE, J. D. (1982). Diurnal variations in clinical depression and accessibility of memories of positive and negative experiences. *Journal of Abnormal Psychology, 91*, 87–95.

CLARK, E. V., & HECHT, B. F. (1983). Comprehension, production and language acquisition. *Annual Review of Psychology, 34*, 325–350.

CLARK, H. H. (1977). Inferences in comprehension. In D. Laberge & S. J. Samuels (Eds.), *Basic processes in reading: Perception and comprehension*. Hillsdale, NJ: Lawrence Erlbaum Associates.

CLARK, H. H., & CLARK, E. V. (1977). *Psychology and language.* New York: Harcourt Brace Jovanovich.

CLARK, H. H., & GERRIG, R. J. (1984). On the pretense theory of irony. *Journal of Experimental Psychology: General, 113*, 121–126.

CLARK, H. H., & HAVILAND, S. E. (1977). Comprehension and the given-new contract. In R.O. Freedle (Ed.), *Discourse production and comprehension.* Norwood, NJ: Ablex.

CLIFFORD, B. R., & LLOYD-BOSTOCK, S. (Eds.). (1983). *Evaluating witness evidence: Recent psychological research and new perspectives.* Chichester, UK: John Wiley.

CLUTTON-BROCK, T. H., & HARVEY, P. H. (Eds.). (1978). *Readings in Sociobiology.* San Francisco: W. H. Freeman.

COHEN, D. (1979). *J. B. Watson.* London: Routledge & Kegan Paul.

COLLINS, A. M., & LOFTUS, E. F., (1975). A spreading-activation theory of semantic processing. *Psychological Review, 82*, 407–428.

COLLINS, A. M., & QUILLIAN, M. R. (1969). Retrieval time from semantic memory. *Journal of Verbal Learning and Verbal Behavior, 8*, 240–247.

COLLINS, A., WARNOCK, E. H., AIELLO, N., & MILLER, M. L. (1975). Reasoning from incomplete knowledge. In D. Bobrow & A. Collins (Eds.), *Representation and understanding: Studies in cognitive science.* New York: Academic Press.

COLWILL, R. M., & RESCORLA, R. A. (1986). Associative structures in instrumental learning. *Psychology of learning and motivation, 20*, 55–104.

CONDON, W. S., & SANDER, L. (1974). Neonate movement is synchronized with adult speech: Interactional participation and language acquisition. *Science, 183*, 99–101.

CONLEY, J. M., O'BARR, W. M., & LIND, E. A. (1978). The power of language: Presentation style in the courtroom. *Duke Law Journal*, 1375–1399.

CONRAD, R. (1964). Acoustic confusions in immediate memory. *British Journal of Psychology, 55*, 75–84.

COOPER, J. (1981). Ubiquitous halo. *Psychological Bulletin, 90*, 218–244.

COOPER, L. A., & SHEPARD, R. N. (1973). Chronometric studies of the rotation of mental images. In W. G. Chase (Ed.), *Visual information processing.* New York: Academic Press.

CORBETT, A. T., & DOSHER, B. A. (1978). Instrument inferences in sentence encoding. *Journal of Verbal Learning and Verbal Behavior, 17*, 479–491.

CORCORAN, D. W. (1967). Acoustic factors in proofreading. *Nature, 214*, 851.

COSS, R. G. (1985). Comparative restraints on learning: Phylogenetic and synaptic interpretations. In Weinberger and others (1985).

COTMAN, C., & MCGAUGH, J. E. (1980). *Behavioral neuroscience: An introduction.* Orlando, FL: Academic Press.

COTTON, J. W. (1955). On making predictions from Hull's theory. *Psychological Review, 62*, 303–314.

COUGHLIN, W. J. (1953, March). The great *mokusatsu* mistake. *Harper's.*

COX, J. R., & GRIGGS, R. A. (1982). The effects of experience on performance in Wason's selection task. *Memory and Cognition, 10*, 496–502.

CRAIK, F. I. M. (1979). Human memory. *Annual Review of Psychology, 30*, 63–102.

CRAIK, F. I. M., & LOCKHART, R. S. (1972). Levels of processing: A framework for memory research. *Journal of Verbal Learning and Verbal Behavior, 11*, 671–684.

CRAIK, F. I. M., & MCINTYRE, J. S. (1986). Age differences in memory for facts and their sources. Paper presented at meeting of the Psychonomic Society, New Orleans, November 1986.

CRAIK, F. I. M., & TULVING, E. (1975). Depth of processing and the retention of words in episodic memory. *Journal of Experimental Psychology: General, 104*, 268–294.

CRAWFORD, C. (1983). Sociobiology: Of what value to psychology? Paper presented at the annual meeting of the APA, Anaheim, CA.

CROMER, R. F. (1974). The development of language and cognition: The cognition hypothesis. In B. Foss (Ed.), *New perspectives in child development.* Baltimore: Penguin.

CROMER, R. F. (1981). Reconceptualizing language acquisition and cognitive development. In R. L. Schiefelbusch & D. D. Bricker (Eds.), *Early language: Acquisition and intervention.* Baltimore: University Park Press.

CROWDER, R. G. (1982). The demise of short-term memory. *Acta Psychologica, 50*, 291–323.

CURTIS, H. (1968). *Biology.* New York: Worth.

DALE, P. S. (1976). *Language development* (2nd ed.). New York: Holt, Rinehart & Winston.

DALY, M., & WILSON, M. (1978). *Sex, evolution and behavior: Adaptations for reproduction.* North Scituate, MA: Duxbury Press.

DALY, M., & WILSON, M. (1982). Abuse and neglect of children in evolutionary perspective. In Alexander and Tinkle.

DALY, M., WILSON, M., & WEGHORST, S. (1982). Male sexual jealousy. *Ethology and Sociobiology, 3,* 11–27.

DANIELS, D. (1983). The evolution of concealed ovulation and self-deception. *Ethology and Sociobiology, 4,* 69–87.

DARWIN, C. (1965). *The expression of emotion in man and animals* (1872). Chicago: University of Chicago Press.

DARWIN, C. J., TURVEY, M. T., & CROWDER, R. G. (1972). The auditory analogue of the Sperling partial report procedure: Evidence for brief auditory storage. *Cognitive Psychology, 3,* 225–267.

DASEN, P. R. (1972). Cross-cultural Piagetian research: A summary. *Journal of Cross-Cultural Psychology, 3,* 23–39. Reprinted in J. Berry & P. Dazen (Eds.), *Culture and cognition: Readings in cross-cultural psychology.* London: Methuen, 1974.

DAVIS, W. J. (1986). Invertebrate model systems. In Martinez & Kesner (1986).

DAWKINS, R. (1976). *The selfish gene.* New York: Oxford University Press.

DAY, R. (1986). Cognitive consequences of different representations. Paper presented at the Psychonomic Society Meeting, New Orleans, November 1986.

D'AZEVEDO, W. L. (1962). Uses of the past in Gola discourse. *Journal of African History, 3,* 11–34.

DEFFENBACHER, K. (1980). Eyewitness accuracy and confidence: Can we infer anything about their relationship? *Law and Human Behavior, 4,* 243–260.

DE GROOT, A. D. (1965). *Thought and choice in chess.* The Hague: Mouton.

DELGADO, J. (1969). *Physical control of the mind.* New York: Harper & Row.

DELGADO, J. (1976). New orientations in brain stimulation in man. In A. Wauquier & E. Rolls (Eds.), *Brain-stimulation reward.* Amsterdam: North Holland.

DELSON, E. (Ed.). (1985). *Ancestors: The hard evidence.* New York: Alan R. Liss, Inc.

DENISI, A. S., CAFFERTY, T. P., & MEGLINO, B. M. (1984). A cognitive view of the performance appraisal process: A model and research propositions. *Organizational Behavior and Human Performance, 33,* 360–396.

DENNETT, D. (1978). Skinner skinned. In D. Dennett, (Ed.), *Brainstorms.* Cambridge, MA.: Bradford/MIT.

DENNIS, M. (1980). Language acquisition in a single hemisphere: Semantic organization. In Caplan.

DERWING, B. L. (1973). *Transformational grammar as a theory of language acquisition.* Cambridge: At University Press.

DEUTSCH, J. A. (1956). The inadequacy of the Hullian derivations of reasoning and latent learning. *Psychological Review, 63,* 389–399.

DE VILLIERS, J. G., & DE VILLIERS, P. A. (1978). *Language acquisition.* Cambridge, MA: Harvard University Press.

DEWSBURY, D. A. (1981). Effects of novelty on copulatory behavior: The Coolidge Effect and related phenomena. *Psychological Bulletin, 89,* 464–482.

DICKEMANN, M. (1982). Paternal confidence and dowry competition: A biocultural analysis of Purdah. In Alexander & Tinkle.

DIXON, T. R., & HORTON, D. L. (Eds.). (1968). *Verbal behavior and general behavior theory.* Englewood Cliffs, NJ: Prentice-Hall.

DOLLARD J., DOOB, L., MILLER, N., MOWRER, O., & SEARS, R. (1939). *Frustration and aggression.* New Haven: Yale University Press.

DOLLARD J., & MILLER, N. (1950). *Personality and psychotherapy.* New York: McGraw-Hill.

DOMJON, M. (1980). Ingestional aversion learning: Unique and general processes. *Advances in the study of behavior* (Vol. 11). New York: Academic Press.

DONALDSON, M. (1978). *Children's minds.* New York: Norton.

DONDERS, F. C. (1969). Over de snelheid van psychische processen. Onderzoekingen gedaan in het Psychologish Laboratorium der Utrechtsche Hoogeschool: 1868–69. Tweede Reeks, II, 92–120. In W. G. Koster (Ed. and trans.), Attention and performance II. *Acta Psychologica, 30,* 412–431.

DOOLING, D. J., & LACHMAN, R. (1971). Effects of comprehension on retention of prose. *Journal of Experimental Psychology, 88*, 216–222.

DOOLING, D. J., & MULLET, R. L. (1973). Locus of thematic effects in retention of prose. *Journal of Experimental Psychology, 97*, 404–406

DOOLITTLE, W., & SAPIENZA, C. (1980). Selfish genes, the phenotype paradigm and gene evolution. *Nature, 284*, 601–603.

DOWNING, D. J., STERNBERG, R. J., & ROSS, B. H. (1985). Multicausal inference: Evaluation of evidence in causally complex situations. *Journal of Experimental Psychology: General, 114*, 239–263.

DUBITSKY, T. M. (1980). *The effects of contextual knowledge on drawing inferences from conversation.* Master's thesis, Kansas State University.

DURHAM, W. H. (1976). Resource competition and human aggression. *Quarterly Review of Biology, 51*, 385–415.

DURHAM, W. H. (1978). Toward a coevolutionary theory of human biology and culture. In Caplan.

DURHAM, W. H. (1982). Interactions of genetic and cultural evolution: Models and examples. *Human Ecology, 10*, 289–323

EBBINGHAUS, H. (1964). *Memory* (1885). New York: Dover.

EDWARDS, B. (1979). *Drawing on the right side of the brain.* Los Angeles: J. P. Tarcher, Inc.

EIBL-EIBESFELDT, I. (1975). *Ethology* (2nd ed.). New York: Holt, Rinehart & Winston.

EILERS, R. E. (1980). Infant speech perception: History and mystery. In Yeni-Komshian et al.

EIMAS, P. D., SIQUELAND, J. R., JUSCZYK, P., & VIGORITO, J. (1971). Speech perception in infants. *Science, 171*, 303–306.

ELIOT, A. J. (1981). *Child language.* New York: Cambridge University Press.

ELKIND, D. (1981). Recent research in cognitive and language development. In L. T. Benjamin (Ed.), *The G. Stanley Hall lecture series* (Vol. 1). Washington, DC: American Psychological Association.

ELKIND, D., & FLAVELL, J. H. (1969). *Studies in cognitive development.* New York: Oxford University Press.

ELLISON, K. W., & BUCKHOUT, R. (1981). *Psychology and criminal justice.* New York: Harper & Row.

ERICKSON, B., LIND, R. A., JOHNSON, B. C., & O'BARR, W. M. (1978). Speech style and impression formation in a court setting: The effects of 'powerful' and 'powerless' speech. *Journal of Experimental Social Psychology, 14*, 266–279.

ERICKSON, T. D., & MATTSON, M. E. (1981). From words to meaning: A semantic illusion. *Journal of Verbal Learning and Verbal Behavior, 20*, 540–551.

ERIKSON, E. (1939). Observations on Sioux education. *Journal of Psychology, 7*, 101–156.

ERIKSON, E. H. (1963). *Childhood and society* (2nd ed.). New York: Norton.

ERON, L. (1982). Parent-child interaction, television violence, and aggression of children. *American Psychologist, 37*, 197–211.

ESPER, J. A. (1986). *The processing of information about rape victims: Schematic distortions as a function of attitudes.* Doctoral dissertation, Kansas State University.

ESSOCK-VITALE, S. M. (1984). The reproductive success of wealthy Americans. *Ethology and Sociobiology, 5*, 45–49.

ESTES, W. K. (1950). Toward a statistical theory of learning. *Psychological Review, 57*, 94–107.

ESTES, W. K. (1972). Reinforcement in human behavior. *American Scientist, 60*, 723–729.

ESTES, W. K., KOCH, S., MACCORQUODALE, K., MEEHL, P., MUELLER, C. G., SCHOENFELD, W. N., & VERPLANCK, W. S. (1954). *Modern learning theory.* New York: Appleton-Century-Crofts.

EVANS, J. ST. B. T. (1982). *The psychology of deductive reasoning.* London: Routledge & Kegan Paul.

EVANS, J. ST. B. T., & WASON, P. C. (1976). Rationalization in a reasoning task. *British Journal of Psychology, 67*, 479–486.

FALK, D. (1987). Hominid paleoneurology. *Annual Review of Anthropology, 16*, 13–30.

FALK, J. L. (1961). Production of polydipsia in normal rats by an intermittent food schedule. *Science, 133*, 195–196.

FALK, J. L. (1971). The nature and determinants of adjunctive behavior. *Physiology and Behavior, 6*, 577–588.

FALK, J. L. (1981). The environmental generation of excessive behavior. In S. J. Mule (Ed.), *Behavior in excess*. New York: Free Press.

FALLON, J. J., JR., ALLEN, J. D., & BUTLER, J. A. (1979). Assessment of adjunctive behaviors in humans using a stringent control procedure. *Physiology and Behavior*, 22, 1089–1092.

FARB, P. (1978). *Humankind*. Boston: Houghton Mifflin.

FARBER, S. (1981, January). Telltale behavior of twins. *Psychology Today*, 15 (1) 58–62, 79–80.

FARLEY, J., & ALKON, D. L. (1985). Cellular mechanisms of learning, memory, and information storage. *Annual Review of Psychology*, 36, 419–494.

FARNHAM-DIGGORY, S. (Ed.) (1972). *Information processing in children*. New York: Academic Press.

FAUX, S. F., & MILLER, H. L. (1984). Evolutionary speculations on the oligarchic development of Mormon polygyny. *Ethology and Sociobiology*, 5, 15–31.

FELDMAN, J. M. (1981). Beyond attribution theory: Cognitive processes in performance appraisal. *Journal of Applied Psychology*, 66, 127–148.

FERSTER, C. B., & SKINNER, B. F. (1957). *Schedules of reinforcement*. Englewood Cliffs, NJ: Prentice-Hall.

FIELDING, G., & EVERED, C. (1980). The influence of patient's speech upon doctors: The diagnostic interview. In R. N. St. Clair & H. Giles (Eds.), *The social and psychological contexts of language*. Hillsdale, NJ: Lawrence Erlbaum Associates.

FILLMORE, C. J. (1968). The case for case. In E. Bach & R. Harms (Eds.), *Universals in linguistic theory*. New York: Holt, Rinehart & Winston.

FILLMORE, C. J. (1971). Verbs of judging: An exercise in semantic description. In C. J. Fillmore & D. T. Langendoen (Eds.), *Studies in linguistic semantics*. New York: Holt, Rinehart & Winston.

FISCHHOFF, B. (1975). Hindsight ≠ foresight: The effect of outcome knowledge on judgment under uncertainty. *Journal of Experimental Psychology: Human Perception and Performance*, 1, 288–299.

FISCHHOFF, B. (1977). Perceived informativeness of facts. *Journal of Experimental Psychology: Human Perception and Performance*, 3, 349–358.

FISCHHOFF, B., & BEYTH, R. (1975). 'I knew it would happen'—Remembered probabilities of once-future things. *Organizational Behavior and Human Performance*, 13, 1–16.

FISHBEIN, H. D. (1976). *Evolution, development and children's learning*. Santa Monica, CA: Goodyear.

FISKE, S., & TAYLOR, S. E. (1984). *Social cognition*. Reading, MA: Addison-Wesley.

FLANAGAN, O. J. (1981, June 12). The Freud-Lamarck connections: The philosophical foundations of the penis-envy hypothesis. Paper presented at Cheiron XIII, River Falls, WI.

FLANAGAN, O. (1982a). Virtue, sex and gender: Some philosophical reflections on the moral psychology debate. *Ethics*, 92, 499–512.

FLANAGAN, O. (1982b). A reply to Lawrence Kohlberg. *Ethics*, 92, 529–532.

FLANAGAN, O. (1982c). Moral structures? *Philosophy of the Social Sciences*, 12, 255–270.

FLANAGAN, O. (1983). *The sciences of the mind*. Cambridge, MA: MIT Press.

FLAVELL, J. H. (1971). Stage related properties of cognitive development. *Cognitive Psychology*, 2, 421–453.

FLAVELL, J. H. (1977). *Cognitive development*. Englewood Cliffs, NJ: Prentice-Hall.

FLAVELL, J. H. (1979). Metacognition and cognitive monitoring. A new area of cognitive-developmental inquiry. *American Psychologist*, 34, 906–911.

FLAVELL, J. H. (1982). On cognitive development. *Child Development*, 53, 1–10.

FLAVELL, J. H., & WELLMAN, H. M. (1977). Metamemory. In R. Kail & J. Hogen (Eds.), *Perspectives on the development of memory and cognition*. Hillsdale, NJ: Lawrence Erlbaum Associates.

FLAVELL, J. H., & WOHLWILL, J. (1969). Formal and functional aspects of cognitive development. In Elkind & Flavell.

FLETCHER, P., & GARMAN, M. (Eds.). (1986). *Language acquisition* (2nd ed.). Cambridge: Cambridge University Press.

FLINN, M. (1982). Uterine *vs.* agnatic kinship variability and associated cousin marriage preferences: An evolutionary biological analysis. In Alexander & Tinkle.

FLINN, M. V., & ALEXANDER, R. D. (1982). Culture theory: The developing synthesis from biology. *Human Ecology*, 10, 383–400.

Foss, D. J., & Hakes, D. T. (1978). *Psycholinguistics.* Englewood Cliffs, NJ: Prentice-Hall.

Fouts, R. S., & Rigby, R. L. (1980). Man-chimpanzee communication. In Sebeok & Umiker-Sebeok.

Fox, J. L. (1983). Debate on learning theory is shifting. *Science, 222,* 1219–1222.

Frederiksen, C. H., & Dominic, J. F. (Eds.). (1981). *Writing: Process, development, and communication.* Hillsdale, NJ: Lawrence Erlbaum Associates.

Freedman, D. G. (1974). *Human infancy: A biological perspective,* Hillsdale, NJ: Lawrence Erlbaum Associates.

Freud, A. (1979). *Psychoanalysis for teachers and parents.* (1935). New York: Norton.

Freud, S. (1920). *Beyond the pleasure principle.* New York: Norton, 1961.

Freud, S. (1949). *An outline of psychoanalysis* (Rev. ed.). (1940). New York: Norton.

Freud, S. (1950). A note upon the 'Mystic-Writing Pad' (1925). *Collected Papers* (Vol. V). London: The Hogarth Press.

Freud, S. (1950). Some psychological consequences of the anatomical distinction between the sexes (1925). *Collected Papers* (Vol. V).

Freud, S. (1952). *A general introduction to psychoanalysis* (1920). New York: Washington Square Press.

Freud, S. (1962). *Three essays on the theory of sexuality* (6th ed.) (1925). New York: Basic Books.

Freud, S. (1962). *The ego and the id* (1923). New York: Norton (1962).

Freud, S. (1962). *Civilization and its discontents* (1930). New York: Norton.

Freud, S. (1965). *The interpretation of dreams* (1900). New York: Avon.

Furth, H. G. (1969). *Piaget and knowledge: Theoretical foundations.* Englewood Cliffs, NJ: Prentice-Hall, (2nd ed.). Chicago: University of Chicago Press, 1981.

Gabriel, M., Sparenborg, S. P., & Stolar, N. (1986). The neurobiology of memory. In LeDoux & Hirst (1986).

Galef, B. (1983, April 10). Tradition and social learning in animals. Paper presented at the second National Zoological Park Symposium, Animal intelligence, Washington, DC.

Galizio, M. (1979). Contingency-shaped and rule-governed behavior: Instructional control of human loss avoidance. *Journal of the Experimental Analysis of Behavior, 31,* 53–70.

Gallagher, J. M., & Reid, D. K. (1981). *The learning theory of Piaget and Inhelder.* Monterey, CA: Brooks/Cole.

Gallup, G. G. (1977). Self-recognition in primates: A comparison approach to the bidirectional properties of consciousness. *American Psychologist, 32,* 329–338.

Garbarino, J., & Bronfenbrenner, U. (1976). The socialization of moral judgment and behavior in cross-cultural perspective. In Lickona.

Garcia, J. (1981). Tilting at the windmills of academe. *American Psychologist, 36,* 149–158.

Garcia, J., Clarke, J., & Hankins W. (1973). Natural responses to schedule rewards. In P. Bateson & P. Klopfer (Eds.), *Perspectives in ethology.* New York: Plenum (1973).

Garcia, J., McGowan, B., & Green, K. (1972). Biological constraints on conditioning. In Seligman & Hager.

Garcia, J., Quick, D., & White, B. (1984). Conditioned disgust and fear from mollusk to monkey. In Alkon & Farley (1984).

Gardner, B. T., & Gardner, R. A. (1980b). Two comparative psychologists look at language acquisition. In Nelson.

Gardner, R. A., & Gardner, B. T. (1969). Teaching sign language to a chimpanzee. *Science, 165,* 664–672. Reprinted in Seligmann & Hager, 1972.

Gardner, R. A., & Gardner, B. T. (1980a). Comparative psychology and language acquisition. In Sebeok & Umiker-Sebeok.

Geis, M. L. (1982). *The language of television advertising.* New York: Academic Press.

Gelman, R. (1972). The nature and development of early number concepts. In H. Reese (Ed.), *Advances in child development and behavior* (Vol. 7.). New York: Academic Press.

Gelman, R. (1978). Cognitive development. *Annual Review of Psychology,* Vol. 29.

Gelman, R. (1983). Recent trends in cognitive development. In G. Scherrer & A. M. Rogers (Eds.), *The G. Stanley Hall Lecture Series,* Vol. 3. Washington, DC: American Psychological Association.

Gentner, D., & Collins, A. (1981). Studies of inference from lack of knowledge. *Memory & Cognition, 9,* 434–443.

Gewirtz, J. L., & Stingle, K. (1968). Learning of generalized imitations as the basis for identification. *Psychological Review, 75,* 374–397.

GHISELIN, M. (1974). *The economy of nature and the evolution of sex*. Berkeley: University of California Press.

GIBBS, R. W. JR. (1984). Literal meaning and psychological theory. *Cognitive Science, 8*, 275–304.

GIBBS, R. W., JR. (1986). On the psycholinguistics of sarcasm. *Journal of Experimental Psychology: General, 115*, 3–15.

GIBSON, E. J., BISHOP, C., SCHIFF, W., & SMITH, J. (1964). Comparison of meaningfulness and pronounceability as grouping principles in the perception and retention of verbal material. *Journal of Experimental Psychology, 67*, 173–182.

GIBSON, E. J., & LEVIN, H. (1975). *The psychology of reading*. Cambridge, MA: MIT Press.

GIBSON, K. (1985). Has the evolution of intelligence stagnated since Neanderthal man? In Butterworth and others (1985).

GILLIGAN, C. (1977). In a different voice: Women's conception of self and morality. *Harvard Educational Review, 47*, 481–517.

GILLIGAN, C. (1979). Woman's place in man's life cycle. *Harvard Educational Review, 59*, 431–446.

GILLIGAN, C. (1982). *In a different voice*. Cambridge, MA: Harvard University Press.

GILLIGAN, S. G., & BOWER, G. H. (1984). Cognitive consequences of emotional arousal. In C. E. Izard, J. Kagan, & R. B. Zajonc (Eds.). *Emotions, cognition, & behavior*. Cambridge, U.K.: Cambridge University Press.

GINSBERG, A. (1954). Does Hullian theory provide the adequate foundations for a comprehensive theory of human behavior? *Journal of General Psychology, 51*, 301–330.

GITTELMAN-KLEIN, R., KLEIN, D. F., ABIKOFF, H., KATZ, S., GLOISTEN, A. C., & KATES, W. (1976). Relative efficacy of methylphenidate and behavior modification in hyperkinetic children: An interim report. *Journal of Abnormal Child Psychology, 4*, 361–379.

GLASS, A. L. (1984). Effect of memory set on reaction time. In J. R. Anderson and S. M. Kosslyn (Eds.), *Tutorials in learning and memory*. San Francisco: W. H. Freeman. Pp. 119–136.

GLASS, A. L., & HOLYOAK, K. J. (1986). *Cognition* (2nd ed.). New York: Random House.

GLASSMAN, R., PACKEL, E., & BROWN, D. (1986). Green beards and kindred spirits: A preliminary mathematical model of altruism toward nonkin who bear similarities to the giver. *Ethology and Sociobiology, 7*, 107–115.

GLENN, C. G. (1978). The role of episodic structure and story length in children's recall of simple stories. *Journal of Verbal Learning and Verbal Behavior, 17*, 229–247.

GLUCK, M. A., & THOMPSON, R. F. (1987). Modeling the neural substrates of learning: A computational approach. *Psychological Review, 94*, 176–191.

GODDEN, D. R., & BADDELEY, A. D. (1975). Context-dependent memory in two natural environments: on land and underwater. *British Journal of Psychology, 66*, 325–331.

GOLDING, E. (1981, April). The effect of past experience on problem solving. Paper presented at the annual conference of the British Psychological Society, Surrey University.

GOODWIN, D. W., POWELL, B., BREMER, D., HOINE, H., & STERN, J. (1969). Alcohol and recall: State-dependent effects in man. *Science, 163*, 1358.

GOSS, A. (1961). Early behaviorism and verbal mediating responses. *American Psychologist, 16*, 285–298.

GOUGH, P. B., & COSKY, M. J. (1977). One second of reading again. In N. J. Castellan, D. G. Pisoni, & G. R. Potts (Eds.), *Cognitive theory* (Vol. II). Hillsdale, NJ: Lawrence Erlbaum Associates.

GOULD, J. E., & GOULD, C. (1981, May). The instinct to learn. *Science 81, 2*, 44–50.

GOULD, J. L. (1982). *Ethology*. New York: Norton.

GOULD, J. L., & MARLER, P. (1987, January). Learning by instinct. *Scientific American, 256* (1), 74–85.

GOULD, P., & WHITE, R. (1974). *Mental maps*. Harmondsworth, UK: Penguin.

GRAESSER, A. D., & CLARK, L. F. (1985). The generation of knowledge-based inferences during narrative comprehension. In G. Rickheit & H. Strohner (Eds.), *Inferences in text processing*. Amsterdam: Elsevier (North-Holland). Pp. 53–94.

GRAF, P., & SCHACTER, D. L. (1985). Implicit and explicit memory for new associations in normal and amnesic subjects. *Journal of Experimental Psychology: Learning, Memory, & Cognition, 11*, 501–518.

GRAHAM, D. (1972). *Moral learning and development: Theory and research*. New York: Wiley-Interscience.

GRANGER, R. H., & SCHLIMMER, J. C. (1986). The computation of contingency in classical conditioning. *Psychology of learning and motivation, 20*, 137–192.

GREEN, S., & MARLER, P. (1979). The analysis of animal communication. In P. Marler & J. G. Vandenbergh (Eds.), *Handbook of Behavioral Neurobiology* (Vol. 3): *Social behavior and communication*. New York: Plenum.

GREENE, E., FLYNN, M. S., & LOFTUS, E. F. (1982). Inducing resistance to misleading information. *Journal of Verbal Learning and Verbal Behavior, 21*, 207–219.

GREENSPOON, J. (1955). The reinforcing effect of two spoken sounds on the frequency of two responses. *American Journal of Psychology, 68*, 409–416.

GREENWALD, A. G. (1981). Self and memory. In G. H. Bower (Ed.), *The psychology of learning and motivation* (Vol. 15). New York: Academic Press.

GREGG, L., & STEINBERG, E. (Eds.). (1980). *Cognitive processes in writing*. Hillsdale, NJ: Lawrence Erlbaum Associates.

GREGORY, M. S., SILVERS, A., & SUTCH, D. (Eds.). (1978). *Sociobiology and human nature*. San Francisco: Jossey-Bass.

GRICE, J. P. (1975). Logic and conversation. In P. Cole & J. L. Morgan (Eds.). *Syntax and semantics III: Speech acts*. New York: Academic Press.

GRIGGS, R. A. (1983). The role of problem content in the selection task and THOG problem. In J. St. B. T. Evans (Ed.), *Thinking and reasoning: Psychological approaches*. London: Routledge & Kegan Paul.

GRIGGS, R. A., & COX, J. R. (1982). The elusive thematic materials effect in Wason's selection task. *British Journal of Psychology, 73*, 407–420.

GRIGGS, R. A., & COX, J. R. (1983). The effect of problem content on strategies in Wason's selection task. *Quarterly Journal of Experimental Psychology, 35*, 519–534.

GROSJEAN, F. (1982). *Life with two languages*. Cambridge, MA: Harvard University Press.

GROTEVANT, H., SCARR, S., & WEINBERG, R. (1978, March). Are career interests inheritable? *Psychology Today, 11* (10) 88–90.

GROVES, P. M., & REBEC, G. V. (1988). *Introduction to biological psychology* (3rd ed.). Dubuque, IA: Wm. C. Brown.

GRUBER, H. E., & VONECHE, J. J. (Eds.). (1977). *The essential Piaget*. New York: Basic Books.

GRUEN, G. E. (1966). Note on conservation! Methodological and definitional considerations. *Child Development, 37*, 977–983. Reprinted in Sigel & Hooper (1968).

GRÜSSER, O.-J. (1983). Mother-child holding patterns in Western art: A developmental study. *Ethology and Sociobiology, 4*, 89–94.

GURIN, J. (1976). Is society hereditary? *Harvard Magazine, 79* (2), 21–25.

GUTHRIE, E. R. (1930). Conditioning as a principle of learning. *Psychological Review, 37*, 412–428.

GUTHRIE, E. R. (1933). Association as a function of the time-interval. *Psychological Review, 40*, 355–367.

GUTHRIE, E. R. (1934). Reward and punishment. *Psychological Review, 41*, 450–460.

GUTHRIE, E. R. (1939). The effect of outcome on learning. *Psychology Review, 46*, 480–484.

GUTHRIE, E. R. (1940). Association and the law of effect. *Psychological Review, 47*, 127–148.

GUTHRIE, E. R. (1952). *The psychology of learning* (2nd ed.). New York: Harper & Row.

GUTHRIE, E. R., & HORTON, G. (1946). *Cats in a puzzle box*. New York: Rinehart Press.

HABER, R. N. (1979). Twenty years of haunting eidetic images: Where's the ghost? *Behavioral and Brain Sciences, 2*, 583–594.

HAGEN, J. W. (1972). Strategies for remembering. In Farnham-Diggory.

HAHN, M., JENSEN, C., & DUDEK, B. (Eds.). (1979). *The development and evolution of brain size: Behavioral implications*. New York: Academic Press.

HALEY, A. (1976). *Roots*. New York: Doubleday.

HALLPIKE, C. R. (1985). Social and biological evolution. I. Darwinism and social evolution. *Journal of Social and Biological Structures, 8*, 129–146.

HAMES, R. B. (1979). Relatedness and interaction among the Ye'kwana: A preliminary analysis. In Chagnon & Irons.

HAMILTON, D. (1979). A cognitive-attributional analysis of stereotyping. In L. Berkowitz (Ed.), *Advances in experimental social psychology* (Vol. 12). New York: Academic Press.

HAMILTON, D. (1981). *Cognitive processes in stereotyping and in-group behavior.* Hillsdale NJ: Lawrence Erlbaum Associates.

HAMILTON, D. L., KATZ, L. B., & LEIRER, V. O. (1980). Organizational processes in impression formation. In R. Hastie, T. Ostrom, E. Ebbesen, R. Wyer, D. Hamilton, & D. Carlston (Eds.), *Person memory.* Hillsdale, NJ: Lawrence Erlbaum Associates.

HAMILTON, W. D. (1964). The genetic evolution of social behaviour. Reprinted in Caplan (1978) and Hunt (1980).

HAMMERSLEY, R., & READ, J. D. (1986). What is integration? Remembering a story and remembering false implications about the story. *British Journal of Psychology, 77,* 329–341.

HAMMOND, K. R., & GRASSIA, J. (1985). The cognitive side of conflict: From theory to resolution of policy disputes. In S. Oskamp (Ed.), *Applied social psychology annual* (Vol. 6). Beverly Hills CA: Sage, Pp. 233–254.

HANEY, C., BANKS, C., & ZIMBARDO, P. (1973). Interpersonal dynamics in a simulated prison. *International Journal of Criminology and Penology, 1,* 69–97.

HARNAD, S. R., STEKLIS, H., & LANCASTER, J. (1976). *Origins and evolution of language and speech. Annals of the New York Academy of Sciences* (Vol. 280). New York: The New York Academy of Sciences.

HARRIS, B. (1979). What ever happened to Little Albert? *American Psychologist, 34,* 151–160.

HARRIS, R. J. (1974). Memory and comprehension of implications and inferences of complex sentences. *Journal of Verbal Learning and Verbal Behavior, 13,* 626–637.

HARRIS, R. J. (1977a). The comprehension of pragmatic implications in advertising. *Journal of Applied Psychology, 62,* 603–608.

HARRIS, R. J. (1977b). The teacher as actor. *Teaching of Psychology, 4,* 185–187.

HARRIS, R. J. (1978). The effect of jury size and judge's instructions on memory for pragmatic implications from courtroom testimony. *Bulletin of the Psychonomic Society, 11,* 129–132.

HARRIS, R. J. (1981). Inferences in information processing. In G. H. Bower (Ed.), *The psychology of learning and motivation* (Vol. 15). New York: Academic Press.

HARRIS, R. J. (1982, January). The use of student journals in teaching psychology. ERIC Clearinghouse on Higher Education, *Resources in Education,* #ED206223.

HARRIS, R. J. (Ed.) (1983). *Information processing research in advertising.* Hillsdale, NJ: Lawrence Erlbaum Associates.

HARRIS, R. J. (1989). *A cognitive psychology of mass communication.* Hillsdale, NJ: Lawrence Erlbaum Associates.

HARRIS, R. J., DUBITSKY, T. M., & BRUNO, K. J. (1983). Psycholinguistic studies of misleading advertising. In R. J. Harris (Ed.), *Information processing research in advertising.* Hillsdale, NJ: Lawrence Erlbaum Associates.

HARRIS, R. J., DUBITSKY, T. M., CONNIZZO, J. F., LETCHER, L. E., & ELLERMAN, C. S. (1981). Training consumers about misleading advertising: Transfer of training and effects of specialized knowledge. In J. H. Leigh & C. R. Martin, Jr. (Eds.), *Current issues and research in advertising.* Ann Arbor: University of Michigan Graduate School of Business Administration, Division of Research, 1981.

HARRIS, R. J., DUBITSKY, T. M., & THOMPSON, S. (1979). Learning to identify deceptive truths in advertising. In J. H. Leigh & C. R. Martin, Jr. (Eds.), *Current issues and research in advertising.* Ann Arbor: University of Michigan Graduate School of Business Administration, Division of Research, 1979.

HARRIS, R. J., HENSLEY, D., LEE, D. J., & SCHOEN, L. M. (1988). The effect of cultural script knowledge on memory for stories over time. *Discourse Processes,* in press.

HARRIS, R. J., LAHEY, M. A., & MARSALEK, F. (1980). Metaphors and images: Rating, reporting, and remembering. In R. P. Honeck & R. R. Hoffman (Eds.), *Cognition and figurative language.* Hillsdale, NJ: Lawrence Erlbaum Associates.

HARRIS, R. J., & MONACO, G. E. (1978). Psychology of pragmatic implication: Information processing between the lines. *Journal of Experimental Psychology: General, 107,* 1–22.

HARRIS, R. J., SCHOEN, L. M., & HENSLEY, D. (in press). A cross-cultural study of story memory. *Journal of Cross-cultural Psychology.*

HARRIS, R. J., SCHOEN, L. M., & LEE, D. J. (1986). Culture-based distortion in memory for stories. In J. L. Armagost (Ed.), *Papers from the 1985 Mid-America Linguistics Conference.* Manhattan, KS: Kansas State University Department of Speech. pp. 84–91.

HARRIS, R. J., STURM, R. E., KLASSEN, M. L., & BECHTOLD, J. I. (1986). Language in advertising: A psycholinguistic approach. *Current Issues and Research in Advertising, 9*, 1–26.

HARRIS, R. J., TESKE, R. R., & GINNS, M. J. (1975). Memory for pragmatic implications from courtroom testimony. *Bulletin of the Psychonomic Society, 6*, 494–496.

HASHER, L., ATTIG, M. S., & ALBA, J. W. (1981). I knew it all along: Or did I? *Journal of Verbal Learning and Verbal Behavior, 20*, 86–96.

HASTIE, R. (1983). Social inference. *Annual Review of Psychology, 34*, 511–542.

HASTIE, R., & KUMAR, P. A. (1979). Person memory. Personality traits as organizing principles in memory for behaviors. *Journal of Personality and Social Psychology, 37*, 25–38.

HAVILAND, S. E., & CLARK, H. H. (1974). What's new? Acquiring new information as a process of comprehension. *Journal of Verbal Learning and Verbal Behavior, 13*, 512–521.

HAWKINS, R. D., & KANDEL, E. R. (1986). Steps toward a cell-biological alphabet for elementary forms of learning. In Lynch, McGaugh, & Weinberger (1986).

HAYES, J. R. (Ed.). (1970). *Cognition and the development of language.* New York: John Wiley.

HAYES, J. R. (1978). *Cognitive psychology.* Homewood, IL: Dorsey Press.

HEAD, H. (1920). *Studies in neurology.* Oxford: Oxford University Press.

HEARST, E. (1975). The classical-instrumental distinction: Reflexes, voluntary behavior, and categories of associative learning. In W. K. Estes (Ed.), *Handbook of learning and cognitive processes* (Vol. 2.). Hillsdale, NJ: Lawrence Erlbaum Associates.

HEDIGER, H. K. P. (1981). The Clever Hans Phenomenon from an animal psychologist's point of view. In Sebeok & Rosenthal.

HEIL, J. (1982). Speechless brutes. *Philosophy and Phenomenological Research, 42*, 400–406.

HEILBRUN, A. B. (1981). *Human sex-role behavior.* New York: Pergamon Press.

HEIMAN, J. R. (1975, April). The physiology of erotica: Women's sexual arousal. *Psychology Today, 8*, 90–94.

HEWES, G. W. (1975, August 30). The evolutionary significance of pongid sign language acquisition. Paper presented at the Annual Meeting of the American Psychological Association, Chicago.

HEWES, G. W. (1976). The current status of the gestural theory of language origin. In Harnad and others.

HILGARD, E., & BOWER, G. (1975). *Theories of learning* (4th ed.). Englewood Cliffs, NJ: Prentice-Hall.

HILL, E., NOCKS, E., & GARDNER, L. (1987). Physical attractiveness: Manipulation by physique and status displays. *Ethology and Sociobiology, 8*, 143–154.

HILL, J. H. (1980). Apes and language. In Sebeok & Umiker-Sebeok.

HINDE, R., & STEVENSON-HINDE, J. (Eds.). (1973). *Constraints on learning:* New York: Academic Press.

HINELINE, P. (1981). The several roles of stimuli in negative reinforcement. In P. Harzen & M. Zeiler (Eds.). *Advances in analysis of behaviour* (Vol. 2). Chichester, UK: John Wiley.

HOCHBERG, J. E. (1978). *Perception.* Englewood Cliffs, NJ: Prentice-Hall.

HOFFMAN, M. (1976). Empathy, role-taking, guilt and development of altruistic motives. In Lickona.

HOFFMAN, M. (1979). Development of moral thought, feeling and behavior. *American Psychologist, 34*, 958–966.

HOFFMAN, M., & SALTZSTEIN, H. (1967). Parent discipline and the child's moral development. *Journal of Personality and Social Psychology, 5*, 45–57.

HOLBROOK, M. B. (1978). Beyond attitude structure: Toward the informational determinants of attitude. *Journal of Marketing Research, 15*, 545–556.

HOLDEN, C. (1980a). Identical twins reared apart. *Science, 207*, 1323–1328.

HOLDEN, C. (1980b, November). Twins reunited. *Science 80, 1* (7) 1–8, 54–59.

HOLDING, D. H. (1979). Does being "eidetic" matter? *Behavioral and Brain Sciences, 2*, 604–605.

HOLLAND, P. C. (1981). Acquisition of representation-mediated conditioned food aversion. *Learning and Motivation, 12*, 1–18.

HOLLAND, P. C. (1984). Origins of behavior in Pavlovian conditioning. *The Psychology of Learning and Motivation, 18*, 129–174.

HOLLIS, K. L. (1982). Pavlovian conditioning of signal-centered action patterns and autonomic behavior: A biological analysis of function. In J. Rosenblatt, R. Hinde, C. Beer, and

M.-C. Busnel (Eds.) *Advances in the study of behavior* (Vol. 12). New York: Academic Press.

HOLLOWAY, R. L. (1976). Paleoneurological evidence for language origins. In Harnad and others.

HONIG, W. K., & THOMPSON, R. K. R. (1982). Retrospective and prospective processing in animal working memory. *Psychology of learning and motivation, 16*, 239–283.

HORTON, D. L., & TURNAGE, T. W. (1976). *Human learning*. Englewood Cliffs, NJ: Prentice-Hall.

HOSCH, H. M. (1980). A comparison of three studies of the influence of expert testimony on jurors. *Law and Human Behavior, 4*, 297–302.

HOSCH, H. M., BECK, E. L., & McINTYRE, P. (1980). Influence of expert testimony regarding eyewitness accuracy on jury decisions. *Law and Human Behavior, 4*, 287–295.

HOVLAND, C. I. (1938a). Experimental studies in rote learning. II. *Journal of Experimental Psychology, 22*, 338–353.

HOVLAND, C. I. (1938b). Experimental studies of rote learning. III. *Journal of Experimental Psychology, 23*, 172–190.

HOWARD, D. V. (1983). *Cognitive psychology: Memory, language, and thought*. New York: Macmillan.

HOWE, M. J. A. (1983). *Introduction to the psychology of memory*. New York: Harper & Row.

HRDY, S. B. (1979). The evolution of human sexuality: The latest word and the last. *Quarterly Review of Biology, 54*, 309–314.

HRDY, S. B. (1981). *The woman that never evolved*. Cambridge, MA: Harvard University Press.

HUBEL, D. H., & WIESEL, T. N. (1962). Receptive fields, binocular interaction, and functional architecture in the cat's visual cortex. *Journal of Physiology, 160*, 106–154.

HUBEL, D. H., & WIESEL, T. N. (1968). Receptive fields and functional architecture of monkey striate cortex. *Journal of Physiology, 195*, 215–243.

HULL, C. L. (1930a). Simple trial-error learning: A study in psychological theory. *Psychological Review, 37*, 241–256.

HULL, C. L. (1930b). Knowledge and purpose as habit mechanisms. *Psychological Review, 37*, 511–525.

HULL, C. L. (1931). Goal attraction and directing ideas concerned as habit phenomena. *Psychological Review, 38*, 478–506.

HULL, C. L. (1934). The concept of the habit-family hierarchy and maze learning. *Psychological Review, 41*, 33–54; 134–152.

HULL, C. L. (1935). The conflicting psychologies of learning—A way out. *Psychological Review, 42*, 491–561.

HULL, C. L. (1937). Mind, mechanism and adaptive behavior. *Psychological Review, 44*, 1–32.

HULL, C. L. (1943). *Principles of behavior*. New York: Appleton-Century.

HULL, C. L. (1952). *A behavior system*. New Haven: Yale University Press.

HULL, C. L. & BAERNSTEIN, H. (1929). A mechanical parallel to the conditioned reflex. *Science, 70*, 14–15.

HULL, C. L., FELSINGER, J., GLADSTONE, I., & YAMAGUCHI, H. (1947). A proposed quantification of habit strength. *Psychological Review, 54*, 237–254.

HUMPHREY, N. K. (1976). The social function of intellect. In P. P. G. Bateson & R. A. Hinde (Eds.), *Growing points in ethology*. Cambridge: Cambridge University Press.

HUMPHREYS, L. G. (1939). Acquisition and extinction of verbal expectations in a situation analogous to conditioning. *Journal of Experimental Psychology, 25*, 294–301.

HUNT, E. (1983). On the nature of intelligence. *Science, 219*, 141–146.

HYDE, J. S. (1981). How large are cognitive gender differences? *American Psychologist, 36*, 892–901.

ILGEN, D. R., & FELDMAN, J. M. (1983). Performance appraisal: A process in focus. In B. M. Staw & L. L. Cummings (Eds.), *Research in organizational behavior* (Vol. 5). Greenwich, CT: JAI Press.

INHELDER, B. (1972). Information processing tendencies in recent experiments in cognitive learning-empirical studies. In Farnham-Diggory.

INHELDER, B., & PIAGET, J. (1958). *The growth of logical thinking*. New York: Basic Books.

INHELDER, B., SINCLAIR, H., & BOVET, M. (1974). *Learning and the development of cognition*. Cambridge, MA: Harvard University Press.

IRONS, W. (1982). Why lineage exogamy? In Alexander & Tinkle.

ISAAC, G. L. (1976). Stages of cultural elaboration in the pleistocene: Possible archaeological indication of the development of language capabilities. In Harnad and others.

ISAACS, E. A., & CLARK, H. H. (1987). References in conversation between experts and novices. *Journal of Experimental Psychology: General, 116*, 26–37.

ISEN, A. M. (1984). Toward understanding the role of affect in cognition. In R. S. Wyer & T. K. Krull (Eds.), *Handbook of social cognition*, Vol. 3. Hillsdale, NJ: Lawrence Erlbaum Associates.

IZARD, C. E., KAGAN, J., & ZAJONC, R. B. (Eds.). (1984). *Emotions, cognition, and behavior.* Cambridge U.K.: Cambridge University Press.

JAKOBOVITS, L. A., & MIRON, M. S. (Eds.). (1967). *Readings in the psychology of language.* Englewood Cliffs, NJ: Prentice-Hall.

JAMES, W. (1890). *The principles of psychology* (Vols. 1 & 2). New York: Henry Holt.

JANIS, I. (1980). The influence of television on personal decision making. In S. B. Withey & R. P. Abeles (Eds.), *Television and social behavior: Beyond violence and children.* Hillsdale, NJ: Lawrence Erlbaum Associates.

JAYNES, J. (1976a). *The origin of consciousness in the breakdown of the bicameral mind.* Boston: Houghton Mifflin.

JAYNES, J. (1976b). The evolution of language in the late Pleistocene. In Harnad and others.

JEFFREY, W. E. (1980). The developing brain and child development. In M. C. Wittrock (Ed.) *The brain and psychology.* New York: Academic Press.

JEFFRIES, R., TURNER, A. A., POLSON, P. G., & ATWOOD, M. E. (1981). The processes involved in designing software. In J. R. Anderson (Ed.), *Cognitive skills and their acquisition.* Hillsdale, NJ: Lawrence Erlbaum Associates.

JENKINS, J. M. (1970). Sequential organization in schedules of reinforcement. In W. N. Schoenfeld (Ed.), *The theory of reinforcement schedules.* New York: Appleton-Century-Crofts.

JERISON, H. J. (1973). *Evolution of the brain and intelligence.* New York: Academic Press.

JERISON, H. J. (1976). The paleoneurology of language. In Harnad and others.

JERISON, H. J. (1982). The evolution of biological intelligence. In R. J. Sternberg (Ed.) *Handbook of human intelligence.* Cambridge: Cambridge University Press.

JOHANSEN, D. C., & EDEY, M. A. (1981). *Lucy: The beginnings of humankind.* New York: Warner Books.

JOHNSON, M. K., BRANSFORD, J. D., & SOLOMON, S. K. (1973). Memory for tacit implications of sentences. *Journal of Experimental Psychology, 98*, 203–205.

JOHNSON, M. K., DOLL, T. J., BRANSFORD, J. D., & LAPINSKI, R. J. (1974). Context effects in sentence memory. *Journal of Experimental Psychology, 103*, 358–360.

JOHNSON-LAIRD, P. N., & TRIDGELL, J. (1972). When negation is easier than affirmation. *Quarterly Journal of Experimental Psychology, 84*, 87–91.

JOHNSTON, T. (1981). Contrasting approaches to a theory of learning. *Behavioral and Brain Sciences, 4*, 125–139; Open Peer Commentary 139–161; reply, 161–169; references 169–173.

JOHNSTON, W. A., & DARK, V. J. (1986). Selective attention. *Annual Review of Psychology, 37*, 43–75.

JONES, D. M. (1979). Stress and memory. In M. M. Gruneberg & P. E. Morris (Eds.), *Applied problems in memory.* London: Academic Press.

JORGENSEN, J., MILLER, G. A., & SPERBER, D. (1984). Test of the mention theory of irony. *Journal of Experimental Psychology: General, 113*, 112–120.

JUNGERMANN, H. (1983). The two camps on rationality. In R. W. Scholz (Ed.), *Decision making under uncertainty.* Amsterdam: Elsevier. Pp. 63–86.

KAHNEMAN, D. (1973). *Attention and effort.* Englewood Cliffs, NJ: Prentice-Hall.

KAHNEMAN, D., SLOVIC, P., & TVERSKY, A. (Eds.). (1982). *Judgment under uncertainty: Heuristics and biases.* Cambridge: Cambridge University Press.

KAHNEMAN, D., & TVERSKY, A. (1973). On the psychology of prediction. *Psychological Review, 80*, 232–251.

KAHNEMAN, D., & TVERSKY, A. (1982). The simulation heuristic. In Kahneman, D., Slovic, P., & Tversky, A. (Eds.), *Judgment under uncertainty: Heuristics and biases.* Cambridge: Cambridge University Press.

KAIL, R. (1979). *The development of memory in children.* San Francisco: W. H. Freeman.

KAIL, R. V. (1984). *The development of memory in children* (2nd ed.). San Francisco: W. H. Freeman.

KAIL, R., & BISANZ, J. (1982). Information processing and cognitive development. In H. W. Reese (Ed.), *Advances in child behavior and development*. New York: Academic Press.

KAMIL, A. C. & ROITBLAT, H. L. (1985). The ecology of foraging behavior: Implications for animal learning and memory. *Annual Review of Psychology, 36*, 141–170.

KAMIN, L. (1968). Attention-like processes in classical conditioning. In M. Jones (Ed.), *Miami Symposium on the prediction of behavior: Aversive stimulation*. Miami, FL: University of Miami Press.

KAMIN, L. (1969). Predictability, surprise, attention, and conditioning. In R. Church and B. Campbell (Eds.), *Punishment and aversive behaviors*. New York: Appleton-Century-Crofts.

KANT, I. (1963). *Critique of pure reason*. London: Macmillan. (Originally published, 1781.)

KASPRZYK, D., MONTANO, D. E., & LOFTUS, E. F. (1975). Effect of leading questions on jurors' verdicts. *Jurimetrics Journal, 16*, 48–51.

KASSIN, S. M. (1984). Eyewitness identification: Victims vs. bystanders. *Journal of Applied Psychology, 14*, 519–529.

KATCHADOURIAN, H. A. (Ed.). (1979). *Human sexuality: A comparative and developmental perspective*. Berkeley: University of California Press.

KAUSLER, D. H. (1974). *Psychology of verbal learning and memory*. New York: Academic Press.

KEEHN, J. D. (1979). *Psychopathology in animals: Research and clinical implications*. New York: Academic Press.

KEEN, S. (1981, February). Eros and Alley Ooop: An interview with Donald Symons. *Psychology Today, 15*, (2), 52–61.

KEENAN, J. M., MACWHINNEY, B., & MAYHEW, D. (1977). Pragmatics in memory: A study of natural conversation. *Journal of Verbal Learning and Verbal Behavior, 16*, 549–560.

KEIL, F. C. (1981). Constraints on knowledge and cognitive development. *Psychological Review, 88*, 197–227.

KEIL, F. (1984). Mechanisms in cognitive development and the structure of knowledge. In Sternberg (1984).

KELLOGG, R. T. (1987). Effects of topic knowledge on the allocation of processing time and cognitive effort to writing processes. *Memory and Cognition, 15*, 256–266.

KENDLER, H. H. (1952). What is learned?—A theoretical blind alley. *Psychological Review, 59*, 269–277.

KENDLER, H., & KENDLER, T. S. (1962). Vertical and horizontal processes in problem solving. *Psychological Review, 69*, 1–16. Reprinted in R. Harper (Ed.), *The cognitive processes: Readings*. Englewood Cliffs, NJ: Prentice-Hall, 1964, and Staats (1964).

KENNEDY, A. (1973). Decision latencies to thematic and nonthematic distractors in prose. *Journal of Experimental Psychology, 98*, 432–434.

KENRICK, D. T., STRINGFIELD, D. O., WAGENHALS, W. L., DAHL, R. H., & RANSDELL, H. J. (1980). Sex differences, andrognyny, and approach responses to erotica: A new variation on the old volunteer problem. *Journal of Personality and Social Psychology, 38*, 317–324.

KERN, L., MIRELS, H. L., & HINSHAW, V. G. (1983). Scientist's understanding of propositional logic: An experimental investigation. *Social Studies of Science, 13*, 131–146.

KESNER, R. P. (1986). Neurobiological views of learning and memory. In Martinez & Kesner (1986).

KIERAS, D. (1978). Beyond pictures and words: Alternative information-processing models for imagery effects in verbal memory. *Psychological Bulletin, 85*, 532–554.

KINTSCH, W. (1974). *The representation of meaning in memory*. Hillsdale, NJ: Lawrence Erlbaum Associates.

KINTSCH, W. (1977). On comprehending stories. In P. Carpenter & M. Just (Eds.), *Cognitive processes in comprehension*. Hillsdale, NJ: Lawrence Erlbaum Associates.

KINTSCH, W., & BATES, E. (1977). Recognition memory for statements from a classroom lecture. *Journal of Experimental Psychology: Human Learning and Memory, 3*, 150–159.

KINTSCH, W., & VIPOND, D. (1979). Reading comprehension and readability in educational practice and psychological theory. In L. G. Nilsson (Ed.), *Perspectives on memory research*. Hillsdale, NJ: Lawrence Erlbaum Associates.

KIPARSKY, P., & KIPARSKY, C. (1970). Fact. In M. Bierwisch & K. Heidolph (Eds.), *Progress in linguistics*. The Hague: Mouton.

KIRKPATRICK, E. A. (1894). An experimental study of memory. *Psychological Review, 1*, 602–609.

KITCHER, P. (1985). *Vaulting ambition: Sociobiology and the quest for human nature.* Cambridge, MA: MIT Press.

KITCHER, P. (1987). Precis of *vaulting ambition: Sociobiology and the quest for human nature. Behavioral and Brain Sciences, 10,* 61–100.

KJELDERGAARD, P. M. (1968). Transfer and mediation in verbal learning. In Dixon & Horton (Eds.).

KLAHR. D. (1980). Information-processing models of intellectual development. In R. H. Kluwe & H. Spada (Eds.), *Developmental models of thinking.* New York: Academic Press.

KLAHR, D. (1984). Transition processes in cognitive development. In Sternberg (1984).

KLAHR, D., LANGLEY, P. & NECHES, R. (Eds.). (1987). Production system models of learning and development. Cambridge, MA: Bradford/MIT Press.

KLAHR, D., & WALLACE, J. G. (1973). The role of quantification operators in the development of conservation of quantity. *Cognitive Psychology, 4,* 301–327.

KLAHR, D., & WALLACE, J. G. (1976). *Cognitive development: An information-processing view.* Hillsdale, NJ: Lawrence Erlbaum Associates.

KLATZKY, R. L. (1980). *Human memory: Structures and processes* (2nd Ed.). San Francisco: W. H. Freeman.

KOCH, S. (1951). Theoretical psychology, 1950: An overview. *Psychological Review, 58,* 295–301.

KOCH, S. (1954). Clark L. Hull. In W. K. Estes and others, *Modern learning theory.* New York: Appleton-Century-Crofts.

KOHLBERG, L. (1958). The development of modes of thinking and choice in the years 10 to 16. Unpublished doctoral dissertation, University of Chicago.

KOHLBERG, L. (1971). From is to ought: How to commit the naturalistic fallacy and get away with it in the study of moral development. In T. Mischel (Ed.), *Cognitive development and epistemology.* New York: Academic press.

KOHLBERG, L. (1976). Moral stages and moralization: The cognitive-developmental approach. In T. Lickona (Ed.), *Moral development and behavior,* New York: Holt, Rinehart & Winston.

KOHLBERG, L., & KRAMER, R. (1976). Continuities and discontinuities in childhood and adult moral development. *Human Development, 1969, 12,* 93–120. Reprinted in N. Endler, L. Bolter, & H. Osser (Eds.), *Contemporary issues in developmental psychology* (2nd ed.). New York: Holt, Rinehart & Winston.

KOLERS, P. (1972). Experiments in reading. *Scientific American, 227(1),* 84–91.

KOPPEL, S. (1979). Testing the attentional deficit notion. *Journal of Learning Disabilities, 12,* 52–57.

KOSSLYN, S. M. (1983). *Ghosts in the mind's machine: Creating and using images in the brain.* New York: Norton.

KOZMINSKY, E. (1977). Altering comprehension: The effect of biasing titles on text comprehension. *Memory and Cognition, 5,* 482–490.

KRAFKA, C., & PENROD, S. (1985). Reinstatement of context in a field experiment on eyewitness identification. *Journal of Personality and Social Psychology, 49,* 58–69.

KRANTZ, G. S. (1980). Sapienization and speech. *Current Anthropology, 21,* 773–779.

KRECHEVSKY, I. (1932). Hypotheses in rats. *Psychological Review, 49,* 516–532.

KUHN, T. S. (1970). *The structure of scientific revolutions* (Rev. ed.). Chicago: University of Chicago Press.

KURTINES, W., & GREIF, E. (1974). The development of moral thought: Review and evaluation of Kohlberg's approach. *Psychological Bulletin, 81,* 453–470.

LABERGE, D. (1975). Acquisition of automatic processing in perceptual and associative learning. In P. M. A. Rabbit & S. Dornic (Eds.), *Attention and performance* (Vol. 5). New York: Academic Press, Pp. 50–64.

LAKOFF, G., & JOHNSON, M. (1980). *Metaphors we live by.* Chicago: University of Chicago Press.

LAMENDELLA, J. T. (1976). Relations between the ontogeny and phylogeny of language: A neorecapitulationist view. In Harnad and others.

LANGDON, J. H. (1985). Fossils and the origin of bipedalism. *Journal of Human Evolution, 14,* 615–635.

LANGER, J. (1970). Werner's comparative organismic theory. In P. Mussen (Ed.), *Carmichael's Manual of Child Psychology* (3rd ed., Vol. 1). New York: John Wiley.

LARKIN, J. (1981). Enriching formal knowledge: A model for learning to solve textbook physics problems. In J. R. Anderson (Eds.), *Cognitive skills and their acquisition*. Hillsdale, NJ: Lawrence Erlbaum Associates.

LARSEN, S. F. (1987). Remembering and the archaeological metaphor. *Metaphor and Symbolic Activity, 2*, 187–199.

LASCH, C. (1978). *The culture of narcissism: American life in an age of diminishing expectations.* New York: Norton.

LASHLEY, K. S. (1923). The behavioristic interpretation of consciousness. *Psychological Review, 30*, (I) 237–272; (II) 329–353.

LASHLEY, K. S. (1950). In search of the engram. In Symposium for the Society for Experimental Biology 4: 454–482. New York: Cambridge University Press.

LAVINE, L. O. (1972). The development of perception of writing in pre-reading children: A cross-cultural study. Unpublished doctoral dissertation, Department of Human Development, Cornell University.

LAZARUS, R. (1977). A cognitive analysis of biofeedback control. In G. Schwartz & J. Beatty (Eds.), *Biofeedback: Theory and research.* New York: Academic Press.

LEAHEY, T. H. (1977a). Training reasoning with implication. *Journal of General Psychology, 96*, 63–73.

LEAHEY, T. H. (1977b). The effect of sentential and abstract rules on implicational reasoning and judgment. *Journal of General Psychology, 97*, 185–191.

LEAHEY, T. H. (1977c). The development of conservation abilities: An intertask analysis of continuous quantity. *Merrill-Palmer Quarterly of Behavior and Development, 23*, 215–225.

LEAHEY, T. H. (1978). Adult strategies in two conservation related tasks. *Journal of General Psychology, 98*, 133–143.

LEAHEY, T. H. (1979). A cognitive reanalysis of anagram solution set learning. *Journal of General Psychology, 100*, 133–141.

LEAHEY, T. H. (1980). *A history of psychology*, 2nd ed. Englewood Cliffs, NJ: Prentice-Hall.

LEAHEY, T. H. & LEAHEY, G. (1983). *Psychology's occult doubles: Psychology and the problem of pseudoscience.* Chicago: Nelson-Hall.

LEAHEY, T. H., & WAGMAN, M. (1974). The modification of fallacious reasoning with implication. *Journal of General Psychology, 91*, 277–285.

LEAKEY, R. E., & LEWIN, R. *People of the lake.* Garden City, NY: Anchor Press/Doubleday.

LEDOUX, J. E., & HIRST, W. (Eds.). (1986). *Mind and brain: Dialogues in cognitive neuroscience.* Cambridge: Cambridge University Press.

LEE, W. (1971). *Decision theory and human behavior.* New York: John Wiley.

LENNEBERG, E. H. (1964). A biological perspective of language. In E. Lenneberg (Ed.), *New directions in the study of language.* Cambridge, MA: MIT Press.

LENNEBERG, E. H. (1965). The natural history of language. In G. Miller & F. Smith (Eds.), *The genesis of language.* Cambridge, MA: MIT Press.

LENNEBERG, E. H. (1967). *Biological foundations of language.* New York: John Wiley.

LENNEBERG, E. H. (1972). On explaining language. *Science, 1969, 164*, 635–643. Reprinted in Seligman & Hager.

LEPLEY, W. M. (1934). Serial reactions considered as conditioned reactions. *Psychological Monographs, 46*, #205.

LEPPER, M., & GREENE, D. (Eds.). (1978). *The hidden costs of reward.* Hillsdale, NJ: Lawrence Erlbaum Associates.

LE ROY LADURIE, E. (1978). *Montaillou: The promised land of error.* New York: George Braziller.

LEVINE, C., KOHLBERG, L., & HEWER, A. (1985). The current formulation of Kohlberg's theory and a response to critics. *Human Development, 28*, 94–100.

LEVINE, F. J., & TAPP, J. L. (1973). The psychology of criminal identification: The gap from *Wade* to *Kirby*. *University of Pennsylvania Law Review, 121*, 1079–1131.

LEWIN, R. (1981). Do jumping genes make evolutionary leaps? *Science, 213*, 634–636.

LEWIS, D. J. (1979). Psychobiology of active and inactive memory. *Psychological Review, 86*, 1054–1083.

LIBEN, L. S. (1977). Memory from a cognitive developmental perspective: A theoretical and empirical review. In W. F. Overton & J. M. Gallagher (Eds.), *Knowledge and development* (Vol. 1, *Advances in research and theory*). New York: Plenum.

LIBERMAN, A. M., HARRIS, K. S., EIMAS, P. D., LISKER, L., & BASTIAN, J. (1961). An effect of learning on speech perception: The discrimination of durations of silence with and without phonemic significance. *Language and Speech, 4*, 175–195.

LICKONA, T. (Ed.) (1976). *Moral development and behavior.* New York: Holt, Rinehart & Winston.

LIEBERMAN, P. (1975). *On the origins of language.* New York: Macmillan.

LIEBERMAN, P. (1984). The biology and evolution of language. Cambridge, MA: Harvard University Press.

LIEBERMAN, P. (1985). On the evolution of human syntactic ability. *Journal of human evolution, 14,* 657–668.

LIEBERT, R., & POULOS, R. (1976). Television as a moral teacher. In Lickona.

LIEBLICH, I. (1979). Eidetic imagery: Do not use ghosts to hunt ghosts of the same species. *Behavioral and Brain Sciences, 2,* 608–609.

LIMBER, J. (1980). Language in child and chimp? *American Psychologist,* 1977, *32,* 280–295. Reprinted in Sebeok & Umiker-Sebeok.

LINDE, C., & LABOV, W. (1975). Spatial networks as a site for the study of language and thought. *Language, 51,* 924–939.

LINDEN, E. (1981). *Apes, men, and language* (Rev. ed.). New York: Penguin.

LINDSAY, P. H., & NORMAN, D. A. (1977). *Human information processing* (2nd ed.). New York: Academic Press.

LINGLE, J. H., GEVA, N. OSTROM, T. M., LEIPPE, M. R., & BAUMGARDNER, M. H. (1979). Thematic effects of person judgments on impression formation. *Journal of Personality and Social Psychology, 37,* 674–687.

LIPTON, J. P. (1977). On the psychology of eyewitness testimony. *Journal of Applied Psychology, 62,* 90–95.

LOCKHART, R. S., & CRAIK, F. I. M. (1978). "Levels of processing": A reply to Eysenck. *British Journal of Psychology, 69,* 171–175.

LOEHLIN, J., WILLERMAN, L., & HORN, J. (1988). Human behavior genetics. *Annual Review of Psychology, 39,* 101–134.

LOEVINGER, J., & KNOLL, E. (1983). Personality: Stages, traits, and the self. *Annual Review of Psychology,* Vol. 34.

LOFTUS, E. F. (1974). On reading the fine print. *Quarterly Journal of Experimental Psychology, 27,* 324.

LOFTUS, E. F. (1979). *Eyewitness testimony.* Cambridge, MA: Harvard University Press.

LOFTUS, E. F. (1980a). Impact of expert testimony on the unreliability of eyewitness identification. *Journal of Applied Psychology, 65,* 9–15.

LOFTUS, E. F. (1980b). *Memory.* Reading, MA: Addison-Wesley.

LOFTUS, E. F. (1983). Silence is not golden. *American Psychologist, 38,* 564–572.

LOFTUS, E. F., & LOFTUS, G. R. (1980). On the permanence of stored information in the human brain. *American Psychologist, 35,* 409–420.

LOFTUS, E. F., & MESSO, J. (1987). Some facts about "weapon focus." *Law and Human Behavior, 11,* 55–62.

LOFTUS, E. F., MILLER, D. G., & BURNS, H. J. (1978). Semantic integration of verbal information into a visual memory. *Journal of Experimental Psychology: Human Learning and Memory, 4,* 19–31.

LOFTUS, E. F., & PALMER, J. C. (1974). Reconstruction of automobile destruction: An example of the interaction between language and memory. *Journal of Verbal Learning and Verbal Behavior, 13,* 585–589.

LORENZ, K. (1966). *On aggression.* New York: Harcourt Brace Jovanovich.

LOVEJOY, C. O. (1981). The origin of man. *Science, 211,* 341–350.

LUBEK, I., & APFELBAUM, E. (1981). The hidden injuries of classical conditioning: An historical and psychological look at editorial taste in taste-aversion learning. Paper presented at the Annual Meeting of the Cheiron Society, River Falls, WI, June 10–13.

LUBOW, R. E., WEINER, I., & SCHNUR, P. (1981). Conditioned attention theory. *The Psychology of Learning and Motivation, 15,* 1–50.

LUMSDEN, C. J., & WILSON, E. O. (1981). *Genes, mind, and culture.* Cambridge, MA: Harvard University Press.

LUMSDEN, C., & WILSON, E. O. (1983). The dawn of intelligence. *The Sciences, 23* (2, March/April), 22–31.

LURIA, A. R. (1968). *The mind of a mnemonist.* New York: Basic Books.

LYNCH. G. (1985, September/October). What memories are made of. *The Sciences,* 38–43.

LYNCH, G. (1986). *Synapses, circuits and the beginnings of memory.* Cambridge, MA: MIT Press.

Lynch, G., McGaugh, J. L., & Weinberger, N. M. (Eds.). (1986). *Neurobiology of learning and memory*. New York: Guildford Press.

Lynch, K. (1960). *The image of the city*. Cambridge MA: M.I.T. and Harvard University Press.

Lyons, J. (1970). *Noam Chomsky*. New York: Viking Press.

Maccoby, C. E., & Jacklin, C. N. (1974). *The psychology of sex differences* (2 Vols.). Stanford, CA: Stanford University Press.

MacCorquodale, K., & Meehl, P. (1954). Edward C. Tolman. In W. K. Estes and others, *Modern learning theory*. Appleton-Century-Crofts.

MacDonald, K. (1984). An ethological-social learning theory of altruism: Implications for human sociobiology. *Ethology and Sociobiology, 5*, 97–109.

MacFarlane, D. A. (1930). The role of kinesthesis in maze learning. *University of California Publications in Psychology, 4*, 277–305.

Mackintosh, N. J. (1978). Cognitive or associative theories of conditioning: Implications of an analysis of blocking. In S. Hulse, H. Fowler, and W. Honig (Eds.), *Cognitive processes in animal behavior*. Hillsdale, NJ: Lawrence Erlbaum Associates.

Mackintosh, N. J. (1985). Varieties of conditioning. In Weinberger, McGaugh, & Lynch (1985).

Macnamara, J. (1976). Stomachs assimilate and accommodate, don't they? *Canadian Psychological Review, 17*, 167–173.

MacWhinney, B., Keenan, J. M., & Reinke, P. (1982). The role of arousal in memory for conversation. *Memory & Cognition, 10*, 308–317.

Mahoney, M. J., & DeMonbreun, B. G. (1978/1981). Problem solving bias in scientists (1978). Reprinted in Tweney, Doherty, & Mynatt.

Maier, S. (1970). Failure to escape traumatic shock: Incompatible skeletal responses or learned helplessness? *Learning and Motivation, 1*, 157–170.

Maier, S., & Seligman, M. (1976). Learned helplessness: Theory and evidence. *Journal of Experimental Psychology: General, 105*, 3–46.

Malcolm, N. (1964). Behaviorism as a philosophy of psychology. In T. W. Wann (Ed.), *Behaviorism and phenomenology*. Chicago: University of Chicago Press.

Malmi, W. A. (1976). Chimpanzees and language evolution. In Harnad and others.

Maltzman, I. (1955). Thinking: From a behavioristic point of view. *Psychological Review, 66*, 367–386.

Maltzman, I. (1977). Orienting in classical conditioning and generalization of the galvanic skin response to words: An overview. *Journal of Experimental Psychology: General, 106*, 111–119.

Maltzman, I. (1979). Orienting reflexes and significance: A reply to O'Gorman. *Psychophysiology, 16*, 274–282.

Maltzman, I., & Morrisett, L. (1952). Different strengths of set in the solution of anagrams. *Journal of Experimental Psychology, 44*, 242–246.

Maltzman, I., & Morrisett, L. (1953a). The effects of single and compound classes of anagrams on set solutions. *Journal of Experimental Psychology, 45*, 345–350.

Maltzman, I., & Morrisett, L. (1953b). Effects of task instructions on solutions of different classes of anagrams. *Journal of Experimental Psychology, 45*, 351–354.

Maltzman, I., Raskin, D., and Wolff, C. (1979). Latent inhibition of the GSR conditioned to words. *Physiological Psychology, 7*, 193–203.

Mandler, J. M., & Murphy, C. M. (1983). Subjective judgments of script structure. *Journal of Experimental Psychology: Learning, Memory & Cognition, 9*, 534–543.

Marcel, A. J. (1983). Conscious and unconscious perception: An approach to the relations between phenomenal experience and perceptual processes. *Cognitive Psychology, 15*, 238–300.

Marek, G. R. (1975). *Toscanini*. London: Vision Press.

Markus, H. (1980). The self in thought and memory. In D. M. Wegner & R. R. Vallecker (Eds.), *The self in social psychology*. London: Oxford University Press.

Markus, H., Crane, M., Bernstein, S., & Saladi, M. (1982). Self-schemas and gender. *Journal of Personality and Social Psychology, 42*, 38–50.

Marler, P. (1970). A comparative approach to vocal learning: Song development in white-crowned sparrows. *Journal of Comparative and Physiological Psychology, 71*, 1–25. Reprinted in Seligman & Hager (1972).

MARLER, P. (1976). An ethological theory of the origin of vocal learning. In Harnad and others.

MARLER, P., & PETERS, S., (1981). Sparrows learn adult song and more from memory. *Science, 213*, 780–782.

MARSCHARK, M., & PAIVIO, A. (1977). Integrative processing of concrete and abstract sentences. *Journal of Verbal Learning and Verbal Behavior, 16*, 217–231.

MARSCHARK, M., RICHMAN, C. L., YUILLE, J. C., & HUNT, R. R. (1987). The role of imagery in memory: On shared and distinctive information. *Psychological Bulletin, 102*, 28–41.

MARSHACK, A. (1972). *The roots of civilization.* New York: McGraw-Hill.

MARSHACK, A. (1976). Some implications of the Paleolithic symbolic evidence for the origin of language. In Harnad et al.

MARSHALL, J. C. (1980). On the biology of language acquisition. In Caplan.

MARTINEZ, J. L., & KESNER, R. P. (Eds.). (1986). *Learning and memory: A biological view.* Orlando, FL: Academic Press.

MARTLEW, M. (Ed.). (1983). *The psychology of written language: A developmental approach.* New York: John Wiley.

MASSARO, D. W. (1988). Some criticisms of connectionist models of human performance. *Journal of Memory and Language, 27*, 213–234.

MASSON, M. E. J. (1979). Context and inferential cuing of sentence recall. *Journal of Verbal Learning and Verbal Behavior, 18*, 173–186.

MATLIN, M. (1983). *Cognition.* New York: Holt, Rinehart & Winston.

MAYNARD SMITH, J. (1971). What use is sex? *Journal of Theoretical Biology, 30*, 319–335.

MAYNARD SMITH, J. (1978). *The evolution of sex.* London: Cambridge University Press.

MAYNARD SMITH, J. (1982a). The evolution of social behaviour: A classification of models. In King's College Sociobiology Group (Eds.), *Current problems in sociobiology.* Cambridge: Cambridge University Press.

MAYNARD SMITH, J. (1982b). *Evolution and the theory of games.* Cambridge: Cambridge University Press.

MAYNARD SMITH, J. (1984). Game theory and the evolution of behavior. *Behavioral and Brain Sciences, 1*, 95–126.

McCLELLAND, J. L. (1988). Connectionist models and psychological evidence. *Journal of Memory and Language, 27*, 107–123.

McCLELLAND, J. L., & RUMELHART, D. E., and the PDP Research Group. (1986). *Parallel distributed processing: Explorations in the microstructure of cognition* (Vol. 2): *Psychological and Biological Models.* Cambridge, MA: Bradford Books, MIT Press.

McCLOSKEY, M. (1983, April). Intuitive physics. *Scientific American, 248*, (4), 122–130.

McCLOSKEY, M., & EGETH, H. E. (1983). Eyewitness identification: What can a psychologist tell a jury? *American Psychologist, 38*, 550–563.

McGEOCH, J. A., & IRION, A. L. (1952). *The psychology of human learning* (2nd ed.). New York: Longman.

McHENRY, H. M. (1982). The pattern of human evolution: Studies on bipedalism, mastication and encephalization. *Annual Review of Anthropology, 11*, 151–173.

McINTYRE, P., BARNETT, M. A., HARRIS, R. J., SHANTEAU, J., SKOWRONSKI, J. J., & KLASSEN, M. L. (1987). Psychological factors influencing decisions to donate organs. *Advances in consumer research, 14*, 331–334.

McKEITHEN, K. B., REITMAN, J. S., REUTER, H. H., & HIRTLE, S. C. (1981). Knowledge organization and skill differences in computer programmers. *Cognitive Psychology, 13*, 307–325.

McKOON, G., & RATLIFF, R. (1981). The comprehension processes and memory structures involved in instrumental reference. *Journal of Verbal Learning and Verbal Behavior, 20*, 671–682.

McNAMARA, H., LONG, J., & WIKE, E. (1956). Learning without response under two conditions of external cues. *Journal of Comparative and Physiological Psychology, 49*, 477–480.

McNEIL, B. J., PAUKER, S. G., SOX, H. C. JR., & TVERSKY, A. (1982). On the elicitation of preferences for alternative therapies. *The New England Journal of Medicine, 306*, 1259–1262.

McNEIL, D. (1970). *The acquisition of language.* New York: Harper & row.

MEALEY, L. (1985). The relationship between social status and biological success: A case study of the Mormon religious hierarchy. *Ethology and Sociology, 6*, 249–257.

MECKLENBRAUKER, S., & HAGER, W. (1984). Effects of mood on memory: Experimental tests of a mood-state-dependency retrieval hypothesis and of a mood congruity hypothesis. *Psychological Research, 46,* 355–376.

MEDIN, D., ROBERTS, W., & DAVIS, R. (Eds.). (1976). *Processes of animal memory.* Hillsdale, NJ: Lawrence Erlbaum Associates.

MERIKLE, P. M. (1980). Selection from visual persistence by perceptual groups and category membership. *Journal of Experimental Psychology: General, 109,* 279–295.

MEYER, D. E., SCHVANEVELDT, R. W., & RUDDY, M. G. (1974). Loci of contextual effects on visual word recognition. In P. Rabbitt & S. Dornic (Eds.), *Attention and performance V.* New York: Academic Press.

MIDGLEY, M. (1978). *Beast and man.* Ithaca, NY: Cornell University Press.

MILGRAM, S. (1974). *Obedience to authority.* New York: Harper & Row.

MILLER, G. (1981). *Language and speech.* San Francisco: W. H. Freeman.

MILLER, G. A. (1956). The magical number, seven, plus or minus two: Some limits on our capacity for processing information. *Psychological Review, 63,* 81–97.

MILLER, G. A., & GILDEA, P. M. (1987, Sept.). How children learn words. *Scientific American,* 94–99.

MILLER, J. L., & EIMAS, P. D. (1983). Studies on the categorization of speech by infants. *Cognition, 13,* 135–165.

MILLER, N. E., & DOLLARD, J. (1941). *Social learning and imitation.* New Haven: Yale University Press.

MISCHEL, T. (1971). *Cognitive development and epistemology.* New York: Academic Press.

MISCHEL, W., & MISCHEL, H. (1976). A cognitive social learning approach to morality and self-regulation. In Lickona.

MISHKIN, M., & APPENZELLER, T. (1987, June). The anatomy of memory. *Scientific American,* 80–89.

MITROFF, I. (1974). Scientists and confirmation bias. Reprinted in Tweney, Doherty, & Mynatt (1981).

MOATES, D. R., & SCHUMACHER, G. M. (1980). *An introduction to cognitive psychology.* Belmont, CA: Wadsworth, 1980.

MODGIL, S., & MODGIL, C. (Eds.). (1982). *Jean Piaget: Consensus and controversy.* London: Holt, Rinehart & Winston.

MODGIL, S., & MODGIL, C. (Eds.). (1986). *Lawrence Kohlberg: Consensus and controversy.* Philadelphia: Falmer Press.

MONEY, J., & ERHARDT, A. (1972). *Man & woman: Boy & girl.* Baltimore: The Johns Hopkins University Press.

MONTAGUE, A. (1976). Toolmaking, hunting, and the origin of language. In Harnad and others. (1976).

MONTAGUE, A. (Ed.). (1980). *Sociobiology examined.* New York: Oxford University Press.

MONTAGUE, M. F. A. (Ed.). (1968). *Man and aggression.* London: Oxford University Press.

MOORE, J. (1984). The evolution of reciprocal sharing. *Ethology and Sociobiology, 5,* 1–14.

MORRIS, C. D., STEIN, B. S., & BRANSFORD, J. D. (1979). Prerequisites for the utilization of knowledge in the recall of prose passages. *Journal of Experimental Psychology: Human Learning and Memory, 5,* 253–261.

MOSKOWITZ, B. A. (1978). The acquisition of language. *Scientific American, November, 239,* 92–108.

MOWRER, O. H. (1954). The psychologist looks at language. *American Psychologist, 9,* 660–694. Reprinted in Jakobovits & Miron (1967).

MUELLER, C., & SCHOENFELD, W. (1954). Edwin R. Guthrie. In W. K. Estes and others. *Modern learning theory.* New York: Appleton-Century-Crofts.

MÜNSTERBERG, H. (1908). *On the witness stand.* New York: Boardman.

MYERS, R. E. (1976). Comparative neurology of vocalization and speech: Proof of a dichotomy. In Harnad and others.

MYNATT, C. R., DOHERTY, M. E., & TWENEY, R. D. (1981). A simulated research environment (1978). Reprinted in Tweney, Doherty, & Mynatt.

NEISSER, U. (1976). *Cognition and reality.* San Francisco: W. H. Freeman.

NEISSER, U. (1981). John Dean's memory: A case study. *Cognition, 9,* 1–22.

NEISSER, U. (Ed.). (1982). *Memory observed.* San Francisco: W. H. Freeman.

NELSON, K. E. (Ed.). (1980). *Children's language* (Vol. 2). New York: Gardner Press.

NEWELL, A., & SIMON, H. (1972). *Human problem solving.* Englewood Cliffs, NJ: Prentice-Hall.

NEWPORT, E. L., GLEITMAN, H., & GLEITMAN, L. R. (1977). Mother, I'd rather do it myself: Some effects and non-effects of maternal speech style. In C. Snow & C. A. Ferguson (Eds.), *Talking to children: Language input and acquisition.* Cambridge: Cambridge University Press.

NICKERSON, R. S., & ADAMS, M. J. (1979). Long-term memory for a common object. *Cognitive Psychology, 10,* 287–307.

NISBETT, R. E., & ROSS, L. (1980). *Human inference: Strategies and shortcomings in social judgment.* Englewood Cliffs, NJ: Prentice-Hall.

NORMAN, D. A. & RUMELHART, D. E. (1975). *Explorations in cognition.* San Francisco: W. H. Freeman.

NYSTRAND, M. (1986). *The structure of written communication.* Orlando, FL: Academic Press.

O'BARR, W. M. (1982). *Linguistic evidence: Language, power, and strategy in the courtroom.* New York: Academic Press.

OBRIST, P., SUTTERER, J., & HOWARD, J. (1972). Preparatory cardiac changes: A psychobiological approach. In A. Black and W. Prokasy (Eds.), *Classical conditioning II.* New York: Appleton-Century-Crofts.

O'KEEFE, J., & NADEL, L. (1974). Maps in the brain. *New Scientist, 62,* 749–751.

O'KEEFE, J., & NADEL, L. (1978). *The hippocampus as a cognitive map.* Oxford: Clarendon Press.

O'KEEFE, J., & NADEL, L. (1979). Précis of The hippocampus as a cognitive map. *The Behavioral and Brain Sciences, 2,* 487–533.

OLDS, J. (1960). Differentiation of reward systems in the brain by self-stimulation techniques. In E. Ramey & D. O'Doherty (Eds.), *Electrical studies on the unanesthetized brain.* New York: Paul B. Hueber.

OLDS, J., & MILNER, P. (1954). Positive reinforcement produced by electrical stimulation of the septal area and other regions of rat brain. *Journal of Comparative and Physiological Psychology, 47,* 419–427.

ORGEL, L., & CRICK, F. (1980). Selfish DNA: The ultimate parasite. *Nature, 284,* 604–607.

OSGOOD, C. E. (1963). On understanding and creating sentences. *American Psychologist, 18,* 735–751. Reprinted in Jakobovits & Miron (1967).

OWENS, J., BOWER, G. H., & BLACK, J. B. (1979). The 'soap opera' effect in story recall. *Memory & Cognition, 7,* 185–191.

PAIVIO, A. (1971). *Imagery and verbal processes.* New York: Holt, Rinehart & Winston.

PAIVIO, A. (1975). Coding distinctions and repetition effects in memory. In G. H. Bower (Ed.), *The psychology of learning and motivation* (Vol. 9). New York: Academic Press.

PAIVIO, A., & BEGG, I. (1981). *Psychology of language.* Englewood Cliffs, NJ: Prentice-Hall.

PARKER, S. T. (1985). Higher intelligence as adaptation for social and technological strategies in early Homo sapiens. In Butterworth and others. (1985).

PARKER, S. T., & GIBSON, K. R. (1979). A developmental model for the evolution of language and intelligence. *Behavioral and Brain Sciences, 2,* 367–408.

PARSONS, C. (1960). Inhelder's and Piaget's the growth of logical thinking II: A logician's view. *British Journal of Psychology, 51,* 75–84.

PATTERSON, F. (1980). Innovative uses of language by a gorilla: A case study. In Nelson.

PATTERSON, F., & LINDEN, E. (1982). *The education of Koko.* New York: Holt, Rinehart & Winston.

PATTERSON, T. E., & McCLURE, R. D. (1976). *The unseeing eye: The myth of television power in national politics.* New York: Putnam's.

PAVLOV, I. P. (1927). *Conditioned reflexes.* New York: Dover.

PAVLOV, I. P. (1928). *Lectures on conditioned reflexes* (Vol. 1). London: Lawrence and Wishart.

PAYNE, T. J., CONNOR, J. M., & COLLETTI, G. (1987). Gender-based schematic processing: An empirical investigation and reevaluation. *Journal of Personality and Social Psychology, 52,* 937–945.

PEARCE, J. A., & HALL, G. (1980). A model for Pavlovian learning: Variations in the effectiveness of conditioned but not of unconditioned stimuli. *Psychlogical Review, 87,* 532–552.

PENDERY, M., & MALTZMAN, I. (1977). Instructions and the orienting reflex in "semantic conditioning" of the galvanic skin response in an innocuous situation. *Journal of Experimental Psychology: General, 106,* 120–140.

PENFIELD, W. (1969). Consciousness, memory, and man's conditioned reflexes. In K. Pribram (Ed.), *On the biology of learning*. New York: Harcourt Brace Jovanovich.

PENFIELD, W., & ROBERTS, L. (1959). *Speech and brain mechanisms*. Princeton, NJ: Princeton University Press.

PETERS, R. (1980). *Mammalian communication*. Monterey, CA: Brooks/Cole.

PETERSON, L. R., & PETERSON, M. (1959). Short-term retention of individual items. *Journal of Experimental Psychology, 58*, 193–198.

PFEIFFER, J. E. (1976). *The emergence of man*. New York: Harper & Row.

PFEIFFER, J. E. (1977). *The emergence of society*. New York: McGraw-Hill.

PIAGET, J. (1963). *The origins of intelligence in children* (1952). New York: Norton.

PIAGET, J. (1965). *The child's conception of number* (1941). New York: Norton.

PIAGET, J. (1967a). Cognitions and conservations: Review of J. S. Bruner and others, *Studies in cognitive growth*. *Contemporary Psychology, 12*, 530–533.

PIAGET, J. (1967b). *Six psychological studies* (1964). New York: Random House.

PIAGET, J. (1969). *Psychology of intelligence* (1947). Totowa, NJ: Littlefield, Adams.

PIAGET, J. (1970a). *Genetic epistemology*. New York: Norton.

PIAGET, J. (1970b). Piaget's theory. In P. H. Mussen (Ed.), *Carmichael's manual of child psychology* (3rd ed., Vol. 1.) New York: John Wiley.

PIAGET, J. (1971a). *Biology and knowledge* (1967). Chicago: University of Chicago Press.

PIAGET, J. (1971b). *Psychology and epistemology*. New York: Viking.

PIAGET, J. (1971c). *Structuralism* (1968). London: Routledge & Kegan Paul.

PIAGET, J. (1972). *The principles of genetic epistemology* (1970). London: Routledge & Kegan Paul.

PIAGET, J. (1973). *The child and reality* (1972). New York: Grossman, 1973.

PIAGET, J. (1976). *The grasp of consciousness* (1974). Cambridge, MA: Harvard University Press.

PIAGET, J. (1978). *Behavior and evolution* (1976). New York: Pantheon.

PIAGET, J., & INHELDER, B. (1969a). Intellectual operations and their development. In P. Fraisse & J. Piaget (Eds.), *Experimental Psychology: Its scope and method* (Vol. VII, *Intelligence*) (1963). London: Routledge & Kegan Paul.

PIAGET, J., & INHELDER, B. (1969b). Mental images. In P. Fraisse & J. Piaget (Eds.), *Experimental Psychology: Its scope and method* (Vol. VII, *Intelligence*) (1963). London: Routledge & Kegan Paul.

PIAGET, J., & INHELDER, B. (1969c). *The psychology of the child* (1966). New York: Basic Books.

PIAGET, J., & INHELDER, B. (1971). *Mental imagery in the child* (1966). New York: Basic Books.

PIAGET, J., & INHELDER, B. (1973). *Memory and intelligence* (1968). London: Routledge & Kegan Paul.

PICHERT, J. W., & ANDERSON, R. C. (1977). Taking different perspectives on a story. *Journal of Educational Psychology, 69*, 309–315.

PILBEAM, D. (1984, March). The descent of hominoids and hominids. *Scientific American*, 84–96.

PILBEAM, D. (1985). Patterns of hominoid evolution. In Delson (1985).

PILBEAM, D. (1986a). Distinguished lecture: Hominoid evolution and hominoid evolution. *American Anthropologist, 88*, 295–312.

PILBEAM, D. (1986b). The origin of Homo sapiens: The fossil evidence. In Wood, Martin, & Andrews (1986).

PINARD, J., & LAURENDEAU, M. (1969). 'Stage' in Piaget's cognitive-developmental theory: Exegesis of a concept. In Elkind & Flavell.

PINES, M. (1979, June). Good samaritans at age two? *Psychology Today, 13*, (1), 66–77.

PISONI, D. B. (1978). Speech perception. In W. K. Estes (Ed.), *Handbook of learning and cognitive processes* (Vol. 6). Hillsdale, NJ: Lawrence Erlbaum Associates, Pp. 167–234.

PLOMIN, R., & DANIELS, D. (1987). Why are children in the same family so different from one another? *Behavioral and Brain Sciences, 10*, 1–60.

PLOTKIN, H. C., & ODLING-SMEE, F. J. (1979). Learning, change, and evolution. *Advances in the study of behavior* (Vol. 10). New York: Academic Press.

POHL, R., COLONIUS, H., & THURING, M. (1985). Recognition of script-based inferences. *Psychological Research, 47*, 59–67.

PORTER, J. H., & ALLEN, J. (1977). Schedule-induced polydipsia contrast in the rat. *Animal Learning and Behavior, 5*, 184–192.

POSNER, M. I., & SNYDER, C. R. R. (1975b). Attention and cognitive control. In R. L. Solso

(Ed.), *Information processing and cognition: The Loyola symposium*. Hillsdale, NJ: Lawrence Erlbaum Associates, Pp. 55–85.

POSTMAN, L., & KEPPEL, G. (1968). Conditions determining the priority of new items in free recall. *Journal of Verbal Learning and Verbal Behavior, 7*, 270–273.

POSTMAN, L., & SASSENRATH, J. (1961). The automatic action of verbal rewards and punishments. *Journal of General Psychology, 65*, 109–136.

PREMACK, A. J. (1976). *Why chimps can read*. New York: Harper Colophon.

PREMACK, D. (1959). Toward empirical behavior laws: I. Positive reinforcement. *Psychological Review, 66*, 219–233.

PREMACK, D. (1962). Reversibility of the reinforcement relation. *Science, 136*, 255–257.

PREMACK, D. (1965a). Preparations for discussing behaviorism with a chimpanzee. In Smith & Miller.

PREMACK, D. (1965b). Reinforcement theory. In M. R. Jones (Ed.), *Nebraska Symposium on Motivation*: Lincoln: University of Nebraska Press.

PREMACK, D. (1983). Animal cognition: *Annual Review of Psychology* (Vol. 34). Palo Alto, CA: Annual Reviews, Inc.

PREMACK, D., & PREMACK, A. J. (1982). *The mind of an ape*. New York: Norton.

PREMACK, D., & WOODRUFF, G. (1978). Does the chimpanzee have a theory of mind? *Behavioral and Brain Sciences, 1*, 515–526.

PRESTON, I. L. (1975). *The great American blow-up: Puffery in advertising and selling*. Madison: University of Wisconsin Press.

PRESTON, I. L. (1977). The FTC's use of puffery and other selling claims made 'by implication.' *Journal of Business Research, 5*, 155–181.

PRESTON, I. L., & RICHARDS, J. I. (1986). Consumer miscomprehension as a challenge to FTC prosecutions of deceptive advertising. *The John Marshall Law Review, 19*, 605–635.

QUIATT, D., & KELSO, J. (1985). Household economics and hominid origins. *Current Anthropology, 26*, 207–222.

RAPAPORT, D. (1960). Psychoanalysis as a developmental psychology. In B. Kaplan & S. Wapner (Eds), *Perspectives in psychological theory*. New York: International Universities Press.

RATLIFF, F. (1976). On the psychophysiological bases of universal color terms. *Proceedings of the American Philosophical Society, 120*, 311–330.

REICHER, G. M. (1969). Perceptual recognition as a function of meaningfulness of stimulus material. *Journal of Experimental Psychology, 81*, 275–280.

REID, B. V. (1984). An anthropological reinterpretation of Kohlberg's stages of moral development. *Human Development, 27*, 57–64.

REITMAN, J. S. (1971). Mechanisms of forgetting in short-term memory. *Cognitive Psychology, 2*, 185–195.

REITMAN, J. S. (1974). Without surreptitious rehearsal, information in short-term memory decays. *Journal of Verbal Learning and Verbal Behavior, 13*, 365–377.

RENSBERGER, B. (1986). Getting another line on evolution. *Washington Post* (August 7), p. A3.

RENSBERGER, B. (1987). Startlingly apelike early human. *Washington Post* (May 21), p. A3.

RESCORLA, R. (1968). Probability of shock in the presence of CS in fear conditioning. *Journal of Comparative and Physiological Psychology, 56*, 1–5.

RESCORLA, R. (1975). Pavlovian excitatory and inhibitory conditioning. In W. K. Estes (Ed.), *Handbook of learning and cognitive processes*, (Vol. 2). Hillsdale, NJ: Lawrence Erlbaum Associates.

RESCORLA, R. (1978). Some implications of a cognitive perspective on Pavlovian conditioning. In S. Hulse, H. Fowler, & W. Honig (Eds.), *Cognitive processes in animal behavior*. Hillsdale, NJ: Lawrence Erlbaum Associates.

RESCORLA, R. (1980). Simultaneous and successive associations in sensory preconditioning. *Journal of Experimental Psychology: Animal Behavior Processes, 6*, 207–216.

RESCORLA, R. A. (1984). Comments on three Pavlovian paradigms. In Alkon & Farley (1984).

RESCORLA, R. A. (1985). Associative learning: Some consequences of contiguity. In Weinberger, McGaugh, & Lynch (1985).

RESCORLA, R. A., & HOLLAND, P. C. (1982). Behavioral studies of associative learning in animals. *Annual Review of Psychology, 33*, 265–308.

RESCORLA, R., & WAGNER, A. (1972). A theory of Pavlovian conditioning: Variations in the effectiveness of reinforcement and nonreinforcement. In A. Black and W. Prokasy (Eds.), *Classical conditioning II*. New York: Appleton-Century-Crofts.

REST, J. R. (Ed.) (1986). *Moral development: Advances in theory and research*. New York: Praeger.

RIBBACK, A., & UNDERWOOD, B. J. (1950). An empirical explanation of the skewness of the bowed serial position curve. *Journal of Experimental Psychology, 40*, 329–335.

RICHARDS, G. (1986). Freed hands or enslaved feet? *Journal of Human Evolution, 15*, 143–150.

RICKHEIT, G., SCHNOTZ, W., & STROHNER, H. (1985). The concept of inference in discourse comprehension. In G. Rickheit & H. Strohner (Eds.), *Inferences in text processing*. Amsterdam: Elsevier (North-Holland). Pp. 3–49.

RICKHEIT, G., & STROHNER, H. (Eds.). (1985). *Inferences in text processing*. Amsterdam: Elsevier (North-Holland).

RIECHMANN, P. F., & COSTE, E. L. (1980). Mental imagery and the comprehension of figurative language: Is there a relationship? In R. P. Honeck & R. R. Hoffman (Eds.), *Cognition and figurative language*. Hillsdale, NJ: Lawrence Erlbaum Associates.

RILEY, D. A., COOK, R. G., & LAMB, M. R. (1981). A classification and analysis of short-term retention codes in pigeons. *The Psychology of Learning and Motivation, 15*, 51–80.

RINDOS, D. (1985). Darwinian selection, symbolic variation, and the evolution of culture. *Current Anthropology, 26*, 65–88.

RINDOS, D. (1986a). The genetics of cultural anthropology: Toward a genetic model for the evolution of culture. *Journal of Anthropological Archaeology, 5*, 1–38.

RINDOS, D. (1986b). The evolution of the capacity for culture: Sociobiology, structuralism, and cultural selectionism. *Current Anthropology, 27*, 315–332.

RISTAU, C. A., & ROBBINS, D. (1982). Language in the great apes: A critical review. In J. S. Rosenblatt, R. A. Hinde, C. Beer, & M. C. Busnel (Eds.), *Advances in the study of behavior* (Vol. 12). New York: Academic Press.

ROAZEN, P. (1976). *Erik H. Erikson: The power and limits of a vision*. New York: Free Press.

ROBBINS, D. (1980). Mathematical learning theory: W. K. Estes and stimulus sampling. In G. Gazda & R. Corsini (Eds.), *Theories of learning*. Itasca, IL: F. E. Peacock.

ROBERTS, D., & BACHEN, C. (1981). Mass communication effects. *Annual Review of Psychology, 32*, 307–356.

ROBINSON, B. W. (1976). Limbic influences on human speech. In Harnad and others.

ROEDIGER, H. L. (1980). Memory metaphors in cognitive psychology. *Memory and Cognition, 8*, 231–246.

ROEDIGER, H. L. III, & BLAXTON, T. A. (1987). Effects of varying modality, surface features, and retention interval on priming in word-fragment completion. *Memory and Cognition, 15*, 379–388.

ROGERS, T. B. (1981). A model of the self as an aspect of the human information processing system. In N. Cantor & J. F. Kihlstrom (Eds.), *Cognition, social interaction and personality*. Hillsdale, NJ: Lawrence Erlbaum.

ROSEN, H. (1980). *The development of sociomoral knowledge*. New York: Columbia University Press.

ROSENFELD, A. (1980, September). Sociobiology stirs a controversy over the limits of science. *Smithsonian*, 73–80.

ROSS, M., & SICOLY, F. (1979). Egocentric biases in avialability and attribution. *Journal of Personality and Social Psychology, 37*, 322–336.

ROTFELD, H. J., & PRESTON, I. L. (1981). The potential impact of research on advertising law. *Journal of Advertising Research, 21*(2), 9–18.

ROTHBART, M., EVANS, M., & FULERO, S. (1979). Recall for confirming events: Memory processes and the maintenance of social stereotypes. *Journal of Experimental Social Psychology, 15*, 343–355.

ROTHBART, M., FULERO, S., JENSEN, C., HOWARD, J., & BIRRELL, P. (1978). From individual to group impressions: Availability heuristics in stereotype formation. *Journal of Experimental Social Psychology, 14*, 237–255.

ROTHWELL, J. D. (1982). *Telling it like it isn't: Language misuse and malpractice/what we can do about it*. Englewood Cliffs, NJ: Prentice-Hall.

ROZIN, P. (1976). The evolution of intelligence and access to the cognitive unconscious. In J. Sprague & A. Epstein (Eds.), *Progress in psychobiology and physiological psychology* (Vol. 6). New York: Academic Press.

ROZIN, P. (1977). The significance of learning mechanisms in food selection: Some biology, psychology, and sociology of science. In L. M. Barker, M. R. Best, & M. Domjan (Eds.), *Learning mechanisms in food selection*. Waco, TX: Baylor University Press.

ROZIN, P., & KALAT, J. (1971). Specific hungers and poison avoidance as adaptive specializations of learning. *Psychological Review, 78*, 459–486.

ROZIN, P., & KALAT, J. (1972). Learning as a situation-specific adaptation. In Seligman & Hager.

RUBENSTEIN, H., LEWIS, S. S., & RUBENSTEIN, M. A. (1971). Evidence for phonemic recoding in visual word recognition. *Journal of Verbal Learning and Verbal Behavior, 10*, 645–657.

RUBIN, D. C. (Ed.). (1986). *Autobiographical memory*. Cambridge: Cambridge University Press.

RUMBAUGH, D. M. (1980). Language behavior of apes. In Sebeok & Umiker-Sebeok.

RUMBAUGH, D. M. (1981). Who feeds Clever Hans? In Sebeok & Rosenthal.

RUMELHART, D. E. (1980). Schemata: The building blocks of cognition. In R. Spiro, B. C. Bruce, & W. F. Brewer (Eds.), *Theoretical issues in reading comprehension*. Hillsdale, NJ: Lawrence Erlbaum Associates.

RUMELHART, D. E., MCCLELLAND, J. L., & and the PDP Research Group. (1986). *Parallel distributed processing: Explorations in the microstructure of Cognition*. (Vol. 1): *Foundations*. Cambridge, MA: Bradford Books/MIT Press.

RUSE, M. (1979). *Sociobiology, sense or nonsense?* (*Episteme*, Vol. 8). Dordrecht, Holland: D. Reidel.

RUSHTON, J. (1982a). Altruism and society: A social learning perspective. *Ethics, 92*, 425– 446.

RUSHTON, J. (1982b). Moral cognition, behaviorism and social learning theory. *Ethics, 92*, 459–467.

RUSHTON, J. P. (1985). Differential K theory: The sociobiology of individual and group differences. *Personality and Individual Differences, 6*, 441–452.

SAHLINS, M. D. (1976). *The use and abuse of biology*. Ann Arbor: University of Michigan Press.

SAMELSON, F. (1980). Little Albert, Cyril Burt's twins, and the need for a critical science. *American Psychologist, 35*, 619–625.

SAMUELSON, P. A. (1983). Complete genetic models for altruism, kin-selection and like-gene selection. *Journal of Social and Biological Structures, 6*, 3–15.

SAVAGE-RUMBAUGH, E. S. (1986). *Ape language: From conditioned responses to symbols*. New York: Columbia University Press.

SAVAGE-RUMBAUGH, E. S., RUMBAUGH, D. M., & BOYSEN, S. (1980a). Linguistically mediated tool use and exchange by chimpanzees. In Sebeok & Umiker-Sebeok.

SAVAGE-RUMBAUGH, E. S., & RUMBAUGH, D. M. (1980b). Language analogue project, phase II: Theory and tactics. In Nelson.

SAVAGE-RUMBAUGH, S., MCDONALD, K., SEVCIK, R., HOPKINS, W., & RUBERT, E. (1986). Spontaneous symbol acquisition and communicative use by pygmy chimpanzee. *Journal of Experimental Psychology: General, 115*, 211–235.

SCARR-SALAPATEK, S. (1976). An evolutionary perspective on infant intelligence. In M. Lewis (Ed.), *Origins of intelligence*. New York: Plenum.

SCHACHTER, D. L. (1985). Multiple forms of memory in humans and animals. In Weinberger, McGaugh, & Lynch (1985).

SCHACHTER, D. L. (1986a). The psychology of memory. In LeDoux & Hirst (1986).

SCHACHTER, D. L. (1986b). A psychological view of the neurobiology of memory. In LeDoux & Hirst (1986).

SCHACHTER, D. L. (1987). Implicit memory: History and current status. *Journal of Experimental Psychology: Learning, Memory, and Cognition, 13*, 501–518.

SCHANK, R. C., & ABELSON, R. P. (1977). *Scripts, plans, goals, and understanding*. Hillsdale, NJ: Lawrence Erlbaum Associates.

SCHATZ, C. (1954). The role of context in the perception of stops. *Language, 30*, 47–56.

SCHEFFLER, I. (1967). *Science and subjectivity*. Indianapolis: Bobbs-Merrill.

SCHNEIDER, W., DUMAIS, S. T., & SHIFFRIN, R. M. (1984). Automatic and control processing and attention. In R. Parasuraman & D. R. Davies (Eds.), *Varieties of attention*. Orlando, FL: Academic Press, Pp. 1–27.

SCHNEIDER, W., & SHIFFRIN, R. M. (1977). Controlled and automatic human information processing: I. Detection, search, and attention. *Psychological Review, 84*, 1–66.

SCHOEN, L. M. (1986). Changes in context and changes in meaning: A study of semantic verification. In J. L. Armagost (Ed.), *Papers from the 1985 Mid-American Linguistics Conference*. Manhattan: Kansas State University Department of Speech. Pp. 210–221.

SCHOEN, L. M. (1988). Semantic flexibility and core meaning. *Journal of Psycholinguistic Research, 17*, 113–123.

SCHOOLER, J. W., GERHARD, D., & LOFTUS, E. F. (1986). Qualities of the unreal. *Journal of Experimental Psychology: Learning, Memory, & Cognition, 12*, 171–181.

SCHRANK, J. (1977). *Analyzing advertising claims*. Palatine, IL: The Learning Seed Company.

SCHWARTZ, B. (1978). *Psychology of learning and behavior*. New York: Norton.

SCHWARTZ, B. (1982). Reinforcement-induced behavioral stereotyping: How not to teach people to discover rules. *Journal of Experimental Psychology: General, 111*, 23–59.

SCHWARTZ, B. (1984). *Psychology of learning and behavior* (2nd ed.). New York: Norton.

SCHWARTZ, J. H. (1984). Hominoid evolution: A review and a reassessment. *Current Anthropology, 25*, 655–672.

SEAMON, J. G. (1980). *Memory & cognition*. New York: Oxford University Press.

SEBEOK, T. A. (1980). Looking in the destination for what should have been sought in the source. In Sebeok & Umiker-Sebeok.

SEBEOK, T. A., & ROSENTHAL, R. (Eds.). (1981). *The clever Hans phenomenon. Annals of the New York Academy of Sciences* (Vol. 364). New York: New York Academy of Sciences.

SEBEOK, T. A., & UMIKER-SEBEOK, J. (1979, November). Performing animals: Secrets of the trade. *Psychology Today, 13* (6), 78–91.

SEBEOK, T. A., & UMIKER-SEBEOK, J. (Eds.). (1980). *Speaking of apes: A critical anthology of two-way communication with man*. New York: Plenum.

SELIGMAN, M. (1975). *Helplessness*. San Francisco: W. H. Freeman.

SELIGMAN, M. E. P., & HAGER, J. L. (Eds.). (1972). *Biological boundaries of learning*. New York: Appleton-Century-Crofts.

SELIGMAN, M., & JOHNSTON, J. (1973). Cognitive theory of avoidance learning. In F. McGuigan & D. Lumsden (Eds.), *Contemporary approaches to conditioning and learning*. Washington, DC: Winston.

SEM-JACOBSEN, C. (1976). Electrical stimulation and self-stimulation in man with chronic implanted electrodes. Interpretation and pitfall of results. In A. Wauquier & E. Rolls (Eds.), *Brain-stimulation reward*. Amsterdam: North-Holland.

SENNETT, R. (1977). *The fall of public man: On the social psychology of capitalism*. New York: Vintage.

SEWARD, J. P., & LEVY, N. (1949). Sign learning as a factor in extinction. *Journal of Experimental Psychology, 39*, 660–668.

SEWARD, J. P., & SEWARD, G. (1980). *Sex differences: Mental and temperamental*. Lexington, MA: Lexington Books.

SHEEHAN, P. W. (1982). Psychology and the law: Some pitfalls of verbal testimony. *Queensland Law Society Journal, 12*, 107–112.

SHEPARD, R. N. (1978). The mental image. *American Psychologist, 33*, 125–137.

SHEPARD, R. N., & FENG, C. A. (1972). A chronometric study of mental paper folding. *Cognitive Psychology, 3*, 228–243.

SHEPARD, R. N., & METZLER, J. (1971). Mental rotation of three-dimensional objects. *Science, 171*, 701–703.

SHETTLEWORTH, S. (1972). *Constraints on learning: Advances in the study of behavior* (Vol. 4). New York: Academic Press.

SHIELDS, W. M., & SHIELDS, L. M. (1983). Forcible rape: An evolutionary perspective. *Ethology and Sociobiology, 4*, 115–136.

SHIFFRIN, R. M. (1973). Information persistence in short-term memory. *Journal of Experimental Psychology, 100*, 39–49.

SHIFFRIN, R. M. (1985). Attention. In R. C. Atkinson, R. J. Herrnstein, G. Lindzey, & D. R. Luce (Eds.), *Stevens' handbook of experimental psychology*. New York: John Wiley.

SHIFFRIN, R. M., & SCHNEIDER, W. (1977). Controlled and automatic human information processing: II. Perceptual learning, automatic attending, and a general theory. *Psychological Review, 84*, 127–190.

SHIMP, C. P. (1976). Organization in memory and behavior. *Journal of the Experimental Analysis of Behavior, 26*, 113–130.

SHIMP, C. P. (1984). Cognition, behavior, and the experimental analysis of behavior. *Journal of the Experimental Analysis of Behavior, 42*, 407–420.

SHIMP, T. A. (1979). Social-psychological (mis)representations in television advertising. *Journal of Consumer Affairs, 13*, 28–40.

SHIMP, T. A. (1983). Evaluative verbal content and deception in advertising: A critical review. In R. J. Harris (Ed.), *Information processing research in advertising*. Hillsdale, NJ: Lawrence Erlbaum Associates.

SHUY, R. W. (1981). Toward a developmental theory of writing. In C. H. Frederiksen & J. F. Dominic (Eds.), *Writing: Process, development, and communication*. Hillsdale, NJ: Lawrence Erlbaum Associates.

SHUY, R. W., & LARKIN, D. (1978). Linguistic consideration in the simplification/classification of insurance policy language. *Discourse Processes, 1*, 305–321.

SIEGEL, S. (1979). The role of conditioning in drug tolerance and addiction. In Keehn (1979).

SIEGLER, R. S. (1983). Five generalizations about cognitive development. *American Psychologist, 38*, 263–277.

SIEGLER, R. S. (1986). *Children's thinking*. Englewood Cliffs, NJ: Prentice-Hall.

SIMON, H. A., & GILMARTIN, K. A. (1973). A simulation of memory for chess positions. *Cognitive Psychology, 5*, 29–46.

SINGER, M. (1979). Processes of inference during sentence encoding. *Memory and Cognition, 7*, 192–200.

SINGER, M. (1981). Verifying the assertions and implications of language. *Journal of Verbal Learning and Verbal Behavior, 20*, 46–60.

SINGER, M. (1984). Inferences in reading comprehension. In M. Daneman & P. A. Carpenter (Eds.), *Reading research: Advances in theory and practice* (Vol. 6), New York: Academic Press.

SINGER, P. (1981). *The expanding circle*. New York: Farrar, Straus & Giroux.

SINGULAR, S. (1982, October). A memory for all seasonings. *Psychology Today, 16*(10), 54–63.

SISSON, J. C., SCHOOMAKER, E. B., & ROSS, J. C. (1976). Clinical decision analysis: The hazard of using additional data. *Journal of the American Medical Association, 236*, 1259–1263.

SKELTON, R. R., McHENRY, H. M., & DRAWHORN, G. M. (1986). Phylogenetic analysis of early hominids. *Current Anthropology 27*, 21–43.

SKINNER, B. F. (1938). *Behavior of organisms*. Englewood Cliffs, NJ: Prentice-Hall.

SKINNER, B. F. (1948a). 'Superstition' in the pigeon. *Journal of Experimental Psychology, 38*, 168–172.

SKINNER, B. F. (1948b). *Walden II*. New York: Macmillan.

SKINNER, B. F. (1950). Are theories of learning necessary? *Psychological Review, 57*, 193–216.

SKINNER, B. F. (1957). *Verbal Behavior*. Englewood Cliffs, NJ: Prentice-Hall.

SKINNER, B. F. (1961a). A case history in scientific method (1956). Reprinted in *Cumulative Record* (3rd ed.) Englewood Cliffs, NJ: Prentice-Hall.

SKINNER, B. F. (1961b). Pigeons in a pelican (1960). Reprinted in *Cumulative Record* (3rd ed.). Englewood Cliffs, NJ: Prentice-Hall.

SKINNER, B. F. (1969). *Contingencies of reinforcement*. Englewood Cliffs, NJ: Prentice-Hall.

SKINNER, B. F. (1972a). *Beyond freedom and dignity*. New York: Bantam.

SKINNER, B. F. (1954/1972). A critique of psychoanalytic concepts and theories (1954). In Skinner (1972b).

SKINNER, B. F. (1959/1972). A case history in scientific method. In Skinner, B. F. (1972).

SKINNER, B. F. (1960/1972). Pigeons in a pelican. In Skinner (1972).

SKINNER, B. F. (1972). *Cumulative record*, 3rd ed. New York: Appleton-Century-Crofts.

SKINNER, B. F. (1974). *About behaviorism*. New York: Knopf.

SKINNER, B. F. (1976). *Particulars of my life*. New York: Knopf.

SLOBIN, D. I. (1973). Cognitive prerequisites for the development of grammar. In C. A. Ferguson & D. I. Slobin (Eds.), *Studies of child language development*. New York: Holt, Rinehart & Winston.

SLOVIC, P., & FISCHHOFF, B. (1977). On the psychology of experimental surprises. *Journal of Experimental Psychology: Human Perception and Performance, 3*, 544–551.

SLOVIC, P., FISCHHOFF, B., & LICHTENSTEIN, S. (1982). Facts versus fears: Understanding perceived risk. In Kahneman, D., Slovic, P., & Tversky, A. (Eds.), *Judgment under uncertainty: Heuristics and biases*. Cambridge: Cambridge University Press.

SLOVIC, P., & LICHTENSTEIN, S. (1971). Comparison of Bayesian and regression approaches to the study of information processing judgment. *Organizational Behavior and Human Performance, 6,* 649–744.

SMEDSLUND, J. (1961/1968). The acquisition of conservation of substance and weight in children, I-VI. *Scandinavian Journal of Psychology, 2,* 11–210. I, III, V, & VI reprinted in Sigel & Hooper.

SMITH, E. E. (1978). Theories of semantic memory. In W. K. Estes (Ed.), *Handbook of learning and cognitive processes* (Vol. 6). Hillsdale, NJ: Lawrence Erlbaum Associates.

SMITH, E. E., SHOBEN, E. J., & RIPS, L. J. (1974). Structure and process in semantic memory: A featural model for semantic decisions. *Psychological Review, 81,* 214–241.

SMITH, F. (1985). A metaphor for literacy: Creating worlds or shunting information? In D. R. Olson, N. Torrance, & A. Hildyard (Eds.), *Literacy, language, and learning.* Cambridge: Cambridge University Press. Pp. 195–213.

SMITH, F., & MILLER, G. (1965). *The genesis of language.* Cambridge, MA: MIT Press.

SMITH, F. H., & SPENCER, F. (Eds.). (1984). *The origins of modern humans: A world survey of the fossil evidence.* New York: Alan R. Liss, Inc.

SMITH, L. J. (1986). *Behaviorism and logical positivism: A revised account of the alliance.* Stanford, CA: Stanford University Press.

SMITH, P. (1974). Ethological methods. In B. Foss (Ed.), *New perspective in child development.* Baltimore: Penguin.

SNOW, C. E. (1972/1978). Mother's speech to children learning language. *Child Development, 43,* 549–565. Reprinted in C. Bloom.

SNOW, C. E. (1986). Conversations with children. In Fletcher & Garman (1986).

SNOWDEN, C. T. (1983). Ethology comparative psychology and animal behavior. *Annual Review of Psychology* (Vol. 34). Palo Alto, CA: Annual Reviews.

SNYDER, M., TANKE, E. D., & BERSCHEID, E. (1977). Social perception and interpersonal behavior: On the self-fulfilling nature of social stereotypes. *Journal of Personality and Social Psychology, 35,* 656–666.

SNYDER, M., & URANOWITZ, S. W. (1978). Reconstructing the past: Some cognitive consequences of person perception. *Journal of Personality and Social Psychology, 36,* 941–950.

SOLANTO, M., & KATKIN, E. (1979). Classical EDR conditioning using a truly random control and subjects differing in electrodermal lability level. *Bulletin of the Psychonomic Society, 14,* 49–52.

SOLOMON, R. (1964). Punishment. *American Psychologist, 19,* 239–253.

SPELKE, E., HIRST, W., & NEISSER, U. (1976). Skills of divided attention. *Cognition, 4,* 215–230.

SPENCE, K. (1944). The nature of theory construction in contemporary psychology. *Psychological Review, 51,* 47–68.

SPENCE, K. (1956). *Behavior theory and conditioning.* New Haven: Yale University Press.

SPENCER, H. (1897). *Principles of psychology* (3rd ed.) (1855). New York: Appleton & Co.

SPERLING, G. A. (1960). The information available in brief visual presentation. *Psychological Monographs, 74,* Whole No. 498.

SPILICH, G. J., VESONDER, G. T., CHIESI, H. L., & VOSS, J. F. (1979). Text processing of domain-related information for individuals with high and low domain knowledge. *Journal of Verbal Learning and Verbal Behavior, 18,* 275–290.

SPIRO, R. J. (1980). Constructive processes in prose comprehension and recall. In R. J. Spiro, B. C. Bruce, & W. F. Brewer (Eds.), *Theoretical issues in reading comprehension.* Hillsdale, NJ: Lawrence Erlbaum Associates.

SQUIRE, L. (1987). *Memory and brain.* New York: Oxford University Press.

STADDON, J. (1975). Learning as adaptation. In W. K. Estes (Ed.), *Handbook of learning and cognitive processes* (Vol. 2). Hillsdale, NJ: Lawrence Erlbaum Associates.

STADDON, J. E. R. (1984). *Adaptive behavior and learning.* New York: Cambridge University Press.

STADDON, J. E. R. (1985). Inference, memory, and representation. In Weinberger, McGaugh, & Lynch (1985).

STADDON, J., & SIMMELHAG, V. (1971). The 'superstition' experiment: A reexamination of its implications for the principles of adaptive behavior. *Psychological Review 78,* 3–43.

STANLEY, G. (1975). Visual memory processes in dyslexia. In D. Deutsch & J. A. Deutsch (Eds.), *Short-term memory.* New York: Academic Press.

STEKLIS, H. D., & HARNAD, S. R. (1976). From hand to mouth: Some critical stages in the evolution of language. In Harnad and others.

STERN, L. (1985). *The structures and strategies of human memory.* Homewood, IL: Dorsey.

STERNBERG, R. J. (Ed.). (1984). *Mechanisms of cognitive development.* San Francisco: W. H. Freeman.

STERNBERG, S. (1966). High-speed scanning in human memory. *Science, 153,* 652–654.

STERNBERG, S. (1975). Memory scanning: New findings and current controversies. *Quarterly Journal of Experimental Psychology, 27,* 1–32.

STILLINGS, N. A., FEINSTEIN, M. H., GARFELD, J. L., RISSLAND, E. L., ROSENBAUM, D. A., WEISLER, S. E., & BAKER-WARD, L. (1987). *Cognitive science: An introduction.* Cambridge, MA: Bradford/MIT Press.

STONEBREAKER, T. B. (1981). Retrospective and prospective processes in delayed matching to sample. Unpublished doctoral dissertation, Michigan State University.

STRATTON, G. M. (1917). The mnemonic feat of the 'Shass Pollak,' *Psychological Review, 24,* 244–247.

STROMEYER, C. F. (1970, November). Eidetikers. *Psychology Today,* 76–80.

STROMEYER, C. F., & PSOTKA, J. (1970). The detailed texture of eidetic images. *Nature, 225,* 346–349.

SULIN, R. A., & DOOLING, D. J. (1974). Intrusion of a thematic idea in retention of prose. *Journal of Experimental Psychology, 103,* 255–262.

SULLOWAY, F. J. (1979). *Freud: Biologist of the mind.* New York: Basic Books.

SYMONS, D. (1979). *The evolution of human sexuality.* New York: Oxford University Press.

SYMONS, D. (1983). Another woman that never evolved. *Quarterly Review of Biology, 57,* 297–300.

TALBOTT, J. A. (1982). Development. In S. Gilman (Ed.), *Introducing psychoanalytic theory.* New York: Brunner/Mazel.

TART, C. (1975). *Learning to use extrasensory perception.* Chicago: University of Chicago Press.

TARTTER, V. C. (1986). *Language processes.* New York: Holt, Rinehart & Winston.

TAYLOR, I., & TAYLOR, M. M. (1984). *The psychology of reading.* Orlando, FL: Academic Press.

TAYLOR, S. E. (1982). The availability bias in social perception and interaction. In Kahneman, D., Slovic, P., & Tversky, A. (Eds.), *Judgment under uncertainty: Heuristics and biases.* Cambridge: Cambridge University Press.

TAYLOR, S. E., & CROCKER, J. (1981). Schematic bases of social information processing. In E. T. Higgins, C. P. Herman, & M. P. Zanna (Eds.), *Social cognition: The Ontario Symposium* (Vol. 1). Hillsdale, NJ: Lawrence Erlbaum Associates.

TERRACE, H. (1963a). Discrimination learning with and without errors. *Journal of the Experimental Analysis of Behavior, 6,* 1–27.

TERRACE, H. (1963b). Errorless transfer of a discrimination across two continua. *Journal of the Experimental Analysis of Behavior, 6,* 223–232.

TERRACE, H. S. (1979a). *Nim: A chimpanzee who learned sign language.* New York: Washington Square Press.

TERRACE, H. S. (1979b, November). How Nim Chimpsky changed my mind. *Psychology Today, 13* (6), 65–76.

TERRACE, H. S. (1979c). Is problem-solving language? *Journal of the Experimental Analysis of Behavior, 31,* 161–175.

TERRACE, H. S. (1982, December). Why Koko can't talk. *The Sciences, 22*(9), 8–10.

TERRACE, H. S., PETITTO, L. A., SANDERS, R. J., & BEVER, T. G. (1979). Can an ape create a sentence? *Science, 206,* 891–902.

TERRACE, H. S., PETITTO, L. A., SANDERS, R. J., & BEVER, T. G. (1980). On the grammatical capacity of apes. In Nelson.

TETLOW, P. E. (1986). Psychological advice on foreign policy. *American Psychologist, 41,* 557–567.

THISTLETHWAITE, D. (1951). A critical review of latent learning and related experiments. *Psychological Bulletin, 48,* 97–129.

THOMPSON, C. P. (1982). Memory for unique personal events: The roommate study. *Memory and Cognition, 10,* 324–332.

THOMPSON, C. P. (1985a). Memory for unique personal events: Some implications of the self-schema. *Human Learning, 4,* 267–280.

THOMPSON, C. P. (1985b). Memory for unique personal events: Effects of pleasantness, *Motivation and Emotion*, *9*, 277–289.

THOMPSON, R. F., & DONEGAN, N. H. (1986). The search for the engram. In Martinez & Kesner (1986).

THOMSON, D. M., & TULVING, E. (1970). Associative encoding and retrieval: Weak and strong cues. *Journal of Experimental Psychology*, *86*, 255–262.

THOMSON, R. H. (1930). An experimental study of memory as influenced by feeling tone. *Journal of Experimental Psychology*, *13*, 462–467.

THORNDIKE, E. L. (1965). *Animal intelligence* (1911). New York: Hafner Press.

THORNDIKE, E. L. (1968). *Human learning* (1928–1929). New York: Johnson Reprint Corp.

THORNDIKE, L. (1923–1958). *History of magic and experimental science* (8 Vols.). New York: Columbia University Press.

THORNDYKE, P. W. (1984). Applications of schema theory in cognitive research. In J. R. Anderson & S. M. Kosslyn (Eds.), *Tutorials in learning and memory*. San Francisco: W. H. Freeman, Pp. 167–191.

THORNDYKE, P. W., & HAYES-ROTH, B. (1982). Differences in spatial knowledge acquired from maps and navigation. *Cognitive Psychology*, *14*, 560–589.

THORNHILL, R., & THORNHILL, N. W. (1983). Human rape: An evolutionary analysis. *Ethology and Sociobiology*, *4*, 137–173.

TINBERGEN, N. (1951/1972). The innate disposition to learn. In Seligman & Hager.

TOLMAN, E. C. (1933). Sign-gestalt or conditioned reflex? *Psychological Review*, *40*, 391–411.

TOLMAN, E. C. (1938). The determiners of behavior at a choice point. *Psychological Review*, *45*, 1–41.

TOLMAN, E. C. (1948). Cognitive maps in rats and men. *Psychological Review*, *55*, 189–208.

TOLMAN, E. C. (1959). Principles of purposive behaviorism. In S. Koch (Ed.) *Psychology: A study of a science* (Vol. 2). New York: McGraw-Hill.

TOLMAN, E. C. (1932, 1967). *Purposive behavior in animals and men*. New York: Irvington. (Originally published, 1932).

TOLMAN, E. C., HALL, C. S., & BRETNALL, E. P. (1932). A disproof of the law of effect and a substitution of the laws of emphasis, motivation, and disruption. *Journal of Experimental Psychology*, *15*, 601–614.

TOLMAN, E. C., & HONZIK. (1930). 'Insight' in rats. *University of California Publications in Psychology*, *4*, 215–232.

TOULMIN, S. (1971). The concept of 'stages' in cognitive development. In Mischel.

TOULMIN, S. (1972). *Human understanding* (Vol. I). *The collective use and evolution of concepts*. Princeton, NJ: Princeton University Press.

TREISMAN, A. M. (1964). Monitoring and storage of irrelevant messages in selective attention. *Journal of Verbal Learning and Verbal Behavior*, *3*, 449–459.

TREISMAN, A. M., & GELADE, G. (1980). A feature-integration theory of attention. *Cognitive Psychology*, *12*, 97–136.

TRIVERS, R. L. (1971). The evolution of reciprocal altruism. Reprinted in Clutton-Brock & Harvey (1978); Hunt (1980); and Caplan (1980).

TRIVERS, R. L. (1972). Prenatal investment and sexual selection. Reprinted in Clutton-Brock & Harvey (1978).

TRIVERS, R. L. (1974). Parent-offspring conflict. Reprinted in Clutton-Brock & Harvey (1978); and Hunt (1980).

TRIVERS, R. L. (1983). The evolution of sex. Review of G. Bell, *The masterpiece of nature: The evolution and genetics of sexuality*. *Quarterly Review of Biology*, *58*, 62–67.

TRIVERS, R. L., & HARE, H. (1976). Haplodiploidy and the evolution of social insects. Reprinted in Hunt (1980).

TRIVERS, R. L., & WILLARD D. E. (1973). Natural selection of parental ability to vary the sex ratio of offspring. *Science*, *179*, 90–92.

TULVING, E. (1972). Episodic and semantic memory. In E. Tulving & W. Donaldson (Eds.), *Organization and memory*. New York: Academic Press.

TULVING, E., SCHACTER, D. L., & STARK, H. A. (1982). Priming effects in word-fragment completion are independent of recognition memory. *Journal of Experimental Psychology: Learning, Memory, & Cognition*, *8*, 336–342.

TULVING, E., & THOMSON, D. M. (1973). Encoding specificity and retrieval processes in episodic memory. *Psychological Review*, *80*, 352–373.

TURIEL, B. (1973). Adolescent conflict in the development of moral principles. In R. L. Solso (Ed.), *Contemporary issues in cognitive psychology*. Washington, DC: V. H. Winston.

TVERSKY, A., & KAHNEMAN, D. (1973). Availability: A heuristic for judging frequency and probability. *Cognitive Psychology, 5*, 207–232.

TVERSKY, A., & KAHNEMAN, D. (1974). Judgment under uncertainty: Heuristics and biases. *Science, 185*, 1124–1131.

TVERSKY, A., & KAHNEMAN, D. (1981). The law of small numbers (1971). Reprinted in Tweney, Doherty & Mynatt.

TWENEY, R. D., DOHERTY, M. E., & MYNATT, C. R. (Eds.). (1981). *On scientific thinking*. New York: Columbia University Press.

UZGIRIS, I. C. (1968). Situational generality of conservation. *Child Development, 1964, 35*, 831–841. Reprinted in Sigel & Hooper.

VAN DEN BERGHE, P. (1979). *Human family systems: An evolutionary view*. New York: Elsevier.

VAN DEN BERGHE, P. (1983). Human inbreeding avoidance: Culture in nature. *The Behavioral and Brain Sciences, 6*, 91–124.

VAN DEN BERGHE, P., & BARASH, D. (1977). Inclusive fitness and human family structure. In Hunt (1980).

VELTEN, E. (1968). A laboratory task for the induction of mood states. *Behavioral Research in Therapy, 6*, 473–482.

VERPLANCK, W. (1955). The control of the content of conversation: Reinforcement of statements of opinion. *Journal of Abnormal and Social Psychology, 51*, 668–676.

VESTERGAARD, I., & SCHRODER, K. (1985). *The language of advertising*. Oxford: Basil Blackwell.

VINING, D. R. (1986). Social vs. reproductive success: The central theoretical problem of human sociobiology. *Behavioral and Brain Sciences, 9*, 167–211.

VIROSTEK, S., & CUTTING, J. E. (1979). Asymmetries for Ameslan handshapes and other forms in signers and nonsigners. *Perception & Psychophysics, 26*, 505–508.

VOEKS, V. (1950). Formalization and clarification of a theory of learning. *Journal of Psychology, 30*, 341–363.

VOEKS, V. (1954). Acquisition of S-R connections: A test of Hull's and Guthrie's theories. *Journal of Experimental Psychology, 47*, 137–147.

VOSNIADOU, S., & BREWER, W. F. (1987). Theories of knowledge restructuring in development. *Review of Educational Research, 57*, 51–67.

VOSS, J. F., GREENE, T. R., POST, T. A., & PENNER, B. C. (1983). Problem solving skill in social sciences. In G. Bower (Ed.), *The psychology of learning and motivation* (Vol. 17). New York: Academic Press.

VOSS, J. F., TYLER, S. W., & YENGO, L. A. (1983). Individual differences in the solving of social science problems. In R. F. Dillon & R. R. Schmeck (Eds.), *Individual differences in cognition*. New York: Academic Press.

WADDINGTON, C. H. (1968). The theory of evolution today. In A. Koestler & J. R. Smythies (Eds.), *Beyond reductionism*. New York: Macmillan.

WAGNER, A. (1978). Expectancies and the priming of STM. In S. Hulse, H. Fowler, and W. Honig (Eds.), *Cognitive processes in animal behavior*. Hillsdale, NJ: Lawrence Erlbaum Associates.

WALLACE, A. R. (1980). On the tendency of species to depart indefinitely from the original type. Reprinted in A. C. Brackman, *A delicate arrangement*. New York: Times Books. (Originally published, 1858.)

WALLACE, I., KLAHR, D., & BLUFF, K. (1987). A self-modifying production systems model of cognitive development. In Klahr, Langley, & Neches (1987).

WARREN, J. M., & NONNEMAN, A. J. (1976). The search in cerebral dominance in monkeys. In Harnad and others.

WARREN, W. H., NICHOLAS, D. W., & TRABASSO, T. (1979). Event chains and inferences in understanding narratives. In R. O. Freedle (Ed.), *New directions in discourse processing*. Norwood, NJ: Ablex.

WASHBURN, S. L. (1981). Language and the fossil record. *Anthropology UCLA, 7*, 231–238.

WASON, P. C., & JOHNSON-LAIRD, P. N. (1972). *Psychology of reasoning*. Cambridge, MA: Harvard University Press.

WASSERMAN, E., NELSON, K., & LAREW, M. (1980). Memory for sequences of stimuli and responses. *Journal of the Experimental Analysis of Behavior, 34*, 49–60.

WATSON, J. (1930). *Behaviorism*. New York: Norton.

WATSON, J., & RAYNER, R. (1920). Conditioned emotional reactions. *Journal of Experimental Psychology 3*, 1–14.

WEIGEL, R. M. (1984). The application of evolutionary models to the study of decisions made by children during object possession conflicts. *Ethology & Sociobiology 5*, 229–238.

WEINBERGER, N. M., MCGAUGH, J. L., & LYNCH, G. (Eds.). (1985). *Memory systems of the brain: Animal and human cognitive processes.* New York: Guildford Press.

WEINER, H. (1970). Instructional control of human operant responding during extinction following fixed-ratio conditioning. *Journal of the Experimental Analysis of Behavior, 13*, 391–394.

WEINER, S. L. & GOODENOUGH, D. R. (1977). A move toward a psychology of conversation. In R. O. Freedle (Eds.), *Discourse production and comprehension.* Norwood, NJ: Ablex.

WEINGARTNER, H., COHEN, R. M., MURPHY, D. L., MARTELLO, J., & GERDT, C. (1981). Cognitive processes in depression. *Archives of General Psychiatry, 38*, 42–47.

WEISBERG, R. W. (1986). *Creativity: Genius and other myths.* New York: W. H. Freeman.

WELDON, M. S., & ROEDIGER, H. L. III. (1987). Altering retrieval demands reverses the picture superiority effect. *Memory and Cognition, 15*, 269–280.

WELLS, B. W. P. (1980). *Personality and heredity.* London: Longman.

WELLS, G. L., LINDSAY, R. C. L., & TOUSIGNANT, J. P. (1980). Effects of expert psychological advice on human performance in judging the validity of eyewitness testimony. *Law and Human Behavior, 4*, 275–285.

WELLS, G. L., & LOFTUS, E. F. (Eds.) (1984). *Eyewitness testimony: Psychological perspectives.* Cambridge: Cambridge University Press.

WERNER, H. (1957). The concept of development from a comparative and organismic point of view. In D. Harris (Ed.) *The concept of development.* Minneapolis: University of Minnesota Press.

WERNER, H. (1978). *Developmental processes* (2 Vols.). S. S. Barten & M B. Franklin (Eds.). New York: International Universities Press.

WEXLER, K., & CULLICOVER, P. W. (1980). *Formal principles of language acquisition.* Cambridge, MA: MIT Press.

WHEELER, D. D. (1970). Processes in word recognition. *Cognitive Psychology, 1*, 59–85.

WHITEMAN, M. F. (Ed.). (1981). *Variation in writing: Functional and linguistic-cultural differences.* Hillsdale, NJ: Lawrence Erlbaum Associates.

WHITING, J., & CHILD, I. (1953). *Child training and personality.* New Haven: Yale University Press.

WICKELGREN, W. A. (1965). Size of rehearsal group and short-term memory. *Journal of Experimental Psychology 68*, 413–419.

WICKENS, D. (1938). The transference of conditioned excitation and conditioned inhibition from one muscle group to the antagonistic muscle group. *Journal of Experimental Psychology 22*, 101–123.

WICKLER, W. (1973). *The sexual code*, Garden City, NY: Anchor Books.

WIEGELE, T. (Ed.) (1982). *Biology and the social sciences: An emerging revolution.* Boulder, CO: Westview Press.

WILCOXON, H., DRAGOIN, E., & KRAL, P. (1971/1972). Illness-induced aversion in rats & quail. In Seligman & Hager.

WILLIAMS, G. C. (1980). Kin selection and the paradox of sexuality. In Barlow and Silverberg.

WILSON, E. O. (1975a). *Sociobiology.* Cambridge, MA: Harvard University Press.

WILSON, E. O. (1975b). *Sociobiology: The new synthesis* (Abridged ed.). Cambridge, MA: Harvard University Press, 1980.

WILSON, E. O. (1979). *On human nature.* New York: Bantam Books.

WILSON, E. O. (1980). *Sociobiology: The new synthesis* (Abridged ed.). Cambridge, MA: Harvard University Press. (Originally published, 1975).

WILSON, J. Q., & HERRNSTEIN, R. J. (1985). *Crime and human nature.* New York: Simon & Schuster.

WINGFIELD, A., & BYRNES, D. L. (1981). *The psychology of human memory.* New York: Academic Press.

WISPE, L. G., & THOMPSON, J. N. (Eds.). (1976). The war between the words: Biological *vs.* social evolution and some related issues. *American Psychologist, 31,* 341–384.

WITTIG, A. F., & WILLIAMS, G. (1984). *Psychology: An introduction.* New York: McGraw-Hill.

WOLF, T. (1976). A cognitive model of musical sight-reading. *Journal of Psycholinguistic Research 5,* 143–171.

WOLL, S. B., WEEKS, D. G., FRAPS, C. L., PENDERGRASS, J., & VANDERPLAS, M. A. (1980). Role of sentence context in the encoding of trait descriptors. *Journal of Personality and Social Psychology, 39,* 59–68.

WOLL, S., & YOPP, H. (1978). The role of context and inference in the comprehension of social action. *Journal of Experimental Social Psychology, 14,* 351–362.

WOOD, B., MARTIN, L., & ANDREWS, P. (Eds.). (1986). *Major topics in primate and human evolution.* New York: Cambridge University Press.

WOODRUFF, D. S. (1983). A review of aging and cognitive processes. *Research on Aging, 5,* 139–153.

WOODS, B. T. (1980). Observations on the neurological basis for initial language acquisition. In Caplan.

WOODY, C. D. (1986). Understanding the cellular basis of memory and learning. *Annual Review of Psychology, 37,* 433–494.

WRANGHAM, R. W. (1982). Mutualism, kinship, and social evolution. In King's College Sociobiology Group (Eds.), *Current problems in sociobiology.* Cambridge: Cambridge University Press.

WREN, T. (1982). Social learning theory, self-regulation and morality. *Ethics, 92,* 409–424.

WUNDT, W. (1973). *The language of gestures.* The Hague: Mouton.

WYER, R. S., & CARLSTON, D. A. (Eds.). (1979). *Social cognition, inference, and attribution.* Hillsdale, NJ: Lawrence Erlbaum Associates.

YARMEY, A. D. (1979). *The psychology of eyewitness testimony.* New York: Free Press.

YATES, A. (1980). *Biofeedback and the modification of behavior.* New York: Plenum.

YATES, F. (1966). *The art of memory.* Chicago: University of Chicago Press.

YENI-KOMSHIAN, G. H., KAVANAUGH, J. F., & FERGUSON, C. A. (Eds.). (1980). *Child phonology* (Vol. 2): *Perception.* New York: Academic Press.

YUILLE, J. C., & CUTSHALL, J. L. (1986). A case study of eyewitness memory of a crime. *Journal of Applied Psychology 71,* 291–301.

ZALKIND, D. L., & SHACHTMAN, R. H. (1980). A decision analysis approach to the swine influenza vaccination decision for an individual. *Medical Care, 18*(1), 59–72.

ZECHMEISTER, E. B., & NYBERG, S. E. (1982). *Human memory.* Monterey, CA: Brooks/Cole.

INDEX